NORTHERN EUROPE
IN THE EARLY MODERN PERIOD
1492–1772

NORTHERN EUROPE IN THE EARLY MODERN PERIOD

The Baltic World 1492–1772

David Kirby

Longman
London and New York

Longman Group UK Limited
Longman House, Burnt Mill, Harlow
Essex CM20 2JE, England
and associated Companies throughout the world.

Published in the United States of America
by Longman Inc., New York

First published 1990

British Library Cataloguing in Publication Data
Kirby, D. G. (David Gordon) *1942–*
    Northern Europe in the early-modern period: the Baltic world 1492-1772.
    1. Baltic region, history
    I. Title
    948

ISBN 0-582-00410-1 CSD
ISBN 0-582-00411-X PPR

Library of Congress Cataloguing-in-Publication Data
Northern Europe in the early-modern period: the Baltic world 1492-1772/David
Kirby.
    p.   cm.
    Includes bibliographical references (p.   ).
    ISBN 0-582-00410-1 – ISBN 0-582-004011-X (pbk.)
    1. Europe, Northern–History.   2. Sweden–History–1523-1718.
    3. Baltic States–History.   I. Title
    DL78.K57   1990
    948–dc20   89-28311
                                                                          CIP

Set in Bembo

Produced by Longman Singapore Publishers (Pte) Ltd.
Printed in Singapore

Contents

Contents

List of maps

Preface

In writing this first of two volumes on the history of the Baltic world
from the late Middle Ages to the present, I have been painfully aware
of the towering presence of Ferdinand Braudel's magnificent and
monumental work on the Mediterranean. Before the inevitably unfavourable comparisons are made, therefore, I have to declare that my
work has been primarily conceived of as a general introduction to the
history and historical controversies of the Baltic region. It must also
be said that the general European perception of the two seas has
always been strikingly different. The Mediterranean is regarded as the
cradle of civilisation, the teeming meeting-ground of cultures from
time immemorial. The Baltic by contrast is usually seen as a chilly,
peripheral backwater on the very edge of the civilised world. The
Mediterranean world is an integral part of the culture of Europe, in
every meaning of that word. Its artefacts adorn museums, its shores
attract hundreds of thousands of sun-seekers every year. The Baltic
cannot compare on these terms. Even its most famous son, Thomas
Mann, was drawn irresistibly to the south, leaving only a fleeting
glimpse of his Baltic childhood in *Buddenbrooks*.

The Baltic area has indeed been the recipient, not the creator of
civilisation, if that is taken to mean the cultural heritage of urban life.
Much of the history of the peoples who inhabit its shores is one of
adaptation to the impulses and pressures of a more vigorous outside
world. Adaptation, not slavish submission: for although the peoples
of the north may have lacked the superior skills and techniques of
those who imposed their mark at various times – German knights,
Dutch traders, Scottish mechanics – they were not without their own

talents; above all, a canny ability to make the most out of the unpropitious circumstances of their surroundings.

The Baltic has long been an area of conflict between 'East' and 'West'. Hostility and fear of Russia – 'enemy to all liberty under the heavens' as a sixteenth-century king of Poland put it – is nothing new. Russia's neighbours have often been deceived in their expectations of assistance from the West. The frequent appeals of the Livonian Order to the German Empire for financial and military aid in the 1550s and the dire warning *hodie mihi cras tibi* (me today, you tomorrow) fell on deaf ears. Peter the Great's determination and military strength proved too much for the Swedes after Karl XII's defeat at Poltava in 1709, and the hesitant policy of Hanoverian England could neither preserve the 'Ballance of the North' nor save Sweden. British and French offers of military intervention in the winter of 1939–40 to aid Finland may have persuaded the Soviet Union to take up peace negotiations with the Finns; but the Finns would have been most unwise to rely on the Allied promises, since intervention was primarily intended to cut off Swedish iron ore supplies to Germany. The Baltic has always been an expendable zone in the policies of the Western powers. British policy-makers voiced grave doubts about the survival of Estonia, Latvia and Lithuania as independent states in the 1920s, and could offer no comfort when their existence was imperilled in 1939. The United States would have been prepared to employ a battery of sanctions against Italy had the communists won the elections of 1948. A communist coup in Finland would not have provoked such a response.

For much of the period covered by this volume, Sweden was the dominant power in the Baltic. The kingdom of Sweden included the Finnish provinces, and controlled for much of the seventeenth century the land between lake Ladoga and the Bay of Riga. Gustav II Adolf's intervention in Germany during the Thirty Years' War brought new territorial acquisitions in Pomerania, Bremen and Verden, and established Sweden as a major military force in Europe. The story of Sweden's rise and decline therefore constitutes the backbone of this present volume. Rather more attention is paid to the domestic history of the two northern kingdoms which resulted from the break-up of the Union of Kalmar than to the internal affairs of Poland–Lithuania, Russia and the kingdom of Prussia, since Sweden and to a lesser extent Denmark are pre-eminently Baltic countries. The zone of exclusion must inevitably be somewhat arbitrary, and I apologise for consigning Norway to the margins and for doing less than justice to Poland and Lithuania.

The struggle for existence in a harsh and unyielding environment is, however, the underlying theme of this work. The emancipation of the inhabitants of the continent of Europe from the scourge of famine, disease, pain and poverty is perhaps the greatest achievement a historian has to record, but is all too often lost in general surveys. In writing this history, I have been acutely conscious of the sombre and often hopeless circumstances in which generations have been conceived, have laboured and died. It is difficult to evoke the basically humdrum and mundane tenor of life in past centuries, to feel the scratchy reality of homespun fustian and coarse linen, the pangs of constant hunger or the fears and fantasies which flourished in an unilluminated world. We live in an altogether different age, and the material and spiritual gulf which divides us from our ancestors is truly great. Their song will never be sung, but will remain forever a background hum accompanying the doings of the great and powerful, upon whose written records history is so dependent. But I hope nevertheless that the bass ground of the common people is heard occasionally in my survey.

I have attempted to tackle the problem of place names in the following manner: the Swedish version is used for all parts of the Swedish realm, i.e. Sweden (including Skåne) and Finland; the German for places in Estonia, Livonia, Kurland, Prussia and Holstein (but not Slesvig). I have preferred to use the native rather than the English version of the names of sovereigns, with one or two exceptions, and in one case, Sigismund of Sweden becomes king Zygmunt of Poland. This may seen unnecessarily pedantic. My only excuse is that years of witnessing the steady diminution in the numbers of English-speaking students able and willing to read in any other language prompt me to pepper my text with foreign names and phrases in the hope of stirring an awareness that life is ordered rather differently outside these blessed isles.

My thanks are due to Roger Bartlett, Michael Branch, Max Engman, Robert Frost, Janet Hartley, Bill Mead, Rudolf Muhs, Thomas Munch-Petersen, Thomas Munck, Stewart Oakley and Tony Upton for their helpful advice and suggestions.

For my parents

PART ONE

The Baltic at the End of the Middle Ages

CHAPTER ONE
The Baltic in the European Economy

THE RISE OF THE DUTCH TRADE IN THE BALTIC

The land mass of Europe is flanked by two seas, running from east to west, where they disgorge their waters through narrow straits into the Atlantic Ocean. The name given to the southern sea, the Mediterranean, is in itself testimony to its importance as the cradle of civilisation and as a major thoroughfare. The northern waterway, seven times smaller than the Mediterranean, has appealed far less to the European imagination. The smell of tar and salted herring cannot really compare with the sweet scent of the lemon blossom, nor have the sparsely populated plains and uplands of northern Europe given poets and painters the same inspiration as the mountains and islands of the south. The sandy and infertile moraine of the north European plain and the vast coniferous forests which covered Scandinavia were, before the age of mass travel, the chilly hyperborean periphery of the European continent, isolated and remote.

Insignificant in comparison with the Mediterranean, the Baltic was nevertheless a vital element in the economy not only of those around its shores, but also of the hinterland. Into its brackish waters flowed the great rivers which drained the Russo-European plain, and along these waterways, trade flourished. The Vikings had already established trading routes along these waterways down to the Caspian and Black Seas. Not without good reason was the Baltic known as the East Sea, for it gave access along the waterways of central Russia to the fabled riches of the Orient. The lure of silks and spices continued to draw traders to the Baltic long after the Vikings, though it was to be the more mundane necessities of life such as furs, skins, wax and tallow which brought the Baltic into the ambit of the western European market. During the thirteenth and fourteenth centuries, the loose confederation of Westphalian and north German towns known as the Hanseatic League had built up a trading network which stretched from Novgorod in the east to Bruges and London in the west. The sturdy, clinker-built cog, capable of carrying a cargo of over 100 lasts (roughly 200 metric tons), was a familiar sight in the Atlantic waters, its white-rimmed hull betraying its Baltic origin on the more saline waters of the ocean. From the fourteenth century onwards, the Hanseatic towns favoured the larger, flat-bottomed and broader-beamed hulk, and – at the end of the Middle Ages – the three-masted carvel, with its smooth hull and high fore- and aftdecks. The hinterland of the Baltic ports offered all that was required for shipbuilding – timber, pitch and tar, flax and hemp for sails and rope – and there were shipyards in most of the ports, with repair facilities in the major harbours such as Lübeck and Danzig.

Of the men who sailed these ships, we know rather little, though the wood sculptures and altarpieces which still grace many of the former Hanseatic towns provide us with an excellent pictorial record of medieval seacraft. Navigational aids were few; the compass and sea chart appear to have been virtually unknown in the Baltic until early modern times. The *Seebuch*, a Flemish manual translated into Low German in the fifteenth century, offered sparse, if succinct navigational instructions, relying very much on landmarks and the use of the lead in shallow waters. This is how it describes the passage from Bruges to the tip of Jutland:

> Item alse gy willen seghelen ute den Swene na dat Reff, unde gy komen buten landes uppe 27 vadem, so sole gy gan nortnortost bet uppe dat Reff, unde dat kors sole gy holden so lange, dat gy uppe 40 vadem ghene grunt en hebben, dan ghaet nortosten osten, bet dat gy Jutlant seyn, unde dan moge gy juwe kors setten, dar na dat gy dat lant vorvellen bet to den Schlagen.[1]

> (If you wish to sail from the Zwijn to the Riff of Jutland, come from the shore to a depth of 27 fathoms, then sail north-north-east towards the Riff, and you should hold that course so long as you find no bottom at 40 fathoms, then set a north-north-east course until you espy Jutland, and then you may set a course which will keep you in sight of land as far as Skagen.)

The mariner passing through the narrow stretch of water known as

1. Koppmann K 1876 *Das Seebuch*. Bremen, pp 52ff.

the Sound, which separates the island of Sjælland from the province of Skåne, was advised to take his course by the church tower in Helsingør. Along the flat southern coast of the Baltic, there were a series of high church spires to guide the mariner – the 126-metre tower of St Peter in Rostock could be seen at a distance of over twenty miles on a clear day. The felling of trees on Cape Domesnäs, a vital sighting for ships sailing to Riga and the Livonian ports, by 'peasants and malicious persons' provoked a storm of protest from seafarers, and led to the erection of a tower at this crucial landmark by the Livonian towns.[2] The town council of Reval provided two barrels to guide sailors through the shoals off the port, for which a toll was levied. The council also had built a lighthouse on the westernmost tip of the island of Dagö, to warn sailors of the treacherous shoal of Neckmansgrund.

Journeys were often slow, depending heavily upon favourable winds. With a following wind, a cog could cover sixty to eighty sea miles in around twenty hours. The average duration of a voyage from Lübeck to Danzig was four days, but in bad sailing conditions, could last two weeks. Sailing in 1591 on board the *Antelope*, an English vessel of 150 tons, Fynes Moryson reached Elbing after a five days' voyage from Helsingør. It was in this East Prussian port that the English merchants of the Eastland Company settled in 1579, but they soon found it unsuitable, for reasons that Fynes Moryson noted: 'The Port of Melvin [sic] is scarce ten foot deepe, but our ship passed through the mud, like a plow upon land'.[3] In addition to the hazards of grounding in the silt washed into the Frisches Haff and the mouth of the Vistula, mariners could also be caught in the ice which made navigation in the eastern Baltic impossible from November to April. Maurauding privateers were a further hazard to navigation in the brackish waters of the 'East Sea'.

The origins of the Hanseatic League are not easy to reconstruct. German merchants trading on the island of Gotland organised themselves into a community in the latter half of the twelfth century. A century later, this Gotland community had virtually ceased to exist with the decline in importance of Visby as a trading centre, and its role was taken over by the trading towns of the southern Baltic. Urban leagues came into being during the Middle Ages to safeguard the peace and protect trade, which declining Imperial power could no longer guarantee. The league of Wendish towns, of which Lübeck was the most important, dated from the 1260s, the Prussian and Livonian

2. Goetze J 1975 Hansische Schifffahrtswege in der Ostsee *Hansische Geschichtsblätter*, **93**: 71–88.

3. Moryson F 1907 *An Itinerary* (reprint edn) (4 vols). Glasgow, vol.1 pp. 129.

leagues from the fourteenth century. The merchants of the Hanse always sought to deny that they were anything other than 'a firm *confederatio* of many cities, towns and communities for the purpose of ensuring that business enterprises by land and sea should have a favoured and desired outcome'; but they wielded considerable political power, as the rulers of England, the Low Countries and the Northern kingdoms found to their cost.[4]

By the end of the fifteenth century, however, the Hanse was no longer the political power it had been, though Lübeck was still capable of playing a crucial role in the conflict between Denmark and Sweden over the union of the three Scandinavian crowns during the fifteenth and early sixteenth centuries. The Hanse's dominance of the sea routes of northern Europe was also coming to an end. The first recorded Sound Dues – the toll levied by the king of Denmark on ships passing into and out of the Baltic through the narrow stretch of water between Helsingør and Hälsingborg – show that already by 1497, the bulk of the vessels were from the Zuider Zee towns. With their superior ships and trading techniques, the Dutch were to become the undisputed masters of the Baltic's international trade during the sixteenth century. The Hanse towns also suffered from the competition of the big south German merchant families such as the Fuggers. Their methods of conducting business were often antiquated, and inadequate, and their cohesion began to decline under pressure from the rulers around the Baltic. The penetration of Baltic markets by the Dutch also caused the towns to fall out. Lübeck and its neighbours in the Wendish league strove to exclude the Dutch as much as possible, since the Sound route took trade away from the overland route across the Holstein peninsula, which Lübeck had controlled for centuries. For the towns of the eastern Baltic on the other hand, the appearance of the Dutch fleet in the spring was a welcome sight, and the actions taken by the Lübeckers to stop the Dutch trade aroused much resentment. Even her neighbours and allies began to weary of the hectoring tone of Lübeck's emissaries, urging them to join the fight against the interlopers from the Low Countries. In 1533, for example, the city of Hamburg quietly detached itself from the anti-Dutch coalition to make a secret agreement with Amsterdam, which was an excellent customer for Hamburg-brewed beer. In the end, only the small and relatively insignificant towns of the Mecklenburg coast remained obedient to Lübeck's call.

4. Reply of the Hanseatic League to the English Privy Council, after the arrest of Hanseatic merchants in London, cited in Dollinger P 1970 *The German Hansa*, pp. 411–3.

The mainstay of Lübeck's medieval prosperity had rested on two commodities – the fine salt pumped to the surface at Lüneburg, and the shoals of herring caught off Skåne. By the early sixteenth century, the herring fisheries, though still bountiful, were no longer as the Danish chronicler Saxo Grammaticus had portrayed them – so teeming with fish that nets were unnecessary to catch them. The Dutch, with their supplies of cheaper salt from the Bay of Bourgneuf, and their superior gutting and preserving techniques, had begun to oust the Lübeckers from the market. But in spite of this competition, the Lübeckers were still capable of opening up new markets, particularly in Spain. Much of the trade between the ports of the Baltic remained in the hands of the Lübeckers. In 1593, Lübeck had a fleet of 253 ships, and the shipyards were turning out fifteen to twenty new vessels annually. The great historian of the Hanse, Walther Vogel, estimated the total tonnage of the Hanseatic towns at the end of the sixteenth century to be 90,000 metric tons, 50 per cent greater than one hundred years previously. With a mercantile fleet of around one thousand ships, the Hanse was by no means a spent force, even if it no longer exercised supreme control over the Baltic trade.

During the late Middle Ages, the focus of international trading activity in the Baltic had begun to shift eastwards. German merchants had established a trading post in Novgorod, the Peterhof *Kontor*, in the thirteenth century. By the fifteenth century, the Lübeckers had lost control over the Novgorod *Kontor* to the Livonian towns. Trade in Novgorod was already in decline, however. In 1494, when Ivan III, grand duke of Muscovy, closed the Peterhof, there were only forty-nine German merchants left in the town. The trade for Russian goods had to a large extent shifted to the Livonian towns, which derived much benefit from this. Their refusal to permit direct trading between foreign merchants within their walls irritated the Wendish towns, who were thereby prevented from negotiating directly with the Russian merchants. The reopening of the Novgorod *Kontor* in 1514 was not a success. Non-Hanseatic merchants were permitted to trade in the town, and the Russian merchants continued to use the overland route to the main ports of Estonia and Livonia.

The Russian hinterland could be reached along the waterways, by the river Neva into Lake Ladoga and then down the river Volchov, or down the Narova river to Pskov. In both cases, however, waterfalls were an obstacle to transport, and the overland route via Reval, Riga or Pernau was preferred by most merchants. In 1346, the right of emporium was guaranteed to these three ports by the Hanse, which meant that all goods destined for the Russian market had to be unloaded, weighed and reloaded in these towns. To avoid this delay, most foreign traders preferred to sell their goods directly to the *koplude* (merchants) of the town. The burghers of these towns jealously guarded their rights as intermediaries. The *bursprake*, a catalogue of the principal rules and regulations of the town which was proclaimed annually from a window of the town hall in Reval, declared unequivocally: 'Ein borger cope als ein borger, ein gast als ein gast' (a burgher trades as a burgher, a guest [foreign merchant] as a guest). The towns of Estonia and Livonia also tried to exclude the indigenous peoples, whom they referred to as 'non-Germans' (*undutsche*) from trading activities. But in spite of regulations and prosecutions, many merchants engaged natives as agents for the trade with the hinterland. Most of the petty trading in these towns was in the hands of non-Germans, who hawked fish and peddled buttons, chains, pins and other gewgaws.[5]

The main commodities from the Russian hinterland during the Middle Ages were wax and furs, though train-oil, leather, sturgeon, isinglass and even Oriental goods were traded. The growth of the shipbuilding industry in the west during the age of maritime exploration and expansion stimulated demand for materials which grew in abundance in the hinterland of the Baltic ports. Flax and hemp from White Russia and Lithuania were transported in barges down the river Düna to be exported from Riga. By the end of the sixteenth century, these two commodities had become the mainstays of Riga's trade. Riga also developed a brisk trade in masts to the west, preparing them from tree trunks floated down the Düna. Flax and hemp were also exported from the Prussian ports, principally Königsberg, which also sold large quantities of pitch and tar, and ash, used for soap manufacture and glass-making.

Before the fifteenth century, the Dutch were little seen in Baltic waters. The first mention of Dutch traders in Novgorod is in 1432, when they appeared in the town, selling herring, cloth and French salt. By the middle of the century, they were becoming frequent visitors. The importance of the Dutch trade to the towns of the eastern Baltic may be gauged from a report to the Regent of the Netherlands by Maximilian Transilvan, the Imperial emissary to Hamburg, in 1534:

> The whole profit and increase of the kingdom of Poland and the said town of Danzig lies in this, that the Hollanders come every year once or twice to

5. Johansen P, von zur Mühlen H 1973 *Deutsch und Undeutsch im mittelalterlichen und frühzeitlichen Reval*. Cologne–Vienna, pp. 140–54, 434.

Danzig with two or three hundred ships, to buy and take off in fourteen days all the grain that they find in the said town of Danzig. For in the past twenty-five years all the great lords of Poland and Prussia have discovered therein the means of sending by certain rivers all their grain to Danzig and there to have it sold to those of the said town. And for this reason the kingdom of Poland and the great lords have become mightily rich. For before this time, they knew not what to do with their grain and left their lands uncultivated, and the town of Danzig, which was nothing but a village, is at this time the most powerful and richest city in all the Eastland sea.[6]

In the summer of 1481, a Danzig shipowner recorded that over one thousand ships, great and small, laden with corn, sailed westwards from the port, bound for Holland, Zeeland and Flanders. A century later, the port was regularly visited by over two thousand ships annually, carrying off quantities of grain from the Polish hinterland to the Amsterdam market. Almost half of the entire trade of the city of Amsterdam was with Danzig, which was also the port of origin of nearly 80 per cent of the rye imported into the Dutch city in the sixteenth century. So important was the trade that Dutch merchants refused to stop re-exporting Baltic grain to the Iberian peninsula during the war against Habsburg Spain. Small wonder that the Dutch saw the grain trade as 'the source and root of the most notable commerce and navigation of these lands'.[7]

But if the Dutch prospered, so did the city of Danzig. Its merchant fleet, which had rivalled that of Lübeck in the Middle Ages, had dwindled to a few dozen small ships by 1600. The Danzig merchants preferred to amass safe profits, thanks to their monopoly of trade in the town, rather than risk their capital on overseas ventures in competition with the Dutch, with their cheaper freight rates, modern commercial methods and sophisticated credit system. The city attracted large numbers of immigrants from the surrounding districts, and from further afield. The religious wars drove many hundreds of refugees out of the Low Countries to settle in Danzig, bringing with them skills and new techniques. Danzig became a manufacturing centre, producing cheap goods for the mass market, and higher-quality items such as furniture, glass, paper and spinning-wheels, which were in demand all over the Baltic area. By the end of the

6. Häpke R (ed.) 1913 *Niederländischen Akten und Urkunden zur Geschichte der Hanse und zur deutschen Seegeschichte* (2 vols). Munich–Leipzig, vol. 1. p. 200.
7. Faber J 1966 The decline of the Baltic grain trade in the second half of the seventeenth century *Acta Historica Neerlandica* **1**: 108. See also Malowist M 1959 The economic and social development of the Baltic countries from the fifteenth to the seventeenth centuries *Economic History Review* Second Series, **12**: 177–189.

sixteenth century, the town council claimed a population of one hundred thousand in the city and its suburbs. This may have been a pardonable exaggeration, but even at half that number of inhabitants, Danzig was the largest city by far in Poland, five times greater than Warsaw, the royal capital.[8]

Danzig's export trade was dominated by two products: timber and grain. The dense forests of oak and pine, which stretched deep into Lithuania, provided the wood which was converted into deals, boards, *Klappholz*, used for making barrels, and *Wagenschoss*, or split oak used in shipbuilding, pitch and tar. The demand for Mazovian timber was so great that large numbers of peasant foresters settled in the area. Timber and grain were transported to the ports along the rivers, and here Danzig was fortunate, since trade along the Oder was disrupted by the constant feuding of the nobility of Brandenburg and Pomerania, and the rivers Niemen and Düna had a shorter floating season, and were made hazardous to boatmen by hidden rocks and shoals. Much of the Polish grain trade by the middle of the sixteenth century was in the hands of the gentry, who were able to secure favourable legislation in the Polish diet, the *sejm*, to protect their interests. It was common for the Danzig merchants to pay in advance for deliveries to be made at the producer's own risk and expense. This had the advantage for the merchant of ensuring control over supplies, though it has also been argued that it may have helped force up the price of grain on the Amsterdam market.

English merchants had managed to establish a trading company in Danzig during the reign of Richard II, but this did not prosper, and England remained largely dependent on the Hanse for its Baltic supplies until well into the sixteenth century. Richard Chancellor's discovery of a new route to Russia in 1553 via the White Sea opened up the possibility of new markets for English cloth. Almost one-third of the founding members of the Muscovy Company were cloth exporters, and great hopes were entertained of the new route. It was believed that the English merchants had stolen a march on their rivals. Richard Chancellor's companion, John Hasse, reported in 1554 that:

> Our merchants may doe well to provide for the Russes such wares as the Dutch nation doth serve them of, as Flanders and Holland clothes, which I believe, they shal serve better and with lesse charge than they of Rye or Dorpt or Revel: for it is no smal adventure to bringe their clothes out of Flanders to either of these places and their charge not a litle to carry them over lande to Novgorode which is from Rye 900 Russian miles.[9]

8. Bogucka M 1984 Danzig an der Wende zur Neuzeit: von der aktiven Handelstadt zum Stapel und Produktionszentrum. *Hansische Geschichtsblätter*, **102**: 1–103.

The opening up of the White Sea passage certainly appears to have alarmed the rivals of the newly founded Muscovy Company, but it never developed into a major trade route. The voyage around the North Cape was hazardous: of the three vessels which set off from London on 20 May 1553, two stranded on the coast of Lapland, and their crews perished. Port facilities were virtually non-existent, even after the founding of Archangel, and the supply of goods for export was always unreliable. The capture of Narva by the Russians in 1558 opened up a new point of access to Russian markets, which the Livonian towns were no longer able to control (although they strove mightily to hinder the passage of vessels to the town). The following year, the governor of the town of Viborg could report to the king of Sweden that an English merchant was about to return home to tell his fellow countrymen that they no longer needed to sail the long route around Norway, since they could get all the goods they wanted in the tsar's new staple port of Narva. In 1564, Sir Nicholas Bacon opined that the Narva trade was 'the best traffique for the commoditie of the realme that hath bene founde in our age'. Unfortunately for the Muscovy Company, however, non-members or 'outleapers' were busily trading in Narva, and in spite of the Privy Council's injunctions, continued to do so.[10]

Trade in the Baltic was extremely sensitive to sudden fluctuations in the market and to political instability. The surviving commercial correspondence between factors and principals offer a rich illustration of this. Heavily interlarded with pious phrases, the letters of the agents of Lübeck merchants in Riga and Königsberg record the arrival of ships, the fluctuation of prices and of market demand. Writing to Albert Bischof of Lübeck on 4 June 1458, Hinrik May in Riga praised God for the safe arrival of the *Bayvar*, the ships carrying salt from the Bay of Bourgneuf, but immediately fell into gloomy speculation on what would happen to prices if the Dutch arrived. The prospect of war between the Order and the king of Poland also threatened trade. The letter concluded:

> I and my wife thank you greatly for your barrels of berries and the barrel of apples. God let me serve. I know of nothing special to write to you concerning trade; there is nothing much doing here. The cloths will not sell, the Russians will have no cloths, especially Flemish cloths which they

do not now ask much after, that makes good business for English cloths...[11]

A century later, the Danzig agent of Thomas Sexton had to try and sell a consignment of 3,800 coney skins. He complained that the price in the town had fallen and that most of the skins were 'so ettyn with worms...that I cane get no mony for them'.[12] As his ability to buy commodities in the local market was largely determined by the price he could obtain for consignments from England, his anxiety was clearly understandable. Further insights into the rumour-laden and fiercely competitive world of sixteenth-century commerce can be found in the dealings of the Muscovy Company. In 1567, having heard of a rumour that peace was about to be concluded between Denmark and Sweden, the Company instructed its agents in Russia to

> send our seruuntes to Nougorode the grett, Plasco [Pskov] and the townes of the trade adioyning, to engrosse and buy vpp all, or as much as they can, of wax, fflax, Tallowe &c goods, commodities for these partes, to staye the Russes from Rie and Reuell... ffor our speciall entent is to preuent the Russes trade to Rie and Reuell, if it were possible the trade of ye Nerue [Narva] being shutt vp from vs by any meanes.'[13]

Faced with increasing competition from the North Sea traders, the merchants of the Hanseatic towns strove vigorously to uphold their trading privileges. In particular, they sought to eliminate direct trade between foreigners in their towns, and to prevent the rural population engaging in active trade. In this they were not always successful. The towns of Pomerania and Mecklenburg were unable to halt the encroachments upon their liberties by the rulers and nobility, or to prevent the widespread illicit trading between nobles and foreign merchants in the *Klipphäfen* or cliff harbours, along the coast. The island of Fehmarn, close to the Danish islands, for example, was much favoured as a market for the corn trade. In the Northern kingdoms, where towns were few and extremely small, active trade was largely in the hands of the rural population. It has been estimated, for example, that the seaborne peasant trade from the Danish islands to the north German coast constituted the most important element of active Danish trade at the end of the Middle Ages. In spite of the hostility of the Swedish regents to rural trade, the sheer absence of

11. Stein W 1898 Handelsbriefe aus Riga und Königsberg. *Hansische Geschichtsblätter*, **4**: 90–1.
12. Zins 1972 p. 303.
13. Attman A 1973 The Russian and Polish Markets in International Trade 1500–1650 Publications of the Institute of Economic History of Gothenburg University 26, Göteborg, p. 27.

towns within the Swedish kingdom meant that any sanctions were ineffective. Finnish peasants preferred to sail across the Gulf of Finland to Reval, rather than trade with their own towns. The church was also actively engaged in trade. The activities of the dean of Åbo cathedral were so vigorous that they provoked complaints from the town's merchants. Påvel Sckeel, the cathedral dean in the 1470s, had business connections from Lübeck to Reval, selling butter, salmon, hides and furs, and buying salt, hops, wine, herrings and cloth. He also bought plate and altarpieces for the cathedral. Even parish priests along the Finnish coast appear to have been actively involved in trade. Surplus produce of monastic and cathedral lands was also sold: the cathedral estates at Linköping in central Sweden traded throughout the region, even selling to Dutch merchants at the mouth of the Göta river. In Holstein, the monks of Preetz abbey fattened cattle for export, as did the local nobility. The Danish nobles were also actively engaged in commerce, and were sufficiently powerful to be able to compel Christian II to renew their right of free trade with foreign merchants in 1513. Considerable numbers of winter-fed cattle were driven along the drove roads of the heaths of Jutland to Hamburg, a trade in which the Danish nobilty was heavily involved.

The publication in the early decades of this century of tables listing the passage of ships and their cargoes through the Sound has provided historians with a major source for the study of Baltic trade, though it is a source which needs to be treated with some caution. The nationality of the skipper recorded in the registers is not necessarily a clear indication of his port of origin; many ships may well have called at more than one port in the Baltic, though this is not shown in the toll-books. The Sound dues also record only the trade passing through one entrance into the Baltic; the overland trade from Lübeck across the Holstein peninsula, and shipping through the Belts is totally omitted. In all likelihood, there was a considerable amount of smuggling or illicit avoidance of the tolls.

In spite of these reservations, the registers of the Sound dues are still the best general indicator of the volume and nature of trade into and from the Baltic. The registers for the period 1557–88 reveal that an annual average of 1,690 ships sailed westward from the ports of Prussia and Livonia, reaching a peak of over two thousand in the early 1580s. Over two-thirds of these vessels had traded with Danzig: Königsberg and Riga were the only other ports regularly visited by more than one hundred ships a year.[14]

14. See Christiansen A 1935 Der handelsgeschichtliche Wert der Sundzollregister *Hansische Geschichtsblätter* **59**: 28–142. Jeannin P 1964 Les comptes du Sund comme

The evidence of the toll registers would also suggest that the value of exports from the Baltic was on average double the value of imports, of which salt, wine and cloth were the most important commodities. Salt was used in great quantities to preserve food. The northern lands lacked natural salt deposits and the sudden cutting off of supplies from the west could spell disaster. In the 1550s, Gustav Vasa of Sweden prudently laid by large quantities of salt in a few central locations, and these stores were to prove a godsend to Sweden during the Northern Seven Years' War (1563–70), when access to supplies was severely restricted by the Danish enemy. In 1566, with stocks running dangerously low, the Swedish navy managed to capture the entire Dutch salt fleet of fifty-two ships. The cargo of 84,000 barrels of salt was the equivalent of a year's supply for the entire kingdom, and the success of the Swedish fleet enabled the king to continue the war and to avoid a potentially explosive situation at home.[15]

Salt was virtually the only commodity for which there was a mass market in northern Europe. Cloths, foodstuffs, spices and wines were unlikely to appeal to a largely self-sufficient and impoverished peasantry, though they did find a better market in the towns of the southern Baltic. But the balance of the Baltic trade was very heavily tilted in favour of the bulky export goods to the West. Taking all other factors into account, it would seem that large sums of ready money were brought into the Baltic area to pay for commodities, though the amounts and their impact on the economy of the region have been hotly disputed. The Livonian Diet in 1529, for example, in deciding to set up a system of quality inspection for Russian flax and hemp, noted that there had been many complaints about the impure quality of these goods, whilst the Russians received 'reyne sulver, besegelde lake, wichtlicke gulde, gewracheden heringk und ander vaste guder', in other words, certified bona fide commodities and precious metals. The inventories of cargoes of ships bound for the Russian market from Lübeck also reveal that large quantities of coin and precious metals were on board.[16]

source pour la construction d'indices généraux de l'activité économique en Europe (XVIe–XVIIIe siècles). *Revue Historique* 231: 55ff. Schildhauer J 1972 Zum Handel der Seestädte des südostichen Küstengebietes der Ostsee in der Zeit des Beginns des Kampfes um das Dominium maris Baltici, in Siilivask K (ed.) *Problemyi razvitiya feodalizma i kapitalizma v stranakh Baltiki.* Tartu, pp. 21–46.

15. Hildebrand K-G 1954 Salt and cloth in Swedish economic history. *Scandinavian Economic History Review* 2: 74–102.

16. Attman 1973 pp. 103–114, 119ff.

THE LAND

The economy of the sparsely populated regions on the northern shores of the Baltic was to a very great extent determined by the forces of nature. Clearings had to be hacked out of the dense bush and forest, and could easily revert to wilderness if left for even a short period. The harsh winter climate and poor soil made cultivation of the land a hazardous business. Grain yields were poor, even in good years: summer droughts or early frosts could spell disaster. Well into the nineteenth century, peasants in eastern and northern Finland and the remoter parts of Sweden regularly mixed ground tree bark with their flour in order to make bread. Beyond the settled areas of the Bothnian coastal plain and south-west Finland stretched vast expanses of forest, into which settlers only began to penetrate in any numbers in the sixteenth century. The forest was a vital and integral part of the natural economy of the peasantry. It provided fuel and building material; barrels, tubs, drinking vessels, platters, spoons and furniture were fashioned out of wood; even the bark of the birch tree was utilised in the making of bast shoes and baskets. The wildlife of the forests supplemented the meagre everyday fare of hard bread and salt fish; and the plentiful waters of northern Europe teemed with fish, which were smoked, dried, salted and pickled for domestic consumption and sale.

North of 58° latitude, the climate made stock-rearing a risky venture for the small farmer, since cattle had to be overwintered indoors for many months, consuming quantities of fodder and yielding little in return which could be consumed by the family. On the other hand, animal manure was essential for arable cultivation, though other methods of fertilisation were resorted to. In forested areas, trees were felled and burned, and crops sown in the ash-enriched soil. Yields were often high, but the land was rapidly exhausted, and the method was also extremely wasteful. Ash was also obtained by the burning of twigs and straw, and in coastal regions, seaweed was also used on the land.[17]

The main cereals grown were rye and barley. Indeed, in Denmark, the yield of 'hard grain' (*hartkorn*) was the yardstick by which land was measured. Much of this barley was malted for brewing; the consumption of beer appears to have been prodigious, though in view of the salty diet, hardly surprising. Beer flavoured with herbs and spices was

---

17. An exposition of the various methods of burn-beat cultivation can be found in Soininen A 1964 Burn-beating as a technical basis for colonisation. *Scandinavian Economic History Review* **12**: 143–62.

consumed to ward off illness and aid digestion; it was mixed with stale bread to make a thick soup; a pot of ale broke the fast in the morning and sent the weary worker to bed. A daily consumption of three or four litres was considered normal, even for children; the beadles in the workhouse for children in Copenhagen were instructed to lock the wells when they were not in use to prevent the inmates drinking the unwholesome waters. Rye was the principal bread grain in the southern Baltic; barley bread and oatmeal cakes and gruel were the staple food in Sweden and Finland, though the cultivation of rye was beginning to make headway in these northern lands by the sixteenth century.

The vastness of the forests and the lack of human habitation – few indeed were the places where one could stand in sight of a church tower denoting the presence of a village – the difficulty of the terrain, which could vary from stony outcrops of rock to bogland within a matter of miles, and the harsh climate made travelling a hazardous business. Roads were few, and ill-kept. Town streets were mired with mud and filth so deep that horses sank up to their haunches in wet weather. The swiftest means of transport in winter was by horse-drawn sledge, over the frozen waterways, which were also the safest and best means of communication in the summer. Military campaigns were usually conducted either in the depths of winter, or in the high summer, since army commanders could be reasonably sure that their troops, baggage and artillery would be able to move about, and not get bogged down in the floods and mire of the spring thaw or autumn rains.

In the vast tracts of the Swedish realm, which stretched from the stony province of Småland through the more fertile central plains of Östergötland and Uppland along the long arm of the Gulf of Bothnia, and reached across to embrace the Finnish provinces as far as the Karelian isthmus, there lived fewer than one million people in 1500. The great majority were peasants. The towns were little more than overgrown villages. Even Stockholm, with a population of six to seven thousand, was insignificant in comparison with Lübeck and Danzig, both of which had over twenty thousand inhabitants in 1500, and its small merchant community was largely German. There were relatively few monastic foundations, and these were poor in comparison with the houses in western Europe. The church in 1500 owned about one-fifth of the land in Sweden, about the same proportion as the nobility. The crown owned a meagre 5 per cent. The remaining half of the land was owned by freehold peasants (in Finland, 95 per cent). It was the continued existence of a numerically strong class of freehold, tax-paying peasants (*skattebönder*) more than anything else, which ensured that Sweden would not go the way of Denmark or the lands colonised by the Germans, where the status and rights of the peasantry were under severe threat.

The causes of the imposition of neo-serfdom on the peasantry of eastern Europe have been the subject of much intense debate amongst historians. Some have suggested that the demand for grain, which could only be kept at a competitive price level by the use of cheap, servile labour, was the stimulus to the enserfment of the peasantry. Others have argued that the noble landlords east of the Elbe were able to deprive the peasant of his rights and liberties because these had been received as inducements to colonise the area, not won in long struggles against the landowner. The security of the peasantry was thus fragile, and once disturbed by the ravages of war, plague and famine, it was lost.[18]

Historians are in general agreement that the process of colonisation in the lands between the Oder and the Niemen was beginning to slacken during the late Middle Ages, and that tracts of land brought under the plough were being abandoned. There is evidence of deserted villages in Brandenburg as early as 1337; plague and incessant warfare further increased the flight from the land. In Prussia, the decline in population seems to have set in during the fifteenth century, as the supply of immigrants from Germany dried up, and a series of bloody wars between the Order and Poland broke out. In 1412, the Grand Master issued ordinances decreeing that no peasant or cottager should be received into any town unless he could prove that he had left the land with his lord's consent. Further regulations, fixing the maximum level of wages and seeking to arrest the flight from the land, were passed in subsequent years. The peasants also were obliged to perform more labour services, which limited the amount of time they could spend in cultivating their own holdings. The Thirteen Years' War (1453–66) between Poland and Prussia, which ended in defeat for the Order and the loss of Culmerland, Pomerelia, and the city of Danzig, caused further devastation and depopulation. In Prussia and Poland, the position of the peasant had deteriorated considerably by the beginning of the sixteenth century. From 1521, Polish peasants no longer had the right to appeal against their lords in royal courts: the ordinances of 1494 in Prussia stipulated that runaway peasants were to be handed back to their masters, who could have them hanged; a run-

---

18. Cf. Brenner R 1976, 1982 Agrarian class structure and economic development in pre-industrial Europe *Past and Present* **70**: 53–59, and **97**: 66–76. Criticisms of Brenner's views may be found in the same journal, **78**, 1978: 24–55.

away servant was to be nailed by the ear to the pillory, with a knife to free himself. The position of the peasantry had also begun to worsen in Pomerania, Brandenburg and Mecklenburg, though there were still many who enjoyed a degree of independent prosperity, such as the peasants on the island of Rügen. The Pomeranian chronicler Thomas Kantzow observed in the 1540s that the status of the peasants in the duchy was by no means equal. Some possessed the right of inheritance for their farms, paid moderate dues and had to render limited services. They could also sell their farms, paying the lord a tithe of the sale price, and depart freely. Others were less fortunate, as Kantzow noted:

> They have no heritage to their farms and must serve the lord as often as he wants them, and often they cannot do their own work because of these services and thus they become impoverished and abscond. And amongst these peasants there is a saying, that they only serve six days in the week, on the seventh they have to carry letters. And verily these peasants are little more than villeins, for the lord drives them away as he pleases.[19]

There were pockets of free and prosperous peasants elsewhere, such as the *Cölmische Freie*, who owned over 15 per cent of the land in Prussia, and who had the right to present their grievances to the Diet, and the so-called 'Curonian kings' in Livonia, who performed military service but were exempt from other obligations to the Order. The general obligation of the Livonian peasants to render military service was however ended in 1498 in favour of a special tax, and nine years later, they lost the basic right of the freeman to bear arms. The term 'hereditary peasant' (*erfbur*) was increasingly used in Livonia in the fifteenth century. The agricultural crisis following the Black Death had plunged many peasants into debt to their landlords, who were willing to lend cattle, draught animals and seed-corn in order not to lose their main source of revenue, the tithes and other contributions paid by the peasantry. By the end of the fifteenth century, the assumption had taken root that every peasant was a debtor of the manor, and could not leave the estate without the consent of his landlord. He was also obliged to render labour service on the manorial estate. *Adscriptus glebae*, the attachment of the peasants to the estate, did not deprive them of all rights: but in the words of the Latvian historian Arnolds Svabe:

---

19. Kosegarten H (ed.) 1817 *Pomerania oder Ursprunck, Altheit und Geschicht der Völcker und lande Pomern, Cassuben, Wenden, Stettin, Rhügen...von Thomas Kantzow* (2 vols). Greifswald, vol. 2, pp. 418–19. On developments in Prussia, see Carsten F 1954 *The Origins of Prussia*. Oxford, pp. 101–16.

The serf established in the domain of a fief lost his direct subjection to the paramount power, he became in some sort mediatised. Between the sovereign and himself the vassal had stepped in, and now began to consider the fief as a separate territory and its inhabitants as his subjects. Thus serfdom became a real and personal dependence; the hereditary peasant had not only become an appurtenance of the fief but to a certain degree was bound to the person of his hereditary lord.[20]

A not dissimilar trend can be observed in Denmark and the duchies of Slesvig and Holstein, though with certain significant differences. During the fifteenth century, in the area covered by Sjælland Law (i.e., the islands of Sjælland, Møn, Lolland and Falster), the system of *vornedskab* became established. This obliged all rural commoners to remain on the estate where they were born and to accept whatever holding the landowner allotted to them. If they left the estate without permission, the lord was entitled to fetch them back, if necessary by force. Demographic decline, the subsequent shortage of labour, and falling agricultural prices may well have prompted the landowners of the fifteenth century to tie the peasantry to the land, at a time of weak central power. But the peasants still retained their legal status and rights. In the fertile parts of Holstein, where noble estates were generally cohesive units, the lords had their own courts and the right to administer corporal and capital punishment upon their peasants (*Hals- und Handrecht*). In Denmark, where estates were often widely dispersed, there were fewer manorial courts, and justice was largely administered by the *herredsting*, in which the peasants played an active role. The Danish nobility sought on several occasions to extend their control over the peasantry. In 1513, they demanded of the newly elected Christian II the same rights over their servants and tied peasants (*vornede*) as the 'good men' of Holstein. Christian II sought to secure the rights of tenants in his Land Law of 1521, which decreed that tenancies should be for a minimum of eight years, and that tenants should not be evicted as long as they maintained the farm, paid the annual rent and performed labour services, and were 'obedient' towards their landlords. Article Three of this law denounced the 'evil and unchristian custom' of *vornedskab* and would have permitted tenants who had suffered ill-usage or injustice at the hand of their landlord to move freely. Most of the provisions of this law, however, were revoked after Christian II was overthrown two years later. In his electoral pact (*håndfæstning*), the new king Frederik I agreed to the right of landowners to compel peasants to take up any tenancy they were offered, and to evict 'after the customs and the law of the land'.[21]

20. Schwabe A n.d. *Agrarian History of Latvia*. Riga, p. 45.

The rights of the nobility to exploit the labour of the tenants upon their estates was given firm force in the Recess of Kolding in 1558. However, manorial estates constituted only a small proportion of the cultivated land in Denmark: small-scale peasant tenant farming was the principal characteristic of Danish agriculture.

In the less fertile parts of Slesvig and along the marshy coastline of the North Sea, there were few noble estates and the peasantry here were mostly freeholders or tenant-farmers with relatively light obligations. In the fertile eastern half of Holstein, however, there were many rich and extensive estates, and here the peasants were burdened with labour services and subject to the lord's rule. On their estates, the landowners fattened cattle and pigs, produced grain, and developed enterprises such as hop-growing, bee-keeping, lumber-milling and glass-blowing. The principal city of the region, Kiel, was very much a centre for aristocratic entrepreneurs, not least as a money market. The annual fair, the *Kieler Umschlag*, attracted hundreds of noblemen and institutions strapped for cash; even the emperor sought to raise a loan in the 1590s to finance the war against the Turks. The sight of impoverished Danish noblemen begging on the streets of Kiel moved the Danish cleric and historian Anders Vedel to anger in 1591. In 1604, the Danish state council argued strongly against war with Sweden on the grounds that 'the nobility of this realm are greatly impoverished, so they are unable to bear any extraordinary costs, and a great part of them are heavily in debt to the land of Holstein'.[22] The only ones to cock a snook at the wealthy magnates were the peasants of Dithmarsch, who managed to inflict a sharp defeat on the heavily armoured *Lansknechte* of king Hans of Denmark in 1500. Safe in their fenny fastness on the North Sea coast, which they defended by cutting the dykes and flooding out incursors, they 'long preserved a rude or rurall libertie', as Fynes Moryson observed in the 1590s.[23] The wealthier peasants of the marshland were active traders, fattening cattle in

21. For a discussion of the system of *vornedskab*, see Skrubbeltrang F 1979 *Det danske landbosamfund 1500-1800*. Copenhagen, pp. 18–25. Munck T 1979 *The Peasantry and the Early Absolute Monarchy in Denmark 1660-1708*. Copenhagen, pp. 175f. See also Ladewig Petersen E 1980 *Fra standssamfund til rangssamfund 1500-1700* (Dansk social historie, vol. 3). Copenhagen.

22. Erslev K 1883 *Aktstykker og Oplysninger til Rigsraadets og Stændermødernes Historie* (3 vols). Copenhagen, vol. 1. p. 127. See also Ladewig Petersen E 1968 La crise de la noblesse danoise entre 1580 et 1660 *Annales*, **23**: pp. 1237–61; and Kellenbenz H 1954 German aristocratic entrepreneurship. Economic activities of the Holstein nobility in the sixteenth and seventeenth centuries *Explorations in Entrepreneurial History* **6**: 103–114.

23. Moryson 1908 vol. 4, p. 65. The peasants of Dithmarsch and Fehmarn were also actively involved in the Baltic trade: see Reuter C 1912 *Ostseehandel und Landwirtschaft im sechzehnten und siebzehnten Jahrhundert*. Berlin, pp. 18–29.

their meadows and exporting them to Holland and the East Frisian ports. With their ornate, two-storeyed houses, they constituted a kind of lesser gentry during the prosperous decades of the sixteenth century.

The recovery of agriculture from the crises of the late Middle Ages, and the rise of the Baltic grain market should not blind us to the fact that this recovery was uneven, and fragile. There was no take-off to sustained growth. Techniques remained primitive, and the evidence would suggest that the expansion of demesne estates was not accompanied by a rise in productivity; if anything, levels of output declined. Cereal yields throughout the Baltic region were poor. Whereas in western Europe, the ratio of grain yield per seed sown seems to have been between 6 to 8, the figure in much of eastern Europe was around 3. The livestock was scraggy and underweight: pigs in sixteenth-century Slesvig-Holstein weighed 42–48 kilogrammes, compared with weights of 55 to 90 kilogrammes in Lombardy. In the seventeenth century, the average annual butter yield of a cow in Livonia was a mere 12½ kilogrammes, one-tenth of the yield of a twentieth-century milch cow. The cattle which managed to survive the long northern winter were often so weak that they had to be carried out to the spring pastures.

The opening up of new trade routes across the Atlantic, the growth of the towns and manufactories of western Europe, and the general upsurge in economic activity also affected the Baltic region. The demand for northern European commodities shifted from the products of a hunting economy to grain, timber and naval stores, for which the traders were willing to pay ready cash. We know rather little about the effects of this influx of money and precious metals, some of which doubtless found its way into the pockets of the more prosperous peasant farmers and craftsmen. A tenant farmer on the island of Lolland in 1505, for example, was the owner of fifteen milch cows, and a fortune of 14 Rhine guilders, 16 Danish marks and 4 German marks, two gold rings and numerous silver ornaments, and clothes made from Flemish, Dutch and English cloth. Peasant wills on the island of Rügen also reveal a degree of modest prosperity. A middle-ranking merchant or tradesman might possess a fortune of between 2,000 and 5,000 thousand marks, a wealthy wholesale merchant engaged in long-distance trade might be worth far more. Johann Bussmann of Lübeck had a capital of over 40,000 marks in the early sixteenth century, large by northern European standards, but tiny in comparison with the Fuggers' fortune of 375,000 marks in 1511. Even the fortunes of the noble landowners were relatively modest in comparison with those of the great magnates of the more prosperous lands in western Europe. The further north one travelled, the less money played a part in the economy. Peasants in Sweden and Livonia usually paid their rent and dues in kind – barrels of butter, herring, even furs and skins. This had the advantage of protecting the landlords from price inflation, and may have been one reason why serfdom took longer to establish itself in Livonia. But it also caused problems for ambitious monarchs whose costs were rising, and who needed ready cash with which to pay their mercenary soldiers.

The most striking feature of the Baltic economy in the sixteenth century was the growth of the grain trade. Given that seed ratios were low, and that there appears to have been a declining rate of productivity, at least in the seventeenth century, it can only be imagined that the producers were operating on very narrow margins, which bad harvests, storms, drought and especially the ravages of war could easily destroy. Although there appears to have been a general upward trend in the volume of grain exported through the Sound from the middle of the sixteenth century to the 1620s, there were periods in which exports slumped, such as the 1580s. In the peak years of the 1590s, the annual total volume of grain sent through the Sound varied between 50,000 and 80,000 thousand lasts (a last is roughly 2.3 tons), of which Danzig and Königsberg supplied by far the greatest share. That the producers of the southern Baltic hinterland could export such quantities was due in large measure to their exploitation of cheap, servile labour (which was by no means a permanent advantage, as the landowners of the seventeenth century were to discover), and the smallness of the domestic market. It has been estimated, for example, that 30–35,000 lasts annually would have been needed to feed the entire population of Estonia (slightly over a quarter of a million people) in the mid-sixteenth century; at about the same period, the total volume of grain exported from Estonian ports has been estimated at around 10,000 lasts – a considerable surplus, in other words. Most of the corn was grown on peasant farms, which far outnumbered the holdings of the nobility, though it was mostly marketed by the nobles. It was generally reckoned that the yield of the grain sown was fourfold, of which the peasant paid one-quarter to the lord in corn-tax, reserving another quarter as seed, leaving half of the crop for sustenance and profit.[24] In other words, the export drive in the grain market came from an area of Europe where agricultural yields were low, and the

---

24. Doroshenko V *et al.* 1974 *Trade and Agrarian Development in the Baltic Provinces 15th-19th Centuries*. Tallinn, pp. 5–7.

circumstances of soil and climate not favourable. It was achieved at the cost of tying the peasant to the estate of his lord, and depriving him of most of his rights and liberties: and it probably weakened the independence and vitality of the domestic market. In seeking to overcome the problem of falling real income by the use of unfree labour to produce a crop for which there was a demand in western markets, the landowners were building upon foundations already laid in place by their colonising forefathers; but they were also creating a social and economic problem of immense dimensions, the repercussions of which form one of the major themes of this book.

CHAPTER TWO

Rulers and Ruled

THE PEOPLE

For almost three hundred years, the lands bordering the Baltic attracted to their shores militant crusaders, who sought to impose the Catholic faith upon the pagan peoples they encountered. On the southern shores, the impetus for this eastwards expansion came from within the German Empire. Settlers from Saxony and Westphalia followed in the wake of crusading knights, who had hacked their way through the dense undergrowth to force Christianity upon the reluctant natives – the Wends in the twelfth century, the Livs, Latvians, Estonians and Prussians in the thirteenth. The only pagans powerful enough to resist were the Lithuanians, whose rulers not only kept the Teutonic knights at bay, but also managed to build up a vast state, which by the fifteenth century stretched from the ethnic heartland around the river Nemunas (Niemen) to the Black Sea. In 1385–6, the pagan prince Jogaila embraced Christianity in return for his election to the Polish throne, thereby laying the foundations for the Polish–Lithuanian union, and the Jagiełłionian dynasty. The conversion of Jogaila (whom the Poles christened Władysław) and his subjects to Christianity deprived the Teutonic Order of a legitimate excuse to sally forth from the Prussian lands to do battle with the pagan: henceforth, the struggle between the Order and Poland-Lithuania was over territory, not souls. To the east, the Order had come up against the Orthodox church. The Livonian Knights of the Sword (from 1237 a branch of the Teutonic Order) failed to extend their domain into the lands of the medieval city-republics of Novgorod and Pskov; lake Peipus marked the boundary between Catholic and Orthodox Christianity. The Orthodox church had also extended its influence into the vast forested tracts of Karelia, at the same time as the Finnish tribes in the west were being converted to Catholicism in a series of crusades mounted from Sweden. At the beginning of the fourteenth century, the Swedes pushed into the Karelian isthmus, where they built the castle of Viborg. The treaty of Nöteborg, concluded between Sweden and Novgorod in 1323, was the first attempt to delineate the frontier, but its terms were extremely vague and imprecise. It is generally assumed that the frontier ran from where the river Sestroretsk enters the Gulf of Finland, curving north-west through the lakes and forests of Savo–Karelia to reach the sea again at the northern end of the Gulf of Bothnia. Neither traders from Karelia nor settlers from the Finnish side paid much heed to it. Raiders and rustlers waged an almost incessant border warfare, and the rulers of Sweden and Novgorod continued to wrangle over the precise location of the boundary for the next century and a half.[1]

Low German was the *lingua franca* in the Baltic, the language of commerce and navigation, and on occasion of diplomacy. It was also the language of a colonising ruling class on the southern shores of the sea. By the sixteenth century, the coastline between the Elbe and the Oder had been fairly thoroughly Germanised. A mid-sixteenth century writer claimed that the last speaker of Pomeranian on the island of Rügen had died a hundred years earlier, and that only a few Wends and Cassubians still lived in Hither Pomerania. Further east, the numbers of Prussian speakers were also diminishing, and the language died out in the eighteenth century. The influx of settlers from Germany into the eastern Baltic lands was much weaker, and the rigid exclusivity of the German urban upper classes and the landowners placed obstacles in the way of any wholesale Germanisation of the native population. From the fourteenth century onwards, there was a gradual erosion of the rights of the indigenous Latvians and Estonians to participate in the major trading and commercial activities of the towns. Classified by the German-speaking rulers as 'non-Germans', the natives were excluded from membership of the Great Gild of Riga, and were also banned from many of the craft gilds of the city. Attempts were also made to prevent intermarriage: the German mer-

1. For a splendid account of this period, see Christiansen E 1980 *The Northern Crusades. The Baltic and the Catholic Frontier 1100–1525*. A more detailed study of Prussia is offered by Burleigh M 1984 *Prussian society and the German Order. An aristocratic corporation in crisis c.1410–1466*. Cambridge. For the Polish–Lithuanian union, see Davies N 1981 *God's Playground. A History of Poland* (2 vols). Oxford, vol. 1. pp. 115–155. The history of medieval Karelia is covered by Kirkinen H 1970 *Karjala idän ja lännen välissä*. Historiallisia Tutkimuksia 80. Helsinki.

chants of Reval around 1400, for example, were forbidden to marry non-German women.

The many regulations and ordinances designed to keep the non-Germans in their place could not however prevent a considerable intermixing of peoples and languages. The German spoken in Reval, for instance, was heavily interlaced with Estonian and Swedish words and phrases. In 1556, a foreign apprentice was fined for questioning whether the town councillors could actually speak German; and other visitors from Germany were to find themselves baffled by the mishmash of languages they encountered here. Young men sent out from Lübeck as factors were encouraged to learn the local languages; it was generally reckoned that a course of seventeen weeks was needed in order to acquire reasonable proficiency. There was no shortage of linguistically talented middlemen and fixers either, much to the annoyance of the town authorities, who sought to curb their activities.[2]

The exclusivity of the German ruling class, and the arrogance which this fostered, undoubtedly caused tension. The German minority still remembered the Estonian peasant uprising of 1343, when many of their number had been slaughtered: they were determined not to let slip their political dominance over the subject peoples. The imposition of the yoke of servitude in the sixteenth and seventeenth centuries caused further bitterness amongst the non-Germans, as numerous folk poems testify:

Kui mina pääsen mõisa'asta,	When I escape out of the manor,
siis mina pääsen põrgu'usta,	I leave behind the gates of hell,
pääsen kui soe suusta,	From the wolf's mouth free myself,
halli hundi hamba'asta,	From the fangs of the grey wolf,
lõvi lõugade vahelta.	From between the lion's jaws.[3]

For the sharp-witted and able, however, there were always ways to beat the rules and regulations, and the frequency of fines imposed on merchants for employing non-German apprentices and assistants suggest that Baltic–German apartheid rules were not always observed by those whom they were meant to protect.

The general appearance and features of the towns of northern Europe varied a great deal. The traveller Fynes Moryson found Lübeck a fair, well-built city, clean and with courteous inhabitants;

2. See Johansen, von zur Mühlen 1973 *Deutsch und Undeutsch im mittelalterlichen und frühzeitlichen Reval*. Cologne–Vienna, pp. 149–51, 373–87, and pp. 471–3 for a good example of the mixture of languages spoken in the town.
3. Nirk E 1970 *Estonian Literature*. Tallinn, p. 25.

but nearby Lüneburg was 'very filthy and full of ill smells', whilst Copenhagen was unbeautiful, consisting largely of timber and mud dwellings, the inhabitants of which 'as if they had never seene a stranger before, shouted at mee after a barbarous fashion'. Thomas Kantzow declared that the food and drink was better in Stettin than in the other towns of Pomerania, and praised Stolp for its school, which attracted pupils from as far away as Hamburg and Denmark. The city of Danzig, with its fine public buildings and busy wharves strung out along the river Mottlau, impressed most visitors. The towns of Sweden, (collections of wooden houses, rather than towns, according to a French diplomat) were rather less impressive.[4]

The standard building material for substantial houses and edifices was brick. The merchants' houses which lined the main thoroughfares were tall and narrow-fronted, with high gables, sufficiently deep to act as commodious warehouses. In the lesser thoroughfares were the crowded wooden huts of the poor, a constant fire hazard. The main showpiece of the town was its market-place, usually flanked by an impressive town hall. Here would be the weighhouse and the instruments of public chastisement – the stocks and the whipping-post. The town would be contained within a strong wall, with massive exit gates; and above this teeming temporal world, dominating the skyline, would rise the spires of the churches – the solid double-towered edifice of the church of the Virgin Mary in Lübeck, the copper-sheathed cupola spire of St Nicholas in Stralsund, the slim, graceful needle of St Olai in Reval.

Rude and uncouth in comparison with the sophisticated centres of culture, commerce and education of southern Europe, the towns of the Baltic were nonetheless capable of producing skilled woodcarvers, masons and painters whose works convey something of the emotions and salty humour of their surroundings. The altarpiece for Bordesholm church, now in the cathedral of Schleswig, which was completed by Hans Brüggemann in 1521, is crowded with expressive figures: a ragged-trousered man, grimacing with the effort of binding a bundle of faggots, a voluptuous Eve, stroking her ample left breast with the apple, and a Christ on the Cross, his eyelids drooping, his beard and hair bedraggled with the sweat of agony. The work of the Lübeck painter and sculptor Berndt Notke can still be seen throughout the Baltic, from the altarpiece of Århus cathedral to the Dance of

4. Moryson 1903 vol. 1 p. 121. Kosegarten (ed.) 1817 *Pomerania oder Ursprunck, Altheit und Geschicht der Völcker und lande Pomern, Cassuben, Wenden, Stettin, Rhügen... von Thomas Kantzow.* Greifswald, vol. 2 pp. 437–44. Andolf S (ed.) 1980 *Relation du Royaume de Suède par Monsieur de sainte-Catherine, 1606.* Gothenburg, p. 22.

Death in the church of St Nicholas in Reval. In the Great Church in Stockholm stands his masterpiece, St George and the Dragon, a work of considerable nationalistic overtones commissioned by Sten Sture after the defeat of the Danish army at Brunkeberg in 1471. The cathedral in Lund was graced by a series of sculptures and reliefs executed by Adam van Düren. In one, an old woman is being admonished by a well-fed monk. The text surrounding the relief reads: 'Many give others good advice without following it themselves.' At the foot of a column, van Düren left a final personal message. On one side, we see an ass which has collapsed under its burden; on the other, a man is about to begin flaying the poor beast's skin. A little verse in Danish ruefully regrets man's inability to comprehend his own frailties and limitations. The artists, many of them from Lübeck (which did a brisk export trade in altarpieces) were master craftsmen in wood and stone: they were less impressive as painters. The one artist of Baltic origin who did make an impact on a wider world was Michael Sittow (c.1470–1525) from Reval, who painted many of the crowned heads of Europe of his day.

The towns along the southern coast of the Baltic, with their tall-spired churches, crow-stepped brick-built town halls, and stout defences, were doubtless a fearsome and wonderful sight to the countryman who approached them. Fearsome, for here dwelt bailiffs, tradesmen, hucksters and whores who would rob and cheat him if they had half the chance, people who scorned the rude manners and simplicity of the bumpkin; but wonderful if he were fleeing from an oppressive lord, for the towns would protect him and resist efforts to claim him back. Small and modest in comparison with the big cities of southern Europe, these towns were nevertheless teeming concentrations of humanity in an otherwise densely forested, infertile landscape, seemingly devoid of other habitation.

The runaway peasant would join the ranks of the unprivileged majority, the *inwaner*. He would probably find casual work, carrying or hawking goods, and would find accommodation in a wooden shack or in a cellar. In the town of Stralsund, with a population in 1500 of around 10,000, there were, according to Thomas Kantzow, 1,400 men engaged in loading and unloading ships and carrying goods, and several thousand living in cellars. The Lutheran pastors of Reval in 1572 complained that they had to seek out many of their flock in 'stinking cellars and hovels within and without the town'; the lower down the social scale one descended, the more overcrowded and noisome was the accommodation.[5]

At the very bottom of the pile were the sick and infirm, the beggars and tramps, who lived on the streets. Those who were fortunate might find shelter in a charitable institution, such as the St Johannis-Spital in Reval. The rules of this hospital were strict – couples were forbidden to sleep together on pain of expulsion, and fines were levied for misdemeanours, such as drunken vomiting and staying up late – but such institutions did help provide a safety-net for the indigent. In Lübeck, there were fourteen poorhouses, primarily intended for travelling paupers. Town councils often issued licences and sought in other ways to regulate begging.[6]

Those who really counted in the affairs of the town were its citizens, or burghers. To become a burgher (*borger*), one had to be of age, married and of independent means, of free and honourable lineage, and able to pay burgher-money. In the north German towns under Lübeck law, the possession or enjoyment of the emoluments of property were not prerequisites for citizenship; but citizenship was a necessary means of acquiring and inheriting property, and of pursuing the more privileged trades. The citizens swore to respect the peace and ordinances of the city, which was in effect an oath of loyalty to the town council. Those excluded from citizenship were denied any say in the affairs of the town, though they were expected to mount watch and defend it alongside the burghers.

The principal administrative and judicial body in the town was its council (*Rat*). Membership of this body was for life, and new councillors were co-opted from the narrow circle of great merchants in the town. The number of councillors varied between twelve and twenty-four, sometimes more; a small number were chosen as leaders, or *Bürgermeister*. The council supervised the defences of the town, represented it in dealings with other towns and princes, collected taxes and tolls, looked after law and order, and dispensed justice. Councillors took on administrative duties, which ranged from the supervision of tax-collection to the provisioning of the town hall's wine cellar. The council also appointed salaried officials, such as town clerks, cellarers, watchmen and supervisors of weights and measures, doctors, apothecaries and barber-surgeons.

The closed and oligarchic nature of the town council often led to conflict, particularly in times of financial or political crisis. To avoid this, councils could consult the community (*communitas, gemenheit*). Membership of the community was acquired through payment of burgher-money, though in matters of grave importance, other inhabi-

5. Kosegarten (ed.) 1817, vol. 2, pp. 437–9. Johansen, von zur Mühlen 1973 p. 111 ff.
6. Johansen, von zur Mühlen 1973 pp 448–9. Schildhauer J 1985 *The Hanse. History and Culture*. Leipzig, pp. 166–7.

tants of the town also seem to have been admitted to the public meetings. It was at these meetings that the artisans and small merchants, resentful of their exclusion from the council, could voice their protests. These internal squabbles did the towns little good, for they offered a golden opportunity to the princes to interfere and impose their rule. In 1525, for example, an attempt by the council in Danzig to arrest the leaders of the Reformed party in the town backfired, and in the ensuing tumult, the council was overthrown. Its members sought assistance from the town's overlord, the king of Poland, who arrived before the walls with an impressive force of troops and had the new council and many of the community arrested. Large and powerful cities such as Danzig were still able to resist the efforts of the ruler to impose his authority: but the smaller towns of the north German coast were less resilient. The margrave of Brandenburg, for example, was able to intervene in the squabbles of a number of towns during the fifteenth century, reinstating deposed patrician councils and making them dependent on his support.

The towns which fell within the territorial ambit of the Teutonic Order were often two entirely separate units within one enclave – in Danzig and Königsberg there were in fact three towns, each with its own administration. The town of Marienburg was dominated by the massive fortifications of the castle, the headquarters of the Grand Master from 1309 until 1466. In Riga and Reval, the castle of the Order loomed over the lower town, though in neither city did the Provincial Master exercise much authority. There was bitter conflict for centuries between the Order and the archbishop for the right to exercise overlordship in Riga. The town itself, with a population of around 8,000 in 1500, exercised full autonomy over its own affairs, and acted as the court of appeal for seventeen Livonian towns. Reval on the other hand was under Lübeck law. Here, the authority of the Provincial Master was confined to settling disputes between the town and the Estonian nobility or within the gilds, though in the 1440s he intervened to compel the town council to abandon its attempt to govern without consulting the opinions of the community.

The economic and social life of the town was also ordered on corporate and hierarchical lines. At the bottom of the pyramid of the economically active population were the unskilled and casual workers, hired hands and servants, who sold their labour where they could, without benefit of organisation. The next layer consisted of organised craftsmen. The right to form gilds was one of the most prized privileges of the towns. By the mid-fourteenth century, there were between forty and seventy different craft gilds in the larger towns of the Baltic, although this number declined as associated trades fused together. The painters' gild in Reval, for example, included painters, glaziers, woodcarvers and carpenters: by 1500, the trades of the town had been grouped into thirteen gilds. The artisan gilds also came together in two associations originally established for religious and charitable reasons – the gilds of St Knud and St Olai. The merchants of the Lower Town in Reval had separated themselves from the artisans of the gild of St Knud in the early fourteenth century, organising their own exclusive Great Gild. The artisans of the Gild of St Knud and the semi-skilled members of the less important Gild of St Olai fought a long, losing battle against the Great Gild, which by 1547 had managed to exclude the artisans from the trade in salt and grain, and to stop them brewing beer for sale.

What happened in Reval occurred in other towns: the wealthy merchants and tradesmen drew apart from the more humble artisans, creating new exclusive clubs and societies, such as the *Zirkelkompanie* in Lübeck, or the *Artushof* in Danzig. Those involved in trade with a particular country or area formed fraternities. A study of one such fraternity in Lübeck, the *Holmevarer*, or traders with Stockholm, has shown how closely interrelated these merchants were. A dense and complex web of family connections, carefully preserved by judicious selection of marriage partners, extended not only over the houses and club-rooms of the wealthy in the western quarter of Lübeck, but also throughout the Baltic. It was nevertheless still possible for a sharp young man to rise into the ranks of the patriciate, especially in times of intense economic activity, when fortunes could be made by new ventures. The growth of the legal profession in sixteenth-century Germany also opened up opportunities for social advancement. On the other hand, the known instances of poor men making it to the top are relatively few.

In many respects, the towns of the Baltic survived and prospered in spite of themselves. Carried to their logical conclusion, the restrictive regulations and practices would have stifled enterprise and ultimately would have sapped the vitality of urban life. We have seen that the Hanse tried to meet the threat of the new and dynamic trading practices of the Dutch by resorting to further restrictions and a crab-bed defence of privileges, and how these measures failed to stem the tide. The pressure to adapt and to survive in business compelled the individual to ignore such corporate strictures, or to move out of active seafaring trade into more lucrative ventures, such as investment in property or land. The merchants of the Livonian towns were prepared to break the regulations forbidding the employment of non-German

31

apprentices and agents, since they needed such people to further their affairs. But the frequent breaches of the regulations do not mean that they were wholly ineffective, or that they were seen as tiresome impositions. The lengthy catalogue of rules (*bursprake*) sonorously proclaimed each year at gild meetings or to the populace outside the town hall was the binding which held urban society together. The regulations proclaimed by the aldermen of the gilds determined standards of quality for goods produced and ensured the livelihood of the members. The *bursprake* sought to ensure that the town walls were maintained, and not pilfered for stone, that the citizens' cows and pigs did not run wild in the streets, that weights and measures were kept to a certain standard, and that prescribed trading practices were observed. The gilds, fraternities and the town council also tried to lay down standards of morality, behaviour and sobriety, and they attempted to prescribe how each social category should dress. These were not simply rules imposed upon an unruly and dissolute people by an authority which had, in the end, rather limited, if brutal, sanctions at its disposal; they were a reflection of the social order, in which patriarchal authority and notions of a hierarchy sanctioned by God were firmly rooted.

The village community was also held together by an intricate mesh of institutions and familial relationships, although the former had been weakened in the colonised lands of the southern Baltic by the gradual imposition of regulations tying the peasant to the soil and whittling away his legal status. In certain areas, however, the peasantry retained a fair degree of autonomy, as in the villages of East Pomerania. Here, a series of '*conditiones*' governed the conduct of local government, which was in the hands of a peasant aristocracy, the *Schultzen*, or mayors and the *Schöppenbank*, which constituted the local court. This court met every quarter, and dealt with questions of property and inheritance as well as the maintenance of order. The authorities looked after streets and bridges, built dams, maintained a fire-fighting service and even used funds to defend the village's privileges against noble encroachment. The village also provided for the upkeep of priests and teachers. The relative absence of feudal lords, and a strongly entrenched peasant community with an acute awareness of its rights and liberties, gave to the peasantry of this low-lying area in the hinterland of Danzig a control of their own affairs not dissimilar to that enjoyed by the free peasantry of Dithmarsch, on the marshy North Sea coast.

In the Scandinavian lands the peasantry also played an active role in the running of local affairs. Each village in Denmark had its own communal organisation, the *bystævne*, which discussed and decided

practical matters such as grazing rights or the appointment of herds-
men. In some localities, this was called a gild. At Herslev, near
Roskilde, the 1515 statutes of the villagers' Gild of the Virgin Mary
laid down rules for helping the sick and poor, provided funds for
those wishing to go on pilgrimage, and decreed punishments for
misdeeds, such as drawing a knife in anger, or spitting on a gild
brother or guest. The wealthier farmers of the hundred (*herred* in
Danish, *härad* in Swedish) served as jurymen on the local court (*ting*),
sitting on wooden benches, often in the open air, to dispense justice.
Several jurymen in southern Finland amassed large fines for wounding
or inflicting bruises on their neighbours, but criminal acts of violence
were no disqualification from the bench – only the bearing of false
witness and illicit removal of boundary markers could cause the
offender to be removed.[7]

Although the absence of reliable statistics makes it difficult to reach
firm conclusions, it would seem that the peasants of southern Finland
at least were a remarkably lawless lot. Ylikangas has estimated that the
rate of fines levied in western Nyland in the 1550s was the equivalent
to one punishment every three-and-a-half years for each peasant
household. The majority of offences were committed against the
person. Most offences were punished by a 3-mark fine, a paltry sum
for a prosperous farmer, though a year's wages for a farmhand.
Ylikangas has suggested that many incidents of violent assault may
have been provoked by verbal abuse: the church's Christian precept of
'he who strikes always offends' seems not to have erased the pagan
concepts of honour from the hearts and minds of the Finnish peasantry. Something of the same boastful self-confidence of the free peasantry is echoed in Thomas Kantzow's portrayal of the wealthy farmers
of Rügen:

> There is no nobleman or peasant in the land so mean that he will not have
> his say, or does not know the customary law of his land. And none will
> give way to another in such presumptuousness, which leads to much
> discord and mayhem: and they are especially fond of arguing in the taverns
> and inns, and when one of them says: as God wills, and in cold iron, that
> means the talking is over and it is time for fisticuffs... And so many fights
> and other injuries occur in the taverns that often a nobleman who owns an
> inn collects as many fines in a year as he does from half or even an entire
> village.[8]

By the seventeenth century, the incidence of crimes of violence in

7. Ylikangas H 1971 Väkivaltarikosten motivaatiopohja 1500-luvulla Suomessa *Historiallinen Arkisto* **65**: 144.
8. Kosegarten (ed.) 1817, vol. 2, p. 434.

southern Finland was in decline. Ylikangas attributes this to a growing impoverishment of the peasantry, caused by the ravages of war and the exhaustion of the burn-beat lands of the area, but more especially to the spread of noble estates in Finland and the erosion of the status of the free peasantry. The pattern of crimes coming before the courts also altered, with sexual and moral offences far more prominent, an indication of the growing strength and supervisory authority of the Lutheran church.[9]

In the absence of detailed studies on peasants and crime in other parts of the Baltic, it is impossible to say how typical the farmers of Nyland were. Court records for the southern Swedish region of Småland in the early seventeenth century suggest this was an area with a high rate of violent crime; around fifty murders are recorded in Konga, a district with a population of eight to nine thousand, between 1614 and 1629. On the other hand, studies of two districts in Uppland indicate that murder was a comparatively rare crime there; as in Nyland, most crimes of violence sprang from insults, and were often committed on occasions when drink was in plentiful supply. There are also numerous instances of drunken behaviour disrupting court sessions. In 1593, Christian IV (no mean toper himself in later life) was obliged to issue instructions for court sessions to begin early in the morning, in the hopes of avoiding disruption from drunken litigants.[10]

It is fairly clear, however, that the peasants of northern Europe were prepared to go to law, and to complain to the king, a practice which the demagogic Vasa kings in Sweden were to encourage when it suited them. The peasant-miners of Dalarna occupied an important position in the mythology of Vasa sovereignty, for it was here that Gustav Vasa found his first support in the revolt against king Christian in the 1520s. Although by no means yet a fully fledged estate of the realm, the Swedish peasantry had managed to establish their claim to be consulted, and were never to lose that right, as did the peasants of Denmark.

The erosion of status and the exactions of landlords and the royal bailiffs provoked unrest, though not on the scale of western and central Europe. The imposition of new taxes sparked off a peasants' revolt in Jutland in 1440–1, and again in the 1530s. There was a rash of

9. Ylikangas 1971, and his 1976 article Major fluctuations in crimes of violence in Finland *Scandinavian Journal of History* 1: 82-91.

10. Larsson L-O 1982 *Småländsk historia. Stormaktstiden.* Stockholm, pp. 47–55. Österberg E 1983 Violence among peasants: Comparative perspectives on the 16th and 17th century Sweden *Europe and Scandinavia: Aspects of the process of integration in the 17th century* (ed. G Rystad), Lund Studies in International History 18. Lund, pp. 261–75.

manor-burning in Skåne in the mid-1520s, and German mercenaries had to be brought in to restore order. The reign of Gustav Vasa (1523–60) was punctuated by peasant uprisings, of which the most serious was the revolt in Småland in 1542. Here, religious and economic grievances were intertwined. The visitation conducted by the bishop of Västerås in 1541 had caused grave offence to the staunchly Catholic Smålanders, who objected to the removal of church plate and other valuables. The king's insistence on his hunting rights in the oak and beech woods of the region caused annoyance amongst the farmers, already chafing under increased taxation. Even more irksome was the royal attempt to divert the time-honoured trade in cattle, butter, hides and skins from the Danish-held southern provinces of Halland, Blekinge and Skåne to the Swedish town of Kalmar. The rebellion, led by Nils Dacke, a prosperous farmer who had already been outlawed for murdering a royal bailiff, soon assumed serious proportions, attracting the attention of Gustav Vasa's enemies abroad. The king was forced to conclude a truce with the rebels, and to rally support elsewhere in the realm, which he did with his usual mastery of propaganda. In a brilliant evocation of the 'good old times' of twenty years previously, Gustav Vasa forcefully reminded his subjects of the chaos and rapine from which he had delivered them, and of the necessity to bear with increased taxation for the good of the fatherland. In the spring of 1543, he launched an offensive into Småland, and succeeded in defeating the rebels in battle. Dacke himself was betrayed and slain, and hundreds of his supporters were deported to Finland as a punishment.

The Peasants' War which raged in southern Germany during 1525 had few echoes in the north. The only serious outbreak of peasant unrest occurred in the province of Samland, in Prussia. The sudden secularisation of the Order in 1525 by the last Grand Master, Albrecht von Hohenzollern, and the ferment of religious change which affected the towns and the surrounding countryside played a part in the revolt, though it was principally directed against noble exactions. Trouble had simmered throughout the summer in this relatively densely populated area. The leaders of the revolt appear to have been more prosperous and independent members of the community, such as the miller of Kaymen and an innkeeper in Schaaken, and they were in contact with sympathisers in the nearby town of Königsberg. Both Prussians and Germans took part in the revolt. The peasants protested their loyalty to the new duke, who was absent in Germany: their hatred was reserved for the 'crows', whose nests they wished to destroy, i.e., the nobility. Their principal demands were for the abolition of recent impositions and a restoration of the old tax of two marks per *Hufe* (roughly forty acres). On his return, Albrecht summoned the peasants to appear in the field, where he had them surrounded by armed men. Shitting their breeches for fear of being put to the sword, in the words of the chronicler, they offered no resistance. The ringleaders were arrested, and several executed. The ordinances issued in the following year tied the peasants still further to their lords, though the unrest by no means ceased with the defeat of the Samland rebels.[11]

The spread of socially radical ideas which accompanied the Reformation caused anxiety in Estonia, where a Low German version of the Twelve Articles of the rebellious German peasantry was circulated amongst the townsfolk of Reval. In 1527, the knights of Harrien and Wierland warned the Provincial Master of the dangers of their peasants picking up this new doctrine of disobedience on their visits to the town. The spiritual condition and welfare of the rural population left much to be desired: a mid-sixteenth century verse put into the mouth of a Livonian peasant the following couplet: 'Ick gewe dem Pastor de Pflicht/ Vnd weth van Gott und sin Worde nicht' (I obey the priest, and of God and His Word know nothing).[12] The Estonian chronicler Balthasar Rüssow, himself a Lutheran clergyman, complained of the poor quality and lack of trained clergy, most of whom could not speak Estonian. The Catholic church had used a combination of Christianity and pagan practices to win over the local population. Pagan customs such as the 'feeding of the souls' at the graveside and the worship of forest and bush gods, were still widespread throughout the colonised lands. The Prussian peasants continued to meet at night to consume the roasted flesh of the sacred goat, invoking the ancient gods Perkunos, Potrimpos and Patollu as they drained the ceremonial vessel. The Lutheran church waged a fierce battle against all aspects of what its ministers regarded as pagan practices. Bishop Mikael Agricola singled out eleven ancient Finnish deities and heroes for condemnation in his 1551 psalter, and the preface of Jacobus Finno's hymn book of 1582 thundered against the singing of shameful, lewd and foolish songs inspired by the devil. Writing in the 1570s, Balthasar Rüssow mournfully conceded that there were many places in Livonia where little was known of the Word of God or of church attendance; the peasants preferred to visit neighbours and drink good

11. Carsten F 1938 Der Bauernkrieg in Ostpreussen 1525 *International Review of Social History* 3: 398–409. Meckelburg F (ed.) 1848 *Preussische Chronik des Johannes Freiberg*. Königsberg, pp. 192–6.

12. Wittram R 1956 Die Reformation in Livland *Baltische Kirchengeschichte* (ed. R Wittram). Göttingen, p. 53.

beer. The scattered population often had to travel many miles to attend church, and this offered a fine opportunity for a social gathering:

> Numerous barrels of beer were brought to the church for sale to the peasants, and when they with their wives, maids and servants, having travelled some miles, began to gather in great numbers on the Saturday evening, they forthwith began tippling and gorging themselves, and with their great bagpipes which on an eventide could be heard over a mile away, they began to make merry throughout the night until daybreak: and when the sermon had begun, the peasants came into the church half-drunk, and there chattered and made such a din that the priest could neither see nor hear for their bellowing. And then, no wiser than they were before, they left the church and started up again, feasting, dancing, singing and running...[13]

Not until the eighteenth century, when Pietism began to spread amongst the rural population of Livonia and Estonia, did the peasantry begin to abandon the pagan practices, and the dancing and bagpipe music which so scandalised the clergy. The tenacity with which the rural people had clung to their old customs can be gauged by the claims of one early eighteenth-century pastor that there were sixty to eighty sacrificial sites in his parish alone, twenty-four of which he destroyed with his own hands. In Finland, it was customary for couples to become betrothed at the beginning of autumn, at the same time as the ancient festival of Kekri, named by Agricola as the ancient god of fertility. Jumi, the god of marriage, also lived on in popular memory. As late as 1758, a parish priest reported that young people in the northern parish of Muhos dressed up in their finery on All Saints' Day and 'with scandalous games, dancing, music and entertaining, in a most outrageous and indecent fashion, celebrate marriage which they call Jumi-marriage, and they presume that they have an ancient right to such liberties'.[14]

This co-existence of paganism and Christianity should not surprise us: there is plenty of evidence to show that popular religion in all European countries could accommodate quite happily a very broad range of beliefs and superstitions. In the darkness of the night or in the pain of sickness, the common people preferred to hedge their bets: the priest might be called upon to intercede with the Almighty, the local witch-doctor might be asked to mutter an incantation. The riotous sociability of the peasantry, so deplored by the more genteel, was a

13. Rüssow B 1967 *Chronica der Provintz Lyfflandt* (reprint edn). Hannover, p. 43.
14. Webermann O 1956 Pietismus und Brüdergemeinde *Baltische Kirchengeschichte* (ed. R Wittram). Göttingen, pp. 159–60. Suolahti G 1927 *Finlands prästerskap på 1600- och 1700-talet*. Helsingfors, pp. 210–11.

necessary release of feelings in what was otherwise a desperately marginal existence. The Pomeranian peasantry, for example, were accustomed to offer a bath, beer and bread to their friends and the poor after a funeral, and a good time seems to have been had by all. They also preferred to wear their best and most colourful clothes on such occasions.

The life of the common people in the late Middle Ages is not easy to recapture. Folk-poetry, of which there is a very rich record in the eastern Baltic, offers many fascinating insights of the spiritual and everyday world.[15] So do contemporary illustrations, such as the woodcuts in Olaus Magnus' *Historia de gentibus septentrionalis* (1555), or paintings on church walls, many of which can still be seen in Scandinavia. Horned devils are ubiquitous figures, partnering the king, the bishop, the nobleman and the peasant with his mattock in a dance of death on the wall of Nørre Alslev church in Denmark, or, at Sæby church in northern Jutland, stealing away the naked corpse from a marriage bed in which a lascivious young man is already embracing the dead man's wife. On the wall of Estuna church in Uppland, there is a scene portraying a gambler about to seize his knife, whilst the innkeeper grabs his hair and prepares to hit him over the head with a jug. In the next scene, cold water is being poured over the luckless gambler's head, whilst the innkeeper is dragging the shirt off his back.

Strong drink has always featured prominently in the life of the people of northern and eastern Europe. 'Ivrogne comme un danois' was a byword amongst the supercilious French in the sixteenth century. Jean Bodin blamed the gluttony and intemperate drinking habits of the northerner on the cold climate. Fynes Moryson found that the Danes surpassed their Saxon neighbours in the excess of their drinking. 'Their dainties are bacon and salt meats, but the common people feede much on divers kinds of dried fishes, which at the first view of them a stranger may wel perceive, by their leane and withered faces, and they likewise feede on bread very black, heavy and windy.'[16] The better-quality products – fresh butter and meat, the fat herrings of the Skåne fisheries – were usually sold; the peasant family had to make do with inferior salt herring and whatever the cottage garden could provide in the way of green vegetables. Contemporaries were acutely conscious of food and drink: popular literature is full of allusions to a good meal, and good cheer. A sixteenth-century Danish folk-verse poked fun at the inhabitants of Fyn, who preferred porridge to Rhenish gold: but there was doubtless sound wisdom in their wishing to fill

15. See Kuusi M, Bosley K, Branch M (eds) 1977 *Finnish Folk Poetry: Epic*. Helsinki.
16. Moryson 1903, vol. 4 p. 67.

their bellies with this nutritious, if rather dull form of sustenance. In the far north, the basic diet was even more meagre: dried fish and sour milk, with hard, flat loaves of barley seemed to constitute the entire stock of the Finnish peasants' nourishment, according to a French traveller in the 1730s. The French actor and playwright Regnard, on his madcap journey to the North Cape in 1687, noted that bread grain was a rarity in northern Finland. The persons of quality in northern and eastern Europe also struck the sophisticated courtiers of France and Italy as outlandish and barbarous. Clumsy in their skins and furs, more accustomed to the saddle and the tilt-yard than to the intricacies of courtly dances, they attracted much mockery whenever they ventured into the sophisticated outside world. Their houses were still grim fortresses, bereft of any comfort or ornament, like the castle of Glimmingehus in Skåne, built at the end of the fifteenth century. But the gentler rays of the Renaissance were beginning to penetrate the north by the middle of the sixteenth century. The sons of the higher nobility were often sent to university and on a grand tour of Europe. Ivar Juel, after ten years of school, attended the university of Copenhagen for three years, and continued his studies in Cologne, before travelling in the Low Countries and Italy: Hogenskild Bielke was educated at the cathedral school of Odense and the university of Wittenberg, obviously picking up a relish for the law, which he was to use with good effect in his constitutional battles with the Swedish monarchs. Heinrich Rantzau, who succeeded his father as royal governor in Slesvig-Holstein, corresponded with the leading humanists of his day and found time to compose a history of the war against Dithmarsch, a topographical description of the duchies and to collaborate in the production of a multi-volume atlas. His principal seat at Breitenburg contained one of the best libraries in northern Europe, unfortunately destroyed by Wallenstein's soldiers in 1627.

The new manners and tastes which the young nobleman picked up undoubtedly included a heightened sense of his own status and the prestige of gentle birth. Before the sixteenth century, the rules and gradations of nobility in northern Europe had been rather rough and ready. The term 'noble' (*adel*) does not appear to have been employed before that time. Danish usage preferred *riddere/milites* and *svende/militares*, which denoted the military origins of the aristocracy. The most common Swedish designation was '*herr*': titles were first introduced in Sweden in the 1560s, in Denmark a century later.

The basic division in Swedish society was between *frälse* and *ofrälse*. Those of the first category were 'delivered' from the obligation to pay tax, in return for equipping an armed horseman for royal service (*rusttjänst*). (Peasants on *frälse* land were also exempt from ordinary taxation, but had to perform a number of obligations to the crown, such as the provision of fodder and transport for travellers.) The nobility and the church enjoyed *frälse* status, but there were also isolated groups of freemen, especially on the islands, who could claim similar privileges by virtue of services performed, such as shore-watch. During the fifteenth century, the crown had attempted to impose restrictions on the expansion of *frälse* land. This restrictive policy at a time of general agricultural crisis caused the wealthier nobility to rationalise their holdings, which were often scattered across the country. The church was also active in the land market, where the losers appear to have been the lesser nobility. Although a good half of the land was owned and farmed by freehold, tax-paying peasants (*skattebönder*), there were wide regional differences in patterns of land ownership. Tax-peasants were more numerous in the less fertile areas such as Norrland and Finland, but in the grain-growing central plains of Svea- and Götaland, the proportion of *frälse* land was much higher.[17]

The nobility formed a small but by no means closed social grouping. Officials such as bailiffs, castellans and stewards could acquire *frälse* status through patronage or hard work, and secure this by an advantageous marriage. Successful non-nobles could also rise in rank by virtue of marriage; the Finnish burgher Jöns Rengonpoika married into the Djäkne family, and his sons into the Fincke and Tavast clans. It was also possible for families, or branches of them, to sink into poverty. On the whole, however, the late-medieval nobility of Sweden seems to have been remarkably close-knit, using the marriage market to consolidate and expand their land holdings.

Ownership of *frälse* land was thus a distinguishing feature of nobility in Sweden, but it was not the only means of exercising social and political power. The inadequacies of the crown's revenues and services had compelled the rulers to allot fiefs to the nobility, who undertook to administer them. *Frälse* men also held a variety of local offices. In fifteenth-century Finland, many of the sheriffs' offices were virtually family fiefs, until the regent, Sten Sture the Elder, began appointing his own men in the 1460s. Office-holding, therefore, could procure social advancement, but it never became a hereditary possession.

In Denmark, the balance between crown and magnates tilted sharply in the latter's favour during the last decades of the union of the crowns. The royal charter of 1483 established the principle that 'free'

17. Larsson L-O 1985 Jordägofördelningen i Sverige under Gustav Vasas regering *Scandia* **51**: pp. 61–90.

noble and church lands could not be alienated. Peasants on these lands were exempted from ordinary taxation, and in 1526, the right of the noble demesne to exemption from extraordinary taxes was extended to all tenant-farms in the parish where the demesne farm was situated. During the reign of Frederik I (1523–33), the nobility also acquired the right to collect fines levied in royal courts on their land, certain fines imposed by church courts, and established their claim to exact punishment on their peasants. By 1536, the nobility had virtually established full autonomy within their estates, which probably accounted for one-quarter of the land in Denmark.[18]

Office-holding was also an attractive and necessary means of social advancement for the Danish nobleman. The holder of a large fief (*len*) or a bishopric could also exercise patronage. A number of new recruits to the ranks of the aristocracy owed their elevation to the grace and favour of a high-born patron. In 1536, there were around 250 noble families in Denmark, rather fewer than a century earlier. A number had perished in the wars, but many had sunk into impoverishment. The lesser nobility, with limited resources at their disposal, had been particularly hard hit. The high nobility showed an increasing tendency towards exclusivity, distinguishing themselves by adopting names from their coat-of-arms, and seeking to man the highest and most prestigious offices in the realm.

THE UNION OF KALMAR

Monarchy under the formal union of the three Scandinavian crowns concluded at Kalmar in 1397 was elective. This offered considerable scope for bargaining between the nobility and the would-be king. The highest administrative and judicial authority was the council of state (*rigsråd* in Danish, *riksråd* in Swedish), whose members were drawn from a limited circle of the high nobility and churchmen. The principle that the king should govern with the advice and consent of his council was well established. During the reign of king Hans (1481–1513), a document circulated to all the cathedrals of Denmark proclaimed in unequivocal terms the constitutional view of the council. Warning of the dangers of servitude which would follow if the king could claim a hereditary right to rule, it asserted that in an elective commonwealth, the rightful owners of the realm were the council and

18. Dahlerup T 1971 Danmark *Den nordiske Adel i Senmiddelalderen*. Reports to the conference of Nordic historians, Copenhagen, p. 59.

the inhabitants. The charter granted by the king at Halmstad in 1483 stipulated that he would not rule Denmark without the council's consent and included the right of the nobility to renounce their oath of fealty if the king exceeded his powers. An earlier elected monarch, Eric of Pomerania, so aroused the hostility of the Danish and Swedish nobility that he had been deposed in 1439. For the rest of the century, a succession of rulers struggled to establish control in Denmark, and to persuade the Norwegian and Swedish magnates to accept their rule. In the Swedish case, a succession of regents (*riksföreståndare*) strove long and hard to obstruct this objective. In the course of the long and exhausting struggles between king and regent, the practice of summoning representatives of other sections of society to discuss matters of national importance with the council developed; and out of these *herredagar* was to emerge the Swedish parliament (*riksdag*).

The council nobility in Sweden took advantage of these feuds to try and alter the balance of power in their favour. In 1441, king Kristoffer was obliged to concede that no new member should be added to the council without its consent. Christian I had to agree in 1457 that the crown should not be permitted to acquire *frälse* land: and 1483, king Hans was faced with a programme of demands which, had they been put into force, would have turned Sweden into a nobleman's paradise.[19] Whoever desired to rule Sweden needed a firm hand and a strong head, both of which were possessed by the young man who succeeded in winning the support of the populace and magnates in the early 1520s.

THE DUCHIES OF SLESVIG AND HOLSTEIN

In 1460, the estates of Slesvig and Holstein had acknowledged Christian I as their elected lord, and consented to elect one of his sons or legitimate heirs as his successor. When Christian died in 1481, his widow attempted to promote the election of her younger son Frederik, and this enabled the estates to frustrate the efforts of Hans, the elder son and king of Denmark, to enforce an hereditary claim to the duchies. A compromise was arrived at in 1482, when both men were elected joint rulers. Eight years later, the duchies were divided into 'royal' and 'ducal' parts, and in 1544, Christian III pushed through a new repartition of the duchies against the strong opposition

19. Roberts M 1968 *The Early Vasas. A History of Sweden 1523–1611*. Cambridge, pp. 41–2.

of the estates. This partition was to have fateful consequences, for the king's half-brother Adolf – who was granted the ducal parts of the duchies – founded the Holstein-Gottorp branch which was to prove a thorn in the flesh of the Danish kings in the next century. The king of Denmark was overlord in the duchy of Slesvig, but held Holstein as a fief of the Empire: the duke was a liegeman of the king in Slesvig, and of the emperor in Holstein. The 'ducal' parts of which he was regent were interspersed with the 'royal' parts, and there were also districts jointly administered by the king and the duke.

The nobility in this patchwork of districts (*Ämter*) enjoyed considerable privileges. A twelve-man council, composed of the bishops of Lübeck and Slesvig, and five nobles from each duchy, was to advise the ruler and govern in his absence. The united *Landtag* of the duchies met twice annually, at Flensborg and Kiel and acted as the supreme court. In 1524, the nobility were granted almost unlimited juridical rights over their peasants, and the right of appeal to Denmark was abolished. Peasants were not allowed to leave their holdings without the permission of their lord, who could also forbid them to marry.

THE TEUTONIC ORDER

Ever since the defeat of the knights at the hands of the Polish army in 1410, the fortunes of the Teutonic Order in Prussia had been in decline. The Treaty of Thorn (1466) which ended the disastrous Thirteen Years' War deprived the Order of the western half of its territory, including Danzig and the Order's headquarters of Marienburg. East Prussia, the rump state of the Order, became a Polish fief. (Unlike Livonia, Prussia had never been a part of the Holy Roman Empire). The loss of Danzig gravely weakened the joint front of the Prussian towns, and Königsberg was left to fight a losing battle against the encroachments of the nobility. The smaller Pomeranian towns had come under pressure from duke Bogislaw X at the end of the fifteenth century; even the proud city of Stralsund had to make concessions. Here too the nobility succeeded in wresting important privileges from the dukes. Councillors (*Landräte*) were to be members of the Pomeranian aristocracy, and were to supervise the appointment of all important office-holders.

The Teutonic Order was a model of centralised efficiency in comparison with the neighbouring secular states. A sophisticated electoral procedure ensured smooth succession to the post of Grand Master and

Provincial Master. Those chosen had usually spent many years as senior administrators. At the height of the crusading era, the monastic Order stretched its tentacles across Europe and into Palestine, where it had headquarters in Acre. After the loss of this base in 1291, the activities of the Order focused upon Prussia: from 1309, the Order's headquarters were located in Marienburg. What had been originally a hospitallers' order for German knights in the Holy Land now became a well-organised administrative machine which could offer careers and prospects for the sons of poor gentlemen in the Holy Roman Empire. This continued to be the case in Livonia. In Prussia, however, the last two Grand Masters were well-connected aristocrats. In 1498, Duke Friedrich of Saxony was elected Grand Master in the hope that a German prince of standing might help revive the fortunes of Prussia in the conflict with Poland. His successor, Albrecht von Hohenzollern, led the Order into a disastrous war with Poland in 1519. Lutheranism was beginning to make inroads in the towns of Prussia, and Albrecht himself was in touch with the Wittenberg reformer. In 1525, Albrecht swore fealty to the king of Poland as the first duke of a secularised Prussian state. By contrast, the Provincial Master in Livonia from 1494 to 1535 was from a poor Westphalian noble family. Wolter von Plettenberg had been in Livonia for thirty years before he was appointed in 1481 to the post of chief financial administrator of the Order. Eight years later, he became *Landmarschall*, or commander of the armed forces. Plettenberg was rather more successful in the field than the princely Grand Master, though his reputation as a doughty defender of Livonian independence against the incursions of the Russians acquired a posthumous aura in the writings of the chroniclers who were writing at the time of the Order's demise.

Livonia was a patchwork quilt of territorial fiefs, in which the knightly vassals had acquired a strong position from their warring overlords. The lands of the Order stretched from Kurland – located between the river Düna and the Lithuanian frontier – to the Gulf of Finland. The knights of Harrien and Wierland in Estonia had succeeded in establishing a powerful corporation during the decades of weak Danish rule, and though owing fealty to the Master from 1347, they preserved their privileges intact. As in Prussia, the Order had created a strongly centralised administrative structure, with some thirty districts, five of which provided the members of the inner council of the Master. Within the territory controlled by the Order, the Master rarely granted fiefs. Most of the land was administered by functionaries of the Order. Unlike Prussia, however, where the bishops were relatively insignificant territorial lords, the bishops of

Dorpat, Kurland, Ösel-Wiek and the archbishop of Riga possessed extensive territories. Here, the need for military support compelled the bishops to concede in fief large tracts of land. The Tiesenhusen family, for example, held in tenure from the bishops of Dorpat and Riga about 1,000 *Haken* in the fourteenth century. (The *Haken*, or a household managed by one horse and a hook-plough, was the basic unit of land taxation.)

The bishops and the Order wrangled incessantly throughout the Middle Ages, much to the advantage of the vassals of the bishops and the knights of Harrien and Wierland, who succeeded in forcing extensive concessions over their rights of inheritance. The Livonian diet (*Landtag*) also acquired political significance. The diet of Walk in 1422 ordained that henceforth, the four estates (bishops and their chapters, the Order, the knights and the towns) should meet annually. After the defeat of the Order at the hands of the Lithuanians in 1435, the diet obliged the Master to consult the estates in future before embarking on a foreign war, and to submit territorial disputes to the diet for arbitration. In 1472, the right to resist the Master, should he encroach upon the liberties of his subjects, was proclaimed. In 1526, however, the most powerful men in the land assembled at Wolmar and offered to follow the Prussian example and accept the Master, Wolter von Plettenberg, as their ruler. Plettenberg, well aware of the internal plottings and suspicious of the archbishop of Riga's motives, refused the offer, as he had refused to follow the example of Albrecht von Hohenzollern a year earlier. A prince in Livonia, argued Plettenberg, would have too few subjects to rely on for the defence of the country, and this would fatally expose it to the attacks of its neighbours. Before reinforcements could be recruited in the Empire, the entire country would be lost. An old and intensely conservative man, Plettenberg remained loyal to Catholicism and the already outmoded ideals of the crusading Order.[20]

The entire land was dotted with stoutly fortified castles, from which the vassals ruled their territorial empires. The increased demand for grain led to an expansion of demesne farming in the sixteenth century. It has been estimated that there were some 500 noble demesnes by the middle of the century, many of them extended by cultivation of hitherto virgin land. The intensification of grain cultivation on noble estates led to further erosion of the rights of the peasantry. Runaways were pursued and pressure brought to bear on the

20. Hellmann M 1985 Wolter von Plettenberg. Bedingungen und Beweggründe seines Handelns *Wolter von Plettenberg. Der grösste Ordensmeister Livlands* (ed. N Angermann). Lüneburg, p. 59.

towns to surrender those who had taken refuge within the walls. The burden of labour-service also increased. The few dozen days a year demanded at the end of the fifteenth century had become several days a week fifty years later. Justice was dispensed by the lords, a right which was extended to the landowners in the territories of the dissolved Order in 1561. Well might the chronicler Balthasar Rüssow portray old Livonia as a land which offered strong attractions for the immigrant from Germany. The German minority constituted a privileged elite, much as did the whites in colonial Africa.

The heyday of the Order was nevertheless long past as the fifteenth century drew to a close. The monastic rules appealed less, and the opportunities for an exciting frontier life in the field against the heathen were no longer there. The moralists of course were to attribute the final demise of the Order to the waning of its militant spirit. During the lengthy interval of peace between Plettenberg's victory over the Russians and the onslaught of Ivan IV's troops fifty years later, declared Rüssow, the devil sowed his tares – carnal pride, opulence, arrogance, extravagant living and self-indulgence. A similar verdict of divine punishment for the woeful neglect of the manly virtues of war was reached by other chroniclers.[21] A more prosaic explanation for the decline and fall of the crusading Order in the Baltic might be that it had outlived its function, and was now faced with aggressive and expansionist powers against which its limited resources could not hold out for long. Albrecht von Hohenzollern was canny enough to realise that it was better to keep Prussia as a fief of the king of Poland than lose it altogether. In the long run, the 1525 treaty of Cracow turned out to be a worse bargain for Poland than it was for the Prussian Hohenzollerns. Wolter von Plettenberg, an elderly and loyal servant of the Order, refused to follow Albrecht's example, and the Order in Livonia continued to pursue a rather aimless course, bickering with the archbishop of Riga to the very end.

The fate of Livonia involved all the major territorial states of northern Europe. In taking Narva in 1558, Ivan IV seemed to be opening up his landlocked Muscovite state to the sea and hence the West. Sweden and Denmark staked claims in Estonia, Poland–Lithuania in Kurland and Livonia. 'The rise of the Baltic question', to borrow the title of Walther Kirchner's study of this conflict, was manifold in its ramifications, for much more was involved than dynastic ambition or territorial greed on the part of the rulers. The Baltic question could also have

21. Rüssow 1967 p 4. Henning S 1967 *Lifflendische Churlendische Chronica* (reprint). Hannover, pp. 20–1. Hausmann R, Höhlbaum K (eds) 1876 *Johannes Renner's Livländische Historien*. Göttingen, pp. 131–139.

arisen half a century earlier, when Ivan III made a major thrust towards the Baltic.

When the final disintegration of the Order in Livonia occurred, it sparked off a conflict which was to last for over half a century. At the end of it, Sweden emerged as the victor. At first sight, this seems a strange outcome. Sweden in 1523 was a poor country, with a small population scattered over a vast area of land, and a new ruler with many problems, not least financial. The tsars of Muscovy and the kings of Poland–Lithuania had far better resources at their disposal, and yet neither succeeded in establishing a strong presence on the Baltic. The reason for this may lie in the fact that both Muscovy and Poland–Lithuania had powerful and persistent enemies on other frontiers. The state of Muscovy which Ivan III inherited in 1462 was entirely landlocked. Within twenty years, Ivan had conquered the weak states of Novgorod and Tver, which allowed him for the first time access to the Baltic and the White Sea. It also brought him into conflict with his new western neighbour, Lithuania. Between 1500 and 1537, in a series of savage wars, the Russians pushed westwards into the Lithuanian lands, seizing the fortress-city of Smolensk in 1514. The union of Poland with Lithuania through the Jagiełłionian dynasty created a vast territorial bloc in eastern Europe, which the election of king Kazimierz IV's eldest son Władysław to the thrones of Bohemia (1471) and Hungary (1490) extended still further. Moreover, the rulers of Poland–Lithuania and Muscovy had to contend with the Tatars in the south and east.

This is not to say that the rulers of Muscovy and Poland–Lithuania had no interest in acquiring territory on the Baltic littoral, or that such a move was of secondary importance in their considerations. Ivan III and Ivan IV were certainly interested in extending their influence into Livonia, as was the last Jagiellon king, Zygmunt II August. But any move by one party invariably provoked the other into hostilities, and both had to keep looking over their shoulders in case the Tatars were about to launch an attack in the south. The history of Russian and Polish–Lithuanian involvement in the long series of Livonian wars is marked by a curious caution and reluctance to become deeply engaged. It is as if, having entered the ring, both fighters realised that a more troublesome or worthy opponent was elsewhere; thus they pulled their punches and saved their forces for war on other fronts. The inability of the Swedish forces to make much headway once a bridgehead had been established in northern Estonia in the 1560s indicates how weak the resources of the Vasa kings really were. It was not until the Swedes began cooperating with Stefan Batory's Polish forces in the late 1570s that the Russians were driven out of eastern Estonia. It took another thirty years before the Swedes were able to take and sustain an offensive southwards against the Poles, thus beginning that spectacular rise to European prominence when 'what the Swede intends' was of prime concern to all European statesmen.

The Livonian wars cannot therefore be seen simply as a localised conflict, involving neighbours in a dogfight over a relatively small territorial area. The 'Baltic question' is also part of a much greater, interlocking series of events, in which the rise of Russia to dominance in eastern Europe must be the major theme. With this in mind, we may begin at the beginning, so to speak, and consider the first moves on the Baltic chessboard.

CHAPTER THREE

The Decline of the Order, 1492–1558

UNION AND DISUNION

At first glance it seems remarkable that, at a time when dynastic rivalries and civil wars brought chaos and territorial disintegration to the kingdoms of the Atlantic seaboard, vast territorial unions were being created in north-eastern Europe during the fifteenth century. The kingdoms of Denmark, Norway and Sweden, united in the Kalmar Union of 1397, stretched from the north Atlantic islands to the Karelian isthmus. The Polish–Lithuanian union was equally impressive in territorial terms, and was given an extra dimension by the ambitions of the Jagiełło dynasty in central Europe. At the end of the fifteenth century, the lands under the rule of the Jagiełło family extended from the Danube to the Dnieper, the Black Sea to the Baltic.

In reality, however, the underpinnings of the two unions were never very secure. The terms of the original Union between Poland and Lithuania at Krewo in 1385 have been fiercely debated by Polish and Lithuanian historians. The latter contend that the union was intended to be nothing more than a purely voluntary association of the two lands, the former argue that the *terrae Lithuaniae et Russiae* were permanently attached to the kingdom of Poland.[1] Whatever interpretation may be made of the text of the agreement, it is fairly certain

---

1. A translation of the text of the Union of Krewo is to be found in Vernadsky G *et al.* (eds) 1972 *A source book for Russian history from early times to 1917* (3 vols). New Haven and London, vol. 1, p. 91. See also Dembkowski H 1982 *The Union of Lublin. Polish federalism in the golden age.* Boulder, p. 24. Zmuidzinas J 1978 *Commonwealth polono-lithuanien ou l'Union de Lublin (1569).* Paris, p. 105.

that the nobility of the Lithuanian lands were unwilling to submit to close control from Cracow. The different territorial interests of the two halves of the union caused much mutual recrimination; the Polish nobility grumbled about the unwillingness of the Lithuanians to give military aid, though they demanded Polish assistance in their wars against Muscovy. The dynastic ambitions of the various members of the Jagiełło dynasty loosened the bonds of union; for much of the fifteenth century, the grand dukes of Lithuania were virtually independent rulers. The union was restored in 1447 when grand duke Kazimierz was elected to the Polish throne, but there was no renewal of the old agreements between the two states. On the death of king Kazimierz in 1492, the union split once more, with the Poles electing one son, Jan Olbracht, as their king, the Lithuanians choosing another, Alexander, as grand duke. Although the grand duchy adopted many Polish institutions during this early period of union, the indigenous nobility were jealous of their privileges and the united commonwealth eventually created at Lublin in 1569 owed more to the determination of king Zygmunt August and the Polish nobility to push it through than to the good will of the Lithuanians. The Polish–Lithuanian union was given a firmer foundation with the Union of Lublin, however, and survived until the partitions of the eighteenth century put an end to the commonwealth, or *Rzeczpospolita*.

The union of the three northern crowns established at Kalmar in 1397 proved even more difficult to maintain. For three decades, the regent Karl Knutsson Bonde mounted a fierce resistance to the efforts of Kristoffer of Bavaria (1439–48) and Christian I (1448–81) to impose their claims to the throne of Sweden. In 1471, the unionist forces of king Christian I suffered a bloody defeat at Brunkeberg, outside the walls of Stockholm, a victory which the new regent Sten Sture was not slow to use for propaganda purposes. Christian I, the founder of the Oldenburg dynasty of Danish kings, had to struggle with other enemies, such as the Hanse towns and the English merchants who had begun to trade extensively with the inhabitants of Iceland. After several decades of privateering warfare, Christian's successor was compelled in 1490 to concede extensive fishing and trading rights to the English. Christian I also pawned away the Orkney and Shetland islands, remnants of the medieval Norwegian Atlantic empire, to cover the dowry of his daughter Margrethe on her marriage to James III of Scotland in 1469.

In spite of long and wearisome negotiations, Christian I failed to impose his will on the Swedes, and Sten Sture was still sufficiently powerful to be able to hold at bay the growing number of opponents to his regency in Sweden. Christian's son Hans was recognised as heir to the Norwegian and Swedish thrones in 1458; but on his father's death in 1481, Hans had little option but to enter once more into negotiations with the Swedish lords. A meeting of representatives of the three councils of the northern kingdoms at Kalmar in 1483 produced a new basis for the union, in which the power of the high nobility and the church was evident. Sten Sture was however able to avoid the application of the decisions of this meeting (summed up in the Recess, or agreed statement), and to break the power of his most powerful rival, Ivar Axelsson Tott.

The fate of the two unions was to be heavily influenced by a third state which began to make its presence felt at the end of the fifteenth century. Under Ivan III (1462–1505), the landlocked principality of Muscovy began a phase of expansion which was to push its boundaries westward towards Lithuania, Livonia and Finland. In the 1470s, the vast territory of Novgorod was brought under Muscovy's control; the principality of Tver fell in 1485, and the khanate of Kazan suffered a decisive defeat two years later. The grand prince of Muscovy also engaged in diplomatic intrigue on an international scale. In the early 1490s, Ivan III's Greek legate Yury Trakhaniot conducted a series of protracted, and ultimately abortive discussions with Maximilian, king of the Romans. The Imperial legate Jörg von Thurn concluded an anti-Jagiełło treaty in Moscow in 1490, and on a return visit a year later, sought to persuade Ivan to extend the truce with Sweden. By the end of 1491, however, Ivan no longer had need of Maximilian's uncertain support, nor was he prepared to entertain any intercession on behalf of the hard-pressed regent in Sweden, Sten Sture.[2]

The Finnish-Karelian border was a constant source of bitter dispute, which a new and energetic overlord in Novgorod could hardly ignore. In 1475, the castellan of Viborg, Erik Axelsson Tott, began building a massive castle (Olofsborg) on an island commanding the main east–west waterway in Savo, in an attempt to block the raids of the Karelians. After the death of Erik and his brother Lars, these two frontier fortresses came under the direct control of Sten Sture. Aware of the vulnerability of his position in Finland, Sten Sture was anxious to extend the peace with Novgorod's new master, in 1482 and again in 1487. The rulers of Denmark for their part had not been slow to recognise the potential value of pressure exerted upon the regent by Sweden's new eastern neighbour. In 1474, Christian I had contem-

---

2. Fennell J 1961 *Ivan the Great of Moscow* Oxford, pp. 117–31. Suvanto S 1952 *Suomen poliittinen asema Sten Sture vanhemman valtakautena vuosina 1483–97*. Historiallisia Tutkimuksia 38. Helsinki, pp. 95–107.

plated a grand alliance against Sten Sture, embracing Ivan III, the king of Poland and James III of Scotland. Nothing came of this grandiose plan, but king Hans was to have rather more success than his father in seeking to assemble a coalition against his Swedish rival and the Hanse towns. In 1490, he concluded alliances with Henry VII and Maximilian, king of the Romans. Three years later, he was to enter into negotiations with Muscovy, in an attempt to encircle Sten Sture.

In 1492, the five-year frontier truce between Sweden and Novgorod was due to run out. Negotiations during the winter of 1492–3 failed to reach any satisfactory conclusion. According to Suvanto, the Russians threatened war in order to force the Swedish negotiators to accept the 1323 frontier. The Swedish side refused to be browbeaten, and, knowing that open war with Lithuania was imminent, the Russians were willing to accept a short-term extension of the truce. The bishop of Åbo, Magnus Stiernkors, an ardent advocate of the crusade against the Russians, had cast doubts upon the advisability of reaching a durable agreement with Ivan III in a letter to the regent. Sten Sture was, however, disposed to prolong the peace as long as possible.[3]

In the end, a short-term truce of eighteen months was signed by the two sides. The conclusion in October 1493 of an alliance between Denmark and Muscovy directed against Sten Sture was a considerable blow to the Sture party, already beset with troubles from domestic opposition led by the archbishop of Uppsala, Jakob Ulfsson. Frantic efforts were made to discuss a prolongation of the truce with Muscovy and the council of the realm in Sweden forced a reluctant Sten Sture to negotiate with king Hans. At the meeting of the estates in Linköping in March 1495, however, Sten Sture was able to rally popular opinion against the idea of union. He was less successful in securing Finland from attack. Having made peace with grand duke Alexander of Lithuania in 1494, and with the Livonian Order neutralised by means of a ten-year extension of the truce, Ivan III launched a major attack across the Finnish frontier in the autumn of 1495. The fortress of Viborg was besieged for three months. On the last day of November, the besieging forces attempted to take the citadel by storm, but were driven off after a tower had collapsed upon them. By the time Sten Sture's relief army had reached the scene, the Russians had withdrawn. In February 1496, Russian troops raided deep into Finland. Northern Finland was ravaged in the summer, whilst Svante Nilsson and Knut Posse led a successful counter-raid across the Gulf of

3. Suvanto 1952 pp. 147–57. Schybergson M 1903 *Finlands historia* (2 vols). Helsingfors, vol. 1, p. 138. Westergaard W 1937 Denmark, Russia and Sweden 1480–1503 *Slavonic and East European Review* **16**: 129–40.

Finland, burning Ivangorod, the fortress erected by Ivan III in 1492 on the eastern bank of the Narova river. Plans for a further campaign in the autumn collapsed when Sten Sture's rival Svante Nilsson returned to Sweden, pleading lack of funds, and the unpaid troops in Finland threatened to mutiny. In his desperate search for allies, Sten Sture even promised the crown of Sweden to grand duke Alexander. Although Alexander declined this offer, he did act as mediator with his new father-in-law in Moscow. Ivan, facing the threat of renewed Tatar attacks, was disposed to peace, and a truce of six years was concluded in Novgorod in March 1497.

The terms of the truce included a provision for further discussion of the frontier, but reminders of this obligation by Ivan III drew little response from the Swedes or king Hans. Although the alliance between Denmark and Muscovy stated that the Finnish–Karelian frontier should remain as of old, it was rumoured that Hans had promised three Finnish parishes to Ivan. In 1501, Ivan's emissaries to king Hans caused some embarrassment by reminding him of this promise. The threat of renewed warfare on the Karelian border continued to hang in the air, though Ivan's attention was drawn to the more pressing need to deal with his neighbours further south. The bringing together of the Russian lands under his rule, and the recognition of his claim to be sovereign of all Russia (*gosudar' vseya Rusi*) was Ivan's primary objective: but he was also eager to establish his ascendancy over other frontier areas. In 1481, after an unsuccessful military campaign into Russian lands, the Livonian Order was obliged to conclude a peace agreement with Ivan, which explicitly recognised his superior authority. In 1494, representatives of the Hanse towns of Reval and Dorpat returning from negotiations in Moscow were arrested, together with the German merchants in Novgorod. The arrests were made, according to the governor of Novgorod, in order to press demands for financial compensation for the damage caused to the retinue of Yuri Trakhaniot during his stay in Reval, and as a protest against the execution of two Russians in Reval.[4] In Reval, there were fears that the arrests presaged an attack on Livonia, and it was widely believed that the closure of the Hanse *Kontor* was a direct result of the Danish–Russian alliance.

Soviet historians have been prone to see Ivan's actions as part of a

4. One was executed for forgery, the other for committing an unnatural act with a mare. Other Russians in the town apparently defended the man by claiming that such practices were commonplace even amongst the high-born in their own country, according to an early piece of anti-Russian propaganda: see von Schirren C (ed.) 1861 Eynne Schonne Hysthorie van vnderlyken geschefften der heren tho Lyfflanth myth der Rüssen unde Tartaren *Archiv für Geschichte Liv- Esth- und Kurlands* **8**: 138–41.

plan to breach the trade barrier imposed by the Livonian towns and to establish direct links with western merchants. Western historians, on the other hand, have tended to reject this idea, focusing instead on Ivan's efforts to impose his will and juridical control upon foreign merchants trading in his domains.[5] Ivan was also well aware of the internal conflicts in Livonia. In 1487, representatives of the Livonian towns were asked by the Russians what they would do in the event of an attack on the Order: the reply was that the merchants would observe neutrality. Riga had been in conflict with the Master of the Order and the archbishop for decades. The new Master, Wolter von Plettenberg (1494–1535), soon found that in moments of crisis, Livonia could not count upon support from outside. In spite of Maximilian's appeals for aid for Livonia at the Imperial Diet in 1495, none was forthcoming. The Grand Master in Prussia was preoccupied with Poland, the Wendish Hanseatic towns failed to rally to the aid of their Livonian rivals, and the Pope's erratic appeals for a crusade against Orthodoxy and the sale of indulgences to finance such a venture were of little practical help. Although Plettenberg managed to negotiate the release of the imprisoned men in 1497, the situation remained tense. In 1500, war broke out between Muscovy and Lithuania, and in the following year, Plettenberg concluded an offensive alliance with grand duke Alexander. The Livonian forces were to receive little help from their ally, whose attention was diverted towards securing the Polish throne on the death of his brother, king Jan Olbracht. In August 1501, Plettenberg's forces won a major victory over the Muscovite and Pskov armies on the Seritsa river, south of Izborsk. After burning and sacking the town of Ostrov, the Livonian army, afflicted by an outbreak of dysentery, withdrew, thus failing to link up with the Lithuanian forces fifty miles to the south.

The Muscovites responded by mounting a major invasion of Livonia in November, winning a crushing victory at the battle of Helmed and ravaging the surrounding countryside: according to Rüssow, 40,000 were either killed or taken prisoner. In 1502, however, Ivan's war plans received a setback, for he failed to capture the crucial fortress of Smolensk, and his forces suffered defeat at the hands of Plettenberg at lake Smolino, south of Pskov. One of Plettenberg's officers, in a letter written just after the battle, boasted that any Russians who fell into the hands of the invaders were throttled and

5. See for example Vassar A, Naan G 1961 *Istoriya Estonskoy SSR* (3 vols). Tallinn, p. 270. Tiberg E 1970 Moskau, Livland und die Hanse, 1487–1547 *Hansische Geschichtsblätter,* **93**: 13–33. Raba J 1978 Russland-Livländische Beziehungen am Anflang des 16 Jahrhunderts: Partnerschaft oder Konfrontation? *Zeitschrift für Ostforschung* **27**: 577–9.

slain. The invading Muscovites were accused of spitting infants on sharp poles and subjecting women to all kinds of bestiality. The atrocities supposedly committed by the invading Russians and Tatars in 1501 were graphically portrayed in a pamphlet written in 1508, and widely circulated in Germany to support the sale of indulgences intended to raise money for Livonia's defence. That it was deemed necessary to mount such a campaign is an apt measure of how vulnerable and enfeebled Livonia now was, faced with a powerful and aggressive eastern neighbour.[6]

The main thrust of Muscovy's war effort in the west was directed against Lithuania. During the reign of Vasily III (1505–33), the fortress of Smolensk was captured, and a number of dissatisfied Lithuanian nobles, such as the Glinsky family, transferred their alliegance to Muscovy. Vasily also maintained the grip his father had established upon Livonia. The truce concluded in 1503 was renewed in 1509, but the Livonians were obliged in future to abstain from alliances directed against Muscovy. The grand duke of Muscovy, for his part, refused to make a similar undertaking, claiming that he was well able to deal with his enemies without assistance from mortal allies. The Muscovites also resorted to trade embargoes and pressure on the Livonian towns. In 1514, after long and exhausting negotiations, an agreement was reached with the Livonian Hanse towns, which allowed the Novgorod *Kontor* to reopen, whilst guaranteeing freedom of trade for Russian merchants in Livonia. This was not a success, and the treaty was not renewed in 1524. The towns also resented the commercial clauses included in agreements made between the Master and the Russians, and refused to acknowledge their validity. Although Livonia was spared the horror of invasion from the east for over fifty years, the truce with Muscovy was at best an uneasy one; and the continued wrangling of the estates which made up the confederation did nothing to ensure that Livonia would be better prepared in future to resist such an onslaught.

In Sweden, the threat of Muscovite attack had temporarily stilled the opposition to Sten Sture. In 1496 however, relations between the regent and the council of the realm deteriorated, and in February of the following year, the council declared Sten Sture's regency to be at an end. In the ensuing civil war, Hans took the opportunity to invade Sweden and besiege Sten Sture's forces in Stockholm. Realising the

6. von Bunge F (ed.) 1905 *Liv- Est- und Kurländisches Urkundenbuch* (12 vols). Riga, part 2, vol. 2, p. 278. Benninghoven F 1961 Russland im Spiegel der livländischen Schonnen Hysthorie von 1508 *Zeitschrift für Ostforschung* **11**: 601–25. Rüssow 1967 Chronica Provintz Lyfflandt (reprint edn). Hannover, p. 33. Fennell 1961 pp. 239–42.

hopelessness of his military position, the deposed regent opened negotiations with the king. In return for a full pardon, he renounced his
claims to the regency and swore fealty to Hans, receiving generous
fiefs in Finland. Hans was finally crowned king of Sweden in the great
church of Stockholm in November 1497.

His triumph was short-lived. Within four years, Sten Sture had
patched up his differences with his enemies and had been hailed as
regent once more. The royal castle in Stockholm was captured and
Hans's queen made prisoner. The death of Sten Sture in 1503 brought
no noticeable improvement in the fortunes of king Hans, for the
deceased regent was immediately succeeded by his relative and former
enemy, Svante Nilsson. A delegation sent by the Swedish council to
negotiate in Copenhagen managed to conclude a truce, and preparations were made once more for joint discussions of the union question. The Swedes failed to turn up at the Kalmar meeting in 1505. The
Norwegian and Danish council members, constituted as a court,
adjudged Sten Sture, his successor and eight of their supporters guilty
of lese-majesty, and declared them deprived of their honour, privileges and lands. This verdict was upheld by the Imperial high court
in 1506, and pressure was brought to bear on the Wendish Hanse
towns to cease trading with Sweden. The trade blockade proved to be
an effective means of forcing the Swedes to reopen negotiations,
though the 1509 Copenhagen agreement, which recognised the rights
of the king and promised him an annual tribute of 12,000 marks, was a
truce rather than a settlement. Peace was finally reached at Malmö, a
month after the death of Svante Nilsson in 1512; the Swedes now
consented to observe the provisions of the Copenhagen agreement.
An attempt by the war-weary council to elect a non-member of the
Sture clan as regent came to nothing: Svante's son, Sten Sture (the
younger) was chosen in the summer of 1512, after promising to obey
the instructions of the council. The corpulent Hans, whose private life
had prompted much scandal (he once appeared at a meeting with the
Hanseatic delegates with a mistress on either arm), died in 1513,
recognised but not accepted as king of Sweden.

The new king of Denmark, Christian II, was a man of different
mettle. In 1515, he married into the powerful Habsburg family, and
embarked upon a vigorous diplomatic offensive to isolate Sweden.
King Zygmunt I and Danzig agreed to observe neutrality, and the
treaty with Muscovy was renewed. In the meantime, the regent had
clashed with archbishop Gustav Trolle, who fought back by appealing
for papal protection. The Sture party was placed under papal ban by
the archbishop of Lund, but Danish invasions in 1517 and 1518 failed

to dislodge the regent. Gustav Trolle's castle of Almare-Stäket was stormed and razed to the ground, and the archbishop deprived of office by a meeting of the estates, which also swore to accept common responsibility for their decision, and to resist any attempt by the papal court to institute punitive measures. In 1519, Sten Sture was excommunicated and Sweden placed under an interdict. Christian II could thus begin a new campaign in January 1520 with the full might of the church and Empire behind him. This time, his troops, ably led by Otto Krumpen, were successful. The Swedes were defeated at Åsunden, Sten Sture dying of his wounds a fortnight later. A section of the council nobility hastened to make peace with Christian, whilst the Sture party grimly held out in Stockholm.

All three Sture regents possessed an uncanny ability to confuse their enemies and rally support by intrigue and openly demagogic tactics. They succeeded in building up their power through the accretion of fiefs and lands, and were able to eliminate potential rivals such as the Tott clan in the 1480s. The aristocratic and ecclesiastical opposition was often outwitted or forced to accede to the demands of the regent; but it did lay down the basis of a constitutional programme which later generations were to develop. Interestingly, when Hans did at last briefly succeed in establishing his claims to the Swedish throne in 1497, he was generous in his treatment of Sten Sture, whom he may have seen as a potential ally in his attempts to overturn the principles of aristocratic conciliar control established in the 1483 Kalmar Recess. Sten Sture had managed to resist the full implementation of these principles, and Hans also sought to set aside the provisions of the Kalmar Recess. In March 1520, the Swedish aristocracy secured a temporary victory when Christian II agreed to rule in accordance with the advice of the council. Events in Stockholm later that year were to show how little the king's word could be relied on. The defenders of the castle surrendered in September, in return for a full amnesty which covered any misdeeds committed against the church. On 1 November, surrounded by Krumpen's men-at-arms, the estates assembled on Brunkeberg, where they were obliged to acknowledge Christian as their lawful and hereditary monarch. The council had made the same submission a day earlier, thereby surrendering the ground won in March.

There still remained the claims of the vengeful archbishop Gustav Trolle to be satisfied. Three days after the king's coronation, according to three canons of Uppsala, who later wrote down their eye-witness accounts for Gustav Vasa, as the king was seated on the throne in the great hall of Stockholm castle, archbishop Trolle came in and began levelling bitter accusations against those who had molested the property of his diocese:

> After a little while, the king went out and the council remained investigating these complaints until it fell dark. Then lights were asked for and, like Judas Iscariot seeking to trap Christ and betray him, Claus Bille and Søren Norby at the bidding of the most cruel king came in with tapers and torches and with a sizeable company of armed men who surrounded the entire hall.[7]

A special court of prelates, convened by the king, pronounced judgement the following day. Throughout the murky November afternoon, on the square outside the castle, eighty-two persons were beheaded, their bodies left in the blood-soaked gutters. Later, with the corpses of the exhumed Sten Sture the younger and his son, they were burnt outside the city walls. Further executions were carried out in Finland and during the king's return journey to Denmark.

The 'Stockholm bloodbath' has caused endless controversy amongst historians. The motives of the chief participants, the nature of the charges and the validity of the sentences have all been hotly debated. It is probable that Christian II seized upon Trolle's complaints as an instrument with which to defeat the Sture party; but as an ambitious prince seeking to establish hereditary rule, he could hardly have wished the full restitution of power to an ambitious and ruthless man known for political intrigue. In terms of canon law, the trial, if it was for heresy (Trolle's original charge against his enemies), was highly irregular. The turning-point probably came during the preliminary investigation, when Sten Sture's widow revealed the existence of the estates' conjuration of 1517. This was used by the court to prove that the conjurors were guilty of having banded together to resist papal authority. The executions removed not only leading members of the Sture party, but several members of the council and the episcopacy. The victims were selected for execution in a highly arbitrary manner which bore little relation to the sentence of the court: and this tends to strengthen the argument that Christian, if not the instigator of the process, certainly saw in it an opportunity to get rid of real or imagined opponents.[8]

Whether Christian was merely the loyal executioner of the blood-thirsty will of the archbishop, or a ruthless opportunist, his reputation

---

7. Hildebrand E 1918 Dokumenter till Stockholm blodbads förhistoria *Historisk Tidskrift* **38**: 118–9.

8. Roberts 1968 *The Early Vasas* pp. 16–18, 478. In addition to the major studies of the bloodbath cited by Roberts, mention may be made of the articles by C Weibull and N Skyum-Nielsen in *Scandia*, 1969, pp. 272–352; 1970, pp. 121–50; 1971, pp. 248–70.

was forever stained. The misdeeds of the 'bloody tyrant and cruel unchristian' king Christian were shouted from the rooftops by the propagandists of the young Gustav Vasa. Gustav, a relative of the Sture family, had been taken to Denmark as a hostage in 1518, but had escaped in 1519 and made his way to Lübeck. Although Lübeck's enmity of Denmark had not abated, the burghers were still sufficiently cowed by the pressure brought to bear by Christian's brother-in-law the emperor Charles V to remain prudently at peace with Denmark. Gustav left the city in the spring of 1520, and after initial failure, succeeded in raising revolt amongst the traditional supporters of the Sture clan, the peasants of Dalarna. By the summer of 1521, Gustav's army had captured Uppsala, and Gustav himself, with aristocratic support, was elected regent. The turning-point in the war came in 1522, when Lübeck, angered by Christian II's breach of an agreement not to raise the Sound dues, and fearful of the Danish king's grandiose plans to create a Scandinavian merchant company, gave its backing to the Swedish rebels. In Denmark, discontent with king Christian amongst the nobility led to revolt, and the election of his uncle, duke Frederik of Holstein, as king in March 1523. Three months later, Gustav Vasa was elected king of Sweden by the council. Christian fled in April to the Low Countries, where he sought in vain to rouse his Imperial brother-in-law to provide him with assistance.

The threat of an attempt to regain the thrones of Denmark and Norway by the exiled Christian drew the two new northern sovereigns together. They were also at one in their desire to shake off the shackles of Lübeck, which had played a major role in elevating the two men to their respective thrones. Lübeck initially backed Frederik's claims to the throne of Sweden, but quickly realised the value of a broken union. On 7 June 1523, two representatives of the Hanse town flanked Gustav Vasa at a solemn mass to celebrate his acclamation as king in Strängnäs cathedral the previous day. The new king of Sweden made extensive concessions to Lübeck and for the first eight years of his reign struggled to discharge his debts to the town, and to escape from its relentless grip upon the national economy. King Frederik I had to rely heavily on Lübeck's assistance in dealing with Christian II's commander, the wily Søren Norby. Norby had ensconced himself on the island of Gotland and turned it into a haven for privateers. A Swedish attempt to evict Norby in 1524 failed, and Lübeck was able to impose a settlement, much resented by Gustav Vasa, at the first meeting of the two kings at Malmö. Søren Norby was obliged to surrender his fief and evacuate the island in Frederik's favour. This he refused to do. During the winter of 1524–5, he busied himself in plots with a variety of Swedish malcontents. The troublesome Norby was finally defeated at sea by the Lübeckers and driven to flight in 1526, but not before he had incited a rebellion in favour of Christian II in Skåne – where the peasantry resented the heavy tax burden imposed by the new king – and resumed his old piratical habits from the ports of Blekinge.

Gustav Vasa was also plagued by troublesome subjects. In the autumn of 1525, the king had to go in person to Dalarna to suppress an incipient rebellion. Eighteen months later, two leading members of the Sture party were executed for plotting against the king. Gustav Vasa was also faced with a new rebellion in Dalarna, led by a young man who claimed (falsely) to be Nils Sture. Most of the grievances of the peasantry were attributable to the heavy burden of taxation imposed by the new king to meet his debts. In the midst of these troubles, the king struck back in masterly fashion. In a lengthy Proposition submitted to the *riksdag* he had summoned to Västerås in 1527, Gustav Vasa disclaimed responsibility for the current hard times and directed the estates' attention towards the wealth of the church. He concluded his peroration with a threat to abdicate. The prospect of a renewal of conflict and the return of the hated Gustav Trolle and king Christian was sufficient to persuade the estates to come up with a series of proposals, incorporated into the final Recess of the *riksdag*. The king was assured of the support of the estates against all traitors. The powers of the church were to be drastically curtailed: episcopal castles were to be surrendered to the crown, which was also authorised to relieve the cathdrals and canonries of 'superfluous' revenue. The nobility's backing for these measures was ensured by a stipulation that all property donated to the church since 1454 could be reclaimed without compensation by the families of the noble donor. Gustav's summary of the Recess went even further, allowing the king to interfere in the appointment of the clergy, and appropriating to the crown many of the fines hitherto payable to church courts. In 1528, Gustav was crowned, and his coronation oath significantly omitted the pledge to safeguard the rights and property of the church.[9]

Gustav's prime concern in 1527 was the elimination of ecclesiastical power and the distribution of church wealth; the injunction to the clergy to preach the pure word of God which was included in the Recess was in no way an unqualified endorsement of the new faith, which had just begun to make inroads in Sweden. The Reformation

---

9. Roberts 1968 pp. 75–84. The course of the Reformation in Sweden will be considered more fully in Chapter Four.

had made more headway in Denmark, and especially in the duchies, where Frederik's son Christian openly championed the new faith. The death of Frederik in April 1533 led to a serious crisis and war, in which religious alignments in the Baltic played a part. Threatened by an invasion of Norway at the end of 1531 by Christian II, Frederik had concluded a new alliance with Lübeck, which the Hanse town hoped would close the Sound to their Dutch rivals, who had financed Christian's return. Christian's military campaign proved a disaster. In the summer of 1532, he agreed to negotiations with his uncle, who promptly had him imprisoned, in spite of guarantees of safe conduct. The luckless Christian was incarcerated in Sønderborg castle, though he remained a potential threat in the continuing atmosphere of political uncertainty.

Neither Frederik I nor Gustav Vasa was willing to accede to the demands of Lübeck to cease trading with the Dutch. A trade war broke out in 1533 between Sweden and the Hanse town, now controlled by a Protestant faction led by Jürgen Wullenweber, and in September of that year the Danish council entered into a defensive alliance with the Low Countries. The conservative nobles of the council had postponed the election of a successor to Frederik: the estates could not agree upon a successor. The burghers of Copenhagen and Malmö rose in support of the imprisoned Christian, and succeeded in attracting the support of Lübeck, whose commander, count Christoffer of Oldenburg, invaded Denmark. The Danish council responded to this threat by signing an alliance with Gustav Vasa, whose position was also threatened by the bellicose Lübeckers. Led by Mogens Gøye, the nobility of Jutland turned to duke Christian with the offer of the Danish throne, in return for promises of restraint in matters of religion. The so-called 'Count's War' continued for two more years before Christian III could claim undisputed mastery over his new kingdom. At the end of 1534, Lübeck made a truce with Christian III, whose Holstein forces had imposed a tight blockade on the mouth of the river Trave. The Jutland peasants who had risen on behalf of the imprisoned Christian were left to their fate, and were ruthlessly crushed. Swedish forces cleared Skåne, and in the summer of 1535, the Lübeck fleet suffered a heavy defeat at the hands of the combined navies of Sweden, Denmark and Prussia. In August 1535, the Wullenweber faction was overthrown, and the restored council sued for peace with Christian III. Finally, the towns of Malmö and Copenhagen surrendered to Christian III in the summer of 1536. Christian prudently concluded a three-year truce with the regent of the Low Countries and associated himself with the princes of the anti-Imperial Schmalkaldic League, in order to shield himself from further attack from the supporters of ex-king Christian.

The confused episode of the Count's War had several important consequences. Lübeck's prestige and ability to dictate terms to its economically weak northern neighbours was severely bruised; even though the town managed to retain a very strong influence upon Swedish trade, it was unable to maintain the privileges conceded by Gustav Vasa in 1523. The heavy cost of the wars against Denmark and the Dutch had compelled the conservative town council in 1528 to agree to the creation of a commission of sixty-four, upon which the Wullenweber faction soon gained control. Wullenweber and his allies were by no means the spokesmen for the unrepresented lower orders. Wullenweber himself was a senior member of the Novogorod traders' club, and many of his supporters were men of high social standing, who resented the increasing exclusivity of the patriciate in control of the town's affairs. The victory of these men in 1533, although short-lived, established the reformed faith in the town, as did Christian III's eventual accession to the throne in Denmark. Christian took the opportunity of the civil conflict to have his ecclesiastical opponents arrested, and their lands confiscated. The church ordinance of 1539 placed Denmark firmly on the road to a Protestant church order. In Sweden, a royal decree in the same year subordinated the church to state control, though in matters of faith, the king continued to pursue a non-committal policy. Both monarchs were deeply involved in the process of consolidating their power and strengthening their finances. The zealous activities of Gustav Vasa's equivalent to Thomas Cromwell, the church *superattendent* Georg Norman, provoked an uprising in Småland in 1542, which the king's many enemies abroad sought to use to their advantage. Fears of foreign invasion were used by the king at the *riksdag* of 1544 to persuade the council and estate of nobles to agree to a succession pact, which converted Sweden into an hereditary monarchy. Christian III's chancellor Johan Friis was able to introduce a number of significant administrative and legal reforms, and to restore many alienated fiefs to royal control. The towns were also placed under tighter royal fiscal supervision. But Christian, like his father, was heavily dependent upon the nobility for his throne, and had to make concessions in his *håndfæstning* which would have driven the choleric king of Sweden to apoplexy.

The demands of domestic policy and the threat of common enemies tended to draw the two kings together in times of crisis. At Brömse-bro in 1541, they concluded a defensive alliance for fifty years. Several of the provisions of this agreement bore the legacy of the now dissolved union. Thus, judges from both kingdoms were to be appointed to investigate cases brought by subjects of either realm who had fallen foul of their king and had been exiled as a result. Christian III, a committed opponent of the Habsburgs, was anxious to have Sweden by his side in the event of a major conflict erupting in Europe. A Franco–Swedish alliance was forged in 1542, at Denmark's instigation, and Sweden was also admitted to the ranks of the Schmalkaldic League. In the subsequent hostilities which erupted between the emperor and his enemies, Sweden played little part, and Gustav Vasa refused to send a representative to the peace talks at Speyer in 1544. The Danes, having closed the Sound to the Dutch in 1542, were obliged to agree to a mutual restoration of seized goods and ships, and to the reopening of the Sound to Dutch vessels. Christian III was also obliged to alleviate the conditions of his prisoner in Sønderborg castle, and concluded in 1546 an agreement with Christian whereby the latter renounced on his own behalf and that of his heirs all claims to the three northern kingdoms in return for a cash settlement and honourable confinement in Kalundborg, where he died in 1559.

The survival of Christian and the vigorous campaigning of his daughter and her husband, Friedrich of the Palatinate, did much to establish Gustav Vasa as sovereign ruler of Sweden, even if the kings of Denmark never fully renounced their claims. As long as the deposed king was alive, neither Frederik I nor Christian III were likely to risk their tenure of the Danish throne by pursuing the vanished chimera of the union. Christian III in particular seems to have been genuinely anxious to uphold the agreement reached at Brömsebro in 1541, even if the suspicious king of Sweden obstinately preferred to go his own way. The long period of relative amity between the two kingdoms did not survive the deaths of Christian III in 1559 and Gustav Vasa a year later, but then a new and intense period of warfare in north-eastern Europe was about to begin. In some respects, the histories of Denmark and Sweden during the first half of the sixteenth century resemble that of another peripheral European country, whose sovereign was also preoccupied with a church settlement and the consolidation of his authority. In temperament and character, indeed, Gustav Vasa shared many of the characteristics of Henry VIII – tetchy, inordinately suspicious, he was a man of energy and talent who could on occasion overreact to his mistakes, with unpleasant consequences for those around him. Both men had a proud and imperious nature. Gustav Vasa's reply to peasants from the Finnish parish of Lappvesi, who grumbled about high taxes – 'It astonishes us not a little that you should trouble yourselves with that of which you ought not to meddle with. And you should know, that we are your true lord and master, and the governance and rule lies with us, and not with you' – is reminiscent of Henry VIII's outburst against the presumptions of the 'rude commons' of Lincolnshire in 1535.[10] But the parallel has its limits. Though by no means an uneducated man, Gustav Vasa was no match for Henry VIII in intellectual or artistic accomplishment; in this regard, Christian II was a much better example of the talented Renaissance prince. There was a world of difference between the rough-and-ready Swedish court (and even rougher manners of the courtiers) and the more refined milieu of Whitehall. The pace of the Reformation was a good deal more leisurely, and far less fraught by religious strife, in the northern kingdoms. Above all, the social and economic problems faced by the Vasa and Oldenburg dynasties were of a different scale and dimension to those of Tudor England. In spite of the size of their domains, the rulers of Denmark–Norway and Sweden–Finland are best described as modest princes, lacking the resources of a fertile soil, prosperous cities and a large manpower reserve with which to pursue their ambitions.

These deficiencies were one reason for the break-up of the union of the three northern crowns. Time and time again, the kings of Denmark were simply unable to muster sufficient military strength to enforce their claims to the crown of Sweden, and had to resort to protracted bargaining. The successful campaign mounted by Christian II was costly, and the fiscal measures taken by the king to meet these costs provoked unrest at home and alienated Lübeck, whose role in the overthrow of king Christian was crucial. The Hanseatic towns had been able to frustrate the efforts of the Oldenburgs to enforce their rule in Sweden. The union, which had been partly effected to challenge the grip of the Hanse, proved to be a golden opportunity for the Wendish towns, led by Lübeck, to maintain their commercial dominance in Scandinavia. Hanseatic support for the regents undoubtedly helped them to hold out against the efforts of the monarchs in Copenhagen to maintain the union. On the few occasions when the Danish monarchs were able to compel the Hanse towns to stop supplying Sweden, as in the last years of the reign of king Hans, the Swedes experienced real difficulties and were obliged at least to negotiate.

The regents of Sweden were thus able to use the Hanse to good effect in their struggles with the Oldenburgs. As those struggles intensified, the Danish kings looked to Muscovy for assistance. The

10. Schybergson 1903 vol. 1, p. 263.

alliance concluded by king Hans in 1493 proved to be a mistake, for Ivan III was not content simply to play the role of a loyal supporter of the rights of a fellow–sovereign and Hans was not prepared to cede away territory on the Finnish frontier. The threat of a Russian attack may also have strengthened Sten Sture's position; and it certainly served to emphasise, at least to those with estates in Finland, the danger from the east which the king seemed prepared to encourage in order to press his claims.

The Muscovite threat may be adduced as one reason for the pre-servation of the union of Lithuania and Poland; the making of alliances with Muscovy by Hans and his successor did little to encourage the Swedish and Finnish nobility to remain loyal to union under the Oldenburgs.[11] The unionist party in Sweden was essentially interested in preserving aristocratic power through the council; it disliked the quasi-monarchical pretensions of the Stures, but it was not willing to see imposed the kind of monarchical rule that Christian II had in mind. Christian attempted to impose the union by force, aided by men such as Didrik Slagheck and Gustav Trolle who were widely feared and hated in both countries. Unlike Zygmunt August in 1569, who was able to push through the union of Lublin with the eager backing of his Polish nobles, the king of Denmark could not count on the unqualified support of his own nobility. There can be little doubt that the events in Stockholm in the autumn of 1520 sounded the death-knell of the union idea, for they destroyed the credibility not only of the king, but of the most powerful figure of the unionist party, archbishop Trolle. The leaders of the church had been amongst the most fervent supporters of the union. The savagery of the executions in Stockholm and elsewhere left the church in disarray, and utterly incapable of offering any effective resistance to the onslaught launched on its wealth and privileges in 1527. The few who opposed the new order were fated to spend their years in futile exile. The church became an obedient servant of the state, and no monarch after Gustav Vasa was ever seriously troubled by fractious prelates.

---

11. For the position and importance of Finland as a base for the Stures, see Suvanto 1952, pp. 300–9, 325–31 (German summary) and Pohjolan-Pirhonen H 1953 *Suomen poliittinen asema pohjoismaisen unionin loppuvaiheissa 1512–1523* Historiallisia Tutkimuksia 40. Helsinki, pp. 31–55, 410–16 (German summary).

THE LIVONIAN QUESTION

The introduction of the reformed faith in Prussia was to have repercussions outside the confines of the newly secularised duchy. The last
Grand Master and first duke of Prussia, Albrecht von Hohenzollern,
was able to institute a new church order with relative ease, with little
opposition from the knights of the Order or the bishops; but in doing
so, he put himself at odds with the German Master of the Order and
the emperor. To secure his position, Albrecht had to engage in diplomatic and political intrigue, which had the effect of destabilising
still further an already weakened polity in Livonia. The bitter conflicts
between the Livonian bishops, their vassals and the towns, and the
rivalry between the archbishop of Riga and the Master of the Order,
offered the duke of Prussia ample opportunity to fish in troubled
waters.

By 1525, the supporters of the reformed faith had managed to
secure the upper hand in Riga, and were making headway in Reval
and Dorpat. The further progress of the Reformation, however, was
heavily dependent upon the willingness of the rural nobility to join
forces with the towns in their struggle against the episcopacy. At the
diet of Wolmar in 1522, an informal alliance had been forged between
the towns and the diocesan vassals to protect their privileges against
the claims of Johann Blankenfeld, the bishop of Reval and Dorpat.
The lay estates refused to give way to the bishops' demands for the
proclamation in Livonia of the papal bull and the edict of Worms,
which denounced Luther and all his works. The reason for this refusal
was not religious conviction, but anti-clericalism: the estates justified
their position by claiming that Livonia had been conquered by the
secular sword, and not by papal bans.[12] This alliance was renewed
two years later, after Blankenfeld's election as archbishop of Riga. In
August 1524, Riga threw off its allegiance to the archbishop and
appealed to the Master of the Order to assume sole lordship over the
town. Blankenfeld, who had developed the techniques of intrigue and
duplicity to a fine art during his earlier years in the papal curia, sought
to drive a wedge into the alliance of the towns and diocesan vassals. In
the autumn of 1524, he abandoned his struggle with his vassals over
the reversion of fiefs by escheat and other contested rights; similar
concessions were also made by the bishop of Ösel.

This move weakened the alliance, but Blankenfeld's position was

---

12. Arbusow L 1964 *Die Einführung der Reformation in Liv-Est- und Kurland* (reprint
edn). Aalen, pp. 221–2. Wittram R 1956 Die Reformation in Livland, in Wittram R
(ed.) *Baltische Kirchengeschichte*. Göttingen, p. 38.

still precarious. He was suspected, with some justification, of having dealings with the Russians, and he also clashed with the magistracy of Dorpat in January 1525. On the other hand, the news of peasant unrest in Germany alarmed the Livonian nobility, who complained that their peasants were imbibing dangerous ideas from the reformers in the towns. The provocative preaching of Sylvester Tegetmeier, whom the Riga delegation brought with them to the diet in July 1525, may well have tipped the balance. Tegetmeier was warned beforehand by Plettenberg not to incite an insurrection. His preaching on Matthew 19: 27–29 and 21:13, was an unmistakable attack on the episcopacy, and his inflammatory words drew upon his head the wrath of the noblemen from Harrien and Wierland, who denounced him as a rabble-rouser and traitor. Forced to withdraw, Tegetmeier preached in the open on a text from Isaiah 1 which included such choice verses as: 'Thy princes are rebellious, and companions of thieves'.[13] The towns were abandoned by their allies, who agreed with the bishops and Master to impose a ban on any further changes in the church. Although the reforms already carried out were permitted to remain in force, the decision of the majority at the diet effectively isolated the towns, already coming under pressure from the Hanse diet not to permit radical preachers in their midst. The radical waves of the Reformation had already lapped against the walls of the Livonian towns, and warnings against such excesses were probably unnecessary for the magistracy. The Reformation in the towns was not put under threat by the decisions of the diet of 1525 – the arrest of Blankenfeld at the end of the year on suspicion of treasonable dealings with the Russians distracted any attention which might have been focused on the doings of the evangelical preachers – but the towns were compelled to look elsewhere for allies.

In this quest, a major role was played by Johannes Lohmüller, the town secretary of Riga. On the eve of the 1525 diet, Lohmüller had addressed an appeal to Plettenberg, in which he had denounced the pretensions of the spiritual estate to exercise secular rule, and urged the Master to assume sovereign authority in Livonia.[14] Lohmüller entertained few illusions about the willingness of Plettenberg to take on such a task. After the towns' defeat at the 1525 diet, he entered into negotiations with agents of the duke of Prussia. Fear of the towns passing under the protection of Prussia, and distrust of the archbishop

13. Arbusow 1964 pp. 438–43. Packull W 1985 Sylvester Tegetmeier, father of the Livonian Reformation: A fragment of his diary *Journal of Baltic Studies* **14**: 348–53.

14. Quednau H 1939 *Livland im politischen Wollen Herzog Albrechts von Preussen.* Leipzig, pp. 14–16.

prompted Plettenberg to act. In September 1525, he agreed to assume sole lordship over Riga. The town's privileges were confirmed, and the Master also agreed to permit the free exercise of the reformed faith in Riga.

The arrest of Blankenfeld seemed to open up once more an opportunity for the Master to assume sovereign powers in Livonia, as he was in fact urged to do by the burghers of Riga. Plettenberg does seem momentarily to have contemplated such a step. In a letter to the German Master of the Order in October 1525, he expressed a desire to be named in the documents confirming his regalian rights as 'lord and prince of Livonia'.[15] But at the decisive moment at the 1526 diet, perhaps fearing the consequences of aligning himself with the urban party of reformers, the aged Master declined to accept the role of secular sovereign. The crafty Blankenfeld saw his chance once more, and entered into secret negotiations with the Master. At a second diet in June 1526, the archbishop and Plettenberg were reconciled, and the prelates placed themselves under the protection of the Master. Blankenfeld undertook to further Plettenberg's claims to exercise supreme authority in Livonia and to the vacant post of Grand Master of the Order, but eventually his intrigues were finally terminated by his death in Spain in 1527. Though Plettenberg failed to secure the titular leadership of the Order, he acquired for himself and his successors the rank of an imperial prince in 1526. Livonia thus formally became part of the Holy Roman Empire.

Alignment with the Empire did nothing to resolve the internal problems of Livonia, nor did it hinder the intrigues of duke Albrecht. Blankenfeld's successor, Thomas Schöning, was drawn into a web of secret dealings with the duke of Prussia, the outcome of which was the election of Albrecht's brother, Wilhelm von Brandenburg as the new archbishop's deputy, or coadjutor. Attempts by Plettenberg's supporters in the diet to block the entry of Wilhelm into Livonia proved futile. The agents of Prussia had built up a formidable array of clients in the towns and amongst the nobility of Kurland and Ösel. Wilhelm, however, proved to be a costly disappointment to his ambitious brother. He became involved in an unsuccessul conflict with the bishop of Ösel in 1532, and his efforts as archbishop (to which office he acceded in 1539) to institute a Lutheran church order came to grief in the face of determined resistance, not only from the Catholics, but also from the estates, who feared the establishment of a secularised

15. Dopkiewitsch H 1967 Die Hochmeisterfrage und das Livlandproblem nach der Umwandlung des Ordenlandes Preussen *Zeitschrift für Ostforschung* **16**: p 205.

princely authority. The diet of 1546 resolved that in future, all the estates would have to consent to the appointment of any foreign coadjutor. Ten years later, this resolution was to be put to the test.

In the autumn of 1555, the ailing archbishop persuaded his chapter to adopt as coadjutor Christoffer, duke of Mecklenburg. It has been argued that this was part of a plan by duke Albrecht to provoke internal conflict in Livonia, which would offer his liege lord, the king of Poland, an opportunity to intervene and impose his authority over Livonia. Zygmunt August had expressed a wish to incorporate Livonia into his lands in secret discussions with the duke of Prussia in 1552–3. Albrecht was willing to provide an excuse for Polish intervention, since he hoped thereby to strengthen his own position within the Jagełłionian realm. He also hoped for support from Christian III of Denmark, to whom he offered the prospect of the restoration to Danish rule of Harrien, Wierland and the town of Reval.[16] The Livonian estates agreed to confirm the election of duke Christoffer, if he accepted a number of conditions. Amongst other things, he was to promise not to secularise his diocese, and he was forbidden to enter into any agreements with the king of Poland. These conditions were rejected by the archbishop and duke Christoffer, and denounced by the king of Poland. Heinrich von Galen, the Master of the Order, sought military assistance in Germany and Sweden, and took the offensive against the archbishop and duke Christoffer, both of whom were soon captured.

The conflict which erupted in 1556 was to have fatal repercussions for Livonia. Relations with Muscovy had worsened noticeably, though Ivan IV was probably content at this stage to use the threat of trade sanctions and the old Russian claim to payment of tribute from the diocese of Dorpat as a means of keeping pressure on Livonia. Ivan was also at loggerheads with Lithuania, whose representatives had refused to recognise his new title of tsar in 1553. The conquest of Kazan in 1552 was a notable success for Muscovy, but the Crimean Tatars continued to pose a serious threat on the south-eastern frontier. Anxiety over this question seems to have prompted Muscovy to seek to extend the truce with Lithuania in February 1556. Ivan IV did not raise objections to Zygmunt August's activities in Livonia, which has led one commentator to suggest that the possibility of a peaceful division of Livonia between the two might have been in the mind of

16. Rasmussen K 1973 *Die livländische Krise 1554–1561*. Copenhagen, pp. 28–33. For a different view, see Gundermann I 1966 Grundzüge der preussisch-mecklenburgischen Livlandpolitik im 16 Jahrhundert *Baltische Studien* **52**: 43–4. These lands had been sold to the Order by Denmark in 1346.

the Polish king.[17] The Lithuanian nobility were unwilling to risk a war against Muscovy, which would necessitate Polish support, the price of which might be demands for closer union. Zygmunt August proceeded cautiously after the arrests of the archbishop and duke, seeking to release them by diplomatic means. The Master preferred to seek the arbitration of the emperor Ferdinand I, though he received little support from that quarter. Christian III was disposed to favour a peaceful settlement of the dispute, and a Danish mission negotiated a compromise agreement with the Livonian estates in February 1557. Zygmunt August refused to accept this, however, and mustered troops on the Livonian frontier. The new Master, Wilhelm von Fürstenburg, bowed to this pressure and ratified the agreement reached with the Poles at Poswol in September 1557. The archbishop was restored and duke Christoffer recognised as his coadjutor, on condition that he refrained from secularising the archbishopric. In addition, a military alliance against Muscovy was concluded, to come into force upon the expiration of existing truces with that state.

The treaty of Poswol has been seen as marking the establishment of a Polish protectorate over Livonia, obliging the latter to assist Poland–Lithuania against Muscovy. The Danish historian Rasmussen, on the other hand, is inclined to see Poswol as a compromise which reflected the prestige won by Zygmunt August as arbitrator.[18] The caution displayed by the king may be attributed to domestic considerations. Although the Polish *sejm* had agreed to Zygmunt August's request for troops, there was some reluctance to become involved in Livonian affairs. The Polish chancellor, for example, feared that the forces of the reformation in Poland–Lithuania would be strengthened if Livonia were taken into the union. The Lithuanian nobles sought to exclude their Polish counterparts from Livonian affairs, and strove to prevent the signing of an alliance between the Order and Poland in 1558–9.[19] From the Livonian point of view, Poswol was perhaps little more than a brutal reminder of how dependent the warring estates had become on external forces to settle their affairs. Had Plettenberg taken the plunge in the 1520s and established a secular state, he would still have had to face the problem of seeking the protection of a powerful overlord, for Livonia was too small and weak to survive alone.

17. Tiberg E 1984 *Zur Vorgeschichte des Livländischen Krieges. Die Beziehungen zwischen Moskau und Litauen 1549–1562* Studia Historica Upsaliensia 134. Uppsala, pp. 92–5.

18. Kirchner W 1954 *The rise of the Baltic question* University of Delaware Monograph Series 3. Newark, pp 205–6. Donnert E 1963 *Die livländische Ordenritterstaat und Russland. Der livländische Krieg und die baltische Frage in der europäischen Politik 1558–1583.* Berlin, p. 223ff. Rasmussen 1973 pp. 88–9.

19. Rasmussen 1973 p 87. Tiberg 1984 p 89. Dembkowski 1982 pp. 71–4.

Albrecht von Hohenzollern was undoubtedly fortunate in having the king of Poland as his liege lord, for within the loose framework of the Jagiełłonian realm, it proved possible for the dukes of Prussia to retain control over their internal affairs, and ultimately to break free of Polish overlordship. Plettenberg, a true believer in the medieval notions of a universal Christian empire, made an unfortunate choice, for the Holy Roman Empire failed to respond effectively to Livonia's desperate appeals for help in the 1550s. A pro-Polish party began to emerge during these crisis years, but by then, it was too late. In August–September 1559, Zygmunt August agreed as grand duke of Lithuania to take Livonia under his protection, but only after the land had been ravaged by Muscovite armies, and Denmark and Sweden were beginning to show an interest in acquiring territory in Estonia.

In the 1550s, there occurred a good deal of scene-shifting on the stage of the European theatre. The emperor Charles V, unable to accept the permanent split in the church, authorised his brother Ferdinand to conclude the peace of Augsburg in 1555. This religious settlement shattered the last hopes of preserving the universal church. Charles, having failed to persuade the German princes to accept his son Philip as his successor, laid down the burdens of office later that year and retired to the monastery of Yuste in Estremadura. His loyal but dull brother Ferdinand succeeded him as emperor, whilst Philip inherited the growing swell of discontent in the Netherlands, which was to break out in open revolt against Spanish rule in the 1560s.

By the middle of the sixteenth century, the Baltic trade was providing the vital sustenance for the Dutch economy. Any disturbance in the flow of heavily-laden grain ships westward through the Sound had severe consequences, forcing up the cost of living in Holland, and affecting the entrepôt trade of the Amsterdam merchants. War in the Baltic and the closure of the Sound in 1565 by the Danes contributed to a sharp rise in grain prices and food shortages in the Netherlands, which led to riots and the spread of revolt against the government of the regent. The Wendish Hanseatic towns had been unable to stop or hinder the passage of Dutch vessels through the Sound. Lübeck could no longer rely on the unqualified support of the other north German towns. Attempts to reorganise the Hanseatic League met with little success; the constitution adopted in 1557 did little more than codify already existing regulations. However, the towns did agree to create a common fund, and a general secretary or syndic was appointed in 1566. In the eastern Baltic, the Wendish towns no longer exercised any political influence, and were often at odds with the Livonian towns over trade with Russia.

71

The Russian trade attracted the interest of the English merchants who formed the Muscovy company during the reign of queen Mary. Although the early high expectations of these merchants were never realised, and the extensive privileges granted by Ivan IV were gradually whittled away, the Elizabethan public was given ample opportunity to learn about the 'barbarous Russe' from those who spent many years in the tsar's domains.[20] Queen Elizabeth was also bombarded with the protests of Muscovy's neighbours, who accused English merchants of supplying the tsar with arms and munitions. In 1559, for example, Zygmunt August complained that:

> ...we knowe and feele of a surety, the Muscovite, enemy to all liberty under the heavens to grow dayly mightier by the increase of such things as be brought to the Narve, while not only wares but weapons heeretofore unknowen to him, and artificers and arts be brought unto him: by meanes whereof he maketh himselfe strong to vanquish all others... We seemed hitherto to vanquish him onely in this, that he was rude of arts, and ignorant of policies. If so be that this navigation to the Narve continue, what shall be unknowen to him?[21]

Ivan IV had attempted to acquire western European technicians in 1547, but had been frustrated by the Livonian towns, who refused to allow passage to the men recruited by the tsar's agents. The failure of this mission may well have brought home to Ivan the vulnerability of his land-locked state to such pressure, and in the negotiations with the Livonian towns in 1554, he was able to exact his revenge by forcing the towns to allow the merchants of Novgorod and Pskov to trade freely with the inhabitants of Livonia and foreign merchants. There is, however, little conclusive evidence to suggest that commercial interests were uppermost in the tsar's mind during the negotiations of 1557, when the question of the tribute payable by the diocese of Dorpat was the main bone of contention.

The final act in Livonia as far as the Order was concerned occurred at the end of 1561. Having signed on behalf of the Order a treaty of submission to the king of Poland, the last Master, Gotthard Kettler, was confirmed as duke of Kurland by Zygmunt August. Thirty-six years after the secularisation of the Order in Prussia, the Livonian branch of the crusading German knights followed suit. In truth, the spirit which had inspired the Order's original founders had long since expired. The Catholic church withered and died of neglect in Livonia,

20. See *Anderson M 1958 Britain's discovery of Russia 1553-1825*. London, and Willan T 1956 *The early history of the Russia Company 1553-1603*. Manchester.
21. Hakluyt 1903, vol. 2. p. 486. Zins 1972, *England and the Baltic in the Elizabethan Era*. Manchester, pp. 44–6, for details of further correspondence.

destroyed by political intrigue. The last masters of the Order were openly tolerant of the reformed faith, though it must be said that after 1530, the Reformation did little to breathe a new spirituality or sense of purpose into the inhabitants of that remote and isolated outpost of the Holy Roman Empire. In certain parts of Europe, protestantism, as an instrument of princely rule or as an ideology in religious conflict, could be used to good effect in defining identity. This was never the case in Livonia. Furthermore, unlike Prussia, there were too many disparate and mutually hostile elements within the Livonian confederation. The towns were suspicious of the motives of the Order, and locked in constant conflict with the episcopacy. The vassals of the bishops might have made common cause with the towns on this score, but wrangling over trade and the towns' protection of fugitive peasants drove the two sides apart. There was indeed little love lost between the rural gentry and the townspeople. High-spirited young noblemen were in the habit of riding through the streets of Reval, singing their intention of breaking the heads of the burghers and making the streets flow with blood:

> Wie willen dee Börger up dee Köppe schlan
> dat Blodt schal up dee Straaten stahn.[22]

The landowning nobility's fear of the social consequences of the Reformation during the years of peasant unrest in Germany effectively dissolved the political alliance forged against bishop Johann Blankenfeld in the early 1520s. After the diet of 1525, the cause of the reformation in Livonia was pursued by the agents of duke Albrecht, who built up a clientele for their lord amongst the rural nobility and undermined still further the already weakened authority of the Master. When the crisis erupted, the jigsaw puzzle of the confederation fell apart as each piece sought to save itself the best way it could.

22. Kelch C 1695 *Liefländische Historia*. Frankfurt and Leipzig, p. 184.

PART TWO
The Livonian Wars

CHAPTER FOUR

New Currents

EDUCATION AND CULTURE

The septentrional regions have always been regarded by Europeans of more southerly latitudes as cold and forbidding. A French delegation sent to Denmark in 1512 to negotiate with King Hans arrived in March to find the country snow-bound and frozen. A fearful cold assailed the Frenchmen, and the sight of their hosts, wrapped in voluminous and outlandish garments of bearskin, did little to make them feel at ease. Almost a century and a half later, Réné Descartes confessed ruefully to a friend that he was not in his element in Stockholm, whence the ambitious Queen Christina had lured him. Christina's hopes of building up a circle of witty French poets and writers foundered in the cold and darkness of the northern winter, which drove most of her recruits back to the comforts of Paris. It was a commonplace view on mainland Europe that the north was inhabited by a rude and barbarous people, lacking in wit and manners, inured to cold and able to survive on meagre rations of hard bread and salt herring. The image of the North was given a broader dimension with the publication in 1555 of *Historia de gentibus septentrionalis*. This lavishly illustrated and at times comically patriotic account of the history, customs and habits of the northern peoples, written by Olaus Magnus, an exiled Swedish prelate, was to become a standard work of reference in early modern Europe. But if the work of Olaus Magnus did something to broaden the knowledge of northern Europe amongst the book-reading public, it is unlikely that the overall image changed very much. The lands on the northern shores of the Baltic, rocky, infertile, forest-covered, remained very much on the outer limits of the European consciousness.

The educated minority of these northern parts, especially those who had studied at the centres of European scholarship and learning, could not fail to be unaware of the intellectual and cultural poverty of their surroundings. The Reformation probably caused a decline in the already meagre level of education, and the few significant centres of learning such as the Birgittine monastery in Vadstena fell into decay. Priceless medieval manuscripts were used as gun-wads, or to bind bailiffs' account-books. Monastic schools were closed, and cathedral schools had to struggle to keep going. Though contemporaries who cared about such things deplored the general decline, many were indifferent. Archbishop Jasper Linde of Riga attempted on several occasions between 1512 and 1519 to persuade the Livonian *Landtag* to accept a programme of educational reforms, with little success: 'such things do not concern us' was the reply of the knights and the towns in 1516. Balthasar Rüssow attributed the poor standards of religious observance in the land to the lack of schools which might train a native clergy, and he also blamed the Order and the episcopacy for their indifference to the spiritual welfare of the peasantry. The Finnish reformer Mikael Agricola complained in 1547 that the peasantry did not wish to send their children to school, and were hostile to the importunings of wandering students, seeking funds for their upkeep. The reformers in Sweden also worried about the poor state of the country's education system, as did Gustav Vasa, who was made aware of the problem by a lack of trained personnel for his administration.[1] During the early years of Gustav Vasa's reign, the number of Swedes studying abroad fell sharply, and the king attempted to remedy this situation by providing scholarships from the sale of confiscated monastic property. By the end of the century, there were generally between seventy and eighty Swedish students registered annually in the German universities. In Sweden itself, there were fourteen grammar schools by 1561; by the 1580s, the school in Stockholm had some two hundred pupils, that in Uppsala over one hundred. Melanchthon's Saxon school ordinance was used as the model for Georg Norman's *Articuli ordinantiae* of 1540 and the school ordinance of 1571, and his grammar went through two impressions, in 1573 and 1584. Essentially medieval in concept, the school ordinance did not change until 1611, when the Swedish education system entered upon a new era.

To acquire a good education, the subjects of the king of Sweden had to travel abroad. A university had been founded in Uppsala in the

1. Tarkiainen V 1985 *Mikael Agricola, Suomen uskonpuhdistaja*. Helsinki, p. 312. Lindroth S 1975 *Svensk lärdomshistoria (3 vols)*. Stockholm, vol. 1, pp. 208–10.

afterglow of the victory over the Danes at Brunkeberg, but it had led a tenuous life at best, and seems to have expired during the final phases of the Union struggle. It was revived in 1566 by Erik XIV, but teaching petered out in the 1580s. In 1576, Johan III founded a royal college in Stockholm. Under the supervision of the rector Laurentius Nicolai, a secret member of the Order of Jesus, the school provided a valuable recruiting-ground for the Society's seminaries in Braunsberg or Olmütz, until the growing anti-Catholic mood in the country obliged the rector and sixteen proselytes to leave the country. Under Lutheran auspices, the college survived a few more years. Several of its pupils were later to enjoy distinguished academic careers in the reign of Gustav II Adolf, when the university of Uppsala finally came into its own. The university in Copenhagen fared little better. In the mid-sixteenth century, there was only one professor of jurisprudence, two of medicine, three of theology and one philosopher, who was also obliged to teach Hebrew, Greek, Latin, rhetoric and dialectics, for a miserable salary. Talented foreign scholars could not be attracted to the university because of poor pay and conditions, and attempts to found grammar schools in the towns were hampered by lack of money. The nobleman Tycho Brahe was given the island of Hven, with an endowment to build his observatory, by Frederik II, and spent twenty years here carrying out his observations: in the end however, he fell into disfavour and died in exile in Bohemia. For those with the means or ability, the universities of central Europe offered an incomparably better education than could be provided at home. Leipzig, Rostock and Greifswald were amongst the most favoured universities for northern European students, though Prague enjoyed a brief period of popularity during the early years of the fifteenth century, whilst Wittenberg was an obligatory destination for any serious student of theology in the sixteenth century.

The growing demand for educated personnel to administer the affairs of state, and the claims of the nobility to such offices, gradually led to an increase in the numbers of young noblemen undergoing an academic education. It was not until the last decades of the sixteenth century, however, that it became common practice for Swedish and Danish noblemen to send their sons abroad for an education. For all but the very wealthy, it was a costly matter, and for that reason, the sons were often sent in groups, the eldest having to wait until his younger brothers were old enough to join him. Those who entered the service of a foreign nobleman or petty prince in order to learn the arts of war often spent many years abroad, gaining experience on the battlefields of the Low Countries or even against the Turk in central

Europe. The martial virtues, though still considered essential for any gentleman, were no longer regarded as the sole prerequisite: indeed, in Denmark, it was usually the less academically gifted sons who were packed off to the fencing-master, whilst the brighter boys studied law. At the beginning of the seventeenth century the Danish nobleman Godske Lindenov argued that a career in state service was the only real option for the aristocracy; in a barbarous state, the warrior-knight was necessary, but in a civilised, peaceful state, he was redundant. Nevertheless, in spite of the civilising influences of the grand tour and observation of courtly life elsewhere in Europe, the northern noblemen still had much to learn from their more refined French or Italian cousins, especially in their table manners. The aristocracy of Denmark were prodigious trenchermen, and formidable drinkers. Cornelius Hamsfort, the court doctor to Frederik II, believed that most Danes, especially the nobility, were inordinately given to strong drink, and that drunkenness was regarded as a sign of manliness. Those who could not hold their liquor were deemed cowardly and dishonourable. Violent and unseemly brawls not infrequently accompanied the prolonged drinking sessions of the aristocracy. Not even the innocent revels celebrating the christening of prince Christian in 1577 were spared. The students playing the part of the Philistines were unwilling to yield to David and his countrymen, as the plot demanded, and a general free-for-all ensued when the octogenarian admiral Peder Skram enthusiastically joined in on the side of the Israelites.

The lack of a sizeable book-reading public made northern Europe an unattractive proposition for the printer seeking to set up business. A number of printers from northern Germany and the Low Countries tried their hand, but usually left after a few years. The pioneer was Johann Snell, who set up a press in Odense in the 1480s, moving briefly to Stockholm in 1483. During the sixteenth century, there was never more than one printer in the whole of Sweden, and for periods of Gustav Vasa's reign, there appears to have been none at all. Livonia was without a printing-press for much of the sixteenth century. The growing reliance of the crown on the printed word and the gradual emergence in Denmark and Sweden of an educated nobility ensured work for the printer there. The rude country gentry of Harrien and Wierland were less likely customers. It is indicative of their slothful barbarity that the elegant missives of king Sigismund to his liegemen in Estonia had to be translated into German, since none could understand Latin. The Swedish nobility would at least have had the grace to pretend to understand, and several would have been eminently capable of comprehension.

THE CHURCH AND THE REFORMATION

The state of the late-medieval church in northern Europe, as else-where, was a mixture of vigour and decay. There were disreputable prelates, such as bishop Fabian Tettinger Merkelingrode von Los-sainen of Ermland (1512–23), 'a miserable fellow, severely stricken with the "French disease", an avaricious wastrel [who] was absolutely indifferent to religion and only once in his eleven-year tenure of office as a bishop said a mass and then only on the day of his consecration': but there were many others who strove valiantly to implant the precepts of Christianity, often against great odds.[2] A provincial coun-cil of the church in Riga in 1428 decreed a campaign to ensure a basic knowledge of the Lord's Prayer and the Credo amongst the peasantry and there is evidence that these fundaments of the Christian religion were translated into the native languages. The bishops of Ösel, Johann Orgas (1491–1515) and Johann Kievel (1515–27), attempted for many years to improve the work of the clergy and to raise standards. The visitations conducted by Kievel in 1519–22 left him in little doubt about the sorry state of affairs in his diocese. The vicar of Karmel had fled to Reval during the plague of 1520, leaving the dead unburied. A year later, he went on a business trip to Prussia, leaving more corpses to moulder in open graves. The vicar of St Thomas in Alt-Pernau was implicated in the theft of property from his own church. Even when such men were dismissed, they were easily able to find employment elsewhere, such was the crying shortage of clergymen. Kievel's efforts to set up a school in Alt-Pernau came to nothing. In 1523, he wrote despairingly to a Dutch colleague, a fellow-member of the Brethren of the Common Life:

> Everywhere the people make tumult without end. We know not what kind of demon it is which pricks them on to rage and fulminate against the clergy. Nowhere is there peace.[3]

The problems of the church were, in fact, not so much caused by avarice, worldliness and corruption, but were a consequence of in-adequate resources. The sparse population of the northern lands was scattered over a vast area, and there were large tracts in which not even a minimal physical presence of the Christian religion – a wayside cross, a rough-hewn chapel of rest, or a hermitage – could be

2. Zins H 1960 The political and social background of the early Reformation in Ermeland *English Historical Review* **75**: 592.

3. Arbusow 1964 *Die Einführung der Reformation in Liv-Est und Kurland* (reprint edn). Aalen. p. 255, and pp. 115–33 for the attempts of archbishop Linde and others to push through reform.

observed. In south-west Finland for example, a number of solid stone churches had been erected in the late Middle Ages, but the hinterland was a virtual wilderness. Bishop Magnus Tavast (1412–50) was obliged to sleep under the stars when he visited the few and far-flung chapels of this forested interior, so utterly devoid of settlement. The fine altarpieces and wood carvings, which provided steady employment for many master craftsmen of the Hanse towns, testify to a spirit of piety in the towns and large villages; but beyond the houses lay a thick layer of paganism which the church had hardly yet begun to penetrate, even less to dissipate.

The impetus for church reform was given explosive force at the end of the second decade of the sixteenth century by Martin Luther and his colleagues at the university of Wittenberg. Within twenty years of Luther's defiant proclamation of faith, much of central and northern Europe had broken with the Roman Catholic church. Rulers and magistrates seeking to extend their control over the church and to acquire some of its wealth played a crucial role in this reformation, though they did not always see eye to eye with (or even understand) the reformers.

The Reformation in the north may best be described as a process of maturation over several decades. The fifteenth-century convulsions in the church had also reached into northern Europe. A number of the works of John Hus were brought back to Sweden in manuscript form, and Hussite doctrines were carried into Prussia, causing some anxiety to the Order. In Rostock, Hussite works were translated into Low German by the priest Nikolaus Rutze. The seeds of heresy were also waterborne; a woman was burnt at the stake in Rostock for being a follower of John Wyclif.[4] On the southern shores of the Baltic in the 1520s the towns were caught up in the ferment of religious change which bubbled throughout Germany and central Europe. The larger towns of Denmark and Sweden were also soon drawn into the turmoil, but they were few in number and their influence over the rest of the two kingdoms was minimal. The Swedish church was stripped of its power and wealth in 1527, the Danish church in 1536, but the break with Catholicism was a gradual process. In both kingdoms, monastic institutions were allowed to survive for several decades. The nobility in particular was anxious to maintain nunneries to which they could send their superfluous daughters. As late as 1552, king Christian III was petitioned to found two nunneries in Jutland so that the daughters of the local gentry need not be obliged to marry peasants or other

---

4. On late-medieval heresies in the Baltic, see Arbusow 1964, pp. 157–67.

'unfree folk', with the attendant risk of noble estates passing out of the family's possession. The reformers were conservative in their approach to church ritual, preserving the basic structure of the Catholic service. There were few original contributions to the theological debates of the epoch from northern Europe, and the apocalyptic pyrotechnics which threatened to set alight parts of Germany and the Netherlands in the reign of Charles V sent few sparks northwards. Grave and earnest, rather than fiery and zealous, the reformers in the northern lands preferred to channel their intellectual energies into translation of the Bible and the major works of Luther and Melanchthon. They were faithful followers, not innovators.

The strong connections between the Hanseatic coastal towns and the central European hinterland ensured that the tremors of religious change would soon be felt on the southern shores of the Baltic. The rays of humanism also reached these lands, although they shone rather wanly. The first university in the Baltic area was founded in Rostock in 1419, followed by Greifswald in 1456, but the most influential centre of humanist scholarship was the Marienkirche school of the Premonstratensian order in Treptow, where the young Johann Bugenhagen was appointed rector in 1504. This Pomeranian school attracted students from as far afield as Poland and Hungary, and around Bugenhagen there developed a circle of young and enthusiastic scholars, many of whom were later to play important roles in the early Reformation. In 1521, Bugenhagen enrolled as a student in Wittenberg. He was succeeded as rector in Treptow by Andreas Knopken, a former student who had spent a miserable two years ministering to the spiritual needs of the porters' gild in Riga. Fired with enthusiasm, members of the Treptow circle openly began preaching the new doctrines. This was too much for the duke of Pomerania, Bogislaw X, and the school was forced to close, an action which helped scatter the seeds of the reformed faith around the Baltic. Knopken returned to Riga in the summer of 1521, and began preaching on the epistle to the Romans, that favourite text of the reformers. The reformed party soon won ground in Riga, but was slow to reach the other towns of Livonia. The citizens of Reval and Dorpat were engaged in bitter dispute with Johann Blankenfeld, who occupied both bishoprics, and this conflict surfaced at the *Landtag* of 1522. The towns and the vassals of the bishops joined forces and sought to impose strict controls on the future election of prelates. This mood also persuaded the lay estates to reject the bishops' demand that the papal bull *Exurge domine* and edict of Worms be published in Livonia: opposition to the pretensions of the church, rather than sympathy for Luther, lay behind this decision.

The estates believed that a council of the church was the best means of settling the present turmoil, a clear echo of medieval conciliarist thinking.

The Reformation in Riga was given new impetus by the town secretary Johannes Lohmüller, who established contact with Luther in the summer of 1522, imploring him to be a Paul unto the citizens of the town. Lohmüller was a clever party man, and maintained a network of contacts with duke Albrecht of Prussia, whose secularised Lutheran state was the model which the Protestants in Livonia sought to emulate. In 1522, Andreas Knopken was appointed public preacher at the Petrikirche in Riga. He was to be joined in the September of that year by Sylvester Tegetmeier, a somewhat unruly spirit who had fallen under the influence of Carlstadt whilst in Wittenberg. An even more combustious figure turned up in Livonia during the crisis-laden years of 1524–5: Melchior Hoffmann, the furrier and apocalyptic preacher. There is little evidence to link Hoffmann with peasant unrest in Livonia, though an attempt by the bishop's bailiff to arrest him in Dorpat in January 1525 sparked off a riot, which offered the magistracy an opportunity to end the bishop's dominance over the town. The first outburst of iconoclasm in Livonia had occurred a year earlier in Riga. The instigators of this orgy of destruction were the young, unmarried German trade apprentices of the *Schwarzhäupter* fraternity, amongst whom the reformed faith had won support. The incident which provoked the attack was the revelation of Franciscan complicity in secret dealings between the hated archbishop Blankenfeld and Rome. As a result of the riots, the town council expelled the Franciscans, and embarked upon an administrative reform of the church's functions.[5]

By the end of the decade, Riga, Reval and Dorpat had all adopted a new church order, but a good deal of doctrinal confusion still prevailed. The experiences of 1525 in Germany and Livonia and the decision of the Hanse diet in July 1525 to persuade the Livonian towns not to admit preachers who incited the masses to disobedience seem to have prompted the urban patriciate to impose a reformed church order from above. In 1527, Johann Briesmann, a colleague of Luther who had been instrumental in effecting the Reformation in Prussia, arrived in Riga. Under his guidance, the Reformation took a more conservative turn, returning to the more ornate rituals and ceremony of the

5. In addition to the work of Arbusow, see also Deppermann K 1979 *Melchior Hoffmann*. Göttingen; and Packull W 1985 Sylvester Tegetmeier, father of the Livonian Reformation: A fragment of his diary *Journal of Baltic Studies* **14**: 343–56, for recent work relating to Livonia.

Catholic church. Whereas the 1524 Reval church ordinance had allowed the council and the congregation an equal voice in the election of pastors, the towns gathered in Wolmar in 1533 decided to confine this right to the council alone; and only approved orthodox priests were to be appointed to office.

The imposition of a conservative church order, after a period of crisis in the 1520s, was a characteristic feature of the urban reformation along the Baltic coast. The exactions of the church had long been a source of complaint, and the fund-raising activities of the Papal legate Arcimboldus in northern Germany in 1516–17 aroused storms of protest. The burden of taxation and the expensive maritime campaigns waged by the patriciate of cities such as Danzig and Lübeck caused much discontent amongst the smaller merchants and craftsmen, and it was amongst these groups that the new ideas found ready support. In certain towns, the new faith won the day with relative ease: in others, there was a fierce struggle between the middle stratum of merchants and craftsmen, backed up by the crowds of the urban proletariat, and the ruling patriciate before victory was finally won by the adherents of Protestantism. The medium used to exercise pressure on the town councils was the citizens' committee. In Danzig, a committee of forty-eight was set up in 1520 to assist the council in sorting out the financial mess caused by heavy involvement in the war against the Order. The new faith soon secured a footing in Danzig; as early as 1520, a work by Luther was printed in the city, and two years later, the committee of forty-eight compelled the town council to accede to a demand for a church to be set aside for adherents of the new faith. The cost of equipping a fleet against Christian II of Denmark in 1522 occasioned further discontent amongst the less wealthy, already in a state of religious ferment. In 1525, the council was overthrown in a popular uprising and the new rulers of the city embarked upon a full-blooded reformation. This prompted the intervention of Zygmunt I, with the subsequent dispersion of the leaders of the Reformation and the imposition of the anti-reformist *Statuta Sigismundi*. In spite of royal protests, however, the Reformation continued to gain ground in the city. By the middle of the century, all the churches were staffed by Lutheran clergy. In 1557, in return for a hefty loan, the king allowed communion to be celebrated in both kinds, thereby virtually conceding the triumph of the Reformation in Danzig. Similar concessions were made to Elbing and Thorn.

In Lübeck and Rostock there were powerful opponents of religious change. The university of Rostock was a bastion of the Catholic faith, and the Catholic party was strong enough to force Joachim Slüter, the ducal appointment to the chaplaincy of the Petrikirche, to leave town in 1525. The Catholic party was weakened the following year, when its leading figure Professor Barthold Müller left for Hamburg. The return of Slüter and the appointment of another reformer, Johann Oldendorp, as town secretary and teacher at the university, tilted the balance in favour of the reformed party. The council finally broke with Catholicism in 1531, though it was careful to ensure the exclusion of Zwinglians and other radicals from preaching appointments. In Lübeck, the chapter of the cathedral granted prebends to sons of councillors, thus creating a strong bond of common interest between church and council in defending the old order. In 1524, the council issued a decree banning the sale, possession, printing or copying of Luther's writings, and it was not until the end of the decade that a new order could be pushed through, largely as a result of the financial crisis which forced the council to negotiate with a citizens' committee. The Reformation was carried through under pressure from this committee, led by Jürgen Wullenweber, and although Wullenweber's party was ultimately overthrown as a result of its disastrous policy of involvement in the Count's War, the restored patriciate were careful not to interfere in the church settlement drawn up by Johann Bugenhagen.

Johann Bugenhagen was a key figure in the northern Reformation. He visited Denmark in 1537 at the king's request, ordained seven superintendants to replace the deposed bishops and drew up a church ordinance. Bugenhagen was also responsible for the church ordinance in Pomerania in 1534, and conducted a visitation in the duchy the following year. He was, however, barred from entering episcopal territory, since the bishops remained loyal to Catholicism. The last Catholic bishop of Kammin died in 1544, but visitations did not begin here until 1552. This pattern of co-existence between the old and new orders persisted for several decades; not until the last decades of the sixteenth century was there any noticeable tightening of the religious dividing lines.

The most spectacular case of conversion to the new order in the Baltic area occurred in Prussia. The new faith had already gained firm footing in Königsberg, where Johann Briesmann had been invited to preach in the cathedral by the reform-minded bishop of Samland, Georg Polentz. The Grand Master, Albrecht von Hohenzollern, was in contact with leading reformers in Germany, and in April 1525, followed Luther's advice; in a public act of submission on the market square in Cracow, he became the first duke of the secularised state of Prussia and liegeman of the king of Poland. Within a year, the foundations of a reformed church had been laid in the duchy. Luther was unable to take up Albrecht's invitation to attend the diet in Königsberg, though he sent a detailed account of his own views on ecclesiastical organisation. Albrecht was undoubtedly aided in his efforts to convert the duchy into a Lutheran state by the voluntary surrender of secular authority by the bishop of Samland in August 1525. A gratified Martin Luther hailed Polentz as the only bishop in the world who praised the Lord and who had freed himself from the clutches of Satan: whilst the cause of evangelism in Germany struggled to make itself heard against a storm of blasphemy and indignation, 'vide mirabilia, ad Prussiam pleno cursu plenisque velis currit evangelium'.[6] Two years later, bishop Queiss of Pomesania also surrendered all secular authority to the duke. There was little opposition from the knights, whose number had shrunk to a mere fifty-six, and most of whom Albrecht was able to win over by granting them court office or putting them in charge of administrative districts.

Little was done to alter the fundamental administrative structure inherited from the Order. The duchy of Prussia was divided into three regions, Samland, Natangen and Oberland, each of which was further subdivided into districts (*Hauptämter*). At the head of each district was the *Amtshauptmann*, a ducal appointee, with administrative, fiscal and judicial functions. Each district was divided into smaller units (*Kammerämter*). The Revenue Chamber supervised receipts and expenditure, and controlled the activities of the district administrators. It formed a part of the Supreme Council, which was responsible for all affairs of state with the exception of foreign and ecclesiastical affairs. Albrecht employed a leading German lawyer, Johann von Schwarzenberg, to assist in the revision of the judicial system, and was able to divert much of the business of the old regional courts to the ducal supreme court – though he did not succeed in preventing his subjects appealing to the Polish supreme court. The treaty of Cracow had also stipulated that Prussia was to cease minting its own coins, but Albrecht was able to persuade the Polish king to allow small-scale minting. The principal sources of revenue, in addition to the natural produce of the ducal estates, were from ground rents, petty fines and dues paid for the use of mills, ducal ponds and forests. Although Prussia began to recover from the ravages of the previous decades, the expenses of the ducal state continued to rise faster than ordinary

6. 'Behold a miracle, the evangel hastens at full speed and with full sail towards Prussia.' Tschackert P 1890 *Urkundenbuch zur Reformationsgeschichte des Herzogthums Preussen. Publicationen aus den Königliche Preussischen Staatsarchiven*, vol. 43 (3 vols). Leipzig, vol. 1, p. 108.

revenue. Albrecht was compelled to mortgage a number of districts, and to make concessions to the nobility in return for their agreement to extraordinary taxation.

In a minor way, ducal Prussia became something of a Geneva of the north during the early years of the Reformation. Königsberg was a centre for the printing of evangelical literature in German and Polish. The university founded there in 1544 was a centre of Protestant teaching, and, with the arrival of the tempestuous and uncompromising Andreas Osiander in 1549 to take up an academic appointment, it was also to become a centre of controversy and dispute.

Duke Albrecht maintained close contacts with leading reformists in Poland–Lithuania and Livonia, and built up a clientele of gentry sympathetic to Protestantism in neighbouring Kurland. In Royal Prussia, the area ceded to Poland in 1466, the influence of ducal Prussia was also strong. Lutheranism in Royal Prussia was closely linked to local particularism and hostility to the idea of closer union with Poland; it was also identified with German, and as such enjoyed relatively little support amongst the Polish-speaking population outside the towns. No church ordinance or synodal structure was ever created, and the Protestant nobility were isolated from their Polish counterparts by virtue of their Lutheranism and German particularism. In 1563–4, the execution of the domains, i.e., the restoration to the crown of lands alienated to the magnates since 1504, was extended to Royal Prussia. Five years later, the closer union of Royal Prussia with the Polish crown was decreed by Zygmunt August. The protests of the local Lutheran gentry at the nomination of a leading Polish Catholic as bishop-elect of Ermland in 1570 went unheeded, and Catholics were systematically appointed to official posts by that great champion of the Counter-Reformation, Zygmunt III. Although the number of Lutherans declined significantly, and the corporation of nobility of Royal Prussia at the end of the seventeenth century declared itself to be Catholic, there were still some eighty Lutheran parishes in 1772, when the area passed under the control of Frederick the Great. The influx of German refugees from the Thirty Years' War swelled the local Protestant congregation, though the continued adherence of neighbouring Pomerania and Prussia to Lutheranism also helped maintain this largely German-speaking dissident community.[7]

In Denmark, Christian II's ordinances of 1521-2, though never fully implemented, were designed to curb some of the abuses of the church

7. Schramm G 1965 *Der polnische Adel und die Reformation 1548–1607* Wiesbaden, pp. 116–36.

and to improve the quality of the clergy. In exile, the erratic king veered briefly towards Lutheranism and it was on his instructions that the New Testament was translated into Danish in 1524. His uncle who replaced him on the throne was cautiously favourable to the new doctrines which were being preached in the towns: although he promised in his *håndfæstning* not to permit heretics to preach against the Pope or the Catholic church, he refused to revoke his letters of protection given to evangelical preachers. The king also promised not to allow foreigners to hold bishoprics without the consent of the council, nor to permit cases to be sent to Rome unless they had first been considered by the Danish episcopacy. During the reign of Frederik I, Denmark began quietly to detach itself from Rome. The council agreed to Frederik's proposal in 1526 that bishops be henceforth confirmed in office by the archbishop of Lund, and that money usually sent to Rome for this purpose be used for the defence of the realm. The vacant see of Lund was filled by the king against the wishes of the Pope, and the bishopric of Odense was occupied by a man who paid the king for his confirmation of office. The Danish episcopacy maintained a strong conciliarist tradition, though they were also staunch opponents of the new doctrines which were seeping into the kingdom. These doctrines began to take root in the larger towns, such as Malmö, where the council obtained permission from the king to dissolve the monasteries and use the house of the Holy Ghost for a town hall, the Greyfriars building for a hospital and school for the clergy. It was in Malmö that the first Danish mass was printed in 1529. A second centre of reformist activity in Denmark was the town of Viborg in the Jutland peninsula, where Hans Tausen, a monk educated in Rostock, Copenhagen and Wittenberg, began preaching in 1525. The reformers in Denmark encountered few real obstacles from the crown. Indeed, Frederik's children married into Lutheran dynasties, and his son Christian encouraged the Reformation in the duchies.

Many of the Danish reformers were former Carmelite monks, such as Frans Vormordsen, the first Lutheran archbishop of Lund, and Peder Laurenssen, the teacher of divinity at the evangelical school for the clergy in Malmö. (The only serious opponent of the reformers, Povel Helgesen, was also a former Carmelite and early critic of the abuses within the church.) In 1530, the reformers were invited to put their views at a debate with the episcopacy in Copenhagen, and the subsequent *Confessio Hafnica* was a summary of their position, which bore some of the features of the teachings of Zwingli. The tension produced by this confrontation led to iconoclastic riots in

Copenhagen, and the closing of the church of Our Lady by royal order.

The election of Frederik I's son Christian as king of Denmark, and his ultimate victory in the Count's War, placed Denmark firmly on the road to an evangelical church order. Sweden's path to a national Protestant church was somewhat more tortuous. At the same time as Bugenhagen's church ordinance was published in Denmark (1539), Gustav Vasa was seeking to impose his own version of church government, and in so doing, clashed with the reformers. A charge of high treason was brought against two leading evangelicals, Lars Andreae and Olaus Petri, and though their sentences were commuted to heavy fines by the king, the cause of the doctrinal reformation suffered a setback. The fragmentary church ordinance drawn up around 1540 by Georg Norman, a professor of Greifswald university recruited by the king on Luther's recommendation, bore the mark of Melanchthon's teaching, but its main purpose was organisational, not doctrinal, as was Archbishop Laurentius Petri's church ordinance of 1571.

The elimination of the power of the church and the strengthening of royal authority were the driving forces behind the reformation instituted by Gustav Vasa; but the king was not unsympathetic to the new doctrines. He provided scholarships for bright young men to study in Wittenberg, and his royal mandate of 1540, authorising Georg Norman to carry out a visitation of the whole country to ensure a thorough reform of church doctrine and ceremonies, was firmly Protestant in tone. During his long reign, the essential works of Lutheranism had appeared in Swedish translation. Olaus Petri, who had studied in Leipzig and Wittenberg between 1516 and 1519, incorporated much of Luther's Large Catechism in his 1530 *Postilla*, and his other works of this period (*The Swedish Handbook* of 1529, the *Swedish Mass* of 1531) were to remain standard works of the national church. His brother Laurentius, elected archbishop of Uppsala in 1531, was largely responsible for the translation of the Bible, which appeared in 1541. A Finnish translation of the New Testament was published in 1548, and the translator, Mikael Agricola, also produced a church handbook and mass in Finnish.

The literary work of the reformers did not transform the kingdom overnight into a bastion of orthodox Lutheranism, however. Gustav Vasa's sons were all, in their different ways, amateur theologians with pronounced views on matters of doctrine, and the church leadership had several tussles with their royal masters. Erik XIV came under the influence of his Calvinist French tutor Dionysus Beurreus, and urged the clergy to forsake 'papist and ungodly ceremonies'. His brother Johan, in the words of Daniel Rogers, was regarded as 'very ticklish and unconstant in matters of religion, for he causeth many superstitions and popish ceremonies to be reared into the church, which breedeth offence towards many'.[8] Johan was an assiduous reader of the works of the early fathers, and had come under the influence of contemporary syncretist theologians, such as Georg Cassander. The *Nova ordinantia* of 1575, although impeccably Lutheran in its emphasis on preaching and education, also contained elements of Cassander's mediatory theology. Johan urged the clergy to read the fathers in preference to Luther, and in 1576 caused further disquiet with his *Liturgia svecanae ecclesiae*, or the 'Red Book', as it came to be known. The emphasis placed on ceremony and ritual aroused the opposition of the clergy, many of whom refused to conform and were dismissed for their pains. Some of those who were dismissed found refuge in duke Karl's domains, others went to Germany, from where they showered Sweden with anti-liturgical tracts, denouncing the Red Book as a 'peppered viper'. Johan dallied with the idea of a union with Rome, but the terms on which he was prepared to bring the Swedish church back into the fold were unacceptable to Gregory XIII. By the end of the reign, the anti-liturgists were in the ascendancy, and the brief interlude of Catholic teaching at Johan's royal college in Stockholm had come to an end. The endorsement of the Augsburg Confession by the church assembly in 1593 finally gave official confirmation of Sweden's status as a Lutheran land, and subsequent legislation during the reign of Karl IX enforced strict religious uniformity.

In the Polish–Lithuanian commonwealth, the high point of Protestantism coincided with the movement amongst the lesser nobility for the execution of the laws in the mid-sixteenth century. By the end of the reign of Zygmunt II August, the Protestant nobility held a majority of both houses of the *sejm*; within forty years, however, the Catholic church had regained the ascendancy, and Protestantism was in retreat. Evangelical doctrines did not strike deep roots in Poland; the towns and the peasantry were largely unaffected, and the reconversion of many of the leading magnates to Catholicism, which began as early as the 1560s, steadily reduced the Protestant cause to a minority. By 1609, only nine Protestants remained in the Senate, where there had been fifty-eight less than forty years before.

One of the areas most affected by Protestantism was northern Lithuania, culturally backward, sparsely populated and only super-

8. *Calendar of State Papers Foreign Vol XXII. July–December 1588*. London 1938, p. 79.

ficially Christian. The lesser gentry of the area were less attached to the conservative values of the magnates, and many sent their sons for an education to Königsberg, a regional centre for Lutheranism. Conversions to Lutheranism began in the late 1530s, and the adhesion of the powerful Radziwiłł brothers to the new faith in the 1540s gave to Protestants in Lithuania a degree of protection lacking in Poland: indeed, a number of Polish Protestants sought service with the Radziwiłłs, bringing to Lithuania Calvinist and anti-trinitarian ideas. There was also a significant conversion rate amongst the leading Orthodox noble families, such as the Sapieha and Chodkiewicz clans, often as a result of young men picking up Protestantism during their studies in western universities. In 1563, the king was obliged to grant religious freedom in Lithuania. For the leaders of the Order of Jesus, Lithuania was seen as a veritable India, where conversion had to begin *ab initio*. The Catholic church was poorly staffed and organised, and lacked the funds which the wealthy Protestant magnates were able to provide for the building and upkeep of the ministry. It was not until 1576 that the Jesuits could open their college in Vilna, though it soon had an intake of 700 pupils, and was elevated to university status in 1578. In spite of the vigorous missionary work of the Jesuits in Lithuania, Protestantism survived well into the eighteenth century in Samogitia, where Catholics were in a minority even as late as 1622.

Much of the success of the Catholic church can be attributed to the efforts of vigorous men such as Martyn Cromer and Piotr Skarga, but in the city of Riga they faced a stiff challenge. The *Corpus privilegiorum Stephanum* granted to the citizens of Riga in 1581 by king Stefan Batory lacked any guarantee of religious freedom, and during his stay in the city the following spring, the king made it plain that Lutheranism was to occupy a strictly subordinate position. Pressure was put on the town council to hand over two churches and a nunnery to the Catholics, and a bishopric was created at Wenden in 1583. Piotr Skarga was authorised to press ahead with the work of reconversion in Riga, but as one of his assistants confessed 'adeo immersa est haeresi civitas haec, ut parvus de ea sperari possit fructus'.[9] The opening of a Jesuit college in 1584 sparked off a riot, as did the arrest of the rector of the Protestant cathedral school, and attempts to impose the Gregorian calendar. Between 1584 and 1589, Riga was effectively under the control of a radical Protestant faction, and the Jesuits were driven out of the city. After their return, they were able to work without further

9. 'The citizenry are steeped in heresy, and little can be hoped of them.' Staemmler K-D 1953 *Preussen und Livland in ihrem Verhältnis zur Krone Polen 1561 bis 1586.* Marburg, p. 75.

disturbance, and could claim a congregation of 6,500 Catholics in the city by 1613. The Protestants responded vigorously to this challenge, setting up a school, a press and a library, founding pious charitable institutions and even building a new church. Before Riga fell to the Swedes in 1621, the Protestants, though operating under constraints, more than managed to hold their own.

By the end of the sixteenth century, then, the evangelical Lutheran church had been officially established in the northern kingdoms, the duchies of north Germany, Prussia and Kurland, and was proving resistant to the efforts of the Jesuits in Polish-held Livonia. How deeply the new faith had impressed itself upon the minds of the inhabitants of these lands is open to doubt. There were no dramatic popular manifestations of religiosity, such as occurred in the Lowlands of Scotland or south-western France. On the outer periphery – ranging from the fells of Lapland to the forests of Lithuania – pagan customs and beliefs continued to frustrate the efforts of the clergy, who were usually poorly paid and far too few in numbers to be effective. Such circumstances demanded men of great vigour and energy: but all too often, the clergy were uneducated and inadequate. On the islands off the Estonian coast and in parts of Lettgallen, the Catholic church ceased to exist, but nothing replaced it, and the peasantry lapsed into a state of paganism alleviated by a hazy folk-memory of mariolatry. Duke Magnus utterly neglected the spiritual needs of his bishopric of Pilten; when it passed under Prussian control in 1585, there were only four priests to be found in the nine parishes. In spite of the efforts of the visitation commission set up under Salomon Henning in 1567, and the church reforms of the superintendant Alexander Einhorn, the state of the church in Kurland left a great deal to be desired. Only four of the eight schools proposed in 1567 were set up, and efforts to establish preaching posts for Latvian congregations met with little success. Of the hundred or so priests in the duchy in 1600, three-quarters came from Germany, and of the seven who can be positively identified as native Kurlanders, all were sons of immigrant German pastors.

A similar situation obtained in the Estonian lands, where the native gentry stubbornly defended their *jus patronatus* in the face of attempts by the Swedish crown and its agents to inaugurate a thorough reform of the church. A visitation conducted in 1586 observed that the Estonians had sunk into heathen darkness. Balthasar Rüssow, himself an Estonian, made many forthright comments about the lack of priests capable of conducting services or catechising in Estonian. The lack of suitable candidates for the priesthood prompted the town council in Reval to contemplate setting up a university in the 1540s, and a school for poor children was set up in 1553. The council in Riga was rather more forward in these matters, engaging the Dutchman Jacobus Battus as Latin master in 1527. Battus reopened the *Domschule* as an evangelical school, based on Melanchthon's *Praeceptor Germaniae curriculum.* The town council also offered university scholarships in the 1530s, though few of those who went to study in Rostock or Wittenberg returned to enter the ministry. Like most other young men, they preferred the more lucrative study of the law, which guaranteed a career and offered the prospect of social advancement.

The reformers placed great stress on the use of the vernacular, though they were not pioneers in this field. The Dominicans who worked in the eastern Baltic had used texts in the native languages, fragments of which survive, and it has been suggested that a number of the works published by the reformers owe a great deal to medieval antecedents. There are also still extant a number of printed religious works in Swedish, Danish and Low German which pre-date the Reformation. However, the Reformation did mark the first appearance of books in Finnish, Estonian and Latvian. A mass in Latvian, Estonian and Livonian (a Finno-Ugric language spoken around the Düna) was printed in Lübeck as early as 1525, but destroyed by order of the authorities. Ten years later, a Lutheran catechism with parallel texts in Estonian and Low German was published, though this too fell foul of the authorities, and was not rediscovered until 1929. A catechism in the South Estonian dialect was printed in Lübeck in 1554. The Commandments and some hymns are known to have been translated into Latvian, and there was probably a Latvian handbook for divine service, though no copy survives. The first Latvian book was the *Cathechismus Catholicorum*, printed in Vilna in 1585, followed a year later by the Lutheran Little Catechism, printed in Königsberg. Full translations of the Bible into Latvian and Estonian had to wait until the next century, though the Little Catechism was generally regarded as containing the essentials of the Christian religion – 'the common man's bible', as the Swede Laurentius Paulinus Gothus put it in 1631.[10]

The reformers were also concerned to improve the manners and morals of their barbarous flock. Bishop Peder Palladius in Denmark and Olaus Petri in Sweden both inveighed against blasphemy and swearing, and funeral orations became a favourite method of attacking

10. Pleijel H 1967 Katekesen som svensk folkbok *Våra äldsta folkböcker*, (ed. H. Pleijel). Lund, p. 68.

the upper classes for lax and immoral living. Heavy drinking was a particular target of Danish churchmen: Peder Palladius wrote of the 'demon drinker' starting the day off with *brændevin*, going on to German ale and ending with Prussian beer. Frederik II set the pace. In 1560, he fell into the water with his horse when trying to cross a bridge in a drunken stupor: two years later, he caused a scandal by coming to blows with Johann von Mecklenburg at his sister's wedding. The king's almanac is heavily scored with crosses denoting the days when he was drunk. Small wonder that Anders Vedel, in his funeral oration over the king, hinted that his majesty would have lived longer had he not ruined his health through drink.

The greatest enemy of all, however, was the devil, the lord of darkness whose earthly form was represented in scores of church wall-paintings across northern Europe. In Scandinavian church paintings, the devil frequently appears alongside or helping a woman churning butter: women supposedly in league with the devil were often called 'milkmaids'. Witches were accused of a variety of crimes: they were blamed for the disastrous Danish naval expedition against Zeeland in 1543, for the loss of ships in a storm off Visby in 1566 and for the premature death of the Danish state councillor Iver Krabbe in 1561. Erik XIV was reputed to have engaged four witches to assist his war efforts against the Danes. The Lapps had a reputation for conjuring up winds, and for killing their enemies with the aid of a ball sent whizzing through the air. As late as the eighteenth century, sophisticated travellers visiting northern Europe would regale their readers with tales of Lapp magic.

As elsewhere in Europe, those accused of witchcraft in Scandinavia tended to be old, poor and the most defenceless members of society. In Estonia, men were far more frequently accused of sorcery than was generally the case elsewhere in Europe, which may suggest that the aim of witchcraft trials here was the eradication of a pagan priesthood, rather than the persecution of lonely old women with a reputation as soothsayers. A study of witchcraft in Estonia written at the beginning of this century by pastor Winkler concluded with a personal testimony that sorcerers were still resorted to, and belief in werewolves, love potions, reading the cards, etc., was still prevalent amongst his parishioners. In Poland–Lithuania, the persecution of witches did not get under way until the seventeenth century, and it has been suggested that this had a lot to do with the decline of religious toleration. The competition between Catholic and Protestant churches in the sixteenth century meant that the forms and institutions of medieval worship – ritual, religious symbols, social welfare – were maintained on both sides of the divide, and that pagan habits were also tolerated. Excavations carried out in 1974 in the cemetery of a Calvinist community in Samogitia revealed, for example, that well into the seventeenth century, the dead were buried in heathen fashion. When the Catholic church took the offensive in the early seventeenth century, it directed its fire as much against paganism as Protestantism. The decline of social welfare and the social dislocation caused by wars, famine and plague fuelled the 'witch craze': landowners often blamed witches for crop failures, for example.[11]

The persecution of witches, which did not die out until the eighteenth century in Poland–Lithuania, is the dark side of an age which also laid great emphasis upon the need for education, learning and refinement of manners. Many who were strong advocates of the necessity of creating institutions of learning, or who fulminated against the rude and uncouth manners of the aristocracy, were also zealous in their pursuit of witches; the glee with which bishop Peder Palladius recorded the numbers of witch trials in his Visitation Book makes distasteful reading today. In Sweden, the tightening of religious orthodoxy in the seventeenth century also produced an increase in the persecution of witches, though the most obvious practitioners of magic, the Lapps, were largely left alone.

Crazed poor folk who babbled under torture of consorting with the devil and dancing at the witches' sabbath could expect no mercy. The upper class could indulge their passion for the occult under the guise of scientific enquiry. Portents and natural phenomena were eagerly observed and analysed, and there appeared a constant stream of apocalyptic prophesies in the last two decades of the sixteenth century. The Danish astronomer Tycho Brahe interpreted the eruption of a new star in Cassiopeia in 1572 as marking the end of the Roman world-monarchy and the beginning of a new era. Several leading intellectual figures in Sweden, such as Johannes Bureus and Johan Skytte, drew inspiration from the mystical prophesies of Paracelsus, whose vision of a golden lion arising in the north and defeating the Imperial eagle was to enjoy enormous vogue in the early seventeenth century.

---

11. Winkler R 1909 Ueber Hexenwahn und Hexenpozesse in Estland während der Schwedenherrschaft *Baltische Monatsschrifte* **67**: 355. Kahk J 1985 Heidnische Glaubensvorstellungen, Zauberei und religiöser Eifer in Estland um 1700 *Zeitschrift für Ostforschung* **34**: 522–35. Tazbir J 1980 Hexenprozesse in Polen *Archiv für Reformationsgeschichte* **71**: 280–307.

THE EXERCISE AND LIMITATIONS OF PRINCELY AUTHORITY

By the end of the sixteenth century, the initial triumphs of the Reformation in central Europe had faded. In the Habsburg lands and Poland–Lithuania, the Catholic church was rapidly regaining lost ground. The tide of reform, which at one stage had threatened to engulf the whole of Europe north of the Alps, was now ebbing fast. From their seminaries in Braunsberg and Olmütz, the Jesuit fathers sent young men back to their northern homelands to work for the restoration of Catholicism. The northern kingdoms responded by proclaiming strict Lutheran orthodoxy and uniformity. Little wonder that the hard-pressed Protestants of Germany in the late 1620s looked to Gustav II Adolf as their great deliverer; after Christian IV's defeat on the Elbe, the king of Sweden was virtually the only hope of the Protestant cause.

The implantation of the evangelical faith in northern Europe was, however, a slow process, and it would be unwise in the extreme to attribute Gustav II Adolf's successes in Germany to the religious fervour of Protestantism. Sweden's rise to the status of a major European power in the seventeenth century owed a good deal more to the structural changes and reforms carried out within the Vasa kingdom than it did to the inspiration of godliness or the virtues of the king's supposed Gothic valour.

The most serious problem facing Gustav Vasa as king of Sweden was the crown's lack of resources. The principle that the king should 'live of his own', that is, from the income, rents and fines from his lands, was not a practical proposition, even though contemporaries continued to pay lip service to it. Gustav Vasa was faced in 1523 with a heavy debt to be paid off to Lübeck, and a run-down domestic economy. The extensive and untaxed lands of the church offered a tempting way out of difficulty, and the king took it. In 1527, the estates of the realm were summoned to Västerås, where they were presented with a royal proposition (backed by a threat of abdication if it were not granted) which sought to deprive the church of most of its wealth, land and power. The nobility were also granted the right to reclaim all land donated (without compensation), sold or mortgaged to the church by their families since 1454. By one act, the power of the church was ended: but although the sequestration of church land and property augmented the crown's sources of revenue, this was insufficient to meet rising expenditure. The king appointed bailiffs to supervise the royal estates: their number almost trebled during the course of

97

the reign. Through his servants, he sought to rationalise the assessment and collection of taxes. New methods of book-keeping and
fiscal administration were introduced by the king's German advisers,
most notably Conrad von Pyhy, whose attempts to reconstruct the
central administrative system on German cameral lines were only
partially successful.

By the end of Gustav Vasa's reign in 1560, Sweden was on the way
to becoming a more efficiently run, centralised state, in which the
crown assigned the annual tax revenue of the fiefs (*län*) in return for
specific services. But there were also decentralising tendencies. In
addition to increasing the terms of knight-service, Gustav Vasa
attempted to set up a native standing army, which would diminish his
reliance on costly mercenaries. This system was based on the land.
Those conscripted were to remain on their farms during peacetime,
and were to be paid by a remission of taxes. Problems still arose when
war broke out, for troops had to be provisioned and paid. Gustav
Vasa always had a marked preference for a natural economy, which,
although inelastic and clumsy in its workings, avoided the problems
of price depreciation through inflation or currency debasement which
so plagued rulers elsewhere in Europe. Exchange was largely effected
without money, though currency units were used to determine value.
The voluminous correspondence of Gustav Vasa is full of examples of
this. In 1547, for example, he permitted the peasants of Dalarna to go
to the Norwegian coast to trade for salt and fish, first having exchanged their butter and cheese for iron in Värmland. In the same
year, he instructed his bailiff in Sunnerbo to purchase a consignment
of Dutch heavy cloth with Swedish butter so that the recently recruited soldiers could have something to wear. By dint of careful
management, the king managed to store up a modest treasury of silver
which quickly disappeared to meet the more extravagant costs of his
sons. The expensive wars in Livonia and against Denmark in the 1560s
and 1570s brought the kingdom to the verge of bankruptcy, and
underlined the old king's conviction that an expansionist foreign
policy would cost Sweden dear.[12]

The burdens of war finance also drained the resources of the Danish
crown. The royal decree of 1525 was the first systematic attempt to
establish the basis for knight-service. To ensure that valuable currency
stayed in the realm and that the crown would not have to tax its poor
subjects each year to pay for foreign soldiers, it was decreed that all

---

12. Hecksher E 1931 Natural and money economy *Journal of Economic and Business
History* **3**: 1–29. Odén B 1967 Naturaskatter och finanspolitik *Scandia* **33**:1–18.

owning landed estates exempt from taxation should provide a fully armed cavalryman for each 100 marks of revenue, or a musketeer for each 50 marks of income. A panel of commissioners was set up to prepare a register of incomes. The Count's War in the early 1530s devastated the crown's finances, and this was a powerful incentive to Christian III to strip the church of its wealth, as Gustav Vasa had done a decade before. Christian III and his chancellor Johan Friis also pushed through a number of administrative and fiscal reforms, reducing the number of administrative fiefs (*len*), restoring many to crown control, and creating an exchequer to deal with the revenues of the *len* and oversee the work of the aristocratic *lensmænd*.

The seven years' war against Sweden (1563–70) imposed severe strains upon the finances of the crown. Frederik II had to resort to borrowing from his Saxon in-laws and to clipping the currency. In 1566, he turned for help to the brilliant jurist and administrator Peder Oxe, who had fallen from favour and been obliged to go into exile in 1558. Oxe persuaded the Danish nobility to pay an extraordinary tax on their estates, and levied a variety of impositions and taxes. Above all, Oxe reversed the disastrous policy of closing the Sound to shipping, and transferred the method of payment of duties from ships to weight of cargo. Within a year, revenue from the Sound dues had risen from 45,000 daler in 1566 to 132,000 in 1567. The war debt was virtually eliminated by the end of Frederik II's reign, and the crown had been able to recall fiefs and consolidate its holdings. In the wealthy *len* of Kronborg, Frederiksborg and Copenhagen, for example, the nobility in 1559 held more than four hundred tenancies. Twenty years later, that amount had shrunk to eighty.

The crown's policy of rationalising its land holdings was successful in certain parts of the kingdom, most notably on the island of Sjælland. It reduced the number of *len* (as was the case in Sweden during the reign of Gustav Vasa, when a similar policy of land consolidation was pursued) and augmented royal income, though the king's love of hunting was wasteful and led to loss of revenue. The crown was also capable of a flexible response to the fluctuations of the international market. After 1576, the rate of conversions of *len* into fiefs of account, administered by a salaried *lensmand*, began to decline. Instead, at a time of international instability which could affect exports such as oxen, the crown preferred to lease out its fiefs, thereby shifting the risk to the fief-holder.

A good deal of the crown's income appears not to have passed through the exchequer, especially payments in kind. The customs of Gottorp and Rendsborg went to meet expenses in the duchies, the cattle duty in Ribe was used to make direct purchases, and most of the Sound dues went straight into the king's personal account. The crown's fiscal policies were sufficiently effective to give Christian IV the reputation of being the richest king in Europe at the end of the sixteenth century: the king himself estimated his fortune at around one million daler in 1618.

The offices and revenues granted by the crown were of considerable importance to the nobility. In 1588, at the funeral of Frederik II, a protest was staged by a number of noblemen, seventy-one of whom signed a petition addressing their grievances to the council. Most of the signatories were owners of medium large estates. Notably absent from the list of petitioners were administrators of the most lucrative fiefs, or *hovedlen*, the revenues of which were considerably greater than the incomes of most noblemen. The evidence would suggest that, at a time of general instability and economic crisis, hard-pressed landowners sought to secure their income through crown office – and that the richest pickings were confined to a small circle of wealthy families. An assessment of knight-service obligations in 1625 showed that one-quarter of noble land was owned by a mere 5 per cent of the high aristocracy, members of the inner circle of office-holders, the very people whose wealth was used to erect the splendid houses which still grace the Danish countryside.[13]

The efforts of sovereigns to assert princely authority and the primacy of crown interests over the privileges and liberties of noble subjects met with only limited success in northern Europe. Christian II's wide-ranging programme of reforms, which encroached significantly upon the exclusive privileges of the nobility, never came to fruition. Though certain Danish historians have detected a good deal of aristocratic resistance to the crown's reforms after 1536, more recent interpretations have suggested that the entrusting of the sovereignty of the crown to the king and the estates at the 1536 *rigsdag* forged a 'dyarchy' of mutual interests between the king and the council nobility. The Swedish nobility, badly shaken by the Stockholm bloodbath, remained docile during the reign of Gustav Vasa, but were roused to opposition by the absolutist pretensions of Erik XIV, whom they helped overthrow. In 1569 they presented a wide-ranging programme of demands to the new king, whom they had helped to the throne.

13. Ladewig Petersen E 1980 Rigsråd og adelsopposition 1588: en socialhistorisk studie *Rigsråd, adel og administration 1570–1648* (K Jespersen, ed.). Odense, pp. 123–68. Enevoldsen P 1981-2 Lensreformerne i Danmark 1557–96 *Historisk Tidskrift* **81**: 343–99. Ladewig Petersen E 1975 From domain state to tax state *Scandinavian Economic History Review* **23**: 116–48.

In some measure these demands sought to reassert noble privileges, and to define aristocratic exclusivity more sharply. At the heart of these demands was the wish to prevent the imposition of extraordinary taxes and aids upon the peasantry on noble estates. The main concession made by Johan III was the exemption from conscription of peasants living within a Swedish mile of the manor, the so-called *frihetsmil*, or mile of liberty. The programme also claimed that, in accordance with ancient and well-tried custom, the king should fill the high offices of state from the ranks of the nobility, and should staff his chancery with members of the aristocracy, who were to receive permanent salaries. Although the kings of Sweden were loath to submit to any demand which effectively circumscribed their powers, they were in practice not averse to employing nobles. Three high-born men were appointed by Gustav Vasa to the reorganised exchequer in 1539, the first Swedish noblemen to become permanently employed functionaries. By the end of the century, the numbers of university-educated nobles had significantly increased, and there was thus less need for the king to employ foreigners with the requisite skills to run the chancery. After 1560, the number of fiefs in Sweden shrank considerably, which meant that the nobility had to be compensated in other ways, if social peace was to be secured. They became intimately involved in the administration of the state, for which they received direct payment in the form of revenue assignments (*förläning*), thereby taking a decisive step towards becoming a salaried service nobility.[14] Karl IX even proposed legislation which would have stripped of his title any nobleman who did not have his sons educated in a manner suitable for crown service.

The promoters of the 1569 programme hotly denied that they were proposing anything new, and rested their case on good old custom which time and tyrannical government had eroded. The nobility were not slow to reassert their own rights and privileges, both as landowners and as the foremost estate of the realm. They possessed a keen, if somewhat one-sided sense of the past, and were quick to condemn the attempts of rulers such as Christian II and Erik XIV to curb their privileges. In his *Oeconomia*, written in the 1570s, Per Brahe spoke of the usurpation of noble rights by 'that old tyrant, king Christian'. Amongst these privileges was the exemption of peasants on *frälse* land from ordinary taxation: no new taxes were to be levied without the consent of the nobility and the commonalty, according to Swedish law, nor was war to be declared or waged without the advice of the

14. Nilsson S 1947 *Krona och frälse i Sverige 1523-1594*. Lund, p. 380.

council.[15] A far more sophisticated statement of aristocratic constitutionalism was made by Erik Sparre in his *Pro lege, rege et grege*, written in the 1580s.[16] Sparre argued that the Swedish people had freely and voluntarily consented to the transformation of an elective to an hereditary monarchy, and that Gustav Vasa had sworn a solemn oath to be bound by the law. He was also concerned to show that the king had not allowed the royal dukes more rights than were specified in his testament; no alienation of regalian rights had occurred, and the dukes enjoyed only *dominium utile* in their duchies.

Pro lege, rege et grege, and Sparre's Oration delivered before king Sigismund at the meeting of the estates in 1594 were a clear statement of a cardinal principle embodied in the medieval Land Law, that of consent, but they also bore some similarity with the contractual theories of the French monarchomachs, and the writings of Sparre's Danish contemporary, Arild Hvidfeldt. In his chronicle of the reign of Christian II, Hvidfeldt declared that the terms of government were renewed and reaffirmed at every royal election and coronation. The task of the *ephori regni*, the king's councillors, was to advise the ruler and hold him to the fulfilment of his sacred oath. Hvidfeldt borrowed extensively from *De jure magistratuum* and *Vindiciae contra tyrannos* in his judgement of Christian II, who was indeed replaced as ruler by his magnates. Hvidfeldt's chronicle was written to teach the young Christian IV how the good governance of the realm depended upon the division of power between king and the representatives of the nobility in the *rigsråd*. The *rigsråd* was highly conscious of its powers, and Christian IV was frequently frustrated in his efforts to pursue a more vigorous and aggressive foreign policy. The Swedish *riksråd* suffered a heavy defeat in the power struggle with duke Karl, though the high nobility was still able to impose an accession charter on the young Gustav Adolf in 1611. The young king seems to have been very conscious of the revolutionary way in which his father had come to the throne, and of the necessity to work with his subjects for the good of the realm. In a speech delivered to the estates in 1617, he provided a lengthy justification for his governance of the realm, and ended by declaring that the oaths which ruler and subjects swore to each other were the very foundation of a well-ordered government, and for the sovereign's part, obliged him to rule by the law of the land.[17]

15. Brahe P 1971 *Oeconomia eller Hushållsbok för ungt adelsfolk* (J Granlund and G Holm, eds). Lund, pp. 166–8.
16. Sparre E 1924 *Pro lege, rege et grege* Historiska Handlingar **27**/1: 64.
17. Hallendorff C (ed.) 1915 *Tal och skrifter av konung Gustav II Adolf.* Stockholm, pp. 55–65.

The guiding principle which underlay the claims of the noble estate was that of consent. This was pushed to its furthest limits in Poland–Lithuania, where Stanisław Orzechowski could claim that the king could ordain no laws affecting the person, financial or juridical status of the aristocracy without noble consent. From 1505, no decision concerning the realm could be taken by the king without the joint agreement of the two chambers of the *sejm*.[18] How far the power of the monarch was already circumscribed before the Jagełłionian line was extinguished in 1572 is a matter of some debate amongst historians. Although the monarchy was formally elective under the Jagełłionian kings, the succession of the king's heir to the throne was tacitly accepted by the magnates, as was the case in Denmark after 1536. The opportunity for a contested and divisive election was thereby avoided, and an element of dynastic continuity maintained. The full-blooded institution of an elective process in Poland after 1572, with each royal candidate having to agree to a *pacta conventa*, or a series of promises made to the aristocratic electorate, undoubtedly weakened the authority of the crown. The articles signed by Henri of Anjou in 1573, subsequently presented to every king-elect for confirmation, decreed that the royal candidate would promise to call the *sejm* at least once every two years, would consult his senators on questions of war or peace, and would consult the *sejm* before imposing any new taxes or calling the nobles to arms. The principle of elective monarchy was to be accepted by the king-elect, and the nobles were guaranteed the right to renounce their allegiance should they deem the king guilty of illegal or extra-legal actions. This right was exercised in 1606, when Protestant nobles seeking to defend their religious liberties joined forces with the opposition to Zygmunt III's attempts to curb the powers of the *sejm*. The powers and authority of the monarchy did not disappear after 1572: in their different ways, Stefan Batory and Zygmunt III showed themselves to be vigorous defenders of royal prerogative. But as Antoni Maczak has pointed out, the continuity provided by the Jagełłionian dynasty was broken, and each new monarch therefore inherited his predecessor's problems without being able fully to benefit from any advantages he might have built up through intrigue or negotiation. The element of continuity thus passed from the monarchy, and was to some extent taken up by the *sejm* and the magnates. The Polish–Lithuanian commonwealth thus

18. Grodziski S 1977 Les devoirs et les droits publiques de la noblesse polonaise *Acta Poloniae Historica* **36**: 163–76.

'achieved not so much balance of political forces as a paralysis, which eventually led to stagnation and then catastrophe'.[19]

The reasons for the political decline of Poland–Lithuania are many and complex, and it is certainly unwise to assume that because the commonwealth finally disintegrated in the eighteenth century, its downward path began with the ill-fated election of Henri of Anjou in 1573. Indeed, if any state appeared to be on the verge of utter collapse in the first decade of the seventeenth century, it was Russia, the ultimate inheritor of most of the Polish–Lithuanian lands. The powers of the Polish–Lithuanian nobility were certainly no greater than those exercised by the junkers of Prussia and Brandenburg. In 1539, the duke of Prussia had to concede that no noble properties could revert to him until both the male and female line of the possessing family had died out. A further levy of taxation to pay for the war against the Turks prompted further concessions in 1542. In return for the re-affirmation of the right of succession of his house, the duke conceded that the highest officials of the land, with the possible exception of the chancellor, should be native-born noblemen. In the duke's absence from the duchy, or in the event of a minor succeeding him, the governance was to rest with the supreme council (*Oberräte*). In 1566, further concessions were made, extending the powers of the supreme council, and granting the estates the right to seek aid from the king of Poland if the duke violated their rights and liberties. By 1609, the agreement of the estates was required for every step affecting the status of the duchy. Any ducal commands infringing noble privileges were to be regarded as automatically null and void. The mental incapacity of duke Albrecht's successor certainly strengthened the hand of the noble estate in Prussia, but elsewhere along the southern Baltic coast, from Mecklenburg to Kurland, the nobility were effectively in charge of the government and firmly entrenched behind a wall of privileges by the end of the sixteenth century.

In Poland–Lithuania, political power tended to devolve upon the local assemblies, the *sejmiki*. Within the *sejmiki*, power was exercised by the nobility; a numerous class, probably encompassing as much as 10 per cent of the population, within which there were very wide differences of wealth, but which had a common ethos and notion of political status, albeit fragmented by religious or ethnic divisions. Although the differences within this large and disparate estate could be exploited by the crown, the king had no other organised social forces

19. See the articles by Andrzej Wyczański and Antoni Maczak in Fedorowicz J 1982 *A republic of nobles. Studies in Polish history to 1864*. Cambridge, pp. 91–134. The citation is from Fedorowicz's introduction to the essay by Maczak, p. 111.

which he could employ as a check to noble pretensions and demands. The largest cities such as Danzig preferred to fight for their own particularist interests and played no part in political decision-making within the commonwealth, and the peasantry had been largely reduced to servility and dependence upon the nobility. Not for nothing did Stanisław Stadnicki, the 'devil of Łancut', boast that more than any other peoples or in any other lands, the Polish nobleman was born to liberty.

In Sweden, on the other hand, the gradual emergence of the multi-estate *riksdag* was an important element in the creation of a balance between king and subject. The origins of the *riksdag* can be traced back to the Middle Ages, though no fixed pattern of representation had been established.[20] For the crucial meeting at Västerås in 1527, the king ordered the councillors of state and nobility to attend, with six peasants from each law district, and a burgomaster and councillor from each town. The bishops were to attend with leading members of their chapters. The next meeting summoned by the king, in 1544, established the corporate structure more firmly: the medieval 'assembly of magnates' (*herremöte*) gave way to a meeting of the estates (*ständermöte*). Gustav Vasa had deemed it expedient to found his royal power upon the consent of the estates: it was at Västerås in 1527 that the king proposed the elimination of the secular authority of the church, and again in 1544, the hereditary monarchy was established with the consent of the estates. In 1569, the leading estate shook off the passivity with which it had accepted the measures of king Gustav, and the nobility was to assert itself on other occasions during the reign of Johan III. During the constitutional crisis of the 1590s, duke Karl was to use the non-noble estates as a weapon against the council aristocracy, and an ingrained suspicion of these estates remained within the ranks of the nobility for several decades thereafter. The desire of the high nobility to limit the functions and role of the estates, which found expression in Gustav Adolf's accession charter of 1611, was never fulfilled. The Danish estates never acquired a permanent consultative role; the nobility alone exercised infuence over government. In Sweden however, the four estates of the clergy, nobility, burghers and peasants were to become an integral feature of the polity during the seventeenth century.

Although the powers of the *riksdag* were modest compared with those of the English parliament, its continued existence and develop-

20. On the origins of the *riksdag*, see Scott F 1978 *Sweden. The nation's history.* Minneapolis, pp. 111–12 and Schuck H *et al.* 1985 *Riksdagen genom tiderna.* Stockholm, pp. 7–36.

ment was a powerful and essential acclamation of the right of the nobility and commonalty to be consulted. Equally, it was a useful instrument whereby the sovereign might acquire the solemn and binding consent of the representatives of his subjects to ambitious policies, and it could also be used to curb the powers of the nobility. Duke Karl had shown in the 1590s that the aristocratic maxim culled from Roman law – 'quod omnes tangit, ab omnibus approbatur debet' (that which concerns all must be approved by all) – could be given a rather different twist. The 'herr omnes' of the peasantry summoned up by the duke was by no means to the liking of the aristocratic constitutionalists. It has been suggested that the political rights of the freehold peasantry in Sweden approximated to those of the poorest stratum of the gentry in Poland: but the *szlachta zagrodowa* were still linked to the magnates by the common ethos and status of nobility.[21] Between the peasantry and the noble estate in Sweden, there were many barriers, not least the distinction between noble and non-noble land. The mutual suspicion of the two estates, which surfaced in times of crisis as in 1650, could be used by the crown to stem any incipient constitutional challenge to its authority. There was, in other words, a degree of balance between crown and estates, resting upon the institutional structure of the realm, a balance which was lacking in Poland–Lithuania.

The crucial difference between the two branches of the Vasa dynasty which ruled in Sweden and Poland–Lithuania during the first half of the seventeenth century was that the hereditary monarchs in Sweden were able to work with the estates and forge an effective national partnership. The elective rulers of the *Rzeczpospolita* had to contend with a far more diverse mixture of peoples, religion, customs and particularist liberties, which evaded all attempts to provide a strong centralised state administration. It is one of history's ironies that the direct line of the Vasa dynasty in both countries terminated in abdication. Queen Christina, however, could successfully overcome a constitutional crisis and arrange for the succession of her cousin in 1654 without any diminution in royal power. The last Vasa king of Poland, Jan Kazimierz (1648–68), had to abandon all attempts to reform the system in the face of a noble rebellion, and ultimately renounced the throne, leaving his noble subjects with the prophetic warning that the commonwealth would be partitioned by its neighbours unless the system were radically changed.

21. Fedorowicz 1982, p. 100 (article by Wyczański).

CHAPTER FIVE

The Struggle for Dominion: The First Phase, 1558–1621

THE LIVONIAN WARS

The series of wars in northern Europe which began with the irruption of Russian and Tatar troops into Livonia in January 1558 falls into two main periods. In the first, lasting until the 1580s, two of the four main contenders for territory in Livonia were effectively eliminated. In the second, Sweden and Poland fought for hegemony in Livonia, and even attempted to extend their influence into the crisis-ridden state of Muscovy. A turning-point was reached in 1621, when Riga fell to the Swedish army. Within five years, Gustav II Adolf (1611–32) was able to transfer his military activities to Prussia and Poland and ultimately to Germany, where he was to meet his death on the battlefield of Lützen. During the first ten years of Gustav II Adolf's reign, therefore, Sweden succeeded in establishing control over most of Livonia and over the mouth of the riva Neva, thereby laying the foundations for a remarkable ascendancy in northern Europe for the remainder of the century.

The first period of hostilities may further be divided into four distinct phases: 1558–61; 1561–70; 1570–77; and 1577–83. In the first phase, the old Livonian confederation disintegrated in the face of Muscovite aggression, and its constituent elements sought protection from a variety of foreign rulers. In the second, the focus for hostilities shifted from Livonia to the Baltic sea and Scandinavia during the seven years' northern war (1563–70). Ivan IV had observed a watchful neutrality during this conflict, but returned to the arena in the early 1570s. The Danish presence in Estonia was virtually eliminated, and Sweden's possessions seriously threatened: after 1577, however, the tide of war turned dramatically. Swedish forces recovered most of the fortified places lost to the Russians, and managed to capture Narva in 1581. Polish–Lithuanian troops marched deep into Ivan IV's lands, capturing a string of fortresses, and compelling the tsar to sue for peace. Ivan IV's reign thus ended ignominiously for Muscovy, forced to abandon virtually all territory in Livonia gained since 1558.

During negotiations in Moscow in 1554, the demand for payment of a tribute in recognition of Russian sovereignty for the use of certain lands by the see of Dorpat was made a central issue by the Russians. Although the Livonian delegates denied all knowledge of such a tribute having been paid in the past, they were compelled to acknowledge the tsar's claim. Three years later, a new Livonian delegation to Moscow was faced with a renewed demand for payment of the tribute. After a good deal of haggling, agreement was finally reached on the sum: but, as the Livonian emissaries had not brought the money with them, negotiations were broken off. On 22 January 1558, Muscovite troops commanded by the Tatar prince Shig-Aley crossed the border. Mild weather hindered the movements of this army, which seems to have been intended as a demonstration of Ivan's power rather than a fully coordinated campaign. The Livonian estates were woefully ill-prepared to meet the foe, and the diet which met at Wolmar in March decided to sue for peace. Ivan IV let it be known through Shig-Aley that he was willing to make peace if the tribute was paid without delay. A new embassy bearing the desired amount set off for Moscow: but Ivan refused to receive it. The violation of the armistice by soldiers of the Narva garrison caused the Russians to renew hostilities, and to capture Narva on 11 May. Dorpat surrendered to the invading forces at the end of July. The army hastily thrown together under the command of the Master of the Order inspired little confidence in the panic-stricken estates, who sought salvation as best they could. The king of Poland was urged to meet his obligations under the treaty of Poswol: the emperor and the Hanseatic League were bombarded with requests for assistance. Other possible saviours were canvassed. Peasants from the island of Ösel sought the protection of duke Johan of Finland: several Livonian noblemen tried to persuade Henri II to send a military expedition to conquer Livonia for France. The garrison of the castle in Reval was persuaded to accept Danish protection by Christoffer von Münchhausen, whose brother, the bishop of Ösel, was busily trying to sell his bishopric to Magnus, the younger son of Christian III. As the chronicler Johann Renner observed, Livonia was in such a state of chaos that the Russian invader could easily have occupied the entire country.[1]

Although the Master was able to regain control of Reval at the end of the year, he was compelled to look for assistance wherever he could find it. The emperor Ferdinand, bombarded with pleas for help, was unable to do very much. An Imperial embassy dispatched to Moscow in 1559 was a miserable failure: the 100,000 gulden voted by the diet of Augsburg in 1559 to finance the Livonian war effort was never collected: and an Imperial ban on trade with Russia was largely ineffective. The best defenders of the Livonian cause in the Empire were certain princes of northern Germany, such as the duke of Mecklenburg; the southern German princes, who saw in Muscovy a potential ally against the Turkish threat, were largely indifferent. The Hanse towns were cool in their response to the pleas of the Livonians: Lübeck contemplated the establishment of a protectorate over Livonia, but this ambitious plan never materialised. The seizure of Narva by the Russians gave new scope for direct trading with Muscovy, which the Wendish towns – for many years at loggerheads with the Livonian towns on this question – were not slow to exploit. Complaints that arms and munitions were being supplied to the 'enemy of Christendom' via Narva failed to stem the traffic: the God of the merchants was in their money-chests, according to the satirist Hans Hasentöter.[2]

The possibility of the restitution of Danish sovereignty over Harrien and Wierland – after more than two centuries – had been contemplated by Christian III during the conflict over the coadjutorship of Christoffer von Mecklenburg. In the autumn of 1558, Christian offered a sizeable subsidy to the Order if the Master ceded the two Estonian districts to Denmark. Furthermore, there would be an additional six-month subsidy should Danish mediators sent to Moscow fail to persuade Ivan IV to accept peace. The Danish embassy failed to make much headway with the Master, and the armistice which they managed to secure in Moscow simply enabled Ivan to disengage troops from Livonia to meet a renewed invasion by the Tatars. The only consolation for Denmark was that the bishop of Ösel was still anxious to sell his bishopric. The new king of Denmark, Frederik II, clinched the deal in September 1559, and persuaded his troublesome brother Magnus to renounce his claims in Holstein in return for the territory, which embraced the western islands and district of Wiek on

1. Tiberg 1984 *Zur Vorgeschichte des livländischen Krieges. Die Beziehungen zwischen Moskau und Litauen 1549–62* Studia Historica Upsaliensa 134. Uppsala, p. 137. Henning 1968, p. 31.

2. For details, see Kirchner 1954 *The rise of the Baltic question* University of Delaware Monograph Series 3. Newark, pp. 40–7,66–7. Donnert 1963 *Die livländische Ordenritterstaat und Russland. Der livländische Krieg und die baltische Frage in der europäischen Politik 1558–83*. Berlin, pp. 160–6.

the mainland. Magnus also purchased the bishopric of Pilten in Kurland in May 1560.

In September 1559, Wilhelm von Fürstenburg was replaced as Master of the Order by Gotthard Kettler. As coadjutor to Fürstenburg, Kettler had been the driving force behind the alliance with Zygmunt August, reached at Vilna in August 1559. Zygmunt August was reluctant to commit himself in Livonia, and the troops he sent were inadequate to deal with the renewed invasion of the forces of Muscovy in November 1559. In February 1560 the Russians stormed the castle of Fellin; in August, they inflicted a heavy defeat on the Livonian army at the battle of Ermes. The burghers of Reval sought to save their town from the growing chaos and their trade from ruin by negotiating with the new king of Sweden. In the summer of 1561, Erik XIV received the submission of the town and the knights of Harrien and Wierland. The final act in the disintegration of the Livonian federation took place in November 1561, when the archbishop, the representatives of the nobility and the towns of Wenden and Wolmar, and Gotthard Kettler (who became duke of Kurland), signed the treaty of submission to the Polish crown in Vilna. Only Riga remained nominally independent, a state of affairs brought to an end in 1581 when the city swore fealty to the king of Poland.

The invasion of 1558 had precipitated the collapse of Livonia. Although the size and military efficiency of the forces under Shig-Aley's command has probably been exaggerated, there can be little doubt of the unwillingness of the Livonian estates to fight. A number of nobles were evidently prepared to acknowledge Ivan as ruler in return for a guarantee of their privileges. The burghers of Narva and Dorpat demanded that their towns be spared the dangers of prolonged siege, and were able to secure extensive privileges from Ivan. The imposition of a war tax and the forced recruitment of peasants for the army in 1559 provoked great discontent, which flared up into a major revolt in Harrien and Wierland in 1560. Swedish observers noted that the peasantry hated their German overlords more than the Russians, and that the lords were reluctant to arm the peasants for fear that they would turn the weapons against them.[3]

The invading armies thus faced a disunited and pathetically weak enemy. Why then did Ivan IV not occupy the whole of Livonia? It has been argued that the campaign launched under the command of the Tatar prince Shig-Aley was improvised, and that it was not until the

3. Schirren C 1861 *Quellen zur Geschichte des Untergangs livländischer Selbständigkeit* Archiv für die Geschichte Liv- Est- und Kurlands, Neue Folge. Reval, vol. 1 pp. 185, 242–3.

late spring of 1558, when Ivan realised the weakness of the opposition and became aware that Zygmunt August was not prepared to take the field in defence of his Livonian allies, that a more purposeful campaign was mounted. Ivan also faced opposition at home from those who preferred a vigorous campaign against the Crimean Tatars.[4] The fall of Narva and subsequent Russian occupation of much of eastern Estonia may have prompted Ivan to contemplate the incorporation of territory into his lands. On the other hand, Svensson's conclusion that the conquest of Narva opened up the way for the realisation of a deep-seated Russian desire to establish direct trading links with the West has not found much favour amongst historians who find that Ivan was less interested in pursuing an active commercial policy than he was in asserting his patrimonial rights in Livonia.[5]

In general, Western historians have tended to interpret the policies of Zygmunt August and Christian III towards Livonia as hesitant and vacillating: the East German historian Erich Donnert, however, is inclined to believe that the Lithuanian nobility harboured aggressive intentions, and that the treaty of Poswol was, in Ivan IV's eyes, a *casus belli*. Under pressure from his adviser Alexey Adashev, who favoured war against the Crimea, Ivan agreed to the six-month truce in 1559. As a result of the truce, Donnert argues, the Order was able to secure Polish assistance, which in turn prompted a more active intervention in Livonian affairs by Denmark and Sweden. The Marxist–Leninist historians tend to see the war against Livonia as a 'progressive' one, essential for the economic and political development of landlocked Muscovy: war against the Tatars could only satisfy the 'reactionary' feudal element at the court. Vernadsky rejects the idea of such alternatives. In his view, there was no choice between the Crimean Tatars and Livonia, for the former were implacable enemies of the Muscovite state with whom no durable peace was possible. The choice before Ivan IV therefore was whether to confine hostilities to the south-eastern front, or to fight on two fronts by attacking Livonia. The tsar chose the latter alternative: in Vernadsky's view, the results proved disastrous.[6]

4. Tiberg 1984, p. 134. Rasmussen 1973 *Die livländische Krise 1554–61*. Copenhagen, pp. 93–102. Svensson S 1951 *Den merkantila bakgrunden till Rysslands anfall på den livländska ordensstaten 1558* Skrifter utgivna av vetenskaps-societeten i Lund. Lund, vol. 35, pp. 149–57.

5. See for example the arguments of Angermann N 1972 *Studien zur Livlandspolitik Ivan Groznyjs* Marburger Ostforschungen. Marburg, vol. 32; and Esper T 1966 Russia and the Baltic 1494–1558 *Slavic Review* 25: 458–74.

6. Donnert 1963, pp. 43–8. *Istoriya Estonskoy SSR* vol. 1, pp. 339–40. Vernadsky G 1969 *A history of Russia*. New Haven–London vol. 5: 1, p. 95. It is not certain for whom the results were a disaster.

Ivan IV's policy towards Livonia must be seen in the broader context of the internal politics of the Muscovite state and the complex interrelationship of Muscovy, the Tatar khanates and Poland–Lithuania. His motives in launching a sudden attack on Livonia in January 1558 continue to attract speculation, as does the seeming reluctance of Zygmunt August to become involved in war over Livonia. It is probable that neither ruler wished to become tied down in what was essentially a minor area of concern. They wished to assert their power and authority, but were unwilling to become involved in the troublesome task of reaching settlements with new subjects who were bound to demand confirmation of privileges and rights. Zygmunt August also had to pay heed to the growing tension between his Polish and Lithuanian subjects, and the machinations of the duke of Prussia. In other words, there were as many reasons for caution as for decisive action in Livonia: and this hesitancy goes a long way to explaining why the Livonian question remained on the agenda for decades after 1558.

During the 1560s, the main area of conflict was the Baltic sea and Scandinavia. The war in Livonia continued as a struggle between Sweden and Poland–Lithuania for the possession of fortified places. Ivan IV's policy in Livonia was to a large extent determined by the relationship between Muscovy and Lithuania. In a series of negotiations in 1559, the Russians sought to convert the truce with Lithuania into a perpetual peace. Since this would have meant the abandonment of Lithuanian claims to Smolensk (which had fallen to the Russians in 1514), the Lithuanian negotiators refused to countenance the idea. A renewed attempt to secure the perpetual peace was made in 1560, this time as part of a proposed marriage contract between one of Zygmunt August's sisters and the recently bereaved tsar. It may be that Ivan IV was endeavouring to reconcile the Lithuanians to the loss of Smolensk by agreeing to a partition of Livonia – though the evidence is not very conclusive – but in the event, nothing came of the discussions. The tsar married a Circassian princess, and refused to prolong the truce with Lithuania in 1562. Having concluded a truce with Sweden and a treaty of amity with Denmark, Ivan launched a major offensive against Lithuania in 1563, capturing the fortress of Polotsk on the upper reaches of the river Düna. The threat to Lithuania may have prompted the nobility of that country to adopt a more conciliatory attitude towards closer union with Poland, though victory over the Muscovite army at the battle of Chasniki in January 1564 caused them to have second thoughts. The Muscovite offensive was now blunted. A stream of defections to Lithuania, led by the commander of the

Muscovite forces in Livonia, prince Andrey Kurbsky, was indicative of growing discontent with the rule of Ivan IV. For the next six years, Muscovy was in the throes of Ivan's *oprichnina*, a massive reorganisation of the state which effectively reduced the Russian war effort to a bare minimum.

The disintegration of Livonia offered an opportunity for the sons of Gustav Vasa to satisfy their dynastic ambitions. Gustav Vasa had preferred to follow a low-key foreign policy. His main concern during the early years of his reign had been to secure the kingdom from renewed attack from Denmark, and to break free of Lübeck's economic grip. His first marriage to Katarina of Saxe-Lauenburg brought him in contact with the German princes, but he avoided binding entanglements with the Schmalkaldic League, and after the death of his wife in 1535, Gustav looked to the daughters of the Swedish nobility for consorts. His sons were more ambitious. Erik was a serious contender for the hand of the young queen Elizabeth of England, whilst Johan married Katarina, the daughter of Zygmunt August, in 1562. This marriage was to bring Johan into serious conflict with his brother the following year, at the same time as the long peace with Denmark was broken.

The king of Denmark, Frederik II (1559–88), who began his reign with a victory over the peasant-republic of Dithmarsch, showed little inclination to continue his father's conciliatory policy towards Sweden. By 1563, relations had deteriorated to the point where open conflict was only a matter of time. In May 1563, a dispute over naval signals off the island of Bornholm led to a battle and the capture of the Danish admiral by the Swedish fleet. Lübeck and Poland–Lithuania joined forces with Denmark, in a war which was to last seven years. To compensate for the loss of Sweden's only outlet to the Atlantic – the fortress of Älvsborg, captured by the Danish army in 1563 – Erik XIV sought to cut a way through to the coast of Norway. Trondheim was captured in 1564, but soon lost again: in 1567, Swedish forces invaded southern Norway. The seizure in 1565 of Varberg, on the coast of Halland, gave Sweden an outlet to the west, though the fortress was regained by the Danes three years later.

The most serious problem faced by the Swedes was the allied blockade, which threatened to deprive Sweden of vital salt supplies. Gustav Vasa had had the foresight to stockpile salt, but by 1566, supplies were running dangerously low. The capture of the Dutch salt-fleet by admiral Klas Kristersson Horn enabled the government to restore morale and confidence, and to continue the war. At sea, the Swedish fleet held the edge over the Danes and Lübeckers. On land, the German mercenaries employed by Frederik II were usually more than a match for Erik's native troops, though they were unable to strike a decisive blow. Rantzau's army managed to advance as far as Norrköping in the autumn of 1567, but lacking reinforcements, was compelled to retreat in atrocious winter conditions. By 1568, both sides were exhausted, and sought to negotiate. However, the war was to drag on for two more years before a peace settlement was reached, through the mediation of the emperor, at Stettin. Sweden renounced her claims to Gotland and the Norwegian provinces of Härjedalen and Jämtland, and recovered Älvsborg on payment of an indemnity of 150,000 riksdaler. Frederik II abandoned his claim to the Swedish throne, but the contentious question of the three crowns borne on the royal Danish coat-of-arms was referred to arbitration. Lübeck was to be paid compensation for claims outstanding since the days of Gustav Vasa, and the trading privileges of 1523 were restored, though Lübeck's merchants were no longer guaranteed the monopoly of Swedish foreign trade in the Baltic. The trade with Narva, which Erik XIV had vainly tried to stop, was declared free to all nations. Danish- and Swedish-held territories in Livonia were to be handed over to the emperor, who would reimburse the two countries for their efforts in defending Livonia against the Russians. Reval and Weissenstein would then be entrusted to the king of Sweden, with Frederik II obtaining the rest in fief from the emperor.

The hollowness of this last attempt to assert Imperial authority in Livonia was soon exposed. The Imperial estates insisted that Maximilian II reimburse Sweden from funds which they knew were non-existent. The Swedes insisted on payment, and finally, in 1577, Johan III cancelled his obligations under the treaty of Stettin and refused to recognise Imperial claims to Livonia. In spite of the evident unwillingness of the Imperial estates to provide meaningful aid, fanciful plans for the recovery of Livonia were still concocted by the German friends of the old order in Livonia. The Count-Palatinate Georg Hans von Veldenz-Lützelstein put forward a scheme for the creation of an Imperial Baltic fleet in 1570. There was a rumour that Reval had fallen to the Russians, and the tsar was about to unleash a fleet of privateers against ships from the Low Countries, which may have secured the backing of the duke of Alba for this project. The Imperial diet, however, was less impressed and turned down the plan as too costly. The Count-Palatinate, nothing daunted, came up with a new scheme in 1578 for the invasion of northern Russia, which would also involve the resurrection of the Order in Livonia. There was a strong undercurrent of such schemes and plots running beneath the surface of conventional diplomacy in late sixteenth-century Europe, grandiose in scope and design but destined to remain confined to the fertile imagination of their progenitors.[7]

Prolonged warfare in the Baltic coincided with the wars of religion in France, the revolt against Spanish rule in the Netherlands, and the struggle between Turk and Christian in the Mediterranean and central Europe. These conflicts frequently became intertwined. In his later years, Ivan IV sought to interest the emperor and the Pope in a joint crusade against the Turk as a means of countering his enemies in the Empire. The prospect of such an alliance persuaded Gregory XIII in 1580 to authorise his legate Antonio Possevino to mediate in the war between Muscovy and Poland. In 1576, Johan III's legate to Rome entered into negotiations with Philip II's representative Zuñíga, offering troops and ships to aid the Spanish armies in the Netherlands in return for money for mercenaries to fight in Livonia. These discussions developed into a plan for an anti-Danish alliance, involving Sweden and Poland, but nothing ever came of this scheme.[8] The western European countries were in general poorly informed about events in northern Europe, lacking any permanent embassies in the region. The one exception was France, whose long-term resident in Copenhagen, Charles de Dançay, worked tirelessly, though with little reward, to promote French commercial and political interests in the north.[9]

The fate of Livonia was to be decided by those who already had staked their claim through the occupation of the strategic strong places of that war-torn land. The ambitions of Erik XIV's younger brother Johan, duke of Finland, caused a rupture between the two in 1563. In 1561, Erik had persuaded the council and estates to agree to a revision of his father's testament. This revision, known as the Articles of Arboga, effectively subjected the king's brothers to tight royal control. Duke Johan's wooing of the king of Poland's daughter, at a time when his brother was trying in vain to persuade Riga to accept Swedish protection, set the two men on collision course. In October 1562, Johan married Katarina Jagiellonica; and in return for a loan to his new father-in-law, received in pledge seven castles in Livonia, one of which the Swedish army was about to besiege. Erik now took steps

7. Donnert 1963, pp. 116–26. Kirchner 1954, pp. 82–3. There is an interesting essay on unoffical diplomacy in Andersson I 1943 *Svenskt och europeiskt femtonhundratal*. Lund.

8. Andersson 1943, pp. 66–78. Molbech C 1845 Philip IIs Planer mod Danmark *Historisk Tidskrift* **6**: 609–16.

9. Kirchner W 1966 *Commercial relations between Russia and Europe 1400–1800*. Bloomington, pp. 100–4.

to summon the *riksdag*, which pronounced the duke in breach of the Arboga Articles and condemned him to loss of life, property and hereditary rights. After a brief siege of Åbo castle, Johan was captured, and kept in confinement for the next four years.

In the meantime, there was no respite for the unfortunate inhabitants of Livonia. 'At this time', wrote the chronicler, 'the German and Swedish soldiers had ravaged the area around Hapsal and in the Wiek so terribly, that some poor peasants had to set their wives to the plough, for all their oxen and horses had been stolen.'[10] In 1562, the Polish–held town of Pernau was taken by the Swedes, Three years later, the garrison – consisting mainly of locally recruited sons of the gentry – mutinied and murdered their Swedish commander. In August, they marched against Reval, but were driven off. A fresh attempt to detach Reval from Swedish control occurred in 1569, when two Livonian nobles, Johann Taube and Eilert Kruse, tried to persuade the council to submit to Ivan IV. Using the argument that the deposition of Erik XIV in 1568 absolved Reval from any obligation to the Swedish crown, the two men promised a glowing future under the benevolent protection of the tsar, or, if the citizens preferred, a German prince who might swear fealty to the tsar like a free German knight in the Empire. The transfer of the staple for Russian trade from Narva to Reval was added as a further inducement. The Revalers were not, however, to be persuaded to switch their allegiance.

These abortive talks marked the return of Ivan IV to active involvement in Livonia. In 1564, he had concluded agreements with Sweden and Denmark, acknowledging their possessions in Estonia, but seeking recognition of his own claims on Livonia. Having failed to obtain by stealth and subversion further territory in Livonia, and with his alliance with Sweden in ruins after the deposition of Erik XIV, Ivan turned to duke Magnus as a stalking-horse for his ambitions. In May 1570, Magnus was hailed as 'king of Livonia' in Moscow, a vassal and ally of the tsar. In August of that year, Magnus led an army of 25,000 men against Reval. The citizens were offered the same terms as in the previous year, but they had little faith in the Russians' promises (the sad experience of the citizens of Dorpat under Russian rule may have stiffened their resolve). Reinforced by sea, the town held out until the the siege was broken off in March 1571. An attack on Moscow by the Crimean Tatars forced Ivan to withdraw troops. Magnus soon proved ineffective and unreliable. In 1575, Ivan IV launched a major offensive

---

10. Rüssow 1967 *Cronica der Provintz Lyfflandt* (reprint edn). Hannover, p. 69.

in Livonia, taking Pernau. In the winter of 1576–77, Reval had to endure the rigours of a second siege. Hostilities had also flared up on the Karelian frontier. In Estonia, the Swedish grip was beginning to weaken. The king was unable to pay his Scottish and German mercenaries, who mutinied: Johan was forced to surrender three castles to the mercenaries as pledges for payment, and when the money was not forthcoming, the disgruntled soldiers handed them over to Frederik II's commander in Ösel. The Swedish king even contemplated handing over his remaining possessions and titles to Frederik in return for the provinces of Bohus or Jämtland.

It was, nevertheless, Denmark and not Sweden which was to be virtually eliminated from the contest in Estonia. In 1576, Russian troops invaded the province of Wiek and even launched an attack on Ösel. Magnus, contemptuously abandoned by his erstwhile protector, gave up his meaningless crown and withdrew into obscurity in Kurland. Frederik II's ambassador Jakob Ulfeldt exceeded his instructions and surrendered the province of Wiek to Ivan IV. Although Frederik II refused to ratify the treaty and had his unfortunate ambassador disgraced, Denmark had for all practical purposes withdrawn from the contest. Only the island of Ösel remained. The mainland possessions were either abandoned to Sweden or sold to the king of Poland.

The truce between Erik XIV and Ivan IV had been at best an uneasy one. Ivan's demand for the surrender of Katarina Jagiellonica, the wife of the imprisoned duke Johan, caused some embarrassment for Erik, for it was widely rumoured that the tsar intended to make her his mistress. Erik's ambassador Nils Gyllenstierna was forced to agree to a treaty in February 1567, according to which the unfortunate Katarina was to be handed over to the tsar. In April a Russian embassy turned up in Stockholm to demand fulfilment of this agreement. Erik's attempts to secure a German ally in the shape of Johann Friedrich, duke of Weimar, had aroused the anger of the emperor Maximilian II. Harassed by the demands of the Russian and Imperial legates, increasingly suspicious that a plot was afoot, the balance of the king's mind became disturbed. In May 1567, Erik had members of the Sture clan arrested and condemned to death. On 24 May , the king visited Svante Sture in his cell in Uppsala castle, and seemed to effect a reconciliation with him. Two hours later, however, the king returned in great haste to the castle, and after a brief exchange of words, stabbed Svante's son Nils. Rushing from the castle, Erik shouted that all the prisoners 'except herr Sten' were to be executed – as the executioner could not tell which of the two Stens the king meant, both were spared. The king killed his former tutor who happened to cross his path, and vanished into the forest. For the remainder of the year, the king was mentally incapable of ruling. The council managed to persuade him to agree to a reconciliation with his brother, who was released in October. The king's favourite, Jöran Persson, was also arrested and condemned to death. In the new year, Erik seemed to have recovered. Persson was released and ennobled. Erik defied aristocratic opinion and married his mistress, a woman of peasant origin. The king now sought to justify the May murders as just punishments for traitors. These actions pushed his brothers into rebellion. In September 1568, Erik surrendered to his brothers. Early in the new year, he was deposed and imprisoned, and Johan was hailed as the new king by the estates.[11]

During the entry of the dukes' army into Stockholm, the tsar's delegation had been roughly treated by the mob. Ivan exacted revenge by throwing the members of a Swedish mission to Moscow into jail. In an exchange of letters, the two rulers traded insults. Ivan declared that Johan's father was of peasant descent, and that Sweden was merely a former province of Denmark, worthy only to negotiate with Novgorod. Johan gave as good as he got: the tsar, he declared, was an unchristian liar and a tyrant, who knew nothing of honour or the truth. These were brave words, for the war in Livonia was going badly for Sweden. Johan III might have expected a closer relationship with Poland: but the death of his father-in-law in 1572 plunged the *Rzeczpospolita* into an interregnum which only effectively came to an end in 1576, with the death of Maximilian II and the establishment on the Polish throne of his rival, the Transylvanian prince Stefan Batory. There was no formal alliance between Sweden and Poland, but from 1578 to 1581, the two cooperated in driving the Russians out of Livonia.

On 21 October 1578, having forged a deep stream under cover of their field-guns, the Swedes and Poles attacked and inflicted a heavy defeat on the Muscovite force which was besieging the castle of Wenden. The battle of Wenden was worthy of its name; it was indeed the turning-point in the war. Within three years, the Polish–Lithuanian army had launched an offensive deep into enemy territory, taking Polotsk, Veliki Luki and besieging Pskov in 1581. In the autumn of 1580, Swedish forces took the town of Kexholm on lake Ladoga. Early in the new year, an army commanded by the resourceful French mercenary Pontus de la Gardie crossed the frozen Gulf of Finland, and

11. Andersson I 1963 *Erik XIV* (revised edn). Stockholm, pp. 145–59. Roberts 1968 *The early Vasas. A history of Sweden 1523–1611*. Cambridge, pp. 235–42.

seized the Russian-held fortress of Wesenberg. De la Gardie crowned a year of success in September 1581 by storming the town of Narva. The war was now carried over the frontier, and Johan III entertained hopes of a campaign against Novgorod. In this he was to be disappointed, for his ally concluded a ten-year truce at Yam Zapolski in 1582, forcing Ivan IV to surrender to Poland all remaining areas under his control in Livonia. The king of Sweden had little option but to follow suit and seek a respite in the fighting. The three-year truce concluded in 1583 left the Swedes in possession of their recent conquests in Karelia and Ingria, but they were obliged to comply with Polish demands for the withdrawal of their troops threatening the port of Pernau.

In 1587, the conflict between Poland–Lithuania and Sweden acquired a new twist, for in the August of that year, a majority of the Polish estates elected Johan III's son Sigismund as their king. The military defeat of the rival candidate archduke Maximilian in January 1588 left Zygmunt III (to give him his Polish title) the undisputed ruler of the Polish–Lithuanian commonwealth. Johan III, however, had ensured that Swedish interests would not be jeopardised by the elevation of his son to the Polish throne. Sigismund had been obliged to accept the terms of the 1587 Statute of Kalmar, which were intended to maintain Sweden's independence and the Lutheran faith, and which specifically declared Estonia to be a Swedish possession. This last provision plainly ran counter to the claims of Poland–Lithuania to sole dominion over the whole of Livonia, and was to prove a major bone of contention between the two countries.

Zygmunt III's first years of rule were unhappy ones, but he was unable to detach himself from his new kingdom as had Henri of Anjou in 1574. In Sweden, a complex game of power politics was played out during the 1590s, the end result of which was to be the deposition of Sigismund Vasa as king of Sweden in 1600 in favour of duke Karl, the last surviving son of Gustav Vasa. Though Karl made a great show of refusing to accept the crown (he was finally persuaded to do so in 1604), he had been *de facto* ruler since the last two years of Johan III's reign. As a political manipulator, he was cast in the mould of his illustrious father. As a military leader and diplomat, however, he was not an unqualified success. The gains made by Sweden at the expense of Muscovy were soon whittled away. In 1590, the Russians resumed the war and retook Ivangorod and Koporye. A Swedish attempt in 1591 to besiege Novgorod ended in failure. The guerrilla war which had been simmering throughout the truce on the Karelian–Finnish frontier flared up again. In the late autumn of 1592, the wooden fortress of Orivirta, built by the Swedes as an advance post in disputed territory at the end of the fifteenth century, was totally destroyed by a raiding party from Karelia. The war even extended to the far north. A peasant army from Ostrobothnia sacked the monastery of Pechenga and attempted to take the town of Kola on the White Sea coast in 1590; a further unsuccessful attempt to take Kola was made in 1591, and the fortress of Soma was attacked the following summer. A truce concluded at the end of 1592 eventually led to peace in 1595. By the terms of the treaty of Teusina, Muscovy abandoned claims to Estonia and Narva, but Sweden was obliged to return Kexholm town and province and Ingria. For the first time, a frontier was drawn which marked the boundary between Finland and Karelia from the isthmus to the White Sea. Thus, although Swedish claims to the Kola peninsula had to be abandoned, much of Lapland was now acknowledged to be part of the Swedish realm.

Whereas the first phase of warfare had been essentially concerned with the fate of Livonia, the second major period of hostilities in northern Europe had far wider ramifications. The virtual disintegration of the state of Muscovy after the death of tsar Fedor in 1598 allowed Sweden and Poland–Lithuania an opportunity to interfere in Russian affairs. Both countries endeavoured to place candidates on the throne in Moscow, and sent troops deep into Russia to promote their objectives. At the same time, both were locked in a dynastic and territorial conflict consequent upon the election of Sigismund Vasa to the Polish throne. The internal repercussions of this conflict will be examined later; at this stage, we must endeavour to thread our way through the incredible complexities of the 'Time of Troubles' which afflicted the state of Muscovy.

After the death of tsar Fedor in 1598, the Kalita line died out. The weak-minded Fedor had fallen under the sway of the boyar Boris Godunov, who effectively ruled the land. Although Godunov was elected tsar by the national assembly (*Zemsky Sobor*), he failed to establish a firm grip on a country suffering from the effects of decades of war, and devastated by famine. Heavy rains and early night frosts in August 1601 ruined the harvest, forcing prices up and compelling the population to eat their seed corn. People were found dying on the streets of Moscow, with grass stuffed in their mouths. Horseflesh was a delicacy, and there were rumours of human flesh baked in pies being sold in the city's markets. Violent disturbances erupted throughout the land, and a march on Moscow by a peasant army in 1603 was only with difficulty halted. In 1604, a man claiming to be Dmitri, the son of Ivan IV (the real Dmitri had died of an epileptic fit in 1591), crossed the frontier at the river Dnepr, accompanied by a thousand Polish volunteers and a few dozen Cossacks. Though heavily defeated in battle, the false Dmitri succeeded in winning over disaffected troops and boyars, and entered Moscow in triumph some two months after the death of Boris Godunov in 1605. Dmitri did not long survive his elevation to the throne. His dependence upon his Polish backers and his marriage to a Catholic aroused opposition, and he was overthrown and murdered in May 1606. Prince Vasily Shuisky was hailed as the new tsar, but he failed to quell the rumours that Dmitri was still alive. Another pseudo-Dmitri appeared in the western borderlands, where an ex-serf, Ivan Bolotnikov, had raised the standard of revolt against the tsar. Bolotnikov's army laid siege to Moscow for a time, but was finally defeated at Tula. The remnants joined the new false Dmitri, who had established a rival government in Tushino, just north-west of Moscow.

By 1608, most of northern Russia had accepted the authority of the impostor, whose armies were a constant menace to the beleaguered Shuisky. In these dire straits, the tsar finally turned to Sweden for help. Shuisky secured an eternal alliance against Poland–Lithuania with Karl IX as the result of negotiations in Viborg: but the price was high. The tsar renounced all claims to Livonia and promised to hand over the province of Kexholm in return for 5,000 troops. These troops soon broke the grip of the motley crew at Tushino, entering Moscow on 12 March 1610, and scattering the remains of the insurrectionary forces. This was by no means the end of Shuisky's troubles, however, for Zygmunt III regarded the treaty of Viborg as a breach of the truce he had made with the tsar in 1608. A Polish–Lithuanian army crossed the frontier and laid siege to Smolensk in September 1609. The erstwhile supporters of the second false Dmitri now began to turn to Zygmunt, proposing the election of his son Władysław as tsar. Defeated by the Polish–Lithuanian army at Klushino on 24 June 1610, Shuisky was overthrown by his boyars a month later. The way now seemed open for Władysław's election as tsar. The fortunes of Karl IX, on the other hand suddenly seemed to have passed behind a menacing cloud. The bedraggled remnants of the Swedish forces, which had been cut to ribbons at Klushino, limped back to Finland. The town of Kexholm obstinately refused to acknowledge Swedish overlordship. Attempts to capture Russian strongholds on the White Sea coast had come to nothing. On top of all this, Christian IV of Denmark declared war in April 1611, and his armies captured the strategically vital town of Kalmar a month later. Karl IX, quarrelsome and defiant to the last, though afflicted in speech by a stroke, died at the end of October 1611, leaving his sixteen year-old son and heir with a near-bankrupt treasury, a discontented people, an alienated nobility, and war on three fronts.

In the confused struggle for control in Russia, the Swedish forces commanded by Jakob de la Gardie succeeded in occupying Novgorod in July 1611, where, according to the chronicler, they pillaged and destroyed churches and inflicted various forms of unpleasant treatment upon the inhabitants. Zygmunt III's attempts to impose his own rule upon the Russians had provoked a national uprising. De la Gardie sought to persuade the leaders of this national movement to elect Karl IX's younger son Karl Filip as tsar. The Russians, hard-pressed and desperate for any assistance, seemed willing to consider the idea; but the murder of the leader of the national army caused the plan to fall through.

In the meantime, the Swedish drive into Karelia continued. Kexholm was taken in 1611 after a lengthy siege, and new attacks were mounted, with the usual lack of success, against the Russian strongholds on the White Sea coast. The main aim of Swedish policy was revealed in Gustav II Adolf's instructions to his negotiators, sent to Viborg in February 1613 to press Karl Filip's claims upon the Russians. Although the possibility of Karl Filip's election as tsar was not excluded, the king was primarily interested in territorial acquisitions, which would have given him control of the White Sea coastline as far as Archangel and the hinterland of Narva as far as Pskov. The election of Mikhail Romanov in 1613 by the *Zemsky Sobor* and resistance to Swedish and Polish occupation put an end to the ambitions of the Vasa cousins. Zygmunt III's garrison in the Kremlin had been forced to surrender in October 1612; although Władysław launched an attack in 1618 which took him almost to the gates of Moscow, the Poles were never again to enjoy such dominance over their eastern neighbour. By the terms of the truce made in 1618, Poland–Lithuania retained Smolensk and refused to abandon Władysław's claim to the throne. Peace between Muscovy and Sweden had been concluded a year earlier at Stolbova. The Swedish army was to evacuate Novgorod on payment of an indemnity by the Russians, but the provinces of Kexholm and Ingria were surrendered to Sweden. As Gustav Adolf boasted to the Swedish estates, Finland had now been made secure from the attacks of the 'false foe', a land bridge to Livonia had been secured, and the Russians could not now launch a single vessel on the Baltic without Sweden's permission.[12]

12. Roberts M (ed). 1968 *Sweden as a great power 1611–97*. London, pp. 134–6.

The Swedish king had not been so fortunate in his war against Denmark. The treaty of Knäred in 1613 obliged Sweden to renounce claims of sovereignty to the Arctic coast and to the fortress of Sonne-burg on Ösel, and to raise a hefty indemnity of 1,000,000 riksdaler for the return of Älvsborg and Göteborg, captured by Denmark in 1612. The war in Livonia was not making much headway, either. Swedish forces had achieved some success in 1600–01, advancing as far as the river Düna: but by 1603, they had been driven back, losing Dorpat and Weissenstein and suffering heavy defeats in battle against the skilled Lithuanian commander, Jan Chodkiewicz. The Zebrzydowski revolt in Poland probably saved Sweden from utter humiliation, for the preoccupation of the Poles with their internal affairs led to a virtual ceasefire in Livonia. From 1606 onwards, both sides were engaged in the tangled web of Muscovite affairs, and the Livonian front was relatively peaceful. In 1617, Gustav Adolf took advantage of con-tinued Polish–Lithuanian involvement in Russia to launch an offensive against the line of the Düna, only to lose most of his conquests as a result of the defection of one of his commanders. The real turning-point in the war occurred in 1621, when the Swedes took Riga and advanced into Kurland. Although hostilities were renewed in 1625, the Polish–Lithuanian forces could not turn the tide. The Swedes won a decisive victory at Wallhof in 1626, and later that year, the war against Zygmunt III was transferred to Prussian territory, the first step of a campaign which was to take Swedish troops to the heart of Europe five years later.

THE RISE OF SWEDEN

After more than six decades of warfare, Sweden had emerged as the dominant power in the eastern Baltic. The persistence and obstinacy of Sweden's rulers, their careful husbanding and utilisation of the country's meagre resources, occasional good military leadership and an element of good fortune all contributed to this success. The acquisi-tion of territory in the eastern Baltic area was the principal aim of Swedish policy during the reigns of Gustav Vasa's sons. In this respect, Swedish policy had a consistency which the other contenders for dominance in the eastern Baltic lacked. Poland–Lithuania and Muscovy were essentially continental powers, constantly drawn into conflict with each other along the long land frontier which stretched from the upper reaches of the Düna river to the steppes. Denmark–

Norway had considerable commercial interests in the Atlantic, and its rulers were also heavily involved in north German politics. Nevertheless, Denmark controlled the key to the Baltic sea, the Sound: not until the middle of the seventeenth century was Sweden able to mount a successful challenge to Danish control of the western Baltic. Denmark was able to demand stiff ransoms in 1570 and 1613 for the return of the fortress of Älvsborg, which commanded Sweden's only significant outlet to the western oceans. On the other hand the Danish presence in the eastern Baltic was considerably diminished during the sixteenth century.

The underlying motives of Swedish policy in the Baltic have been a cause of much debate. In an article published in 1890, the German historian Fritz Arnheim attempted to rehabilitate the reputation of Erik XIV. Arnheim praised Erik's action in taking Reval under Swedish protection as a far-sighted step towards the ultimate goal of Baltic dominion, and laid the blame for the seven years' northern war firmly at the door of Frederik II. Nearly three decades later, Arnheim drew parallels between that conflict and the great war then raging in Europe. Like the Entente powers, Denmark, Lübeck and Poland sought to encircle and starve their foe (Sweden) into submission. Swedish historians, much influenced by the resurgence of patriotism in the wake of the crisis over the Swedish-Norwegian Union and the vogue for geopolitics, also took up the idea of Danish-Norwegian encirclement, which was seen as a permanent threat to Sweden's independence. In 1933, for instance, Curt Weibull declared that the goal of Gustav Vasa and his successors was to secure Sweden from Danish encirclement by breaking through the ring, giving Sweden room to breathe and unhindered economic and political links with the rest of Europe. The strong fortifications erected by Christian IV across Skåne and Bohuslän meant that it was virtually impossible for Sweden to crack Danish domination of the Sound by direct assault: but conquests in the eastern Baltic were feasible, and profitable, and could also counter Danish influence and claims to Baltic dominion.[13]

The importance of the Baltic trade for the combatants in the Livonian wars is a central theme in the writings of Swedish historians of what Michael Roberts has called the 'New School'. For Sven Svensson, the dominance of the Russian market was the alpha and omega of Swedish Baltic policy, whilst Attman sees control of the Russian trade

13. Arnheim F 1890 König Erich XIV als Politiker *Historische Zeitschrift* **64**: 430–75. Weibull C 1933 Gustaf II Adolf *Scandia* **6**: 1–22. For a vigorous refutation of the idea of Danish encirclement, see: Jensen F 1976 Den danske 'indkredsning' af Vasa-tidens Sverige *Historisk Tidskrift* **76**: 1–24.

as a consistent objective of Swedish policy after 1562.[14] Excessive emphasis upon the primacy of economic aims does lead historians to ignore or play down other, equally important considerations such as the security of the realm or the prestige of an ambitious monarch. Thus, Attman regards the treaty of Stolbova as something of a setback for Sweden, which abandoned hopes of controlling the Arctic coastline and was frustrated in its desire to control the Russian trade via the communication centres of Novgorod and Pskov: virtually all that was acquired was 'waste land around the Neva'.[15] Seen in the light of earlier plans to acquire control of northern Russia, there is perhaps some substance in this assertion. But the incessant raids of the Russians and Karelians across the frontier into Finland had posed a major security problem for decades, and the pushing back of the frontier beyond lake Ladoga was undoubtedly a significant strategic victory, as Gustav Adolf made clear in his speech to the estates in 1617. It is also worth noting the comment of the Polish historian Kazimierz Lepszy that trade, which should have been the foundation of and an inducement to the union of Sweden and Poland–Lithuania, 'was pushed back to a place of third-rate importance' in the statute of Kalmar.[16]

Arguments emphasising the importance of commercial considerations in Swedish policy paradoxically highlight the lack of commercial and entrepreneurial skills which an economically backward country such as Sweden could command. In 1558, for example, Gustav Vasa endeavoured to develop the trade of Viborg, which had experienced a sudden influx of Russian merchants. The Reval merchants immediately responded by imposing a blockade on the port. The local merchants lacked the capital to finance large-scale transactions, and Swedish

---

14. Roberts M 1979 *The Swedish imperial experience 1560–1718*. Cambridge, pp. 26–34. Svensson 1951, pp. 9–10. Attman 1979 *The struggle for Baltic markets. Powers in conflict 1558–1618*. Acta Regiae Societatis Scientarium et Litterarum Gothoburgensis. Humaniora 4. Göteborg, pp. 63, 98. Attman A 1985 *Swedish aspirations and the Russian market during the 17th century* Acta Regiae Societatis Scientarium et Litterarum Gothoburgensis. Humaniora 24. Göteborg, pp. 6–9.

15. Attman 1979 p. 207.

16. Lepszy K 1960 The union of the crowns between Poland and Sweden in 1587 *Poland at the eleventh international congress of historical sciences in Stockholm*. Warsaw, p. 174. Zernack K 1981 Schweden als europäische Grossmacht der frühen Neuzeit *Historische Zeitschrift* **232**: 338, argues that Stolbova marked the beginning of a new epoch of expansion along the lines of the three principles which motivated Sweden's initial involvement in Livonia in 1561: security on the eastern frontier, a counterweight to Danish dominance in the Baltic, and commercial-economic benefits.

merchants were unable to provide the goods required by the Russians. An attempt to impose a 5 per cent duty on the goods brought for sale by Hanseatic merchants simply drove the merchants away, and the creation of a staple for Russian trade in Narva in 1559 effectively brought to an end Viborg's brief moment of activity.[17]

The rulers of Sweden were undoubtedly interested in devising schemes to control the Russian trade: but their ambitions were fated to remain unrealised. In the reign of Erik XIV, for example, the construction of a canal across Sweden – which would thus avoid the Sound – was proposed, and there was some talk of an Anglo-Swedish company to exploit the Russian market. When the Swedish crown sought to put into practice its ambitions, however, the limitations soon became apparent. Erik XIV's attempts to control the Narva trade were not a success. He sought to compel foreign merchants to buy Russian goods from ports under Swedish control, but veered between allowing certain foreign vessels to pass to Narva on payment of dues to patrolling Swedish ships and imposing a total ban on shipping with the Russian-held port. The 1567 treaty negotiated by Gyllenstierna was a sharp rebuff to Erik's hopes, for the tsar insisted that ships from Lübeck and Denmark – then at war with Sweden – be allowed to pass freely to and from Narva, irrespective of what they were carrying. Although Erik eventually refused to accept the treaty, his successor was obliged to accept the terms of the peace of Stettin, which freed the Narva trade. Johan III endeavoured to blockade the mouths of the Narova and Neva rivers, but had to instruct his admiral in 1572 to act diplomatically in order not to provoke unnecessary hostility.

The capture of Narva by the Swedish forces in 1581 brought to an end that town's brief period of intense commercial activity. At the height of its prosperity, in 1565–7, Narva had exported over three times as much flax and hemp as the great staple port for these commodities, Riga. Giles Fletcher, Elizabeth's special envoy to Muscovy, noted in 1588 that formerly, over one hundred shiploads of flax and hemp had been exported annually from Narva: now only five shiploads a year left the port. Johan III attempted to make Narva the staple for the Russian trade, but over nine-tenths of the commodities exported had to be fetched from the Russian hinterland. Swedish Narva became little more than a transit port and customs port for Russian goods. Although effectively cut off from direct access to the Baltic, the Russians were able to distribute goods from the trading centre of Pskov to Riga, Reval or even further afield, via Lithuania and Poland, to reach western markets. They were also able to use the White Sea

17. Attman 1979, pp. 15–32.

port of Archangel, though it never succeeded in attracting large numbers of foreign vessels.[18]

Sweden's emergence as a great power upon the stage of central Europe during the last years of Gustav II Adolf's reign is all the more remarkable in view of the parlous condition of state finances and the legacy of political and constitutional conflict which the young king inherited in 1611. The meagre resources of the realm were strained to their uttermost in order to pay off the Älvsborg ransom to Denmark. In the early 1620s, the Danish legate Peder Galt painted a gloomy picture of famine and pestilence, and discontent amongst the people, not too different from the reports submitted by Samuel Laski to Zygmunt III in the winter of 1597–8.[19] Much of Sweden was afflicted by crop failures between 1596 and 1603. A graphic description of the famine year of 1596, preserved in the parish register of Örslösa in western Sweden, described the situation in the country as akin to the plagues of Egypt or the fall of Jerusalem.[20]

These years of exceptional hardship coincided with the most serious political crisis to face Sweden since the establishment of the Vasa dynasty upon the throne. During the last years of Johan III's reign, the council (*råd*) had begun to assert itself in matters of state policy. The possibility that the king's heir would be elected king of Poland allowed the council magnates a chance to establish their claim to play a leading role in the governance of the realm. After discussions between the king and leading members of the *råd*, a plan for an aristocratic council to govern the country in Sigismund's absence was drawn up in 1587. Although both Johan and Sigismund appended their signatures to this statute of Kalmar, it was never brought into force. The *råd* also worked with the Polish senators at the Reval meeting in 1589 to thwart Johan III's efforts to release his son from his misery as king of Poland, and to bring him back to Sweden.

An assertive *råd* aristocracy, led by men of erudition such as Erik Sparre, and a grievously missed son were not the least of Johan's worries. He had come into conflict with the church over his attempts to introduce a new liturgy: his brother Karl, who had created virtually a state within a state in his duchy of Södermanland, was a constant challenge to royal authority. In 1590, the two brothers made common

18. Attman 1979, pp. 114–30. Öhberg A 1956 Russia and the world market in the seventeenth century *Scandinavian Economic History Review* **3**: 123–62.

19. Ahnlund N (ed.) 1922 Peder Galts depescher 1622–24 *Historiska Handlingar* **26** (1): 5–122. Palme S 1944 Samuel Laski om Sveriges tillstånd vintern 1597–98 *Historisk Tidsskrift* **64**: 118–21.

20. Utterström G 1955 Climatic fluctuations and population problems in early modern history *Scandinavian Economic History Review* **3**: 28.

cause and attempted to destroy the opposition on the *råd*. For two years, the leading figures were silenced, and duke Karl was effectively in charge of the kingdom. An anonymous pamphlet of 1592 accused the duke of behaving like 'all tyrants and wilful persons' and warned him of the fate of king Christian who 'died like a simple malefactor in prison', Erik XIV and even Henri III of France, assassinated three years earlier.[21]

Johan III died in November 1592: his son and heir was deeply embroiled in the political affairs of the *Rzeczpospolita* and since the Statute of Kalmar had been rescinded, there was no procedure laid down for the government of the country in his absence. Duke Karl seized the opportunity; after a hasty reconciliation with his enemies, he established a joint government with the *råd*. The new interim government immediately summoned a church council to meet in Uppsala, an action of doubtful legality but great political astuteness, for the defence of 'God's pure word' against the pretensions of a Catholic sovereign was the one sure way of rallying the non-noble estates behind the new government. The resolution of the Uppsala assembly declared unequivocally Sweden's adherence to the Augsburg Confession. No other faith would be tolerated in the realm. The resolution was printed and circulated throughout the realm, and was signed by almost two thousand representatives of the estates, towns and provinces. When Sigismund finally arrived in Sweden, at the end of September 1593, he was told bluntly by the government that acceptance of the Uppsala resolution was a condition for his coronation as king of Sweden. His efforts to play off the duke against the *råd* came to nothing; the *riksdag* which met in February 1594 stood firmly behind the Uppsala resolution. In his accession charter, Sigismund confirmed the supremacy of the Lutheran church in Sweden, promised to rule with the advice of duke Karl and the *råd*, and declared that the government of Sweden in his absence would be decided in consultation with duke Karl and the *råd*, acting on behalf of the non-noble estates.

In his proposals for the ordinance of government, duke Karl deemed it politic to make concessions to the aristocratic constitutionalists. The *råd* on the other hand was prepared to allow the absent monarch a considerable degree of authority in order to counter the influence of duke Karl. Sigismund, however, preferred to put his trust in his office-holders and commanders, who could not be removed

21. Sjödin L 1930 En pampflett av år 1592 *Historisk Tidskrift* **50**: 330. The author of the pamphlet was probably Axel Leijonhufvud, a member of the *råd*.

without his permission. Unfortunately, Sigismund pinned his faith in men who were deeply unpopular, such as the arrogant and brutal Klas Fleming in Finland, or were suspected of Catholic leanings, like Erik Brahe, the governor of Stockholm. In their hostility towards such men, the *råd* and duke Karl were united. They sought to undermine the powers and authority of Sigismund's appointees, and to bring Fleming to heel. The two parties also agreed after negotiation to bestow upon Karl the title of regent (*riksföreståndare*), albeit with carefully circumscribed powers. This uneasy alliance soon began to show signs of cracking. The *råd* was reluctant to cause a breach with Sigismund. Its members informed the king at the end of 1594 that they had been compelled to agree to appoint Karl as regent in view of the pressing circumstances of the war with Muscovy and the financial difficulties of the kingdom. As the most wealthy and powerful land-owner in the land, Karl was able to exercise considerable pressure upon his fellows in government. In 1595, he used the threat of resignation to persuade the *råd* to agree to the calling of a *riksdag*. The most the *råd* could hope for was that the summoning of the estates might finally persuade the king to devise a balanced form of government, which would effectively circumscribe the powers of duke Karl.

The proposition submitted by the duke to the estates at Söderköping was designed to give him effective royal powers as regent. Although the peasants' estate endorsed it, the burghers of Stockholm, the clergy and nobility were far less enthusiastic. In the end, the archbishop and Erik Sparre produced a reply which went some way to meeting Karl's demands. He was recognised by the estates as regent, but he should govern with the advice and consent of the council. Those who dissociated themselves from the Söderköping resolution were to be regarded as 'unruly and lopped-off members', and such persons holding office were to be proceeded against by lawful and proper means.

The Söderköping resolution may be interpreted as a victory for council constitutionalism, a national binding agreement which allowed the *råd* a controlling influence in the governance of the kingdom; but it also gave duke Karl an opportunity to pursue his own goals, in the first instance, to proceed against the king's officers. Karl was a ruthless and unscrupulous politician. His aggressive and peremptory manner contrasted sharply to the hesitant balancing act of the *råd* members, anxious not to cause a breach with the absent king, and yet unable to resist duke Karl's demands for a resolution of the question of authority in the kingdom. The king's men in Sweden were effectively isolated by the end of 1595, but Klas Fleming, the admiral of the fleet and royal governor in Finland, was a much tougher proposition. He had successfully countered Karl's efforts to undermine the loyalty of his troops, and in January 1596 subjected the hapless emissaries of the duke to a torrent of abuse when they tried to explain the Söderköping resolution to the Finnish estates. The exactions of Fleming's officials and the continued burden of the quartering system, which was still maintained even though peace had been reached with Muscovy, provoked a stream of complaints from an exasperated Finnish peasantry. The *råd*, although it disapproved of Fleming's excesses, refused to support Karl's demands for a military expedition to Finland, fearing this would be seen as an act of rebellion against the king. The opinion of the upper estates was broadly similar, and they refused to be browbeaten by Karl's old trick of threatening to resign.

During the winter of 1596–7, duke Karl conducted what can only be described as a rabble-rousing electoral campaign. He accused the council of seeking to sabotage the Söderköping resolution, though he was careful not to attack the absent king, whose return to the land, he maintained, was the best means of sorting out the misgovernment of the royal officials. Karl also freely handed out letters of protection to the peasantry of Finland, who complained bitterly about the exactions of Fleming's troops, and he was not averse to inciting rebellion there. The peasants' revolt in Finland which erupted at the end of 1596 was certainly to the duke's advantage, since it prevented Fleming sending troops to Sweden. Karl was also prepared to tell horror stories of the fate of the Finnish peasantry and to hint at measures to be taken against the nobility in his harangues to the peasants' estate at the *riksdag* which met at Arboga in February 1597. But, even though the members of the council were absent from the meeting, the upper estates refused to give way entirely to Karl's demands, insisting that he should continue to govern with the council's consent and should endeavour to settle the dispute with Fleming in a peaceable manner. The members of the *råd*, few in number and lacking in determination or cohesive purpose, were helpless to resist the vigorous onslaughts of the duke. A further meeting of the upper estates in Stockholm later that year agreed to a suspension of the council, and consented to a military expedition to Finland.

The situation at the end of 1597 was extremely finely balanced. Virtually all the members of the *råd* had been driven by Karl's ruthlessness into siding with the king. Most of the nobility, the burghers of Stockholm and the archbishop took the king's part. Klas Fleming had died in April, but his successor as royal governor in Finland,

Arvid Stålarm, was a firm upholder of the king's rights, and succeeded in recapturing Åbo castle from the inadequate garrison left behind by duke Karl. Karl had managed to extract from the Finnish estates a recognition of his authority as regent, but he had miserably failed to impose that authority during his brief autumn campaign. His efforts to win the support of the estates in Estonia were equally fruitless, although he constantly played upon the fears of the local gentry and burghers by warning them of evil Polish designs and the threat to their religion posed by Sigismund's Catholic advisers. Although the Estonian nobility and the governor Jöran Boije remained loyal to Sigismund, they were noticeably reluctant to offer themselves in the king's service outside their own frontiers. After much negotiation in 1598, the Estonian levy joined the forces being assembled by Stålarm in Finland, but returned home at the end of July after Stålarm had retreated before the threatening presence of duke Karl's fleet. A month later, Stålarm heard the news of the king's landing at Kalmar, and sought to regroup his forces. The Estonian levy procrastinated, and by the time the expedition reached the Stockholm archipelago, it was too late. Sigismund had been defeated in battle at Stångebro (25 September 1598), and had signed a treaty in Linköping with the victorious duke three days later. At the end of October, he left Sweden, never to return.[22]

Sigismund's tardiness in returning to Sweden, and his general lack of political aggression – in contrast to the methods employed by his uncle – gravely weakened his own cause. He was unable to offer inspiration or encouragement to those who were troubled by the excesses of the duke. His most prominent supporters alienated rather than attracted the uncommitted. He was beset with troubles in Poland, where his pro-Habsburg policy aroused the hostility of powerful noblemen such as Jan Zamoyski. His unwavering devotion to the Catholic faith probably helped turn the tide in Poland–Lithuania, although the high point of Protestantism was already over. In Sweden, however, the Lutheran faith had been elevated to supremacy at Uppsala, and the suspicion that Sigismund would seek to subvert this order was cleverly used by duke Karl.

Duke Karl's triumph was by no means an unqualified one, however. The treaty of Linköping failed to determine the crucial question of how the royal power was to be exercised in the king's absence; with the *råd* in political disarray, the only alternative was duke Karl. The

22. For details, see Roberts 1968, pp. 372–84. Federley B 1946 *Kunglig majestät, svenska kronan och furstendömet Estland 1592–1600*. Helsingfors, pp. 133–65.

king refused to answer the request of the upper estates to return, and in 1599, the estates took the plunge and renounced their allegiance. One year later, they offered the crown to Karl, who had in the meantime disposed of the remaining royalist strongholds of Kalmar and Åbo, executing his principal enemies in the process. The 'blood-bath' in Åbo was repeated at Linköping in 1600, where the duke's opponents on the *råd* were executed after trial.

Opinions over duke Karl have been sharply divided. He has been castigated as an unscrupulous autocrat by some, and portrayed by others as sharing many of the basic constitutionalist notions of his opponents. It has even been suggested that his reluctance to accept the crown offered by the estates was motivated by a genuine concern for legitimacy. In 1604, his nephew duke Johan renounced his claims to the throne, and the succession was fixed upon Karl's eldest son Gustav Adolf. The 'elected king', as Karl preferred to style himself, was not crowned until 1607. Karl was curiously reluctant to impose a more permanent settlement upon the kingdom; his was essentially a personal regime, in which administrative reforms were planned but never realised. The council of the realm was re-established in 1602, though its powers were somewhat muted, and Karl was careful to ensure that the estates should act as a possible check upon the council's activities. The estates were bound to the duke by virtue of their rejection of Sigismund, but they were by no means obedient ciphers. There was much dissatisfaction amongst the non-noble estates at the cost of the war against Sigismund in Livonia, and the estates also managed to defeat Karl's attempts to co-opt six members of the Estonian nobility to the council. Plans to reform the medieval Land Law also had to be abandoned in the face of opposition from the estates. The constant sessions of the *riksdag* and the involvement of the estates in the affairs of the realm – especially matters of taxation – gave the institution a greater cohesion and sense of purpose, even if it was still strictly subordinated to the king's command.

The death of Karl IX in 1611 threatened to provoke a new crisis, for the king's eldest son was technically a minor by the terms of the 1604 agreement, which prescribed the establishment of a regency government until he should attain his eighteenth birthday. Large numbers of the aristocracy were in exile; the clergy had been angered by Karl's meddling in religious affairs; the burden of taxation to pay for war was a constant source of grievance for the peasantry. On the other hand, the country was hard-pressed by Denmark, and there was no desire to submit to the mercies of the Catholic ruler of Poland–Lithuania. The estates, summoned to Nyköping, preferred to invest the young Gustav Adolf with the full powers of kingship, subject to one condition: he would have to grant an accession charter, spelling out the terms and conditions of his rule.

The accession charter of 1611 was a major milestone in Swedish history. It reaffirmed religious uniformity; bound the king to rule in accordance with the law of the land; without the consent of duke Johan, the council of the realm and the estates, no new law could be made nor any old and accepted law rescinded, nor could the king embark upon any war. make peace or conclude any alliance. The charter was a forthright condemnation of the excesses of Karl IX's reign, and a reassertion of the constitutionalist principles contained in the *Postulata nobilium* of 1594, and outlined by Erik Sparre in his oration which introduced this programme. The *Postulata* sought to give the council a mediating role between king and subject, and it also embodied certain decentralising features, such as the request that no statutes be decreed without the unanimous consent of the estates and prior negotiation in each province. Karl's unscrupulous manipulation of the non-noble estates had aroused the hostility of the nobility, and this was reflected in the sixth clause of the accession charter. No legislation was to be made nor taxes levied without the knowledge and advice of the council 'and the consent of those who are concerned'. The king promised not to burden the estates with too many meetings, and the council would have to consider and approve the reasons for summoning the *riksdag*.

The charter also laid down the basis for reconciliation between king and subjects, in particular the aristocracy, whose privileges were to be extended in 1612. The fifth clause stated that the five high offices of the realm (steward, marshal, admiral, chancellor and treasurer), the council and exchequer council, the offices of judge and governor in each province and the command of the main fortresses of the kingdom were to be filled by 'inborn men of the nobility', and competent native Swedish men were to be appointed to lower offices. The *Postulata nobilium* had requested that the offices of state should be filled by native nobles, not foreigners or low-born men, and in his coronation oath, Sigismund had been obliged to revive the late-medieval promise not to take any but native Swedes into the council.[23]

During the first decade of Gustav II Adolf's reign, the administra-

---

23. A translation of the accession charter can be found in Roberts M (ed.) 1968, pp. 7–10. On the constitutional conflict, see Rystad G 1963 Med råds råde eller efter konungens godtycke? *Scandia* **29**: 157–249. Hermansson Å 1962 *Karl IX och ständerna. Tronfrågan och författningsutvecklingen i Sverige 1598–1611*. Uppsala. Runeby N 1962 *Monarchia mixta. Maktfördelningsdebatt i Sverige under den tidigare stormaktstiden*. Uppsala.

tive structure of Sweden was transformed. The responsibility for much of this work lay with the man appointed chancellor in 1612, Axel Oxenstierna. A supreme court, composed of four members of the *råd* and nine assessors, five of whom were to be noblemen, headed by the high steward, was established in 1614. The court was to hold its sessions for five months of the year in Stockholm, which was thereby acknowledged as the capital of the realm. Three more supreme courts were later established, in Åbo (1623), Dorpat (1630) and Jönköping (1634). In 1618, the treasury was reorganised as a *collegium*, or board with collective responsibilities. All accounts except those of the admiralty and ordnance, were to be submitted in the first instance to this body, which comprised the treasurer and five treasury counsellors. The introduction of double-entry book-keeping by the Dutchman Abraham Cabeljau enabled the treasury to draw up statements of the national account and to prepare proper budgets from the 1620s. The keystone of Oxenstierna's administrative reforms was the chancery, over which he presided for more than forty years. In 1618, its establishment and the duties of its members were prescribed, and eight years later, it was transformed into a *collegium*. Local government was also placed on a more efficient footing. By 1634, the number of provinces, each administered by a governor (*ståthållare*), had been fixed at twenty-three. A memorandum issued in 1620 ordered these governors to provide secretaries, supervise crown bailiffs and to forward regular reports to the treasury.

The system of government established in the reign of Gustav II Adolf had its flaws. Officials were often overworked and poorly paid, and certain central institutions were understaffed. There were also large areas of the kingdom, such as the fiefs held by the high nobility and the mining areas, which remained outside the system. But measured against the more prosperous and powerful countries of Europe, such as France, where Richelieu's attempts at reform foundered on intransigent noble opposition, the achievements of the Swedish king and his chancellor are impressive. Above all, the expansion and definition of the system of government provided an effective means of national integration, involving not only the nobility, with its claims to the lion's share of offices, but also the clergy and able low-born men and foreigners. Had Sweden suffered disastrous reverses abroad, like Christian IV's Denmark, the story might well have been different and we will have to look in more detail at the economic and military foundations of Sweden's age of greatness in later chapters. In closing this survey of the decades of war in the eastern Baltic which were the prelude, as it were, to the great campaigns in central Europe by the

'Lion of the North', it would nevertheless seem appropriate to establish some of the reasons for Sweden's success. The fact that the country was able to recover so well from the crises of the 1590s may be one indication of internal durability and strength. Although the kingdom was riven by internal strife, the Uppsala declaration, proclaiming uniformity of religion, and a strong sense of national identity against the external foe proved to be a powerful salve for the wounds of civil turmoil. Karl may have been an unscrupulous politician, but he was no absolutist, and his son was well versed in the principles of *monarchia mixta* by his tutors. Balance, rather than excess, was the keynote of Gustav II Adolf's governance, and this allowed potentially threatening elements an opportunity to channel their energies into working with the crown, rather than against it. There was also a deep-seated respect for the law, and a firmly-established principle of the necessity of consent on the part of those under the rule of the sovereign. The glorious past of the Swedish people was constantly evoked by royal propagandists. In 1626, Peder Eriksson was sent into Uppland, Norrland and the mining districts to raise money for the war. He addressed peasant assemblies, treating them to a recital of the glorious exploits of their Gothic ancestors, finally urging them not to let the valour and manliness of their ancient forebears go to waste:

> Let us yet be Swedish, Gothic men, let their high fame and renowned exploits cheer our minds and give us the same courage to defend our dear wives, children and our Christian religion, and to this end have we pledged to His Royal Majesty all our estates, life and blood...[24]

Against this patriotic exhortation we must set the sour and undoubtedly biased observations of the Danish legate Peder Galt, who reported in 1622 that all the estates opposed increased taxation to meet the costs of the unpopular war in Livonia. Clearly, the strains of war and the ravages of sickness and famine which Galt also recorded did tax the resources of Sweden's meagre population. The Vasas were highly adept at getting the most out of their subjects without pushing them into rebellion. The period of expansion did offer opportunities for men of humble origins to advance up the social scale, as it also gave the high-born even more scope for amassing estates and offices. But Sweden's 'age of greatness' was not achieved without a great deal of strain and effort, which in the long run a country of few human or material resources could never hope to sustain.

24. Nordström J 1934 *De yverbornas ö*. Stockholm, p. 72.

CHAPTER SIX
War and Society

WARFARE

The conduct of war in the terrain of trackless marshy moorland, scrub and dense forest which covered most of northern Europe called for very different tactics and methods to those employed on the battle-fields of northern Italy and the Low Countries. The wars fought in Livonia and on the Finnish–Karelian frontier were largely a series of raids and counter-raids, with few pitched battles. The massed pha-lanxes of pikemen and musketeers – the famous Spanish *tercio* – would have been too expensive to equip, and probably ineffective, in the northern wars of the second half of the sixteenth century. Whereas mud and rain drove troops in central and southern Europe to seek winter quarters, the hard frosts and snows of the north facilitated speedy movement. On one famous occasion in 1658, it enabled the Swedish army to cross the frozen sea between the Jutland peninsula and the Danish islands. One hundred years earlier, Ivan IV's troops invading Livonia had run into problems because of the exceptional mildness of the winter, which kept the waterways open and the ways miry. Ski-troops were regularly employed during the wars between Sweden and Muscovy along the Finnish–Karelian frontier, and Karl IX's Finnish skiers mounted surprise night attacks on Polish camps in Livonia. Johann von Nassau, who spent some time in 1601 trying unsuccessfully to knock the Swedish army into shape, was quick to notice that the Finns were able to ski long distances, fully equipped, over terrain impassable to the horseman or ordinary foot soldier. Skis were not the only form of winter transport used: during the unsuc-cessful Swedish campaign mounted in the winter of 1611 against the fortress of Kola, on the White Sea, thirty Lapps and four hundred reindeer were drummed into service as a transport corps.

The formidable natural hazards of the climate and land could pose severe problems for professional soldiers, as a troop of *Lansknechte* recruited by king Hans to cow the peasants of Dithmarsch into submission found to their cost. On a bitingly cold, wet day in February 1500, the heavily armoured soldiers were attacked by their adversaries in a miry, narrow lane running between deep dykes. The horsemen were unable to manoeuvre, and total chaos reigned as the Dithmarschers ran alongside the dyke, stabbing the horses milling about in the mire. 'The horses, wounded and injured, began to rear up, throwing off their riders, trampling upon them; many were pitched into the dyke and drowned...The steam and smoke rising from the horses, the snow, hail and rain blinded the eyes of the troops, so that they could see nothing...'[1] In the steep, wooded defiles of Tiveden and Holaveden, which barred the way to the plains of central Sweden, ambushes made from felled trees (*bråtar*) were effective barriers to any advancing army. One of the arguments advanced by the *rigsråd* when it turned down Christian IV's plans for war against Sweden in 1604 was that the vast distances between the Danish–Swedish frontier and Stockholm, and the inhospitable country which any invading army had to traverse had caused difficulties for the past eighty years, to the great cost and discomfort of the realm.[2]

Although peasants armed with spears and bows, with their intimate knowledge of the trackless forests, continued to play an important part in the guerrilla wars on the Finnish–Karelian frontier, the days when a peasant army could defeat trained professionals in pitched battle (as a Swedish peasant levy had done in 1466) were numbered. Peasants could not be used in the long campaigns which were essential if the sovereign's ambitious plans for expansion were to be realised. Their modest skills and unsophisticated weaponry were no match for firearms and pike. The Danish crown increasingly relied on mercenaries to fight its campaigns. Otto Krumpen's army, which successfully invaded Sweden in 1520, was composed largely of German and Scottish troops; the Count's War of 1534–6 was mostly waged by foreign mercenaries, who inflicted a severe defeat on the rebellious peasantry of Jutland. Peasant militiamen were still used for guard duty and shore-watch in Denmark, but Frederik II relied primarily upon pro-

1. Huitfeldt A 1599 *Kong Hansis Kronicke*. Copenhagen (1977 reprint edn), p. 166.
2. *Aktstykker og Oplysninger til Rigsraadets og Stændermødernes Historie*, I, p. 128.

fessional *Lansknechte* for his war against Erik XIV. In 1614, however, a standing army based on conscripted peasants was instituted by Christian IV. Seven years later, the system was revised to group all peasants on crown or church lands into files of nine: each file was to provide a soldier, who would serve for three years and would work for a wage on one of the farms within the file.

Gustav Vasa also employed mercenaries, but the cost of maintaining what could turn out to be an unreliable professional army persuaded him in 1544 to begin a system of conscription (*utskrivning*). The system was given a more efficient administrative structure in the 1620s. Peasants were grouped in files (*rotar*) of ten (twenty in the case of peasants of the nobility), and each file was obliged, as a rule, to supply one foot soldier aged between eighteen and forty, and to contribute towards the cost of fitting out the man selected. A commission supervised the annual conscription, which all inhabitants were obliged to attend: all absentees were automatically drafted. The commissioners preferred to take men who could be spared from agricultural work, such as the younger sons of farmers, though they excluded certain categories, such as workers in the mines or armament industries and the only sons of widows, and avoided ne'er-do-wells and persons of unsavoury character. The men conscripted were paid a small wage by the crown, and provided with small plots of land made over to them by the members of the file. The reluctance of peasants to make available parcels of land, and the constant alienation of crown lands to the nobility – which reduced the number of files – caused problems, as did the unwillingness of many of those selected to serve in the armies of His Majesty. The draft imposed serious strains upon the meagre manpower resources of the kingdom, and on numerous occasions the commissions failed to reach the target set for conscription. In Norrland, the vast tract of land stretching northwards from the fertile plains, the 7,820 peasants assessed in 1566 provided 391 foot soldiers, a number which seems to have been increased considerably during the Livonian campaigns of Johan III's reign, when several troops (*fänikor*), each with a strength of 400–500 men, were recruited from Norrland. For an impoverished region, the constant drain of manpower to the wars, and the heavy losses sustained through disease or in battle – half of Måns Gudmundsson's Norrland troop perished at Narva in 1593, for example – could have serious demographic consequences.

Lacking a truly systematic administrative structure, the conscript army inaugurated by Gustav Vasa soon ran into difficulties. The overseas wars of the king's sons necessitated the employment of mercenaries, whose unreliability was dramatically demonstrated during the reign of Johan III. Already hard-pressed to raise the money needed to pay Denmark for the redemption of the Älvsborg fortress, and with his German cavalry demanding payment, Johan managed with great difficulty to pay the first instalment of the wages of some four thousand Scots, commanded by Archibald Ruthven, and to get them across to Estonia. Here, they failed to take the town of Wesenberg by storm, and on 17 March 1573, staged a mutiny, fighting a pitched battle against the king's German soldiers outside the town. The involvement of certain Scottish officers in plots against the king led to arrests and investigations, whilst the unpaid troops were left to make their way back home as best they could. The men recruited to fight in Estonia were not the only ones to suffer from royal disfavour and chronic lack of pay. Of the 1,500 Scottish arquebusiers recruited by Frederik II in 1568, over half had died of wounds or sickness three years later. Those remaining were confined to garrison duty on the coast of Jutland, expressedly forbidden to cross over to Sjælland without royal permission. Some, hoping to find a ship bound for Scotland in Helsingør, crossed the frozen sea on foot, a desperate venture in which several drowned or died of exposure.[3]

Erik XIV had endeavoured to stiffen the fighting capacity of his troops, developing linear tactics and insisting on the pike as an offensive weapon: but during the reign of his successor, these reforms were largely forgotten, as the poorly trained conscripts discarded their cumbersome pikes and heavy armour. Erik had also striven to enforce the nobles' obligation to provide him with horsemen, but Johan was obliged to lower the quota and to reduce the period of unpaid service overseas. Commutation was a common practice, and musters were usually poorly attended. Karl made valiant efforts to restore noble cavalry service, the *rusttjänst*, ordering the Finnish nobility on pain of forfeiture of their estates to perform service in Livonia in 1601, and roundly declaring three years later than those who did not fulfil their obligations were traitors; but it was all in vain. His son met with a similar lack of success. In 1623, fewer than two hundred men, of whom only twenty-eight were fully equipped, turned out at the muster. Unwilling to alienate the nobility, Gustav Adolf did not press

3. Dow J 1965 *Ruthven's Army in Sweden and Esthonia* Historiskt Arkiv 13. Stockholm. Bricka C. (ed.) 1901 *Indberetninger fra Charles de Danzay til det Franske Hof om Forholden i Norden 1567–73*. Copenhagen, p. 122. As the French ambassador further informed the king, 'l'hyver a esté si grand et vehement pardeca, que nul n'est peu sortir de ceste isle de Zeland ne y venir sans se mectre en tres evident danger que depuis peu de jours'.

his claims, and resorted instead to new methods of taxation as a means of ensuring that the nobility paid a contribution to the war effort. The light cavalry, which earned such a fearsome reputation on the battle-fields of Germany, was raised by offering tax exemption to any farmers willing and able to provide a fully equipped trooper.

Although Gustav II Adolf had to use mercenaries for his overseas campaigns, the reforms he put into effect in the 1620s ensured that the core of his armies was Swedish, and was firmly based in the scattered provinces of the realm. The kingdom was divided into eight recruit-ing areas, each comprising two to three provinces. Each province was to raise one regiment (*landsregiment*). Each provincial regiment was to furnish three field regiments, or six squadrons of 408 men plus offic-ers, a system in which the administrative and tactical structures of the army neatly dovetailed together.

The success of Gustav Adolf in perfecting an effective system of conscription was not emulated by his Danish rival, Christian IV. The burden of conscription fell upon the crown peasantry (although the nobility agreed in 1638 to recruit peasants from their estates, to be trained and maintained in special companies): it was highly unpopular, and the quality of the recruits left a good deal to be desired. Three days of exercises thrice a year was hardly enough to instil more than the basic rudiments of the soldier's craft, nor was it a good idea to store rifles in damp churches for fear that the peasant-recruits might take a potshot at the game in the royal forests. The national militia proved to be no match for the battle-hardened veterans of the Thirty Years' War who invaded Denmark in 1626 and again in 1643, and attempts to make the system more effective after 1646 were frustrated by adminis-trative incompetence and the unwillingness of the nobility to allow their tenants to be taken as conscripts.

Gustav Adolf was also concerned to ensure that his armies were properly equipped. His infantry were supplied with pike, muskets replaced the antiquated arquebus favoured by the troops, and the cavalry were equipped with swords as well as pistols. His most far-reaching innovations, however, were in tactics; for well over a decade before the Swedish armies seized the attention of the whole of Europe, Gustav Adolf strove to improve upon the practices favoured by leading tacticians of the day, such as Johann von Nassau. The war fought against the Poles in Livonia and Prussia gave him ample scope for innovation, for in many crucial respects, tactics favoured in west-ern Europe were of little use against the highly mobile light cavalry of eastern European armies. Gustav Adolf's father, for example, had remained loyal to the caracole, which obliged horsemen to advance at a trot upon the enemy and discharge their pistols, thereupon retiring as best they could. This tactic was ineffective against the Polish cavalry, which relied on a lance charge at full gallop, striking terror into the hearts of their opponents. At the battle of Kirchholm in 1605, Chodkiewicz had managed to lure the superior Swedish forces into attack. The Swedish cavalry, which had been placed in the gaps between the squares of infantry, were drawn out to the flanks, where they broke under the charge of the Polish lancers and were driven back, with appalling carnage, upon their infantry. The experience of campaigns against the Polish armies taught Gustav Adolf the value of the cavalry as an offensive weapon. Combined with detachments of musketeers, whose task it was to repel the enemy horse by concentrated fire, the Swedish cavalry was used to devastating effect on the battlefields of Prussia and Germany, charging upon the disordered ranks of their enemies, whilst the musketeers reloaded for another volley. The same combination of steel and firepower was used for the infantry: Gustav Adolf's musketeers unleashed a terrifying salvo of concentrated fire as the prelude to a decisive push of the pike. Gustav Adolf's unceasing attention to detail, his insistence on the vital importance of drill, and his many innovations, especially in field artillery, transformed the Swedish forces from a third-rate army into the finest units upon the battlefields of Europe.[4]

Gustav Adolf's naval reforms are rather less well known, though the Swedish navy played a vital role in transporting troops and munitions to the southern shores of the Baltic. Gustav Vasa had recognised the importance of a navy, and his son Erik had built upon his inheritance. By the end of the century, however, the navy was in a state of disarray, and in spite of Karl IX's efforts to rebuild, the Danish fleet had the upper hand during the War of Kalmar. The effectiveness of the Swedish war effort against Christian IV depended upon free access to foreign troops: two armies in Russia had been lost as a result of defeat and mutiny, and Karl IX had only 472 mercenaries at his disposal when the war began in 1611. The loss of Älvsborg deprived Sweden of its only port of access to the west, and the war had thus to be fought by ill-trained conscripts, hastily drafted into the army. The administration and organisation of the Danish navy had been put on a sound footing during the reign of Frederik II, and Christian IV devoted

4. For details of Gustav Adolf's army reforms, see Roberts M 1958 *Gustavus Adolphus. A History of Sweden 1611–32* (2 vols) London, vol. 2, p. 169ff. On the Swedish armed forces before 1611, see Artéus G 1986 *Till militärstatens förhistoria. Krig, professionalisering och social förändring under Vasasönernas regering* Militärhistoriska studier 8. Stockholm.

much attention to building up the fleet – largely financed by the revenue from the Sound dues – and to strengthening Danish fortifications in Skåne and on the Sound. Although the fleet created by Gustav Adolf, which was nurtured by the guiding genius of Klas Fleming for over two decades, proved to be more than a match for Christian IV's navy in 1644, Sweden's triumph over the Jutish arch-enemy was ultimately achieved by Lennart Torstensson's brilliant military campaign, launched from Germany into the Jutland peninsula. The fleet was an indispensable auxiliary, rather than a decisive offensive weapon, in Swedish military strategy. It carried out valuable surveillance work off the southern Baltic ports during the 1620s, and effective blockades were mounted on the Pomeranian coast at a crucial time in the winter of 1629–30. The earlier blockade of Danzig was perhaps less effective, and the Swedish fleet suffered a defeat at the hands of the Polish navy in November 1627. Under the supervision of Klas Fleming, sixteen warships were built between 1620 and 1630, and the money spent on the navy more than quintupled between 1616 and 1632. There were setbacks however. In 1625, ten vessels foundered on the rocks at Domesnäs, off the Livonian coast, and three years later, the *Vasa* went to the bottom during trials off Stockholm. The crown resorted to a variety of expedients to make good these losses, including the formation of a Ship Company by the towns to provide and maintain sixteen armed merchantmen.

The shipbuilding programmes inaugurated by Christian IV and Gustav Adolf, by the king of Poland and the 'General of the Oceanic and Baltic Seas', Albrecht von Wallenstein, were impressive, but it may be argued that in the end they achieved rather little. Wars in the Baltic were won on the land, not at sea. In this respect, the shoals of light, shallow-draught oared vessels which could negotiate the shallow coastal waters of the Scandinavian skerries and Prussian lagoons – and the extensive inland waterways leading into the Gulf of Finland – were to prove rather more useful and effective than heavily armed and costly sailing ships.

It is indeed rather ironic that these expensive ships of the line which were built by the two ambitious northern sovereigns did not clash in battle until the last years of Christian IV's long reign, when Swedish ascendancy in the Baltic had already been assured. Christian's attempts to pursue a vigorous aggressive policy against Sweden in the early seventeenth century were opposed by the *rigsråd*, which preferred to abide by the arbitration procedures laid down in the 1570 peace of Stettin to settle disputes between the two kingdoms. The members of the council also feared that war would tax their resources, would make the king less dependent on their grants, and would in the long run reduce their status and power. Christian managed to persuade the council reluctantly to support his war against Sweden in 1611, and at Knäred, the king succeeded in excluding Sweden from the disputed Arctic coastline from Titisfjord to Varanger. Tandrup argues however, that the *rigsråd* helped the Swedes during the peace talks, forcing Christian to give up his plan of annexing Älvsborg. What, according to the Swedish historian Curt Weibull, 'was a Versailles peace...intended to cripple Sweden, economically and politically, for decades', is seen by Tandrup as a poor peace for Denmark.[5]

The peace treaty contained provisions for freedom of trade between the two countries. The friction caused by Sweden's imposition of a sales tax on exports to Denmark led to a crisis in relations between the two countries ten years later. Frustrated by the reluctance of the *rigsråd* to grant him the necessary supplies and permission to recruit troops for a war against Sweden, Christian IV had to back down. After a month of hard bargaining on the frontier, Denmark failed to persuade the Swedes to abandon the sales tax, and had to reaffirm the principle of exemption from the Sound dues of any Swedish-owned vessels and cargoes. The agreement reached in June 1624, according to Michael Roberts, marked a turning-point in relations between the two Scandinavian kingdoms, though the same author has also made the point that fear of Denmark continued to haunt Swedish policy-makers throughout the century.[6]

The eruption of conflict in central Europe in 1618, a war which rapidly engulfed much of the continent, greatly altered the dimensions of the struggle for Baltic supremacy, as contemporaries readily noted. In May 1617, an agent of Richelieu in Danzig, reporting on Zygmunt III's plans to recruit 12,000 men in Austria and Bohemia to recover Sweden, observed that as no naval preparations were being made for the invasion, 'tout le monde subçone quil y ait quelq'autre desseign cache'. Prime suspicion fell on Spain, and it was feared that the plan was directed against Holland. Aware of Zygmunt's overtures to the Dunkirk pirates and the Spanish in 1619, Christian IV feared that the threat of a Polish–Habsburg alliance might provoke the United Provinces to resist, and the subsequent naval conflict in the Baltic would pose a direct challenge to Danish claims of dominion.[7] 'Matters are now come to such a pass', Gustav Adolf wrote to his chancellor in

5. Tandrup L 1979 *Mod triumf eller tragedi* (2 vols). Aarhus, vol 1. Weibull C 1933 Gustaf II Adolf *Scandia* **6**: 5.

6. Roberts M 1973 *Gustavus Adolphus and the Rise of Sweden*. London, p. 58. Roberts M 1979 *The Swedish Imperial Experience 1560–1718* Cambridge, pp. 4–9.

April 1628, 'that all the wars being conducted in Europe are mingled one with another and become as one'.[8] It was to be the Swedish king's good fortune that Sweden enjoyed greater success in this war than did Denmark. This in turn allowed the Swedish armies to overcome the formidable frontier and naval defences of Denmark by attacking the king of Denmark through his weak back door – the Jutland peninsula.

Denmark's claims to be a serious contender for supremacy in the Baltic region suffered a major setback when Gustav Adolf captured Riga in 1621. Gustav Adolf justified his aggressive policy by claiming that his intention was to prevent the domination of the Baltic by any one state. He protested that his enemies suspected him of wishing to drain the whole sea because necessity had obliged him, as he put it in a letter to duke Adolph Friedrich of Mecklenburg, to draw off a pail of water.[9] His commands and actions, however, spoke a different language. Immediately after the conquest of Riga, Lars Eskilsson, sailing with a cargo of copper for Lübeck, was ordered not to strike topsails, even if the Danes commanded him to do so, unless there were more than seven or eight Danish ships, and only then under protest. This challenge to Denmark's claims of dominion over the Baltic south of the Bornholm–Gotland–Ösel line was reinforced by constant talk of 'the great design' of shifting the war against Poland southwards, a plan which Gustav Adolf finally realised in 1626.

At first sight, it seems strange that Christian IV did not make better use of the quarrel between the Vasas. Sigismund had tried to win Danish support in 1599; his emissary, Samuel Łaski, insinuated that Karl had seized power by egging on the peasantry, and was an enemy of the Augsburg confession. Christian, possibly influenced by the peace-loving nobles of the *rigsråd*, refused military assistance, though he allowed Sigismund's fleet to sail through the Sound. Although Christian was a strict legitimist, and had his own quarrels with Karl IX, he was also disturbed by the militant Catholicism of the king of Poland, and the web of intrigue stretching from Cracow to Madrid, which threatened the Protestant cause. Nothing came of negotiations for a Polish–Danish alliance in 1617, though Christian IV also turned down the idea of an anti-Polish alliance floated by Gustav Adolf. In

7. Forsten G 1889 *Akty i pis'ma k istorii Baltiyskago voprosa v XVI i XVII stoletiyakh* (2 vols). St Petersburg, vol. 1, pp. 224–5. *Aktstykker og Oplysninger til Rigsraadets og Stændermødernes Historie*, I, pp. 247–50. Zygmunt had also tried to make an alliance with Denmark, but had been rebuffed.

8. Hallendorff C. (ed.) 1915 *Tal och skrifter av konung Gustav II Adolf. Ett urval.* Stockholm, p. 99.

9. Ahnlund N 1956 *Tradition och historia.* Stockholm, p. 121–2.

the complex diplomatic game of the 1620s, Christian IV proved to be a poor player. At the end of 1624, the Swedish council was reluctant to break the truce with Poland–Lithuania as long as there was a threat of attack from Denmark, and Gabriel Oxenstierna was sent to Copenhagen to test the ground. He found Christian IV preoccupied with preparations for intervention in Germany, and received assurances of friendship. Secure in the knowledge that an attack from Denmark was not to be expected, Gustav Adolf was able to persuade the council to support the continuation of the war against Poland–Lithuania. The great design in Prussia was not an unmitigated success, but it did bring Sweden nearer the centre of the European war at a time when Denmark was suffering humiliation at the hands of the armies of Tilly and Wallenstein.

Frustrated by Swedish advances in the eastern Baltic, Christian IV sought compensation by expanding his influence in northern Germany. One son was installed as bishop of Schwerin, another as coadjutor of Halberstadt, and Christian also engaged in a lengthy struggle with Hamburg for control of the lower Elbe. The waning fortunes of the evangelical cause in Germany gave Christian an opportunity to strengthen his position in the Lower Saxon circle, and to outmanoeuvre his Swedish rival. Although the Dutch had concluded defensive alliances with Lübeck (1613) and Sweden (1614), and had aided Brunswick against the duke of Brunswick–Wolfenbüttel and Denmark in 1616, the approaching expiry of the twelve-year truce with Spain persuaded the States-General to secure their lifeline to the Baltic. The Orangist faction, in the ascendancy after the fall of Oldenbarnevelt in 1618, began to steer the ship of state into Danish waters, and sought to persuade Christian IV to part with some of his fortune on behalf of the Protestant cause. In 1621, Christian managed to increase his grip on the Lower Saxon circle by acquiring control of the bishopric of Bremen and Verden for his son Frederik; but his proposed evangelical alliance, backed by the Dutch and James I, failed to get off the ground. His activities in northern Germany aroused resentment there, which allowed Sweden an opportunity to bid for friends who might prove useful in future. Cautioned by his council against going to war in Germany with inadequate guarantees and unreliable partners, Christian IV plunged to disaster in 1626.

The judgement of the Danish historian J. A. Fridericia, writing in the aftermath of Denmark's loss of Slesvig-Holstein in 1864, that the king should have heeded the advice of the *rigsråd*, which favoured a peaceable defensive policy based upon alliance with the Hanse towns, England and the United Provinces, has recently been challenged by

Leo Tandrup. Tandrup argues that Christian IV sought to safeguard the primary security interests of the kingdom, whilst the council of the realm allowed their own narrow economic interests to take precedence, and sought to avoid any active foreign policy which might make the king less dependent upon them. The crown's income came mainly from tolls and duties, and in interest on loans put out by the king on the Kiel money market. Increased revenue from the Sound dues, king Christian's income from his dealings in the Kiel money market and the windfall of the Älvsborg ransom allowed the crown to maintain liquidity until the German war, and afforded Christian IV relative independence in his governance of the realm. At the same time however, it was no longer possible to increase revenue from the *len* system, the power base of the nobility. Any attempt by the crown to do so would and did arouse fierce opposition from the noble possessors of the administrative posts of *lensmænd*. When the money began to run out in the 1620s, the council was able to demand control over war finances, and engaged in a long battle with the king which brought the kingdom to near bankruptcy by 1660.

An ambitious foreign policy without the financial resources to sustain it, or any means to make war pay for itself, ruined the fortunes of Christian IV, though it ultimately destroyed the power of the high nobility in Denmark. How then did the kings of Sweden cope with the problem of spiralling military expenditure? Gustav Vasa had attempted to reduce his dependence on expensive and unreliable mercenaries by the introduction of a standing army based on the land, but the brief war against Muscovy in 1556–7 exposed the shortcomings of this system. The silver hoarded in the royal treasury could not easily be minted for use, and the small amounts of money paid to the troops on active service were insufficient to purchase supplies. Erik XIV failed to realise the revenue he had hoped for from customs duties, and had to resort to depreciating the currency, for he feared unrest if heavy taxes were imposed. His successor inherited an empty treasury, and embarked on a programme of pawning or enfeoffing crown lands and raising loans from his wealthier subjects. By 1574, the crown was unable to pay its troops in Estonia, and they mutinied. Johan rejected the alternative solution to his difficulties advanced by the council, which was for the crown to rent out its lands and other enterprises in return for a cash revenue, though his financial situation was so bad that he had to allow the council a measure of control over the fiscal administration in the 1580s. Duke Karl used mercenaries and raised taxes to pay for them. 'The peasants are to be tempted with peace and threatened by a Russian attack', was his justification for levying a new imposition.[10] The rapid alienation of crown lands to the nobility meant that the burden of taxation fell even more heavily upon a shrinking number of freehold and crown peasants. This was particularly the case in Finland, where the number of farms in noble hands rose from a few hundred in the 1560s to over two thousand by 1600. In 1604, the *riksdag* at Norrköping attempted to define the terms on which the crown could make donations of land and revenues. All grants were to be at the king's pleasure, and had to be reconfirmed at the beginning of each new reign. They were also to revert to the crown on the extinction of the male line of the possessor, an unfortunate stipulation which tended to confirm the nobles' belief that this sanctioned hereditability. Gustav Adolf confirmed the holders of the so-called Norrköping estates in their possession in 1612, and added to their number, mainly in the conquered territories in Estonia and Livonia. He also resorted to farming out revenues in return for an annual payment to the crown, a practice which increased the flow of cash into the royal coffers, but which was gradually discontinued after 1629 as inflation eroded the true value of the tariff established in 1623. The social consequences of the sale and wholesale alienation of land by the crown were potentially explosive: Peder Galt reported in 1624 that the Swedish peasantry were beginning to mutter that they were being forced into the position of the Livonian peasantry.[11] The revenue raised from the sale of lands was moreover relatively modest, and the new taxes and impositions levied by Gustav Adolf, which affected peasant and noble alike, also failed to meet the crown's urgent need for cash to fight its wars.

The opening up of a new theatre of war in Prussia in 1626 afforded Gustav Adolf an opportunity to put into practice his belief that war ought to pay for itself; in the winter of 1627–8, over a million daler was collected from the occupied lands. Sweden also began levying tolls on ships visiting the ports of the southern Baltic, from Danzig to Narva – the so-called licence system – and the retention of these tolls was a major victory for the negotiators of the six-year truce of Altmark, concluded with Poland in 1629. The annual income from the Prussian ship tolls averaged 600,000 riksdaler (rdr), and this cash revenue was to play a vital part in financing the Swedish war effort. The licence system in Prussia yielded a revenue of 329,843 riksdaler in 1628, and over half a million riksdaler in 1629, a sum which covered

10. Odén B 1967 Naturaskatten och krigspolitik, ett finansiellt dilemma *Scandia* **33**: 13.
11. *Peder Galts depescher 1622–24*, p. 107.

around one-third of the costs of the military budget. The subsidies paid by France after 1631 never equalled the level of income from the Prussian ports. As Michael Roberts observes, 'it was not Richelieu's gold that financed Breitenfeld; far more was it the reluctant contributions of Dutch and English skippers, the tribute of the conquered, the plunder of the occupied areas, and the copper mines of Falun'.[12]

THE SINEWS OF WAR

The Falun mine was one of the wonders of the pre-industrial world, capable of supplying enough copper to satisfy European demand. The changeover in Spain to copper *vellón* currency in 1599 sharply increased the demand for copper, which reached its highest price level on the Amsterdam exchange in 1625. The *Spanienfahrer* company, established in Lübeck in 1575, was authorised to carry Swedish copper to Spain. In 1619, Gustav Adolf established his own trading company, *Svenska Handelskompaniet*, to control the production and sale of copper. The company was to pay a toll of 22 rdr per skeppund (150 kg mine-weight), a source of revenue which the king unwisely milked too heavily. By 1625, the toll had risen to 60 rdr, just as the bottom was about to fall out of the copper market in Amsterdam. In renewing its privileges in 1625, the company agreed to convert into coin any copper they could not sell above a fixed minimum price. The collapse of the market, and the destruction of Sweden's only copper mint by spring floods, meant that the company could neither sell nor mint its copper. The company fell back on the device of appointing the great Dutch financier Louis de Geer as their commissioner for the sale of copper, but prices continued to fall, and in 1628, the company was finally wound up. In a vain attempt to bolster prices, Gustav Adolf resorted to minting vast quantities of copper coin, which he tried to stuff into the pockets of his troops, officials and allies alike. The consequence of this was rapid depreciation of the overvalued copper coinage against the silver riksdaler, and the ludicrous efforts of the Swedish crown and the master of the mint to maintain parity through weight meant that a six daler copper coin in the reign of queen Christina weighed nearly twenty kilos.

The Swedish iron industry enjoyed rather more consistent fortunes.

12. Roberts 1958, p. 85. See also Lundkvist S 1966 Svensk krigsfinansiering 1630–35 *Historisk Tidskrift* **86**: 377–421.

The creation of the General Office of Mines in 1630 as an overall coordinating body for the scattered iron-mining industry epitomised the spirit of entrepreneurial consolidation and development encouraged by the Vasas. In the 1580s, Wellem de Wijk had been authorised to organise the development of the iron industry, and had begun to import skilled workers from Germany. A generation later, Wellem de Besche and Louis de Geer came together to lease the Finspång works, a partnership which was to lay the basis for the Swedish armaments industry. The Walloon craftsmen, engaged under contract, brought with them new techniques of forging, smithing and smelting. Their innovative practices had a spin-off effect on other branches of production, and in this way, helped reshape the structure and outlook of Swedish manufacturing industry. By 1629, Louis de Geer could recommend to the king that Sweden no longer needed to import arms. In 1629–30, he was able to furnish 20,000 muskets, 13,670 pikes and 4,700 suits of armour for the Swedish armies, and was exporting considerable quantities of cannon. Although the crown resumed control of the arms factories in 1631, de Geer continued to run a commercial empire which included ropewalks, wireworks, brass foundries, textile mills, shipbuilding and banking.

The development of the iron industry by foreign entrepreneurs was matched in other fields of production. Only small quantities of tar had been exported from Sweden before the end of the sixteenth century, but by 1637, pitch and tar exports had risen to around 88,000 barrels, and constituted the third most important item, after copper and iron, of Sweden's foreign trade. Sweden supplanted Prussia as the principal producer of pitch and tar in the Baltic, and it was from Prussia that experts were recruited and sent into the Finnish forests to teach the natives the subtleties of tar-burning. Foreigners also played a major role in the development of Swedish trade. Dutch merchants were encouraged to settle in the new town of Göteborg by Karl IX and his son. In 1624, Gustav Adolf authorised the Dutchman Willem Usselincx to set up his grandly named 'General Company for Commerce and Navigation with the Lands of Africa, Asia, America and Magellanica', a venture which failed to live up to its prospectus, even if it provided the inspiration for a new company which established a Swedish colony on the Delaware in the reign of queen Christina. Both northern kingdoms suffered from a lack of means to compete with the Dutch. An anonymous Danish pamphleteer in the middle of the seventeenth century complained that wealthier merchants set up companies without knowing how to run them, and that most of these enterprises had collapsed as a result of this incompetence. The trading activities of the nobility undermined the competitiveness of the burghers, so that 'there are hardly any burghers in our country who can obtain a good living from trade alone, but all our neighbours and all the foreigners who visit us become rich and fat on our wretchedness and poverty'. The one advantage Sweden had over its Scandinavian rival was its mineral wealth: as Claude Nordmann remarks, copper and iron were truly the driving force of Swedish expansion and the basis for Sweden's military power.[13]

LORDS AND PEASANTS

The decades of warfare that followed the collapse of the Livonian Order exacted a terrible toll in human lives. The population of Estonia, estimated at around a quarter of a million in 1558, was reduced to fewer than seventy thousand by 1625. Three-quarters of the peasant farms in southern Estonia were deserted, and the situation was little better in the north. Over half of the peasant homesteads in central Livonia were destroyed in the course of the Polish–Swedish war. Those who could fled to the comparative safety of the islands; thousands perished in a land stripped bare by marauding bands of troops and ravaged by pestilence and famine. Johann von Nassau, commanding the Swedish armies in the bitterly cold winter of 1601–2, reported that:

> Everything and everyone is demolished, burnt or killed, and for many miles no living person is seen, and one does not know whether people have ever lived here. Those who have not been killed have so much suffered from the famine that, among the poor peasants, parents and children, children and parents, husband and wife, kill and eat up one another. The bodies of criminals are taken from the gallows and the wheel, and in many places even the dead are taken out of their graves by the poor in their extremity.[14]

The abandonment of peasant holdings on such a large scale noticeably worsened the legal status of the peasantry. Deserted farms were taken over by landlords and either incorporated into their own demesnes, or resettled by peasants with no rights of tenure. The land-

13. Fridericia J 1894 *Adelsvældens sidste Dage. Danmarks Historie fra Christian IV's Død til Enevældens Indførelse (1648–60)*. Copenhagen (1975 reprint edn), pp. 80–1. Nordmann C 1971 *Grandeur et liberté de la Suède (1660–1792)*. Paris, p. 22.
14. Cited in Schwabe A n.d. *Agrarian History of Latvia*. Riga, p. 62.

owners argued that the peasants in general had no rights of tenure, having lost such rights with the conquest of Livonia in the thirteenth century, and they also claimed that the peasant had no right to free movement, but was bound to his master. These claims were contested, though with little success, by the new rulers of the Baltic lands. In 1561, Erik XIV gave orders that the peasantry of Harrien and Wierland should henceforth be properly tried and punished in strict accordance with the prescribed sentence. In 1601, duke Karl laid a series of radical propositions before the *Landtag* in Reval, inviting the estates to consider union with their Swedish counterparts, the introduction of Swedish law, the foundation of churches, schools and hospitals in a land notably bereft of such institutions, and the education of peasant children. Not surprisingly, the hard-bitten gentry protested loud and long against a series of proposals which would have effectively undermined their privileges. They claimed that they already had their own laws, and they defended serfdom on economic and social grounds, even arguing that the peasants themselves had expressed a preference for the ancient usage of corporal punishment when Stefan Batory had earlier tried to replace this custom with fines. The continuing war and the need to retain the loyalty of the Baltic nobility rendered nugatory any plans to introduce Swedish law into the Baltic lands, though Ingria – where there were few noble land-owners – was brought under Swedish law, and Axel Oxenstierna also introduced Swedish law in his vast complex of estates around Wenden and Wolmar. Oxenstierna enjoyed the reputation of being a considerate and fair-minded landlord. As a rule, however, the Swedish nobles, who by 1680 owned over half of the land in Livonia, tended to follow the practices of the indigenous gentry in keeping the peasantry in bondage.

North of the Gulf of Finland, the Finnish peasantry were also experiencing hard times. The number of farms declined from 33,543 in 1566 to 29,000 in 1593, at a time when the nobility was increasing its land holdings through donations and service fiefs (*förläningar*). The nobility managed to evade their military obligations, and their tenants were also not obliged to quarter men-at-arms or to provide horses for transport. These and other burdens and impositions fell upon the tax-paying peasantry. There were numerous instances of violence and rapine, and the aggrieved farmer was by no means assured of justice when the judges and their clerks were noblemen and their servants. A particular source of complaint was the misbehaviour of those who, in return for serving the crown as soldiers, obtained exemption from taxation on their farms. These *knapar*, several hundred in number, came in for bitter criticism in a petition by three hundred commoners, addressed to the king in 1589. 'Many sons of burghers and priests' sons who have left school have got themselves a horse, young lads who know nothing of warfare but only the freedom of being in camp, robbing and raping their own country.' The petitioners addressed the king 'in great distress, for we fear that our country will be ravaged and made as desolate as Livonia by these unjust acts'.[15] Clashes between peasants and troops had occurred in south-western Finland in the 1570s, and there was a minor uprising at Christmas 1592 at Rautalampi, when peasants attacked a contingent of cavalry. The harsh regime of the royal governor Klas Fleming prompted a flood of complaints to Stockholm, where duke Karl was only too happy to issue letters of protection to the petitioners and to declare them free of the exactions of quartering and unjust levies. At the end of 1596, revolt flared up in Ostrobothnia, where the imposition of quartering was seen as a breach of king Johan's 1592 instruction, freeing the region of this burden. The homes of local *knapar* were attacked and burned, and the peasant forces decided to advance southwards. The object of the peasants' ire was Klas Fleming; all nobles believed to oppose him were to have their estates spared and attempts were made to persuade several of them to join the peasants. The army advancing along the coastal route was defeated, and Klas Fleming was able to break up the main rebel camp at Nokia. The fleeing peasants were pursued and cut down, their leaders captured and executed. There was a second uprising in Ostrobothnia in February 1597. The rebels were better armed than their predecessors, and had an agent of duke Karl in their ranks; but they too suffered defeat at the hands of Fleming's troops, at Santavuori on 24 February 1597.

The 'Club War' has long been a contentious issue in Finnish historiography. The nationalist historians of the nineteenth century and their later disciples believed that, as a result of the acquisition of lands and offices, and of the experience of long years of war on the eastern frontier, the nobility in Finland developed a sense of separate identity. The blame for the peasant revolt is placed on duke Karl, who incited a 'backward' peasantry to rise. Writing in the immediate aftermath of war and defeat in 1945, Pentti Renvall blamed a collapse in morale, rather than the burdens of quartering, for the revolt. The gullible peasants, instead of gritting their teeth and bearing the burdens 'which society had to impose upon its members', were seduced by 'forces

15. Juva M *et al.*, (eds). 1968 *Suomen historian dokumentteja* (2 vols). Helsinki, vol. 1, pp. 209–212.

which sought to promote objectives alien to Finland's needs'.[16] The theory first advanced by Gustav Adolf, that the nobility 'made the poor Finns so desperate that they preferred death to life' and they were thus driven to revolt by 'the two evil influences, poverty and ignorance', has recently been endorsed by Heikki Ylikangas, for whom the revolt was primarily an act of desperation provoked by the exactions and oppression of the nobility and their servants. The notion of a separate and conscious Finnish identity in the ranks of the nobility has been contested by Finnish–Swedish historians such as Eric Anthoni. In Anthoni's view, Klas Fleming was animated by loyalty to king Sigismund, not a sense of Finnish consciousness. Although Anthoni agrees that there was a notable diminution in the numbers of noblemen primarily resident in Finland in the seventeenth century, he attributes this less to the loss of life at the hands of Karl's soldiers and his executioner than to the centralisation of the bureaucracy of the realm and the shifting of Sweden's foreign policy interests away from the eastern frontier, which lessened the importance of the Finnish estates for their owners, many of whom began transferring their residences to Sweden.[17]

Although geographically isolated from Sweden, Finland was regarded as an integral part of the realm. The newly acquired territories south of the Gulf of Finland posed a different problem. As the armies of Johan III began to advance eastwards into the district of Wierland in 1578, the nobility of that region deemed it expedient to seek confirmation of their privileges from the king. They were joined by the nobility of Harrien and Jerwen, whose privileges had been confirmed by Erik XIV in 1561. Johan mistrusted the Estonian nobility, many of whom, as he put it, 'had borne the cape on both shoulders' (i.e., had been less than loyal to the Swedish cause), and he preferred to entrust office to Finns and Swedes rather than to the native nobility.

The *Landtag* summoned by Pontus de la Gardie in 1584 was the first to define the territory of the duchy of Estonia. The knights of the four districts of Harrien, Jerven, Wierland and Wiek declared themselves to be a united *corpus*, and the privileges and institutions long established in Harrien and Wierland gradually spread to embrace the entire nobil-

16. Renvall P 1945 Eräitä huomioita 1500–luvun loppuvuosikymmenien talonpoikaislevottomuuksista *Historiallinen Aikakauskirja* **43**: 50.
17. Hallendorff 1915, p. 165. The comments were made by the king in his unfinished history of Sweden. Ylikangas H 1977 *Nuijasota*. Helsinki. Anthoni E 1937 *Konflikten mellan hertig Carl och Finland. Avvecklingen och försoningen* Skrifter utgivna av Svenska Litteratursällskapet i Finland 262. Helsingfors, esp. pp. 366–76. For a different interpretation, see Lehtinen E 1961 *Hallituksen yhtenäistämispolitiikka Suomessa 1600–luvulla* Historiallisia Tutkimuksia 60. Helsinki, pp. 38–45.

ity of the duchy of Estonia in Livonia (*Ritter- und Landschaft des Fürstentums Esten in Livland*). Those who, according to the privilege of 1452, lived on their estates and 'ate their bread' in the provinces were entitled to attend the *Landtag*. The *Landtag* debated matters of noble concern, such as the upkeep of roads and bridges, punishment of the peasantry and broader issues, such as measures of defence and taxation. Together with the twelve-man *Landrat*, it formed the court of highest instance (*Oberlandgerichte*). In spite of the efforts of the crown to force appointments on the *Landrat*, that body maintained its right to select its own members, and it also appointed local judges. However, the boundary between royal and local authority was vague and often ambiguous, and the *Landrat*, chaired by the royal governor, embodied this ambiguity: on the one hand, it was an instrument of royal authority, on the other, the mouthpiece of the local nobility.

Although Johan was willing to confirm privileges, he refused to give way to demands that only the indigenous nobility should be appointed to the administration, or be allowed to own land in the duchy. Johan argued that all land held in fief could in principle be recalled by the crown, unless it had been granted *in perpetuo*, and it was during his reign that the process of granting estates to non-native nobles was begun. The land revision of 1586 nevertheless confirmed all who could prove their loyalty to the crown in possession of their estates, and the prospects of Estonia passing under the control of the Polish crown prompted the nobility to send a delegation to Stockholm in 1588 to ensure that Johan had no intention of allowing Estonia to pass from Swedish into Polish hands.

The *Privilegium Sigismundi Augusti* of 1561 had granted the Livonian nobility almost unrestricted freedom of disposition over their land and subjects, and had guaranteed the Lutheran faith and the indigenous rights of the nobility in matters of administration and justice. Its twenty-seven points were the model for the privileges conceded by Gotthard Kettler in his duchy of Kurland in 1570, and were held by later generations to be the Livonian constitution. As such, they formed the basis for negotiations with Peter the Great in 1710. There are, however, some grounds to support the view that the *Privilegium* was a reflection of the desire of the nobility to consolidate their old privileges rather than a codification for all time of the rights of the *Ritterschaft*. The *Cautio* issued by Zygmunt August in 1562 was far less generous, especially in matters of trade, and reflected more closely the ambitions of the Lithuanian nobility. In 1566, Kettler was replaced as the king's governor by Jan Chodkiewicz, and the duchy of Livonia (*ducatus ultradunensis*) was incorporated into Lithuania. The *Indigenats-*

recht of the Livonian nobility was strengthened in the diploma of union, though the Livonians were unable to exact confirmation of those rights from the king in 1569.[18] The irruption of Russian troops into Livonia in 1576 caused widescale panic, and many small towns such as Wenden ejected Polish garrisons and received duke Magnus as their ruler in an attempt to save themselves from Muscovite occupation.

The threat posed by Ivan IV may have persuaded the citizens of Riga to negotiate with Stefan Batory, though the talks in Vilna dragged on for two years before final agreement was reached. The *Corpus privilegiorum Stephanus* confirmed the town's rights and privileges, but it lacked any guarantee of religious freedom. In May 1582, the king made it clear that he intended to restore Catholicism in the city and the rest of Livonia, which he felt was his right by virtue of conquest. His *Constitutiones Livoniae* only allowed Lutheranism inferior status to Catholicism, and divided the land into three *praesidia*, on the Polish model. The *starosti* who were to be appointed to administer the subdivisions of the three provinces were to be Poles, Lithuanians or native Livonians (in 1589, the last-named category was omitted altogether). A biannual *Gerichtslandtag* was to meet in Wenden, under the chairmanship of the royal governor, and was to function as the court of highest instance, recognising only Livonian land law. The *Landtag* was to be summoned by the king, and was to elect six deputies to the *sejm*. During his stay in Riga in 1582, Stefan Batory made it clear that the nobility would have to prove title to the estates which they had abandoned in the wars, and on several occasions he intimated a desire to put an end to the flogging of peasants by their lords. Grants of land were made to Polish and Lithuanian nobles, and attempts were made to establish colonies of peasants from Poland and Lithuania. Although Zygmunt III's 1598 ordinance for Livonia once more permitted Livonians access to appointments to office and authorised the drafting of a land law, many nobles were attracted by duke Karl's offers, and negotiated with him in 1601. Those who went over to the Swedish side had their estates confiscated, though they were compensated by Karl with lands in Finland.

'God grant that we will understand how to proceed with what God has delivered into our hands. We have indeed gained a small kingdom,

18. Cf. Spekke A 1951 *History of Latvia*. Stockholm, p. 195. Seraphim E 1908 *Baltische Geschichte im Grundriss* Reval, p. 170. Staemmler K-D 1953 *Preussen und Livland in ihrem Verhältnis zur Krone Polen 1561 bis 1586*. Marburg, p. 17. Donnert E 1963 *Der livländische Ordenritterstaat und Russland. Der livländische Krieg und die baltische Frage in der europäische Politik 1558–83*. Berlin, pp. 86–90.

but I doubt that we will understand how to deal with it.'[19] Such was the verdict of the Polish field commander Zamoyski in 1582, an apt prediction of the problems which the duchy of Livonia posed for its new rulers. The dukes of Kurland had to wrestle with an even more intractable set of vassals. After the death of Gotthard Kettler in 1597, the duchy was divided between his two sons, Wilhelm and Friedrich, each with his own court, treasury and chancery. The ambitious but headstrong Wilhelm aroused noble opposition with his demands for the fulfilment of knight-service, and his appointments of foreigners to high office, but he was forced to give way on these points in 1606. The lengthy feud between duke Wilhelm and the Nolde brothers, who had appealed successfully to the Polish courts for restitution of their lands, reached a tragic climax in 1615, when the two brothers were murdered in the streets of Mitau as the dukes were treating with the assembled *Landtag*. A commission appointed by Zygmunt III declared duke Wilhelm deposed, and his elder brother Friedrich was confirmed in possession of the entire duchy. The recommendations of the commission were incorporated in the 1617 *Formula regiminis*, which effectively created a republic of nobles in Kurland. The *Ritterbank*, which commenced its work in 1620, was given exclusive rights to determine who was to hold the title of nobility. Noble deputies from twenty-seven parishes were to assemble once every two years in the *Landtag*, from which the towns were excluded. The members of the supreme council (*Oberrat*) and the four regional governors (*Oberhauptmänner*) were to be native noblemen, and could only be replaced with the consent of their colleagues. The supreme council would govern the duchy in the absence of the duke, or in cases of a minority or infirmity. All the rights of the landlord over his peasants were confirmed and codified in statute form. The Polish overlord also succeeded in establishing his rights in the duchy. In the case of disputes between the duke and his vassals, the royal courts would arbitrate: Polish and Lithuanian nobles were to enjoy the same rights as the indigenous nobility, and Catholicism was given equal status with the Augsburg Confession.

The situation of the dukes of Kurland was in some ways analogous to that of the dukes of Prussia. Albrecht had been forced to make extensive concessions to his nobility in the 1540s. Because of his perilous financial position, he had to admit the right of the estates to determine the way in which taxes were raised, and to agree to the principle that high officials should only be appointed from the indige-

19. Seraphim 1908, p. 185.

nous nobility. In the 1560s, an adventurer named Professor Paul Skalich succeeded in gaining the confidence of the ailing duke, and this prompted the nobility to appeal to the king to intervene. The commission set up by Zygmunt August effectively acted as the ruling body, for the duke was incapacitated by a stroke, and unable to govern. The *Landtag* took over the appointment of bishops and strengthened its own privileges. Albrecht's successor was mentally unstable, and the governance of the duchy remained in the hands of the council until 1577, when Stefan Batory, without consulting the estates, confirmed Georg Friedrich, margrave of Ansbach, as regent and successor to the infirm duke Albrecht Friedrich. Stefan Batory forged a close liaison with Georg Friedrich, who had to battle to restore the parlous finances of the duchy and to regain ducal lands alienated by his predecessor. That Prussia did not gradually disappear into the yellowing pages of long-forgotten histories, as did Kurland, owes a great deal to the fortuitous circumstances of marriage. In 1591, the eldest grandson of the elector of Brandenburg, Johann Sigismund, married the eldest daughter of the duke of Prussia, who had no male heirs. The regency government of Prussia was taken over by Brandenburg in 1603, and when Albrecht Friedrich died in 1618, the duchy passed to Johann Sigismund, elector of Brandenburg, who continued to hold it as a vassal of the king of Poland. The acquisition of the duchy of Cleves and the counties of Mark and Ravensberg on the Rhine in 1610 also gave Brandenburg a foothold in western Germany, the first step towards the final unification of Germany under the Hohenzollern sceptre in 1871.

The nobility of the lands on the southern shores of the Baltic, from Holstein to Estonia, are usually portrayed as selfish, rapacious, cruel landlords, forming a solid corporate body of privilege against which the weak rulers could do very little. The petty landowners of the eastern Baltic seem to have been a particularly unpleasant lot, indulging in bouts of litigation with neighbours, and occasionally ending up in court themselves on charges of incest or adultery.[20] The Baltic nobility believed they had a time-honoured right to beat their peasants, though they were also fearful of what might happen should they revolt. Gustav Vasa's agent in Reval wrote in 1558 that the nobility did not wish to allow the peasants to offer armed resistance to the Russians 'for they fear that when the peasants have dealt with the Russians, they will also drive out the nobility'. Gotthard Kettler

20. Helk V 1985 Zwei Öseler Kleinadelsfamilien in dänischer und schwedischer Zeit (1559–1710) *Zeitschrift für Ostforschung* **34**: 504–21.

feared that the exactions of the soldiery would drive the peasants into the arms of the Russians, and indeed the invading armies did attempt to present themselves as liberators and blood-brothers of the peasantry.[21] There were signs of nervousness amongst the Estonian junkers in the 1590s, as news of peasant disturbances in Finland began to reach them: the *Landrat* proposed that the rod should not be spared, and that peasants caught possessing weapons should be punished with death.

In their dealings with the Swedish or Polish crown, the German-speaking nobility fought long and hard to maintain the privileges of their estate. Duke Karl's attempts to persuade the Livonian nobility to allow themselves to become an integral element of the Swedish realm, even his offers of seats in the *riksråd*, failed to move those stolid gentlemen. In their view, it was the duty of higher authority to defend and protect noble liberties, an assertion which says a great deal about their particularist mentality.[22]

The evil reputation of the Livonian landlords, and the wretched condition of the peasantry, was well known on the other side of the Gulf of Finland, where the epithets 'Livonian dog' and 'son of a Livonian tramp' were regular terms of abuse. Nevertheless, large numbers of Finns moved to Estonia in the early seventeenth century as settlers; by 1637, they comprised 20 per cent of the peasant population of Wierland. These settlers came as freemen, though as the century progressed, this status became badly eroded. In 1626, Axel Oxenstierna established 142 Finnish families in the deserted and ruined town of Wolmar, in order to meet his obligation to provide a garrison. In 1641, they were resettled, and in 1659, they were being described as *Erbcolonier*, little different from the hereditary peasantry (*Erbbauer*). Finns also settled the forests of northern Sweden and Dalarna, where their burning of the forest to provide fertile land for cultivation brought them into conflict with the conservationist state authorities after 1640. Numbers of Finns, some transported for offences against the forest laws, found their way to New Sweden on the Delaware from their settlements in the high forests of Medelpad. In Amsterdam, the Swedish representative was shown a letter from the brother of one of a party of 140 Finns from Medelpad, assuredly one of the first 'American letters', which declared that 'New Sweden was a so beauti-

21. Schirren C. (ed.) 1861 *Quellen zur Geschichte des Untergangs livländischer Selbstständigkeit* (8 vols). Riga, vol. 1, pp. 242–3. Donnert 1963, pp. 65–71, 97.

22. Federley B 1963 *Konung, ståthållare och korporationer. Studier i Estlands förvaltning 1581–1600* Societas Scientiarum Fennica. Commentationes Humanorum Litterarum 30. Helsingfors, p. 59.

ful and priceless land in which to live, for everything there grows in abundance'.[23]

The life of the common man in northern Europe was to a very great extent dominated by darkness, superstition, inadequate diet, disease and death, much as it had been for centuries: but it was not entirely immune to external influences and change. The increased European demand for grain and animal products brought benefits to many peasant farmers as well as to noble landowners. The free peasantry of Dithmarsch developed a system of husbandry, in which land enriched by four years of grazing was used for cereal growing for two or three years, and reaped rich profits from the sale of dairy products to the cities of north-western Europe. It was said that the farmers of Eider-stedt, a region which exported over two million pounds of cheese annually at the end of the sixteenth century, covered their roofs with copper, and that silver and gold were more common than iron or brass. The frequency with which sumptuary legislation was breached by the peasants of eastern Pomerania would suggest that they had money enough to buy the forbidden velvet and satin. A German visitor to Sweden in the 1580s noted that many peasants owned silver spoons, and the Frenchman Charles Ogier declared in 1634 that the peasants of Sweden were more prosperous than those of France. Johannes Bureus observed that the wealthier farmers in the Tornio valley had guest-rooms in their houses, which were also furnished with glazed windows. These observations do not of course constitute proof of an overall improvement in living conditions, and there is a formidable array of evidence to suggest the opposite. Though some prospered, many fell into destitution, and all were afflicted by the hardships of crop failure and the ravages of the plague. The margin between health and hardship, survival and death was always exceedingly thin.

MIGRANTS, ALIENS AND THE PROBLEM OF RELIGIOUS DIVERSITY

The growth of trade links with western Europe brought an influx of merchants and craftsmen into the ports of the Baltic. Settlers from the Low Countries brought with them capital and new techniques, as we have seen in the case of the mining industry in Sweden. In Danzig, the

23. Gothe R 1945 *Medelpads Finnar*. Stockholm, p. 127.

settlers introduced Dutch bread and founded distilleries: Anthony Cuiper from Amsterdam planned the first public bank, though his scheme was dashed by the opposition of the city's private bankers. There were also colonies of Scots and English traders in all the ports of the Baltic which shipped commodities to the East Coast ports. Across the vast lands of the Polish–Lithuanian commonwealth, a great variety of cultures and religions could be encountered. Further north, howeverer, a much greater degree of ethnic and religious homogeneity prevailed. The only exotic outsiders, who seem to have found their way to northern Europe by the sixteenth century, were gypsies. As elsewhere, they were persecuted. According to a law of 1637, all male gypsies found in Sweden were to be hanged without trial, a decree which appears not to have been put into practice, at least not on gypsies innocent of any offence. Per Brahe even attempted to settle gypsies on abandoned farms on the Finnish–Russian border in 1662, though his intentions seem to have been to train them as soldiers. Occasionally, of course, multi-ethnic bands of mercenaries traversed the native heath, stealing the peasants' chickens and abusing their womenfolk. In August 1561, prince Radziwiłł's army of Armenians, Tatars, Turks, Podolians, Russians, Wallachians, Germans, Poles and Lithuanians marched through the streets of Riga, an episode recorded years later by Balthasar Rüssow:

> Many pious souls of Riga, when they saw such strange nations and peoples, each with their own habit, weapons and music, were greatly troubled that their fatherland and the streets of the Christian city of Riga should be trodden by such unusual, strange and barbarous nations and people.[24]

Rüssow was also scandalised by the behaviour of the Scots mercenaries in Reval. Citizens who ventured to stick their heads out of doors were liable to be robbed of the money from their purses, or the coats off their backs by the unpaid soldiery, and 'in sum, it was not much better than an enemy occupation'. The Scots had their own Calvinist preacher, which prompted the Lutheran pastor to confide in his chronicle that it was a blessing of the Lord that they were ignorant of the German language 'for otherwise they would have smitten many people with their zealotry'.[25]

Although for economic reasons, foreigners of another faith were tolerated in Sweden, as long as they refrained from proselytising, any subject of the king of Sweden who abandoned Lutheranism for

24. Rüssow B 1967 *Chronica der Provintz Lyfflandt*. Hannover (reprint) p. 67.
25. Rüssow 1967, p. 100. Dow 1964, pp. 33–4.

another faith stood to lose his rights of inheritance, and could be banished in accordance with the decision of the 1604 Norrköping *riksdag*. The acquisition in 1617 of territory inhabited by adherents of the Orthodox faith thus posed a problem which the Swedish authorities wrestled with for many decades. Luther and Philipp Melanchthon had been generally positive in their view of Orthodoxy. Swedish theologians at the beginning of the seventeenth century accepted that Orthodoxy was a Christian faith, even if they disliked its ritual, and shared the general prejudice that the Orthodox priesthood was drunken and incompetent. For economic and political reasons, the Swedish authorities sought to assure the merchants of the towns of Ingria that they would be allowed free exercise of religion. They were, however, unwilling to allow Russian-trained priests to take up appointments in the parishes of Ingria and Karelia. At one stage, it was proposed that qualified Ingrians be sent at the state's expense to be trained in Constantinople. From the 1630s, a more active policy of conversion was followed, aided by the influx of Lutheran settlers, and numbers of Karelians fled from the over-zealous activities of the pastors to the region around Tver, where their descendants remain to this very day.

By the end of the sixteenth century, Lutheranism had become the established religion of the Scandinavian states, and rigid uniformity of faith was consistently enforced until well into the nineteenth century. The catechism was used as the basis of popular instruction, and as a means of ensuring that the Christian knew his duty towards God and higher authority. It ranked higher than the Augsburg Confession in the list of confessional writings included in the Swedish 1634 Form of Government: psalms and hymns were moulded around the text of the catechism: examination of the common people's knowledge of the catechism was deemed more important than preaching by the clergy. The Swedish state and church expended enormous effort in trying to impose a Swedish church order upon the Baltic lands, and when the Danish lands on the eastern side of the Sound finally passed to the Swedish crown in 1660, it was upon the church that the policy of swedification was focused.

The Lutheran faith was not the only means of establishing an identity for the Swedish people. Great attention was paid to the glorious past of the nation. The Gothic origins of the Swedish people had been forcefully declaimed by Nicolaus Ragnvaldi at the Council of Basel in 1434, and an anonymous chronicler in the 1520s boasted of the Mediterranean conquests of the Goths from the north. Olaus Petri, in his *Swedish Chronicle*, poured scorn on the notion that the ancient Goths had their origins in Sweden: but his work was condemned by Gustav Vasa as seditious, and it was to be the work of an exiled Catholic prelate, Johannes Magnus, which was to grip the Swedish imagination in subsequent decades. Erik XIV had copies of Magnus' history of the Goths distributed to the English court; Johan III and Karl IX both authorised translations. On the traditional perambulation of the kingdom (*eriksgata*), Karl IX reminded his subjects that their Gothic forebears had conquered Rome; in 1611, the aged king challenged Christian IV to a duel, according to 'the lawful usage and custom of the ancient Goths'. At a tournament celebrating his coronation, Gustav Adolf played the part of Berik, the supposed conqueror of the lands of the south, and in his farewell address to the estates in 1630, he urged the nobility to spread the fame of their Gothic forefathers, who had once ruled the world.[26] Gustav Adolf and Christian IV were keen patrons of antiquarian research, and the nobility of both kingdoms shared a passion for deciphering runic inscriptions. Both royal courts had their official historiographers, though perhaps the most famous work of the age – *Scondia illustrata* – was produced in prison by Johannes Messenius, convicted of treasonable activity in the cause of Catholicism in 1617. Sovereigns were well aware of the value of the printed word in propagating their views. The plans of the house of Habsburg for establishing their presence in the Baltic were first advanced by the Jesuit Ofondi in his *Classicum paciferum Daniae* (1619); Christian IV's claims to Baltic dominion were stated in *Mare Balticum* (1638). Christian IV and Gustav Adolf released floods of pamphlets and flysheets, justifying their intervention in the German war. In the conflict between Sigismund and duke Karl, the 'Russian threat' was employed by both sides to rally support. Many of the negative characteristics attributed to the Danes during the last phase of the Kalmar Union were to be used by Swedish propagandists in describing the Russians a century later.[27]

The nobility of Sweden and Denmark at the beginning of the seventeenth century were undeniably more refined, better educated and living in rather more luxurious surroundings than their grandfathers. Latin phrases adorned their speech, and they affected much of the military and diplomatic terminology of their continental counterparts. If their manners still caused foreign eyebrows to be raised, and their cuisine left a good deal to be desired, they were making great

26. Nordström J 1934 *De yverbornas ö*. Stockholm, pp. 61ff. Lindroth S 1975 *Svensk lärdomshistoria. Medeltiden. Reformationstiden*. Stockholm, pp. 169–72.
27. Tarkiainen K 1974 *'Vår Gamble Arffiende Ryssen'. Synen på Ryssland i Sverige 1595–1621 och andra studier kring den svenska Rysslandsbilden från tidigare stormaktstid* Studia Historica Upsaliensia 54. Uppsala, pp. 70–1.

efforts to catch up. The fashions of French cuisine were taken up, though by the time the north had learnt that meals should begin with a soup, the meat in the broth had been replaced by herbs or vegetables. Tarts and pies also gained favour: Erik XIV's coronation was the first occasion pastries had ever been made in any quantity in Scandinavia, and the cookbook published in 1581 by Max Rumpelt, cook to the Danish royal court, listed 66 different types of pastry and 46 recipes for baking tarts. The high fashions of Europe were also imitated, though moralists such as Peder Palladius fulminated against the immorality of the cod-piece, padded breeches and the slashed doublet. Closer contact with the main centres of culture and education, and with the courts of Europe, fostered an aristocratic spirit which more than justified the placing of Minerva as well as Mars on the house of the estate of nobles (*riddarhus*) in Stockholm. The acquisition of land, office and power also led to greater exclusivity on the part of the high aristocracy, though in neither of the Scandinavian kingdoms did the nobility ever seek to exclude the common people from the body of the nation, even though they sometimes regarded the peasantry as unconscionably rude and barbaric, and were ashamed of their surroundings when distinguished foreign visitors paid a call. Defiant patriotic pride, mingled with a desire to bring the trappings of civilisation – if needs be, by plundering the libraries and collections of conquered cities – to their impoverished native land helped motivate the Swedish nobility during the age of greatness. It was not in vain that Gustav Adolf bade them in his farewell speech to the estates on 19 May 1630 to go to war to restore the ancient honour of their Gothic ancestors, though his hint at broad acres to be won was probably a more powerful inducement.

Sweden as a Great Power

PART THREE
Sweden as a Great Power

CHAPTER SEVEN

The Central European Wars (1618–79)

GERMANIA

Since the Peace of Augsburg, the German lands had been largely spared the ravages of religious war which had afflicted France and the Low Countries. This relative tranquillity was not to last. The revolt of the Bohemian estates in 1618 precipitated an era of general European conflict, in which all the major Christian potentates were to become directly or indirectly involved. At one level, the wars became merely a new variant on the old Franco-Habsburg rivalry, fought on a wider stage than heretofore. For the German princes, the struggle for 'German liberties' against Imperial pretensions was a major issue, given an additional dimension by what was perceived to be an attempt by the emperor to overturn the religious settlement of 1555. The turmoil in central Europe also drew in the northern kingdoms, and their involvement was to have great bearing upon the struggle for dominion in the Baltic.

For those who had to suffer the depredations of the marauding soldiery, the Thirty Years' War was a nightmare. Scarcely any region of the German lands was left untouched. Even those places where the hand of war pressed less heavily, such as Dithmarsch, experienced hardship. The occupation of the region by Imperial troops in the late 1620s caused a veritable guerrilla war between the local inhabitants and the soldiers. To add to these miseries, the plague ravaged the marshy lands. In 1629, the air around Heide was said to be so foul that swallows were the only birds seen in the vicinity. The experience of war bred further violence; feasts and celebrations in the district of south Dithmarsch were terrorised by young men armed with knives and bent on mayhem and murder. The Jutland peninsula was ravaged by Imperial troops between 1626 and 1629. Many of the inhabitants fled to the safety of the islands, but those who remained, such as the unfortunate priest of Mejrup, on the main road between Holstebro and Viborg, were obliged to act as involuntary hosts to the soldiery. By 1629, the priest's cupboards, chests and doors had been smashed to smithereens, his goods and chattels plundered and his ryefields trampled by the horses of the cavalrymen. The locals suffered worse, if anything, at the hands of the retreating cavalry, commanded by the soldier of fortune Wolf von Baudissin. The 'monstrous and unchristian tyranny' of the cavalry not only laid the peninsula waste, according to the local gentry: it also prompted a peasant uprising in Vendsyssel. Much was made in Protestant propaganda of the saviour-like qualities of Gustav Adolf and his Swedish armies; but as the war dragged on, even the virtuous Swede became the butt of satire. The pamphlet *Rossomalza/ Das ist: Der schwedische Vielfrass* (1644) viciously attacked the voracious appetite of Swedish politicians and generals for German lands: Oxenstierna was portrayed as an ox, or as having a wolf's face. Pamphlets had parents teaching their children to pray that the Swedes would not come. The 'Midnight Lion' might be portrayed chasing the Imperial eagle and the bear of the Catholic League through the 'Priests' Alley' of central Germany, to the plaudits of the propagandists: but to the common people, the deceased lion's troops soon became like all the rest – smashing in the windows, melting down the lead and using it for bullets with which to shoot the peasants.[1]

As tension mounted in central Europe in the second decade of the seventeenth century, the tentacles of Habsburg policy seemed to contemporaries to stretch over the entire continent. The king of Poland, already linked to the Austrian Habsburgs through marriage, concluded an alliance with the emperor Matthias in 1613, and sent troops to help the emperor deal with his rebellious subjects in Silesia in 1616. The Dutch, in the midst of domestic crisis and fearing an agreement between Denmark and Spain which might cut off their

---

1. See Langer H 1978 *Kulturgeschichte des 30jährigen Krieges*. Leipzig, p. 109. On Dithmarsch, Bolten J 1788 *Ditmarsische Geschichte* (4 vols) (reprint edn). Leer 1979, vol. 4, pp. 224–56. On Jutland, Steensberg A (ed.) 1969 *Dagligliv i Danmark i det syttende og attende århundrede*. Copenhagen, pp. 236–8. The myth of the 'agmen horribile haccapellitorum', the Finnish light cavalry whose battlecry was supposed to strike fear into the heart of the enemy, has recently been subjected to close scrutiny: Lappalainen J 1986 'Ex agmine haccapellorum libera nos Domine' *Historisk Tidskrift för Finland* **71**: 98–110. On Protestant propaganda, see Rystad G 1960 *Kriegsnachtrichten und Propaganda während des Dreissigjährigen Krieges*. Stockholm; and Böttcher D 1953–4 Propaganda und öffentliche Meinung im protestantischen Deutschland (1628–36) *Archiv für Reformationsgeschichte* **44**: 181–203, **45**: 83–98.

access to the Baltic, were cool in their response to Swedish requests for assistance in 1617–18. The Swedes had been able to take advantage of Poland's eastern conflicts with the Russians and Turks when they resumed the war in Livonia in 1617: but the initial gains made were soon lost to the Poles, and in the summer of 1618 a two-year truce was signed. Gustav Adolf followed the Bohemian revolt with some interest, occasionally comparing the deposition of Ferdinand to that of Sigismund Vasa, but did little to provide active assistance to the rebels. The Bohemians in fact complained that the king of Sweden's truce with Poland allowed Zygmunt III to provide the Emperor with Cossacks to put down the revolt.

As the battered Protestant forces crumbled before the assaults of Spinola's Spanish troops and the Catholic League, the erstwhile king of Bohemia, the Elector Palatine Frederick V, and his supporters sought to forge an anti-Habsburg alliance in defence of 'German liberties'. The particular interests of the likely allies frustrated these efforts. The Dutch wanted the main war effort to be on their eastern flank to relieve the pressure of Spinola's armies; Christian IV wished first to impose his will upon Hamburg, Lübeck and Bremen; and Gustav Adolf was still primarily engaged in the struggle against Poland. Although the capture of Riga in 1621 was a challenge to the pretensions of Christian IV's claim to dominion over the Baltic, it was not followed by any significant Swedish advances. Gustav Adolf was prepared to return the city to Poland if a durable peace could thereby be guaranteed; but the best that could be obtained was a renewal of the truce for two years. During the winter of 1622–3, relations between Sweden and Denmark deteriorated to the point that the Swedish agent in Helsingør could report that it was commonly rumoured that, were he not occupied with German matters, Christian IV would open hostilities against Sweden. In April 1623, the Danes started to levy tolls on Swedish ships passing through the Sound in reprisal for indirect duties imposed on Danes trading with Sweden. At the same time, Robert Stewart was authorised by the king of Poland to raise a force of 7,000 troops for an invasion of Sweden. To counter this threat, Gustav Adolf mounted a naval demonstration off Danzig, and his diplomats tried to persuade the English and Dutch governments to prevent the recruitment and transport of mercenaries by Robert Stewart. An attempt was even made, via the Dutch envoy to Constantinople, to get the Patriarch to urge Orthodox Christians in Lithuania to rebel and throw in their lot with Sweden.

Little came of these activities, though James I was stirred to initiate talks aimed at bringing the two northern sovereigns into the war in

Germany. Gustav Adolf declared himself willing to accept a subsidy and the sizeable backing of an Anglo-Dutch fleet in the Baltic to secure him against a Danish attack, and proposed to invade Prussia as a prelude to marching into Silesia. The prospect of an invasion of Prussia alarmed the Elector of Brandenburg, whose minister Bellin sought to persuade Gustav Adolf to intervene in north-west Germany. The Swedish king's terms for such an action were also high: an army of 32,000 men, paid in advance, over which he was to have supreme command; bases at Bremen and Wismar; and guarantees for the neutrality of Danzig. Such terms were too much for James I and Georg Wilhelm of Brandenburg. Although Gustav Adolf continued to toy with the idea of involvement in Germany, he was not prepared to play a subordinate role to Christian IV, who in February 1625 concluded an agreement with James I to lead an army into Germany on rather more modest terms than his Swedish rival. As Christian, in his capacity of president of the Lower Saxon Circle, crossed the Elbe and advanced down the Weser valley in the summer of 1625, Gustav Adolf resumed the campaign in Livonia.

Victory at Wallhof in January 1626 enabled the Swedish king to realise an ambition he had long cherished, that of transferring the war to Polish Prussia. The Prussian campaign was not an unmitigated success, though the Swedes more than held their own: Christian IV's campaign was a disaster. Although the remnants of the armies commanded by Count Mansfeld and Christian of Brunswick-Wolfensbüttel joined Christian, there was open discontent in the Lower Saxon Circle, where the towns of Bremen and Lübeck intrigued against the king and Georg of Brunswick-Lüneburg openly sided with the emperor. Denmark's allies were slow in paying subsidies, and Charles I began to lose interest in the whole project. In April 1626, Wallenstein's forces had stopped Mansfeld's advance into Silesia: at the end of August, Christian IV suffered a crushing defeat at the hands of Tilly's Catholic League at the battle of Lutter. With his allies in the Lower Saxon Circle deserting him in droves, the king of Denmark retired beyond the Elbe. In August 1627, Tilly invaded Holstein, to be joined a month later by Wallenstein's Imperial troops. By the end of the year, most of the Jutland peninsula was under their occupation, and the last vestiges of resistance in Germany were being stamped out. The plan hatched in Madrid for a Spanish–German trading company to undermine Dutch trade had also begun to assume more concrete form. Philip IV promised a fleet of twenty-four vessels to reinforce the small Polish navy, and plans for the seizure of the Sound were discussed. Wallenstein, on whom the emperor Ferdinand conferred the titles of duke of Mecklenburg and General of the Oceanic and Baltic Seas in 1628, put pressure on the Hanse towns to furnish ships and to join the planned Spanish–German trading company, and began building ships for the Habsburg navy in Wismar. A French agent in Poland, who urged his government to support Sweden as the one power capable of stopping Habsburg domination of the Baltic, declared in 1626 that the Habsburgs 'wish to make themselves masters of the Baltic sea in order to ruin with one blow all who are opposed to their design'. Three years later, Gustav Adolf told the members of the *råd* that he had long suspected that the emperor 'would be at our throats', and that the events of the previous summer had proved him to be right.[2]

By the autumn of 1629, however, the king of Sweden had already decided upon intervention in Germany. On 12 January 1628, the secret committee of the *riksdag*, to whom the king had spoken at length of the emperor Ferdinand's 'open conspiracy' to deprive Sweden of her trade and sovereign rights in the Baltic, effectively gave Gustav Adolf full authority to take what steps he deemed necessary. The first step to be taken was the conclusion of a three-year alliance with Denmark. In the summer of 1628, the besieged town of Stralsund was relieved by Danish and Swedish troops. This north German port was to become Sweden's first base in Germany, for the Danish troops were withdrawn in the autumn, and the Swedish commander gradually assumed the role of governor of the town.

In the meantime, the war against Poland had encountered several setbacks. Only the vigorous actions of a new commander saved Livonia from falling into Polish hands in the spring of 1628, and the campaign in Prussia was going badly. The financial burden of the war was causing severe discontent at home, and a propagandist had to be sent to tour troubled areas to calm the situation. The problem of financing the war had been raised by the king in a long letter to his chancellor in April 1628. In this letter, Gustav Adolf held out the prospect of creating a powerful base in Prussia, which could sustain the needs of the army and would enable Sweden to command the Baltic coast and to have free access to and from the theatre of opera-

2. Forsten G 1889 *Akty i pis'ma k istorii Baltiyskogo voprosy v XVI i XVII stoletiakh* (2 vols). St Petersburg, vol. 1, p. 236. *Sveriges riksrådets protokoll* (SRP) (18 vols), 1878–1959. Stockholm, Vol. 1: 1621–9, p. 218. The dukes of Mecklenburg were sentenced to be deprived of their title and lands for rebellion against the emperor.

tions. An offensive campaign could thus only be sustained by making war pay for itself (*bellum se ipse alet*).[3]

In the autumn of 1628, however, such notions were far from realisation. The more ambitious of the army estimates in November 1628 spoke of a force of 56,000, of whom 20,000 would be stationed in Stralsund. The chancellor urged the king to finish off the war in Poland, and to remain on the defensive in Stralsund. In a series of meetings of the *råd* at the turn of the year, the arguments for and against intervention in Germany were elaborately debated. The king argued that Sweden had offered the emperor no provocation, for the relief of Stralsund had merely frustrated the unauthorised designs of the emperor's commanders. Ferdinand, however, had aided Zygmunt, impeded the peace in Poland and had threatened Sweden's trade and *dominium maris Baltici*. The threat of war was thus apparent, and the council was asked to discuss three related questions: whether or not the peace should be maintained; if not, whether the Imperialist threat should be met at home or in Germany; and in the latter instance, should the war be conducted defensively or offensively. On 8 January 1629, all the members of the council voted in the king's presence that war should be waged against the emperor in Germany. No Swedish army was to land in northern Germany for a further eighteen months, but the king had successfully manoeuvred the *råd* into a position where they not only endorsed his plans, but assumed collective responsibility for them.[4]

Although a decision in principle had been taken, Gustav Adolf still faced a number of problems. Christian IV concluded peace at Lübeck in May 1629, on terms which obliged him to give up his territorial ambitions in the Lower Saxon Circle, but returned to him all his lands occupied by enemy forces. Although the meeting of the two northern sovereigns at Ulvsbäck parsonage in February conveyed an impression of Nordic unanimity in the face of Imperialist aggression, hard words had been exchanged, and the Swedes continued to harbour deep suspicions of their Jutish arch-enemies. With his forces of occupation now released, Wallenstein was able to send troops to assist the Poles, who had suffered a sharp reverse at Gorzno. These reinforcements did not greatly distinguish themselves, but they did dash any hopes the king of Sweden might have had of opening a campaign

3. *Axel Oxenstiernas skrifter och brevväxling* (AOSB) (27 vols), 1888– (in progress). Stockholm, vol. II:1, pp. 395–400.

4. Ahnlund N 1914 Ófverläggningarna i riksrådet om tyska kriget 1628–29 *Historisk Tidskrift* **34**: 108–23. SRP vol. 1, pp. 123–5. See also the king's letter of 30 December 1628 to Axel Oxenstierna, AOSB, vol. II: 1, pp. 445–53.

in northern Germany in 1629. Sweden's search for allies and financial aid produced meagre results. Above all, the king had still to justify his decision to intervene in Germany to the rest of Europe and to his own people, already weary of the burdens of carrying the costs of war in Prussia. In his concluding speech to the *råd* meeting in November 1629, Gustav Adolf did not shrink from addressing the difficulties of the lack of means with which to fight the war: the sad state of the king of Denmark's realm stood as a warning example to all. The king denied all pretension to glory: he was solely concerned with the welfare and security of the fatherland. At the end of the year, Gustav Adolf suddenly sought to obtain a guarantee of neutrality from Denmark, and proposed a conference in Danzig to settle the differences between himself and the emperor. These manoeuvrings seem to suggest that a degree of uncertainty still hovered in the king's mind about which course to take: but preparations for war continued throughout the winter, and these were 'certeynely not pour faire la monstre nor to conquer the North Pole', as the English ambassador Thomas Roe shrewdly noted.[5]

In one vital area, success was achieved: on 16 September 1629, as a result of French mediation, a truce was finally reached between Sweden and Poland at Altmark. The truce, which was for six years, gave Sweden control of the Prussian littoral; a treaty reached with Danzig the following year allowed Sweden to take the greater share of the 5½ per cent toll collected at that port. The revenue thus gained, when added to the ship-tolls collected from Memel to the Neva, yielded over half-a-million riksdaler in 1629. In the following year, however, the revenue fell to a mere 361,000 riksdaler, largely because of the decline in trade as a result of plague and the threat of war in the Baltic: over two million riksdaler had to be raised at home to keep the army in being. Although the toll revenue rose above the half-million riksdaler mark in 1631 and 1632, this crisis gave added edge to the king's device of making the war self-financing. In order to secure more revenue, even more territory would have to be occupied, which necessitated further recruitment of expensive mercenaries. Even before the German campaign was launched, Gustav Adolf had great problems meeting his dissatisfied troops' demands. Oxenstierna was urged to hold out 'great hopes' of the German war to the unpaid cavalry in Prussia, who could not be paid off because it was not easy to lay hands on ready cash, and who could not be dismissed for fear that their ensuing anger would cause much ill-will and damage to the

5. Cited in Roberts M 1957 *Gustavus Adolphus. A history of Sweden 1611–1632*. London, vol. 2, p. 404.

king's reputation in Germany. The chancellor promised to do what he could, but held out little hope of success.[6]

The control over the harbours of the eastern Baltic which was won in 1629–30 may be seen as supporting that interpretation which sees commercial advantage as the driving force of Swedish foreign policy. It is certainly true that the economic advantages which might accrue from such acquisitions were discussed; but it is also true that military, rather than commercial considerations were usually uppermost in the king's mind. Hence Gustav Adolf visualised the establishment of Swedish control over the Baltic shoreline as a strategic necessity, and the milking of the customs levied in the Baltic ports as a useful means of raising money for the war. Gustav Adolf intervened in Germany to throw back the encroaching threat of the 'universal monarchy'. He wished to put an end to the Habsburg challenge to his claims of *dominium maris*, thereby securing his Swedish realm. On several occasions, he offered to withdraw if adequate security could be provided in northern Germany – by Johann Georg of Saxony, for example, who declined to step into the breach when so asked in September 1630. The shakiness of his finances, the lack of allies and the uncertainties of war clearly persuaded the king of Sweden to adopt cautious and limited objectives in his initial entry into the conflict. There was no mention of freedom of religious conscience in the king's peace programme submitted to the negotiators in Lübeck in January 1629, nor in the proclamation which was issued after the landing at Peenemünde in July 1630. This is not to say that the king was indifferent to the religious issue; but as Axel Oxenstierna told the *råd* in 1637, religion was not the main reason for Sweden's entry into the war, even if it was to be included within the broad framework of the preservation of the security of Sweden and her religious allies. The emperor's Edict of Restitution of 1629, which threatened to destroy the precarious religious settlement in Germany and undermined the particularist rights of the princes, gave new wind to the old rallying-cry of the defence of German liberties. In 1620, Oxenstierna had exclaimed in exasperation that 'truly, with difficulty may a remedy be found, when in the Empire nothing is an empire, nothing is obeyed, there is no authority, and finally, no study of the public good': Gustav Adolf was to discover that there was a great deal of truth in this gloomy assessment of the situation in the Empire.[7]

6. AOSB vol. II: 1, pp. 552–61, vol. I: 5, pp. 158–66.
7. AOSB vol. I: 2, p. 402. Roberts 1957, vol. 2, pp. 417–25. Barudio G 1985 *Gustav Adolf der Grosse. Eine politische Biographie*. Frankfurt-am-Main, pp. 385–404.

Protestant spirits were doubtless lifted by the thunder and lightning which accompanied the landing of the Swedish king at Peenemünde on 26 June 1630: did not the French emissary Charnacé flatter the 'Lion of the North' that he was coming as a Messiah to a land where everyone was his friend? The reality was, however, somewhat different. The Protestant princes of Germany showed little inclination to ally themselves with Sweden: the troops at the king's disposal were too few to force a decisive victory, and yet were costly to maintain. The annual subsidy of 400,000 riksdaler promised by France as part of the five-year alliance concluded in January 1631 was in fact only paid in 1632 and 1633, and was inferior to the sums mulcted from the Prussian tolls: moreover, as the years after 1637 were to show, the payment of such subsidies could also bind Sweden to French designs. The alliance with the aged and childless duke Bogislaw XIV of Pomerania gave Sweden access to the Pomeranian tolls and a cash contribution of 200,000 riksdaler: Gustav Adolf also claimed the right to sequestrate the duchy, as security for compensation for his war expenses, if Georg Wilhelm of Brandenburg (who laid claim to the succession to the title) had not acceded to the treaty on the duke's death. For the time being, however, the Elector of Brandenburg preferred to align himself with the Protestant princes who sought to build up a 'third party' in German affairs.

By the spring of 1631, the Swedish army had succeeded in establishing a bridgehead around the river Oder, and was pushing westwards into Mecklenburg. On 10 May, however, there occurred a catastrophe: the city of Magdeburg, which Gustav Adolf had sworn to relieve, fell to Tilly's army, was mercilessly pillaged and destroyed by fire. The flames which reduced a city of 30,000 inhabitants to ashes seemed also to have consumed the reputation and fortunes of the king of Sweden. In fact, the ultimate loser was Tilly, who was compelled to move his troops away from a once-wealthy city which might have fed and housed his men. During the summer, the Protestant princes began to bestir themselves against the Imperialists. Gustav Adolf forced a passage of the Elbe, literally marching his armies off the maps which they had brought with them: central Germany, with its rich towns, abbeys and churches, lay open to Swedish advance, a tempting new source of supply for the king's growing armies. One by one, the north German princes allied with the Swedish king. In September, Johann Georg of Saxony, his lands invaded by Tilly's men, reached agreement with the Swedes. Electoral Saxony was to be a highly unreliable ally, and the contribution made by the elector's troops at the battle of Breitenfeld on 7 September was an inglorious one: but the

175

day was more than saved by the Swedish forces. As the dusk gathered, over seven thousand of Tilly's army lay dead on the battlefield, thousands more were prisoners-of-war, and Tilly himself was gravely wounded, his reputation as a military commander in tatters.

The victory at Breitenfeld not only established the credentials of the king of Sweden as a supreme military commander; it also gave him political prestige, which enabled him to snap his fingers at Richelieu's attempts to build a new 'third party' around Bavaria, and to impose his own terms upon his German allies. The power which the triumphant monarch appeared to wield from his winter quarters at Mainz was to prove temporary and ultimately, illusory. His opponents had been defeated, but not destroyed. Pappenheim managed to prevent the Lower Saxon circle falling under Swedish control, and threatened Erfurt, a town vital for Swedish communications with the now-distant Baltic coast. The Saxon advance into Bohemia was stemmed by Wallenstein, recalled to command the Imperialist army. The Imperialist advance against Saxony obliged Gustav Adolf to abandon his advance along the line of the Danube, and to dig in outside the walls of Nuremburg. The complex manoeuvres of the armies in the summer of 1632 failed to produce a decisive battle, though disease and desertion reduced the Swedish forces by one-third within a matter of weeks. For a second time, Gustav Adolf was obliged to suspend operations against Bavaria and march north to relieve the pressure on Saxony. On 6 November 1632, battle was joined at Lützen. The armies fought in the fog and smoke until exhausted, and Wallenstein withdrew under cover of darkness. Losses were high on both sides: the Imperialists lost their most brilliant cavalry commander, Pappenheim: but for the Swedes, there was an even greater loss. Caught in a melee, Gustav Adolf had been killed.

The dead king's heir and successor was a six-year-old girl, who was not to assume the reins of power until 1644. The governance of the realm was entrusted to a regency council: the effective ruler of Sweden was the chancellor, Axel Oxenstierna. In contrast to the often impetuous and hot-tempered Gustav Adolf, Oxenstierna had a phlegmatic, even resigned temperament. Whilst the king had occupied centre stage in Germany, the chancellor had played a subsidiary role in Prussia, supervising the collection of the tolls and overseeing the government in Sweden. He had been sceptical of, if not opposed to the king's policy, regarding Denmark and Poland as greater threats than the emperor, and although he came to accept the war in Germany, he did not share Gustav Adolf's vision of a fundamental revision of the constitution of the empire. In the long and wearisome years during which Oxenstierna grappled with the problems of Sweden's involvement in Germany, this vision faded and was replaced by a more straightforward concern for 'satisfaction' and security for Sweden.

In the immediate aftermath of the king's death, Oxenstierna faced two options. Sweden could seek an honourable withdrawal from the conflict, having first obtained the restitution of the pre-1625 status quo in the Upper and Lower Saxon circles, and compensation in the form of the duchy of Pomerania, with a substantial sum of money to pay off the vast armies now under Swedish command: or the chancellor could try to consolidate Gustav Adolf's legacy and secure Swedish hegemony in Germany by means of an evangelical alliance, along the lines indicated in the *Norma futurarum actionum*, drafted in May 1631 at the king's behest, and fleshed out by the king during the last months of his life.[8] Oxenstierna chose the middle way, continuing to follow the general policy and strategic lines laid down by the king, but at the same time reducing purely Swedish involvement. He was particularly anxious to avoid imposing a heavy financial burden upon the homeland, and the loss of the Prussian tolls (which had produced over 600,000 riksdaler annually between 1632 and 1635) in 1635 was a bitter pill for the chancellor to swallow. The constant threat of a resumption of war by Poland also worried the chancellor. 'The Polish war is our own', he wrote in October 1634, 'the German war, I know not what it is, only that we *pro reputatione* spill our blood here, and have nothing more than ingratitude to look forward to.'[9] The League of Heilbronn, concluded with the princes of the four circles of Upper Germany in April 1633, was intended to act as a guarantee against Imperialist aggression and was also a means of shifting the burden of raising and maintaining troops to the German princes: but it was undermined by the very principle it was supposed to uphold, princely particularism. The money was slow to come in, and in the north, Johan Adler Salvius was only able to squeeze 144,000 riksdaler out of the network of client towns and states in 1633, less than a quarter of the sum obtained in 1632. To appease his mutinous troops and discontented officers, Oxenstierna had to resort heavily to donations of lands and revenues, giving away most of Sweden's conquests in the process: and he had to appeal to Stockholm for one million riksdaler to prop up the

---

8. For details of these plans, see Roberts 1957, vol. 2, pp. 504–7, 619–73. Roberts M 1967 The political objectives of Gustav Adolf in Germany, 1630–2 *Essays in Swedish history*. London, pp. 82–110. Barudio 1985, pp. 492–503, 585–601.

9. AOSB, vol. I:12, pp. 632–3.

League, even before the disastrous military defeat suffered at the hands of the Cardinal-Infante at Nördlingen in 1634.

Gustav Adolf's German allies had clung to Sweden out of necessity, not love: and once Swedish military and political hegemony began to founder, they sought their own salvation. Johann Georg of Saxony was especially distrustful of Oxenstierna, whom he rudely dismissed as a *Plackscheisser*: by May 1635, he had made his peace with the emperor at the peace of Prague, an agreement which offered a real possibility for a 'German' settlement of the conflict. Georg Wilhelm of Brandenburg refused to abandon his claim to Pomerania, and was not to be seduced by Oxenstierna's offers of the duchy in return for the cession of Prussia to Sweden. A weakened Sweden had been unable to extend the terms of the Altmark truce: instead, the treaty of Stuhmsdorf obliged the Swedes to relinquish their Prussian bases and the levying of tolls on Prussian ports and Danzig, in return for Poland acknowledging Swedish possession of Livonia. Władysław IV (1632–48), freed of his brief war with Muscovy, was intriguing with Christian IV. The king of Denmark revived the claims of his son to the see of Bremen in 1634, in defiance of the terms of the peace of Lübeck: the chapter, embittered by the high costs of the Swedish occupation, elected prince Frederik, who entered his new see with an armed force. Oxenstierna had no option but to accept this as a *fait accompli*, in order to avoid driving Christian IV into an alliance with Władysław.

By the end of 1635, Sweden's fortunes were at their lowest ebb. The mutinous state of the remaining forces under Swedish control, the lack of effective French support, the parlous financial situation after the loss of the Prussian tolls and the demands of the regency government for peace forced Oxenstierna to negotiate. In adversity, however, he was to prove a formidable opponent. The preliminary round of talks with Johann Georg foundered over the elector's insistence that any settlement would have to be based on the terms of the peace of Prague, which the Swedes believed to be inimical with their desire for security via the restoration of German liberties. A third round of talks began in October 1635, as Swedish troop reinforcements released from Prussia by the terms of the treaty of Stuhmsdorf began to arrive in Germany to stem the Saxon advance against Swedish positions. The cash subsidy offered by France in March 1636 enabled the Swedes to recruit fresh troops, and the victory achieved by Johan Banér at Wittstock redressed the balance in Sweden's favour.

Although Swedish commanders were to achieve further successes in the remaining twelve years of the war, Sweden was no longer perceived as the saviour of the Protestant cause or of German liberties, but rather as a threat to the stability and integrity of the Empire. The peace of Prague offered a possible solution to the conflict between the emperor and the German estates. As Salvius observed, after the peace of Prague Sweden was no longer fighting as a principal, but as an assistant in Germany. It is highly likely that Gustav Adolf, had he lived, would have been compelled to revise or even abandon his plans for a German settlement; but he would have had distinct advantages over his chancellor, who faced increasing opposition to his policies at the court in the 1640s. Gustav Adolf had entered the war with limited objectives. He desired the restitution of the duchy of Mecklenburg to the deposed rulers, and guarantees that the Habsburg plans for a naval presence in the Baltic be abandoned: to this end, he hoped to hold Stralsund and Wismar, which might also check any possible moves by his untrustworthy Danish neighbour. The military campaign to extend the bridgehead around the Oder was accompanied by attempts to force Pomerania and Brandenburg into an alliance which would offer military assistance and sustenance for the king's armies. The former came under Swedish control, but the latter did not, and the claims and counter-claims of the two sides to the Pomeranian lands were to prove a major obstacle to the final conclusion of peace. Military success enabled the king to screw up his terms for alliance, though such high-handed action was not calculated to endear him to the German princes. In the case of Mecklenburg, the king moderated his original demands, but the final treaty in February 1632 was still a stiff one, obliging the dukes to admit Swedish copper at face value, to allow Sweden to collect tolls at the ports, to cede Wismar and Warnemünde for the duration of the war, and entrusting absolute powers of military and political direction to Sweden. During 1632, it became clear that *satisfactio* no longer meant an indemnity, but territorial gains along the Baltic coast, and that *assecuratio* no longer meant security in the form of controls over the Baltic littoral, but a rather ill-defined programme of military and political controls in the heart of Germany.[10]

Undoubtedly, Gustav Adolf's arrogant and at times brutal treatment of those on whom he forced his terms of alliance was ultimately detrimental to the Swedish cause: but his concern for the restoration of German liberties was well founded, since therein lay the best guarantee of Swedish security. Once the aura of victory and the prestige of the Swedes had been tarnished, once the emperor and the princes began to patch up their differences, the notion of security once de-

---

10. Roberts 1957, vol. 2, p. 641. See also Goetze S 1971 *Die Politik des schwedischen Reichskanzlers Axel Oxenstierna gegenüber Kaiser und Reich.* Kiel, pp. 55ff.

scribed by Michael Roberts as 'a sort of miniature NATO for Germany, with Sweden in the role of the United States' was bound to collapse.[11]

The search for security was nevertheless the most intractable of the problems facing Axel Oxenstierna, since, unlike the purely Swedish demands for a *contentement* with which to pay off the troops and territorial *satisfactio*, *assecuratio pacis* was hedged around with time-worn slogans and involved a very large number of states. It took six years before agreement could be reached on the staging of a general peace conference and a further four years of haggling at Osnabrück and Münster before the final terms of the peace of Westphalia could be signed in 1648. Sweden finally settled for an indemnity of five million riksdaler, the western portion of the duchy of Pomerania, the port of Wismar and the secularised bishoprics of Bremen and Verden. Brandenburg acquired the rest of Pomerania and the ecclesiastical lands of Magdeburg, Minden and Halberstadt. The details remained to be worked out, especially the terms upon which the swollen Swedish forces were to be disbanded and paid off. The final terms represented something of a triumph for the aged Swedish chancellor, who had held out against the policy of securing peace by concessions favoured by Salvius and queen Christina: but he was well aware of the enmity Sweden had incurred, not least in regard to the other states on the Baltic. Sweden's new-found status as a European power with a voice in the affairs of the empire was dearly bought.

DANIA

Chief amongst the discontented was the younger son of Christian IV. Until the death of his elder brother in 1647, Frederik had few hopes of succeeding his father to the throne of Denmark, and the loss of his bishopric of Bremen to the Swedes affected him very deeply. This hostility towards Sweden boded ill for future relations between the northern states when Frederik was elected king on his father's death in 1648. Christian's activities after his disastrous incursion into Germany had done little to restore Denmark's prestige or power. His attempts to levy tolls on the upper Elbe angered Hamburg and the maritime states: increased Sound dues alarmed the Dutch, who concluded a fifteen-year defensive alliance with Sweden in 1640: and his naval

11. Roberts M 1973 *Gustavus Adolphus and the rise of Sweden*. London, p. 162.

attack in 1637 on Władysław IV's fleet, which had offended the Danish king's pretensions to *dominium maris* by levying tolls off Danzig, jeopardised any chance of a Polish–Danish alliance. In 1643, Christian began blockading Hamburg, and his emissaries sought to persuade Poland, Muscovy and the emperor to form an anti-Swedish coalition. In May, the Swedish council ordered Lennart Torstensson to launch an attack from the south, through Jutland. Torstensson's armies overran the peninsula, but failed to effect a landing on the islands, and were compelled to withdraw in 1644 by an Imperialist army. At sea, the Danes managed to defeat a fleet equipped by de Geer off the island of Sylt, but were less successful in a battle off Kolberger Heide, the aged king Christian losing an eye in the fighting. Another defeat was inflicted by a Dutch–Swedish fleet off Fehmarn in August, and on land, the Swedes reoccupied the duchies and Jutland in the autumn.

The peace negotiated through Dutch mediation at Brömsebro gave the islands of Gotland and Ösel, and the Norwegian provinces of Jämtland and Härjedalen to Sweden: the province of Halland was also ceded for thirty years. Ships owned by Swedish and Livonian subjects of the queen were to be exempt from the Sound dues, and from inspection of their cargoes. The Dutch, French and English also acquired in subsequent separate negotiations a drastic reduction of the tolls levied upon their shipping. As a result, the revenue from the Sound dues fell from around 405,000 rigsdaler in 1642 to 140,000 rigsdaler in 1646. The loss of territory and the devastation caused by war further plunged Denmark into financial crisis. The sick and ailing king failed in 1647 to push through a reform of the *len* system, and was much afflicted by the sudden death of his eldest son, prince Christian. Christian IV's last years were also plagued by quarrels with his daughters. In spite of these royal wranglings, the husbands of two of these daughters came to occupy central positions in the administration of the realm, Hannibal Sehested as governor of Norway and Korfits Ulfeldt as the High Steward (*rigshofmester*). Ulfeldt had attempted to forge an alliance with France and the United Provinces in 1647, but growing tensions between the Dutch and French nullified this ambition. Christian IV was also reluctant to conclude an alliance with the Dutch, or to agree to Ulfeldt's plan for a redemption treaty, which would have allowed the Dutch free passage through the Sound in return for an annual cash payment. His successor was less hostile, and in 1649 Ulfeldt succeeded in concluding with the Dutch a defensive alliance for thirty-six years, and a redemption agreement, to run for the same period. In return for exemption for Dutch ships from the

Sound dues, the United Provinces were to pay 140,000 rigsdaler annually, with an advance payment of 100,000 rdr, plus a further 200,000 rdr on ratification of the agreement.

Although the redemption treaty was not ratified by the provinces until 1651, and was scrapped two years later, it alarmed the Swedes, already irritated by the Dutch practice of levying duties on foreign shipping leaving their ports for the Baltic. During the first Anglo-Dutch war (1652–4), Sweden fended off Dutch efforts to create a triple alliance of the northern kingdoms and the United Provinces. Bulstrode Whitelocke's embassy of 1653–4 was cordially received, but the Swedes were in no hurry to conclude an agreement with Cromwellian England. The treaty finally signed in the summer of 1654 confined itself largely to professions of amity and promises of better trading relations.

If the Dutch were unable to persuade Sweden to depart from a policy of neutrality, they had rather more success in Denmark. A fleet of English merchantmen awaiting convoy was detained in Copenhagen, provoking the Commonwealth to respond by expelling the Danish minister and seizing Danish and Norwegian vessels in English ports. In 1653, a Danish fleet patrolled the Kattegat and the Sound was closed to English shipping. The prospect of Denmark being drawn into the war caused disquiet in Sweden, where the uncertainties of the domestic situation and the continued deadlock in negotiations with Poland at Lübeck persuaded the government to proceed cautiously. Axel Oxenstierna was dogged by ill-health, and did not enjoy the full confidence of the queen, whose intrigues with the Spanish ambassador did little to inspire confidence amongst the representatives of the other powers. In such circumstances, a policy of neutrality was the wisest option. Nothing came of talks with a Danish embassy to Stockholm (Oxenstierna privately dismissing the leader of the embassy as better suited to understanding stock-rearing than diplomacy). Sweden would not be drawn into a triple alliance with Denmark and the United Provinces, though the inclusion of Denmark as a signatory of the peace treaty between the States-General and the Commonwealth was welcomed in Stockholm as a guarantee of peace in the Baltic.

The acquisition of new territories from Denmark and in the Empire did nothing to quell the Swedes' obsession with security. The policy of consolidation and the maintenance of the status quo pursued during the last years of Christina's reign was only partially successful: settlement with Poland–Lithuania in particular proved impossible to achieve. In the autumn of 1652, in the face of threatened hostilities in the Baltic, the *riksdag* had approved a royal proposition for a programme of rearmament and increased naval and military expenditure. This measure may have been a concrete expression of Sweden's armed neutrality in the Anglo-Dutch war, but it also may be seen as an indication of Sweden's readiness to embark upon an active and aggressive foreign policy at some future date. As Christer Bonde observed in December 1654, peace was costly and did nothing to preserve the security, respect and reputation of the state.[12] That Sweden could not sit quietly by when the clouds of war began massing on the eastern horizon was taken for granted by the council nobility: even those who argued in favour of a pacific policy recognised the need for mobilisation as the Russian–Polish conflict threatened to spill over into the Baltic region.

POLONIA

Since the conclusion of the truce of Altmark in 1629, Sweden and Poland–Lithuania had remained at peace. The Polish–Lithuanian nobility, many of whom owned vast estates on the eastern frontier, were not disposed to endorse their sovereign's quarrel with the Swedish Vasas, and Władysław IV had been obliged to drop his family's claims to the Swedish throne in his *pacta conventa* of 1632. Sweden's relations with Muscovy had also remained good after the peace of Stolbova. Gustav Adolf's agent Anthoni Monier was dispatched to Moscow in 1630 to buy up large amounts of grain which the Swedish crown hoped to resell at a fat profit in Amsterdam: Monier was also instructed to press the tsar to take the offensive against Poland when the truce between the two countries expired. The Swedish king also provided military advice and permitted Scots officers such as Alexander Leslie to enter Russian service. His death at Lützen, however, dashed the prospects of a joint Russo-Swedish assault on Poland. The Russians besieged but failed to take Smolensk in 1633, and were obliged to abandon their claims to the city in the peace treaty with Poland, signed in 1634.

The relative calm in eastern Europe was disrupted in the late 1640s by the revolt against Polish rule of the Zaporozhian Cossacks, led by

12. Olofsson S 1957 *Efter Westfaliska freden. Sveriges yttre politik 1650–1654.* Stockholm, pp. 298ff. Åsard B 1970 Upptakten till Karl X Gustavs anfall mot Polen 1655. Till frågan om krigets mål och medel *Karolinska Förbundets Årsbok*, pp. 7–20. SRP vol. XVI, pp. 13–14.

Bogdan Khmelnitsky. Tsar Aleksey was at first reluctant to support the rebels, whose alliance with the Crimean Tatars he viewed with some suspicion, but by the autumn of 1653 he was prepared to offer protection to the Cossacks and to take the field against Poland–Lithuania. In January 1654, the Ukrainian lands were placed under Muscovy's protection as an autonomous entity by the terms of the agreement of Pereyaslavl. In the spring and summer of that year, Russian troops invaded and occupied large tracts of White Russia, including Smolensk, and began to move towards the upper reaches of the river Düna.

Karl Gustav succeeded his cousin Christina as ruler of Sweden in June 1654, as the eastern crisis was beginning to unfold. Thirty-two years of age, the son of the Count Palatine of Zweibrücken and Gustav Adolf's sister Katarina, Karl Gustav had served with distinction in the Swedish armies during the Thirty Years' War. His military background undoubtedly influenced his ultimate decision to seek a resolution of Sweden's foreign policy needs in expansion by force of arms, though he was sufficiently well-versed in the politics of persuasion to obtain the wholehearted consent of the *råd* for such a policy. Polish historians have been inclined to portray Karl X Gustav as bent on war with Poland from the very outset. The Swedish historian Nils Edén, on the other hand, found nothing in his initial actions to suggest that this was so, a view supported by Bohdan Kentrschynskyj. More recently, however, Birger Åsard has argued that the essential decisions for a war against Poland were taken in 1652, when the secret committee of the *riksdag* approved a programme of increased military expenditure, and that Karl Gustav was merely following a policy already staked out. Troop reinforcements were sent into Livonia and Pomerania even before Christina's abdication, foreshadowing the eventual plan of attack on Poland which was put into operation in 1655.[13]

The meeting of the *råd* in December 1654 has generally been seen as the crucial stage in Sweden's involvement in the eastern conflict, though opinions have differed as to the king's motives. Some historians have claimed that the decision to mobilise was the real issue, not the debate over the future direction of Swedish policy, which others have seen as the crucial feature of the meeting. The king himself did

---

13. See for example Kubala L 1914 *Wojna szwecka w roku 1655 i 1656*. Lwów: Nowak T 1957 Geneza agresij szwedzkiej, in Lepszy K (ed.) *Polska w okresie drugiej wojny północnej 1655–1660* (3 vols). Warsaw, vol. 1, pp. 83–136. Edén N 1906 Grunderna för Karl X Gustafs anfall på Polen *Historisk Tidskrift* **26**: 5–45. Kentrschynskyj B 1956 Karl X Gustav inför krisen i östen 1654–1655 *Karolinska Förbundets Årsbok*, pp. 7–140. Åsard 1970, pp. 34, 53–6.

not participate in the meetings, which were carefully steered along by his senior officials. At the first session, on 8 December, the chancellor constantly reminded the more bellicose members that they were discussing mobilisation, not war. The mood of the meeting was not particularly aggressive, though there was general agreement with the king's opinion, as transmitted by his chancellor, that it was reasonable to make defensive preparations in view of the proximity of hostilities to Swedish territory. Military preparedness, as the Steward Per Brahe reminded his audience, was a costly business. Raising troops at great expense, and then leaving them to stand around idle, was tantamount to waging war on oneself. The members of the council assented to the proposition that Sweden should arm, and acknowledged that the greater danger lay in the east, but failed to arrive at any satisfactory conclusion with regard to the follow-up question of whether Sweden should prepare for a defensive or an offensive campaign in the east. When the debate was renewed on 11 December, a majority of councillors supported mobilisation against Muscovy and Poland, but a number strongly advised against war for financial reasons, and others warned of the continuing threat from Denmark. The general view of the meeting was that Sweden should arm in order to force concessions from Poland. On 12 December, the king went a step further. Through the chancellor, he posed the question of what would happen if Jan Kazimierz agreed to abandon claims to Livonia and the Swedish crown. Should Sweden not seek to obtain something to cover the costs of mobilisation and to provide greater security against Poland in future? The king left the councillors in no doubt that he favoured an aggressive policy, and a majority sided with this view. No decision was taken on war – as the chancellor pointed out, the consent of the estates was needed for this – but by agreeing to mobilisation, the council had effectively committed Sweden to such a course of action.[14]

Against whom it was intended to use the Swedish forces is also a matter of some debate. Kentrschynskyj believes that, in spite of the failure to reach agreement with a Polish embassy sent to Stockholm in the winter of 1654–5, Karl Gustav and the *råd* still sought an accord with Poland, a view which is not generally shared by Swedish historians, for whom the military considerations are of primary importance. Thus, for Birger Åsard, Karl Gustav's plan for a pincer action

14. In addition to the works cited above, see also Landberg H 1968 Decemberrådslagen 1654. Karl X Gustav, rådet och rustningsfrågan *Karolinska Förbundets Årsbok*, pp. 43–68. SRP vol. XVI, pp. 2–36. Roberts 1968, pp. 163–9, for translated extracts of the debate.

designed to control the coastline from Stettin to Riga was 'a decisive step towards the realisation of the old Great Swedish dream of the Baltic Sea as a Swedish lake', a limited objective which was ruined when crushing military victories and the internal disintegration of the Polish–Lithuanian Commonwealth persuaded the king to embark on a more ambitious venture.[15]

In July 1655, field marshal Arvid Wittenberg crossed the Oder with a force of 14,000 men, mostly drawn from units in Bremen and Pomerania. Within a month, Great Poland had fallen under his control, and the magnates had ackowledged Karl Gustav's suzerainty. In Lithuania, the hetman Janusz Radziwiłł signed an act of submission on 18 August: de la Gardie's army occupied most of Samogitia. The royal army, landing at Wolgast and marching through Great Poland, joined up with Wittenberg's troops at Konin on 24 August, and the Swedish forces drove relentlessly southwards. Warsaw was occupied without a fight on 8 September, and the main Polish army was defeated at Zarnów. By the end of autumn, Jan Kazimierz had been driven into Silesia, Cracow had capitulated, and most of the magnates had sworn allegiance to Karl Gustav. Wittenberg had been instructed in August to sound out the possibility of the Polish nobility accepting Karl Gustav as their hereditary monarch, and Schering Rosenhane had included the replacement of Jan Kazimierz by the Swedish king – or another elected by the Poles themselves – as two of the possible options open to Karl Gustav. The king's intentions are by no means clear, though the wholesale desertion of Jan Kazimierz and the flattering approaches of Khmelnitsky evidently tempted him to embark on a far more radical political course than he had originally contemplated. plated.

Jan Kazimierz was not the only prince with whom Karl Gustav had to deal. Frederick William of Brandenburg–Prussia, who disposed of a not inconsiderable army, was attempting to sell his support to the highest bidder. In negotiations at Stettin in July 1655, the Swedes had offered Frederick William sovereignty over Prussia and Ermland, minus the town of Braunsberg, in return for the elector providing an armed force of 8,000 men. Sweden would take Royal Prussia and Pomerelia, which Frederick William not unnaturally feared would cut off his lines of communication between Brandenburg and Prussia.

15. Åsard 1970, p. 53. Wittrack G 1920 Karl X Gustaf och Polen *Karolinska Förbundets Årsbok*, pp. 5ff. Wimmer J 1973 Polens krig med Sverige 1655–1660 – operativ översikt, in Stade A, Wimmer J (eds) *Polens krig med Sverige 1655–1660* Carl X Gustaf-Studier 5 Kristianstad, pp. 332–4.

Karl Gustav was suspicious of the negotiations taking place at the same time between Brandenburg and the Dutch, which resulted in a defensive alliance. Strengthened by this, Frederick William demanded the whole of Ermland and Elbing, part of Samogitia and a guaranteed line of communication across the Vistula. Karl Gustav, at the pinnacle of success in Poland, refused to accept these demands, and the talks were broken off. At the end of October 1655, Karl Gustav, leaving Wittenberg in command in southern Poland, turned north to deal with the elector. Hemmed in by the Swedish armies, Frederick William was obliged to sign an agreement in January 1656 at Königsberg, whereby Sweden assumed sovereignty over Prussia, and the elector promised military and financial aid to his new overlord.

The tide of war had now begun to turn against the Swedish king. A Swedish attempt to seize the monastery of Jasna Góra at Częstochowa provided Jan Kazimierz's propagandists with a welcome opportunity to play upon religious and patriotic sentiment. Guerrilla warfare had already broken out in areas occupied by the Swedes, and in order to hold these regions, Karl Gustav was obliged to scatter his forces in garrisons and strongholds. His campaign against Lublin and Lwów in the early months of 1656 ended in failure, with the army cut down by disease and the incessant attacks of Czarniecki's guerrillas. By the summer, Great Poland was in revolt, and the Swedish garrison in Warsaw had been forced to surrender. In order to preserve the loyalty of Frederick William, Sweden offered the four counties of Great Poland in return for military assistance. In a bloody three-day battle (18–20 July 1656), the Brandenburg–Swedish troops defeated the Polish army outside Warsaw. Frederick William was however unwilling to pursue the war any deeper into southern Poland, and Karl Gustav now faced a new enemy in the east. Annoyed by Karl Gustav's intrigues with Khmelnitsky, tsar Aleksey launched an offensive along the line of the Düna in June, capturing Dünaburg and Kokenhusen, and laying siege to Riga at the end of August. The elector's representatives signed an agreement with the tsar in his camp outside Riga, offering neutrality in return for a Russian promise not to attack Prussia. A truce was also agreed between Poland and Muscovy in October, with both sides promising mutual assistance in the fight against Sweden. The emperor Ferdinand III also concluded a treaty of assistance with Jan Kazimierz. Frederick William took full advantage of Sweden's waning fortunes to obtain a promise of full sovereignty over Prussia from Karl Gustav in return for assistance in Royal Prussia. Karl Gustav's only diplomatic success was an alliance with George Rákóczi, prince of Transylvania, who invaded southern Poland early in 1657. Several fruitless months of campaigning across Poland failed to bring the Swedes a decisive victory. A Russian force had taken Dorpat in October 1656, and Ingria and the province of Kexholm were also attacked. More ominously, Frederik III of Denmark was beginning to prepare for war.

In terms not dissimilar to those presented to the Swedish *råd* in December 1654, Frederik asked the *rigsråd* in September 1656 to agree to a programme of increased military expenditure. The council advised the king to seek to rectify Danish grievances by negotiation, warning him that the approaching winter and the general poverty of the country made recruitment of an army inadvisable. Denmark had earlier joined forces with the Dutch in seeking to maintain freedom of navigation in the Baltic, but the Dutch were unwilling to break with Sweden and obtained assurances of most favoured nation status for their merchantmen and free passage to Danzig from the Swedes in the treaty of Elbing (1 September 1656). Frederik III's attempts to secure allies bore little fruit. The Dutch turned down his request for assistance, Ferdinand III was unwilling to upset the Westphalian settlement by supporting Frederik's claims to Bremen, and an embassy to Moscow returned with little to show for its pains. The estates met at Odense in February 1657, and, fearing an impending Swedish attack, were more than usually generous in voting contributions. However, it was not decided whether these funds were to be used for an offensive war or to defend the kingdom. The council finally declared its willingness to support the king if he resolved 'to use the means which God and nature has placed in His Majesty's hands to seek satisfaction... and bring his land and subjects into a contented and secure state', a less than enthusiastic endorsement for what proved to be a disastrous war for Denmark.[16] Bereft of allies, short of money, with ill-trained troops commanded by officers of poor quality, Frederik III declared war on 1 June. The main objective of the campaign was the seizure of Bremen-Verden. Anders Bille, commanding the army in Holstein, was unsure of what he was supposed to do and believed that the Swedes would not attack. By 9 July, however, the fortress of Bremervörde had been taken, and only Stade held out. Karl Gustav broke up camp in Bromberg on 26 June, and had reached the western border of Pomerania two weeks later. The Holstein frontier was crossed on 22 July by an army of 9,000 men, before which Bille deemed it prudent to retreat. The Jutland peninsula was overrun by

---

16. Fridericia J 1975 *Adelsvældens sidste Dage. Danmarks Historie fra Christian IV's Død til Enevældens Indførelse (1648–1660)* (reprint of 1894 edn). Copenhagen, p. 252.

the Swedish forces in the autumn, whilst the main Danish army lay behind the walls of the Fredriksodde fort. Only in Halland did the Danes enjoy a modest degree of success.

Karl Gustav was anxious to deliver the decisive blow as soon as possible, for his enemies were massing behind him. Rákóczi had been driven out of Poland, and the remaining Swedish forces were confined to Royal Prussia, which was attacked by Imperial and Polish forces in autumn 1657. Swedish Pomerania and Livonia were also invaded, and Frederick William, having achieved the promise of full sovereignty over Prussia at the treaty of Wehlau, allied with Jan Kazimierz. On the Karelian frontier, Gustav Horn sought valiantly to hold the line against Russian attacks, and countermanded several orders to transfer troops from Finland for the defence of Livonia. Oliver Cromwell, having politely declined Karl Gustav's offer of North Jutland, or a share in the partitioned Danish lands, issued a warrant for equipping a fleet to aid Sweden in October, when it appeared as if the Dutch were going to assist Denmark. When it became evident that the Dutch were not going to war, Cromwell backed away, and sought to assuage the Swedish king with vague promises of financial aid. As the Swedes stormed Fredriksodde and prepared to launch an invasion of the Danish islands, the Dutch and English began to draw together in order to mediate in a conflict which threatened to disrupt their trade routes in the Baltic.

An exceptionally hard winter proved to be Sweden's greatest ally. At the end of January, the Swedes crossed the frozen sea to Fyn, and quickly overran the island. At the beginning of February, the army advanced via Langeland to Lolland, a crossing vividly described by the French emissary, de Terlon: 'The many horses which the king had with him had so trampled down the snow along the route that there was at least two feet of water on the surface of the ice. There was a terrible fear of stepping into the open sea...'[17] As Swedish forces began to pour into the island of Sjælland, Frederik III decided to sue for peace. A preliminary truce was signed on 18 February, and was converted into a peace at Roskilde. Denmark was obliged to cede the provinces of Skåne, Blekinge, Halland, Bornholm, Bohus and Trondheim to Sweden. Frederik III also had to restore Korfits Ulfeldt to his titles and estates, to renounce his claims of overlordship over the ducal parts of Slesvig, and provide two thousand horse for the king of Sweden's use.

Denmark had been resoundingly defeated, and a truce concluded

17. Cited in Ellehøj S 1964 *Danmarks historie. 1596–1660.* Copenhagen, p. 478.

with the Russians in the summer of 1658; but there still remained the powerful coalition of Austria, Brandenburg and Poland. After the conclusion of the peace at Roskilde, Karl Gustav planned to direct an offensive against Frederick William, hoping to secure the Prussian ports and their toll revenues. Having lost control of most of Poland–Lithuania, Karl Gustav began to cast around for ways of relieving the burden of maintaining his armies in the field. On 20 June, the king asked the *råd* if the small points of dispute with Denmark should be set aside, or if Sweden should seek to obtain satisfaction by force. Four days later, the *råd* agreed upon action. The maintenance of troops in Denmark was costly, and provisions hard to come by. At a meeting of a section of the council in Gottorp on 7 July, the king raised the prospect of compensation from Denmark if the fortress of Thorn fell to the Austrian and Polish besieging army. It was agreed that if the Swedish commissioners had not reached agreement with the Danes over the terms of the peace treaty, they were not to do so, and Sweden would prepare for war against Denmark. At Wismar on 23 July, plans for the complete subjugation of Denmark were discussed. Two weeks later, the Swedish fleet arrived off Korsør harbour on the west coast of Sjælland. The fortress of Kronborg surrendered to the Swedes in September, and the city of Copenhagen was placed under siege.

The first war against Sweden had aroused much anger and resentment against the king and his councillors in Denmark. Pasquinades nailed to the doors of churches and houses in the capital denounced the councillors as spineless and dishonourable traitors to the realm, and the king himself was deeply unpopular. Karl Gustav's brutal assault in the summer of 1658 wrought a dramatic change. The burghers of Copenhagen rallied to the defence of their city, and pledged their support to the king (for which they were rewarded with sweeping new privileges which breached noble prerogatives). Frederik III was not entirely without external allies. The United Provinces agreed to send a fleet and troops to relieve Copenhagen, a mission which was duly accomplished in October 1658. Frederick William had also crossed the Holstein frontier with an army of 30,000 men in September. These troops, however, failed to effect a crossing of the Belts to eject the Swedish forces from the islands. Relations between the emperor Leopold and the elector became strained, with the former wishing to remove his troops from the Jutland peninsula to attack Swedish Pomerania, a move not favoured by Frederick William. The Dutch also grew cool towards the Danes, and in concert with the English, sought to mediate. By July 1659, the terms of a peace had been worked out in The Hague, and put to the warring sovereigns, with the threat of action by an Anglo-Dutch fleet if one or both refused to accept the terms. Frederik III declared his willingness to abide by them, causing the collapse of preliminary peace talks with Sweden. Although Karl Gustav refused to be bound by the concert, the Anglo-Dutch cooperation began to come apart, as Montague sailed home with the bulk of his fleet to prepare the way for the Restoration. Mazarin, although not officially a party to the concert, did not wish pressure to be brought to bear on Sweden. The Dutch, however, were prepared to resupply Copenhagen and to take action against the Swedes. In October 1659, a Danish–Dutch force assembled in Kiel was landed on Fyn, where the Swedish forces were defeated outside Nyborg. Emboldened by these successes, Frederik III sought to enlist the aid of the Dutch in squeezing concessions from Sweden at the peace talks which began soon after the premature death of Karl Gustav in February 1660. The Dutch were not willing to prolong a costly war, especially in view of the likelihood of conflict with France, now at peace with Spain and working in the Swedish interest.

The peace of Copenhagen restored Trondheim and Bornholm to Denmark, but the Danish provinces on the eastern shores of the Sound were to remain under Swedish rule, and the duke of Holstein-Gottorp's sovereignty over the ducal lands in Slesvig was once more confirmed. Peace between Austria, Brandenburg, Poland and Sweden was restored through French mediation at Oliva in May 1660. Jan Kazimierz abandoned his claims to Livonia and the Swedish throne, and all parties acknowledged the sovereignty of the Elector of Brandenburg over Prussia. Finally, peace was signed in 1661 between Sweden and Muscovy at Kardis, the Russians agreeing to a restoration of the territorial status quo. The war between Muscovy and Poland was finally brought to an end at the treaty of Andrusovo in 1667, Poland ceding Smolensk and territories in White Russia.

Poland and Denmark emerged from the wars with considerable losses of territory and prestige. Frederik III was able to use the experiences of war to his own advantage, however, establishing an absolutist monarchy which was to last for almost two centuries. Jan Kazimierz, the last of the Polish Vasas, ultimately abandoned the Polish crown. His successor, Michael Korybut Wiśniowiecki (1669–73), sought to revise the terms of the treaty of Wehlau, by which Prussia had ceased to be a Polish fief; but the incipient threat of civil war and the ever-present Turkish menace obliged him to give way. Jan Sobieski (1674–96) concluded an alliance with Louis XIV in 1675, and at Danzig two years later reached agreement with the Swedes, promising support in an attack on Prussia, which was to revert to

Poland. A strong pro-Hohenzollern faction in the *sejm* opposed this policy, urging the king to join Sweden's enemies and seize Livonia. The Swedish assault on Prussia in the winter of 1677–8 received no support from Sobieski, whose attentions were now fixed on combatting the Turkish advance.

SUECIA

The immense strain of incessant warfare upon a country poor in resources and manpower now began to tell upon Sweden. In a memorial written in 1661, the treasurer Gustav Bonde advanced a programme of retrenchment and reform. Sweden had:

> learned by experience that no war in past times has brought renown, profit or advantage to king and country, without also exacting large annual expenditure of our resources, and burdening the subject with taxes and conscriptions...so that when our gains are measured against our sacrifices, they appear sufficiently dearly bought. It seems therefore necessary that we make up our minds to a period of peace, and lay aside all thought of war as long as peace is to be had...'.[18]

The problem was that the maintenance of peace also involved the preservation of Sweden's security, which an impoverished country could not easily sustain from its own resources. At first, the regency government attempted to follow a pacific, non-aligned policy. In 1661, a defensive alliance and trade treaty was concluded with England. The Swedes refused to join the Danes and Dutch in closing the Sound to English shipping in 1666, and helped mediate the peace settlement at Breda. In 1668, in spite of the chancellor Magnus de la Gardie's preference for alignment with France, Sweden joined the Maritime Powers. Anglo-Dutch rivalry, the unwillingness of the Dutch to make concessions over trade, and the skilful diplomacy of Louis XIV's ministers served to undermine this triple alliance. By 1672, Charles II had shifted into the French camp, followed by a number of north German princes. Fearing that France would seek the friendship of Denmark if Sweden did not respond favourably to Louis XIV's offers of an alliance, de la Gardie persuaded his fellow-councillors in April 1672 to join France. Something of the decayed state of Sweden is conveyed by the report of Honoré de Courtin to Louis XIV after the conclusion of the agreement:

18. Cited by Roberts 1968, p. 173. See Wittrack G 1913 Riksskattmästaren Gustaf Bondes politiska programm 1661 *Historisk Tidskrift* **33**: 42–54.

Sweden is in the last stages of impotence, one cannot be in Stockholm without being convinced that she is in no state to make herself feared. Her poverty is so great that for the last fortnight they have been reduced to looking for people who can make advances on the subsidy which Your Majesty has promised to pay.[19]

At first, it appeared as if Sweden might avoid direct involvement in the hostilities which began with the French attack on the United Provinces. Within two years, however, Brandenburg and Denmark had joined the growing anti-French coalition, and Louis XIV was pressing his northern ally to intervene, threatening to withhold the subsidies unless Swedish troops attacked Brandenburg. In the end, the expense of maintaining an army in the field drove the Swedish commander in Pomerania to invade Brandenburg. The defeat inflicted on the Swedish forces by the Great Elector's army at Fehrbellin in 1675 persuaded Christian V of Denmark to attack Sweden in an attempt to regain the lost provinces. The duke of Holstein-Gottorp was captured by the invading Danish army, and forced to sign an agreement restoring Danish overlordship over his lands in Slesvig. Wismar was occupied by Danish troops in October, and most of Sweden's north German possessions were overrun by the troops of the Great Elector, the duke of Brunswick-Lüneburg and the bishop of Münster. A Danish–Dutch fleet inflicted a heavy defeat on the Swedes off Öland in June 1676, whilst in Skåne, only Malmö remained in Swedish hands. The only crumb of comfort for Sweden was a military success at the end of the year. The battle of Lund probably saved Skåne for Sweden, and it undoubtedly enhanced the prestige of the young king, Karl XI. A bitter guerrilla war, fought between Swedish troops and local peasants, raged in the province for the next two years. Sweden managed to hang on, but suffered the humiliation of having to accept peace terms dictated by Louis XIV at Fontainebleau. Denmark failed to regain the lost provinces, and had to restore the duke of Holstein-Gottorp to full sovereignty over the ducal possessions in Slesvig: Frederick William managed to obtain the right bank of the Oder in Pomerania.

As had occurred in Denmark twenty years earlier, setbacks in war were laid at the door of the council nobility, and the king of Sweden was able to effect a radical shift in the balance of power. The reforms set in train during the remainder of Karl XI's reign enabled Sweden to pursue a more independent line in foreign policy, though the country still faced the problem of maintaining the security of an empire whose southern outposts were always vulnerable to attack by ambitious

19. Cited in Nordmann C 1971 *Grandeur et liberté de la Suède (1660–1792)*. Paris, p. 66.

rivals. Axel Oxenstierna's dictum: 'when things are going well, we must think of peace, but when things are going badly, we must set our heads against giving way too easily', served Sweden well enough as long as she had the means and resources to manoeuvre.[20] Sweden was able to emerge from the Thirty Years' War with territories in northern Germany, and an indemnity of five million riksdaler to cover her military expenses, by virtue of her military prowess and the weakness and exhaustion of the other states over whose territories the campaigns had been waged. The defence of these acquisitions in peacetime imposed burdens which Sweden alone was unable to bear. The bastions on the north German coast which served Sweden as points of entry into Europe had to be garrisoned and fortified, since they had no natural defences and were vulnerable to attack from all quarters. Karl X Gustav calculated that the defence of Pomerania would require 8,000 men in peacetime and 17,000 in time of war, and yet Pomerania suffered invasion in 1659 and again in 1677. The possession of Pomerania incurred the lasting enmity of the Great Elector and his successors. The see of Bremen also caused problems. In 1671, Gustav Kurck estimated that it might take as long as seven months to reinforce the garrison from Sweden; Karl Gustav had toyed with the idea of handing over Bremen and Verden to Cromwell in return for financial assistance, and a proposal to hand the bishoprics over to England for the duration of the war was mooted in 1675. Sweden enjoyed little political advantage within the Empire; the role of leader of the evangelical cause had already suffered a severe battering during the 1630s, and after 1648, Sweden tended to side with the emperor in upholding the status quo against the particularist pretensions of the princes. The balance of power in Europe had shifted decisively westwards, towards the France of Louis XIV and the Maritime Powers. The latter had shown at the decisive stages of Karl Gustav's wars that they were prepared to intervene in order to safeguard their commercial interests in the Baltic, whilst the former's largesse proved too tempting to an impoverished state striving to keep its enemies at bay.

> Le plus sage au conseil, le premier aux hazards,
> Mes vertus ont esteint le lustre des Cezars.
> Et rendu l'univers estonné de ma gloire.
> Quel siecle void jamais vng si grand conquerant?[21]

20. SRP, vol. VI, p. 621.
21. Forsten 1889, vol. 2, p. 154.

These lines, placed in the mouth of the dead Swedish king by a French admirer, undoubtedly expressed the feelings of many contemporaries, but posterity has been less kind in its judgement. Gustav Adolf's grandiose venture into the heart of Europe may have brought Sweden respect and renown, but it is hard to avoid the conclusion, as did Gustav Bonde, that Sweden had to pay a high price for its reputation. The intricate pattern of alliances constructed in western Europe by Louis XIV ensured that Sweden might at least hang on to her north German possessions, for Sweden was a useful counter-balance to Brandenburg–Prussia and the north German princes. In order to maintain the defences of these German outposts, however, Sweden neglected the defences of the eastern frontier, and it was in the east that the danger now lay. Plans for a Russian fleet in the Baltic had already been discussed in the 1660s, and Ordyn-Nashchokin, the architect of the treaty of Andrusovo, sought to persuade Poland to join forces against Sweden. The conflict in the Ukraine and the threat of the Tatars drew Muscovy's attention southwards, but under a determined ruler eager to bring his country into the orbit of the West, the drive towards the Baltic coastline which had been terminated at Stolbova was to be resumed.

CHAPTER EIGHT

The Military State

ESTATES AND RULERS

'Alliances, to be sure, are good, but forces of one's own still better,' wrote Frederick William, elector of Brandenburg, in 1667: 'Upon them one can rely with more security, and a lord is of no consideration if he does not have means and troops of his own.' This dictum was fervently endorsed by his grandson sixty years later, when he advised his heir always to keep up a large and efficient army: money and a good army ensured the glory and safety of a prince.[1] Frederick William had inherited a parlous situation in 1640. His father's scattered territories had been ravaged and bled dry during the previous decade. Much of Brandenburg was occupied by Swedish troops, revenues had been reduced to a pittance, and the few troops at the elector's disposal were dissolute and unreliable. When he died in 1688, he had an army of around 30,000 men, and his own authority and powers as ruler had been decisively strengthened. His successors were able to double the size of the army, and to establish the principle of universal obligation to serve in the ranks. The Brandenburg–Prussian officer corps was on the way to becoming the first estate in the land, 'not only the soul of the army, but also the training-ground [*Pflanzschule*] for the idea of the Prussian state amongst the hitherto particularist nobility of the scattered territories', in the words of Otto Hintze.[2]

The creation of a large and reliable army by the Great Elector was not achieved without a struggle. The ruinous state of the country and

---

1. Cited in Craig G 1964 *The politics of the Prussian army 1640–1945* (revised ed). New York, p. 2, 7–8.
2. Hintze O 1967 *Regierung und Verwaltung. Gesammelte Abhandlungen zur Staats-Rechts- und Sozialgeschichte Preussens* (3 vols). Göttingen, vol. 1, p. 14.

its administration had offered Frederick William an opportunity to restore a level of confidence between the ruler and the estates, and he was not slow to take it. He acted with vigour to restore some semblance of order, concluding a truce with Sweden and dismissing the unruly mercenary officers who had terrorised his subjects. His father's adviser, Count Schwartzenberg, had been allowed to bypass the privy council in Brandenburg, and his war council was staffed almost exclusively with foreign nobles or commoners. After Schwartzenberg's death in 1641, the war council was dissolved, officials dismissed or retired, and the privy council restored to favour. The estates of Brandenburg were happy to vote the supplies necessary to allow the rebuilding of the army, and by 1648, Frederick William had a small but reliable force of 8,000 men at his disposal. The Brandenburg diet squeezed considerable concessions from the elector in 1653, for in return for a grant of 530,000 thaler, payable over six years, Frederick William made sweeping concessions to the noble landowners, abandoned tax reform and the introduction of an excise. The ultimate victor, however, proved to be the elector, for with the money grant he was able to lay the foundations for a standing army. The outbreak of war in 1655 enabled him to build up a sizeable force, which he financed through extraordinary taxes and levies, imposed against the protests of the Brandenburg estates. Although there were reductions in the size of the army after 1660, Frederick William was still able to maintain a force of between seven and twelve thousand men, which he expanded considerably during the wars of the 1670s.

In seeking to create a reliable standing army, rulers were liable to clash with their subjects, upon whom rested the burden of maintaining such a force. The outcome of the conflicts between ruler and estates varied according to their relative strengths and weaknesses. The Great Elector was able not only to build up a sizeable army; he also gained the upper hand over the estates, asserting his authority and laying the foundations of the Prussian military state. It was his army which enabled him to break free of Polish overlordship in 1657, and it was armed assistance to the emperor which won for his successor the title of king in Prussia in 1701. In Poland–Lithuania, the situation was rather different. There were plans for reform, which might have strengthened the authority of the crown. The elimination of Jan Kazimierz's most obdurate opponents (who defected to the Swedish side) and a willngness on the part of the nobility to accept stronger central authority during the darkest days of the Swedish war seemed to offer an opportunity to effect such plans: but nothing came of them, and the reign of the last Vasa king of Poland ended in revolt, growing chaos in the *sejm* and ultimately, the abdication of the king himself.

The eventual disintegration and partition of the Commonwealth has perhaps led historians to attach too much significance to the lack of a firm and consistent central authority: economic decline and the sheer magnitude of the problems of defending an extensive frontier against a variety of external threats undoubtedly played their part in the demise of Poland–Lithuania. On the other hand, it might be argued that similar problems beset the kings of Denmark and Sweden, and yet Frederik III and Karl XI were able to strengthen royal authority as a result of and in response to fiscal and economic crises. Involvement in the German wars not only ended disastrously for Denmark, which was twice invaded and defeated; it also brought a once-prosperous kingdom to the verge of bankruptcy. Sweden enjoyed much greater success on the battlefield, and was thus able to compel occupied territories, threatened cities and subordinate allies to pay out large sums of money towards the upkeep of the swollen armies under the Swedish flag. Nevertheless, the acquisition of territory on the southern shores of the Baltic also meant an increase in the costs of defence, which in time of peace was to place a severe strain upon the limited resources of a poor and sparsely populated land.

During the latter half of the sixteenth century, the crown in Denmark had sought to maximise its returns through careful rationalisation of estate management, and had been fairly adept at juggling the terms upon which fiefs (*len*) were held in order to reap the maximum benefit. In 1608, annual and irregular income from crown estates comprised 67 per cent of the gross revenue (50 per cent net). Christian IV was also an active money-lender, carefully recording his transactions in an old notebook. The ransom paid by the Swedes for the return of the Älvsborg fortress, paid into the king's own treasury, was also used for loans to the nobility. Christian IV's attempts to build up a power base in northern Germany in the 1620s were financed from his own treasury, or by loans from the dowager queen; but the associated expenditure was then converted into a national responsibility to be covered by extra taxes voted by the *rigsråd*: this would then release the original capital for further use. When the scale of Christian IV's involvement in German affairs became apparent in 1623, the council tried to ensure that taxes granted were not used to redeem the king's debts.[3]

3. Ladewig Petersen E 1975 From domain state to tax state *Scandinavian Economic History Review* **23**: 116–48. Ladewig Petersen E 1982 Defence, war and finance. Christian IV and the council of the realm 1596–1629 *Scandinavian Journal of History* **7**: 277–313. Rystad G (ed.) 1983 *Europe and Scandinavia: aspects of the process of integration in the*

The initial phase of the war in Germany appears to have been financed fairly painlessly from the king's own resources and by underhand manipulation of tax revenue. Army pay in 1626 swallowed up four-fifths of expenditure on the war, and since the inflow of revenue was uneven and had in many instances to be converted into money, there was a perpetual shortage of cash. The flow of subsidies from Christian's allies soon dried up, with the consequence that the duchies and Denmark had to bear the burden of paying for the king's war effort. The disruption to Baltic trade caused by war and economic crisis reduced the opportunities to squeeze extra tolls out of foreign merchantmen passing through the Sound. Christian IV's creditworthiness on the Kiel money market also fell: his income from loans shrank from 108,637 rigsdaler in 1625 to a mere 3,000 two years later. Income was also lost as a result of the occupation of the duchies and the Jutland peninsula by Wallenstein's troops.

The setbacks suffered in 1626 enabled the council to bring pressure to bear on the king to convene a meeting of the estates and to appoint four new councillors. Christian was also obliged to appoint a new marshal of the realm (*rigsmarsk*) and admit him to the council, whose control over military operations was thereby strengthened. The *rigsråd* agreed to extraordinary levies in 1628, but on condition that these should be handled by a general war-payments commissariat, composed of members of the council. Although this was meant to be a temporary measure, it effectively deprived the king of control of war finances.

The war debt was not unduly burdensome, but it was not liquidated. By the end of the reign, the national debt stood at four million rigsdaler, largely as a result of deficit budgeting in the 1630s, when court, military and above all, naval costs (which swallowed over half the budget in the 1630s and 1640s) rose steeply. The renewal in the 1630s of the union agreement between the king of Denmark and the duke of Holstein-Gottorp obliged the kingdom to raise 3,000 infantry, in addition to the 600 horse stipulated in 1623. By 1642, this defence force had swollen into an army of over 7,000 men: in addition, three regiments of recruits, totalling 7,000, were raised in the provinces of Jutland, Skåne and Sjælland. The constant threat of war persuaded the council to agree to increased spending on defence, but the amount of income raised by extra taxation was never sufficient to

---

seventeenth century: Ladewig Petersen E War, finance and the growth of absolutism: some aspects of the European integration of seventeenth-century Denmark. Lund, pp. 40–1.

meet spiralling costs. The union army alone cost between 300,000 and 400,000 rdr annually, at a time when ordinary revenue was just over half a million a year. Christian IV managed to force the council to agree to raise one million rigsdaler in 1629 (though it took eight years to raise this 'ten barrels of gold', largely through extra land taxes) by threatening to refuse to ratify the treaty of Lübeck. The council was unwilling to vote further extra taxes in 1630 to meet the budget deficit, and insisted that the king use the barrels of gold to finance his foreign activities. Christian maintained that this sum was to cover the debts he had already incurred in the defence of the realm, and he cast around for other sources of income. His proposals to squeeze more revenue out of the *len* threatened the economic interests of the noble councillors, most of whom enjoyed sizeable incomes from administering these fiefs. The council would only agree to raise taxes, and insisted on controlling these through the war commissariat. Since the taxes collected went towards the maintenance of the union army, the council-controlled war commissariat had no disposable reserves, and little leeway to raise more money, since taxes were already uncomfortably high. Christian IV was thus tempted to raise customs duties and tolls. By doubling the scale of payments for shipping passing through the Sound, Christian succeeded in pushing up the annual revenue from the tolls from 229,000 rigsdaler in 1637 to 616,000 rdr in 1639: but he also antagonised the Dutch, who concluded a defensive alliance with Sweden in 1640. In 1645, the Dutch threatened to join Sweden in the war against Denmark if the Sound dues were not lowered, and the Danes were eventually obliged to give way. The reduction in the Sound dues obtained by the Dutch by the treaty of Christianopel (similar terms were conceded to the French and English) meant a fall in revenue from 405,000 rdr in 1642 to 140,000 rdr in 1646. In the same year, expenditure on the court and the navy alone had risen to almost one million rigsdaler, far outstripping the crown's ordinary revenues.

As a young man, Christian enjoyed the reputation of being one of the wealthiest kings in Christendom. His personal fortune in 1623 is estimated to have been one and a half million rigsdaler. How then is this spectacular slide into financial crisis to be explained ? Drawing upon the work of J A Schumpeter, the Danish historian E Ladewig Petersen has seen the roots of the crisis lying in Denmark's inability to adapt sufficiently to the exigencies of a situation in which increased military expenditure rendered the medieval demesne economy outmoded and inadequate. Denmark remained in all essentials a 'demesne state' until the later years of Christian IV's reign; in other words, crown revenue was derived mainly from its estates, and royal financial administration resembled that of manorial management. The annual growth rate of between three to four per cent in income from the *len* during the relatively prosperous years of Frederik II's reign was not sustained, but until the mid-1620s, Christian IV had been able to realise a substantial income from other sources, such as the Sound dues and money lending. When however the king sought to devise ways of augmenting his income from the *len*, he encountered vigorous opposition from the aristocratic fief-holders (*lensmænd*), pinched by rising costs and falling incomes from their entrepreneurial activities. J A Fridericia estimated that the average annual income of the *lensmænd* from their fiefs was in the order of 100,000 rdr: small wonder that the council aristocracy resisted the demands of the crown's creditors for royal demesnes to be sold, and the posts of *lensmænd* to be offered to the highest bidder, irrespective of social status.

The growing financial crisis of the Danish state was not helped by the failure of Christian IV's German war, or the invasions of 1626–9 and 1643–5. Wallenstein's army of occupation cost the inhabitants of Jutland around 400,000 rdr a month: Lennart Torstensson's forces extorted hefty sums in the form of forced contributions or protection money. Making war pay for itself was axiomatic for the Swedes. The rueful remark of Frederik III's commander Anders Bille in 1657 that 'we should amuse ourselves with the odd sortie and between whiles live off the provender of our own country' stands in stark contrast to the Swedish experience.[4]

The campaigns waged in Livonia and Prussia in the 1620s were largely financed by Swedish resources and the numerous extraordinary imposts and taxes levied by the crown provoked much discontent. The money thus raised was often inadequate to pay the troops. By the winter of 1627–8, for example, the unpaid troops in Prussia were on the verge of mutiny. The Prussian tolls proved to be a godsend, yielding 329,843 rdr in 1628 and 581,625 rdr in 1629 (the costs of maintaining the cavalry in ducal Prussia during the winter of 1628–9 was 247,056 rdr, and the budget proposal of 1628 estimated that 775,400 rdr would be needed for an offensive campaign). The Prussian tolls were not adequate to cover the huge costs of the campaign planned in Germany, however. The size of the Swedish forces rose from around 10–20,000 men in the Prussian campaign to 150,000 by

4. Fridericia J 1975 *Adelsvældens sidste Dage. Danmarks Historie fra Christian IV's Død til Enevældens Indførelse (1648–1660)* (reprint of 1894 edn). Copenhagen, p. 269.

the time of Lützen (when Swedes and Finns constituted a mere 18 per cent of the king's army). Gustav Adolf recognised the problem of cost in a letter to his chancellor in October 1630, but expressed the hope that the commanders of his forces could find the means of sustenance in the areas which they occupied. The evidence suggests that the cost borne by Sweden declined sharply, from around 2.3 million rdr in 1630 to 0.128 million rdr in 1633. Much of the costs of war were met by forced contributions and extorting a *Brandschatz* from the hapless citizens of threatened cities. The city of Würzburg, for example, paid 80,000 rdr, Munich a staggering 300,000 rdr in order to avoid destruction by the Swedish armies. Army commanders received huge land grants in return for payment: Bernhard of Saxe-Weimar paid 600,000 rdr for lands in Franconia, for example, and the contemporary historian Pufendorf calculated that the crown derived a total income of almost five million riksdaler in this way.

Gustav Adolf was much influenced by the methods developed to a fine art by Wallenstein, though his experiences in the 1620s should have taught him that *bellum se ipse alet* (war nourishes itself) was not always feasible. It presupposed, amongst other things, speedy and decisive victories and the occupation of large areas which could sustain the soldiery, camp-followers and horses. In November 1630, the king was worried that the troops about to go into winter quarters would go short if support were not forthcoming from Sweden: hence the importance of occupying Mecklenburg and parts of Brandenburg. By the end of July 1631, the king was confiding to Oxenstierna that 'we are not a little worried how we are to keep the army in devotion for much longer, since it has had no money for sixteen weeks'. The troops had only the bread supplied by the neighbouring towns, and the king feared imminent mutiny or a shameful and disastrous retreat. The situation was finally relieved by treaties with allied princes – that with Saxony produced a cash inflow of around 40,000 rdr a month – and victory at Breitenfeld opened the floodgates. Gustav Adolf looked forward to squeezing fat contributions out of the bishoprics in Franconia, which would enable him to maintain his army in comfortable winter quarters, ready for the spring campaign.[5]

This happy situation did not last. Defeat at Nördlingen in 1634 and the subsequent withdrawal of Swedish forces from much of southern and central Germany meant that it was more difficult to make the war pay for itself. The loss of the Prussian tolls in 1635, when the Swedish

---

5. Lundkvist S 1966 Svensk krigsfinansiering 1630–1635 *Historisk Tidskrift* **86**: 377–421. *Axel Oxenstiernas skrifter och brevväxling* (AOSB) (27 vols), 1888– (in progress). Stockholm, vol. II:1, 735, 746.

war effort in Germany was going particularly badly, was a severe blow. Income from the tolls in the ports of Pomerania and Mecklenburg was modest, declining from 126,744 rdr in 1639 to a low of 41,206 rdr in 1644. The French subsidy, increased to 480,000 rdr in 1641, provided the cash needed to recruit fresh troops and enabled Lennart Torstensson to launch a new offensive into Saxony and Moravia. The truce concluded between Brandenburg and Sweden in 1641 allowed the Swedes to retain conquered towns and fortresses, whose garrisons were to be maintained by the surrounding districts. The invasion and occupation of the Jutland peninsula in 1644 brought in substantial sums of money, not least the 100,000 rdr paid by the duke of Holstein-Gottorp to ensure the neutrality of his domains. The occupation of Bremen and Verden also augmented Swedish revenues; 202,974 rdr was paid in 1647, an indication that the economy of these territories was sufficiently well protected by the Swedes to allow the payment of such sums.

In the mid-1630s, Sweden was prepared to accept five million riksdaler as the sum required to pay off her armies. Military successes in the 1640s encouraged her negotiators at Osnabrück to raise this sum to twenty-six million, or thirteen million with possession of Pomerania, Bremen and Verden. In the end, Sweden accepted just over five million riksdaler, of which three million went to pay off the troops. The Swedish high command received half a million, the principal negotiators about one hundred thousand riksdaler. The acquisition of territory in Germany was a somewhat dubious advantage, for the economies of these new possessions were incapable of sustaining the high cost of defence. The massive alienation of royal lands and revenues at home had substantially reduced ordinary revenue, and the deficit had to be made up with extraordinary taxation, which bore heavily on a diminishing number of freehold and crown peasants. The non-noble estates had long pressed for the surrender of the nobles' privileges of tax-exemption, but by 1650, the idea of a *reduktion*, or resumption of alienated crown lands and revenues, began to gain ground. Noble exemption had been significantly weakened during the German wars, and in addition, the nobility had agreed to pay extra contributions. In 1655, the alternatives were clearly spelled out by Erik Oxenstierna: 'if the crown is to be helped, this must occur either through the surrender of some of our rights and privileges in perpetuum, or by contributions ad tempus.'[6] A *reduktion* found little favour amongst the high nobility, but they opted for the restitution of

6. *Sveriges riksrådets protsholl* (SRP) (18 vols), 1878–1959. Stockholm, vol. 16: 128.

one-quarter of the estates alienated since 1632 in preference to a contribution equivalent to the tax revenue of the estates to be reduced, which they feared would make them liable to similar taxation in future. In the end, the *reduktion* was postponed for three years in return for a contribution, and was never fully implemented.

The growing tax burden also caused much discontent in Denmark. In August 1629, a meeting of Jutland burghers in Viborg drafted a supplication to the king, in which they complained that 'our dear fatherland, Jutland, is quite laid bare and taxed to exhaustion... there are no supplies to sustain the market towns, credit is enfeebled, the peasants have not the means to till the land, so that there is almost no food left to feed the poor common people'.[7] Pointed criticism of the nobility and noble privileges were made at this and a later meeting in Ry. Although this hostility failed to develop into a full-scale movement, resentment continued to simmer. At the meeting of the estates in 1638, the burghers renewed their complaints against the nobility, and joined with the lesser aristocracy in demanding the revival of the war commissariat. Extra taxes were to be earmarked henceforth for a standing army, and paid into provincial war chests (*landekister*), controlled by provincial commissaries chosen by the nobility.

The last decade of Christian IV's reign has been portrayed by Ladewig Petersen as 'revolutionary', with the privileged status of the council magnates coming under attack. This opposition movement of the burghers and lesser nobility sought to weaken the political power of the council by the establishment of independent, decentralised organs of control. A comparative study of the membership of the council and of the provincial commissaries has revealed, however, that they shared virtually identical social backgrounds, had very similar career structures, and held similar political views. The noble opposition arose in the first instance as a result of tax levies which infringed their privileges. The commissaries sought to lessen this burden by a policy of retrenchment and the building up of a fiscal reserve. For this reason, they favoured the creation of a national militia (much disliked by military experts) on grounds of cheapness.[8]

During the last years of the reign, the estates played a hitherto unaccustomed role in decision-making, and it seemed for a while that

7. Ellehøj S 1964 *Danmarks historie 1596–1660*. Copenhagen, pp. 282–3.

8. Ladewig Petersen E 1980 *Fra standsamfund til rangssamfund 1500–1700* (Dansk social historie, vol. 3). Copenhagen, pp. 390ff. Jespersen L 1981–2 Landskommissærsinstitutionen i Christian IVs tid. Rekruttering og funktion *Historisk Tidskrift* **81**: 69–100. See also Jespersen L 1984 1600-tallets danske magtstat, in Ladewig Petersen E (ed.) *Magtstaten i Norden i 1600-tallet og dens sociale konsekvenser. Rapporter til den XIX nordiske historikerkongres*. Odense, pp. 9–40.

the nobility might force the council to include in Frederik III's accession charter a provision that the consent of the estates was required for new taxes and laws. In the end, class interests prevailed over the new-found sense of solidarity with the burghers. Having been assured by the chancellor, Christian Thomsen Sehested, that the new charter would pay heed to their demands for offices to be filled by Danish nobles and for the unscrambling of the *len* reforms which Christian IV had managed to put through, the nobility abandoned their constitutional programme. As in Louis XIII's France, the estates-general in Denmark sputtered only fitfully: the meeting of 1648 proved to be the last opportunity for the estates to take on a permanent political existence; and that chance was not taken.

By contrast, the estates in Sweden came to play an increasingly important role in the affairs of state. The structure, procedures and protocol of the *riksdag* was given formal recognition in the reign of Gustav Adolf, though the king frequently preferred not to call the peasants to attend, and resorted to the use of a secret committee of selected members of the other three estates to discuss and expedite important or confidential business. Of the four estates which ultimately acquired permanent representation in the *riksdag*, the nobility held prime position. The *riddarhusordningen* of 1626 divided the nobles into three classes: the first, some twelve families in 1626, contained the counts and barons: the second (twenty-two families), the descendants of former members of the council; and the third (ninety-two families), the lesser nobility. All members of the nobility could attend, but only the elected head of each family could speak and vote. Each class had one collective vote, and a majority of two classes determined the final decision of the estate. Members of the council could attend, but were not permitted to vote, an important distinction which undermined the claim of the *råd* to be a separate estate of the realm.

The 1634 Form of Government, in all probability the work of Axel Oxenstierna, has been seen as a victory for the high nobility, placing 'an aristocratic hierarchy of officials at the centre of the affairs of state'.[9] In a document running to sixty-five paragraphs, it outlined the structure and functions of government at national and local level and established the scope and powers of the regency council, which was to rule the realm during the minority of the sovereign. It stated clearly that the five colleges of central government – the supreme court, the chancery, the treasury, the war council and the admiralty – should be staffed primarily by native-born members of the nobility, from whose

9. Hessler C 1935 Den svenska ståndsriksdagen *Scandia* **8**: 34.

number the ruler was also to choose the council of the realm. The monopolisation of office by the nobility caused some discontent amongst the non-noble estates. At the 1634 *riksdag*, the clergy demanded equal right of access to office for all honourable and competent persons of the Swedish nation, and this demand was to be repeated more forcefully in subsequent years. The anti-aristocratic faction, led by Karl IX's illegitimate son Karl Karlsson Gyllenhielm, cavilled at the excessive power wielded by the great magnates, especially the Oxenstierna family, four of whose members belonged to the council in 1647. For his part, Axel Oxenstierna maintained that possession of office was a noble prerequisite, 'the highest *ius* we have, that we are *capaces munerum publicorum*', and he once calculated that there were some 800 civil and military posts which by rights should pertain to the nobility.[10]

The political and economic power of the high nobility came under fierce attack from the non-noble estates and the anti-aristocratic faction during the last years of queen Christina's reign. The rights of the estates, which had seemed threatened by the provision in the Form of Government allowing an annual meeting of officers of state to deal with matters not requiring a special *riksdag*, were vigorously asserted during the period of the regency. The pugnacious bishop of Västerås, Johannes Rudbeckius, claimed in 1635 that the estates had the power and authority to make and change resolutions, whilst the nobility insisted that selection and appointment of the high officers of the realm be done with the agreement and consent of the estates. In the 1640s, demands for an investigation into financial mismanagement by the regency council were raised, and there appeared a series of pamphlets, highly critical of the council.[11] The financial problems of the kingdom were made worse by bad harvests, food shortages and high prices. The mood of the peasantry was distinctly rebellious, and threats of a general uprising were regularly reported. In Hamburg, Johan Adler Salvius noted in December 1649 that travellers from Sweden had detected the glow of a dangerous fire in the ashes. Salvius had already warned the queen that *seditiones populi contra principes* was heard throughout the world, from England to China. It was against

10. Sjödell U 1976 *Infödda svenska män av ridderskapet och adeln* Skrifter utgivna av Vetenskapssocieteten i Lund 72. Lund, pp. 37–40. For details of the familial ties of the high nobility, see Ågren K 1976 Rise and decline of an aristocracy. The Swedish social and political elite in the 17th century *Scandinavian Journal of History* 1: 55–80.

11. See Roberts M 1968 *Sweden as a great power 1611–1697*. London, pp. 29–43; and Runeby N 1962 *Monarchia mixta. Maktfördelningsdebatt i Sverige under den tidigare stormakt-stiden* Studia historica Upsaliensia 6. Uppsala, pp. 329ff.

the lurid background of sedition and uproar that the estates assembled in Stockholm in July 1650.

The *riksdag* of 1650 was, in Michael Roberts's words, 'a flash in the pan, almost a missed opportunity'.[12] The non-noble estates joined forces in demanding a *reduktion*, and their protestation, circulated throughout the land on the conclusion of the session, was an open assault on noble exclusivity and privilege. They refused to respond to the propositions of the government before they had drawn up their own resolutions, and they made frequent appeal to fundamental law. But the principal worry of the estates was not constitutional issues, but the overweening power and greed of the nobility. The nobles' control of the land, argued archbishop Lenaeus, threatened to undermine the power of the crown and to crush the estates, starting with the peasantry. Far from seeking to use their control of supply to further constitutional objectives, however, the estates wished to restore the crown to its own through the wholesale resumption of alienated lands. Queen Christina seized this opportunity to further her own constitutional aims. She had made up her mind to abdicate some time before the session, and now encouraged the lower estates in order to frighten the nobility into accepting her cousin Karl Gustav as hereditary prince and as her successor to the throne. Once this objective had been realised, she abandoned her erstwhile allies, having promised a few emollient reforms to appease them.

The failure of the Danish nobility to develop the kind of constitutional consciousness of their Swedish counterparts was probably crucial in 1660, when the aristocracy meekly surrendered their powers, enshrined in the accession charter, to the king. The Swedish nobility became intimately involved with the affairs of the crown. Its members staffed the administration and judiciary, and were assiduously consulted by the king in the council of the realm and the estate of nobles. They endorsed and were intimately involved with the policy of expansion. They were rewarded with lands and fiefs in the conquered territories. Sweden's military victories reinforced their own prestige, honour and glory. The Danish nobility, on the other hand, found making money more attractive to waging war during the prosperous later decades of the sixteenth century. The council of the realm agreed to *len* reforms in order to ensure that the king did live off his own, and did not try to impose extraordinary taxes on the aristocracy and their peasants. After 1600, however, it was no longer possible to maximise revenue from the *len* without fundamental reform, which would have

12. Roberts M 1967 *Essays in Swedish history*. London, p. 119.

seriously threatened the power base of the nobility. Falling prices and demand for Danish agricultural products after 1620 made possession of *len* even more essential for the nobility, and Christian IV's schemes for reform were all defeated. Wedded to an outmoded system, reluctant to endorse the active foreign policies of the ruler for fear of upsetting the carefuly balanced budget, the Danish nobility never played a consistently active role in the affairs of state. Their control of the king through the council of the realm was essentially a negative one, and the 'dyarchy of mutual interest' which Ladewig Petersen believes was created in 1536 began to founder once those interests diverged.

The accession charter imposed upon Frederik III in 1648 reinforced a number of noble privileges, such as tax exemption for their tenants who lived close enough to the manor to perform weekly labour services (*ugedagsbønder*) and the exclusive right of the nobility to hold the post of *lensmand*. The powers of the *rigsråd* were also significantly extended, and any vacancy was to be filled by the king from a shortlist of three, selected by the council from a list of candidates elected by the nobility of the home province of the previous incumbent. Should the king disregard or break his obligations, the *rigsråd* was empowered to assume sovereign power. The charter of 1648 thus appeared to confirm the ascendancy of the council nobility over a king who had not expected to rule (his elder brother Christian died shortly before their father). How then was Frederik III able so easily to break the political power of the nobility and establish absolutist rule?

Support for strong monarchical power was by no means absent in Denmark. Bishop Jesper Brochmand spoke in his coronation sermon in 1648 of the unlimited powers which God had bestowed upon kings and royalist sentiment appears to have been strong amongst many of the graduates of the noble academy of Sorø. The power and influence wielded during the last years of Christian IV's reign by his sons-in-law aroused jealousy and resentment, which Frederik III was not slow to exploit. Hannibal Sehested, the energetic governor of Norway, was obliged to lay down all his offices and forfeit his estates in 1651, after a committee of investigation found him guilty of mismanagement of Norwegian affairs. Korfits Ulfeldt, falsely implicated in a plot to murder the king, fled the kingdom. The king made increasing use of German advisers well versed in the theories of absolutism, and refused to replace deceased incumbents of high office or council posts. In spite of efforts to introduce the collegial system of government, the administration was poorly managed, with a good deal of overlapping between the different offices of state. The noble secretaries in the

Danish chancery were poorly paid, and often regarded the job simply as a stepping-stone to higher things: by 1658, their records were six years in arrears. The treasury was dependent on the chancery, which controlled all incoming and outgoing correspondence, and it had no control over the king's private treasury. Above all, the antagonism between the burghers and nobility had in no whit abated. The imposition of an excise on beer and spirits in 1650 provoked the burghers of Copenhagen to protest that this was a breach of their privileges; the exemptions from the excise granted to the nobility and clergy also exacerbated feelings. This protest movement revived with new vigour after the conclusion of peace at Roskilde in 1658. A thirteen-point programme submitted in June to the *rigsråd* by the burghers of Copenhagen expressed the wish that non-nobles who came into possession of noble land should henceforth enjoy the same rights of ownership as the aristocracy, and demanded an end to exemptions from taxation. In August, as Karl X Gustav renewed the war, Frederik III granted Copenhagen the status of a separate estate of the realm, and confirmed most of the burghers' demands.

The first clear breach of noble privilege had thus been made, and a tacit alliance forged between king and burghers. Relations between the king and nobility were tense. Henrik Bielke told Karl Gustav that the Danes were heartily sick of their king, who was ruled by his wife. During the first war against Sweden, the balance of power had swung towards the king. Frederik was able to finance his war effort largely with the help of foreign loans raised by his trusted agents; the war commissariat system virtually ceased to function through lack of revenue. The death of the *rigsmarsk* and the prominence given to foreign military commanders such as Ernst Albrecht von Eberstein threatened to deprive the council of control of the army – hence the urgent demand for the creation of a *Krigskollegium* which might allow the nobility to regain overall direction. In May 1658, Frederik seems to have contemplated staging a coup with the connivance of the Swedes. His request for the withholding of some of the cavalry he had been obliged to place at Karl Gustav's disposal was discussed by the *riksråd* on 18–19 May. Karl Gustav clearly felt that 'the king must have something in mind against a part of the estates' and the upshot was that Sten Bielke was instructed to dissuade Frederik from taking such a step, with the threat that Sweden would take the side of the Danish nobility should any coup be staged.[13] Thus baulked, Frederik abandoned any plans he may have had, and ordered field-marshal Eber-

13. Fridericia J 1887 Frederik III og Enevældens Indførelse *Historisk Tidskrift* **5/6**: 729.

stein to return with his troops to Holstein. In return for promising to fill the vacancies on the council, the king was able to obtain the consent of the council for new taxes. Gunner Lind has recently maintained that: 'King and council were clearly on the path to a compromise in the classic model – money for the army, new opportunities for control for the consenting [council] – when the new war broke off negotiations.' Nothing in these negotiations indicated a desire on the part of the monarch to institute absolutist rule: on the contrary, they were directed towards the restoration of the hitherto prevailing balance of forces.[14]

The status of the council nobility suffered a sharp decline during the second war, in which Copenhagen acquired not only a reputation for patriotic valour, but also enhanced privileges, with a thirty-two man committee elected to advise the king through its two delegates. Frederik had managed to obtain full sovereignty over the royal parts of Slesvig, and the island of Bornholm, having freed itself of the Swedish occupation, placed itself under the crown as a hereditary possession of the king. The loss of Skåne, where there were many noble estates, also weakened the ranks of the aristocracy. Frederik ignored the advice of the council to reduce the size of the army after peace had been signed with Sweden, and had the troublesome Korfits Ulfeldt arrested, in defiance of the amnesty which he had agreed to in the peace treaty. In September 1660, a German regiment under the king's confidant, general Lubbes, was called to the capital, where the estates were due to meet.

The meeting was addressed on 10 September by the steward Joakim Gersdorf, who complained that the war had been lost because of the generals' lack of unity and the unwillingness of the nobility to provide the necessary supplies: the land had been saved by the brave king and the valorous burghers of Copenhagen. The purpose of the assembly was to discuss means of paying off the war debt and of restoring the defence of the realm to a sound footing. The king and his council thus proposed to levy a 'consumption tax', to which all estates would be subject. The estate of nobility initially sought exemption from this tax, but finally gave way. At this stage, many of the delegates believed that the main business of the meeting was over; but behind the scenes, an alliance of leading clergy and burghers was being formed, and it

14. Lind G 1984 Den politiske situation i Danmark efter Roskildefreden, in Christiansen G *et al.* (eds) *Tradition og kritik. Festskrift til Svend Ellehøj.* Copenhagen, pp. 307–20. Lind thus takes issue with Fridericia's portrayal of an impotent *rigsråd* giving way before monarchical pressure.

was from these circles on 17 September that a new proposal was launched. This aimed at nothing less than the wholesale reform of the administrative system, with all *len* to be converted to fiefs of account, or leased to the highest bidder. Peasant labour services were to be converted to cash payments (an idea floated by Christian IV in the 1620s), and *vornedskab* commuted for cash; customs duties were to be lowered, and a thorough reform of the tax system on the basis of a land assessment was to be instituted. Burgher and noble commissioners were to control fiscal administration, and in certain towns, burghers were to be allowed to elect their own magistracy.

This radical series of demands, which the nineteenth-century historian Fridericia likened to the *cahiers* of 1789, provided the necessary weapon with which to strike free the fetters upon royal authority. A small coterie of influential figures, including bishop Hans Svane and Hans Nansen, one of the burghermasters of Copenhagen, were deeply involved in secret talks with the king. On 4 October, the burghers put forward a new proposition which called for the king and his heirs to be recognised as hereditary rulers. Four days later, a meeting of the non-noble estates, the thirty-two man committee and magistracy of Copenhagen proposed to invite the king to proclaim the monarchy hereditary, on condition that the rights and privileges of the estates remained inviolate. The *rigsråd* refused to endorse this proposal, whereupon the non-noble estates proceeded to the royal palace, where the king promised to give his reply to the proposal the following day.

Acceptance of this proposal without the consent of the nobility or the council would have been in clear breach of the king's accession charter. There is no clear evidence to show that Frederik and his confidants (who included Hannibal Sehested, now restored to royal favour) were actively plotting the humiliation of the council and the establishment of absolutist rule. Contemporary diarists had no inkling of what was afoot, and the Austrian minister, writing after these events, admitted that he simply did not know if the king, as was suspected, had long striven to fulfil such a plan or had simply grasped the opportunity presented to him. On the night of 10–11 October, the guard was doubled and the gates of the city locked to prevent anyone leaving. Isolated and faced with determined and mounting pressure from the non-noble estates, the *rigsråd* began to give way. Its efforts to retain the inviolability of the privileges of the estates, in return for agreeing to the introduction of a hereditary monarchy, were not enough. On 13 October, when the estates and council were received by the king, Hans Svane went a stage further, announcing that since the kingdom was now declared to be hereditary, the old accession charter was invalid. A commission composed of members of the council and the three estates was set up by the king that same day to consider the implications of this. Although Frederik III was now recognised as sovereign hereditary monarch, it seems clear that the estates did not consider this synonymous with absolute power. The non-noble estates, for example, seemed to have envisaged a kind of Swedish constitution, in which the estates would participate in decision-making, whilst the nobility wished to preserve as much of the old accession charter as possible. In the end, the commission decided to allow the king himself to issue a recess which might be to the benefit of the ruler, the kingdom and the estates, and which would guarantee the privileges of the estates. This reference to privileges was dropped, however, although the estates clearly still hoped that they would be preserved as an institution.

Frederik's main concern in the autumn of 1660 was to ensure the acceptance of hereditary monarchy. Once this had been accomplished, he took steps to establish an absolute government, removing the archives of the council to his palace and replacing the *rigsråd* with a royal council. On 10 January 1661, the instrument of absolute hereditary monarchy was issued, signed by the members of the council and circulated to members of the estates for their signature. This claimed that the estates had freely agreed to transfer hereditary rule and all *iura maiestatis* to the king. The privileges bestowed in June 1661 were a blow to the nobility, who were not assured of any role in government nor guaranteed permanent exemption from taxation for their peasants. The political reforms proposed by the burghers were largely ignored, as were their hopes of relief from the burden of taxation. Copenhagen retained its status as a free city, but the promise to select members of the magistracy for the royal council was abandoned, as was the right to consent to the imposition of the excise duty. The four burghermasters and the city councillors were appointed by the king, who selected loyal members of the patriciate or crown servants. Swedish agents regularly reported dissatisfaction amongst the citizenry. The building of a citadel in the city was especially unpopular: there was much muttering in the taverns that 'It is us who kept the crown on the king's head, and we can tear it off again if we are so minded', and several citizens were haled off to the Blåtårn prison for uttering such sentiments.[15] The collegial system of government introduced after 1660 operated only fitfully, and much of the real work of

15. Olsen G 1970 *Danmarks historie* (vol. 8). Copenhagen, p. 118, citing a report of the Swedish agent, Peter Chambers, in April 1662.

reform was done by special commissions, such as that appointed in the reign of Christian V to prepare a land register. Local administration was also overhauled. From 1662, the *len* were changed into counties (*amter*); the governors (*amtmænd*) were salaried officials and no longer had any military authority or powers over the towns. The responsibility for the collection of taxes was also transferred from the governor to the county clerk (*amtskriver*). Those who enjoyed the king's favour were rewarded with titles and office: Hannibal Sehested was made treasurer, and was also to play an influential role in the conduct of foreign affairs until his death in 1666. The *statskollegie* under the presidency of Joakim Gersdorf took over some of the functions of the now defunct *rigsråd*, but lapsed into inactivity after the accession of Christian V in 1670, when a privy council (*gehejmekonseil*) was set up to advise the king.

The ultimate expression of royal absolutism was contained in the Royal Law, completed in 1665 but not published until 1709. Credit for the final version has been attributed to the king's secretary and librarian, Peder Schumacher. The theocratic overtones of earlier drafts were played down: the powers of the king are seen as resting upon the voluntary agreement of his subjects, grateful to their overlord for saving them from the perils of war. The king was God's representative on earth, with unlimited powers to make and unmake laws (with the exception of the Royal Law), dismiss and appoint officials, levy taxes, and to conduct foreign policy.

The Royal Law was undoubtedly one of the boldest statements of the principles of unadulterated absolutism, but it did nothing to solve the chronic financial difficulties of the crown, nor did it ensure the security of the realm in the form of a strong and effective army. The crown sought to liquidate its debts by selling off land to its creditors. The cost of maintaining an army in the field during the war against Sweden in the 1670s was three million rigsdaler annually, whilst the navy cost four million. The public finances were in such a poor state that it was said that if the president of the treasury failed to return from Holland with a loan, he would not be able to get through Holstein, because there were hundreds of angry creditors waiting to waylay him there. The sale of crown lands inevitably meant an increase in taxation: it has been estimated that the tax burden on peasant tenants on noble land increased four-and-a-half times between 1650 and 1690. Remarkably, perhaps, in a century of peasant revolts, the Danish countryman remained docile, preferring to seek remedies for his grievances in petitions to the king or in the law courts.[16]

The triumph of absolutism in Denmark was made possible by the economic and financial crisis in which the country found itself after the Swedish wars. Several historians have made the point that the control exercised by the nobility was essentially negative, and that the safeguarding of their own narrow interests, rather than the good and welfare of the realm, was their primary concern. Under attack in 1660 for having brought the realm to the verge of disaster by their unwillingness to sacrifice self-interest for the national good, they were incapable of mounting any sort of defence of aristocratic constitutionalism: they meekly agreed to the introduction of a hereditary monarchy, hoping that this would still allow them to keep their privileges. During the early years of absolutism, the old nobility was regarded with some suspicion by the monarchy. The elaborate public 'execution' of an effigy of Korfits Ulfeldt in 1663 (Ulfeldt himself had fled the country) was clearly intended to underline the authority of the sovereign power. Letters-patent of nobility emphasised service; the 1693 table of ranks placed the three highest groups of officials on a par with the traditional aristocracy. The creation of titles in 1671 was based on the size of land-holdings, and only five of the eighteen counts created in the 1670s were members of the old nobility. By 1720, only one-tenth of the higher offices of state were held by members of the old nobility: almost three-quarters were of non-noble birth.

In a number of respects, the status and position of the Danish nobility before 1660 bears comparison with that of the Prussian aristocracy. The administration of the duchy was effectively in the hands of the native nobility, from whose ranks were chosen the twelve *Landräte* and four *Oberräte*. Although the city of Königsberg also had a voice in the affairs of the duchy, with its burghermasters being represented in the consilium which was entrusted with powers of government when the diet was not in session, it could be outvoted by the noble majority. The ruler also tended to side with the rural gentry, who were quite happy to grant supplies in the form of taxes on merchandise and beverages, which bore more heavily on the burghers than on themselves. Königsberg fought back, even refusing to swear fealty to Frederick William in 1642 until the city's grievances were

16. Munck T 1979 *The peasantry and the early absolute monarchy in Denmark 1660–1708*. Copenhagen, pp. 241–2. On the establishment of absolutism and the Royal Law of 1665, see Bøggild-Andersen C 1971 *Statsomvæltingen i 1660* (reprint of 1936 edn). Århus. Fabricius K 1971 *Kongeloven* (reprint of 1920 edn). Copenhagen. Ekman E 1957 The Danish Royal Law of 1665 *Journal of Modern History* **29**: 102–7.

resolved. In Brandenburg, the elector was able to obtain supplies in 1653 at the cost of granting extensive concessions to the nobility. The Prussian estates were also able to wrest important concessions in 1655: an excise on consumer goods and manufactures was to be levied and collected by the estates, and Frederick William had to give an undertaking that the grant was in no way to prejudice the privileges of the estates and would cease after twelve months.

The war of 1655–60 gave the elector an opportunity to assert control over the estates in his scattered lands. He raised taxes without their consent, and was able to coerce the towns of Brandenburg into approving an excise duty in the 1660s. Prussia was badly affected by the war, and there was a strong undercurrent of opposition which threatened to undermine the important political gains made by Frederick William in his treaties with Poland. These grievances surfaced in the *Landtag* which sat from 1661 to 1663. At first, the ruler was forced to back down and reduce the number of troops and the level of taxation. In November 1661, the *Landräte*, the estate of nobles and the aldermen of the towns agreed to recognise Frederick William's sovereignty, The commons of Königsberg, led by Hieronymus Roth, refused to do this, claiming that the transfer of sovereignty from Poland to the duke of Prussia was illegal. The resistance of the burghers had to be broken by force: troops moved into the city and arrested Roth. Having been forced to accept the sovereignty of Frederick William, the burghers now struggled to resist the imposition of the excise. In the end, the ruler had to make concessions, confirming the privileges of the estates, promising not to raise taxes without their consent and permitting Königsberg to raise its own taxes. The granting of supplies, however, allowed Frederick William to maintain an army in peacetime, and this enabled him to win the upper hand. Taxes were imposed without the consent of the estates in the 1670s, and collected forcibly. In 1674, Königsberg was occupied by the army and obliged to provide a contribution. Taxes were collected by a war commissariat, staffed by non-natives, and the estates' powers of control of revenues was whittled away. After 1681, the ruler was able to split the estates by allowing Königsberg to raise its own taxes, which enabled him to impose a different mode of contribution upon the nobility and the peasantry. The growing burden of taxation placed upon a country devastated by war led to widespread desertion of the land by the peasantry, whilst high tolls seriously affected the trading competitiveness of the ports. The nobility, although not exempt from taxation, escaped more lightly, and managed to retain control of most of the high administrative offices.

By employing a policy of divide and rule and favouring the nobility against the urban estates, the Great Elector was able to emasculate representative institutions in his lands. His brother-in-law, the energetic and resourceful duke Jakob of Kurland, was less successful in his efforts to curb the power of his nobles. The *Formula regiminis* of 1617 had in effect created 'a noble oligarchy with a princely head'.[17] The towns were excluded from the *Landtag*, which was to meet biannually. The chief officials were henceforth to be selected from amongst the ranks of the indigenous nobility. The *Oberräte* were to govern during the prince's absence, infirmity or minority, and acted also as a watchdog of noble interests and privileges. It was the task of the *Ritterbank* to define who was to be deemed 'noble', and this institution was extremely reluctant to admit the prince's advisers to these exclusive ranks. Duke Jakob's attempts to build up a degree of financial independence through commerce and industry enjoyed a modicum of success, until ruined by war. He was tempted to follow his brother-in-law's example and seek Swedish support in breaking the links of Polish overlordship, but nothing came of his negotiations, and in 1658, his lands were overrun and he himself was imprisoned by the Swedes. Jakob had tried to make himself independent of the nobles' military service (*Rossdienst*), but his recruits were too few to repel the onslaught of the Swedish armies. Kurland was too small to sustain a sizeable army: its position and prosperity made it a natural target for occupation, and unlike the dukes of Holstein-Gottorp, the rulers of Kurland did not possess a nuisance value which might have made them useful allies.

The nobility in the patchwork quilt of territories which formed the duchies of Slesvig and Holstein managed to retain their privileges and the right to elect their overlord throughout the sixteenth century. The partitions of 1544 and 1564, carried through in the teeth of noble opposition, allowed members of the Oldenburg family to establish their own territorial enclaves; although that of Sonderborg lapsed in 1580, with the death of the childless Johann, the duchy of Holstein-Gottorp survived. In 1616, the estates abandoned their claim to elect the new ruler when Friedrich was formally inaugurated as duke of Holstein-Gottorp in succession to his father. During Friedrich's reign, the estates gradually lost the power to raise taxes, and his council was dominated by non-nobles, who formed a privy council in 1620, based on collegial principles. In 1644, Friedrich concluded a treaty of neut-

17. Seraphim E 1908 *Grundriss der baltischen Geschichte*. Riga, p. 309. Wittram R 1954 *Baltische Geschichte*. Munich, pp. 113ff.

rality with the invading Swedish forces (contrary to the union agreement of 1533, renewed and extended by Christian IV) and he openly
aligned himself with the Swedes against his overlord in 1657. At the
subsequent peace treaty of Roskilde, Frederik III had to surrender his
overlordship over the ducal parts of Slesvig, and the alliance of Holstein-Gottorp and Sweden was to remain a threat to Denmark for the
remainder of the century.

The growth of absolutist rule in Holstein-Gottorp coincided with
the economic crisis which badly affected the local nobility. A number
of leading families sought to repair their fortunes by seeking office and
advancement in Denmark. As in Brandenburg and Prussia, the landowning gentry retained control over the peasantry and enjoyed a
number of privileges and exemptions. The towns were relatively
weak, and had never played any role in the affairs of the united
Landtag, which ceased to meet after 1675. Frederik III had also been
able to persuade the nobility of the royal parts of the duchies to agree
to his succession without election in 1650, and had indeed imbibed
many of the doctrines and practices of absolutist rule during his many
years as administrator of these lands.

SWEDEN AND THE TRANS-BALTIC LANDS

The crisis of 1650 had revealed the strength and flexibility of the
Swedish monarchy. Karl Gustav succeeded to the throne in 1654, and
his accession charter was sufficiently loose to give him freedom of
action in foreign and domestic affairs. The aged chancellor, perhaps
relieved to remain in office under a monarch with whom he had not
enjoyed the closest of relations, argued against those who wished to
bind the new king to the Form of Government and to impose an
accession charter similar to that sworn by Gustav Adolf in 1611.
During his short reign, Karl Gustav made clear his determination to
exercise sovereign powers. The posts of chancellor and marshal were
left vacant upon the deaths of their incumbents, and in his will, the
king decreed that the last-mentioned office should be filled by his
brother, Adolf Johan. The will, which also established a regency
council under the queen-mother to rule during the minority, was
immediately challenged in the estate of nobility as contrary to the
fundamental laws of the land. Adolf Johan was excluded from office
on the grounds that no foreigner was allowed to hold any of the five
high offices of the realm. The *riddarhus* also challenged the council's

right to fill the vacant high offices and won the right to approve appointments. The Addition to the Form of Government was the outcome of a lengthy tussle between council and estates, and within the ranks of the nobility. It marked an extension of the power of the estates, who were to meet at least once every three years and whose resolutions were to have the force of law. The estates were also to approve all future appointments to high office during the minority. Restrictions were placed on the numbers of any one family to be appointed to high office or to the council, and provisions were made to safeguard offices for native-born men.

The regency government was faced with a number of serious problems, not least financial. The austere budget introduced by the treasurer, Gustav Bonde, in 1662 allowed little scope for expansion of income. The chancellor, Magnus de la Gardie, proposed various schemes to make the crown's revenues more productive, but fought shy of the idea of a *reduktion*. There was a groundswell of discontent which grew stronger as the king reached his majority in 1672. Already in 1664, the clergy had retorted to a request for a grant to enable the government to build twelve ships that 'it is astonishing that so many noble gentlemen have land to a breadth of ten to twelve [Swedish] miles and fine oak forests, which all have passed from the crown into private hands, but the king has not even so much as a plank of oak. If the crown be so poor, then it were best that it took back what it had given away'.[18] The *Blue Book*, produced in 1668 by a commission set up by de la Gardie's opponents, was highly critical of his fiscal policies. The chancellor also encountered fierce opposition to his policy of alliance with France. When the *riksdag* assembled in Uppsala in the autumn of 1675, as the news of Sweden's defeat at Fehrbellin and of Denmark's declaration of war became known, de la Gardie's enemies launched a new attack. The commission set up by the estates with the king's consent was to investigate the conduct and fiscal management of the regency council; its findings were ultimately to undermine the foundations of high aristocratic power.

For the remainder of the war, the king spent most of his time in the army headquarters in the south, surrounded by eager young officers with pronounced royalist sympathies and advised by de la Gardie's long-time adversary, Johan Gyllenstierna. The chancellor himself was in Västergötland, supervising the defences; in August 1677, he suffered a defeat at the hands of the Danes, in contrast to the successes achieved in the field by Gyllenstierna. Magnus de la Gardie was no

18. Strindberg A 1937 *Bondenöd och stormaktsdröm*. Stockholm, p. 187.

match for skilled intriguers and political in-fighters such as Gyllenstierna, who succeeded in exercising enormous influence over the king before his untimely death on the eve of the 1680 *riksdag*. Gyllenstierna has indeed been widely seen as the inspiration for the introduction of absolutism, though the evidence for any carefully prepared programme is slight.[19] An attempt to discredit Gyllenstierna in the autumn of 1678 misfired; instead, the chancellor fell into disgrace, and leading opponents of the Gyllenstierna faction were relieved of their offices. By 1680, the council had dwindled to twenty-four members, with an average age of fifty-five. Attendance at meetings was poor, and the conduct of important business was largely taken over by the king's own advisers. The council had already committed one serious political error in pressing for a *riksdag* in 1678, for the estates took this as an occasion to press even more resolutely for a resumption of crown lands. In January 1680, when the council mildly objected that the king had concluded a marriage agreement with Denmark without consulting them, they were curtly informed by Karl that such matters were none of their business.

The political initiative now clearly lay with the king, whose reputation had been enhanced by a vigorous conduct of the war against Denmark; but, like Frederik III twenty years earlier, he seems at the opening of the *riksdag* to have had no definite intention of overthrowing the constitutional framework as defined in his accession charter. The proceedings of the autumn *riksdag* would suggest that the king's friends, led by Hans Wachtmeister, distinguished themselves more by their clumsy and aggressive behaviour than by finesse.[20] The king's own reluctance to show his hand or declare a preference further confused matters, especially in the debate over how to deal with the findings of the commission of enquiry into the regency government. As in the 1650s, the *reduktion* was a central issue, though now the non-noble estates were given full rein to press the attack on the magnates. A joint memorial of the three estates, demanding the resumption by the crown of alienated lands, was presented to the nobility. This was seen as an attack on the privilege of the noble estate, and the *riddarhus* initially closed ranks to rebuff such a move. On 29 October, however, Hans Wachtmeister employed a masterly tactical

19. Rosén J 1966 *Från Sveriges stormaktstid*. Lund, pp. 39–85 argues the case for a programme. Grauers S 1949 *Kring förspelet till 1680 års riksdag. Historiska studier tillägnade Nils Ahnlund*. Stockholm, pp. 138–79 takes a more sceptical view. For a recent summary, see Upton A 1987 The Riksdag of 1680 and the establishment of royal absolutism in Sweden *English Historical Review* **403**: 285ff.

20. Upton 1987, pp. 294–96. Roberts 1968, pp. 72–5.

move which split the nobility. The lesser nobility had for years grumbled about the burden of contributions and had made sarcastic remarks about those who sat tight on vast estates given away by the crown. Wachtmeister hinted that, by agreeing voluntarily to a *reduktion*, those with modest estates might be allowed to keep them. This clearly appealed to the lesser nobility of the third class, and many in the second class as well. Amidst uproar,

> Judge Ulf Bonde and Governor Axel Stålarm leapt to their feet, saying that this was not the opinion of the class, and that the class had not known what was really being proposed. To which Herr Axel Wachtmeister and Col. Soop retorted that this was the class's agreed view. At that Herr Hans Wachtmeister in the first class sprang to his feet, saying: All those of us who are for the reduction gather round, and we'll go up to the king. And therewith took some steps across the floor. Col. Erik Soop then leapt up in the second class, clapped his hat on his head and brandished his stick, shouting: Come on! Let's go! At the same moment, Herr Per Sparre jumped up, saying: We can go to the king just as well as you ! and moved with some others to the door.[21]

Sparre and his friends received little comfort from the king, however, and not much support from the *riksråd* either. The belated objections of the council to the way in which the decision to proceed with a *reduktion* had been taken by the estates gave the king the opportunity he needed to deal the final blow to the *riksråd*. On 10 December, the estates were asked to respond to three questions posed by the king: was he bound by the 1634 Form of Government and the 1660 Addition; was he obliged to govern with the advice of the council; and was the council, as it claimed, a distinct estate of the realm. The reply of the estates was that the king was not bound by the Form of Government, but by Sweden's laws and customs; as such, he had no need to seek the advice of the council, whose claim to be a distinct estate was declared to be incorrect.

The declaration of the estates finally put paid to the notion of the council as a mediatory body between king and estates, though as Upton remarks, the unwillingness of the *råd* to challenge the consensus of the estates suggests that aristocratic constitutionalism was a dead issue by 1680. Writers such as Henning Arnisaeus, a product of Helmstedt university and an advocate of monarchical sovereignty, had already begun to win ground in intellectual circles in Denmark and Sweden: Swedes were also acutely aware of the strong tide flowing in favour of absolutism in Europe.[22] It is also important to

21. Roberts 1968, p. 126.
22. Upton 1987, p. 306. Rystad 1963 Med råds råde eller efter konungens godtycke? *Scandia* **29**: 157–249. Roberts 1967, pp. 226–68.

remember that the estates had never challenged the authority of the ruler, as had the English parliament. The initiative always remained with the crown; the council and estates were all too often merely accomplices in decisions already decided. Karl XI had no need to resort to the crude tactics employed by his earlier namesake in order to destroy the power of the council. The authority and prestige of the council had suffered a serious decline since 1660 and the remaining members were old, tired and clearly unable to mount any vigorous defence of the traditions established by Erik Sparre and Hogenskild Bielke. The nobility was sharply and bitterly divided, and the non-noble estates were growing impatient for a *reduktion* which they believed would compel the nobility to disgorge their ill-gotten gains and so enable the king to live off his own again. The lesser nobility were also persuaded of the necessity of a *reduktion* which would cut most deeply into the land-holdings of the magnates and would relieve the corporate class of the nobility of the burden of contributions. In this they were to be disappointed. Having used the splits and animosities within the estates to reassert the sovereign power of the crown, Karl XI pushed home his advantage. The estates in 1682 were forced to concede that they had no right to circumscribe the king's right to legislate, and their right to grant taxes was eroded after 1689. The ultimate assertion of absolutism, couched in the most servile language, was the resolution of the 1693 *riksdag*, which proclaimed that Karl and his heirs were responsible for their actions to no man on earth, but had power and authority to rule and govern at their pleasure.[23]

The shift in political power was accompanied by considerable changes in the pattern of land ownership as a result of the *reduktion*, from which the lesser nobility were not spared (nor were they released from the imposition of contributions). In Sweden proper, it is estimated that the nobles' share of the cultivated land fell from two-thirds to one-third; elsewhere, where donations and alienation of crown lands had occurred on a larger scale, the returns to the crown were even greater. In total, something like two and a half million silver daler in revenue was restored to the crown. In 1693, the crown's fortunes had improved to such an extent that the king could inform the estates that he had no need to impose any extra taxes.

These new financial resources enabled the crown to free itself still further from dependency on the grants of the estates: the old system of drafting men into the army was now converted into an allotment

23. Roberts 1968, pp. 88–90.

system (*indelningsverket*). Nearly every province of Sweden–Finland concluded a contract with the king to raise a regiment of 1,200 foot. Farms were grouped in pairs, or files, and each file had to furnish a recruit, who was provided with food, clothing, an annual wage and quarters, either a small cottage or lodgings, in return for working for the farmers of the file (a similar system was introduced in the province of Blekinge to recruit crews for the navy). The cavalry regiments were raised by offering exemption from taxes and the file system to any who could provide a fully equipped horseman, a system which brought great benefits to the wealthier farmers, released from the burden of taxation and able to employ their substitutes (*sventjänare*) as labourers on their farms. Officers were provided with housing on crown farms. In addition to this conscript army, totalling some forty thousand men, the crown also employed a further 25,000 mercenaries in the defence of the trans-Baltic territories.

In general, the Swedish crown pursued a cautious policy in regard to the rights and privileges of the indigenous estates of the overseas provinces. As we have seen, the *Ritterschaft* of Estonia jealously clung to their rights and privileges and resisted the efforts of Karl IX to draw them into the Swedish system of justice and government. The position of their Livonian counterparts was less secure, since Sweden could claim that it had acquired Livonia by conquest, not by agreement with the nobility. Gustav Adolf was not averse to claiming *ius belli* as a means of frightening the Livonian and Pomeranian gentry into coughing up supplies, and there were always zealous Swedish churchmen or administrators who sought to enforce Swedish practices in the overseas provinces; but, at least until the 1680s, they had remarkably little success. Gustav Adolf's first governor-general of Livonia, Ingria and Karelia, Johan Skytte, clearly intended to continue where the king's father had left off. If the towns and provinces under his charge could be placed under the supreme jurisdiction of a high court in Dorpat, he argued, 'many *irrationabiles consuetudines, iam absurda* and manifold wondrous legal conceits, of which this land is replete in every scattered corner, can be destroyed and made an end of'. Skytte's attempts to realise the principle of *unus rex, una lex et grex unus* (one king, one law, one community) encountered fierce opposition not only from the indigenous nobility, but also from Swedish magnates such as Axel Oxenstierna, who owned large estates in the Baltic provinces. It was the chancellor himself who reminded a delegation of the Estonian *Landrat* in 1640 that many Swedish nobles had a vested interest in preserving the privileges of the nobility in the

Baltic lands, and his opposition in 1633 was sufficient to persuade Skytte to vacate his office, his plans for reform unfulfilled.[24]

The Swedish government was indeed more interested in the defence and security of the trans-Baltic lands than in pursuing uniformity. Axel Oxenstierna recalled in 1643 that the king had warned against the introduction into the Swedish *riksdag* of a particularist Baltic nobility which would constantly be seeking to promote their own interests. The chancellor's own position was quite clear: the Livonians should either have their own privileges and rights, or they should enjoy the same as their Swedish counterparts. The 1634 Form of Government had already spelled out this distinction. Those who did not reside in Sweden–Finland had no rights of representation in the *riksdag* nor any claim to participate in the government of the realm. A clear distinction was thus made between the kingdom of Sweden proper and its trans-Baltic provinces. This did not apply in the case of the provinces ceded by Denmark in 1645 and 1658, for here the crown initially sought to make full possession of Swedish rights and privileges sufficiently attractive to wean the local nobility away from their rights guaranteed under the terms of the peace treaties. A more rigorous programme of uniformity was embarked upon during the reign of Karl XI, when the Swedish church order and judicial system were introduced in the southern provinces. Uniformity in the former Danish provinces was deemed necessary to weaken the links with the former motherland, especially after the Scanian war of 1676–79. Such reasoning did not apply in the German and Baltic lands, and the Swedish government was content to allow the local nobility to retain their privileges and local administration. Attempts were made at various times to weaken the powers of the nobility over their peasants, and Swedish law was introduced in certain instances, as on the estates of Axel Oxenstierna and in the town of Narva; but on the whole, the Swedish government preferred to leave the provinces to look after their own affairs.

The Livonian nobility, led by the resourceful Otto von Mengden, succeeded in establishing a firm basis for their political hegemony during the reign of queen Christina. The governor-general was to be assisted in the administration of the province by counsellors (*Landräte*), elected by the *Landtag*. Together with deputies elected by the nobility of each district, this twelve-man *Landratskollegium* constituted the watch-dog of aristocratic interest, the *Adelskonvent*. The fact that

24. Rosén J 1946 Statsledning och provinspolitik under Sveriges stormaktstid *Scandia* **17**: pp. 240–4.

many Swedish magnates possessed large estates in Livonia and participated in the government of the province (half of the *Landräte* were
usually Swedish) forged a relatively harmonious community of interests and probably ensured that the privileges and autonomy of the
province remained secure from further interference by the crown until
the 1680s.

The implementation of the *reduktion* in the Baltic provinces challenged many of the fundamental privileges of the indigenous nobility.
In 1690, the Livonian *Landtag* elected a deputation to present their case
in Stockholm. A leading role in this deputation was played by a young
captain, Johann Reinhold Patkul. Patkul's choleric and combative
temper may have made him a doughty defender of Livonian rights,
but his outbursts and personal attacks on the king's governor-general,
Jakob Hastfer, angered the king and his Swedish advisers. The argument advanced by Patkul that Livonia stood in a personal union with
the rulers of Sweden, and that decisions taken by the *riksdag* had no
validity, cut little ice with Karl XI, and the fact that the Livonians
could not produce the original copy of the *Privilegium Sigismundi
Augusti* made their case even less tenable. The deputation returned
empty-handed at the end of 1691, and the Livonian nobility prepared
to dig their heels in and fight for their privileges. A four-man permanent committee was set up at a meeting of the *Adelskonvent*, with
instructions to defend the privileges and liberties of the estate. In a
letter to the king, Patkul spelled out a list of grievances which had
been raised at the meeting of the *Adelskonvent*, attacking Hastfer, the
reduktion and its consequences, and even criticising the tendency towards swedification of the university in Dorpat. The king's council
took an unsympathetic attitude towards complaints that Finnish and
Ingrian priests were replacing Germans. Gyldenstolpe declared that if
any had reason to complain, it was the poor peasants, who had been
enslaved and denied spiritual welfare by the nobility, and Bengt
Oxenstierna compared the conquest of Livonia to the Spanish subjugation of the 'wretched and simple Americans'.[25]

Reinvigorated after a lengthy absence taking the waters in Germany, governor-general Hastfer returned to Riga in 1693. When the
Landtag proved resistant to his demands, he declared the session
concluded. In Stockholm, the council was more than willing to support an investigation and trial of those deemed to be the leaders of the
opposition. An extraordinary court was constituted in Stockholm to
try the ringleaders. Four were condemned to death, though the sent-

25. Isberg A 1953 *Karl XI och den livländska adeln 1684–1695*. Lund, p. 223.

ences were commuted to a term of imprisonment for Vietinghoff, Budberg and Johann Mengden. Complaining that the seizure of his private papers was a breach of the king's letter of safe-conduct, Patkul had prudently fled before the grim sentence of death could be carried out. With him departed the last vestiges of Livonian resistance (Patkul himself was soon to resurface as a leading agent of the anti-Swedish coalition). Hastfer's suggestion that Livonia be incorporated into the Swedish realm found little response in the council, and was not pursued. On 20 December 1694, a royal rescript abolished the *Landräte*, and placed strict limits on the competence and composition of future diets. Preparations were also made for the introduction of Swedish law and law courts, but the outbreak of war in 1700 prevented the implementation of these plans. The Swedish church ordinance of 1686 was also introduced into the Baltic provinces, though it met with some resistance. The 1696 *Ökonomireglement* limited the powers of the lessees of crown lands over their peasantry, and decreed that peasants could complain of unfair treatment to the local courts or even to the governor-general. The crown also embarked on an ambitious prog-ramme to tackle the problem of rural ignorance and paganism by setting up a school in every parish. Hastfer's successor, Erik Dahl-bergh, also proposed the establishment of a regiment of dragoons on the Swedish allotment system, an idea which found favour with the king but which, like so many other plans, was fated to remain still-born with the outbreak of war. Dahlbergh feared that the indigenous nobility, no longer possessed of the land, might prefer to flee in the face of the enemy rather than defend the country. As it turned out, many Baltic nobles remained loyal to the Swedish crown, in whose service they now found lucrative employment: Patkul's exhortations to his countrymen to abandon their allegiance fell on deaf ears. Loyal-ty may have been a matter of expediency rather than of conviction for many, and the peasantry may have preferred to loot abandoned man-ors to fighting the invader; but there was to be no guerrilla war against Karl XII's forces in the Baltic provinces as there had been against the armies of his father in Skåne thirty years earlier.[26]

In Pomerania, the estates and the ruler had achieved a kind of balance of power based on the dualistic notion of sovereignty. This state of affairs was rudely disturbed by occupation, war and the extinction of the ducal line in 1637. By the terms of an agreement concluded in 1529, the Pomeranian duchies were to pass to the elector

26. Schartau S 1924 De svenska östersjöprovinserna vid det stora nordiska krigets utbrott *Karolinska Förbundets Årsbok*. 1924, pp. 1–53.

of Brandenburg in the event of the ducal line dying out. Gustav Adolf had tried to tie the elector to the Swedish–Pomeranian alliance of 1630 by insisting that if Brandenburg had not ratified and confirmed the treaty before the death of the duke, the Swedish crown would sequestrate Pomerania until the right of succession was established and Sweden had been compensated for her war expenses. The Pomeranian estates refused to accept this reservation, and also claimed that the 1630 treaty did not give Sweden the right to exercise civil and ecclesiastical administration in the duchies. They attempted to present their case during the peace negotiations at Osnabrück, but without success. Sweden acquired western Pomerania as a fief in perpetuity, thus effectively blocking the Hohenzollern claim, and was allowed to retain the right to levy tolls on shipping in the Pomeranian ports. A court of appeal for Sweden's German territories was to be established, and the religion, rights and liberties of the queen's new subjects were guaranteed.

In the years immediately following the conclusion of peace, some consideration was given to a plan for the general administration of Sweden's German lands. A *Generaldirektorium* in Wismar was to oversee the administration of the separate provinces, whose powers of local government would be substantially reduced. Nothing came of these plans, however, nor of the efforts to rationalise and reform the chaotic finances of the Pomeranian lands, which would have involved a resumption of alienated ducal demesne lands. The constitutional arrangement arrived at in 1663 was essentially a compromise, which preserved the dualistic principles of the estates whilst allowing the crown the right to maintain a standing army in the duchy and to continue levying taxes originally introduced to meet the costs of war, such as the excise on drink and grain. The strategic importance of Pomerania made the provision of an adequate defence force the primary consideration: having secured this objective (which had largely to be financed by the other parts of the Swedish empire, so inadequate were Pomerania's own financial resources), the crown was wise enough not to push its claims to sovereignty. The court of appeal set up in Wismar was cleverly used by the estates as an instrument for settling internal consitutional matters: since the majority of assessors were appointed (and paid) by the Pomeranian estates, the crown generally found itself on the losing side. Karl XI was anxious to break the grip of the Pomeranian gentry over the Wismar tribunal and an addition to the *Tribunalsordnung* in 1692 sought to confine the scope of the court to purely juridical matters: but this restriction was to be abandoned after 1721. The 1663 settlement survived in all important respects until the end of Swedish overlordship in the early nineteenth century, ensuring the continued existence of the Pomeranian estates at a time when such representative bodies were disappearing elsewhere in Germany.[27]

In Schering Rosenhane's *Hortus regius* of 1645, there is an emblematic representation of the Swedish state as a four-tier building (the estates), capped by a crown and flanked by the scales of justice and a sceptre, both suspended from heaven. David Ehrenstrahl's 1693 portrait of the dowager queen Hedvig Eleanora places the four estates in adulatory postures around an altar-pedestal, upon which the robed Svea, with the symbols of majesty in her hands, stands beside portraits of the royal family.[28] This painting is a clear illustration of the altered relationship between crown and estates; but it is worth noting that the estates nonetheless remain in the picture, albeit in submissive mood. The period of absolutism in Sweden did not survive the childless Karl XII, and the estates were to regain the initiative in 1719–20, until the pendulum swung once more towards strong monarchical rule in 1772. In Denmark, the estates disappeared altogether until the nineteenth century. Absolutism in the northern kingdoms was, however, rather less extreme than the high-flown language of the Royal Law or the 1693 declaration of the Swedish estates might suggest. It was established by consent, rather than by coercion. The political power of the nobility was checked, particularly in Denmark, but the crown did not dispense with the services of the aristocracy. Instead, state service, rather than land ownership, became the determinant of nobility, and was given formal structure through the introduction of tables of ranks. On the other hand, the Scandinavian states did not follow the Prussian path towards a centralised, bureaucratic–military state in which the non-noble estates were crushed into submission, and the yoke of serfdom and *Kadavergehorsamkeit* (blind obedience) in the army were the lot of the wretched peasantry. The bonds which tied the Danish peasants to their landlords were tight, certainly, but they had ready access to the local law courts, and the crown did show a concern for their material and spiritual circumstances – as did the Swedish crown, at home and overseas – which was not the case in the domains of the elector of

27. Back P-E 1955 *Herzog und Landschaft. Politische Ideen und Verfassungsprogramme in Schwedisch-Pommern um die Mitte des 17 Jahrhunderts*. Lund. Gerhard D (ed.) 1974 *Ständische Vertretungen in Europa im 17 und 18 Jahrhundert*: Back P-E Die Stände in Schwedisch-Pommern im späten 17 und im 18 Jahrhundert. Göttingen, pp. 120–30.

28. Dahlgren S (ed.) 1967 *Kultur och samhälle i stormaktstidens Sverige*: Ellenius A Konst och miljö, Stockholm, pp.41–5.

Brandenburg. To a radical Whig such as Robert Molesworth, the Danes had reaped 'the Glory of having forged their own Chains, and the Advantage of Obeying without reserve. A Happiness which I suppose no English Man will ever envy them.' But the Glorious Revolution of 1688 was, after all, something of an exception.[29] Forty years earlier, another Englishman basking in the liberty of revolution drily remarked that the right of the Swedish king to initiate discussion in the *riksdag* by means of a proposition might be a good way to preserve the tranquillity of the realm, but perhaps less beneficial for the rights and liberties of the people. 'This were an inconvenience if the people's rights and liberties were not already settled; but, by our laws, the boundaries of the King's power and of the people's rights are sufficiently known and established,' was the reply of his interlocutor, the aged Swedish chancellor.[30] Axel Oxenstierna was sounding the bass note of much of Swedish political thought, that the laws of the land determined the relationship of king and subject: but, as Karl XI and the estates were to demonstrate in 1680, the law of the land could also be appealed to in order to redefine the nature of that relationship.

29. Molesworth R 1698 *An account of the State of Denmark as it was in the year 1692.* London, p. 74.

30. Whitelocke B 1888 *Journal of the Swedish embassy 1653–54* (2 vols). London, vol. 2, p. 279.

CHAPTER NINE
Trade and the Baltic Economy

FROM GRAIN TO NAVAL STORES

'The trade of the Baltic Sea is as the root of all other marine trades,' wrote Sir Thomas Roe in 1631, 'and lies hid in the baseness of the commodities, yet all the beautiful fruits of navigation are supplied from it, in the materials for shipping and therefore it is of as great importance for England as any other.'[1] The Dutch had long held such sentiments, though for them, the 'soul of all commerce' was the grain trade, rather than the purchase of naval stores. Three-quarters of the rye and wheat carried westward through the Sound in the seventeenth century travelled in Dutch bottoms. Although the Dutch no longer dominated the Baltic trade at the end of the seventeenth century in the way they had done a hundred years earlier, their control of the grain trade remained unchallenged. What did change, however, was the importance of the trade. The average volume of grain shipped to Dutch ports in the first half of the eighteenth century was less than half of what had been carried a hundred years previously. The peak years of the early seventeenth century, when as many as a hundred thousand lasts of rye and wheat a year could be shipped westwards from Danzig, were never to recur.

A number of explanations for the decline of the Baltic grain trade have been advanced. The Polish historian Maria Bogucka places the decline within the context of the general crisis in European agriculture during the seventeenth century. Sharp price rises and the low level of efficiency on Polish farms reduced the competitiveness of Baltic grain

1. Cited in Fedorowicz J 1980 *England's Baltic trade in the early seventeenth century. A study in Anglo-Polish commercial diplomacy.* Cambridge, p 51.

on western markets. Writing about the reasons for the falling-off in Danzig's trade in 1660, Johann Köstner noted that Amsterdam had been able to manage without Polish grain during the recent Polish–Swedish wars and that only crop failure in the West or the cheapness of Polish grain could maintain the level of Danzig's grain exports. Bogucka sees the decline setting in before mid-century, whereas Stanisław Hoszowski believes the widespread destruction and depopulation caused during the wars against the Cossacks and the Swedes in the 1650s accentuated the negative features of intensive demesne farming with servile labour, thus hampering any prospects for regeneration or innovation. Others have argued that there was a decline in demand for grain in western Europe, partly as a result of demographic stagnation. Cultivation of new crops such as rice and maize in southern Europe, and improved methods of fertilisation, drainage and crop rotation, may well have increased the level of self-sufficiency. On the other hand, the slump in grain prices persuaded many landowners in western Europe to go over to more profitable forms of husbandry such as dairy-farming.[2]

The consequences of the decline of the grain trade were serious for Danzig and its hinterland. Grain production on Polish noble estates in 1685 was only 65 per cent of what it had been in mid-century, and exports from Danzig fell from 55,000 lasts in 1651 to fewer than 25,000 lasts in the 1670s. More and more vessels from western Europe now sailed beyond Danzig to the Livonian ports in search of flax, hemp, masts, deals and boards, pitch and tar. The English cloth trade, which had inspired the setting up of the Eastland Company in 1579, became increasingly unprofitable: English merchants often preferred to sail in ballast to ship off the commodities needed for an expanding shipbuilding industry, or turned to the re-export of colonial goods such as tobacco. There is evidence to suggest that Danzig's coastal trade in the Baltic during the seventeenth century grew at a faster rate than did her international trade, but it is unlikely that it produced the same profits as had the grain trade in its heyday. The Lübeck customs accounts for 1672–91, for example, reveal that the value of goods shipped from Riga was more than twice that of commodities sent

2. Bogucka M 1974 Danzigs Bedeutung für die Wirtschaft des Ostseeraumes in der frühen Neuzeit *Studia Historia Oeconomica* 9:95–106. Hoszowski S 1960 The Polish Baltic trade in the 15th–18th centuries *Poland at the 11th International Congress of Historical Science at Stockholm*. Warsaw, pp 117–54. Harder-Gersdorff E 1978 Lübeck, Danzig und Riga. Ein Beitrag zur Frage des Handelskonjunktur im Ostseeraum am Ende des 17 Jahrhunderts *Hansische Geschichtsblätter* 96:100–138. Faber J 1966 The decline of the Baltic grain trade in the second half of the seventeenth century *Acta Historica Neerlandica* 1:108–32.

from Danzig, despite the fact than an average of 30 ships per annum hailed from Danzig, as against 27 from Riga. By the end of the century, smaller ports such as Elbing and Pernau were regarded as acceptable substitutes for Danzig: western European merchants gave instructions that their ships should sail on to these ports if prices were too high, or goods not available, in Danzig. The Polish economy was further weakened by foreign competition, which destroyed native industries, such as the forges producing iron around Danzig. The political power of the Polish nobility enabled them to obtain tax and customs privileges which eventually crippled the trade of hitherto flourishing towns such as Poznań and Cracow. These privileges also diminished the ability of the peasantry to compete in the grain trade, and this lack of competition helped preserve the feudal pattern of agricultural production. High tariffs also affected the overland transit trade, and central European merchants began to use the Elbe in preference to the Vistula. The construction of the Oder-Spree canal in the 1660s by the elector of Brandenburg opened up another route to the Elbe, to the benefit of the towns on the Oder.

The Polish economy, geared to grain production, was unable to adapt to the changing pattern of demand in western Europe. High tariffs and the exhaustion of timber supplies in the Vistula hinterland persuaded traders to look eastward for their potash, boards, deals, pitch and tar. Whereas the great bulk of the Eastland Company's trade during the first decades of its existence was with the Prussian ports, only about one-third of England's Baltic imports came from that area by the 1660s. Johannes Köstner complained in 1660 that the flax and hemp trade had moved from Königsberg to Riga, and the evidence of the Sound dues clearly shows the decline of Danzig's earlier predominance in the Baltic trade. Two-fifths of the ships passing westward through the Sound between 1601 and 1610 had sailed from Danzig. By the last decade of the century, however, that proportion had shrunk to less than one-fifth, and Riga was beginning to challenge Danzig's status as the premier port of the southern Baltic.

Riga's trade was based on flax and hemp, which made up 60 per cent of the city's exports at the end of the seventeenth century. Hemp was in great demand in the naval dockyards of the maritime powers: in 1697, it was calculated that Britain spent £90,000 a year on hemp out of a total sum of £205,000 expended on naval stores from the Baltic. The *Atlas maritimus et commercialis*, recalling the years before the outbreak of the Great Northern War, claimed that 'it is out of doubt that Riga is a Port of a very great Trade, and 'tis usual to have 3 or 400

Sail of Ships of all Nations here together.'[3] In addition to flax and hemp, Riga also exported masts, boards and deals, and a quantity of grain. The city also attracted entrepreneurs. A sawmill and linseed-oil mill were set up with Dutch capital and labour, and after these were destroyed by fire, the owner founded textile mills in the city. Riga merchants also established tanneries, ropewalks and foundries, and a shipbuilding industry was started in the Cronstierna yards. A cluster of industries also grew up along the Narova river, where shipyards, flax and hemp refineries and sawmills were founded, often with foreign capital and expertise. After its conquest by Sweden in 1581, Narva's brief period of commercial prosperity had been extinguished, but by the last quarter of the seventeenth century, its economy had significantly improved with the revival of the Russian transit trade.

English merchants were particularly active in the Narva and Riga trade, importing naval stores to meet the demands of a rapidly growing merchant fleet and the Royal Navy. The tonnage of the Royal Navy more than doubled between the restoration of Charles II and the end of the century, and the maintenance of such a fleet necessitated heavy expenditure on imported naval stores, mostly from the Baltic. As early as the reign of Charles I, the Baltic was supplying over three-quarters of the hemp and flax imported into the port of London. The parlous state of affairs during the early years of the Commonwealth, when the number of English vessels passing through the Sound fell from 130 in 1647 to 22 in 1651, and the Danish–Dutch alliance threatened to close the Baltic entirely to English shipping, clearly brought home the message. As Cromwell warned Parliament just before his death, 'if they can shut us out of the Baltic, and make themselves masters of that, where is your trade? where are the materials to preserve your shipping?'[4] It was to protect these interests that the Navigation Acts of 1650–1 were passed, and a state-financed shipbuilding programme entered upon. Further navigation acts in 1660 and 1662 restricted the import of most Baltic commodities to English or native bottoms, and sought to ban the import of naval stores from Holland and Germany. As a consequence, the Dutch were virtually eliminated from the Anglo–Baltic carrying trade, though a good deal of this trade passed to native vessels, as John Robinson, the English envoy to Sweden, observed:

3. *Atlas maritimus et commercialis*. London, 1728, p. 39. Jepson Oddy J 1805 *European Commerce*, p 138, gives a total of 359 ships sailing with cargo from Riga in 1704; *Paul Jakob Marpergers...Moskowitischer Kauffmann*. Lübeck 1723, pp. 230–1 claims 488 ships visited Riga in 1694, out of almost 1,000 vessels calling at Livonian ports.

4. Cited in Fedorowicz 1980, p. 52.

> When Sueden has been engaged in a War, the English Ships have had the whole Employ: but in Times of Peace, the Advantage is so great on the Suedish side, and Merchants so much encouraged by Freedom in Customs to employ their Ships, that English Bottoms cannot be used in that Trade, but only while Sueden is unprovided with a Number of Ships sufficient for the Transportation of their own Commodities.[5]

Thus, when Sweden was engaged in war against Brandenburg–Prussia in 1675, 90 per cent of loaded vessels passing through the Sound for England were owned by English merchants, but in 1693, during the Anglo-French wars, Swedish and English vessels each accounted for 42 per cent of the traffic.

England's Baltic trade was unfavourably balanced, constituting 10 per cent of the country's imports, but only 5 per cent of exports in 1700. The 'drain of money' which this represented exercised the minds of the pamphleteers. During the 1690s, when commercial relations between England and Sweden were strained, Charles Davenant argued that this unfavourable balance had in the past been offset by the fact that English merchants had imported naval stores in English bottoms, but that 'now they do not employ five Ships: and for a great while, have Exported between Three and Four Thousand Pound per Annum'. To counter this unsatisfactory state of affairs, Davenant strongly advocated the development of a colonial trade in naval stores, a policy which Parliament and the government was already considering.[6]

The French lagged a long way behind the maritime powers in the Baltic trade. Only about ten French ships per annum passed through the Sound during the latter half of the seventeenth century, in comparison with some 500 English and 800 Dutch ships. French goods were exported in increasing quantity, but generally in foreign bottoms. Colbert's Compagnie du Nord (1669–74) failed due to lack of merchantmen, Dutch competition and the depredations of war. By exempting foreign vessels from payment of duties on numerous occasions, the French crown sapped native enterprise. Colbert attempted to preserve French forests for shipbuilding needs, but the quality of the timber was poor and the French still had to rely heavily on foreign-built ships or imported naval stores, which were often of inferior quality. The freighting charges on French vessels were high

5. Robinson J 1694 *An Account of Sueden*, pp. 62–3.

6. Davenant C 1698 *Discourses on the Publick Revenue*. London, vol 2, pp. 87, 189, 195, 238–9. Åström S-E 1962 *From Stockholm to St Petersburg. Commercial factors in the political relations between England and Sweden 1675-1700* Studia Historica 2, Helsinki. Kirby D 1974 The Royal Navy's quest for pitch and tar during the reign of Queen Anne *Scandinavian Economic History Review* **22**: 97–116.

and labour costs were greater than those of the Dutch because larger crews were engaged. As with the English, lack of ready capital and credit and technological backwardness tended to put the French at a disadvantage in competition with the Dutch, who could build a *fluit* in 1669 for £800 (to build a similar vessel in England cost around £1,300). The navigation acts were frequently blamed for forcing up the prices of foreign commodities, though in all likelihood, the conservatism of English shipwrights and the superior experience and organisation of the Dutch meant that English ships cost more to build and equip.

The efforts of the Swedish government to exploit more advantageously the commodities which were in demand, such as iron, pitch and tar, greatly annoyed the English. The trade ordinance of 1673 sought to enforce previous regulations governing aliens, and forbade natives to act as figureheads for foreign merchants, who were permitted to reside in Sweden for no more than two months of the year. English diplomatic pressure brought about the postponement of the ordinance, though new restrictions were introduced in 1684, and three years later, the 1673 ordinance was put into effect, with foreigners being allowed a four months' period of residence. In 1695, most of the English factors in Sweden were expelled as a means of bringing pressure upon the English government to pay compensation for Swedish vessels seized during the war against France, and relations were still poor when the Great Northern War broke out four years later. English merchants also protested against the Swedish tar monopoly, established in 1648. Karl X Gustav, well aware that the English merchants trafficking in the Baltic had 'got a taste of our offer of the tar trade', tried to negotiate loans to the crown in return for allowing Dutch and English merchants to buy up pitch and tar from the Company. These negotiations failed, as did a further attempt to press money out of the Dutch in 1661, in return for the abolition of the monopoly.[7] After a brief period of free trade, the monopoly was restored in 1689. The new company had leading Swedish businessmen on its board, and did not lack capital or credit. It came into being at a time of high demand for pitch and tar, and more than three-quarters of its sales were to English merchants, who continued to agitate for the overthrow of the staple right of Stockholm and for free and unrestricted trade with the suppliers in the towns along the Bothnian coast.

7. Hallberg A 1959 *Tjärexport och tjärhandelskompanier under stormaktstiden* Svenska Litteratursällskapet i Finland, Historiska och Litterära Studier, 371:34, Helsingfors, pp. 112–3.

GOVERNMENT AND THE DOMESTIC ECONOMY

The restrictive commercial policies of the Swedish government also caused much resentment amongst the native merchants and producers. A series of trading ordinances issued in the reign of Gustav II Adolf created a small number of staple towns, which alone had the right to engage directly in overseas trade. Market towns were only permitted to trade with their immediate hinterland and the staple towns. After 1636, all ports north of Stockholm and Åbo, with the exception of Gävle, were forbidden to engage in direct trade with foreign merchants. The creation of the Tar Company in 1648 had serious implications for Finland, where tar-burning had rapidly become an important part of the economy. Tar exports made up half of the volume of exports from the three Finnish staple towns of Åbo, Helsingfors and Viborg by the 1640s. After 1648, however, these towns were obliged to sell their tar to the company at a fixed price of fifteen riksdaler a last. Ostrobothnian tar had to be shipped direct to Stockholm, to the great detriment of the trade of Åbo, which had hitherto taken much of the tar from Ostrobothnia. Bad blood was caused by the company's insistence on setting as a standard measure the Rostock beer-barrel, which was larger than the barrels used along the Bothnian coast. Above all, the foreign trade of the staple towns suffered badly, since they no longer were able to offer for sale their principal commodity. As a consequence, there was soon a lack of vital imports such as salt. At the 1649 *riksdag*, complaints were made by burghers from the towns affected by the new monopoly. Queen Christina was unsympathetic to their grievances, retorting that the merchants of the staple towns were welcome to join the Tar Company if they wished to buy shares. This did in fact take place in 1654, though the control of the company's affairs remained firmly in the hands of Stockholm merchants. The Ostrobothnian towns continued to strive to have the monopoly overturned, but the company had powerful defenders at court and in the College of Commerce.

The defence of the Tar Company which the College of Commerce made in 1660 was in accordance with the principles of the well-regulated state. The company, it was argued, had helped keep prices at a good level, and had amassed a large sum of capital which would provide His Majesty with foreign credit. If the company were abolished, the Dutch would capture the trade, prices would fall, and the peasant would suffer. The company and its successors ceaselessly waged war with the suppliers, who demanded higher prices and tended to overproduce; the efforts of the College of Commerce to regulate the situation by imposing quotas or trying to force peasants to stop production were of little avail.

The ordinances and decrees with which the state sought to control and direct production and trade were frequently broken or ignored. Ships from the Ostrobothnian ports traded illegally with the towns of Livonia, as did peasant traders from southern Finland. The crown's attempts to curb the trading activities of the rural population along the rocky coastline of Halland (which came under Swedish control in 1645) merely encouraged smuggling. In the parishes of Onsala and Tölö, there were over fifty vessels, mostly built locally. These small ships, often setting out in ballast, plied the northern seas, carrying sawn timber from Norway to Denmark, north Germany and even Holland. Crown officials strove long and hard to break up the system of patronage practised by wealthier town merchants, who provided hospitality and other comforts to peasants in order to persuade them to sell their goods directly to the merchant and not offer them for sale in the market. Nobles and clergymen as well as merchants employed agents who toured the countryside, buying up peasants' produce. The crown itself was not always consistent in applying its own policies: thus, the vicar of the Ostrobothnian parish of Kalajoki, who had covered a debt to the crown incurred by a royal bailiff, was allowed to buy up and ship to Stockholm all the tar produced in the parish, much to the distress of the merchants of the nearby towns.

In order to combat illegal trade in the countryside and thus increase the crown's revenue from internal customs duties, the Swedish government tried to promote free markets. The trade ordinance of 1636 established three-week autumn fairs in Stockholm and Åbo, at which foreign merchants were free to buy and traders free to sell their goods. This was not unnaturally opposed by the burghers, who felt that this free trading robbed them of their privileges guaranteed under the staple town system, and they prevailed upon the government to exclude other native traders from the market. The system of free markets tended to favour the burghers of the staple towns and the peasantry, but not the market towns, whose number was greatly increased during the seventeenth century. The creation of new towns, such as Vasa on the Ostrobothnian coast, aroused opposition from the peasantry, who feared that their former rights would be lost. The peasants of Närpes petitioned the king in 1626 to allow them to continue to sail to Stockholm with their cattle and fish, for without this right, granted by Karl IX, they were unable to pay their taxes. The petitioners drew a distinction between their produce and the merchandise of nearby Vasa, and were also evidently annoyed at the order to build a fence around the new town, which they claimed had been issued without the king's knowledge. Popular pressure persuaded the government to establish a free market in Vasa, against the wishes of the burghers of the town. The peasants were not satisfied with this victory, however, for they argued that the period of the market was too short to attract foreign merchants.

The crown's efforts to direct the development of Sweden's major export industry were also frustrated in many ways. An ordinance of 1636 complained that there were too many forges in the mining district of Bergslagen, and banned future replacement of foundries with forges. In spite of the attempts to disperse the industry, the forge tax of 1695 revealed that 40 per cent of all bar-iron was produced in forges established in the Bergslagen after 1636. The government was also concerned about the widespread destruction of the forests. In 1648, there were complaints of a lack of timber in the eastern dales (Österdalarna), whilst twenty years later, the local governor observed that timber was becoming scarce in the river valleys of the whole Dalarna region. The first statute designed to preserve timber stocks was passed in 1647. The destructive habits of the Finnish settlers in the forests of Norrland, Dalarna and the Bergslagen were singled out for attention: anyone who practised burn-beat cultivation was liable to be jailed and to have his farm destroyed.

The Swedish government also faced problems in its attempts to promote domestic industry. The rural population either made their own clothes and household utensils or purchased them from wandering peddlers. Rural handicrafts (*slöjd*) flourished, and in certain areas, home-produced items, such as nails made in Närke and furniture in Halland, earned the peasantry a sizeable income. The upper classes preferred to buy better-quality imported goods, which meant that the only significant customer for native manufactures was the crown. The textile industry was given a boost by the 1686 instruction, which decreed that the army should be fitted out with uniforms made of Swedish cloth, but it failed to make much impact upon the domestic market. Although certain high-ranking personages such as Gabriel Oxenstierna and even Queen Christina favoured opening up or even the abolition of the gilds, the numerous clauses of the 1621 gild regulations were rigorously enforced. The legislation of 1669 was the first systematic attempt to regulate the gild system. In principle, the gilds were to take all willing to learn who could be taught, but in practice, these regulations had a negligible effect. In small towns, gilds were few, and even in the larger cities, the proportion of apprentices to masters was very small. There were also many craftsmen outside the gilds, the so-called *bönhasar*. Although officialdom attempted to curb their activities, they had powerful protectors. Noblemen preferred to employ their own wigmakers and tailors, and public institutions such as the Admiralty employed large numbers of masons and building workers who were not enrolled in any gild. The efforts of the tailors' gild in Copenhagen to drive out the *bønhaser*, most of whom were employed by the court, came to grief in 1662 when the alderman of the gild was packed off to prison for daring to suggest that it was the craftsmen who had saved the city during the siege and had kept the crown on the king's head.

The Swedish roads and the conveyancing system generally aroused the admiration of foreign visitors, though journeys were often long and made hazardous by heavy drifts of snow or floods. Bulstrode Whitelocke's large retinue took three weeks to get to Uppsala from Göteborg in December 1653. The sledge was a more rapid form of transport, conveying de la Motraye from Uppsala to Stockholm in six hours in 1717. A winter without snow posed severe problems: in 1645, the lack of snow in the Bergslagen brought the mines to a halt, since no hay supplies could be sent up by sledge, and the miners had thus been obliged to send their horses into Närike for fodder. A canal-building programme was begun by Karl Bonde, but the Trollhätte canal planned by the polymath Christopher Polhem was abandoned as impracticable, since only flat-bottomed boats with collapsible masts would have been able to use it. In one other form of communication the Swedes excelled: a postal system across the frontier to Hamburg and Stralsund existed in the first decades of the seventeenth century, and the 1636 ordinance provided for agents stationed every two to three Swedish miles (20–30 km) along the main routes, who were to expedite the mails in return for exemption from taxation. Postmasters were appointed in the towns, with a central directorate in Stockholm.

By the middle of the seventeenth century, the bars of copper which were issued to maintain parity through weight with silver coinage had reached monstrous proportions. A six-daler piece in 1655 weighed almost twenty kilos, and the bars given to Whitelocke in recognition of his services filled the hold of a sizeable ship. Such heavy coinage certainly deterred thieves: two men who stole 170 daler from a shop in Viborg were unable to raise the money above knee-height. The impracticability of such coinage, and the difficulties encountered by merchants seeking to clear bills of exchange, led to the establishment of a bank in Stockholm during the reign of Karl X Gustav by a Dutch–Livonian, Hans Wittmacher, subsequently ennobled as Johan

Palmstruch. Palmstruch's bank had two sections, dealing with exchange and credit. Although the note issue was modest, it was impossible to fix it against a bimetallist currency, since silver and copper constantly shifted in value in relation to each other. A rise in the value of copper in the 1660s led to a run on the bank, and despite the efforts of the government, it was declared insolvent in 1663. The unfortunate Palmstruch was jailed for financial irregularities. The bank was however resurrected in 1668 as the bank of the estates (*Riksens Ständers Bank*), directed by six commissioners chosen by the *riksdag*. It was not permitted to issue notes, and its operations remained limited. By the end of the century, the crown had become its largest customer, using it to obtain advances for the treasury.

The governments of the northern European states, poor in native skills and capital, welcomed foreign entrepreneurs, even bending their strict religious laws to accommodate them (though Axel Oxenstierna once told a Swedish merchant that he would rather see his fatherland without trade than corrupted by alien religions). In almost any town with pretensions to commerce there were Dutch, German or Scottish immigrants. Karl IX's new town of Göteborg was in all essentials a Dutch settlement on Swedish soil, and the first council of the new town which rose upon the ashes of the settlement destroyed by the Danes in 1612 included ten Dutchmen, seven Swedes and a Scot. Lists of merchants engaged in overseas trade out of Åbo show a steady increase in the number of foreigners, particularly Germans, between 1616 and 1652, a pattern which was repeated in all coastal towns. Christian IV abolished the privileges of the gilds in 1613 in an effort to encourage foreign craftsmen to settle in Denmark, and his successors sought actively to encourage weavers, spinners and dyers by holding out promises of exemptions from the payment of taxes and imposts. The Danish East India Company, founded in 1616, was largely financed by merchants from Holland and Hamburg, and a Dutch syndicate took over the short-lived Silk Company in 1624. A number of foreign entrepreneurs, such as the Marselis family, managed to establish commercial and industrial empires stretching from Amsterdam to Russia. Others sought to make their fortunes with ambitious projects. In 1653, a Reval merchant decided to set up a silk spinnery, and obtained a ten-year monopoly from the Swedish government for the purchase of Persian silk: financial difficulties and the decline of Reval's trade, however, doomed the enterprise. Another entrepreneur in Livonia, von Rademacher, secured the monopoly of production of certain metal goods, and the imposition of a 25 per cent duty on imported wares to protect his enterprise, a levy which aroused the opposition of the Riga city council.

The Swedish government devoted a great deal of time to considering ways of developing and controlling the Russian trade. The reports prepared by Swedish agents in Russia during the middle of the seventeenth century showed that trade from and into Russia could be directed via the Baltic or the Arctic, depending on the policy of the Russian government and the inclinations of the foreign merchants. Although the volume of trade passing through Archangel was low in comparison with that passing through the Baltic ports, the Swedish government was concerned to divert or destroy that northern trade route. In the 1640s, the government embarked upon a policy of attracting foreign merchants to the Baltic ports by abolishing the border duty into Russia, lowering the transit duty to negligible levels and ending the ban on *Gast-zu-Gast* trading (ban on direct trading between foreign merchants). There was a sharp increase in trading activity, especially in Narva, during the early 1650s, when the Anglo-Dutch war effectively closed off the Archangel traffic. Although the outbreak of war between Muscovy and Sweden in 1656 caused the temporary suspension of trade through Narva, the revival in that port's trade continued during the last decades of the century.

After the *libertas commerciorum* period of the 1640s, Sweden sought to pursue a more active policy of concentrating the Russian trade into the hands of Swedish or naturalised merchants. An ambitious attempt to buy up Russian grain surpluses had been made during the reign of Gustav Adolf, in order to cash in on the high prices commanded by grain on the Amsterdam market. It seems, however, that the profits from this venture were relatively modest, and fell steadily after 1631, when the slump in prices in Amsterdam was not accompanied by a similar fall in prices paid for grain in Russia. The Russians were also unwilling to allow Swedes unhindered rights to monopolise grain supplies and circumscribed the efforts of Swedish agents after 1631.[8] Another grandiose plan was mooted by Johann de Rodes in 1653, for the purchase of the entire year's production of Russian leather, which would cut the Dutch out of the market at a time when they were engaged in war, and would also benefit Sweden's Baltic possessions. The 1655 Krusenstierna embassy was instructed to obtain the right of free trade for Swedish merchants throughout the whole of Russia, and to press the Russian government to lower its customs duties to Swed-

8. Ekholm L 1974 Rysk spannmål och svenska krigsfinanser 1629–1633 *Scandia* **40**: 57–103.

ish levels. The treaty of Kardis (1661) provided for 'free and unhindered trade' between the two countries, but the New Trading Ordinance issued by tsar Aleksey in 1667 obliged foreigners wishing to trade in the Russian hinterland to pay high transit duties in foreign currency. The Swedes were particularly incensed to find that the duty on the Baltic transit trade was higher than the duty payable in Archangel, and negotiations to persuade the Russians to change their policy proved fruitless. The advice proffered to the Swedish government by the secretary to the College of Commerce, J.P. Lillienhoff, was that only the conquest of Archangel would suffice, a recommendation which Karl XII was to try and put into practice in 1701. The increasingly protectionist policy of the Russian government also irritated the Swedes, as it did other nations. The lack of adequate trade regulations and provisions, and currency problems made the development of any form of commerce difficult and provoked storms of complaints from foreign merchants. In these trying circumstances, the Dutch proved to be most adept at surviving: commercially backward countries such as Sweden could do little other than concoct ambitious but unrealisable plans for the development of the Russian trade.[9]

In spite of Sweden's relative commercial backwardness, its volume of trade increased considerably during the seventeenth century. Textiles and foodstuffs were the principal imports. The amount of salt imported rose by 46 per cent between 1560 and 1685, although its share of the total amount of imports declined from around a quarter during the sixteenth century to a tenth by the reign of queen Christina. Salt was still vital for the national economy, however. As Axel Oxenstierna observed in 1643, Sweden's lack of salt was the one thing which the Jute could take advantage of, 'for if we had salt in the country, we would have less need to go to war with him'.[10] The vagaries of the climate also meant that Sweden–Finland had to import grain during periods of bad harvest: not without reason were the Baltic provinces regarded as Sweden's granary. In 1685, for example, after the failure of the harvest in central Sweden, the Baltic provinces

9. On Swedish–Russian trade, see Attman A 1985 *Swedish aspirations and the Russian market during the 17th century* Acta Regiae Societatis Scientarum et Litterarum Gothoburgensis. Humaniora 24. Göteborg. Piirimäe H 1961 *Kaubanduse küsimused Vene-Rootsi suhetes 1661–1700 a*. Tartu Riikliku Ülikooli toimetised 113, Tartu; and the two-volume collection of documents from Swedish and Soviet archives, published in 1978: *Ekonomiska förbindelser mellan Sverige och Ryssland under 1600-talet/Ekonomicheskie svyazi mezhdu Rossiey i Shvedtsiey v XVII veke*. Stockholm–Moscow.

10. Hecksher E 1936 *Sveriges ekonomiska historia från Gustav Vasa* (2 vols). Stockholm, vol. 1:2, p. 551.

supplied Stockholm with 153,145 hectolitres of grain worth almost a quarter of a million riksdaler.

The needs of the court, the magnates, the Admiralty and the military garrison, in addition to the town's growing population – which increased from around 10,000 in the 1620s to over 50,000 by the end of the century – attracted all with goods to sell to Stockholm. The crown's policy of encouraging monopoly companies and of concentrating active trade in the staple towns also fostered the growth of the city's trade. At the end of the seventeenth century, the Swedish merchant fleet probably totalled 750 ships, mostly small coastal craft: the large ships of over a hundred lasts' capacity were nearly all owned by Stockholm merchants organised in trading companies.

Sweden's major asset during the Age of Greatness was its mining industry. Copper and iron accounted for over three-quarters of the value of Swedish exports during the latter half of the seventeenth century, but whereas copper production declined from around 2,000 tons annually in mid-century to 1,200 tons per annum in the reign of Karl XII, the annual output of iron rose. In 1695, there were some 500 forges and 324 foundries spread throughout central Sweden. Exports of bar-iron tripled, from 10,000 tons annually in the 1640s to 33,000 tons by the 1690s. It has been calculated that at least four-fifths of Sweden's iron production was exported. By the reign of Karl XII, England was by far the most important customer, and it is an indication of Sweden's dominance over the market that the bar-iron imported by 'East Country' merchants into England in 1718 (after the government in London had prohibited the direct import of bar-iron from Sweden) had been supplied by Sweden via Königsberg and the Dutch ports.

Christian IV could not trump this Swedish ace, in spite of vigorous efforts to promote the mining industry in Norway. Denmark's export trade was largely dependent upon the demand for agricultural produce, especially beef. Over 30,000 head of cattle were driven annually down the drove roads to the Hamburg market in the early years of Christian IV's reign, reaching a peak figure of 50,000 in 1612. During the last stages of the Thirty Years' War, however, cattle exports began to fall sharply, and Danish farming, already badly afflicted by the devastation of war, entered a period of crisis. Noble interference in trade and the burden of taxation prompted the burghers of Jutland to address a protest to the king in 1629, and the antagonism between urban merchants and the nobility continued to simmer. An anonymous pamphlet written during the early years of Frederik III's reign accused the nobility of ruining the potential trade of the burghers by engaging in trade on their own account, and also attacked the royal policy of favouring monopoly companies. The granting of new privileges to the city of Copenhagen by Frederik III in 1659 not only breached noble privileges regarding land and office-holding: it also gave a powerful fillip to the commercial life of the city, whose population doubled between 1660 and 1690. In 1674, the Swedish agent could report a notable increase in the town's maritime trade, which during the reign of Frederik III yielded something like one-third of all the customs dues paid in the kingdom. Flagging enterprises such as the East India Company were revived, and new industries to supply the needs of the growing consumer market were set up in and around the city. A small group of patrician burghers, often linked by marriage, were actively involved in a variety of enterprises. Hans Nansen, born in Flensborg, had led the Arctic expedition of the *Petsoriske Kompagni* in the 1620s, and his expertise in northern waters secured him a job as secretary to Mikkel Vibe, the city's leading merchant, and a directorship in the Icelandic Company. Jacob Madsen, born on Gotland, was active in the Spanish and Mediterranean trade, and a major supplier to the admiralty and the court. Both men were to become burghermasters of the city. Perhaps the most spectacular entrepreneurial career was that of Henrik Müller, a Holsteiner who had entered state service in the 1630s as a clerk in the king's private treasury and had begun to make money in commercial ventures. Collaboration with Korfits Ulfeldt further advanced his career and fortunes, especially as a supplier to the fleet. During the 1640s, when the royal navy was considerably expanded, Müller supplied almost 40 per cent of the goods and materials for naval construction. His interests ranged from forestry and mining in Norway to ironworks in the Mølle valley north of Copenhagen: in 1660, he was the largest private landlord in the capital. Both Müller and Nansen played prominent roles in the events of 1660, and both men were principal shareholders in the revitalised Icelandic Company.

The wealth and activities of such men were highly dependent upon the crown. It was the growing requirements of the court, the navy and the army which provided men like Müller and Louis de Geer with opportunities. The regulations and decrees of the crown could also influence trade, often adversely. The efforts of the Swedish crown to channel rural trade into the towns were thus weakened by the Little Toll of 1622, an *ad valorem* duty payable on goods brought to market, which led to widespread evasion and illegal trading in the countryside. Attempts to protect native industries by banning the import of competing foreign commodities were rarely successful. Ambitious projects designed to create a native industry often failed because of a lack of skilled workers, raw materials, and above all, the absence of a sizeable domestic market. Christian IV's efforts to promote a textile and silk industry in Copenhagen came to nothing: the one sizeable manufactory, which furnished most of the army's clothing, was the house of correction.

The princes of the era certainly did not lack vision, even if they did not have the resources with which to fulfil their ambitions. Friedrich, duke of Holstein-Gottorp, invited Dutch colonists to his new town of Friedrichstadt on the river Eider, and entertained great hopes of making this a major port for the Persian trade. To this end, an embassy was sent to Russia in the 1640s, but little was achieved. Tracts of land along the Delaware river were bought from the Indians by the Swedes in the reign of queen Christina, but Swedish settlement proved to be short-lived, for the area was seized by the Dutch in 1655. At various times, Sweden, Denmark and Brandenburg–Prussia sought to establish trading posts on the African coastline, though none of the Africa companies set up to develop the colonial trade prospered.

For a brief period, Jakob, duke of Kurland (1642–81) was able to achieve what many of his fellow-rulers dreamed of. During the duke's long reign, his shipyards at Windau built forty-four men-of-war and seventy-nine merchantmen. The native merchant fleet was able to cut back the Dutch predominance over the country's export trade, and the duke's flag was raised on the island of Tobago and in the Gambia. Mitau, the capital of the small duchy, was given staple rights to the colonial trade. Over seventy new enterprises, including sawmills, iron and steel foundries and glass manufactories, were created in the duchy, and there was a flourishing export trade in meat and dairy products. Sudden occupation by Swedish troops in 1658, and the two-year captivity of the duke, largely destroyed these ventures. The loss of much of his fleet meant that the duke was powerless to deal with the pirates who infested the Caribbean and attacked the Tobago trade: the colonies had eventually to be given over to the English.

The rise and fall of the tiny mercantile state of Kurland illustrates many of the problems faced by the northern lands. The promotion of trade and industry was by no means a vain exercise, even if the more grandiose projects ultimately failed due to lack of adequate capital, resources or expertise, and the superior competition of the maritime powers. But all too often, the results were rather meagre in comparison with the achievements of the Dutch and English, who continued to dominate and to a large extent determine the pattern of the Baltic economy.

THE LAND

The expansion of the Swedish state was achieved by a country with very limited human resources. Louis XIV could claim to rule over twenty million Frenchmen; Karl XI's scattered lands sustained fewer than three million souls. Population growth remained sluggish, periodically pruned by the ravages of war, epidemics and famine caused by crop failures. During the seventeenth century, Europe experienced what has been termed a minor ice age, which in northern latitudes could spell disaster for the harvest. Long, intensely cold winters, followed by hot, dry summers, often terminated by sudden and premature night frosts and floods were recorded in contemporary accounts. The Swedish clergyman Petrus Magnus Gyllenius, for example, reported that floods in autumn 1648 hindered the gathering of the harvest and prevented the sowing of winter seed; at Michaelmas, there were heavy snowfalls, and there was no let-up in the harsh winter weather before Christmas. The cold weather lasted well into May 1649, and there was widespread famine in 1650. Gyllenius noted that people were reduced to eating leaves and twigs, and that it was impossible to count the numbers of beggars swarming the streets. Nearly fifty years later, during the great famine years of 1696–7, the Danish resident in Stockholm reported that such misery had not been seen in the kingdom since the time of Gustav Vasa: in Finland, whole parishes were wiped out by hunger, whilst in the capital, bakers' shops were looted by famished crowds.[11] It has been estimated that over a quarter of the population of Finland perished during these years, and that pre-famine population levels were not attained until the second half of the eighteenth century. The kingdom of Sweden was largely spared the ravages of war, but the campaigns conducted by Gustav Adolf and Karl Gustav in Pomerania and Poland wrought immense destruction. The population of Pomerania probably was reduced by 50 per cent, that of Mazovia by 64 per cent. Further east, the mid-century wars, bad harvests and epidemics cut great swathes through Lithuania and White Russia: around Vitebsk, the number of hearths recorded for taxation purposes fell by over 60 per cent between 1648 and 1667, and it is estimated that the population of the region was reduced by one-third during these two decades. The Russo-Swedish war of 1656–8 accelerated the flight into Russia of the

11. Gardberg C, Toijer D (eds) 1962 *Diarium Gyllenianum: eller Petrus Magni Gyllenii dagbok 1622-1667*. Karlstad, pp. 106, 108, 114, 123. Fryxell A 1843 *Utdrag och afskrifter af missiver från danska sändebud i Stockholm till regeringen i Köbenhavn från 11 jan.1696 till april 1700* Handlingar rörande Sverges historia 4. Stockholm, pp 65, 78–9, 91–2.

Orthodox population of the Swedish-held parts of Karelia and Ingria. In 1651, 55 cent of the population of the northern part of Swedish-held Karelia were Orthodox: forty years later, a mere 10 per cent. In spite of efforts to resettle the area with Lutheran Finns, many farms remained deserted.

Denmark also suffered frequent invasions: the wars of 1657–60 were particularly destructive, probably reducing the population by one-fifth. The inhabitants of Jutland were plagued by wolves after 1660, and mass wolf-hunts had to be organised to keep the numbers down. The amount of land under the plough varied from almost half of the land area of Fyn and Falster to less than 10 per cent in the infertile parts of the Jutland peninsula. Here, sand drift posed serious problems along the west coast, whilst inland, there were large stretches of heath and bogland. It has been estimated that almost 5 per cent of peasant farms in Denmark were derelict as late as the 1680s, and modern Danish historians are inclined to believe that this figure is too low. The crown strove to get to grips with the problem by offering tax exemptions and other inducements to any willing to take up the tenancy of a deserted farm. Legislation in 1682 added a note of compulsion to the package of exemptions, placing the burden of restoring abandoned holdings upon the shoulders of the peasant community. Private landlords had long sought to compel their tenants to take up derelict farms. The fiscal policies of the Danish crown after 1660 gave added impetus to these efforts. From 1670, the landowner was responsible for the payment of taxes on all holdings, including derelict land, in return for exemption for demesne land, and it does not appear as if the exchequer was very sympathetic to those land-owners who were unable to find tenants for their vacant farms. Not surprisingly, government policy had the effect of reinforcing the tendency to incorporate abandoned farms into the seigneurial demesne: though the 1682 ordinance prohibited the enclosure of villages and peasant farms within the manorial demesne, arbitrary evictions and the extension of crown or private demesnes still occurred.

In spite of the extension of demesne land, small-scale tenant farmers continued to dominate Danish agriculture. The ordinance of 1523 and the Kolding recess of 1558 appear to have strengthened security of tenure, but the recess also enshrined the nobleman's right to exploit his estate to the fullest advantage. Although it would seem that security of tenure for life was fairly well established as the norm on the islands and Jutland, there are indications that the tenant's freedom of movement was increasingly circumscribed in the early decades of absolutism. Clause 17 of the 1682 ordinance prohibited a tenant or his widow from quitting the tenancy without the consent of the landlord, unless it could be demonstrated that the latter had acted contrary to the law, a restriction which may well have increased the number of illegal desertions. On the other hand, however, the institution of *vornedskab*, which bound all adult males on the large islands to the estate on which they were born, was ultimately abolished in the early eighteenth century.

In Estonia, three-quarters of the peasant farms in 1620 had been abandoned. The recovery here was characterised by a marked extension of demesne land, often by Swedish noblemen and officials, the beneficiaries of the crown's largesse. Conquered territories in Livonia were likewise sold or donated to Swedish nobles: Axel Oxenstierna, for example, received from the king the bishopric of Wenden (established during Polish rule), with all the estates, land, rent and revenues of the area. By the 1680s, over half of the cultivated land in Livonia was owned by Swedish nobles, with the native nobility possessing just over one-third. Resettlement of the land was initially difficult. Landowners hunted peasants who had fled to the safety of the islands, and legislation sought to ensure that landless peasants were either engaged on an annual contract or were settled on peasant farms. Troops and army horses were used to clear overgrown land, and numbers of Finns were brought in as settlers. Within thirty years, however, the landowners were faced with the problem of a labour surplus. The large estates sought to meet this problem by expansion and rationalisation. Simple day labour might be replaced by a specific work assignment, such as ploughing a given area of land, and peasants surplus to needs on the main farm might be moved to new, outlying farms (*Beigüter*). Count Claes Tott doubled his grain yield in the 1660s by creating new farms, to which he sent almost half of the peasants from his two main estates. Magnus de la Gardie also created new farms on his Arensburg estates, and tried to use surplus labour in industries such as flax-spinning, tar-burning and glass-blowing.

During the course of the century, the proportion of peasant farms to demesne holdings in Estonia and Livonia shrank, and the amount of labour service which the peasants were obliged to perform on the estate increased. In addition to providing an ox team for ploughing and horses for harrowing (the estate usually kept an emergency reserve, which could be loaned to those whose own animals had died or were too exhausted), the peasant could be called upon to help with manuring, sowing and harvesting, and for a variety of extraordinary duties. On the Oxenstierna estates, each peasant farm was obliged to provide a worker with a horse for five days of the week the whole year round, or one worker on foot with an extra fieldhand in the summer. Farms with excess manpower had to provide a third worker as an extraordinary service. Each household had to provide in turn a worker to tend the demesne animals or to perform night-watch and cartage duties. Boon work, usually rewarded with food, could be demanded for urgent tasks.

Demesne farming was primarily geared to grain production 'the only thing which the countryman can turn to money', as Bengt Horn observed in 1666. Large-scale farming which depended upon cheap servile labour was not necessarily more efficient or productive than the small peasant farm. The expansion of acreage under the plough which took place on numerous large estates in the Baltic provinces and Prussia brought increased output, but not better yields. On the Oxenstierna estates in Livonia, revenue from the peasantry was almost four times as great as that from the demesne over the period 1624–54, though there were considerable fluctuations in this pattern. Arnold Soom has shown that grain yields appear to have been higher on the poorer soils of north Estonia than in the south, where many of the large estates were to be found, and ascribes this to poor manuring on the larger fields in the south. Dung was the fundament of field husbandry, as Erik Oxenstierna sagaciously observed, and there is evidence to suggest that better manuring may have increased the grain yields on the Oxenstierna estates in Livonia. Even here, however, the peasants probably got higher returns from their seed corn as a result of better manuring ratios. The peasant usually had a pair of draught oxen, and could employ other methods of fertilisation, such as burning twigs and straw, on his small fields: in northern Estonia, burn-beating was still common. On the large estates given over to grain production, animal husbandry was comparatively neglected. Cattle were poorly housed and inadequately fed, and had often to be carried to the pastures in the spring, weak and emaciated after the long winter. Comparatively little attention was paid to improving pasture land, or the provision of more nutritious fodder.

Agriculture in north-eastern Europe thus remained technically backward, dependent upon cheap compulsory labour. Peasants compelled to work on the lord's land were unlikely to have been the most efficient form of workforce, either in terms of their individual work input or of the overall deployment of those obliged to perform labour service. The problem of a labour surplus was summed up by a revision commission for Livonia set up by the crown in 1688, which observed that: 'if a crown estate has too many workers and not enough field work for them, so that the labour greatly exceeds the value of the revenues of the estate, since the fields of the demesne are either too small or of poor quality, then ways must be found to diminish the proportion of labour and increase the revenues.'[12]

Large estates were a feature of the serf economy east of the Elbe. Over half the estates in Mecklenburg, Pomerania and parts of East Prussia were over one hundred hectares in size, whilst the average size of a seigneurial demesne in Poland was even greater. Manorial demesnes accounted for over a quarter of the tilled land in northern Estonia. In the northern kingdoms, the proportion was much less, ranging from 9 per cent in Denmark (1688) to 7 per cent in Finland (1670). In Sweden, where the nobility owned 63 per cent of all cultivated land in 1655, large manorial estates (*säterier*) were comparatively few. The average size of forty-two manorial farms in the relatively fertile regions of Uppland and Södermanland was only 37.5 hectares, and in Kronoberg province, only 7.5 hectares. By comparison, the average size of Danish manorial estates, according to the 1688 land register, was over 100 hectares. The number of *säterier*, however, increased significantly. Acquisition of a manorial estate was important for reasons of prestige and tax evasion. They were to be found in the more fertile areas of the realm, in the plains of central Sweden, on the southern coast of Finland and along the waterways of the hinterland. The extension of noble demesne was particularly great in Finland, where half of the farms in the mid-seventeenth century were in the hands of those who had received donations or had purchased estates from the crown. The greatest increase in the number of *säterier* occurred immediately after the Peace of Westphalia. Most were small, and almost half were farmed by peasants displaced from their land, who paid half the crop as rent. The income from demesne farming was also but a small proportion of the revenue gained from peasant dues.

A succession of bad harvests during the first three decades of the seventeenth century, the constant drain of manpower for military service and the growing burden of extraordinary taxation severely affected Finnish agriculture. Yields were in any event low: a peasant household in south-west Finland could expect in a normal year to harvest around 1,400 kilogrammes of corn, of which a thousand kilogrammes went to feed the household, and the rest in taxes. Between 1630 and the mid-1650s, it appears that annual sowings of grain fell by a fifth in the western part of southern Finland, and by as much as a third in some districts. The amount of livestock appears to have

12. Soom A 1954 *Die Herrenhof in Estland im 17 Jahrhundert*. Lund, p. 234. See also Dunsdorfs E 1981 *The Livonian estates of Axel Oxenstierna*. Stockholm.

declined between 1570 and 1620, and the number of farms fell from 33,991 in the 1560s to 27,486 in 1634–5, rising again to 31,684 in the mid-1690s. Not all were lost through incorporation into manorial estates; many were probably abandoned temporarily by farmers unable or unwilling to pay taxes. The pattern was by no means uniform, for there was an increase in the number of farms in the areas of settlement in Savo, northern Ostrobothnia and along the river valleys of Lapland.[13] Burn-beating was still widely practised in the dense forests of the hinterland. In Ostrobothnia, peatland was drained and then burnt for cultivation from the 1640s, a practice which spread inland in subsequent decades. Ditching and draining techniques were also refined, and stronger and more efficient ploughs introduced; but farming in Finland remained primitive, scarcely able to provide enough food for the indigenous population even in normal years.

The seventeenth century was a period of long-term decline and depression in agriculture over much of Europe, of demographic stagnation and even regression – the population of Poland fell by as much as a third or even a half between the mid-seventeenth and mid-eighteenth centuries. Contemporaries painted often harrowing pictures of misery and impoverishment, which they contrasted with former prosperous times. It is nevertheless difficult to reach firm conclusions regarding the overall standard and patterns of living. Amongst the wealthy magnates and urban patriciate, a more opulent lifestyle is clearly evident from the houses they built, the pictures they commissioned, the clothes and jewellery they wore, and the goods they consumed. Many sank into poverty as a result of injudicious land purchases or overspending, but there were always others to fill their place. By marrying later and restricting the size of the family, men and women might enjoy a better standard of living, and the evidence we have seems to suggest that there was indeed such a trend. The pattern of poor harvests conceals the fact that there were also exceptionally good years, or that there were often wide differences in yields between one farm and another. Famine and plague were disasters for those who perished, but fewer mouths to feed meant more for those who survived. The farmhands on the Oxenstierna estates in Livonia seemed to have lived well during good years: the steward's records suggest an intake of 3,812 calories a day, plus an extra 500 calories in the form of ale. Evidence culled from the wreck of the *Vasa* also indicates that the era of rude plenty, as Eli Heckscher characterised the sixteenth century,

13. Luukko A 1967 *Suomen historia 1617–1721* Suomen historia, vol. 8. Porvoo, pp. 128–41. Jutikkala E 1980 Asutus ja väestö *Suomen taloushistoria* (3 vols). Helsinki, vol. 1, pp. 160–70.

may well have continued longer than the great Swedish historian imagined, at least for those in royal service.[14]

Most historians would nevertheless agree that the rural farming population was having to cope with increased burdens imposed by landlord and ruler alike, and that many sank into wretched impoverishment. The problem of the poor was one of great concern to the authorities. Vagabonds were greatly feared. In 1611, Christian IV advised parishioners to ring the church bells whenever unwelcome hordes of beggars approached, and to use their weapons to drive them off. Towns preferred to expel petty criminals rather than go to the expense of incarcerating them: occasionally, a beggar king might be appointed in an attempt to control the vagrants within the town precincts. Sturdy vagabonds were liable to be be seized and forced to do unpaid work for noblemen or the crown: Christian IV relied heavily on beggars as a labour force for his extensive building programme, and was even prepared to commute the death penalty for thieves who were prepared to join the labour gangs. Estimates of the numbers of vagrants are often unreliable, since the numbers of people tramping the highways varied enormously, according to the season of the year or the result of the harvest. Returning soldiers, men and women seeking farm work, peddlers and agents of various kinds were regular sights on the road, but their numbers could be greatly augmented when the last corn sack was empty. Many sought to shuffle off the burdens of rent, labour services or taxation by quitting the land and fleeing to the towns. One of the reasons why the idea of abolishing *vornedskab* gained ground in late-seventeenth century Denmark was that the crown was interested in promoting urban development. An order issued in 1680, for example, directed local officials to discontinue the practice of pursuing those who escaped their bondage to the towns on the grounds that extra manpower was as necessary in the towns as in the countryside. On the southern shores of the Baltic, however, the towns were alone in their efforts to resist the demands of landowners for the return of runaways. Königsberg protested vigorously against the 1633 regulations which decreed that peasants' children who ran away could be imprisoned or flogged, but the tightening grip of *Leibeigenschaft* and the breaking of Königsberg's independence by the Great Elector seriously undermined the burghers' resistance to noble pressure. Demographic stagnation, and in some cases,

14. Doubt has however been cast on the figures and conclusions reached by Heckscher: see Morell M 1987 Eli F Heckscher, the 'food budget' and Swedish food consumption from the sixteenth to the nineteenth century *Scandinavian Economic History Review* **35**: 67–107.

decline, also meant that town councils were less keen to attract run-aways who might simply swell the ranks of beggars.

Vagrants and the landless poor were at the bottom of the social heap, and could expect little mercy from higher authority, anxious to exert strict social control. The extent to which the farming peasantry were subject to increasing controls and exactions has aroused some controversy. Fussing was of the opinion that the Danish tenant-farmer was bold enough to stand up for his rights, which the courts would protect, whilst Olsen argues that peasants generally thought twice before taking on their landlord. More recently, Thomas Munck has concluded that the records clearly show that local court officers were capable of resisting seigneurial pressure and upholding peasant complaints. Munck also draws attention to the importance of petitioning the king, which could on occasion produce results.[15] Danish tenant-farmers paid an entry fine (*stedsmål, indfæstning*) on conclusion of their contract, and this appears to have been largely determined by the laws of supply and demand. In addition, they were obliged to pay an annual rent, the *landgilde*. Arent Berntsen, in his *Danmarckis og Norgis Fructbar Herlighed*, published in 1656, claimed that this amounted to one-third of the grain sown by the farmer, but it has proved impossible to establish with any certainty the precise amounts paid. What is fairly clear is that there was little attempt by the government to regulate either the entry fines or rent, though it did try to interfere in matters relating to labour and transport obligations, which increased sharply from the mid-seventeenth century, though to little effect. The principal burden fell upon those tenants living in the same parish as the manor, who were obliged to work several days a week on the de-mesne lands without pay. In return, these *ugedagsbønder* were exempt from taxation, a status sanctioned by custom (though terminated in 1662, when the crown introduced a universal land tax).

Although the Danish peasant-farmers formally possessed greater security of tenure than their Swedish and Finnish counterparts, they were subjected to humiliating restrictions upon movement and were ultimately dependent upon a landlord who could always find means of evicting or moving them if he chose. In Sweden, the wholesale transfer of freehold revenues to the nobility which occurred during the

15. On this question, see Munck T 1979 *The peasantry and the early absolute monarchy in Denmark 1660-1708.* Copenhagen, pp. 59–65, 151ff, 242. Skrubbeltrang F 1979 *Det danske landbosamfund 1500-1800* Copenhagen, pp. 70–1. For differing interpretations of the relationship of lord and peasant, see Fussing H 1942 *Herremand og fæstebonde: Studier i dansk landbrugshistorie omkring 1600.* Copenhagen; and Olsen G 1957 *Hovedgård og bondegård: Studier over stordriftens udvikling i Danmark i tiden 1525–1744.* Copenhagen.

first half of the seventeenth century drew cries of anguish from the peasantry. In the words of a pamphlet of 1649, 'the freehold peasant has been forced to accustom himself to accept the same conditions as the peasants of the nobility, or has been driven to surrender his property and his title to his noble landlord, who can then clap a rent upon the land as high as he pleases'.[16] Some historians have however been inclined to dismiss the protests of these *skattefrälsebönder* as exaggerated. Swedish research would suggest that they were not more burdened than other types of peasant. The Uppland nobility often refrained from levying the full burden of impositions, and in the *riksdag* resisted efforts to impose new extraordinary taxes which would have borne heavily on their tenants. Court records reveal few cases of eviction, though landowners did sometimes seek to bind their tenants to remain on the land. The legal precept that the peasants had only the right to live on and cultivate the land (*dominium utile*), and could forfeit this if they failed to pay their taxes for three consecutive years, appears to have been applied with some vigour in Finland. The evidence suggests, however, that the crown was at least as active here as the nobility in depriving the peasants of their rights, and that the possessors of donated lands in the counties and baronies along the west coast were usually unwilling to press for forfeiture when the peasant was unable to pay his taxes.[17]

The former crown and tax-paying peasants who found themselves subject to noble lords may well have fared rather better than an earlier generation of historians believed, though they were often confused about their changed status. Why then did they complain so much, and why were they so eager for a *reduktion*? Ågren and Revera are rather dismissive of the grievances of the peasantry brought before the 1650 *riksdag*, but Jutikkala believes that the sheer volume of complaints from peasants about mistreatment before 1650 cannot simply be regarded as exceptionally successful propaganda. The flood of alienations which occurred during the reign of queen Christina, and the subsequent shift in relations between peasant, crown and nobleman; the exactions of war and the burdens of taxation and increased labour services; and the basic pattern of low productivity, exacerbated to the point of poverty and starvation by poor harvests – all helped create tensions and bad feeling, which the peasant not unnaturally directed against his landlord.

16. Roberts 1968 *Sweden as a great power 1611–1697*. London, pp. 98–9.
17. Ågren K 1973 The *Reduktion. Sweden's age of greatness 1632-1718* (M.Roberts, ed). London, pp. 257–61. Jutikkala E 1983 *Talonpoika – aatelismies- kruunu. Maapolitiikka ja maanomistusoloja Pohjoismaissa 1550–1750*. Helsinki, pp. 68–76. Luukko 1967, pp. 443ff.

The grievances laid before the 1650 *riksdag* by the peasants' estate dwelt at length on the evil consequences of alienation of crown lands, and urged the queen to resume all alienated freehold and crown lands.[18] Christina regarded this as a challenge to her prerogatives, though she used the agitation to ensure the succession of her cousin to the throne. Karl Gustav, however, did make plans to push through a resumption of crown lands, the *reduktion*, partly to finance his war effort, and in 1655, a partial *reduktion* was effected. Eighteen 'inalienable areas' were listed, and within these areas, all former crown lands were to be restored to the crown. A quarter of the estates donated after 1632 were to be handed back, though the nobility were given the option of paying a three-year 'contribution' equivalent to the tax yields of the estates to be reduced. Finally, the principle of conditional tenure for donated lands enunciated in the 1604 Norrköping resolution was reaffirmed, and all lands given away in allodial tenure in breach of this resolution were to be converted accordingly.

Karl Gustav's absence at the wars and his premature death in 1660 meant that the resumption of crown lands dwindled after 1655. The issue was raised once more during the war crisis of the 1670s, and the pressure for a full-blooded *reduktion* came to a head in the *riksdag* of 1680, when the three non-noble estates presented a memorial calling for the resumption of alienated lands. The assent of the nobles was obtained by rather dubious procedural means, with the royalist party led by Hans Wachtmeister exploiting the fears and divisions within the separate classes of the *riddarhus*. The 1680 resolution went much further than the 1655 *reduktion*, for it authorised the crown to resume alienated estates in the overseas provinces, the counties and baronies, and the so-called Norrköping resolution estates, i.e. lands held on conditional, quasi-feudal tenure. Only small properties were to be exempt, though even this concession was brushed aside in 1682, when the king effectively compelled the estates to admit that the medieval Land Law gave him sole rights to dispose of all fiefs as he saw fit.

In the long run, the number of freehold peasants was increased as a result of the *reduktion*, and the landowning capacity of the nobility was appreciably diminished, though the magnates were by no means reduced to beggary, as historians used to believe. In Denmark, the crown preferred to liquidate its debts after 1660 by selling off land. The number of farms in the royal domain shrank from 30,250 in 1650 to 14,679 in 1688, from half to a quarter of the cultivated land. The

18. The supplication of the three non-noble estates is printed in Roberts 1968, pp. 101–5.

principal beneficiaries were the new class of *proprietærer*, men such as Henrik Müller and Gabriel Marselis. Many noble estates were also put on the market to clear off debts, and the abolition of restrictions on non-noble purchase and ownership of demesne land in 1662 allowed the wealthy urban patriciate to acquire landed estates. The old nobility's share of privately owned manor land declined from 95 per cent in 1660 to a mere 38 per cent by 1710: by contrast, the new nobility held 19 cent, the non-noble landowners 43 per cent. The lesser nobility were particularly hard-hit by debt and the agricultural depression, and a number sank into poverty, such as the member of the Urne family found living as a cottar in Vendsyssel in 1730, or Valdemar Daa, who ended his days as a poor tenant in Jutland. Those who managed to hang on, through judicious marriage or prudent husbandry, still enjoyed most of the privileges of the nobility. The export of cattle remained in their hands, their estates were exempt from payment of the tithe, and the higher nobility still possessed the right to hold their own courts and administer chastisement to stiff-necked peasants. Between 1670 and 1682, the nobility even regained the privilege of tax exemption upon their manors, a privilege retained after 1682 by the owners of large estates.

In Sweden, although the nobility's share of the land shrank by almost a half as a result of the *reduktion*, the old nobility was still able to recover. Magnus de la Gardie spent his old age bewailing the state of destitution to which his family had been reduced, but already by the next generation, his heirs were building up the family fortunes once more through successful ventures into the depressed land market. Karl XI sought to prevent *frälsejord* passing into the hands of commoners, and his successor's investigations in 1717–18 revealed that only 7 per cent of *frälse* farms had passed into non-noble ownership, with the highest proportion of such ownership being in the former Danish provinces of Blekinge and Halland. In Finland, where the policy of donations had reached epic proportions by 1655, the recovery of lands by the crown was much greater than in Sweden: by 1725, 70 per cent of the farms were on crown land, 22 per cent were freehold, and a mere 7 per cent were on *frälsejord*. In the frontier province of Kexholm, where almost all of the land had been given away in donations, the crown continued the practice of farming out tax collection. The ruthless behaviour and demands of the tax-farmers provoked unrest, which flared up into open rebellion in 1696–7.

The *reduktion* was also applied to the Baltic lands. One-third of the land in Estonia, and one-quarter of the land on the island of Ösel reverted to the crown. The Livonian lands, which had come under

Swedish rule in the military campaigns of the 1620s, were particularly hard hit. The *starosti* estates created by the Polish crown, which comprised almost half of the cultivated land of Livonia, had been mostly donated by the crown to Swedish magnates. Demands for the resumption of these estates were made at the Halmstad *riksdag* of 1678, and in 1680, a leading royalist had declared that the overseas provinces ought to be self-supporting, a defensive bastion for the realm, and not a burden upon it. For this reason, Wachtmeister concluded, the alienated lands must be taken out of the hands of private persons and returned to the public domain.[19] By 1687, the process of *reduktion* in Livonia was largely completed. The crown initially opted for a policy of leasing the former *starosti* lands on twelve-year leases to the local nobility. By 1693, however, relations between the crown and the indigenous *Ritterschaft* had so deteriorated that the king preferred to offer these lands on perpetual leasehold to loyal members of the Swedish aristocracy, such as Hans Wachtmeister, who received estates with an annual income of over six thousand riksdaler.

Although the *reduktion* was primarily designed to recover for the crown those estates lost or alienated since the time of Gustav Adolf, the investigations of the royal commissioners into rights of possession also threatened to deprive many of the local nobility of their estates. In 1678, a deputation of Baltic landowners had visited Karl XI in camp at Ljungby, and received what they took to be a royal confirmation of their privileges and title to their estates. In the subsequent heated debate, the Baltic nobility clung fast to their belief that the king was bound by his word. Karl, however, had been careful to point out at Ljungby that the nobility were to enjoy their privileges on condition that these were not prejudicial or harmful to the interests of the crown and state. The protests of the Baltic nobility were in vain: the crown commissioners extended the *reduktion* to lands deemed to have been in the public domain (i.e., the lands of the Order and the bishops) but subsequently alienated. By 1687, much of the *reduktion* had been completed. Two years later, a royal resolution decreed that all properties which yielded an annual revenue of up to 1,500 daler were to be let out on hereditary lease to their former proprietors, who could obtain a reduction of one-third on their rent if they provided one soldier for every fifteen *haken* of land. The rents were mostly paid in cash, and may well have brought in over half a million silver daler annually by the 1690s. A major cadastral revision in the 1690s redefined the basic tax unit according to the liabilities of the peasant to the

19. Isberg A 1953 *Karl XI och den livländska adeln 1684–1695*. Lund, p. 11.

demesne, thereby increasing the tax revenues of the crown by at least 25 per cent.

By the end of Karl XI's reign, the Baltic provinces were yielding a healthy profit: by 1696, the annual sum remitted to the treasury in Stockholm had grown to half a million silver daler. In 1699, the surplus of revenue over local expenditure in Estonia was some 334,000 silver daler, in Livonia one year later, 404,598 silver daler. Over one-fifth of the state's revenue in 1699 came from the Baltic provinces and Ingria, and one-tenth of the national budget was made up from the surplus from these lands.[20] The Baltic provinces also supplied Sweden with large quantities of grain, as much as 800,000 tons in the crisis year of 1696. The loss of the Baltic provinces in Karl XII's reign was a severe blow, and one of the few consolations which Sweden was able to obtain at the peace of Nystad was the right to import grain free of duty to the value of 50,000 roubles annually.

The ordinary revenues of the state in 1699 amounted to just over six and a half million silver daler, of which slightly over a half came from Sweden proper. In 1693, the king was able to announce that he did not require the estates to grant any extraordinary aids, and the finances of the kingdom were declared to be in a healthy state. Karl XI's reforms were criticised by Eli Hecksher as a reversion to a rigid natural economy, which weakened liquidity and undermined royal credit. Recent research has challenged a number of these assumptions, though as Sven-Erik Åström points out, the modest reserves which were built up at the end of Karl XI's reign (and virtually exhausted in 1698–9 in paying for the state funeral and his successor's coronation) were largely the fruits of the trade boom during the years of Swedish neutrality. The crown treated its creditors in a rather high-handed manner, and still owed 1.3 million riksdaler in 1693. The great injections of money from abroad which had sustained Sweden in earlier decades – the combined income from the French subsidy and the Prussian ship tolls in 1633 accounted for almost one-third of the total revenue, for example – were no longer available (against this must be set the increase in revenue from the overseas provinces). Pitched into a new war against Denmark, Poland and Russia – the last a formidable and relentless foe – Sweden's economic limitations were soon

---

20. Lundkvist S 1973 The experience of empire: Sweden as a great power *Sweden's age of greatness 1632–1718*, pp. 23–4. Piirimäe H 1976 Rootsi riigi ja Liivimaa finantsisuhted XVII sajandil *Uurimusi läänemeremaade ajaloost* Tartu Riikliku Ülikooli toimetised 371. Tartu, pp. 3–32.

exposed.[21] Taxes paid in barrels of grain, fish or butter may not have been the Achilles' heel of Sweden's Baltic policy, for as Birgitta Odén points out, they were advantageous to the state at times of price inflation: the fatal weakness lay in the limited possibilities which the crown had to increase revenue from taxation and other impositions or to raise loans. 'In Sweden's agrarian society during the Vasa and Caroline era', concludes Odén, 'the resources of the peasantry could not be mobilised for an ambitious foreign policy without causing serious social and political difficulties.'[22]

Denmark failed to reach the level of relative financial stability achieved by Sweden under Karl XI. The national debt in 1660 amounted to over four million rigsdaler, excluding the debt for the duchies. Although five-sixths of the creditors were Danish, over a third of the debt was owed to foreigners: 670,000 rigsdaler was owed to eight Hamburg families alone, whilst Gabriel Marselis claimed 272,000 rigsdaler and Henrik Müller 335,000. Creditors at first were fobbed off with pledged crown lands and notes of assignation on state revenue, especially from the customs dues. In December 1660, the notes of assignation were cancelled in order to allow reform of the revenue system, though the practice was soon resumed. Merchant houses which acquired land in settlement of debts often faced difficulty, since they were unable to convert this asset into cash with which to pay off their own creditors.[23] The liquidation of the debt by the alienation of crown lands eventually solved the immediate financial crisis, but reduced the crown's ability to raise credit. The loss of revenue from crown lands also meant an increase in the tax burden. The *hartkorn* tax of 1662, based upon a hastily compiled land register, which also included hitherto untaxed demesnes and manorial tenants, was expected to yield 280,000 rdr, twice the sum of the double-tax levy of 1640, and by 1668, a revenue of 420,000 rdr was anticipated. Extraordinary taxes were also raised on the basis of the land register, causing much distress to an already overburdened peasantry. The creation of tax-exempt cavalry estates after 1670, the continued alienation of crown lands and incomes and the strains of the Scanian war led the government to undertake a new survey of the land. A land register

21. Cf. Hecksher G 1941 *Svenskt arbete och liv från medeltiden till nutiden*. Stockholm, p. 161. Cavallie J 1975 *Från fred till krig. De finansiella problemen kring krigsutbrott år 1700*. Uppsala. Åström S-E 1973 The Swedish economy and Sweden's role as a great power 1632–1697 *Sweden's age of greatness 1632–1718*, pp. 79–100.

22. Odén B 1967 Naturaskatter och krigspolitik: ett finansiellt dilemma *Scandia* **33**:18.

23. Jørgensen J 1963 Bilantz 1660. Adelsvældens bo *Festskrift til Astrid Friis*. Copenhagen, pp. 153–71. Jørgensen J 1963 Denmark's relations with Lübeck and Hamburg in the seventeenth century *Scandinavian Economic History Review* **11**:73–116.

drawn up in 1664, admittedly inaccurate in a number of respects, came up with a national total of 443,759 *tønder hartkorn* (td.htk., or barrel of hard corn, the basic unit of assessment for tax purposes). Christian V's land register of 1688 produced a total of 349,139 td.htk., in other words, a decline of one-fifth in the gross amount of a potentially taxable source. The decline was particularly serious in Jutland and on Fyn, and on peasant land in general. Even though legislation in 1682 had confined manorial tax exemption to demesnes of more than 200 td.htk. and peasant tenancies within ten miles of the manor, such a sizeable diminution in the gross amount of taxable land posed severe problems. In 1685, the king had agreed to a suggestion from the exchequer that all taxes for the April quarter be reduced by a third, and requested a full list of arrears so that concessions might be considered. On the whole, however, the government appears to have been rather unsympathetic to peasant pleas for a reduction in taxation, and was unwilling to give tax concessions to coastal areas affected by sand-drift.[24] Belt-tightening measures and fiscal reforms were all too often nullified by an ambitious foreign policy and lavish military expenditure, and the exchequer tectered on the brink of bankruptcy for much of the reign of Christian V.

24. Munck 1979, pp. 65–88.

CHAPTER TEN
Society and Culture in the Baroque Age

THE JOYS AND SORROWS OF EVERYDAY LIFE

In his monumental *Atlantica* (1679), the Swedish polymath Olof Rudbeck portrayed the ancestral homeland of the Swedes as a fertile and populous land from whence the ancient Goths had poured forth to conquer Europe. This bold image was sharply at odds with the demographic situation of Rudbeck's own time. Rudbeck's vision of a land blessed by God and Nature, whose bounty had attracted the survivors of the Flood, was primarily intended to conjure up a glorious mythical past. Although later Swedish writers believed that the Creator had blessed their land with a healthy climate and a great variety of flora and fauna, foreign contemporaries found little evidence of this benevolence in seventeenth-century Sweden. William Carr, an English visitor in the 1680s, observed that: 'He that hath read in the histories of this last age the great exploits of Gustavus Adolphus and his Swedes, perhaps may have a fancy that it must be an excellent Countrey which hath bred such warriors; but if he approaches it, he will soon find himself undeceived.' Although travellers did come across fertile tracts – Regnard thought the plains of southern Sweden bore comparison with those of France, for example – Carr's inability to discover little more than barren rocks, forests and lakes summed up the general view of most foreign visitors.[1]

Villages, often consisting of a long row of two-storey wooden houses and farm buildings, were common only in areas of relatively long-established field cultivation, such as the central plains of Sweden,

---

1. Carr W 1688 *Remarks of the government of severall parts of Germanie, Denmark, Sweedland, Hamburg, Lübeck and Hanseatique Towns.* Amsterdam, pp. 171–2. Regnard J 1866 *Théâtre de Regnard, suivi de ses voyages en Laponie, en Pologne, etc.* Paris, pp. 619–20.

though in more infertile regions, such as western and central Jutland, isolated farmsteads were more frequent than village settlements. In the dense and trackless forests which covered so much of northern Europe, settlements also tended to be isolated, the result of much wandering in search of suitable grazing pastures or timber for clearance. Land cleared for cultivation by the burn–beat method was soon exhausted, compelling settlers to move on. Many of these households were inhabited by extended families, often thirty or forty strong, each forming a closely knit community capable of providing sustenance and welfare for the sick and elderly as well as the able-bodied. Such households had to be self-sufficient, for their remoteness often cut them off almost completely from the outside world. The lack of roads meant that the inhabitants had to rely on packhorses, sleds and their own backs to obtain necessities and bring their produce to market, a state of affairs which lasted well into this present century.[2]

The sparse distribution of population meant that the farmer in northern Europe often had to be his own smith and wheelwright, carpenter and mason. Only the most basic of trades were practised in the small towns, whose weak economic position was further undermined by competition from craftsmen engaged by local magnates or living in the countryside. The imposition of customs and excise duties on goods brought into towns for sale meant that smuggling was widespread, and the efforts of burghers to put a stop to rural trade and annual trade fairs which undermined their business were usually frustrated. Long distances and difficult terrain made the transport of goods slow and costly: it cost Abraham Momma as much to transport grain to his ironworks in Lapland as it did to buy it. There was a woeful lack of inns and hostelries able to provide accommodation: Danish priests who were unlucky enough to live near main roads frequently complained that they were eaten out of house and home by travellers who sought hospitality. Bulstrode Whitelocke's large retinue encountered great difficulty in finding food and lodgings as it progressed through Sweden, and on one occasion, the English ambassador suspected that the beef they were served had come from the rotten carcass of a cow found in a ditch.[3]

The diet of the common people was monotonous and often meagre.

2. See Berg G, Svensson S 1969 *Svensk bondekultur*. Stockholm, pp. 51–67 on settlement in Sweden; and Voionmaa V 1969 *Suomen karjalaisen heimon historia* (reprint of 1915 ed). Porvoo, pp. 165–86 and pp. 387ff. on settlement and the extended family households of Karelia.

3. Whitelocke B 1888 *Journal of the Swedish Embassy 1653–1654* (2 vols). London, vol. 1, p. 188.

The peasants of northern Finland subsisted on dried fish, sour milk and a dry, hard barley bread, according to the abbé Outhier; Regnard found that fishbones and bark were ground down to make bread in the far north. The Livonian peasantry ate a bread made of rye and chaff (*Spreubrot*). In Jämtland, where fresh fish and game abounded, the inhabitants preferred to salt or smoke their catch; even in the cattle-raising districts of Sweden, the peasants rarely ate fresh meat. Vegetables were infrequently eaten: as the peasants on the island of Rügen bluntly declared, 'grönfauder ät wi nich' (we don't eat greens).[4] Of the three great seventeenth-century stimulants, tea and coffee remained well beyond the means of the common people because of their price: a half-pound of tea in early eighteenth-century Denmark cost the equivalent of six bottles of wine. Tobacco was more widely consumed, though, if Regnard is to be believed, its soothing virtues were squeezed to the last drop:

> Having finished their repast, the richest [Lapps] take for dessert a small piece of tobacco, which they draw from behind their ears, where they are accustomed to dry it... They chew it for a while, and when they have extracted all the juice, they replace it behind their ears, where it acquires a new flavour: they then chew it again for a time, and replace it as before: and when it has lost all its potency, they smoke it.[5]

Tobacco and alcohol were the comfort and consolation of the poor, and often had to serve as medicaments in an age when medical care was rudimentary. A Danish doctor complained in 1639 that the common people's circumstances were so poor that they could not afford his services; instead, they treated their ailments with Rostock ale. Many Danish peasants were rejected as unfit for military service because of physical disabilities which might have been cured, had they been able to obtain treatment. Travelling quacks offered dubious cures for ailments ranging from ruptures to the 'French disease', and vied with barber-surgeons (and occasionally, the hangman) for the custom of those willing to undergo surgery. The picture was not entirely gloomy, however. The barber-surgeons of Copenhagen instituted training courses in 1684, and provided the first holder of the chair of surgery founded in the city's university in 1718. Thomas Bartholin had earlier won a European reputation as an anatomist, attracting foreign students to his public dissections at the university's Domus Anatomica, founded in 1644 by Simon Paulli. Denmark also led the way in the provision of proper training for midwives, and in estab-

4. Steffen W 1963 *Kulturgeschichte von Rügen bis 1815*. Cologne, p. 300. Berg, Svensson 1969, pp. 97ff.
5. Regnard 1866, p. 580.

lishing controls over the quality and reliability of apothecary's wares. Even so, the country's physicians were quite unable to cope with epidemics such as the plague which ravaged Denmark during the Great Northern War, when over twenty thousand are thought to have perished in Copenhagen alone. Efforts to limit the spreading of the disease often met with resistance. The citizens of Karlshamn, for example, defied the orders of the governor of Blekinge province, recovering bodies from the plague pits and taking them for burial to the churchyard, where they lay exposed for weeks. The governor complained that the sick and healthy continued to live together, feasting and carousing 'as long as life remained to them'.[6]

A life of toil, sustained by a poor and inadequate diet, and bound by a severe moral code which imposed harsh and cruel penalties upon transgressors, left little room for affection and tenderness. Few were the wives who could claim never to have been beaten by their husbands, according to the Livonian chronicler Christian Kelch: the peasants' children were also treated roughly. The peasant was generally portrayed as a rough, coarse-grained brute, on whom force had to be used to overcome his natural laziness and insolence. They were, according to one writer, 'human beings, it is true... but their repulsive habits are known to all ... When they eat, they employ no fork, but stick all five fingers into the bowl.'[7] But there is also another side to the picture, revealed above all in folk song and stories. The young lad or lass who returns home weeping to report the loss of a valuable item – a ring, a cow, or a horse – is consoled; the girl goes to the woods to collect berries for her mother, the son repays his mother for the pains she suffered at his birth. Folk poetry reflects the beauty of life, as well as its pains and torment:

Igav on olla iluta,	Dull is life with nothing fair,
hale olla laulemata,	sad to live and never sing,
kole käo kukkumata,	or to miss the cuckoo's song,
raske rõõmuta elada.	hard to live deprived of joy.
Ma ise ilutegija,	I make my beauty myself
rõõmu kalli kandija.	bringing joy to everyone.[8]

Poetry was also a form of consolation, especially for the oppressed. The tiller of the soil was expected to know his place, and be content.

---

6. Hallerman P 1926 Tillståndet i Blekinge under det stora nordiska kriget *Karolinska Förbundets Årsbok*, p. 248. Estimates of the numbers who perished in Blekinge vary from seven to sixteen thousand.

7. Steffen 1963, p. 287, citing a pamphlet of 1684.

8. Nirk E 1987 *Estonian literature*. Tallinn, p. 24. See also Kuusi M *et al.* 1977 *Finnish folk poetry: epic*. Helsinki.

Those obliged to work on their lord's estate often had to endure the curses and blows of reeves and bailiffs. In Denmark and along the southern shores of the Baltic, the landlord was entitled to administer physical punishment for misdemeanours. The well-meaning efforts of the Swedish crown to curb the worst abuses of serfdom in the Baltic lands met with much local resistance. When Karl XI proposed the abolition of serfdom in 1681, the Livonian nobility's reply was that without the rights of ownership over their peasants, they could not remain in the land. The regulations of 1696 defined the offences for which peasants on leased crown lands could be punished, and allowed the aggrieved the right to complain to the local courts, and even to the governor-general, against unfair treatment; but war intervened before these regulations could be extended to private estates.

In comparison with the indigenous hereditary peasantry of the Baltic lands, the Danish *fæstebonde* still enjoyed a degree of independence from his landlord. Access to the lower courts was readily available and relatively cheap. The quality of the law officers was not always of the highest order – there are recorded instances of stableboys and farm stewards being appointed as judges and clerks in manorial courts, and of irresponsible and incompetent officers in the hundred courts (*herredsting*) – and undoubtedly abuses did occur, especially in the fifty or so manorial courts (*birketing*). But the regularity with which the peasants had recourse to law – causing the *lensmand* of Bøvling, for example, to complain to Christian IV that he had been hounded from court to court by tenants contesting the terms of labour service he had decreed – is an indication of the importance of the law as a means of redress in the eyes of the Danish tenants.

The peasant's sense of justice did not always correspond to that laid down by the law. Danish peasants refused to accept that stealing from the landlord's woods was a crime, in defiance of the provisions of *Danske Lov*, and tended to appeal to time-honoured custom and tradition. The inhabitants of Bornholm regularly appealed to the privileges granted to them by Frederik III in their conflicts with central authority: freehold peasants, whose rights were highly complex, based their arguments on past custom in their disputes with aggressive landowners seeking to force them to render labour service. Custom and tradition also largely determined the relationship between the pastor and his flock. Parishioners often judged a priest by his willingness to overlook their semi-pagan habits, and to repay traditional gifts with small favours. In Finland, the succession of a relative to the living often depended on the ability of the clergyman to ingratiate himself in this way. Semi-pagan customs survived, in spite of the fulminations of bishops and ordinances of the state: even in the nineteenth century, Finnish clergymen were still being asked to drive out evil spirits from the possessed and to use their supposedly magical powers to find cows lost in the wood.

'There is a view prevalent amongst the common people', wrote the rural dean U.A. Plesner in 1832, 'that the higher orders in Denmark are still favoured at the expense of the lower orders. 'The great ones all stick together': that is what the peasant says and believes.'[9] Plesner was writing after the land reforms, recording what was clearly a deep-rooted conviction, founded on decades of bitter experience. Even in Sweden, where the political and social circumstances of the peasantry were far better than on the southern shores of the Baltic, such sentiments were common, as countless sayings and proverbs testify. In general, as Claus Bjørn has argued in his study of the Danish peasantry, there was a tendency to accept the prevailing system and to work within it to improve one's position, rather than engage in violent protest. The opportunities for exploiting the weaknesses of the ruling structure were few, and those who did seek to take collective action to remedy their grievances were swiftly dealt with. If his protesting tenants were not chastised, claimed Henrik Müller in 1665, then neither he, nor any other landowner or authority could be safe amongst 'such rebellious people': the ringleaders were promptly hauled off to the Blåtårn prison in Copenhagen. A similar fate befell the tenants on Hans Schack's estates in 1672. Stewards on the scattered lands of the Swedish magnates also complained that their authority was threatened by malicious and tale-bearing tenants, who did not shrink from inciting others to rebellion.[10]

'The peasant is not a goose, even though he is grey', ran a well-known Danish proverb, and indeed, the grey home-spun garb of the countryman could clothe a wide range of socially distinctive figures. The status of the farmer might be determined by the size of his landholding, the nature of his tax payments, or his relationship (often difficult to determine) to his overlord. The disruptions of war, the burden of tax, rents and labour services, the changes of land tenure introduced by absolutist rulers and the vicissitudes of life could and did have a significant effect upon the peasant household. There seems to have been a sizeable decline in the number of farms on Sjælland in the second half of the seventeenth century, for example, and a sharp

9. Bjørn C 1981 *Bonde, herremand, konge. Bonden i 1700-tallets Danmark*. Copenhagen, p. 43.

10. Bjørn 1981, pp. 27, 32. Jokipii M 1960 *Suomen kreivi- ja vapaaherrakunnat* (2 vols) Historiallisia Tutkimuksia 48:1–2. Helsinki, vol. 2, pp. 199–234.

rise in the number of cottagers (*husmænd*); whereas there were five peasant farmers for three cottagers in 1680, the proportions had risen to three cottagers for every two farmers a hundred years later. There was also an increase in the numbers of landless labourers (*inderster*). The *reduktion* in Sweden drastically reduced the amount of labour available to the estate-owners, and stimulated the creation of new tenant farms, often on cleared land: the tenants (*torpare*) of these farms were obliged to perform labour service on the main estate. Legislation was also enacted to release surplus labour: a law of 1686 sought to limit the number of servants on peasant farms (principally to provide men for the army and navy), and further legislation in the eighteenth century limited the number of hired hands on the peasant farm, and even obliged the farmer's children to find service elsewhere if their numbers were deemed to be too great for the farm to support.

The landless peasant went under a variety of names, even in one area. Derivations of the Russian term *bobyl'* crop up throughout the eastern Baltic region, whilst other names, such as *Badstüber, Katenleute,* or *backstugusittare* derive from the type of accommodation in which the landless were housed. Other groups were named according to their tax status, such as the *Einfüsslinge* or the 'axemen' of eastern Finland, impoverished peasants who were unable to pay the taxes levied on their farms. The landless poor existed on the margins of society, their numbers fluctuating according to circumstances. Those who were unable to cope or had no-one to look after them – the elderly, orphans, the infirm and disabled – were often driven into destitution and vagrancy.

Many sank; but some rose. Erik Andersson began his career in the entourage of Jakob de la Gardie, made himself useful with his knowledge of Russian and trade across the Karelian border, and became de la Gardie's business partner in the sable-fur trade. His Russian expertise attracted the attention of the government, and he ended his days as a royal official and holder of enfeoffed lands, raised to the nobility under the name of Trana. Distinguished service in the royal armies could be rewarded. Per Jonsson, son of a Småland peasant born around 1612, entered the army as a 'baggage boy' to captain Witte, whose daughter he eventually married. A second marriage to a daughter of a petty nobleman in 1647, three years after he had been given his first command, took him further up the social scale, and allowed him to acquire an estate. In 1650, he was ennobled, taking the name of Stålhammar, and he ended his long life as commander of the Småland cavalry regiment. To rise from the plough to the ranks of the aristocracy was, however, comparatively rare, and even more difficult after the zenith of Sweden's age of greatness had passed. There were much better prospects for social advancement within the ranks of the non-noble estates in Scandinavia. Roughly one in five of the clergy in Växsjö diocese came from a peasant home, and the overall proportion for Sweden–Finland was probably higher. Not all prospered, however, for the existence of the curate in a poor parish was little better than that of the most miserable peasant. Literacy and numeracy were important assets, for they enabled the sons of peasants to take up clerical and administrative posts. Even so, career prospects were not always good. Whereas bailiffs in Finland and the Baltic lands were often foreigners, the lower-ranking officials were usually recruited from the indigenous peasantry, able to communicate with the tenants in their own tongue. There is, however, little conclusive evidence to suggest that appointment to a lower office could lead to higher things. Indeed, there was a strong tendency for the upper ranks of estate management to intermarry and found virtual dynasties, in the manner of the higher levels of the clergy, law officers, burghers and the nobility, thus hindering the prospects of advancement for the newcomer.

Marriage and family ties were a crucial part of the social fabric. Weddings were occasions for lavish feasting and celebration at all levels of society. Prince Christian of Denmark's wedding in 1634 took over a year to prepare, and cost several hundred thousand rigsdaler. The costly and sumptuous nuptials of the burghers of Reval outraged the chronicler Balthasar Rüssow, and Paul Fleming's poem *Liefländische Schneegräfin*, a description of a wedding which took place in Reval in February 1636, suggests that not even the sobering effect of decades of war could stifle the desire to celebrate at all costs. Fleming boasted that the celebrations in Germany lasted even longer. In Lübeck, high-society marriages were carefully conducted affairs, with at least three different kinds of roast meat, Elbe salmon, ham and many other delicacies, washed down with copious quantities of beer and wine. Marriages were also alliances, and the degree of endogamy within the urban patriciate was high. Certain trading activities came to be dominated by the kinship ties: nearly every member of the Stockholm traders (*Holmevarer*) in sixteenth-century Lübeck were related to Thomas van Wickede, and similar family connections existed within the city's Greenland traders of the next century. An agreement concluded in 1620 after a long tussle between the councillors and gilds of Königsberg sought to impose limits on the numbers of any one family who could hold office, and there are many other instances of complaints against excessive domination by one or several powerful families. In the small Swedish coastal town of Västervik, for example, only three of the eight magistrates in 1693 were not related to the Bauman family, and an aggrieved party in 1668 complained that all who sat on the council were mostly related to each other. Those who were unwise enough to marry outside their ranks were subjected to scorn and discrimination. The Königsberg vintner Johann Benedict Matthäus was refused admission to the burgherage in 1705 because he had married a daughter of the executioner: the council argued that the presence of his wife at social occasions could well cause embarrassment and bad feeling, which would inevitably lead to brawling. A century later, another Königsberger, writing about the gild system, drily observed that an illegitimate child could become a field marshal or a minister, but not a shoemaker or master-tailor.[11]

Marriage was also an important issue for applicants to church livings, for the widow and dependants of the previous incumbent had to be provided for, and wedlock was often a cheaper alternative than the provision of a pension. On occasion, written contracts promising marriage and maintenance of the relict of the deceased incumbent were extracted from candidates to a vacant living, and there were instances of widows marrying and outliving two or more successors to the post. Marriage could ensure that the living remained within the family for generations – in the case of Døstrup in southern Jutland, from the Reformation to 1865. The bishops of Sjælland were all related to one another between 1590 and 1730, and three men in succession in the eighteenth century succeeded their fathers-in-law to the episcopal seat. The marriage ritual offered a good deal of scope for underhand dealing. A clergyman's widow on the island of Rügen in 1644 resolved initially to offer her daughter to the candidate, but his inaugural sermon aroused such passions in her that she retracted and insisted that the hapless young man marry her instead. A curate in the Finnish parish of Kuortane who obtained the post by promising to marry the incumbent's ugly eldest daughter and then insisted on marrying the prettier younger daughter after he had been appointed was dismissed as soon as his wife died so that the eldest daughter could once more be offered to aspiring candidates.

Larger and more populous parishes could yield a comfortable living

11. Lindberg F 1933 *Västerviks historia 1215–1718*. Västervik, p. 233. von Glinski G 1964 *Die Königsberger Kaufmannschaft des 17 und 18 Jahrhunderts* Wissenschäftliche Beiträge zur Geschichte und Landeskunde Ost-Mitteleuropas 70. Marburg, pp. 15–26. See also Möller S 1954 *Suomen tapulikaupunkien valtaporvaristo ja sen kaupankäyntimenetelmät 1600-luvun alkupuolella* Historiallisia tutkimuksia 42. Helsinki, pp. 72–7 for examples of intermarriage within the patriciate of the Finnish staple towns.

for the clergyman, but remote and impoverished livings were far less rewarding. The life of a country parson in Estonia and Livonia was sufficiently attractive to ensure a ready supply of recruits from the rest of the Swedish empire and Germany. The relatively comfortable life of the clergy on the island of Rügen also attracted immigrants, such as the son of a Viennese Hofrat who came to Pomerania as vicar-general of an Imperial army, but defected from Catholicism, studied in Greifswald and ended as rural dean of Bergen. The sons of the Rügen clergy seem to have been less interested in following in their fathers' footsteps than was the case elsewhere in the Baltic area. Many ventured abroad in search of a career. One of pastor Musselius' six children ended up as a bookkeeper in Halle, another as a merchant in Stockholm: of the ten adult children of pastor von Essen, one became an organist in Prussia, another a merchant in Hamburg, and a third died on active service in the Brandenburg army. On the other hand, many had to content themselves with lesser glories, ending up as bakers and brewers.

Patronage played a not unimportant part in furthering a clergyman's career. Although it was recognised that the right of appointment to a living was not a noble privilege in Sweden, the nobility could and did exercise influence. They could offer jobs as regimental pastors, headmasters or house chaplains, and occasionally provided scholarships for the sons of the clergy. By the eighteenth century, the upper echelons of the clergy had become a part of genteel society: their lesser brethren still clung to the habits of a former age. Thus, tea was the preferred beverage in over half of the vicarages in mid-eighteenth-century Finland, but was drunk by only 4 per cent of the families of the lesser clergy. Curates still caroused with their neighbours and became involved in brawls, in the time-honoured fashion of their predecessors. In the frontier province of Kexholm, many curates and their families had to live in smoky hovels, fighting an unequal battle to keep their threadbare raiment free of soot and grime: in such conditions, as Gunnar Suolahti remarks, there was little wonder that the clerical proletariat was tempted to seek solace in strong drink.[12]

For the fortunate, however, the church, or a clerical background, did offer an avenue for social advancement. In Sweden, the classic route to the top was followed by numerous sons of the clergy who entered royal service and were subsequently elevated to the nobility: some sixty between 1680 and 1699. Between 1611 and 1680, there

12. Suolahti G 1927 *Finlands prästerskap på 1600- och 1700-talen.* Helsingfors, pp. 264–73.

were 845 additions to the numbers of aristocratic families, of whom 485 were of indigenous stock. Crown servants made up the largest single grouping of these ennobled natives. Those from a trading or entrepreneurial background constituted around one-fifth, though most earned their title through service to the crown, rather than by virtue of their enterprise and skill as a trader or manufacturer. During the reign of Karl XI, the ranks of the nobility were significantly augmented, as the king rewarded his faithful servants: over a third of the 331 families ennobled between 1680 and 1699 were in state service. Commoners could also reach the higher ranks of the titled nobility. Almost half of the men elevated to the rank of baron or count between 1632 and 1697 started life as commoners. A large number of foreigners were also elevated to the peerage, especially by queen Christina. The greatest number came from the Baltic lands and Germany, and usually received their titles in reward for military service. In Denmark, the influx of foreigners into the ranks of the nobility was even greater: of the ninety families ennobled between 1536 and 1660, over half hailed from Germany, and nearly a quarter from Holstein: only eight were native-born Danes. Around one-third were ennobled through possession of estates in the kingdom, 42 per cent for service in the royal administration or at court, and 21 per cent by virtue of military service.

The shift from a landed to a service nobility was particularly marked in late seventeenth-century Denmark. Frederik III's 1661 letter patent made entry into office conditional upon qualifications, not birth, and the 1671 table of ranks underlined the shift of emphasis to service as the criterion for nobility. The 1679 ordinance gave noble privileges and rights to non-noble higher officials, and was probably intended to strengthen loyalty to the crown after the Scanian war, the first serious test of the absolutist system. Specific mention was made in the ordinance of faithful and loyal service during the war, and it also spoke of encouraging others to strive to serve fatherland and crown. Christian V was reserved in his attitude towards the old nobility, though he was prepared to encourage them to engage in royal service in order to strengthen his sovereignty. The new titled nobility introduced in 1671 included five members of the old aristocracy, though most of the titles went to members of the royal family, foreigners such as Frederik Ahlefeld and Conrad Reventlow or parvenus such as Peder Schumacher, son of a wine-merchant, who, as Count Griffenfeld, enjoyed a meteoric career as the all-powerful minister and favourite of the king. In the first two decades of absolutism, the old nobility secured half of the posts in the colleges and court of appeal and managed to retain a grip on one of their traditional areas of influence, the administration of the provinces, providing over half of the *amtmænd* in Christian V's reign. By 1720, however, only 12 per cent of the highest offices of state were held by the old nobility, as against 72 per cent occupied by men of non-noble origin. The rise of the parvenus was satirised by Mogens Skeel in his 'Comedy of the count and the baron' (1680), but many, including Skeel himself, accommodated themselves to the new order.

The established nobility sought to defend their position in a variety of ways. On the southern shores of the Baltic, the nobility had succeeded in erecting a formidable barrier of privileges in the course of the Middle Ages. The estates in East Prussia in 1657 defined the right to hold office as the greatest benefice of the indigenous nobility. Magnates such as the Wallenrodts and Tettaus created a dependent clientele through the lavish distribution of offices. Office-holders could and frequently did buy and sell posts, which were regarded as hereditary possessions. Ambitious and resourceful rulers such as the Great Elector deemed it more expedient to soften the erosion of the political liberties of the noble estate by extending landholding privileges. The Great Elector's growing army and civil service also provided career opportunities for the sons of the many impoverished gentry. Although they faced competition from immigrant Huguenots, who comprised over a quarter of the Prussian army officers in 1688, the Junkers still dominated the corps and retained most of the important administrative offices in East Prussia. The importance of office for the nobility was revealed in a complaint of 1682 that many lacked the means to live like gentlemen and 'instead of books and the sword...had to take up the plough and other peasant-like [*bäuerliche*] work'.[13]

The established Swedish nobility frequently voiced their alarm and dissatisfaction at the elevation of thrusting commoners, such as Johan Adler Salvius, or the appointment of foreigners to high office. Gustav Bonde's 1661 programme proposed that the numbers of new noble creations should be drastically reduced in order to ensure a balance between supply and demand for state service. Bonde maintained that the elevation of merchants to the aristocracy had prompted them to abandon useful and necessary occupations and invest their capital in land, thereby ruining the nobility, whose sons were forced to compete for jobs.[14] There were attempts to prevent the Skåne nobility taking

13. Carsten F 1988 *Geschichte der preussischen Junker* Frankfurt-am-Main, p. 38.
14. Wittrack G 1913 Riksskattmästaren Gustaf Bondes politiska programm 1661 *Historisk Tidskrift* **33**: 51.

up their seats in the *riddarhus*, and to debar those who engaged in trade. Some of the resentment and disdain felt by the high nobility towards the lesser ranks was revealed in the 1670s, when Axel Sparre was hauled before the courts for instigating an assault on Crispin Flygge, a minor nobleman and customs official. Sparre's supporters in the ranks of the high aristocracy claimed that the supreme court ought to be able to distinguish between 'a simple and an eminent man' and they suspected Flygge dared not accept reconciliation for fear of what his fellows might do to him at the next *riksdag*. The old-established families succeeded in maintaining their position rather better in Sweden than in Denmark, but the rise of the *noblesse de robe* still posed a serious challenge. Kurt Ågren has suggested that the matrimonial ties which linked the political and social elite of the early seventeenth century were beginning to break down before the introduction of absolutism in 1680 finally ended the dominance of these clans, and Ingvar Elmroth's studies have shown that the growth of the new nobility far outstripped that of the pre-1600 aristocracy from the middle of the seventeenth century onwards.[15]

Service to the crown necessitated education. Gustav II Adolf's privileges for the nobility sought to encourage them to educate their offspring, and a *collegium illustre* to prepare their sons for state service was opened in 1625. Sorø academy in Denmark served a similar purpose, though it was also intended to spare noble families the expense (and risk of spiritual contamination) of sending their offspring abroad for their education. After a solid grounding in religion, bookish arts and studies, wrote Arent Berntsen, the young Danish nobleman undertook the grand tour to acquaint himself with other nations' customs, languages and politics. Although literacy and learning were becoming an essential part of a nobleman's upbringing, there still remained a lingering suspicion that book-learning was somehow demeaning. Stiernhielm's Hercules is urged to set aside paper and ink and let clerks and poor students bury their heads in books, for 'Thou art of nobler blood: thy birth such would disgrace': Fru Dygd (Madam Virtue), however, points out that nobility, properly understood, involves an obligation to seek after wisdom.[16]

An education was also intended to refine the manners of the gentle-

15. Rystad G 1955 *Johan Gyllenstierna, rådet och kungamakten* Biblioteca historica Lundensis 2. Lund, p 62. Ågren K 1976 Rise and decline of an aristocracy *Scandinavian Journal of History* **1**: 79. Elmroth I 1981 *För kung och fosterland. Studier i den svenska adelns demografi och offentliga funktioner 1600–1900* Biblioteca historica Lundensis 50. Lund.

16. Gustafsson L 1967 Litteratur och miljö: Dahlgren S *et al. Kultur och samhälle i stormaktstidens Sverige*. Stockholm, p. 108.

man, as Schering Rosenhane reminded his son, studying in Paris. He should learn to be 'courtois, civil, hardy et galant, d'aimer les bonnes compagnies et de sçavoir ses exercises et honestement entretenir les dames'.[17] The Scandinavian nobleman of the late seventeenth century was certainly more urbane and polished than his ruder forebears, able to converse fluently with foreigners and prone to lapse into French or Latin in his public utterances; but the mask of sophistication could occasionally slip. Axel Oxenstierna had occasion to chastise members of the *riddarhus* for behaving like peasants in the local court (one wonders how he would have reacted to the outburst of the old soldier Anton von Steinberg, who greeted the futile attempts of the marshal of the nobility to keep order at the 1672 *riksdag* by shouting: 'God's death, look not so sour, we are cavaliers, thou needst not treat us like boys').[18]

The social order of pre-industrial Europe was based on a hierarchy of rank, stoutly reinforced by countless laws and regulations. If contemporaries frequently ignored the rules, they rarely challenged the assumptions which underpinned the corporate structure of society. They accepted without question that God had ordered the world according to rank and estate. The society of rank portrayed itself in elaborate imagery: thus, each estate had its own humour – melancholia symbolised the black-garbed clergy, choler the haughty, sword-bearing nobility, with the sanguine burgher and phlegmatic peasant making up the quartet. The social order also determined the quality, colour and cut of the apparel worn. The common man was to be content with grey homespun; the clergy wore black broadcloth (though bishops and the more wealthy preferred silk). Towards the end of the seventeenth century, the colours adopted for the uniforms of the national armies – blue in Sweden, red in Denmark – were much favoured by the fashionable and wealthy. The wearing of a blue suit of clothes, declared Anders Bachmansson in 1730, conferred respect upon the wearer, as did the carrying of a sword. A man who forgot to buckle on his sword or had it taken away went about as if ashamed or embarrassed.[19]

In spite of all the efforts of churchmen and the state to preserve the distinctions of rank and status, the lower orders showed an incorrigi-

17. Runeby N 1983 Barbarei oder Zivilität? Zur Entwicklung einer organisierten Gesellschaft in Schweden im 17 Jahrhundert: Rystad G (ed.) *Europe and Scandinavia: Aspects of the process of integration in the 17th century*. Lund, p. 214.

18. Rystad G 1985 Stormaktstidens riksdag (1611–1718): Schück H *et al. Riksdagen genom tiderna*. Stockholm, pp. 87, 89.

19. Wirilander K 1982 *Herrskapsfolk. Ståndspersoner i Finland 1721–1870* Nordiska museets handlingar 98. Stockholm, pp. 44–7.

ble propensity to buck the rules. Those who dressed in the materials and rayment of a more refined estate soon drew attention to themselves, like the Danish gamekeeper of the 1690s who possessed no fewer than three wigs, or the student of theology at Copenhagen university who drew the wrath of the church authorities upon his bewigged pate in 1657. A royal official in Königsberg complained in 1708 that it was no longer possible to distinguish between 'persons of quality' and members of the burgherage, with their gilded carriages and liveried lackeys. Satirists and foreign travellers commented on the ardent desire of the wives of the bourgeoisie to imitate French fashions. Maidens with modest natural endowments could buy papier-mâché falsies in a shop off the Copenhagen Bourse; but, as the satirist Hans Willmsen Lauremberg revealed in his *Fire Skiæmte Digte* (1652), one young lady at least was betrayed when she bent down too hastily to fasten her garter – the falsies popped out 'like two mustard pots'.[20] Churchmen were constantly being abjured to set a good example and dress modestly. Many of the curates and priests in poor parishes were so impoverished that their dress was hardly distinguishable from that of the peasantry, but in more prosperous areas such as the diocese of Växsjö, priests were regularly exhorted to set aside frivolous dress and long collars, to cut their hair and wear decent hats.

Contemporaries were highly conscious of their status and position in society, and often reacted violently to slurs upon their honour. The term 'executioner' was a particularly foul term of abuse. Those who performed this task were social outcasts, often pardoned criminals, living in isolated parts of the town or countryside. It was difficult to persuade 'honourable' men to have anything to do with the executioner, his assistant or his trade. The executioner had his own stool and mug in the alehouse, and none would sit where his assistant had rested. Workers engaged to repair the gallows outside Copenhagen in 1644 had to be bribed with liberal quantities of ale and music supplied by two drummers and a piper before they would agree to do the work. The redundant gallows at Löbenicht, one of the three towns of Königsberg, could only be dismantled in 1714 after the entire company of carpenters and masons, accompanied by a band and with the symbols of their trade openly displayed, had ritualistically decreed the work to be honourable; and a similar ceremony had to be performed almost a hundred years later before carpenters would begin work on a

20. Steensberg A (ed.) 1969 *Dagligliv i Danmark – det syttende og attende århundrede 1620–1720.* Copenhagen, pp. 392–3. Magalotti L 1968 *Relazioni di viaggio in Inghilterra, Francia e Svezia.* Bari, p. 232, comments on the eagerness of the wives of Swedish burghers to copy French fashions.

mill to be erected on the site of another gallows in the town. Prostitutes and their children were also regarded as social outcasts, the women often being made to wear distinctive headgear as a mark of their shameful profession. Like beggars, they could be whipped and driven out of the village or town, though the efforts of authority seems to have done little to reduce their numbers: in 1634, 170 prostitutes were caught working the streets of the northern suburb of Stockholm alone.

The Lutheran church played an important role in the enforcement of moral discipline and education. The duties of the Christian were spelled out in the text of the catechism as a collection of biblical aphorisms reflecting the social order of the three estates: *politia*, ordained to discipline sin, *ecclesia*, ordained to fight sin, and *oeconomia*, which covered the family and household. Karl XI's church law of 1686 decreed that a basic knowledge of the catechism was to be a condition for taking communion and for entering into marriage. Examination of the catechism was rated more important than preaching, and much of the spiritual literature for popular consumption was based upon its text. The 1686 church law, which was to apply to all Swedish domains, reflected the absolutist power of the monarch, and marked the final subjection of ecclesiastical to secular authority. The king reserved the right to ignore the recommendations of the chapter and to impose his own choice of bishop, and he could install his own candidate in any parish. Although the parishes were to continue to oversee moral discipline, most of the church's judicial powers were abolished or subordinated to secular authority. The 1687 instructions to provincial governors, charging them with the maintenance of religion and the proper forms of worship, illustrates the degree to which the church had been placed under state control. Similar developments occurred in Denmark and Prussia. Under the absolutist ruler, the clergy became servants of the state, responsible for a variety of administrative duties, and the church became the instrument of religious uniformity by the grace of sovereign majesty: as the elector Friedrich reminded the Prussian government in 1695, they should be in no doubt that he alone was supreme bishop in the land.

The inculcation of Christian values was an integral part of what Peter Burke has termed 'the reform of popular culture', a systematic attempt by the godly reformers, generally aided and abetted by the secular authorities, to change the values and attitudes of the rest of the population.[21] Particular attention was paid to the young: during the

21. Burke P 1978 *Popular culture in early modern Europe*. London, pp. 207ff.

reign of Christian IV, each town in Denmark was ordered to appoint two overseers to ensure that parents and guardians allowed their children to go to school, and that the young were set to honourable employment. The legal age of responsibility was also raised. Manuals advised parents not to lose control and call their children names, or to scare them with bogeymen: Christian piety and birching were the best means of disciplining children and saving them from evil. The rude manners and promiscuous habits of the commonalty were also to be eschewed. Erasmus of Rotterdam's *De civitate morum puerilium libellus*, which achieved wide circulation in translation, warned children not to wipe their noses on their hats or sleeves like peasants or fishwives, and recommended that children should not see each other naked and should not have to share beds.

The overall effect of these attempts to reform the habits and morals of the commonalty is hard to judge. There is evidence to show that those who offended against the moral code enforced by the church were shunned by the community: pregnant brides in Sweden, for example, were not permitted to wear the bridal crown. On the other hand, there were areas of conflict between strict Christian morality and local tradition, such as the widespread custom of unmarried young men and women sleeping together. Peasants in general did not regard sorcery as wrong, since they argued that it was intended to ward off evil, not to bring it upon others. Marriage within the prohibited degrees was widespread in Livonia and the church was unable to eradicate this custom, or the habit of seizing the bride by force and marrying without benefit of clergy. Attendance at church was compulsory for the peasantry in Estonia and Livonia, and failure to comply could land the guilty party in the stocks. The clergy nevertheless had a hard job in persuading their flock to come to church. The peasant often had to travel several miles to reach the church, and the landlords' habit of making them work late on Saturdays prevented those in outlying districts from making the journey at all. The nearby inn was also a temptation, and fines were imposed on innkeepers who sold drink during the service. Once inside the church, the rustics could not be relied upon to behave, but – according to one Swedish visitation register – 'hollered and gossiped like uncontrollable goats', rushing out of the church once the parson had finished. In 1686, the Swedish government threatened fines, bread-and-water sentences and running the gauntlet for those guilty of scuffling, wrangling or disturbing the peace in church.[22]

22. Levander L 1933 *Brottsling och bödel*. Stockholm, pp. 185–6.

The clergy were also in the forefront of campaigns to extirpate witchcraft. As late as 1677, a Livonian church committee complained of the immense difficulties of rooting out 'this terrible idolatry and heathen blindness which afflicts so many thousands of poor souls in this land'.[23] The accusation of attendance at the witches' sabbath was comparatively rare in the Baltic lands: here, a high proportion of the accused were men, and many were charged with lycanthropy. In the wave of trials which afflicted parts of northern Sweden in the 1670s, children played a prominent role, complaining that they had been taken by witches to Blåkulla, where they were obliged to consort with the devil. It has been suggested that the children may have been intoxicated by narcotic drugs, such as datura, which was left smouldering at night to ease the pain of toothache, though there also appears to have been a strong element of hysteria in the mass denunciations, especially as many of the witnesses were prevented from sleeping to protect them from the wiles of the witches. This mass outbreak of witchcraft caused the authorities in Stockholm to appoint committees of investigation. As members of these committees lived outside the affected districts, they were often able to reveal the specious nature of the charges. The discrediting of witnesses by the committees brought to an end the wave of persecutions, with the government ordering its officials and the church to take a cautious line on future accusations. A similar outbreak of hysteria in the Danish parish of Thisted in 1695 was investigated by the bishop of Ålborg, who found several girls guilty of deception. The number of trials for witchcraft in Denmark had begun to decline after 1648: the last witch was burnt in 1693, though the peasantry could still exact rough justice, as in 1722 when a women suspected of witchcraft was burned in her home, and as late as 1721, a prisoner on Bremerholm was executed for signing a pact with the devil.

Amongst the educated, a growing scepticism about witchcraft was evident. The eminent physician Thomas Bartholin was inclined to believe that melancholia lay behind the phenomenon. Urban Hjärne, one of the fiercest opponents of the witchcraft epidemic in Sweden, presented a masterful analysis of the tyranny of the denunciators 'whose amusement it has been to wreak revenge on those whom they have long feared or those whom they envy for being richer or of a better station in life. And if any dare oppose them, they are immediately denounced, just as when dogs bark, one begins at first and

23. Kahk J 1985 Heidnische Glaubensverstellungen, Zauberei und religiöse Eifer in Estland um 1700 *Zeitschrift für Ostforschung* **34**: 525.

then the others follow suit....'[24] Villum Lange, who had considerable experience as a judge in Denmark, also expressed doubts about the state of mind of those who freely confessed to witchcraft. The church's obsession with rooting out sorcery and devil worship can be seen as part of an intensified struggle against paganism: Jesuit and Lutheran alike inveighed against heathen practices, from Pomerania to Lapland. Students who dabbled in the black arts also fell under suspicion, and the first professor of Greek and Hebrew at Åbo academy was forced to quit his job because of persistent rumours that he had encouraged his students to read cabbalistic literature. By the end of the century, however, even churchmen were beginning to see sorcery and soothsaying as relatively harmless superstitious survivals of the pagan age.

EDUCATION

The foundation of new universities and academies was part of a general trend towards the better provision of education. The administrative and commercial needs of the state, as much as the ideas of pedagogic reformers such as Jan Comenius (who visited Sweden in the 1640s), stimulated the creation of new grammar schools (*gymnasii*). Like the lower-grade *trivium* schools (where the instruction was based on the three liberal arts of rhetoric, grammar and dialectic), these *gymnasii* were usually located in towns. The quality of education was variable. Inspectors frequently complained that few of the pupils understood even the basic rudiments of Latin, and their teachers were often ill-equipped to provide the necessary instruction. Many dropped out after a few years: others were withdrawn at certain seasons of the year to help with household or farm work. Teaching methods were repetitive and unimaginative, and a harsh regime prevailed. The Danish poet Anders Bording remembered with some feeling the lavish use of the birch and cane, the salty and inadequate food and unheated rooms in which the shivering children tried in vain to sleep at night. Older pupils in Denmark were employed as peripatetic elementary teachers, instructing the children of the parish in the catechism. The church held this practice to be unsatisfactory, and it was banned in 1670: henceforth, each parish was to have a permanent clerk (*degn*). Like the schoolmasters appointed to run the elementary schools which the Danish and Swedish governments strove to establish (particularly in the last decades of the seventeenth century), the clerks were in daily

24. Heikkinen A 1969 *Paholaisen liittolaiset* Historiallisia tutkimuksia 78. Helsinki, p. 59. See also Hildebrand S (ed.) 1923 *Hakvin Spegels dagbok*. Stockholm, pp. 10–11.

contact with the commonalty, from whose ranks they often came. Some were rogues, many were incompetent, all were poorly paid; but they were an indispensable element in the work of the Lutheran church, carrying out a variety of tasks from keeping parish registers to playing the organ.

The number of students enrolled at the universities in the Swedish lands rose from around 200 in the 1620s to some 1,500 by the end of the century. This expansion caused some anxiety in academic circles, and Olof Rudbeck, as rector of the university in Uppsala, attempted to ensure stricter controls over the admission of students. Although the intellectual dominance of the theologians weakened as the century progressed, the orthodox Lutheran church still exercised a tight control over many aspects of the students' life. The principal intellectual activity of the students was the study of Latin, since most were ill-prepared to follow lectures in that language. Evidence suggests that many graduates who entered the church had limited their studies of theology to attendance at compulsory lectures. Other disciplines often had difficulty in attracting sufficient students: the faculty of medicine at Uppsala, for example, rarely reached the minimum level of fifteen students laid down in the statutes. The law faculty at Uppsala, which Axel Oxenstierna sought to expand in order to provide more recruits into public service, was generally under-subscribed, attracting no more than 10-15 per cent of the total student body. Much of the teaching was mediocre in quality: professors regularly changed posts in order to obtain better salaries or more prestige. The most talented scholars often preferred to work outside the universities. The laboratories of Urban Hjärne and Christopher Polhem drew students from the university, and the brilliant anatomists Thomas Bartholin and Niels Steensen found the university of Copenhagen an uncongenial place for their researches. Although the orthodox theologians' dominance of the universities was undermined by the determination of the state to secure a more appropriate education for its future bureaucrats, they were still sufficiently powerful to see off reformers such as Olof Rudbeck and to fight a stiff rearguard action against the natural scientists and Halle-inspired Pietists in the first two decades of the eighteenth century.[25]

25. Strömberg J 1988 Den regionala studentrekryteringen till stormaktstidens svenska universitet, in Villstrand N-E, (ed.) *Kustbygd och centralmakt 1560–1721* Skrifter utgivna av Svenska Litteratursällskapet i Finland 546. Helsingfors, pp. 67–90. Almqvist D 1934 Fackutbildning och humanistisk tradition vid stormaktstidens svenska universitet *Historisk Tidskrift* **54**:1-28. See also von Rauch G 1943 *Die Universität Dorpat und das Eindringen der frühen Aufklärung in Livland 1690–1710* Schweden und Europa 5. Essen.

The academies in Åbo and Dorpat were founded primarily to educate young men in the provinces for the royal administration. The hopes expressed by Johan Skytte in his inauguration speech in 1632 that the *Academia Gustaviania* in Dorpat would be open to all classes was not to be fulfilled. The majority of students were Swedes or Finns, mostly the children of burghers and parsons: the native nobility preferred to send their sons abroad. Skytte's successor as governor-general of Livonia, Bengt Oxenstierna, proposed abolishing the university, which seemed only to attract Smålanders, and to set up an academy for the nobility. The professors seem to have been unhappy in the town, requesting in 1634 that they be allowed to remove to Reval. The occupation of Dorpat by Russian troops in 1656 effectively brought the first phase of the history of the university to an end, and it was not until 1690 that it was reopened as the *Academia Gustavo-Carolina*. There were fewer Swedes and Finns attending the university during this second period (1690-1710), largely because of the rival attractions of Åbo and Lund. The nobility still preferred to send their sons to Königsberg, Rostock and even Leiden, though this did not stop them complaining that Dorpat was being used as a centre for the swedification of the land. (Governor-general Hastfer retorted that although one of the professors, 'a pious and upright man', had said that 'within ten years we will all be good Swedes', he must either have been joking or drunk).[26]

CENTRAL GOVERNMENT AND THE PROVINCES

The strengthening of royal power in Sweden undoubtedly led to an intensification of efforts to subordinate the provinces to tighter central control, though whether or not this also implied swedification is questionable. The Swedish government's attitude towards the overseas provinces had always been somewhat ambivalent. On the one hand, there was a clear desire to impose Swedish institutions, but, after the 1630s, there was also a marked reluctance in the *riksråd* to pursue the policy of incorporation favoured by Karl IX. Johan Skytte's attempts to realise this programme during his brief tenure of office as governor-general of Livonia (1629–34) encountered resistance, not least from the Swedish magnates who were also big land-owners in

26. Siilivask K (ed.) 1985 *History of Tartu university 1632–1982*. Tallinn, pp 18-53. Isberg A 1953 *Karl XI och den livländska adeln 1684–1695*. Lund, p. 222.

the Baltic lands. The requests made in 1643 and 1662 by the Livonian nobility to be incorporated into the Swedish realm were politely declined. The *råd* aristocracy disliked the idea of admitting Baltic Germans to their ranks (Axel Oxenstierna feared that they would constantly be pursuing their own particularist interests), and many were quite happy to enjoy the benefits of separate and distinct local privileges as landowners in the Baltic whilst continuing to exercise power in Stockholm.[27] A plan to incorporate Livonia into the Swedish realm was mooted by governor-general Hastfer in 1694–5, but not taken up. Karl XI was content to reduce the political power of the Baltic nobility and to strengthen his grip on the provinces through the introduction of Swedish church law and the Swedish legal system. The crown also embarked upon an ambitious programme of educational reform, seeking to establish a school in every parish. In Livonia, this objective was vigorously supported by the general superintendant Johann Fischer and clergymen such as Ernst Glück in the Latvian districts and Bengt Forselius in the Estonian areas around Dorpat. The nobility, hoping to secure some concessions from the crown, voted in 1687 to help finance the system, but their long-established opposition to any provision of education for the peasantry tended to override such belated acts of generosity. School buildings were often inadequate; poorly paid schoolmasters were obliged to find lodgings in the parson's sauna or in a wretched hovel; and there was a shortage of teaching materials. The nobility, faced with a shortage of labour as a result of the famine years of 1695–7, also tried to reclaim Estonian and Latvian schoolmasters and parish clerks.

The intentions of central government were all too often frustrated by local resistance or obstruction, at home as well as overseas. The small town of Västervik, for example, seems to have ignored the 1620 instructions to appoint a secretary and to elect officials to supervise good order and seemly behaviour. The nomination of a royal official to the magistracy in the 1650s aroused a lot of hostility, and it was not until the 1670s that the crown really began to take a close interest in the election of burghermasters. By the end of the century, however, the provincial governor regularly appointed his own nominees to the magistracy of the town. Of the Baltic towns, Riga and Reval were strong enough to resist attempts to impose royal administrators upon them, and the government was wise enough to avoid open confrontation. Great hopes were held for Narva, which Axel Oxenstierna

27. Isberg A 1968 *Livlands kyrkostyrelse 1622–1695*. Uppsala; and Isberg A 1970 *Kyrkoförvaltningsproblem i Estland 1561–1700*. Uppsala.

believed could be developed into the second city of the realm. The 1617 privileges decreed that the town secretary should know Swedish and placed the town under the Swedish law code: royal burghermasters were appointed from 1630 onwards. Under the royal burghermaster Jakob Fougt, the town council was reorganised along collegial lines in the 1640s, though popular resistance forced Fougt to resign in 1653 with these reforms half completed. The magistracy received several warnings that they should use Swedish and not German in their dealings with the administration and supreme court, and the government in Stockholm persisted in using Swedish in their correspondence with all the Baltic towns: but no conscious attempt was made to eliminate the use of German.

The use of Swedish was clearly a matter of prestige. Gustav Adolf demanded that the Livonian *Landräte* learn Swedish in order to be able to understand Swedish law; Axel Oxenstierna scolded the Estonian nobility in 1643 for presuming to advise the queen on what language she should use in correspondence with them. But the use of Swedish in the Baltic and north German lands remained confined to official business and correspondence. In the territories acquired from Denmark between 1645 and 1660, however, the Swedish government pursued a more vigorous policy of incorporation. In areas where there were comparatively few privileged groups, such as the upland provinces of Jämtland and Härjedalen, this proved to be a relatively straightforward task; but the nobility of Halland and Skåne posed a more difficult problem. The treaty of Roskilde guaranteed the customary laws and privileges of the estates as long as they did not contravene the fundamental laws of Sweden, and the treaty of Copenhagen in 1660 specifically itemised the privileges of the Skåne nobility. Jerker Rosén has argued that the Swedish crown offered the nobility of Skåne a choice: either they could preserve their privileges and separate status, or they could abandon them and enjoy the full rights and privileges of their Swedish counterparts. The Scanian war of the 1670s marked a turning-point, for although most of the nobility sat the war out, several actively supported the Danish cause, and the peasant *snapphanare* guerrillas wrought havoc amongst the Swedish armies. Karl XI set his face against any pardon for the thousands who fled to Denmark after the cessation of hostilities, preferring to settle the devastated areas with loyal Swedes, and founding the town of Karlshamn as a mark of Sweden's intentions. The right of the Skåne estates to sit in the *riksdag* was revoked in 1679, and was only restored on the crown's terms. The 1678 *riksdag* authorised a programme of swedification for the church. The local clergy were obliged to use the

Swedish language and church ceremonial. The Danish catechism was replaced by that of Sweden, and the young were to be taught in Swedish by Swedish priests and parish clerks. The terms of the peace treaty obliged the crown to proceed with caution, but within two years, the clergy had been persuaded to sue for the introduction of the Swedish church order and admission as an estate into the *riksdag*. Under the energetic direction of Canutus Hahn, the programme outlined in 1678 was put into force. The *Academia Carolina conciliatrix*, founded in Lund in 1668, was also intended to foster Swedish education and culture in the southern provinces.

To the extent that the inhabitants of Skåne remained loyal to the Swedish crown during the Great Northern War, the policies of Karl XI and his servants may be deemed a success. The *snapphanare* – denounced by some as little more than murderous robbers, hailed by others as heroes and patriots – passed into legend, and the inhabitants who remained after the Scanian war gradually accommodated themselves to their new circumstances. The impact of the Swedish language, in spite of the efforts of the church and officialdom, was probably slight. In all likelihood, the natives of Skåne gradually came to regard Swedish as the official language corresponding to their own dialect, in much the same way as they had earlier regarded Danish.[28]

Nationalist historians in Finland have long argued that the status of Finnish declined during the seventeenth century, though their arguments are predicated on the contentious assumption that Finland enjoyed a kind of special position within the realm before that time. There was clearly an increase in the number of appointments to high office in Finland of non-natives, some of whom were indifferent or even hostile towards the Finnish language. On the other hand, there was often a clear awareness of the advantages of appointing officials who understood the local language. A secretary without a knowledge of Finnish in those parts was as hampered in his work as a dancing-master with the cramp, according to governor-general Herman Fleming. The native-born clergy and army officers also used the linguistic argument in their attempts to restrict the appointment of 'foreigners or strangers who do not understand our Finnish tongue'.[29] These arguments are pragmatic, rather than ideological, and it would be as unwise to claim the existence of a clearly defined Finnish 'programme'

28. Rosén J 1946 Statsledning och provinspolitik under Sveriges stormaktstid *Scandia* 17: 224–70. Åberg A 1958 *När Skåne blev svenskt* Stockholm. Fabricius K 1906, 1952 *Skaanes Overgang fra Danmark til Sverige* (3 vols). Copenhagen.

29. Lehtinen E 1961 *Hallituksen yhtenäistämispolitiikka Suomessa 1600-luvulla* Historiallisia tutkimuksia 60. Helsinki, pp. 243, 340.

as to see the government in Stockholm pursuing a consistent policy of linguistic assimilation.

The most evident form of uniformity which the state sought to uphold was that of religion; but even here, exceptions had to be made. Concessions were made to foreigners of a different faith, as long as they refrained from proselytising. The Calvinist Walloons who settled in Sweden tended to form separate and autonomous communities in the countryside, and their co-religionists in the towns were numerically insignificant. The conversion of the Hohenzollerns to Calvinism caused some conflict in Prussia, where the Lutheran estates resisted the attempts of the dukes to give office to their co-religionists. Frederick William caused grave offence when he insisted on his Reformed court preacher conducting the funeral service for his father in the castle church in Königsberg. The influx of Huguenot refugees at the end of the century swelled the ranks of the Calvinists in the towns: by 1703, the French community in Königsberg numbered 500 and there were also congregations of English, Scottish, Dutch and Polish–Lithuanian Calvinists in the city. Danzig too was home to a variety of different faiths, and the town council had to cope with the tensions which this caused. Artisans demanded the reinstatement of a popular preacher in 1673, and appealed to the king two years later to curb the activities of the Mennonites. The Catholics also made demands, and the council had to allow them to build a chapel in the town and to be represented on the committee of one hundred (*Hundertmänner*) as part of a deal struck with Jan Sobieski in 1677.

In sensitive frontier areas, such as Karelia and Ingria, the Swedish crown was as anxious to wean the peasantry away from Orthodoxy as it was to substitute the Swedish for the Danish church order in its southern provinces. There was a noticeable stiffening of attitudes on both sides of the frontier; the measures taken by Patriarch Nikon in 1658 were, like the Swedish church ordinance of 1686, intended to strengthen orthodoxy and the monarchy. In spite of the efforts of zealous church administrators, little progress was made in persuading the Orthodox priesthood to abandon their ways and embrace the Lutheran catechism. Johan Gezelius the younger, appointed superintendant of Ingria in 1681, planned to convert the Ingrians and Votes (who spoke languages akin to Finnish) by segregating them from Russian-speakers. This policy was endorsed by the government, but ran into strong opposition from the local landowners, who refused to stop their peasants attending the Russian Orthodox church or wearing Russian dress. It also came to the notice of the tsars, who dispatched a letter of protest to Stockholm. The Ingrian peasantry soon got wind of this, and sent a representative to lay their grievances before the king. Karl XI, alarmed at the prospect of unrest and the wholesale flight of peasants across the frontier, and embarrassed by the Russian protests, which he admitted were justified according to the terms of earlier treaties, ordered that conversions should henceforth be voluntary. Gezelius manfully stuck to his guns, writing a hostile attack on Orthodoxy which he was later obliged to revise under pressure from the authorities. Though the 1686 church law was introduced in Ingria, Karl XI warned Gezelius' successor not to use it as a means of resuming the policy of forcible conversions.

National identity, as defined by the literate upper echelons of society, was usually a compound of myth, heightened self-awareness and xenophobia, sustained by an uneasy feeling of inferiority. The Sarmatian myth of the Polish nobility was reinforced by a fierce xenophobia and a resurgent Catholicism. The privileges enjoyed by the Polish nobility tended to attract their non-Polish counterparts into what Tazbir has called a kind of political-institutional community: in the course of time, this was accompanied by linguistic polonisation, as occurred amongst the aristocracy of Royal Prussia and the Lithuanian lands. Janusz Radziwiłł, for example, declared in a letter to his brother that, though he was born and would die a Lithuanian, 'we must use the Polish language in our country'.[30]

If, as Tazbir suggests, the myth of the Sarmatian nation provided the historical underpinning, and even the *raison d'être* of the aristocratic Polish–Lithuanian commonwealth, Gothicism helped sustain the self-image of the Swedes. The fame and renown of the Swedes' Gothic ancestors was lauded in verse and prose, most notably in Olof Rudbeck's *Atlantica*. Rudbeck's avowed intention was to demonstrate that Sweden had been the ancient cradle of civilisation, a quest which led him to suppose that Hercules was a variant of Härkalle, and Proserpina was really Frostpina. Rudbeck even applied for state funds to send a researcher to look for Gothic remains in the places which they had supposedly conquered in ancient times. This pride in Swedish ancestry was underlaid with a sense of inferiority. 'Skogekär Bergbo', the anonymous author of *Thet Swenska språketz klagemål* (The lament of the Swedish language, 1658) bitterly bewailed the neglect of Swedish by his contemporaries: whilst other nations valued literature, Swedes preferred the martial arts. Those who were educated interlaced their discourse with French loan-words and Latin tags, whilst German was

30. Tazbir J 1986 *La république nobilitaire et le monde. Etudes sur l'histoire de la culture polonaise à l'époque du baroque* Polish Historical Library 7. Wrocław, p. 39.

an everyday language in the larger towns. Foreigners scorned the idea of learning Swedish, finding no use for it, and proclaimed the superiority of their own tongue. The Danish writer Peder Syv also campaigned for the improvement of the mother tongue, to the honour of the fatherland, and was eventually rewarded in 1683 with the post of *philologus regius danicæ linguæ*.

The inferior status of Swedish as a literary language was reflected in the output of printed books. Three-quarters of the works published within the Swedish realm in the seventeenth century were in classical or foreign languages; those in Swedish were largely directed towards the lesser educated, or served a severely practical purpose. For the educated elite, there was little obvious advantage in a switch from the classical languages, which gave access to the European 'republic of letters'. The Swedish scholar Stina Hansson has argued that the 'lament of the Swedish language' was in fact a political programme, emanating from chancery circles, and that the writing of national history was from the outset promoted by the government. Gothicism, far from being the fantastic outpourings of versifiers seeking promotion, is seen by Hansson as having practical and rational implications, 'supporting and strengthening the idea of the national state, and playing a part in the basic process whereby Sweden became Sweden'.[31] The universities, on the other hand, preferred to remain loyal to the languages of antiquity. In 1677, Olof Rudbeck greeted the academics of Uppsala university by declaring that, 'I have not yet discovered in any book that Aristotle or Cicero ever honoured the Gothic or Scythian tongue (which is the oldest)', and, as they had used their mother tongue in addressing an academic audience, Rudbeck intended to follow their example 'in good, pure Swedish, our mother tongue'.[32] There was much resistance to his efforts to introduce Swedish into the university, though by the end of the century, the language began to creep into the occasional oration, and was used far more extensively in the eighteenth century. Swedish was also employed far more in epithalamia and funeral odes, as the fashion for engaging a poet to pen laudatory verses spread to a broader public.

The invention of a glorious Swedish past also spilled over into Finland. In his *Scondia illustrata*, the Swedish-born historian Johannes Messenius declared the Finns to be descendants of the Wends, and described an ancient Finnish kingdom which had stretched from the

---

31. Hansson S 1984 *Svenskans nytta Sveriges ära. Litteratur och kulturpolitik under 1600-talet* Skrifter utgivna av litteraturvetenskapliga institutionen vid Göteborgs universitet 11. Göteborg, p. 112.
32. Cited in Castrén G 1907 *Stormakttidens diktning*. Helsingfors, p. 82.

Tornio river to the borders of Saxony. A later Swedish writer, Michael Wexionius, gave this an added twist by claiming that the hard-pressed Finns were saved from extinction at the hands of the Russians and Germans by the protective intervention of Sweden. A rather more aggressively patriotic attitude was struck by the unknown author of *Chronicon Finlandiæ* at the end of the seventeenth century, and by Daniel Juslenius in his *Aboa vetus et nova* (1700). Both authors sought to show that their fatherland also had a history, and that, in Juslenius' words, 'bountiful mother nature has not left us desolate here in the cold North, nor gave our forefathers sponges for brains, as is often said'.[33]

The growing interest in antiquity and the origins of the inhabitants of the northern lands, and the process of self-definition set in motion by increased contacts with foreigners, should not however lead us to make too sweeping conclusions about national awareness. All too often, corporate interests and local and regional particularism were dominant. The burghers of Viborg in the 1640s, for example, grieved over the destruction wrought by the recent wars in their dear fatherland of Jutland, whilst the 'fatherland' of the Estonian or Livonian nobility was defined in terms of their privileges, and certainly did not include the 'non-German' peasantry. The degree to which the peasantry perceived of a fatherland beyond the confines of the family or local community is difficult to ascertain, though it is perhaps interesting to note that the descendants of the Orthodox Karelians who fled to the hinterland of Russia in the seventeenth century have only the vaguest folk memories of their historical past, and little sense of national self-awareness. The absolutist state in Denmark and Sweden may in some respects have eroded local particularism, but loyalty to the sovereign as the God-appointed ruler of the realm, and obedient service to his majesty, did not necessarily promote patriotism on a larger scale. Loyalty towards the king as 'father of his people' was inculcated by the church and the authorities, but there was also another image of the kingdom of heaven which featured prominently in the cheap devotional literature which could be found in peasant households. In view of the exactions and impositions which the earthly king laid upon his subjects, they might well have preferred to

33. Juslenius D 1987 *Vanha ja uusi Turku* Suomalaisen kirjallisuuden seuran toimituksia 466. Helsinki, pp. 22–3. Messenius J 1988 *Suomen, Liivinmaan ja Kuurinmaan vaiheita sekä tuntemattoman tekijän Suomen kronikka* Suomalaisen kirjallisuuden seuran toimituksia 467. Helsinki. See also Anthoni E 1943 Den tidigare finländska historieskrivningens syn på de nationella förhållandena och Finlands ställning till Sverige *Historisk Tidskrift för Finland* **28**: 77-103.

bend their daily thoughts to the pleasing prospects offered in the kingdom of God rather than to the blandishments of secular patriotism.

Juslenius' complaint that foreigners foolishly believed that there was no civilisation beyond their own frontiers contains more than a grain of truth. It was the immense force and dominance of nature, rather than human culture, which left the most profound impression on foreign visitors to Sweden. The French poets (and the philosopher Réné Descartes) enticed to the court of queen Christina wrote mournfully of the sad climes of Sweden, where dark, cold and gloomy winters seemingly had banished forever 'l'agreable verdure'. Human endeavour in such climes was regarded at best as rude and mechanical: influential writers from Bodin in the sixteenth to Montesquieu in the eighteenth century characterised the peoples of the north as best suited for warfare, not the polite arts and graces of civilised society. The abbé Dubois could firmly assert in 1719 that 'the whole world knows that only wild poets, rough poetasters and chill colourists come from the far North', whilst in the play *Les entretiens d'Ariste et d'Eugène* (1671), the following dialogue takes place:

> *Ariste* I acknowledge that cultivated minds are somewhat rarer in colder countries, because nature there is somewhat more languid and mournful, so to speak.
> *Eugène* You should rather acknowledge that intellectual culture, as you have defined it, is entirely incompatible with the coarse temperament and clumsy frames of northern peoples. [34]

Those who lived on the periphery of 'civilised' Europe were often painfully aware of the limitations of their surroundings. Sweden's age of greatness did not lead to any fundamental changes in the appearance of the landscape or the circumstances of life of most of the inhabitants of the northern kingdom. The splendid palaces and houses of the great noble families, recorded by Erik Dahlberg in his three-volume *Suecia antiqua et hodierna* (1667–1716), certainly reflect a degree of aristocratic style and self-confidence, even though a number of the illustrations were drawn from plans of buildings which were never erected. The nobility were the arbiters of taste and fashion, and a top-level painter such as David Ehrenstrahl could command high prices for his work; but the circle of wealthy patrons of the arts was exceedingly small. The lack of a market made book publishing and hence writing as such

---

34. Abbé Dubois 1740 *Réflexions sur la poésie et sur la peinture* (2 vols). Paris, vol. 2, p. 148. Texte J 1895 *Jean-Jacques Rousseau et les origines du cosmopolitanisme littéraire*. Paris, p. 11. Examples of verse written by the French poets at the court of queen Christina are provided by Castrén G 1910 *Norden i den franska litteraturen*. Helsingfors, pp. 62ff.

a rather precarious occupation. Books were expensive. A catalogue issued by the College of Antiquities, founded in 1667 to promote antiquarian studies and publish 'Gothic' materials, shows that two volumes of *Scondia illustrata*, printed on cheap paper, cost 18 copper daler; bibles cost six to ten daler. The annual salary of a copyist in government employ at this time was around 50 copper daler, that of a notary, 112 copper daler. Devotional literature enjoyed the best sales, though broadsheets (*skillingtryck*) also sold well. Most poets survived on what they could earn from writing verses for weddings, funerals and feasts. They usually had the verses printed at their own expense, hoping to sell them to the happy bridegroom or the bereaved family. This could be a risky business: the Swedish poet Lucidor was clapped in jail in 1669 for writing verses to which Göran Gyllenstierna took exception. Civil servants marooned in outlandish places such as Pomerania and Livonia penned verses as much in hope of attracting the attention and patronage of the king as to satisfy the Muses. Gunno Dahlstierna's eulogy on the virtues of Karl XI, *Kunga skald*, helped elevate him from the land surveyor's office in Pomerania to become head of the land surveying office in Stockholm; Georg Stiernhielm's intense literary output in the 1640s was rewarded by appointment to the post of state archivist.

Writers such as Stiernhielm, Runius and Dahlstierna laid the foundations for Swedish literature, as did the poets Anders Bording (who produced Denmark's first newspaper, *Den danske Mercurius*, mostly written in alexandrine verse) and Thomas Kingo for Denmark. But in the world of Racine, Molière, Milton and Dryden, their works appear stiff and crude, reflecting the unsophisticated milieu in which they lived. The two Scandinavian towns of any size were modest in comparison with London or Paris, and could not support the kind of cultural activity recorded, for example, in Pepys' diary. The spiteful Molesworth said of the Danes that: 'their Seasons of Jollity are very rare, and since the fatal Opera about four years ago, wherein many hundred Persons were burnt together in the old Queen's House, they content themselves with running at the Goose on Shrove-Tuesdays and taking their pleasure upon Sledds in the Winter, well wrapped up in Wooll or Furr'.[35] The diary of Petrus Magnus Gyllenius, born Peder Månsson, a poor peasant's son from Värmland, chronicles the rather simple pleasures he enjoyed as a student in Karlstad and Åbo between 1636 and 1652. The boy learnt to read from an ABC book

35. Molesworth R 1694 *An Account of the State of Denmark as it was in the Year 1692.* London, p. 96.

bought by his mother from a colporteur sheltering from the weather, and was given a basic education by the local clergyman, with whom he lodged for two years. As a student in Åbo, he took part in plays and visited the holy well at Kupittaa on Midsummer Day to play games around the bonfires lit to celebrate the summer solstice. In summer 1652, he visited the sights in Stockholm – the royal dining room, a concert in the castle chapel, where a castrato Turk sang, the glass-works and the public gardens, where he saw 'beautiful fountains, vines, many other foreign trees and strange herbs', in addition to a lion ('a fierce beast').[36] Not very exciting, perhaps, when set against the pleasures of the big city; but it gives the measure of the difference between rural, isolated Sweden and the centres of European taste and culture. The towns of north Germany were able to sustain a more varied cultural life. Franz Tunder started a series of evening concerts at the church of St Marien in Lübeck, and attracted the great masters of Baroque music, such as his successor Dietrich Buxtehude, to the town. On the other hand, the talented natural scientist Johann Jungius found Hamburg more congenial than his native city, whilst the Knil-ler brothers found fame and fortune (and in the case of Gottfried, a knighthood) in England.

The sense of being on the outer fringes of European civilisation ('in medio scorpionum et barbarorum hominum', as the bishop of Åbo, Isak Rothovius, once complained) prompted two often contradictory reactions. There was a strong desire to integrate into the mainstream, to copy and to emulate the polished manners and customs of the courtiers of Versailles, and to introduce the new cultural fashions of opera, theatre, coffee-house society and newspapers into the native land: but there was also a pronounced sense of inferiority, of having to put up with clumsy and crude imitations, of being laughed at by foreigners, which could on occasion provoke the kind of outburst exemplified by *Thet Swenska Språketz klagemål*, or prompt the Swed-ish *riksråd* to take umbrage at the insolence of the Estonian gentry in asking for letters sent by queen Christina to be written in German. The lack of a literary past was keenly felt, as Samuel Columbus indicated in his draft version of *Den svenske konungsson*: Alexander the Great and Achilles would have remained unknown, were it not for the pen – how many Gothic heroes were condemned to oblivion by the lack of such an instrument?[37] It was perhaps small consolation for the Swedes to be able in turn to regard their Russian neighbours with

36. Gardberg C, Toijer D (eds) 1962 *Diarium Gyllenianum: eller Petrus Magni Gyllenii Dagbok 1622–1667*. Karlstad, p. 141.
37. Castrén 1907, p. 84.

some contempt, for the barbarians were at the door, and under a ruler who was also eager to draw his backward country into the ambit of western culture (and more importantly, to learn from western technology), were ultimately to wrest the supremacy of the Baltic from Sweden's grasp.

The Rise of Russia

PART FOUR

The Rise of Russia

CHAPTER ELEVEN
The Struggle for Dominion –
The Final Phase

THE ROAD TO POLTAVA

As the seventeenth century drew to a close, Sweden's age of greatness seemed to have passed its zenith. The martial reputation of Swedish troops was dealt several fearful blows during the war against Denmark and Brandenburg–Prussia in the 1670s, a war which revealed how woefully subordinate to French interests Sweden had become. The German provinces had proved to be expensive acquisitions, costly and difficult to defend against the designs of neighbouring states, and membership of the Empire brought little benefit to the northern kingdom. The legacy of Gustav Adolf and his chancellor was to weigh heavily on their successors, compelled to uphold Sweden's sagging reputation and committed to the defence of the terms of the Westphalian settlement. To maintain the defences of the overseas territories, the regency government during the minority of Karl XI was obliged to seek French subsidies, and this carried the risk of involvement in Germany. The disastrous consequences of de la Gardie's French alliance helped bring about the downfall of the chancellor and the establishment of absolutism when the king attained his majority. Karl XI's military reorganisation and the restoration of financial solvency through the *reduktion* and taxation measures helped Sweden break away from excessive dependency on foreign subsidies. From 1680 onwards, a policy of cautious neutrality was observed by the king and his president of chancery, Bengt Oxenstierna. In this, Sweden was undoubtedly assisted by the fact that her neighbours were also exhausted by incessant and ruinous warfare. Poland and Muscovy were embroiled in conflict with the Turks, whilst the aggressive foreign policy of Louis XIV occupied the attention of the German states and the maritime powers, England and the Dutch Republic.

The two decades of peace which Sweden enjoyed after 1679 enabled the country to draw second wind, but the dangers of attack on the extended overseas frontiers still remained. Denmark and Brandenburg–Prussia, dissatisfied with the peace terms of 1679, gravitated towards the French camp and planned to attack Sweden's possessions in Germany. Christian V of Denmark copied Louis XIV's example by attempting his own version of a *réunion* in 1684. Having occupied the territories of the duke of Holstein-Gottorp, he issued a Patent declaring the union of the ducal and royal lands in Slesvig, and imposed an oath of loyalty upon the estates. Christian V and Frederick William also planned to divide up Sweden's German lands between them, and attempted to draw the two dukes of Lüneburg into the French alliance. Louis XIV, however, was unwilling to support a war against Sweden: his principal concern was to check his opponents in northern Germany. Christian V agreed in November 1683 to attack Lüneburg if the dukes engaged in hostilities against France, and to fight the Swedes if they sent more than six thousand men to Germany, but relations between France and Brandenburg–Prussia became strained. Christian V's vain attempt to coerce Hamburg into accepting his overlordship in 1686 alarmed the neighbouring north German states and the maritime powers, who joined forces to put pressure on the Danish king to restore the rights and lands of the exiled duke of Holstein-Gottorp.

The duke's rights were eventually returned and guaranteed by the maritime powers in 1689, after protracted negotiations in Altona. Holstein-Gottorp was a vital link in Sweden's defences, affording access to the north German territories. The bitter rivalry between the duke and the king of Denmark was both an advantage and a drawback to Sweden. It offered an opportunity to counter Danish designs on the lost Scanian provinces, but it also called for military commitments. As Karl XI admitted in 1686, Sweden was not in a position to offer military assistance to the duke. The Swedish navy had suffered a crippling defeat at the hands of admirals Tromp and Juel off Öland in 1676, and was in no state to provide the transports and protection necessary to ship troops to Germany a decade later. Even though Karl XI bequeathed to his son a new navy of thirty-four ships of the line and eleven frigates, Sweden's control of the Baltic after 1681 was ultimately dependent on the goodwill of the maritime powers, whose interests Sweden could ill afford to ignore.[1]

1. Roberts M 1979 *The Swedish Imperial Experience 1560–1718*. Cambridge, pp. 133–41.

Cast in the role of guarantor of the peace settlements of 1648 and 1679, Sweden was able temporarily to make common cause with potential enemies, also threatened by the repercussions of the growing conflict between France and the maritime powers. Sweden and Denmark came together in 1691 to oppose the Anglo-Dutch convention on neutral shipping, though Bengt Oxenstierna refused to be drawn into Louis XIV's proposed league of neutral states. The king of Poland, Jan Sobieski, was also brought into contact with the northern kingdoms through French mediation, and in 1694, a plan for Danish protection of Polish shipping in return for Polish diplomatic pressure on the maritime states if Denmark were attacked was put before the *sejm*. The pro-Habsburg party, however, managed to defeat the plan in the Senate, leaving the Danes to make their peace with the Dutch as best they could. In 1686, finally disenchanted with Louis XIV, Frederick William of Brandenburg–Prussia concluded an alliance with Sweden, and eleven years later, joined forces with the guarantors of the Altona agreement in forcing Christian V to abandon a new offensive against the territories of the duke of Holstein-Gottorp.

The scope for collaboration between the northern states was strictly limited. The recurrence of conflict between the king of Denmark and the duke clearly demonstrated the flimsiness of the Altona agreement. Possession of Swedish Pomerania was still an objective of the elector of Brandenburg, who was also busily engaged in advancing his claims to disputed territory along the Prussian–Polish frontier. Jan Sobieski's attempts to forge an alliance with Sweden against the Great Elector met with little success, though it temporarily removed from the list one of the Swedes' potential enemies. Sobieski achieved renown for his part in the relief of Vienna from the Turkish siege, but his adherence to the Holy League imposed impossible strains on the already enfeebled financial and military resources of the *Rzeczpospolita*, and little was achieved from his alliance with Muscovy.[2] On Sobieski's death in 1696, a fiercely contested campaign to elect his successor broke out. Ominously for Sweden, the ultimate victor in this contest, Friedrich August, elector of Saxony, was supported by Denmark and Muscovy. August II (the title bestowed upon the elector as king of Poland) was anxious to restore a Polish presence on the Baltic in order to bypass the high tolls levied on goods in transit through Brandenburg and allow direct access to the sea for the traders of his landlocked state. Initially, August professed a willingness to negotiate a treaty

2. Piwarski K 1962 Das Interregnum 1696/97 in Polen und die politische Lage in Europa, in Kalisch J, Gierowski J (eds) *Um die polnische Krone. Sachsen und Polen während des Nordischen Krieges 1700–1721*. Berlin, pp. 13–14.

guaranteeing Sweden's Livonian possessions and upholding the claims of the duke of Holstein-Gottorp; but whilst these talks proceeded, his agents were concluding a secret treaty with Denmark, with provisions for an anti-Swedish coalition.

On 5 April 1697, Karl XI died at the age of forty-two, leaving as his heir and successor a fifteen-year old boy. The Danish minister to Stockholm, Count Luxdorph, painted a picture of despair and discontent in his reports: hair-raising rumours of revolution abounded, and the common people believed that the torments suffered by the king in his last days (probably cancer of the stomach) were God's punishment for a man who had sucked the marrow from the bones of his subjects, now prostrated by famine. Contrary to Luxdorph's expectations, however, there was no attempt to overthrow the absolutist regime. The supporters of absolutism forestalled any moves the malcontents might make by having Karl XII proclaimed of age by the estates at the end of the year. The omission of the royal oath (*konungsförsäkran*) at the coronation ceremony finally brought home to the estates the significance of what they had conceded in 1680.[3]

The young king's first years of government offer little evidence to support the popular notion of Karl XII as an ambitious madman whose only delight was 'to find, or make, an enemy of all mankind'.[4] The finishing touches were put to his father's finely honed military system, but the underlying mood was defensive. Reinforcements were sent to north Germany and the lands of the duke of Holstein-Gottorp in the autumn of 1699, but at the same time, Sweden sought by diplomatic means to oblige the maritime powers to uphold the Altona agreement. The treaties signed in January 1700 with England and the Dutch Republic were not in fact ratified by Karl XII until he had received the news of the Danish invasion of the ducal lands in Slesvig, so reluctant was he to risk involving Sweden in a possible European conflict.

A fortnight before the news of Frederik IV's attack reached Karl

3. Fryxell A 1843 *Utdrag och afskrifter af missiver från danska sändebud i Stockholm till regeringen i Köbenhavn från 11 Jan. 1696 till April 1700* Handlingar rörande Sverges historia 5. Stockholm, pp. 89–92, 140. In Luxdorph's words, 'that the king did not swear an oath to uphold the law and maintain the privileges of each estate affected them to the very marrow; for, as the kings of Denmark in former times had to swear accession oaths, so too did the kings of Sweden... and now he is exempt from this [obligation] and is as absolute and sovereign as any potentate in the world'. One wonders if Luxdorph, the representative of an absolutist monarchy, realised the irony of these words. On the accession, see Hatton R 1968 *Charles XII of Sweden*. London, pp. 69–81.

4. The line is from Pope's *Essay on Man*, Epistle IV, cited in Olsoni E 1956 Karl XIIs-gestalten genom tiderna *Karolinska Förbundets Årsbok*, p. 194.

XII, he had received word of a full-scale Saxon invasion of Livonia. The final strands of the anti-Swedish coalition had been woven in the autumn of 1699, with the exiled Johann Reinhold Patkul playing a prominent part in its design. Patkul had presented his plan for an attack on Sweden to August at the beginning of 1699. Austrian support was to be sought, the Dutch were to be cajoled and threatened into neutrality, and Louis XIV was to be persuaded to back Denmark. Vital to the success of the design was an alliance with Peter I, though Patkul was also aware of the risk that the tsar might snatch the roast from the spit, in other words, seize Livonia. Patkul was careful not to concede Livonian territory to Peter's sphere of interest when he presented the tsar with a memorial justifying August's plans in October 1699. The tsar was to have Ingria and Karelia, but Narva was to be the frontier town of Livonia.[5]

The expressions of friendship with Sweden which Peter professed concealed a resentment at the treatment he had received in Riga on the first stage of his 'Great Embassy' to the West in 1697. During that journey, Peter made no secret of his desire to acquire an outlet to the Baltic, or his wish to develop Russian trade with the West.[6] He was being wooed by Denmark, with whom he concluded a defensive alliance in the spring of 1699. Peter's active engagement in the planned offensive against Sweden was contingent upon his making peace with the Turks, whom the Swedes were actively encouraging to continue the war. The threat of a Dutch attack on his territory of Cleves dissuaded the elector of Brandenburg from joining the anti-Swedish coalition, though he agreed to allow passage through his lands for Saxon troops whilst denying the same right to the Swedish forces in Pomerania and Wismar.

Faced with the prospect of war on two fronts, Karl XII chose first to deal with Denmark. With the help of an Anglo-Dutch naval squadron, he was able to transport 10,000 troops to Sjælland and force Frederik IV to sue for peace. By the treaty of Travendal, Frederik agreed to evacuate ducal territory and pay compensation for damages caused during their occupation, and promised in the so-called amnesty clause not to help Sweden's enemies (specified as Saxony–Poland by the Swedish negotiators) or to act like an enemy towards Sweden and

5. Wittram R 1952 Patkul und der Ausbruch des Nordischen Krieges *Nachrichten der Akademie der Wissenschaften in Göttingen.I. Philologisch-Historische Klasse* 9: 201–33. See also Erdmann Y 1970 *Der livländische Staatsmann Johann Reinhold von Patkul.* Berlin; and Vozgrin V 1986 *Rossiya i evropeyskie stranyi v godyi severnoy voynyi.* Leningrad.

6. Svensson S 1931 Czar Peters motiv för kriget mot Sverige *Historisk Tidskrift* 51: 456, citing the Danish ambassador's report of 29 July 1698; and Wittram R 1964 *Peter I. Czar und Kaiser* (2 vols). Göttingen, vol. 1 pp. 197–9.

the house of Lüneburg, whose head – Georg Ludwig, later George I of England – he recognised as elector of Hanover. The conclusion of the treaty was indeed a triumph for the diplomatic forces of the anti-French alliance rather than for Swedish arms. Karl XII delayed his evacuation of Sjælland until he was sure that the terms of the treaty and the amnesty clause securely restrained Frederik IV from aiding his erstwhile Saxon ally. The maritime powers, mindful of the impending death of Carlos II of Spain and the question of his successor, had assisted Sweden in the restoration of peace, but could offer little more than goodwill and supplies for the campaign against August, cautioning Karl against invading the king-elector's Saxon lands. Louis XIV offered even less, refusing to honour his guarantee of the peace of Oliva of 1660, which August had infringed by invading Livonia.

The Saxon campaign had not in fact met with much success. An attempt to seize Riga on Christmas Eve 1699 had been beaten off, and the Saxon forces suffered a sharp defeat which drove them back across the Düna in May. The Livonian nobility had failed to throw off the Swedish yoke, as Patkul had hoped, the Sapieha family were still in revolt against August in Lithuania, whilst the Polish Senate dissociated the *Rzeczpospolita* from the actions of the king. August broke off the siege of Riga upon hearing the news that Denmark had left the alliance, and intimated to Louis XIV his willingness to accept an armistice. Karl insisted on the complete withdrawal of Saxon forces from Livonia before he would consent to an armistice, a brusque response which has tended to strengthen the image of the king as an intractable warrior with few diplomatic skills.[7] In the event, he was to turn his attentions to the Russian rather than the Saxon threat when he landed at Pernau at the beginning of October. Peter's forces had taken Dorpat and were laying siege to Narva. (In his terms for capitulation, Peter promised the citizens the maintenance and protection of their privileges and religion, much as Ivan IV had done some hundred and fifty years previously.) After a week's exhausting forced march, the Swedish forces, greatly outnumbered by their opponents, won a decisive victory in a blinding snowstorm. Some eight to ten thousand Russian troops lay dead on the battlefield. Thousands more were captured, together with vast supplies of food, ammunition and field guns.

The tsar had left his army on the eve of the battle to return to Moscow, leaving in command the veteran duc du Croy. It has been suggested that the tsar was all too aware of the deficiencies of his

7. For a discussion of Karl's reaction, see Hatton 1968, pp. 145–8.

troops and the command, and abandoned his army to its fate, banking on being able to fight another day. The losses sustained at Narva were indeed soon made up, even if church bells had to be melted down to cast cannon. The reforms set in motion in 1698 provided a new structure for the army. Between 1699 and 1725, something like 280,000 men were drafted into the army, whose total strength at the end of Peter's reign was around 130,000. The Swedish victory at Narva had demonstrated that numbers alone were not enough: but the troops which Karl XII was to encounter on the battlefield at Poltava nine years later were incomparably better trained and led. Furthermore, they had not been exhausted by years of wearisome campaigning. The Swedish army was extremely well prepared for war in 1700. The plans for mobilisation worked out in advance functioned efficiently, and adequate supplies flowed in to sustain the movement and provisioning of the troops. Even so, the *statskontoret*, the financial nerve-centre of the administration, tried in vain in February 1700 to dissuade the king from plunging into a war which could drain an already impoverished country even more should his designs fail.[8]

At the end of 1700, Denmark had been knocked out of the war, the Russians had suffered a major military defeat, and the position of August II in Poland–Lithuania was increasingly shaky. The trans-Baltic defences had held, despite all the odds. Why then did Karl XII launch an offensive war which was to take his armies deep into central Europe and ultimately, to defeat in the Ukraine? Hatton has suggested that external circumstances played a part in determining Karl's strategy after Narva. The outbreak of the War of Spanish Succession caused Louis XIV to abandon his role as mediator in the Saxon–Swedish conflict for fear that one or both combatants might join the ranks of his enemies. Karl XII was forced to draw closer to the maritime powers in order to ensure the pacification of Denmark, but this necessitated promises of military help as soon the king could be freed of his own war, a war which the maritime powers, absorbed in their own conflict, could do little to end. Karl's freedom of action was thus seriously constrained by the war being waged by the maritime powers.[9] However, this begs the question of what freedom of action the king had in mind. On the morrow of Narva, he seems to have

8. Cavallie J 1975 *Från fred till krig. De finansiella problemen kring krigsutbrottet år 1700* Studia Historica Upsalensia 68. Uppsala, p. 271. The provinces do seem, however, to have borne the initial burden of the war remarkably well: see Schartau S 1915 Tillståndet i Jönköpings län 1697–1721 *Karolinska Förbundets Årsbok*, pp. 207–45 and Hallerman P 1916 Tillståndet i Blekinge under det stora nordiska kriget *Karolinska Förbundets Årsbok*, pp. 240–73.

9. Hatton 1968, pp. 155–7. See also Vozgrin 1986, 91–5.

been persuaded of the desirability of a winter campaign into the Russian heartland, but sickness and the problems of shipping reinforcements from Sweden caused this plan to be abandoned. The revival of August's fortunes – he was able to impose stiff terms on his Russian ally in the treaty concluded at Birsen in February 1701, and was planning a new offensive against Riga – meant that he had to be dealt with first. The plan drawn up at the Swedish headquarters envisaged a crossing of the Düna in order to drive the Saxons back into Kurland: the main army would then turn eastwards against Gdov and Pskov, where it would take up winter quarters. The crossing of the Düna in July 1701 was a brilliant success. The duchy of Kurland was occupied in August, and measures such as the taking of an oath of loyalty from the officials and the levying of port tolls for the use of the Swedish crown hinted at the possible future incorporation of the duchy into the Swedish realm.[10]

Some time during the campaign, the planned operation against Pskov was postponed. Karl now hoped to persuade the Poles to dethrone August, leaving him free to resume his original design of attacking Russia. The Poles, hopelessly riven into factions, failed to respond as the king hoped; the reply of the *sejm* at the end of 1701 was a polite rebuff, leaving Karl with little option but to abandon his Russian campaign and to seek to unravel 'the Gordian knot of our Polish dilemma'.[11] As the king predicted, 'we shall be fighting this side of the water for many a year to come'. The problem of supplies for the army had played a part in the choice of Kurland for winter quarters in 1701-2, but it soon became apparent that the duchy's resources were not sufficient to maintain the troops. The centralisation of the administration of the *generalkrigskommissariat* by Magnus Stenbock after 1703 provided the army with adequate rations, but at the cost of occupying much larger areas of Poland–Lithuania in order to spread the burden of contributions. Sustaining the army thus imposed its own terms on Karl's strategy and policies after 1702.

Five years of campaigning were to pass before Karl finally managed to settle his differences with August. The defeat inflicted on the Saxon and Polish Crown army at Kliszów on 9 July 1702, the subsequent occupation of Cracow, and the capture of Thorn in the autumn of

10. Hildebrand K-G 1949 Ekonomiska syften i svensk expansionspolitik 1700–1709 *Karolinska Förbundets Årsbok*, pp. 15–25, argues that the acquisition of Kurland would have secured Swedish control of the mouth of the Düna and would have thus protected Riga's trade.
11. A phrase coined by Josias Cederhielm, cited (with the king's prediction) in Hatton 1968, p. 178.

1703 seriously weakened August's powers of resistance, but did not bring about a settlement. The conclusion of a new treaty between August and Peter in 1703 – this time on terms more favourable to the tsar, whose forces were beginning to make inroads into Sweden's Baltic possessions – persuaded the neutralist Poles led by Cardinal Radziejowski to agree to the deposition of August in January 1704. The most acceptable candidate for the throne, Jakub Sobieski, was kidnapped by the Saxons, and Karl XII had in effect to impose Stanisław Leszczyński on the divided Polish factions. A treaty of peace and alliance was concluded between the Republic and Sweden in November 1705 and was followed by a winter campaign against the Russo–Saxon–Polish forces in Lithuania, which drew the Swedish forces into the Pripet marshes in their pursuit of the retreating enemy. Momentarily freed from the threat in the east, Karl now turned to deal with August, whose Saxon lands he invaded in August 1706. Unwilling to expose his electorate to the ravages of war, August agreed in the treaty of Altranstädt to accept his dethronement, to recognise Stanisław as king, and to terminate his alliance with Peter. The arch-intriguer Patkul, who had been held prisoner in Saxony after falling out with August in 1705, was handed over to be executed in accordance with the sentence passed in 1694.

Why did Karl XII pursue August with the such unremitting zeal ? His chancery officials frequently urged the wisdom of concluding peace and extricating Sweden from the Polish mire in order to deal with the growing threat of Russian incursions into the Baltic lands. The maritime powers, anxious to secure Swedish assistance in their war against France, grew increasingly irritated by Karl's obstinacy, and were annoyed by his invasion of Saxony. The disruption of trade caused by the war was also unsettling for the English and Dutch, highly dependent upon naval stores from the eastern Baltic. The high prices asked for pitch and tar by the Swedish Tar Company prompted the Navy Board to explore other sources of supply, and the efforts of Peter the Great to attract western merchants to his new port, although marred by clumsiness and much mutual misunderstanding, opened up a new dimension in Baltic trade. Trade considerations were by no means absent from Karl XII's grand design for Poland. The Polish–Swedish treaty concluded in Warsaw in 1705 contained provisions allowing Swedish merchants to trade freely in the Commonwealth, and efforts were made to prevent the transit of Russian goods overland through Poland. (A Swedish expedition against Archangel in 1700–1 was the last vain attempt to cut Russia's access to the West via the White Sea.) But it is hard to avoid the conclusion that ultimately, military considerations swayed the king's judgement, even if they were balanced by a greater awareness of the diplomatic contours of the general European conflict than is usually assumed. Chasing August around Poland whilst the Russians were nibbling away at the Baltic frontier was unwise, certainly; but the gradual erosion of the goodwill of the maritime powers was in the long run more damaging for Sweden's interests. In 1706, it appeared as if Peter I was willing to return most of Sweden's Baltic lands provided he was allowed to keep Ingria and 'his beloved Petersburgh'. Karl XII refused to contemplate such a settlement. Charles Whitworth, the English ambassador to Moscow, knew of several Swedish ministers who thought that England would never consent to a Russian presence in the Baltic, 'and this opinion has partly caus'd the fatal neglect of that province [Livonia], which they imagine whatever may happen, their neighbours will be one day bound to recover for them'.[12] Although the preservation of the 'balance of the North' was to remain a basic tenet of British policy, the willingness and ability to aid Sweden were strictly limited – and more so after the accession of George I, whose Hanoverian interests placed him amongst the potential partitioners of the Swedish lands.

The final triumph over August in no way reduced Sweden's other unresolved problems, nor did the assiduous courting of the Swedish king by French representatives and the duke of Marlborough further his cause. In 1704, Russian troops had taken Dorpat and Narva, whilst on the banks of the Neva, Peter the Great was laying the foundations of a new city, St Petersburg. The Swedes also had to contend with the territorial ambitions of the wily elector of Brandenburg, who had succeeded in acquiring the title of king in Prussia from the emperor in 1700.[13] Although Sweden signed a defensive treaty with Prussia in August 1707, Karl refused to recognise the new king's territorial claims. The flurry of diplomatic activity at the Swedish headquarters in Saxony created a system of checks upon Sweden's potential enemies: but this would hold only as long as it was in the interests of the Grand Alliance to uphold the pacification of Germany, and as long as the Swedish armies remained unbeaten in the field.

The Swedish advance eastwards through the trackless Masurian swamps in the winter of 1707–8 was a bold stroke which took their opponents by surprise. Peter believed the main thrust of the attack would be aimed northwards into the Baltic provinces; but in the

---

12. British Museum, Additional MSS 37 355, Whitworth letter-books 1705–1708. Whitworth to Harley, 13/24 February 1706.
13. See Frey L and M 1984 *Frederick I: The Man and his Times* East European Monographs 166. New York, pp. 228–39.

summer of 1708, general Lewenhaupt moved out of Livonia to join the main Swedish forces encamped at Mohilev, leaving only a residual force to defend the province. This army was defeated at Wesenberg in Estonia, and a plan for a land and sea operation against St Petersburg had to be abandoned. Lewenhaupt's army, bearing supplies, was bogged down by the heavy rains which made the roads virtually impassable; the retreating Russians had devastated the land for miles around; and on 14 September 1708, within striking distance of Smolensk, the main Swedish army was ordered to march south, where food supplies were available. The news of Lewenhaupt's defeat at Lesnaya and the loss of the supply train reached an exhausted army, racing southwards to get to the Ukraine before their enemy. Here, Karl was able to link up with the rebel hetman Mazepa; but the bitter winter cut swathes through his remaining forces. The Russian forces had suffered even heavier casualties during engagements, but these could be replaced. With his weakened forces, Karl XII was obliged to proceed cautiously in the spring of 1709, relying on good news from the Poles, Cossacks, Tatars and the Porte, which had signified its readiness to open hostilities against Peter. This did not come. Stanisław Leszczyński's position had begun to crumble, and the hoped-for Swedish reinforcements had to be moved into Pomerania to forestall a new attack from August. The Sultan forbade the khan of the Crimean Tatars from joining forces with the Swedes. Meanwhile, Peter was massing a large army to relieve the fortress of Poltava. The Swedish plan was to allow a section of the Russian army to cross the river Vorskla so that battle could be joined whilst Peter's forces were still divided. As the Russians began the crossing on the 16–17 June, however, Karl XII was wounded in the foot. Unsettled by the king's injury and believing the Russians to be already too well entrenched on the western bank of the river, the senior Swedish officers decided not to risk a confrontation, thus allowing the entire Russian army to complete the crossing. Outnumbered and outgunned, the Swedes suffered a crushing defeat eleven days later outside Poltava. Almost 7,000 Swedes were slain, and 2,760 were taken prisoner.[14]

SWEDEN AT BAY

The defeat at Poltava, and the surrender of the remnants of the army at Perevolotnya not only set the seal on Sweden's hopes of forcing Peter

14. On the Russian campaign, see Hatton 1968, pp. 231–301.

to sue for peace; it also unleashed a new round of hostilities which carried the war deep into the Swedish realm. Karl, with a few hundred followers, withdrew into Turkish-held Moldavia, where he was to remain for a further five years. The directives and instructions of an absent king placed even greater strains on the harassed government in Stockholm, which had to contend with the ravages of plague and streams of refugees in addition to the burdens of raising money and men to continue the war. The imposition in 1712 of new taxes which drew their inspiration from German cameralist theories was much disliked by the estates, and the *riksdag* summoned by the council in 1713 sought to return to the old system, a decision which the enraged king overruled. The desperate need for cash obliged the king's servants to seek it where they could – from the Sultan, Greek and Jewish merchants in addition to the financiers of western Europe. The burghers of Stockholm were prepared to advance a loan in return for trade advantages, a concession which Karl was unwilling to make. The capital's burghers also objected to plans to quarter refugees on them, arguing that the burden should be borne by all the towns of the realm. According to the council's estimates, there were at least 12,000 refugees in Stockholm in 1715. The king insisted that protection should be offered to all who sought it; but the means to carry out this policy were sadly lacking.[15]

After his victory at Poltava, Peter I occupied the duchy of Kurland and prepared to launch an assault on Riga. The duke of Kurland, Friedrich Wilhelm, was only five years old on his accession in 1698 and had spent the war years in exile in Germany; his uncle Ferdinand had been confirmed as regent by August II and had ruled in this capacity from exile in Danzig. Peter laid down a future claim to the duchy by allowing the marriage of his niece Anna Ivanovna to the young duke in 1710, a union which the duke did not long survive, leaving his widow to rule the duchy with Russian advisers. The assault on Riga in the summer of 1710 was prefaced by a propaganda campaign which promised the Livonian nobility guarantees for the free exercise of their religion and of their privileges, as well as the return of their lands confiscated by the *reduktion*. These promises were to be incorporated in the capitulation agreement after the surrender of the city in July. In return for their oath of loyalty and fealty to the tsar, the Livonian estates regained their old privileges. Similar agreements were later made for the towns of Pernau and Reval and the Estonian *Ritterschaft*.

15. Snellman K 1970 Svensk flyktningspolitik under stora nordiska kriget åren 1711–12 *Karolinska Förbundets Årsbok* pp. 85–132.

By offering such generous concessions, Peter hoped to win over the burghers and nobility and establish a strong position in the Baltic lands, should Sweden seek to regain them or August II assert his own claims. August was in fact in no position to dictate terms to his Russian ally. His Polish supporters were unwilling to have him back unconditionally. Peter replaced the treaty agreement made in Dresden in July 1709 with a new pact which allowed him to station troops in Poland, and recognised his claims to Estonia in return for a Russian guarantee of electoral Saxony and Livonia to be held by August and his successors, as long as they observed the alliance. This treaty of Thorn, with its insistence on August acknowledging that his recovery of the Polish throne was due to Russian arms, marked the ascendancy of Russia in the war over Sweden's Baltic possessions. Not even the series of attacks launched by the Turks against Russia – which culminated in near-catastrophe for Peter when his army was surrounded on the river Prut in 1711 – could deflect the tsar from his aim of achieving mastery over the eastern Baltic. By the end of 1710, Livonia and Estonia were under his control, and the towns of Viborg and Kexholm had fallen to his forces. A sizeable galley fleet had been built up and was augmented by frigates, built in shipyards around lakes Ladoga and Onega. The Russian navy was raw and inexperienced, commanded mostly by foreign officers; but it received a great deal of attention from the tsar, and was to prove a powerful weapon in the invasion of Finland.

Hard-pressed on all sides – Krassow's army had been forced to retreat from Poland into Pomerania, and a Dano-Norwegian force had entered Skåne – the council in Stockholm endeavoured to persuade the maritime powers to abide by their treaty obligations to Sweden. Still preoccupied by their war against France, the allies were more concerned to avoid any breach of the peace in Germany. To this end, a convention was signed in The Hague in March 1710 for the preservation of the neutrality of the Empire. The convention was signed by Sweden's enemies, and approved by the council in Stockholm. The king, however, refused to accept an arrangement which would effectively have interned his army in Pomerania and limited his freedom of action, though he professed that he had no intention of disturbing the peace of the Empire. His chances of returning to take command of his armies were dashed by Peter's failure to observe the terms of the Peace of Prut and withdraw his troops from Poland; a breakout of a reinforced army from the Pomeranian base, thrusting southwards towards the king's camp at Bender, seemed the only feasible alternative.

Seen from the perspective of Bender, the situation in the autumn of 1712 seemed not unhopeful. Magnus Stenbock, having compelled the Danes to withdraw from Skåne two years earlier, had landed with reinforcements on the island of Rügen and was preparing to cross to Pomerania. The Porte was preparing to embark upon a third war against Peter, and the Sultan sent a strong detachment to Bender to escort Karl through Poland. Friedrich I of Prussia was also making overtures for a Prussian–Swedish–Saxon alliance against Russia. Within a matter of weeks, however, the scene had changed dramatically. Stenbock, his transports destroyed by the Danes, was obliged to sue for an armistice, and when ordered to resume the campaign, moved westwards into Mecklenburg. The prospect of a lengthy march through Poland with inadequate supplies may well have encouraged Stenbock to make this move, though he also seems to have believed that cooperation with August in repelling the Russians from Poland and the Baltic territories was feasible. The king-elector was in fact pulling a number of different strings. His agents had managed to persuade the Crimean khan and Ismail Pasha, the Seraskier of Bender, that Karl was standing in the way of the formation of an anti-Russian coalition. The Swedish king's continued presence in the domains of the Sultan was becoming tiresome, and Ahmed III gave orders to the Seraskier in January 1713 to abduct the Swedish king and escort him to a French ship in Salonika. The subsequent skirmish, or *Kalabalik*, at Bender was an embarrassing episode, as well as a breach of hospitality; but it served to underline the impotent position to which the king had been reduced. His insistence on maintaining a blockade on Russian-held ports and his refusal to accept the neutrality convention alienated the British government, which detached itself from the convention in 1711 and began seriously to contemplate an accommodation which would allow Russia at least a foothold on the Baltic. Karl's hopes of persuading the Turks to bring pressure to bear on Peter to withdraw his troops from Poland and allow him free passage home bore no fruit. Above all, he was increasingly at odds with his council back in Stockholm, where the situation appeared far grimmer than it did in the warmer climes of Moldavia.

Karl was to remain in exile for a further twenty-two months after the *Kalabalik*. When he arrived at the gates of Stralsund on 10 November 1714, after a dramatic ride through Transylvania, Hungary, Austria and Germany, little was left of the Swedish empire. Stenbock had been forced to surrender to the Danes in May 1713; Bremen and Verden had been overrun by Danish troops; and by the end of 1714, most of Finland had been lost to the Russians, who now threatened to invade Sweden proper. Russia, Saxony and Prussia were busily engaged in dividing up Sweden's overseas possessions amongst themselves. The seizure of English merchantmen had caused friction in Anglo-Swedish relations at the end of Anne's reign, which the licensing of privateers by Karl on his return to Stralsund did nothing to halt. As a general principle, Britain wished to preserve, as far as it was possible, the territorial status quo in the Baltic, but was unwilling to abide by treaty agreements to assist Sweden militarily. This policy was not significantly altered with the accession of Georg Ludwig of Hanover as king George I of England in August 1714, though the king's Hanoverian interests in north Germany had now to be taken into account. In November 1714, George recognised Prussian possession of Stettin and the southern half of Swedish Pomerania in return for Frederick William I's acknowledgement of his claims to Bremen and Verden. Denmark was to take the remainder of Pomerania in compensation for Bremen. A squadron commanded by admiral Norris was sent to the Baltic in 1715, effectively preventing the Swedish fleet from leaving Karlskrona. On the southern shores, Prussian, Saxon and Danish forces closed in on Wismar and Stralsund, taking the island of Rügen in November and forcing Stralsund to capitulate a month later.

The conquest of Sweden's German possessions – Wismar fell in April 1716 – was not achieved without considerable friction between the allies. Peter's alliance with duke Karl Leopold of Mecklenburg, which gave free and direct access to the ports of the duchy for Russian vessels and allowed the tsar to station a sizeable force there, alarmed George I, who sought to counter the alliance by giving his support to the Mecklenburg *Ritterschaft* in their quarrel with the duke. Dissension between the Russians and Danes also led to the abandonment of a proposed seaborne invasion of Sweden in 1716, though Karl XII's thrust into Norway also played some part in keeping the Danish fleet otherwise occupied.

The invasion of Norway, an improvised campaign which was finally halted by the destruction of Swedish transports by admiral Tordenskjold, was intended not only to force Frederik IV to sue for peace; by encouraging the Jacobites to believe he favoured their cause, Karl hoped also to frighten George I into leaving the alliance. A plan had been floated in 1715 for a Spanish-financed expedition to land a Jacobite force off Newcastle. Although Karl XII wisely decided that his ships and men would be better employed in relieving his garrison in Stralsund, the links with Spain and the Jacobites were maintained. In these complicated diplomatic manoeuvres, a crucial role was played by Georg Heinrich von Görtz. Görtz, an overbearing if impressive figure, whose enamel false eye and colourful background provided plentiful material for the satirists, had acquired ascendancy over the regency council set up to administer the duchy of Holstein-Gottorp after duke Friedrich IV was killed at the battle of Kliszów. He had shown his talent for duplicity in 1713, when Stenbock's troops had been driven into the ducal lands, officially protesting against this encroachment but secretly agreeing to allow the Swedish general to take refuge in the fortress of Tønning. (The Danes soon tired of his prevarications and occupied the ducal lands, which were placed under Danish rule.) Görtz then entered Swedish service, where he soon acquired an all-powerful position, albeit without any formal post. In 1716, Görtz went to Holland and France in search of loans and assistance. The Dutch were interested in acquiring safeguards for the safe passage of their ships to Sweden, but were less willing to grant loans. The regency in Paris was unwilling to abide by the 1715 alliance with Sweden and provide further subsidies. Although Görtz was wary of commitment to the Jacobite cause, he was tempted by the offer of a loan of £60,000 and plans were hatched for an invasion of England. The Spanish minister Alberoni was also active in creating a counter-force which might overthrow the terms of the Treaty of Utrecht, whilst the Jacobites played their part, through the agency of Peter I's doctor Erskine, in trying to procure agreement between Sweden and Russia. In response to these moves, the maritime powers and France concluded the Triple Alliance. Görtz and the Swedish ambassador to London were arrested shortly afterwards on the evidence of their intercepted correspondence.

The publication of the Görtz–Gyllenborg correspondence and their arrest embarrassed the Dutch and compromised a number of leading Frenchmen, imposing a strain on the Triple Alliance. The Townshend-Stanhope ministry discounted the possibility of a Swedish invasion, but sought to use the incident to rally the country behind the king's Baltic policy.[16] Görtz, released by the Dutch in August after Karl XII promised further trade concessions, now sought to play off Russia against England. Peter I had already let it be known that he was willing to negotiate, and in a meeting with Görtz at Het Loo in August 1717, he agreed to the holding of a peace conference on the Åland islands.

The prospect of a separate Swedish–Russian peace drew George I

16. Nordmann C 1962 *La crise du Nord au début du XVIIIe siècle*. Paris; Chance J 1909 *George I and the Northern War*. London; Murray J 1969 *George I, the Baltic and the Whig split of 1717*. London, for details of this episode.

into negotiations with the Swedes, though the terms presented by his emissaries at the king's headquarters in Lund were such as to prove unacceptable to the Swedes. The negotiations with the Russians which began in May 1718 in the village of Lövö on the Åland islands were equally tough, and it is not easy to disentangle the motives and objectives of the participants. At first, the Russians insisted on retaining all their conquests except Finland (minus Viborg), whilst the Swedes were only prepared to consider surrendering Ingria. Secret negotiations between Görtz and Ostermann, however, began to produce results. In June, Ostermann presented two alternatives: the tsar was willing to return Finland, Estonia and Livonia, with the exception of Narva and Viborg, or he was prepared to enter into a military alliance with Karl to help conquer Norway and regain the lost German provinces in return for the Baltic provinces and part of Karelia. The tsar was also prepared to persuade the duke of Mecklenburg to hand over his duchy to Sweden in return for compensation within Peter's lands, and even offered to cede part of the White Sea coastline to Sweden. Görtz attempted to persuade the king to accept this second alternative, but without success. Peter I was also unwilling in the end to make readjustments to the Russo-Finnish frontier, or to offer military assistance against Frederik IV, though he was prepared to support the Swedish king against Hanover and Saxony. This was not enough for Karl, who insisted on military aid against Denmark. Though the Russians were exasperated, they continued to maintain the conference in being, partly through fear that George I might steal a march on them and conclude his own settlement with Sweden.[17]

George I's bargaining position was greatly strengthened by the collapse of Alberoni's grandiose schemes to overturn the Utrecht settlement in the summer of 1718, and the adherence of the emperor – whose prestige had risen with the conclusion of an advantageous peace with the Turks in July – to the Triple Alliance. Peter, who had been prepared in the spring to lend an ear to Alberoni's plans for a Russo-Swedish alliance to keep the maritime powers tied up in the north whilst Spain pushed its Sicilian claims, now deemed it expedient to make overtures towards England. George I responded by sending a mission to Russia to sound out the possibilities of an alliance. In the meantime, preparations were being made in Sweden for a second campaign against Norway. Karl was still able to muster a formidable

17. On the Åland conference, see the detailed study by Hartman K 1921–31 *Åländska kongressen och dess förhistoria* (6 vols); Åbo and Feygina S 1959 *Alandskiy kongress*. Moscow. Hatton 1968, pp. 446–61 offers a useful synthesis and interpretation of the complicated strands of diplomatic manoeuvring in 1718.

army of 60,000 for a two-pronged attack. The Jämtland corps under Karl Gustav Armfelt was to move against Trondheim, whilst the main force under the king's command would invade southern Norway. The prime objective was to force Frederik IV to sue for peace, though it is probable that Karl also considered the possibility of a feint against the Scottish coast as a means of putting pressure on George I. Armfelt's march on Trondheim bogged down in the autumn rains, but the main army forced their opponents to withdraw for fear of encirclement, and in November, laid siege to the fortress of Fredriksten. Here, on 30 November, the Swedish king was killed by a bullet through the head as he was inspecting the siege-works.

Karl XII's death had momentous internal consequences for Sweden; the repercussions on the outcome of the war are more difficult to gauge. It is possible that military success in Norway might have swung the balance once more Sweden's way, or at least have given Karl rather more freedom to manoeuvre; but the fact is that the forces united against him were too numerous, and in spite of their differences, were determined to squeeze concessions out of Sweden. It is true that George I finally broke with Russia in 1719, and was able through his ministers Bassewitz and Carteret to secure the terms of a settlement with the new regime in Stockholm; but this breakthrough was facilitated by the demise of Görtz upon the succession to the throne of Ulrika Eleonora, wife of Friedrich of Hesse, for the Hessian faction had long opposed Görtz's designs and advocated a settlement in the west. Bassewitz obtained a promise of the cession of Bremen and Verden to Hanover in return for assistance against Russia, and Carteret was empowered to offer naval assistance and supplies 'to bring the Czar to reason'.[18] Charles Whitworth in Berlin was also able to detach Frederick William from the Russian alliance, though the Swedes were also obliged to agree to the cession of Stettin to Prussia. Frederik IV was more reluctant to fall in with the British plans, blockading Göteborg and preventing the British squadron under Norris sailing through the Sound. Without the naval protection Norris might have offered, the Swedes were vulnerable to attack from the Russian galleys, which ravaged the archipelago off Stockholm.

The French were anxious to ensure that their ancient Swedish ally still retained a foothold in Germany as a possible future counter to the Habsburgs, and persuaded George I to agree to Sweden retaining the Stralsund region and Rügen, which had been promised to Denmark.

---

18. Instructions to Carteret, 6 May 1719, in Chance J 1922 *British Diplomatic Instructions 1689-1789. Volume 1 – Sweden 1689–1727*. London, pp. 106–112.

The remainder of Pomerania was ceded to Prussia. Frederik IV was finally persuaded to give way, restoring Stralsund and Rügen to Sweden in order to ensure allied guarantees for his incorporation of the ducal parts of Slesvig. His reason for so doing was that duke Karl Friedrich of Holstein-Gottorp had taken refuge in St Petersburg, where his rights were taken up by Peter. Karl Friedrich also provided Peter with a useful weapon against the Swedes, for he was the son of Karl XII's elder sister and as such disputed the succession of the younger sister and her husband, acclaimed king of Sweden in 1720 as Fredrik I. Karl Friedrich's claims were used by Peter to force the Swedes to conclude peace at Nystad in 1721. Promises of assistance from Austria and Prussia did not materialise; domestic problems occupied the Townshend-Stanhope ministry; and a Russian invasion of Norrbotten served to give added strength to Peter's demands. Sweden had to abandon Livonia, Estonia, Ingria and Karelia, including Viborg. Peter returned his Finnish conquests and promised not to interfere in Sweden's internal affairs, nor help anyone contemplating such an intervention. Clause 7 of the peace of Nystad thus effectively shut the door for the time being on Karl Friedrich's hopes, though the claims of the Holstein faction were to remain a useful instrument in Russian policy towards the Scandinavian kingdoms in future years.

The life and death of Karl XII have long provided historians with a rich crop of controversial issues. Rumours that he was murdered, probably at the instigation of the prince of Hesse, began to gain currency almost immediately after his death.[19] There has also been speculation about his sexual proclivities, though there is little hard evidence to suggest that he was either hermaphrodite or a homosexual. It is certain that he revelled in the hard life of the army camp, pushing himself to the point of endurance on many occasions. His simple dress and abstemious habits marked him out in an age of periwigs and pomp. He appears to have been genuinely solicitous for his subjects' welfare on the occasions when he encountered distress and hardship, though he grew impatient with the council's constant tales of misery at home, which he believed would only weaken Sweden's cause should they reach the ears of the enemy. The discipline which was instilled into his soldiers stood them in good stead in adversity, and helped prevent excesses of the kind which had been commonplace during the Thirty Years' War.[20] The nineteenth-

19. Hatton 1968, pp. 495–509 gives a good survey of the theories. Her own conclusion is that the king was killed by a stray shot from the Norwegian fortifications.

20. This did not stop his opponents circulating tales of Swedish cruelty: see the pamphlet produced by Peter's minister P P Shafirov, *A Discourse concerning the Just*

century historian Fryxell's presentation of Karl XII as a self-willed warmonger, who plunged his people into misery and ruined his country has been greatly modified, particularly by the early twentieth-century 'new school' of Swedish historians. Karl XI had managed to avoid war for two decades because those countries which might have challenged Sweden's position on the southern shores of the Baltic were otherwise engaged, and because the maritime powers were prepared to bring pressure to bear on Denmark in the matter of the duchies. His son had to contend with the ambitions of two new rulers, August II and Peter I, both of whom wished to establish their presence in the Baltic, and was not able to secure the active assistance of the maritime powers or of Sweden's old French ally to act as a counter-weight to the Saxon–Russian threat.

In the end, it proved impossible for a country with a small population and meagre resources to sustain the burdens of territorial empire in the face of determined pressure. But might not a more favourable peace settlement have been reached had Karl XII been less obdurate? The evidence of his stiff-necked unwillingness to reach an accommodation which he believed would have been detrimental to Sweden's interests is plentiful. In 1711, for example, he authorised the council in Stockholm to negotiate with Denmark, but not to make any concessions. The king was sure that the council shared his view that no honest patriot would even contemplate buying a dishonourable peace by ceding provinces 'since this would be the quickest way to put the realm in such a position that, at the next breach of the peace...[it] would be obliged entirely to surrender to the will and dictate of its neighbours and accept such law which either the enemy or those who still call themselves friends, wish to prescribe'. The king's refusal to allow the council any leeway in negotiations, in Lundquist's judgement, 'made a peace agreement with Denmark impossible'.[21] On the other hand, it can be argued that the king was more aware of the dangers to the future existence and security of the realm than were his advisers and councillors. The humiliating situation which the king predicted would follow from the abandonment of the overseas provinces did indeed occur in the 'Age of Liberty' which followed his death. Karl has with some justification been accused of

21. Carlson E 1893 *Konung Karl XIIs egenhändiga bref*. Stockholm, p. 369. Lundquist C 1975 *Council, king and estates in Sweden 1713–14*. Stockholm, p. 29.

Reasons which his Czarish Majesty, Peter I ... had for beginning the War against the King of Sweden (1717), reproduced, with Russian text in Butler W (ed.) 1973 *A discourse concerning the just causes of the war between Sweden and Russia: 1700–1721*. Dobbs Ferry, New York, pp 336–7.

allowing military and strategic considerations to take precedence over diplomacy. 'His prevailing passion... the desire of glory and renown' irritated those who sought to persuade him to reach an accommodation with his enemies (though at various times, Peter the Great and Frederik IV of Denmark also provoked similar reactions); but the king of Sweden might well have retorted that, like Henri IV of France, his affairs and those of his kingdom 'étoient dans un tel état que l'honneur l'obligeoit de vaincre ou de mourir'.[22]

Karl inherited from his father the trappings of absolutism, beneath which the traditions of aristocratic constitutionalism still survived. The absence of the king from Stockholm – to which he never returned after 1700 – and the question of the succession occasioned by his unmarried and childless existence tended to undermine the foundations of a system which had relied as much on the estates' willingness to concede power to the king as on the king's own ability to enforce it. On the other hand, the suspicions and rivalries which had allowed Karl XI to restore royal power had not diminished. The desire for peace was not enough to unite the estates and council in 1713–14, for example. The *riksdag* was convened by the council to discuss taxation, and possibly to obtain the support of the estates for a negotiated peace. In the event, the council had to produce the king's letter, two months after receiving it, ordering the disbandment of the estates, in order to stem the tide of opposition. In 1713, a new levy had been introduced, a percentage tax on assets in money and property (which the king's subjects had to disclose). This tax was rejected by the estates, who devised a scheme for raising more revenue through the old taxation system. Aware that the king insisted on keeping the new system, the council was nevertheless forced to go along with the estates' proposals. The estates also tried to influence peace moves, claiming that it would be difficult to continue discussion if the secret committee of the *riksdag* was not permitted to share the council's opinions and thoughts on matters of peace. In January 1714, the estates demanded immediate peace talks through neutral mediators, and declared that they, with the council and princess Ulrika Eleonora, should conclude peace in spite of royal opposition. The princess had been given a seat (with two votes) on the council in October 1713. The president of the chancery, Arvid Horn, a former 'Holsteiner' who had gravitated towards the Hessian camp through dislike of Görtz, probably saw this as a pre-

22. Memoirs of the Swedish officer, Axel von Löwen, cited in Hatton 1968, p. 374. The 'king's prevailing passion' was an expression used by Robert Harley in a letter to John Robinson, minister to Karl XII, in 1704. See Chance 1922, p. 29.

emptive move to prevent Karl naming his sister as regent, which would have weakened the position of the council. In February–March 1714, however, he was faced with a rising tide of demands from the estates for Ulrika Eleonora to be made regent, and had to persuade the princess to dissociate herself from her supporters. The return of the king at the end of the year brought to an end the council's period of government. Karl's reorganisation of the administration into six 'state expeditions', or departments, was intended to expedite business more speedily and effectively. The chancery lost its central role in the administration, whilst the council was virtually ignored by the king.

In spite of the famine of 1696–7 and the disappearance of Karl XI's carefully accumulated reserves into the costs of his own funeral, his daughter's wedding and his son's coronation, Sweden entered the war in 1700, in Gösta Lindeberg's words, with 'an unbelievably well-organised financial system compared with that of other European states'.[23] A decade later, however, the system was beginning to creak under the strain. The loss of the Baltic provinces deprived the crown of valuable revenue; the re-entry of Denmark into the war and the subsequent closure of the Sound to Swedish shipping struck hard at commerce; and the plague which devastated the land in 1711–12 (although its demographic effects were exaggerated by contemporaries) reduced the numbers of tax-paying subjects. The Bank of the Estates (*Riksens ständers bank*), which had granted loans to the crown against the security of the revenues of the customs, was obliged to suspend its lending operations in the aftermath of Poltava for fear of a run on the bank. Thereafter the crown was only able to obtain loans by pledging its revenues in advance to the creditor. By 1713, the crown was beginning to fall behind on its interest payments, and the bank was reluctant to give any more credit.

In his Turkish exile, Karl and his intimate circle of advisers studied the most modern cameralist theories of financial management, and from 1712 onwards, attempted to put some of them into practice in Sweden. Many of the measures which were to be associated with the Görtz regime were in fact considered at this time. What was unique about Görtz was his method of dealing with the financial chaos which threatened to bankrupt the state. In order to restore the crown's credit, loans to the state (*obligationer*) were to be raised, in denominations of 10,000, 5,000, 1,000 and 100 riksdaler, redeemable after four years, with a fixed interest of 6 per cent. The interest was to be paid from the

---

23. Lindeberg G 1946 *Krigsfinansiering och krigshushållning i Karl XII:s Sverige*. Stockholm, p. 4. The findings of James Cavallie have tended to reaffirm this viewpoint.

tax on property, now reintroduced, whilst the debt was to be amortised by a new tax, the loan payment. Those liable for this tax were divided into classes, a principle borrowed from France. To administer this system, a new institution was set up, the *upphandlingsdeputation*. Görtz seems to have envisaged this as a kind of semi-private venture controlled by Swedish merchants, along the lines of the East India or South Sea Companies, but he failed to attract support for this idea, and the deputation was largely managed by his own confidants. Low-value copper and paper tokens or tickets, carrying no interest, were also issued as a short-term device to restore credit. To maintain confidence in this surrogate currency, Görtz lowered the value of the copper coinage, giving holders the choice of seeing their heavy bars of copper (*plåtmynt*) depreciate by a third in value or of exchanging them for *obligationer*, copper or paper tokens. This maintained the value of the new currency, strengthened the credit of the crown and provided it with a valuable export commodity, copper, at one and the same time.

In the last stages of the Görtz regime, the state was exercising unprecedented controls over all aspects of life. Prices of foodstuffs and other goods were fixed, controls were placed over exports and imports and large quantities of bar-iron and copper were compulsorily purchased by the crown, payment being largely in the form of the new currency and *obligationer*. The demand for iron in European markets, and the heavy export duty levied on the purchasers of this commodity, provided a welcome influx of income for the crown: Görtz's policy of 'forced credit', although contributing to inflation, restored monetary stability and confidence and enabled Karl XII to prepare for his great offensive against Norway in 1718. Had the king lived another year, he might well have run into difficulties with his new economic system, which rested on rather shaky foundations. As it was, he perished, and his death sealed the fate of Görtz and his system. The former was beheaded after trial in February 1719, the latter was speedily dismantled and replaced by the old institutions. The coin tokens were reduced to half their nominal value and exchanged for redeemable 'insurance notes', and the highly unpopular regulations and controls over commerce were withdrawn.[24]

The fact that Karl XII could still muster a sizeable and well-equipped army in 1718 testifies to the effectiveness of the reforms which were adopted during the long years of the war, as well as to the

24. The best treatment of Görtz's financial system is: Lindeberg G 1941 *Svensk ekonomisk politik under den görtzska perioden*. Lund.

resilience of the Swedish people. Recent research has shown that the cost of the war in human and material losses was not as great as had previously been assumed. Moreover, the long years of war cast a heavy shadow elsewhere. The duchy of Kurland and large parts of Poland–Lithuania were badly affected by occupation and the disruption of trade. Denmark was also ravaged by the plague, which carried away a third of the population of the capital. The army and navy budget rose from 1.7 million rdr in 1708 to 9.3 million rdr ten years later, and to meet these costs, the Danish crown levied a series of extraordinary taxes and imposts on luxuries; but the chronic fiscal instability which had prevailed since the time of Christian IV continued to frustrate the efforts of the crown's servants for decades.

The one victor of the Great Northern War was Peter the Great. A pro-Swedish pamphlet of 1715 warned English readers of the great potential of Peter's Russia:

> What better Materials are required for a well furnished Yard, than he has within his own Dominions, and may, by means of his Canal, carry to Narva and Petersburg without Expence? Does he want Timber, Planks and Masts? His own Forests might furnish all the Yards in Europe ... Is it Iron he wants? He needs not fetch it from the Dutch, for they can't afford to sell him so Cheap, as he may have it in the Neighbourhood. Is it Rigging and Sails? His Country chiefly supplies all others with Hemp. He has got Workmen enough from England and Holland to direct his Forges and Rope-Yards. Is it Pitch and Tar? The Dutch themselves are supply'd with these Commodities from him...[25]

Peter I laid great emphasis on the need to develop Russia's industry and commerce. He encouraged talented young men to go abroad to learn the skills of commerce, and trade was thrown open to all classes. War stimulated the development of industry, though the lack of capital and entrepreneurial skills meant that the state played a dominant role. By the end of the reign, Russia was exporting commodities which had previously been imported, such as iron, and a total of 178 new manufactories had been set up. In western European terms, Russia remained an economically backward country, in spite of the efforts of the tsar to recruit foreign experts to supervise the building and running of the sawmills, ironworks and shipyards, and draconian legislation intended to enforce improvements. Foreign merchants continued to complain about the inadequate facilities in Russian ports, the lack of quality controls over products such as hemp, and above all, about the tsar's manipulation of the customs dues. The level of agri-

25. *Further Reasons for the Present Conduct of Sweden, in Relation to the Trade in the Baltick...* London, 1715, p. 18.

cultural production was poor, hampered by an inefficient use of manpower and a primitive technology. In 1721, for example, Estonian peasants were sent around Russia to demonstrate the use of the scythe, and all the tsar's subjects were ordered to use this method of harvesting the following summer.

How effective were the stream of decrees and instructions in changing the customs and habits of Peter's subjects is open to question. In a matter of a quarter of a century, Peter drastically reshaped the superstructure of the state, drawing heavily upon German and Swedish models. These reforms were intended to foster and promote the 'common good', though this term tended to be synonymous with the interests of the state. Many of Peter's reforms were pushed through too rapidly, and with little regard for the ability of the Russians to adapt to or to operate the new institutions. Like his great admirer J.V. Stalin, Peter was indifferent to the lives of those who slaved and toiled to erect the magnificent edifices and structures which he believed his beloved St Petersburg merited. The new capital was erected on marshy land, and building materials and supplies had to be fetched from afar. Convicts, Tatars, prisoners-of-war and volunteers were drafted in to undertake the building work, but there was often a shortage of manpower, and mortality rates were frighteningly high. Peter's dream of a city of stone buildings was never realised: most of the houses beyond the main thoroughfares were of wood. The tsar's efforts to promote the trade of St Petersburg encountered difficulties, not least from foreign merchants, who disliked his sudden changes of policy.[26]

The foundation of St Petersburg, and its rapid growth into a city of some 80,000 inhabitants by 1750, symbolises the shift of power in the Baltic. Sweden's Age of Greatness finally came to an end at Nystad, little more than a century after Gustav II Adolf had boasted that the Russians would not lightly jump over the 'ditch' (Lake Ladoga) beyond which they had been confined by the treaty of Stolbova. The offensive waging of war to which Karl XII resorted in order to protect the territorial gains of his forefathers proved to be Sweden's undoing. In pursuing August II deep into Saxony, Karl XII weakened his eastern defences. A settlement with Peter might have been feasible in 1706, but concessions would have had to be made, and this Karl was not prepared to do. An improved Russian army inflicted a decisive defeat at Poltava, giving Peter the freedom of action which Karl was

26. On the effect of Peter's decree of 1713, transferring the trade from Archangel to St Petersburg, see Wittram 1964 *Peter I. Czar und Kaiser* (2 vols). Göttingen, vol. 2, pp. 248ff., and Scheltema J 1817–19 *Rusland en de Nederlanden* (4 vols). 's Gravenhage, vol. 3, pp. 301ff.

never able to achieve. In the end, his enemies were too many, and his resources too few.

The successes in the field which Karl XII's armies achieved at Narva and in Poland owed much to the reforms put in train during the reign of the shy, dyslexic and rather dull Karl XI. Karl X Gustav's spectacular campaigns left the kingdom dangerously over-exposed and in a financially weak state, which the years of the regency did nothing to amend. Had Sweden had to face more formidable foes in 1675, without the protection of France, then the Age of Greatness might well have ended much sooner. Karl XI was no Louis XIV, and it is not easy to determine the king's personal role in the events leading up to the restoration of monarchical power in 1680. The great Swedish historian Eli Hecksher dismissed the fiscal and military reforms as a return to a medieval-type natural economy, whose inadequacies were soon revealed during the war years. More recent research has tended to agree with the eighteenth-century aristocrat, Nils Reuterholm, that Sweden's internal strength and external prestige was greatly augmented by the wise and economical government of the king; and it is worth noting that Peter the Great modelled his administrative reforms on the example of Karl XI's Sweden.[27]

The enhanced power of the monarchy did not survive the death of Karl XII. The Age of Greatness was followed by the Age of Liberty, in which the balance of power swung decisively towards the estates. To a certain extent, this resulted from the problem of the succession and the inability of two foreign-born monarchs to assert their authority (in spite of the promptings of their more strong-minded spouses). Gustav III, like his contemporary George III of England, was anxious to assert his rights as monarch in his native land, and was indeed to have rather more success, even if an assassin's bullet, rather than insanity, was to be his fate. The revival of monarchical authority after 1772 owed as much to the inability or unwillingness of the estates and council to oppose the king as it had done in 1680. Neither Karl XI nor Gustav III had to impose an entirely new system, as did Peter I, or, to a lesser degree, the Great Elector and his successors. They were able to build upon existing foundations, and in partnership with, rather than opposition to their estates.

Much has been made of commercial advantage as a driving-force

27. Hecksher E 1941 *Svenskt arbete och liv från medeltiden till nutiden*. Stockholm, p. 161. See Roberts M 1967 *Essays in Swedish history*. London, pp. 226–68, for an evaluation of the importance of Karl XI; and Peterson C 1979 *Peter the Great's administrative and judicial reforms: Swedish antecedents and the process of reception* Skrifter utgivna av Institutet för rättshistorisk forskning,1:29, Stockholm, for the Swedish model.

behind Swedish expansion. It is undeniable that economic considerations were important, though it was often the necessities of financing the war effort which were uppermost in the thoughts of the king and his council. Swedish maritime trade did expand considerably in the latter half of the seventeenth century, though this was more a result of internal developments than of external expansion. Sweden possessed in abundance those commodities which the western European nations eagerly sought – copper, iron, pitch and tar – and the Anglo-Dutch naval wars of the 1650s and 1660s gave Swedish merchants an opportunity to ship these goods westwards in their own vessels. Much of Sweden's international trade was in the hands of the Stockholm merchants, who could boast an ocean-going fleet of seventy-five large ships with a total tonnage of around 34,000 tons in 1695; but there was also a flourishing coastal traffic, with dozens of barks plying between the small harbours along the Bothnian coastline and Stockholm, Reval, and even Riga.

In common with other parts of northern Europe, Sweden derived much benefit from the skills and capital investment of foreign entrepreneurs. Many of the more grandiose ventures, such as the attempts to open up trade routes to Persia or Usselincx' scheme for an international trading company, were stillborn; but Sweden was possessed of minerals and timber which could be exploited at a profit by men such as de Geer, the Kocks and the Momma-Reenstiernas. Though not all of the immigrants prospered, none found a land of Moab as did the despairing Huguenots on the sandy outskirts of Berlin. The skills and techniques of the immigrants were important, certainly, though they were part of a general dissemination of knowledge and diversification of trade which brought northern Europe within the ambit of a burgeoning world market. In comparison with the mercantile powers bordering the North Sea, Sweden still remained a backwater, lacking sophisticated credit and insurance institutions or indeed a sizeable merchant class. Its towns were small and unpretentious, capable of providing a livelihood only for the most basic of trades. The natural economy still predominated in the rural northern areas, remote and isolated. The Swedish high aristocracy sought to emulate the lifestyle of their contemporaries in France, but their palaces were modest in comparison and few in number, and the court in Stockholm afforded few of the pleasures of Versailles. Of the trades and occupations which were beginning to spring up even in provincial towns such as Bourges or Shrewsbury to cater for the needs of a growing leisured class, Sweden – and indeed, northern Europe – remained largely ignorant. The imposition in 1720 of a tax on chaises and carriages by the Danish government, for example, caused no difficulties for the citizens of Grenå, who went by foot or in a peasant's cart when they had to travel. Although newspapers and coffee-houses were to be found in the larger towns, there were few publishers or bookshops, and no learned public comparable to that of the London of Addison and Steele. It was not until the Age of Liberty, when Sweden's fortunes had waned, that any meaningful discourse and debate on the state of the nation, its economy and commerce, commenced.

Viewed from the perspective of that more elegant age, the era which passed into history with the death of the last warrior-king seemed to be one of barbarous heroism. Count Anders von Höpken acknowledged that king Karl had been 'a hero for the old Goths in their bold wanderings and campaigns', but could only be considered dauntless and bold in the present age 'when war has become a science and demands more knowledge that that of killing people'.[28] Enlightened Swedes preferred to forget about the valorous deeds of their Gothic ancestors, and to play down their immediate past. Sweden's clock had moved from twelve to one with the death of Karl XII, in the words of Cederhielm's famous epigram, and the country had to adjust to the status of a minor power. Two hundred years of Vasa rule had however left an indelible imprint, which lasted long after the Baltic and north German territories had been lost. The territorial empire was transitory, but the mobilisation and organisation of Sweden's scant resources which had permitted its creation also ensured that the northern country did not sink into decay, as did the much mightier Spanish empire, or nearer to home, the Polish–Lithuanian state.

28. Cited in Olsoni 1956, p. 204.

CHAPTER TWELVE
After Nystad: Politics and Diplomacy in the North

THE BALTIC IN THE EIGHTEENTH CENTURY – A EUROPEAN BACKWATER?

The resolution of the 'Baltic question' in Sweden's favour during the early years of the seventeenth century was the prelude to the northern kingdom's dramatic incursion into central Europe, and the acquisition of further territory along the Baltic littoral. Denmark was now out-flanked, its residual claims to Baltic dominion torn to shreds by the armies of Lennart Torstensson and Karl X Gustav. At a critical juncture in the conflict of the major continental powers, Sweden was to play a decisive role; and even though the pinnacle of success achieved by Gustav II Adolf in the winter of 1631–2 was never again to be reached, Sweden's intentions continued to exercise the minds of European statesmen. Unhindered access to the vital naval stores of the Baltic region was a major concern of the English and Dutch in the second half of the seventeenth century. Although prepared actively to intervene in 1658–9 to ensure that Sweden did not upset the balance of power in the western Baltic and secure control of vital access routes, they were content to support the territorial status quo in the eastern Baltic. Sweden's attempts to pursue a more aggressive trade policy in the 1690s, and the disruptions to trade caused by privateers licensed by Karl XII may have annoyed the maritime powers, but did not lead them to abandon this policy.

The collapse of the Swedish territorial empire after 1709 and the prospect of the war spreading into Germany were viewed with alarm in London and The Hague. Russia was an unknown quantity: its unrealised potential had fascinated and worried western Europeans since the days of Ivan IV, and the ambitions of its current ruler were well known. Immediately after the battle of Poltava, captain James

Jeffryes, who had accompanied the Swedish army, wrote of 'the great projects the Muscovites have made to extend their dominance in the East-Sea, all along the Nieper, over Crimm and from the Black Sea to the Mare Caspium; their vast design to enlarge their shipping and commerce, their more than human endeavours to roote themselves where once they gett footing'.[1] Russia, in other words, was regarded as potentially a far greater threat to the established balance of power in Europe than Sweden had or could ever have been. British statesmen talked frequently of the restoration of the 'Ballance of the North', but practical considerations tended to confound their aspirations. The territorial interests of the Hanoverian dynasty made it difficult to reach an accommodation with Karl XII and led to the resignation of Townshend and Walpole in 1717 because George I refused to back Sweden against Russia. Moreover, as Townshend admitted, an open break with Russia could jeopardise supplies of vital naval stores. In spite of attempts to promote production of pitch and tar in the north American colonies and to grow hemp and flax in Ireland, Britain was still heavily reliant on the commodities of north-eastern Europe for its rapidly expanding shipbuilding industry and the Royal Navy. Britain therefore sought to secure its trade with the Russian-held Baltic ports: but as Peter I was only prepared to negotiate a commercial treaty if a defensive alliance were part of the deal, little progress was made. Relations remained tense after the peace of Nystad, with British naval squadrons being sent to cruise menacingly in the Gulf of Finland during the last years of George I's reign. The gradual break-up of the alliance forged in 1725 between Britain, France and Prussia, the fall of the Holstein party in Russia after the death of Catherine I, and the necessity of establishing proper commercial relations with the power in control of the eastern Baltic littoral led thereafter to a gradual improvement in Anglo-Russian relations, culminating in the signing of a commercial treaty in 1734.

The death of the childless Karl XII of Sweden and the failure of the Holstein faction to ensure that the succession passed to duke Karl Friedrich, son of Karl XII's elder sister, was in some ways as significant as the peace settlements of 1720–21. The price of accession for the deceased king's younger sister Ulrika Eleonora in 1719 was the renunciation of absolutism. The transfer of sovereign power to the estates was carried a stage further the following year, after she agreed to step down in favour of her husband, who was crowned as Fredrik I.

---

1. Hatton R (ed.) 1954 *Captain James Jeffreyes's letters from the Swedish army 1707–1709* Historiska Handlingar **35**: 1. Stockholm, p. 76.

Fredrik's involvement in the peacemaking process had aroused mistrust and his inability to mitigate the harshness of the final settlement served only to weaken his authority still further. The royal couple's childlessness kept the question of the succession open, a situation which the Holstein party in Sweden and Russia were not slow to exploit.

Enfeebled by two decades of war, reduced to the status of a minor power but still possessing the residue of empire and its responsibilities in Germany, Sweden was bound to come under pressure from the great powers seeking to enmesh the northern kingdom in their systems of alliances. The factionalism of the 'Age of Liberty', which lasted from 1719 until Gustav III's *coup d'état* in 1772, offered foreign powers ample scope for bribery and manipulation. The Russian ambassador Mikhail Bestuzhev-Ryumin observed shortly after his arrival in Stockholm in the 1720s that the state of affairs in Sweden resembled that of Poland: 'everyone his own master, the subordinates not obeying their superiors, no order in anything' – a situation which Bestuzhev was to exploit in the Russian interest for over three decades.[2] Fearing Russian interference on behalf of the Holstein claimant, the Swedes had requested the insertion of a clause in the peace treaty which obliged Peter and his successors not to intervene or support anyone contemplating intervention in Sweden's internal affairs. The Russians also undertook to prevent any attempt to change the succession or the constitution of 1720, thereby obtaining an invaluable instrument for controlling Swedish affairs in future years. (Guarantees of the liberties of the Polish nobility included in the pacification treaty of 1717 and the agreement signed in 1720 between Peter I and Frederick William of Prussia afforded the Russians a similar opportunity to interfere in the affairs of the Polish–Lithuanian commonwealth.)

Fredrik's efforts to amend the constitution and to pursue his own foreign policy only succeeded in bringing together the defenders of the constitutional status quo and the Holstein faction. The lesser secret deputation of the estates put pressure on the king to receive the emissary of the duke of Holstein-Gottorp and to accord the title of royal highness to Karl Friedrich. It was rumoured that the king's Swedish opponents had even encouraged Peter I to mount a naval and

2. Bagger H 1974 *Ruslands alliancepolitik efter freden i Nystad* Københavns universitets slaviske institut: Studier 4. Copenhagen, p 16. In 1740, Bestuzhev remarked that Russian interests required constant enmity between the two parties in Swedish politics. Misiunas R 1974 The Baltic question after Nystad, in Ziedonis A, Winter W and Valgemäe M (eds). *Baltic history*. Columbus, Ohio, p. 76.

military demonstration in the Baltic in the summer of 1723 as a means of bringing further pressure to bear. Whatever truth there was in these rumours, the marshalling of Russian forces in the Baltic provinces persuaded the king to give way, though it also alarmed the opposition. The claims of the duke of Holstein-Gottorp were a useful device, both for Peter and the opposition in Sweden; but having succeeded in their mutual aim of preventing any resurgence of royal power, and in the conclusion of a defensive alliance, neither side was prepared to allow itself to become an instrument of Karl Friedrich's own ambitions.

The defensive alliance was a decisive victory for Russian diplomacy, creating a counterbalance to the Anglo-Danish *rapprochement*: but it was also a victory for the estates and the defenders of the 1720 constitution, led by the chancery president Arvid Horn. Karl Friedrich had to be content with promises of a satisfactory solution to the question of succession, and support for his claims to the ducal lands in Slesvig. The prospect of marriage to Peter's daughter Anna Petrovna was tempered by the tsar's insistence that the couple renounce all claims to Russia or any of its territories – which was intended to frustrate the Holsteiners' hopes that Livonia would be part of Anna Petrovna's dowry. During the brief reign of Peter's widow, Catherine I (1725–7), the duke's prospects once more seemed bright. The French and Austrian ambassadors believed he exercised great influence. The Holsteiners hoped that Catherine would proclaim Karl Friedrich her heir and would back a campaign against Denmark to restore the duke to his lands in Slesvig, returning Livonia to Sweden as a reward for military assistance. Their hopes were to be disappointed. The prospect of further involvement in war alarmed many in Sweden; and when the English and French ministers sought to win over the Swedes, they found willing listeners. The presence of a sizeable British fleet in the eastern Baltic in 1726 gave further encouragement to Arvid Horn in his battle with the leading Holsteiner, Josias Cederhielm. Sweden's accession to the anti-Habsburg alliance in 1727 was not in itself of great significance; but it was a decisive defeat for the Holstein faction, which suffered a further blow when Karl Friedrich was expelled from St Petersburg after Catherine's death.

The claims of the house of Holstein-Gottorp were to resurface after Karl Friedrich's death in 1739; but for more than a decade, relative tranquillity prevailed in the north. Rather like his contemporary, Robert Walpole, Horn preferred to avoid entanglement in potential conflict. He was shrewd enough to resist French blandishments to assist the luckless Stanisław Leszczyński, driven to take refuge in

Danzig by Russian and Saxon forces during the War of Polish Succession, for he realised that French support for Stanisław was half-hearted at best. He displayed less political acumen in accepting a Russian offer to renew the 1724 treaty, whilst at the same time agreeing to a subsidy treaty of alliance with France, still officially supporting Stanisław Leszczyński against the Russians and Saxons in Poland. Fleury refused to ratify the treaty; and the pro-French party (lavishly funded by the French embassy) used this as a means to drive Horn from office in 1738 (after a subsidy treaty had finally been negotiated with France), and to replace his supporters on the council the following year.

The new men who now directed Sweden's affairs were eager to take advantage of Russia's difficulties in the war against the Turks. In order to fulfil their plans to attack Russia, it was hoped to be able to persuade the French either to pay the whole of the subsidy in advance, or to increase it, and to obtain the neutrality of Prussia and Danish support. The Danes, who were also taking advantage of Anglo-French rivalry by negotiating with both sides, demanded Bohus province in return for support against Russia, and staked their claim to the Swedish succession, terms which were unacceptable to the Swedes. The conclusion of peace between Russia and Turkey in 1739 was a further blow to the hopes of the war party. The situation was changed, however, with the invasion of Silesia by Frederick II. By the end of June 1741, France was in alliance with Prussia, whilst Britain and Russia hastened to the assistance of Maria Theresa of Austria. A Swedish attack on Russia now accorded with French interests, and a new subsidy of 400,000 riksdaler was agreed in March, on condition that Sweden attacked Russia. Similar assistance was not forthcoming from Prussia, and Denmark was distinctly hostile. In St Petersburg, the Swedish minister was in contact with Peter I's daughter Elizabeth: but although she assured him that a Swedish attack would help her carry out a coup against the infant Ivan VI, she was careful not to promise any rewards for such assistance.

The war launched by Sweden in the summer of 1741 proved to be an unmitigated disaster. The crews of the fleet fitted out in Karlskrona were incapacitated by disease, which carried off over 700 men; Wrangel's forces suffered a bloody defeat on Finnish soil in August; and the cautious advance across the frontier in November, which facilitated the planned coup by Elizabeth, was rapidly abandoned upon the conclusion of a truce. The principal beneficiary of Elizabeth's coup was not Sweden, but France. In seeking to win over Russia to the anti-Habsburg alliance, d'Argenson paid little heed to the pleas of his hapless ally, and even began to look towards Denmark as France's principal partner in the north. The death of Ulrika Eleanora in November 1741 opened up the question of the succession once more. The empress Elizabeth offered little encouragement to colonel Lagerkrantz, who was sent to St Petersburg to negotiate in favour of the Holstein succession, and the war was renewed in the spring of 1742. The retreating Swedish army surrendered without a fight in August, leaving Finland once more to the mercy of Russian occupying forces.

Anxiety and fear of the disastrous consequences of a war against Russia had been frequently voiced by the Finnish estates. In Sweden it was widely believed that, exposed once more to danger, the inhabitants of Finland would choose to seek their own salvation by submitting to Russian rule. The flight of many officials and parish priests during the Russian occupation of the Finnish provinces in the Great Northern War had severely dented the image of a protective state authority. The commissions set up in the 1720s to investigate the circumstances of the occupation and postwar conditions in Finland found that they had to proceed with some caution, especially in the eastern frontier areas, for fear of losing the loyalty of the peasantry towards the crown. A number of men arrested early in 1741 for conspiring with Bestuzhev, the Russian minister to Stockholm, were from Finland; and it may be that they persuaded Bestuzhev to report that the Finnish people were prepared to throw off their allegiance to the Swedish crown and to seek Russian protection.[3] The burden of maintaining and supplying an army bore heavily on a region devastated by crop failure. Although the local peasantry could be prevailed upon to defend the frontier in the king's name, their loyalty soon waned when it became obvious that the king was unable to protect their lives and property. The provincial governor Karl Johan Stiernstedt complained bitterly in August 1742 that the common people were already sending deputations to seek Russian protection 'when the enemy is thirty or forty [Swedish] miles from any place'.[4] On 18 March 1742, Elizabeth had issued a manifesto, offering protection to the Finns and holding out the promise of support for an independent Finnish state, should the Finnish estates seek to break with Sweden. Whether Elizabeth had been encouraged by Bestuzhev's reports to issue this manifesto, or whether it was a device inspired by Lager-

3. Juva E 1960 *Kaksi suomalaista vapaudenajan myllerryksissä* Historiallisia Tutkimuksia 56. Helsinki, pp. 70–86. Juva E 1947 *Suomen tie Uudestakaupungista Haminaan 1721–1808*. Helsinki, pp. 76ff. There were other reports of Finnish discontent: a Russian courier reported that several priests he had spoken to on a journey through eastern Finland believed Finland would shortly be united to Russia.
4. Wirilander K 1962 Gränsmarken och rikskärnan. Östfinsk förhållanden och opinioner såsom element i Finlands utveckling till autonom stat *Scandia* **28**: 354.

krantz as a means of ensuring the succession of the Holstein claimant, duke Karl Peter, is a matter of some debate amongst Finnish historians. The most likely explanation, however, is offered by Juva, who believes that it was part of a general Russian policy of creating buffer states. That much was hinted at by the Swedish counter-manifesto, which warned the inhabitants of Finland of the old Russian trick of fomenting rebellion and promising self-government in frontier provinces 'but those selfsame provinces have afterwards found themselves to be deceived in their aspirations, for they have been forcibly placed under the Russian yoke and have been subjected to the unlimited slavery of its governance, to which the fate of Great Novgorod and the Ukraine, with others, still bear sorrowful testimony'.[5]

Whatever may have been the intention of the Russians in issuing the manifesto, the idea of Finnish independence was not taken up by the parish representatives who sought the protection of the invading forces. The Holstein succession was taken up by the provincial estates meeting in Åbo (though no mention was made of it at the meeting of the Ostrobothnian estates in Vasa), but the Russians refused to permit a delegation to ask the empress to support duke Karl Peter's candidature, claiming that, since the duke had been named next in succession to the Russian throne, he would in the course of time also become ruler of Finland.

The question of the succession was thus intimately tied up with the conclusion of the war. The Russian government pressed the candidature of Karl Peter's relative Adolph Friedrich, the prince-bishop of Lübeck; Christian VI promoted the claims of his eldest son. The prospects of a renewed Scandinavian union prompted the Russian negotiators to lower their territorial demands and to settle for a new frontier along the river Kymi in eastern Finland. As the preliminary peace settlement was being signed in Åbo on 16 June 1743, a peasant army from Dalarna was advancing on the capital to press the claims of the Danish prince, whom the estates had threatened to elect successor to king Fredrik in order to force the Russians to conclude peace. The crisis finally subsided when the prince-bishop was elected as successor

5. Juva 1947, pp. 106–8. The British minister Edward Finch, formerly envoy to Sweden, reported from St Petersburg in April 1742 that: 'The tendency or drift [of the manifesto] is to engage those people to withdraw themselves from their allegiance to Sweden, and set up a new form of government among themselves, by which means the duchy of Finland under their own duke or chief might serve as a barrier between Russia and Sweden.' Finch was of the opinion that the manifesto would not produce the desired effect 'nor do I believe this court expects it.' *Sbornik Imperatorskogo Russkago Istoricheskago Obshchestva* **91**. St Petersburg, 1894, p. 458.

by the Swedish estates and Christian VI abandoned plans to invade southern Sweden in the face of likely Russian intervention.

The uncertain waters into which Sweden had been precipitated by the reckless bellicosity of the Hats continued to toss the ship of state: but the storm raging in Europe also affected the courses of the other northern powers. The Russian statesman J.F. Ostermann had sought to counter French influence in the north through an alliance of the 'three eagles', Austria, Prussia and Russia. The defeat of the French candidate Stanisław Leszczyński in the War of Polish Succession further strengthened Russia's grip over Poland. The new Saxon king August III (1734–63) owed his throne to Russian military intervention, and was obliged to accept the protection of the status quo in Poland by the three eastern powers, none of whom favoured reform of the commonwealth's inadequate military-fiscal system. Russian ascendancy also put paid to the realisation of a decision taken by the Polish *sejm* in 1726 to incorporate the duchy of Kurland into Poland on the death of the childless duke Ferdinand. Having valiantly but vainly done his bit to prolong the Kettler line by marrying at the age of seventy-five, the duke died in 1737. Ferdinand had preferred to remain in Danzig, leaving his nephew's widow Anna Ivanovna in charge. Anna Ivanovna became empress of Russia in 1730; and the nobility of Kurland, persuaded that their privileges and autonomy would be safer under Russian protection, unanimously elected her favourite, count Ernst Johann Biron, as Ferdinand's successor. Biron fell from grace on the death of the empress Anna, and he remained in Siberian exile for the next twenty-two years.

The Franco-Prussian alliance of 1741 was a serious setback to Ostermann's system of containment. The successes of Frederick II of Prussia in his war against Austria alarmed the Russians, who were also perturbed by Frederick's proposal of an alliance with Sweden, and Hohenzollern claims to the duchy of Kurland. Mikhail Bestuzhev observed with alarm in 1744 that the Prussian court, once so dependent on Russia, was now a major threat, and with French backing, could reverse the gains of 1721. Above all, the Russians were worried that Frederick II might wrest control of Poland from their grasp, and in alliance with a reinvigorated Polish commonwealth, threaten Russia's position in Livonia and the Ukraine. To counter this threat, Russia sought to detach Saxony and Sweden from the Franco-Prussian camp. An alliance was signed with Saxony in 1744, but Sweden remained within the French ambit. The large sums of money spent by the British and Russian ministers in the elections to the *riksdag* of 1746–7 were not sufficient to counter French influence; by the end of the session, Sweden had concluded a defence treaty with Prussia, and renewed the subsidy treaty with France. France's efforts to bring Sweden and Denmark (with whom a renewed subsidy agreement was reached in 1746) into a northern European alliance with Prussia and Saxony were coolly received in Berlin and Dresden, whilst Denmark sought primarily to exploit the growing rift between Sweden and Russia in order to reduce the threat from the house of Holstein-Gottorp.

With the ending of the War of Austrian Succession in 1748, the Russian chancellor Aleksey Bestuzhev sought to bring pressure to bear on Sweden once more. Denmark appeared willing to support a Russian declaration that any attempt to alter the Swedish constitution by the circles around Adolf Fredrik and his wife (the sister of Frederick II) would justify Russian interference in accordance with the terms of the peace treaties of 1721 and 1743. Bestuzhev's bid to make Russia the dominant diplomatic force in northern Europe was trumped by the French. Adolf Fredrik was persuaded to renounce his claims to the ducal lands in Slesvig in return for financial compensation, and to promise to exchange Holstein-Gottorp for the counties of Oldenburg and Delmenhorst, should he or his heirs inherit the title. Denmark opted for a new subsidy treaty with the French, and a renewal of the 1734 defensive alliance with Sweden, rather than risk further involvement with Russia, where the duke of Holstein-Gottorp had been recognised as Elizabeth's successor in 1741.

Having acquired the eastern Baltic littoral, the Russians were in general content to maintain the status quo in the north, relying on the exploitation of party differences in Sweden, support for the Holstein claimant, and even the idea of creating a Finnish buffer state to counter Swedish revanchism. The acquisition of large expanses of sparsely populated Finnish forests was hardly attractive to a vast country with its own multitude of lands lying empty.[6] Commercial and political considerations also drew Russia's attention to the southern Baltic, where there was a potential challenge from Prussia to be reckoned with. These considerations probably reinforced the Russian desire to build up a 'northern system', in which Sweden was the key element. This was an implicit challenge to France's traditional claim to diplomatic dominance in the north, and gave the Swedish government an opportunity to escape from the grip which the Russians sought to impose. The renewal of the French alliance in the 1730s enabled the Hat-dominated government in Stockholm to counter Russian press-

6. Misiunas 1974, p. 72, citing vice-chancellor Vorontsov.

ure; but the war embarked upon so recklessly in 1741 revealed the inadequacies of the French alliance, and of French subsidies. It also demonstrated that Sweden was no longer a serious military threat, even if the memory of Narva still haunted Russian generals and policy-makers. Sweden's armed strength was less than that of Denmark and paled into insignificance against the vast forces at Russia's disposal: its eastern provinces were almost entirely without defensible fortifications; its fleet was a motley collection of superannuated ships of the line and galleys. The improvement of fortifications at Landskrona, the construction of Sveaborg fortress off Helsingfors, and the building of a fleet of light, swift vessels to defend the skerries went some way to remedy the deplorable state of Sweden's defences after 1750; and the Hats also seemed disposed to follow Ulrik Scheffer's advice, proposed in a memorial to the lesser secret committee of the *riksdag* in 1756, that peaceful inactivity should be the prime objective for Sweden. But, as Michael Roberts has pointed out, 'unlike Denmark, which throve on subsidies paid to her to do nothing, Sweden could never long enjoy this enviable position'.[7] Denmark enjoyed comparative freedom of action and could afford to choose her allies at a time when the Anglo-French conflict obliged the belligerents to be accommodating. A British request for troops in 1755 was turned down on the grounds that this would conflict with Danish neutrality, and the Danes also refused to assist the French even though the 1754 subsidy treaty obliged them to do so if France were attacked. The French for their part preferred Denmark to remain neutral, and were instrumental in bringing about the Swedish–Danish neutrality convention of 1756, in the hopes that this would harm British maritime interests in the Baltic and the colonies (where neutral vessels were essential to maintain France's lucrative colonial trade).

Sweden, on the other hand, was fated to be a kind of military paperweight in the French service. This is not to say that the council obediently danced to the paymaster's tune; but the memory of former greatness continued to haunt Sweden's policy-makers, and made them vulnerable to French persuasion. Carl Scheffer toyed with the idea of Sweden playing a decisive role in Polish affairs in 1751: his brother Ulrik had also qualified his advice of following a policy of neutrality by urging the council to take advantage of any favourable conjuncture to promote Sweden's reputation and possible expansion. The Scheffer brothers played a major part in bringing Sweden into the Seven Years' War as an ally of France against Prussia, at a time when the council

7. Roberts M 1986 *The age of liberty. Sweden 1719–1772.* Cambridge, p. 20.

was hesitant and divided on which course to pursue. Sweden's ambitions in 1741 and 1757 were wholly unrealistic, as their French allies well knew, and as Swedish statesmen themselves were prepared to admit in private. The vain attempts to revive the glories of the past were always tempered by an awareness that the resources and means were no longer sufficient against vigorous and far more powerful neighbours.[8] The divisions and jealousies of party politics undoubtedly weakened Sweden's ability to pursue a truly independent and effective foreign policy; but the decision to embark on war cannot solely be attributed to the reckless bellicosity of the Hats in 1741, or a desire to humiliate Frederick II's sister after the failure of the court *coup* in 1756. Denmark was able to pursue a successful policy of neutrality until the Napoleonic wars because that neutrality was more beneficial to the principal contestants for colonial and maritime power than military support, and because no neighbouring power seriously threatened Danish territorial integrity. Sweden's decline to the status of a second-rate power did not *ipso facto* liquidate the residual burden of empire (as the insistence of the French and Austrian courts in 1757 that Sweden should fulfil its role as guarantor of the peace of Westphalia demonstrated); nor did it remove Sweden from the zone of great-power territorial conflict. The ambitions of Russia and Prussia and the system-makers in Versailles continued to draw the northern Baltic state into the tangled web of European politics and war, and the consequences of the major colonial and European conflict which began in 1755 were to be felt, even on the Baltic periphery.

Alarmed by the territorial ambitions of Frederick II and the revival of French intrigue in Polish affairs, Russia gravitated towards Britain and Austria after the War of Austrian Succession. The imminence of a colonial war with France in 1755 persuaded a hitherto reluctant British government to agree to pay an annual subsidy of £100,000 to Russia for the upkeep of troops to be used to protect Hanover should the electorate be attacked by Prussia or France. The Russians for their part insisted that the troops would only be used against Prussia, and refused to ratify the agreement, which in all probability was intended by the British to detach Frederick II from his French alliance. The king of Prussia was indeed willing to reach an accommodation with Britain, and the conclusion of the convention of Westminster in January

---

8. For a perceptive and comprehensive summary of the 'predicament of a minor power', see Roberts 1986, pp. 15–58. Sweden's relations with France are summarised in detail in Jägerskiöld O 1957 *Den svenska utrikespolitikens historia 1721–1792.* Stockholm, and more concisely by Nordmann C 1971 *Grandeur et liberté de la Suède 1660–1792.* Paris, pp. 254–67.

1756, although little more than an agreement to preserve the neutrality of Germany, was the first step in the 'diplomatic revolution'. Angered by the seeming perfidy of their erstwhile ally, the French signed a defensive alliance with Austria in May. Two months earlier, Russia had begun soundings in Vienna and Paris for support against Frederick II. The proposal laid before the Russian imperial council in March 1756 for a 'rounding-off of the frontier' with Poland–Lithuania envisaged the restoration of East Prussia to Poland, in return for the cession to Russia of Kurland and Polish Livonia and adjustments to the frontier in White Russia.[9] Sweden was to have Pomerania, Saxony Magdeburg, should they join the anti-Prussian coalition. Aware of the forces massing against him, Frederick II decided to strike first, invading Saxony in August. His action outraged the French court, and activated the Franco–Austrian alliance; but it also exposed some of the weaknesses of the coalition of forces now ranged against Prussia. Austria was primarily interested in regaining Silesia, and regarded Russian territorial ambitions with some suspicion. The French were alarmed at the degree of influence exercised in Poland by the Russians, but were unable to prevent either the occupation of Danzig or the imposition of the Russian candidate (a son of August III of Saxony–Poland) as duke of Kurland. The Russian war effort was hampered by the poor organisation of supplies for the army, the ill-health of the empress Elizabeth, and the knowledge that her designated successor was a devoted admirer of Frederick the Great. Sweden's contribution to the war effort was ineffectual: the government in Stockholm spent more time checking the moves of neutral Denmark than it did on prosecuting the campaign in Pomerania.

The coalition of forces marshalled against the king of Prussia was nonetheless formidable, and he faced a major crisis in the autumn of 1757. The French forced the surrender of the Hanoverian forces and advanced into the western provinces of the kingdom, linking up with the Austrians who were driving through Saxony. The Russians invaded East Prussia, capturing Memel and inflicting defeats on the Prussians at Gross Jägerndorf and Wehlau. Abandoning his outlying provinces, Frederick fought a rapid campaign along interior lines, defeating the French and Austrian forces at Rossbach, and crushing a superior Austrian force at Leuthen. News of the illness of the empress Elizabeth and logistical problems caused Apraksin to withdraw his

9. *Sbornik Imperatorskogo Russkago Istoricheskago Obshchestva* **136**. St Petersburg, 1912, p. 33. Mediger W 1968 Russland und die Ostsee im 18 Jahrhundert *Jahrbücher für Geschichte Osteuropas* **16**: 100ff. Müller M 1980 Russland und der Siebenjährige Krieg *Jahrbücher für Geschichte Osteuropas* **28**: 198–219.

forces from East Prussia. The brunt of the war effort was borne by the Russians over the next two years. Much of East Prussia was occupied by Russian forces, who won a decisive victory at Kunersdorf in August 1759. Elizabeth's death in January 1762 produced a dramatic change. Her successor immediately suspended hostilities and began peace negotiations with Frederick II. By midsummer, Russia and Prussia had made an alliance, and Frederick II had agreed to support Peter III's claims to Slesvig. Sweden, which had also managed to make peace with Prussia, was prevailed upon to grant rights of transit for Russian troops through Pomerania. Thirty thousand Danish troops were moved into Mecklenburg in preparation for war. The threat of hostilities between Russia and Denmark disappeared with the deposition and murder of Peter III in July. His wife and successor had secretly opposed his designs, and immediately suspended military operations. The triumph a year later of Nikita Panin over the fiercely anti-Prussian Aleksey Bestuzhev ushered in a new phase of Russian foreign policy. Panin's grand design for a 'Northern system', based on Russo-Prussian cooperation, opened up the possibility for a peaceful settlement of the Holstein-Gottorp claim. The first step on the road to settlement was taken in 1765 with the signing by Russia and Denmark of an eight-year friendship and guarantee treaty to preserve the peace of the north. By April 1767 agreement had been reached on a pro-visional exchange treaty. Holstein-Gottorp was to pass to Denmark in exchange for Oldenburg and Delmenhorst. The treaty was to become valid when Catherine II's son Paul attained his majority in 1772, and was in fact confirmed by Paul in 1773.

The main test for Panin's system was the ailing Polish–Lithuanian state. With Prussian backing, Catherine II succeeded in forcing through the election of Stanisław Poniatowski to the Polish throne in 1764, after the anti-Russian candidate had been driven over the frontier by Russian troops. Although Catherine expressed her general support for reform, the measures taken by the confederated *sejm* (where the obstructive *liberum veto* did not apply, decisions being taken by simple majority vote) aroused her anger. Frederick II opposed any reforms which might strengthen Poland's military forces, and joined the empress in demanding the abolition of the confederation *sejm*. Confederations of non-Catholics were organised and placed under Russian military protection, and under pressure, the *sejm* agreed to a Russian guarantee of the Polish constitution in 1768. The opposition to Russian interference rallied to the noble confedera-tion set up in Bar, and the Turks, backed by France, demanded the withdrawal of Russian troops and the rescinding of the guarantee of the Polish constitution.

The Russo-Turkish war which followed formed the background to the first partition of Poland. Fears of a Russian territorial advance into the Balkans prompted Frederick II to suggest a three-power partition of Polish territory. Although the preservation of Poland's territorial integrity was officially endorsed by Russia, Frederick's advances revived the long-held view of Russian statesmen that a rectification of the frontier was desirable. Catherine preferred to avoid conflict with Austria over the Balkans, and by 1771 was prepared to endorse Frederick's plan, in spite of Panin's opposition. Austria was in no position to oppose Russia militarily in the Balkans, and Kaunitz eventually persuaded Maria Theresa to overcome her moral scruples and join in the partition. The convention signed by the three eastern powers in August 1772 assigned the two-and-a-half million inhabitants of Galicia to Austria, whilst Russia gained Polish Livonia and a substantial part of White Russia. Although he failed to gain Danzig and Thorn, Frederick II's acquisition of West Prussia finally closed the corridor between Brandenburg and East Prussia.

The Annual Register for 1772 characterised the partition of Poland as 'the first very great breach in the modern system of Europe': yet it had been brought about by the workings of that selfsame system. In order to avoid conflict over the Balkans, the three eastern powers agreed to augment their territorial ambitions at the expense of a weakened state. Religious intolerance, regional and class tensions and rivalries gave Poland's neighbours ample opportunity to interfere. The decision of the *sejm* in 1717 drastically to reduce the size of the royal army gravely weakened the Polish state. Attempts to reform the fiscal basis of the army after the War of Polish Succession were defeated by external pressure; suspicious of French intentions, the Russians were not prepared to tolerate a revival of Polish military strength. In order to forestall the revival of Polish claims on Kurland after Biron's fall in 1740, the Russians twice threatened to break up the *sejm*; and this effectively nullified all hopes of military reform. In the end, it was the efforts of the magnates aligned to the Czartoryski family to reform the financial and military institutions of the commonwealth which aroused Russian hostility and ultimately sealed Poland's fate.[10]

10. The extract from the Annual Register is quoted in Müller 1980, p. 214. There is a good survey of recent historiography of eighteenth-century Polish history, albeit from a German perspective, in Müller M 1983 *Polen zwischen Preussen und Russland* Einzelveröffentlichungen der Historischen Kommission zu Berlin 40. Berlin, pp. 1ff.

The notion of partition was not new: the dismemberment of the Polish–Lithuanian state had been considered by its opponents in the 1650s. Nor was it confined to Poland–Lithuania: Karl X Gustav had toyed with the idea of carving up Denmark, and Aleksey Bestuzhev in his more intemperate moments seems to have regarded dismemberment as the best solution to the Prussian problem. But all these schemes envisaged partition as a consequence of victorious war: Poland–Lithuania was not even allowed an honourable defeat.

The partitions of Poland may be seen as a further stage in the struggle for hegemony in the Baltic, particularly if the declining influence of Ottoman and Tatar power (which had undoubtedly affected the outcome of the sixteenth-century struggle for Livonia) is taken into account. The continental interests of the partitioning powers, however, left the Baltic very much on the periphery. And whereas Sweden and Denmark had been very active participants in the struggle for supremacy in the Baltic during the sixteenth and early seventeenth centuries, they were now little more than secondary players in a game dominated by the major European powers. Foreign powers blatantly interfered in Swedish politics, handing out pensions and funding election campaigns. French subsidies had helped the political faction known as the Hats to power in 1738. The failure of the Hats to reach agreement over the payment of subsidy arrears in 1763–4 was a serious blow to their sagging fortunes. The French were in any case beginning to reconsider the value of an unreliable ally, and of feeding the corruption of the estates and council, and Choiseul instructed the French minister to work for the restoration of monarchical power. The Russians, mindful of the council's decision to enter the war in 1757 without consulting the *riksdag*, preferred to weaken the power of the executive still further. The reforms pushed through by the Hat's opponents in the *riksdag* of 1765–6 went some way to establish the control of the estates over the executive. The chancellor of justice was henceforth to be chosen by the estates, not appointed by the king, and candidates for membership of the council to whom the king objected were to be automatically appointed if nominated four times in a row by the estates. However, the Caps were unable to remove Hat supporters from their entrenched positions in the bureaucracy and in 1768, these men struck back, supporting the king's refusal to exercise his royal functions until an extraordinary meeting of the estates was called. The council was forced to back down in the face of royal strike action; and the elections of 1769 returned the Hats to power. For an explanation of the 'Hats' and 'Caps' see p. 347.

The brief period of Cap ascendancy did not lead to any permanent realignment of Swedish foreign policy. A treaty of friendship was concluded with Britain in 1766, but Russian designs on Poland cooled any desire for closer relations with St Petersburg. On the other hand, the French refusal to pay any more subsidies unless a revolution to restore the power of the monarchy was carried out gave food for thought to the Hats and inclined them towards caution in their dealings with Louis XV. News of a Danish mobilisation at the behest of Russia greeted the estates as they convened in April 1769 in Norrköping: the unwillingness of the Hats to push through the constitutional reforms desired by the court meant that no assistance could be expected from the French. At the end of the year, Denmark and Prussia concluded alliances with Russia, promising military assistance should any amendment of the 1720 Swedish constitution occur. The Russians also revived the possibility of creating an independent Finnish state. As Olof Jägerskiöld remarks, contemporaries did not fail to draw parallels with the fate of Poland. More recently, however, Andreas Bode has argued that Catherine harboured no aggressive intentions and feared a war as much as Sweden.[11] The naval expedition to the Mediterranean was a costly venture: plague ravaged Moscow, and peasant discontent flared up into rebellion in 1773. Although crown prince Gustav failed to win much support in France for his plans for a *coup*, news of his father's death in 1771 opened up French coffers. In a marginal note to a dispatch by her minister in Stockholm, Catherine wrote: 'Better to give money than absolutism in Sweden and war with us as a consequence of French money and French intrigue,' but neither the dispensation of funds nor the sending of a squadron to cruise off the Swedish coast was sufficient to prevent the *coup*.[12] Plans for a Russo-Danish assault on Sweden with Prussian and British backing were mooted in 1773, but the crisis faded with the outbreak of Pugachev's revolt, the continuing war against Turkey and the reluctance of Prussia and Britain to countenance war in the north.

POLITICS AND PARTY STRIFE

The treaty of Nystad deprived Sweden of the territories in the eastern Baltic acquired during the previous century, and of a slice of eastern

11. Jägerskiöld 1957, p 237. Bode A 1979 *Die Flottenpolitik Katharinas II und die Konflikte mit Schweden und der Turkei (1768–1792)* Veröffentlichungen des Osteuropa-Instituts München 48. Wiesbaden, p. 79.
12. Bode 1979, p. 87.

Finland held by Sweden since the Middle Ages. These areas had been under continuous Russian occupation since 1710, but whereas eastern Finland had simply been placed under a military administration, the Russians had concluded agreements with the burghers and nobility of the Baltic lands. The 'capitulations' have long been regarded by Baltic German historians as a bilateral treaty between the tsar and the estates, upon which the separate status of the provinces within the Russian empire was founded. Doubts have been voiced as to whether an autocratic ruler would have permitted himself or his successors to be bound by such a treaty; as O-H Elias points out, the capitulations were in the first instance acts of surrender by beleaguered garrisons, provisionally delineating the legal position in a wartime situation. Peter I insisted on receiving the oath of loyalty of the estates before confirming privileges, and explicitly described the capitulation of Riga, for example, as an act of submission. The tsar, in other words, 'spoke as an autocrat', not as a partner in a quasi-feudal agreement.[13]

Nevertheless, the capitulations – which were also affirmed in the treaty of Nystad – amounted to a remarkably generous settlement: guarantees for the Lutheran religion, the maintenance of the university to serve the educational needs of noble youths, the restoration of lands lost to the crown during the *reduktion*, and the confirmation of the rights of self-government for the estates. At the head of the administration of the provinces (*gubernii*) of Livonia and Estonia was a governor, usually a high-ranking officer: each had a Russian chancery dealing with military matters, subordinated to the Senate in St Petersburg, and a German chancery, which dealt with the local executive. In Estonia, the twelve *Landräte* and twelve deputies elected by the four districts of Harrien, Wierland, Jerwen and Wiek represented the *Ritterschaft* as a committee when the provincial diet was not in session. In Livonia, the 'residential *Landräte*' reported back to the *Landtag*, and a deliberative assembly of senior nobles met regularly to prepare items of business for consideration by the *Landtag* and to carry on its work between regular sessions. Both diets had the right to initiate legislation and vote their own taxes; in Livonia, however, landowners who were not on the roll of nobility and the town of Riga also had representation and voting rights in the *Landtag*. The areas of competence of the governor and the local administration were not clearly defined, but until 1775, the indigenous nobility were able to keep a tight grip on the affairs of the provinces, occupying the chief administrative and judicial offices.

13. Elias O-H 1978 *Reval in der Reformpolitik Katharinas II*. Bonn–Bad Godesberg, pp. 63–5. See also Wittram R 1954 *Baltische Geschichte* Göttingen, pp. 106–7, 133–4.

The degree of noble self-government which obtained in Livonia and Estonia before the reforms of Catherine II was greater than it had been during the last years of Swedish rule. The preferential treatment accorded to the Baltic Germans by Peter and his successors stands in marked contrast to the way in which other subject peoples, such as the Ukrainians, were dealt with. As Edward Thaden has pointed out, the Baltic Germans constituted a reliable and competent elite, with valuable links with the outside world and command of a major European language. Unlike the Ukrainians, they were also good lobbyists.[14] They were also virtually unchallenged by any other section of society, able to screw down even more tightly their controls over the peasantry, and virtually excluding the towns from any real say in the running of the provinces.

A similar situation prevailed in the part of Pomerania which remained under Swedish control. Most of the larger towns were lost to Prussia: Wolgast and Greifswald were ruined by war: and the members of the town council of Stralsund were granted noble title in 1720, which reduced any potential opposition to the privileges granted to the nobility in that year. Frederick William, on the other hand, dismissed the pleas of his new Pomeranian subjects for confirmation of their privileges as an impertinence. Prussian policy was to unite the scattered domains of Hither Pomerania and the newly acquired territory. Stettin was made the headquarters of the administration, and the province was divided into tax districts, which gradually assumed administrative functions running counter to the older pattern of noble-controlled districts (*Ämter*). The local nobility soon won the favour of Frederick William for their willingness to enter his officer corps: the East Prussian aristocracy were less well regarded by the Prussian king. In 1740, on the occasion of Frederick II's accession, the East Prussian nobility complained of the ban on travel and study abroad and the obligation to send their sons into the army. Compulsory drafting of their peasants under the provisions of Frederick William's cantonment system of recruitment was a further grievance, for it deprived them of many of their best workers. These complaints are an indication of the loss of political power of the nobility. When the elector had tried to summon a deputation of the estates to Berlin in 1690 to negotiate over taxation, they refused to go, fearing that this would create a bad precedent. Nevertheless, the threat of raising taxes without consent invariably forced the estates to comply, in return for

14. Thaden E 1981 Estland, Livland and the Ukraine: Reflexions on eighteenth-century regional autonomy *Journal of Baltic Studies* **12**: 311–17.

a promise that this would not jeopardise their privileges. The war years finally broke the back of the estates. Regular diets were no longer held: the title of *Oberrat* was abolished, and the holders of this office became royal Prussian privy councillors. In 1712, new instructions for service on the Berlin model were introduced, and new administrative departments set up. The town magistracy became royal town councillors, and many of their functions were taken over by royal officials. The East Prussian *Landtag* expired after 1704, though twelve interim *Landräte* were appointed by Frederick II at the beginning of his reign. Three salaried officials supervised the local taxes in the districts of the duchy. Day-to-day administration in the provinces was controlled by the War and Domains Chambers, which collected and assigned revenues, provided assistance for trade and industry and supervised the victualling and billeting of troops. The accounts of these chambers were examined and checked by the Chief War and Domains Audit Office, which was in turn subordinated to the General Directory. A degree of local control did nevertheless remain: ecclesiastical authorities and courts of law were relatively free from central control, whilst the privileges of the landowning Junkers were preserved.

The ducal lands in Slesvig were placed under Danish royal control in 1720. Although the royal patent spoke of incorporation in accordance with the royal law (*secundum tenorem legis Regiae*), no immediate administrative incorporation took place, nor was the Danish law introduced. The administration of the royal lands in Slesvig-Holstein came under the German chancery in Copenhagen; taxation was dealt with by the treasury, the army and navy by the colleges for war and the admiralty. The chancery in Glückstadt lost most of its administrative functions, though it remained the court of highest instance in Holstein, and Frederik IV created a separate high court in Slesvig. The duchy of Holstein-Gottorp, with a population of some 14,000, was administered by a privy government council in Kiel. During his years in the duchy from 1727 until his death in 1739, Karl Friedrich dispensed with this council, but it was revived after his death by the regent Adolph Friedrich. A series of administrators succeeded Adolph Friedrich after his election as heir-apparent in Sweden, until Caspar von Saldern was given full powers to govern in 1764 by Catherine II, wife of the luckless duke Karl Peter. The energetic Saldern set up a commission to tour the duchy to survey the welfare of its people; his land survey placed the fiscal structure of the duchy on a sounder footing, and field enclosure was vigorously promoted. Though less successful in his attempts to abolish serfdom, Saldern had by the 1770s turned Holstein-Gottorp into something of a model state of enlightened reform, and many of his ideas were to be taken up by Catherine the Great in her programme of reform for the empire.

The absolutist system in Denmark was characterised by Edvard Holm as 'a peculiar mixture of collegial administration and cabinet government'.[15] The chanceries were subordinated to the council after 1703, but the council had little to do with fiscal matters, for the treasury was directly answerable to the king, or with military affairs. Although the pleasure-loving Frederik V left government largely to his officials, his predecessors dealt personally with a great deal of often routine business, such as the appointment of organists or bridge bailiffs. Criticism of the system was muted at best. Klaus Jakobsen Brandt was reprimanded for seeking representation for Norway on the council, and another Norwegian was executed for plotting to detach Norway from Denmark with Russian assistance (Russia was to have Greenland as a reward): but not until the second half of the century did a more consistently articulated campaign for a more favourable deal for Norway develop. Although there was some hostility towards foreigners who were held to have stolen the bread out of the natives' mouths, there was little antipathy towards the German language which most of these outsiders spoke, and which was widely used by all social classes in the capital. Loyalty to the crown was important, though as Edvard Holm pointed out, the increasing emphasis on the 'common good' tended to stifle ultraroyalism and to elevate state and fatherland above the king, diverting attention away from civil liberties and political freedom. Love of the fatherland spread rapidly in academic circles in the 1740s, but the first to attempt a precise definition of patriotism was Tyge Rothe. Rothe's *Tanker om Kærlighed til Fædrenelandet* (Thoughts on Patriotism, 1757) sought to formulate a national programme for the 'crowned patriot', Frederik V. His assertion that the fatherland was 'the country in which we live as citizens' sounded a new note in the public debate encouraged by Frederik V's relaxation of the censorship, but it provoked a response ten years later from the Norwegian Eiler Hagerup. In his anonymous *Brev om Kærlighed til Fædrenelandet* (Letter concerning patriotism), Hagerup challenged Rothe's easy assumption of a common love of the fatherland. Like Holberg before him, Rothe believed that the peasant, bound to the soil by the law, had little desire or incentive to work or defend the fatherland; but he failed to draw any conclusions from this. By insisting that the peasantry would only be patriotic if they were

15. Holm E 1891 *Danmark–Norges historie*. Copenhagen, vol. 1, p. 241.

liberated, Hagerup entered the lists in a struggle for peasant emancipation which was to engage the attentions of 'patriots' throughout the southern Baltic lands for the next four decades.[16]

The peasantry on the northern shores of the Baltic and in Norway had never been reduced to a servile status. Although only a third of the peasantry in Sweden owned their farms, the number of freeholders was growing by virtue of the crown's need to raise cash by the sale of land. Moreover, they participated in the affairs of the realm as a distinct estate. Delegates elected in the parishes would assemble every three years in the hundred (*härad*) to choose their representatives. In some instances, hundreds would combine to send a joint representative; although the non-noble estates received expenses, Stockholm was an expensive city and travel costs from distant regions were high, and this was one way of saving money. The franchise was in theory limited to freeholders and crown peasants, and delegates were supposed to live and farm in the hundred. Although the farmers of central Sweden appear to have jealously guarded the 'purity' of their estate, those on the periphery were less fussy. There is evidence of officials participating in elections to the peasants' estate in the Finnish provinces, for example, and of ex-soldiers, officials and even a nobleman being elected.[17] On average, around 140 peasant delegates attended the *riksdag*. Each of the towns of the realm was entitled to return at least one member, though some chose to combine to send a representative, and the largest cities regularly sent more than one member – Stockholm, for example, returning ten, five of whom usually sat on the all-important secret committee. The 1723 *riksdag* ordinance ·decreed that the towns were to elect representatives 'of their estate', a vague formulation which later laws sought to make more precise. By 1740, the franchise embraced tax-paying burghers and artisans resident in the town, and by the end of the Age of Liberty, widows and daughters who had inherited a business or property were also exercising the right to vote. The burghers' estate varied in size between 86 and 121 members: the estate of clergy was much smaller, no more than 51 members, elected by the beneficed clergy of the diocese. The largest estate was that of the nobility, for every noble family was

16. Holm E 1975 *Kongemagt, folk og borgerlig frihed* (reprint of 1883 ed). Copenhagen, pp. 90ff. Feldbæk O 1984 Kærlighed til fædrelandet. 1700-tallets nationale selvforståelse *Fortid og Nutid* **31**: 270–88. Olsen A 1939 Samtidens Syn paa den danske Stavnsbundne Bonde *Scandia* **12**: 99–139.

17. For details, see Paloposki T 1961 *Suomen talonpoikaissäädyn valtiopäiväedustus vapaudenajalla* Historiallisia Tutkimuksia 57. Helsinki, pp. 70–8, 167–76, and Olsson R 1948 *Riksdagsmannavalen till bondeståndet under den senare delen av frihetstiden (1740–1772)* Skrifter utgivna av Fahlbeckska stiftelsen 33. Lund, pp. 53ff.

entitled to be represented by its head or a proxy. Up to a thousand nobles, rich and poor, no longer divided into three classes for voting purposes, packed into the *Riddarhus* when the *riksdag* was in session. Such large numbers made the efficient conduct of business almost impossible; but the decision taken by the nobility in 1762 not to permit the introduction of newly ennobled members until the total number of those entitled to sit in the *Riddarhus* had fallen to 800 was seen by the non-noble estates as yet another attempt to strengthen noble exclusivity.

As a representative body, the eighteenth-century Swedish parliament could claim several advantages over its British counterpart. The voice of the established church was not confined to the bishops, and the clergy played an active role in pressing for needful reform, as did the burghers in the tumultuous decade of the 1760s. There was no dominating landed interest, no rotten or pocket boroughs; and the presence of the peasants' representatives ensured that a significant section of the population had a direct say in the affairs of the nation.[18] True, the rather arbitrary and often contradictory definitions of 'estate' caused anomalies and excluded important social categories. A group of non-noble officials sought representation in 1719 on the grounds that participation in the *riksdag* was no longer a public duty, but a right and a liberty to be enjoyed by every 'true citizen'; but within a matter of years, two-thirds of the group had in fact obtained access through ennoblement. Office-holding conferred prestige, even if it brought little financial reward: with the exception of the peasants' estate, the *riksdag* was, in Roberts's words, 'a parliament of placemen'.[19] The army had also vainly endeavoured to secure recognition as an estate in 1719, and regiments continued for the rest of the century to elect members to the 'army command' (*krigsbefälet*), which met when the *riksdag* was in session as a kind of unofficial pressure group. The officer corps, however, was a powerful force in the land. Serving and former officers dominated the estate of nobility and commanded almost half of the most senior administrative positions. They played an important role in the constitutional and political crises of 1719–20, 1738–9 and 1772: in the view of Gunnar Artéus it was unlikely that the parliamentary regime would have been dissolved in

18. In Finland, where peasants constituted 91 per cent of the population, it has been estimated that 44 per cent of the adult population in the mid-eighteenth century were enfranchised: Paloposki 1961, p. 33. For a comparison of the British and Swedish parliaments, see Roberts M 1973 *Swedish and English parliamentarianism in the eighteenth century*. Belfast.

19. Roberts 1986, p. 73.

1772 had not the military come to see it as a dangerous threat to their fundamental corporate interests.[20]

The foundations of that regime were laid down in the winter of 1718–19, when the system of absolutism was abandoned stage by stage by queen Ulrika Eleanora. The revolution of 1719–20 has been interpreted as a triumph for a self-seeking upper class, rather than as a constitutional issue. It was certainly a victory for the lesser nobility over the more conservative elements who sought to revert to the old balance between king, council and estates, even if the *riksdag* in 1719 declared its purpose to be the restoration of the government of the realm to its former state. The lingering hopes of the magnates for the dismantling of the *reduktion* found no support amongst the numerous office-holders and army officers dependent for their livelihood on income from the crown and the allotment system. As Lennart Thanner concluded, the transformation which occurred after Karl XII's death was in the first instance a revolution staged by the noble bureaucracy.[21]

The constitution of 1719, amended a year later, effectively transferred power to the estates. They were to meet every three years, and they had the authority to draft necessary laws, raise and apportion taxes, and to propose three candidates to the king, who would select one to fill any vacancy which arose on the council (which consisted of sixteen members after 1720). The king was to rule in accordance with the advice of the council, and he was allowed two votes and the casting say in the event of deadlock. The most important matters were under the purview of a secret committee, comprising fifty members of the estate of nobility and twenty-five nominees of the clergy and burghers appointed at the opening of each parliamentary session: numerous sub-committees, to which the peasants' estate was also admitted, were also set up. The old rhetorical style of debate gave way to the cut-and-thrust of party politicking. The committees conducted inquests and inquisitions into a bewildering multitude of matters,

---

20. Artéus G 1982 *Krigsmakt och samhälle i frihetstidens Sverige* Militärhistoriska Studier 6 Stockholm, pp 331-61.
21. Thanner L 1953 *Revolutionen i Sverige efter Karl XII:s död. Den inrepolitiska maktkampen under tidigare delen av Ulrika Eleanora den yngres regering.* Uppsala, p. 38. See also the classic study by Lagerroth F 1915 *Frihetstidensförfattning.* Stockholm; and the more contentious study by Buchholtz W 1979 *Staat und Ständegesellschaft in Schweden zur Zeit des Überganges vom Absolutismus zum Ständeparliamentarismus 1718–1720.* Stockholm.

leaving many, such as the Hat politician Christoffer Johan Rappe, fervently wishing that their work was done.[22]

The constitution of 1720 severed the link between council and the administrative machinery of the collegial system: only the chancery president and his deputy were permitted to be members of the *collegia*. The council was not to embark on an offensive war without the consent of the estates, which also had the right to review its activities. Members of the council, although appointed for life, could be and were removed by a form of impeachment (*licentiering*), charged with abusing the constitution or failing to comply with the instructions of the previous *riksdag*. The authority of the king, already severely circumscribed, was reduced still further in subsequent decades. When Fredrik I sought to use his fellow-Hessian Ernst von Diemar as an adviser, the *riksdag* had him expelled; after the failure of a royalist plot in 1756, Adolf Fredrik had to agree to an act which declared that the estates could dissolve the tie between king and subject if the monarch broke his oath. Adolf Fredrik's refusal to sign nominations approved by the council was countered by the making of a name-stamp, to be used if the king should prove obdurate again. The Swedish constitution aroused mixed feelings abroad. Admired by Voltaire and Mably, it was regarded as inferior to that of England by Montesquieu, and disliked by French ministers such as Choiseul who believed it rendered the country incapable of pursuing a resolute policy (by the same token, it was welcomed and supported by the Russians). La Beaumelle described the balance of power in the following terms:

> The constitution of Sweden is admirable: the power of the king is checked by the senate, the power of the senate is checked by the diet. The king is not wealthy enough to use corruption, the nobility is not sufficiently powerful to oppress, the people is not strong enough to disobey. The prince is bound by his oaths, the nobles by the laws, the people by their interests. The three powers are judiciously distributed. The diet makes the laws, the senate upholds them, the king carries them out.[23]

La Beaumelle made light of the fact that the balance was heavily tipped towards the estates, and he ignored the disharmony of party politics. In general, 'party' was not perceived in a very positive light:

22. In a letter written at the end of the extremely long session of 1760–2, Rappe talked of not having had a break for a fortnight: 'We have been in committee from five in the morning, in plenary session at nine, dining at four, back to committee at five again, and remaining there until ten, eleven or twelve at night'. Cited by Michael Metcalf in Schuck H *et al.* (eds) 1985 *Riksdagen genom tiderna*. Stockholm, p. 130. See also Tilas D 1974 *Anteckningar och brev från riksdagen 1765–1766* Kungl.Samfundets handlingar 2. Stockholm, for a detailed day-by-day account of the work of the estates.

23. Cited in Nordmann C 1971 *Grandeur et liberté de la Suède 1660–1792*. Paris, p. 238.

suitable only for rogues and fools, according to the sceptic Olof Dalin, a threat to Sweden's internal security and the political and social order according to others such as Carl Otto Lagerkrantz. But when the system was threatened, it did not lack defenders: England ruled the world midst parliamentary strife, declared Jakob Wallenberg in *Min son på galejan*, and even Lagerkrantz believed that *confutio licencia* had preserved the Polish state, and that the curbing of dissent in Sweden would mark an end to liberty.

The political factions, or 'parties', of the 1720s were loose groupings associated with a particular cause or individual. It was not until the 1738 *riksdag* that a fully developed party system emerged. The opposition to the chancery president Arvid Horn had already secured a victory in 1734, when the nobility insisted on secret elections to the committees. Ousted from the post of marshal of the nobility, and no longer able to exercise the degree of control which had crushed the Holstein faction in 1727, Horn found himself under attack four years later from a well-organised political opposition, masterminded by count Carl Gyllenborg. With financial assistance from the French minister, proxy votes were bought up, and the non-noble estates were lavishly 'treated', Gyllenborg himself drinking morning tea with the peasants' delegates and sharing a glass of wine and a pipe with young merchants in their clubs and coffee-houses. Carl Tessin was elected marshal, and the new party secured a safe majority on the all-important secret committee. The aged Horn sought and was granted retirement, and his supporters on the council were purged through the *licentiering* procedure.

The Hat party (so named after the French tricorne favoured by Gyllenborg's young supporters) dominated Swedish politics for the next twenty-seven years. Their opponents, contemptuously referred to as the 'night-caps', were to come into their own during the last phase of the Age of Liberty. The Caps soon imitated the methods of their opponents, but their lack of adroit leadership and experience, and the panic caused by the peasants' revolt in Dalarna in 1743 saved the Hats from political defeat after the calamitous war against Russia. The Caps were outmanoeuvred in 1746 over the appointment of new members to the council; suitably reinforced, the Hats forced the resignation from the council of the Cap leader Samuel Åkerhielm and instituted the trial of a leading Cap burgher, Christopher Springer, for his dealings with the Russian and British ministers. Ten years later, the Hats were still sufficiently powerful to defeat the machinations of the court party, but cracks were beginning to appear and the form and structure of party politics were to undergo a significant transformation in the 1760s.

Given the often imprecise and irregular nature of representation, it is not easy to arrive at any firm conclusions regarding the composition of the parties. Many, probably the majority, were either neutral or shifting in their allegiance. There is little evidence of attempts to influence the elections to the peasants' estate, nor much sign of active politicking in the smaller provincial towns. The agents employed by the parties to travel the country recruiting votes seem to have concentrated their efforts on the nobility. Ingemar Carlsson has been able to establish the party affiliation of 416 members of the *riksdag* between 1731 and 1743, but this is only a small fraction of the total number. Ulla Johansson's study of the elections for the burghers' estate in 1755–6 shows that in 21 of 49 the Swedish towns for which records are still extant, delegates were returned unopposed. The Hats dominated this estate: there were no more than ten Caps, of whom half were adherents of the court party in the first instance.[24]

Carlsson's researches have modified the older view of the Hats drawing their support from the lesser nobility or the newly ennobled, with the older nobility and magnates supporting the Caps. The older nobility in fact seems to have been evenly divided, and there appears to have been no significant age difference, in spite of Hat propaganda that the victory of 1738 owed much to the influence of discontented younger nobles. Both factions were intimately connected by family ties. No fewer than half the Hat nobility recorded by Carlsson were linked to the Gyllenborg and Lewenhaupt families; but almost half of the Caps were also connected by family ties. Guards officers, officials of the central administration, magistrates, large exporters and those involved in manufacturing tended to be the Hats' natural supporters; provincial army officers, navy officers, provincial officials, burghers and craftsmen were more likely to support the Caps. During their long period of ascendancy, the Hats favoured credit to promote manufacturing, expansion of the money supply, protectionist legislation, premiums for the export of manufactured goods and the farming-out of customs to private entrepreneurs. The inflation and the system of patronage which resulted from these policies were to pro-

24. Carlsson I 1981 *Parti – partiväsen – partipolitiker 1731–1743* Stockholm studies in history 29. Stockholm, p. 136. Johansson U 1973 Hattar och mössor i borgarståndet 1755–1756 *Historisk Tidskrift* **93**: 489–529. There is a useful summary of the historiography of the party system in Metcalf M 1977 The first 'modern' party system? Political parties, Sweden's Age of Liberty and the historians *Scandinavian Journal of History* **2**: 270–87.

vide the revived Caps party with a powerful rallying cry in the 1760s.

Sweden's somewhat inglorious involvement in the Seven Years' War had left the country in a financial crisis, and the Hat party, already riven by internal discontent, was hard pressed to maintain control of government. The Hats hoped to relieve the financial situation through the payment of subsidy arrears by the French; but the terms offered were rejected as too binding and inadequate. If France did not provide four million livres by the end of 1763, the council threatened to seek other solutions. The prospect of an alignment of the Hats and the court faction within the Cap party, and of a constitutional reform which would have restored some of the powers of the monarchy, prompted the Russians to take an active role, offering subsidies to support the 'patriots' who opposed such moves. Britain, which had not been represented in Stockholm since 1748, was also alarmed at the prospect of France securing the service of Swedish vessels in the event of a future conflict. In August 1764, Lord Sandwich wrote to Goodricke, appointed envoy extraordinary to Stockholm, that the Swedish navy 'makes our Connexions with that Crown a principal Object to Great Britain', and a sum of £4,000 was earmarked for payment of bribes to the anti-Hat party to counter French plans to secure naval assistance from Sweden.[25]

The sums of money expended by foreign powers in the run-up to the elections of 1764 had little effect on the final outcome. The Caps swept to victory in the three non-noble estates on a tide of general discontent with the Hats' mismanagement of affairs. The Caps built their following on opposition to the conduct of the war, government extravagance and inflationary policies. They attacked the Hats' policy of favouring overseas trade and manufacturing to the detriment of agriculture, mining and internal trade. The former Hat Anders Bachmansson (ennobled as Nordenkrantz) fulminated against the abuse of power by office-holders and the confusion of administrative responsibility with legislative sovereignty. Nordenkrantz held that all power derived from the people, not the government, which had to be made accountable to the legislature, composed of and elected by men of adequate and independent means. His radical views alarmed the moderate Cap leaders, but appealed to those sections of society excluded from power by the coalition of bureaucrats, manufacturers and powerful city merchants. According to P.-E. Brolin, the decisive factor behind the Caps' victory was social, rather than economic: the

25. Metcalf M 1977 *Russia, England and Swedish party politics 1762–1766*. Stockholm–Totowa, NJ, p. 84.

wealthy merchants with their aristocratic connections and the municipal bureaucrats were swept away, replaced by the aspiring middle classes.[26] In Stockholm, the grip of the mercantile plutocracy was shattered, the leadership of the wealthy merchant Gustaf Kierman replaced by that of the tanner John Westrin. Forced by the action of the king and the Hat bureaucracy to summon a new *riksdag* for 1769, and having made themselves unpopular by a variety of harsh measures, the Caps were defeated in the elections; but they were to return to power in 1771. In this last meeting of the estates before the *coup* of 1772 put an end to the Age of Liberty, the onslaught on noble privilege begun in 1765 was resumed. A pamphleteer of 1770 had claimed that party quarrels were far less devastating than internecine strife between the social orders; in a letter to his mother in February 1772, Gustav III claimed that 'there are no longer Caps or Hats; there is the nobility on the one side and the other three orders on the other'.[27]

The degree of class conflict was perhaps not as acute as the king affected to believe: the non-noble estates were no premature Jacobins. Nevertheless, change was in the air. In Denmark, the queen's lover Johann Friedrich Struensee had shunted aside the old guard and had released a veritable avalanche of reforms. Peter III's manifesto on the freedom of the nobility in 1762 had removed the theoretical underpinnings of serfdom in the Russian empire, and, if the Russian peasantry had to wait another century for their final emancipation, the whole issue of land reform was at least placed squarely on the agenda of debate. The propositions laid before the Livonian *Landtag* in 1765 by governor-general Browne and the ideas of land reform advanced by Catherine II's protégé Eisen seemed to threaten the entrenched privileges of the Baltic nobility. Middle-class intellectuals and *literati* took advantage of relaxed press censorship to publish their views, and established associations and societies for the promotion of the 'common good'. Urban traders began to band together to promote their interests against the monopolies and restrictions of the privileged mercantile and manufacturing oligarchies. Even those who hankered for a return to past glories admitted that this was best achieved through reform. The financial crisis which affected all northern European countries after the Seven Years' War revealed the inadequacies of a system which sought on the one hand to maximise the resources of

---

26. Brolin P-E 1953 *Hattar och mössor i borgarståndet 1760–1766.* Uppsala. Söderberg T 1956 *Den namnlösa medelklassen.* Stockholm. For an assessment of Brolin's work, see Metcalf 1977, pp. 274–5.
27. Barton A 1986 *Scandinavia in the revolutionary era 1760–1815,* p. 79.

the state – thereby encouraging individual self-interest – but on the other maintained a rigid system of controls and regulations which threatened to choke all enterprise. As the 'philosophical century' entered its sixth decade, patriots everywhere prepared to launch their onslaught on the closed, corrupt and outmoded world of the regulated state.

CHAPTER THIRTEEN

State and society in the Age of Enlightenment

THE BALTIC ECONOMY

The Four Horsemen of the Apocalypse cut a deep swathe through the lands of the Baltic during the first two decades of the eighteenth century. Hard on the heels of the great famine which afflicted the eastern Baltic region in 1696–7 followed the ravages of war and pestilence. Almost two-thirds of the peasant population of Estonia and Livonia perished during the plague, which, spreading northwards from Constantinople, reached Poland in 1708–9 and the shores of the Baltic a year later. Once it had taken hold, there was little that could be done by the handful of doctors, with only the most rudimentary knowledge of the causes and treatment of the disease. Between September 1709 and April 1710, 9,368 people, a quarter of the population of Königsberg, died of the plague and related illnesses: mortality rates in Riga and Reval were even higher, whilst in the smaller towns of Livonia and Estonia, the population was reduced to a mere handful. The pestilence crossed the Baltic to Sweden in 1710, carrying off as many as 40,000 people in the capital, and entered Denmark in November 1710 in spite of quarantine measures. Helsingør lost 40 per cent of its population, Copenhagen a third.

The tide of war carried before it a flood of refugees. As many as 20,000 fled from Finland during the Russian invasion. The council estimated that there were 15,000 fugitives from the war in Stockholm alone in 1715, with a further 8,000 scattered along the Bothnian coastline. Poland–Lithuania and the Baltic provinces suffered the ravages of war in addition to those of pestilence. Dorpat was virtually razed to the ground in 1708, after the burghers had been ordered by the Russian authorities to evacuate the town, taking with them their valuables and even the lead from the roof of the town hall. The survivors did not return from their exile in Vologda and Ustyug until 1714. Twenty years later, there were still only 69 houses in a town which had boasted 300 dwellings in 1699. Recovery was slow in the other towns of Estonia. The population of Reval had not regained its pre-1710 level by the end of the eighteenth century, in spite of a rising birth-rate and an influx of immigrants, many from Germany. Almost as many of the 1,194 new citizens accepted by Reval town council between 1710 and 1786 came from Germany (490) as from the surrounding region (518). The old urban patriciate, though it suffered grievous losses during the plague years, was by no means replaced by these newcomers: surviving members of leading families such as the Dunckers, Clayhills and Nottbecks in Reval filled the ranks of the magistracy and the town's gilds in the 1720s. The citizens of Dorpat also seem to have opted for continuity, for the first burghermaster appointed after the return from exile, Philipp Kellner, had been town notary and secretary before 1708.[1]

The havoc wrought by war and disease occurred during a period of long-term agricultural depression. Grain prices continued their downward curve which had set in during the Thirty Years' War. In East Prussia and Lithuania, farmers fed grain to their cattle or left it to rot in the fields, so low was the price during the first decade of the century. Exports of grain from Danzig in the early eighteenth century slumped to a mere fraction of what had been sent westwards during the heyday of the trade a century earlier. World cereal prices began to rise again from the 1740s, but Polish grain production in 1800 was still barely two-thirds of what it had been two hundred years earlier. The Danish cattle trade, already in decline, was dealt a further blow in the 1740s by a murrain which carried off some two million beasts over a seven-year period.

Innovations and improvements were slow to penetrate into northern Europe. In Slesvig-Holstein, one of the most advanced regions, a form of convertible husbandry, with regular rotation of fallow and grain crops on enclosed, hedged fields, was practised. The 'Hollander' dairies which dotted the fertile plains of the duchies supplied the cities of northern Germany and the Netherlands with butter and cheese, and the cows provided an adequate supply of manure for the fields. Neglect of animal husbandry was the measure of agrarian backwardness. The protein needs of the peasant family could be supplied more

1. Hartmann S 1973 *Reval im Nordischen Krieg* Quellen und Studien zur baltischen Geschichte 1. Bonn–Godesberg, pp. 82–90. Rauch G von 1983 Der Wiederaufbau der Stadt Dorpat *Zeitschrift für Ostforschung* **32**: 482.

easily by a farinaceous diet, supplemented by fish and game: stock-rearing was generally limited to draught oxen, and the upkeep of even these animals over the long winter months was a drain on meagre resources. Grazing pastures were in short supply: only 5 per cent on average of the land-holding of the Prussian peasantry, for example. The inevitable consequence was inadequate manuring and poor grain yields from land which was poorly drained, broken by the hook plough rather than turned, and harrowed with primitive wooden implements. Improved sowing and harvesting techniques and the use of more efficient implements advocated in manuals such as Johann Heinrich Denffer's *Vernunft- und erfahrungsmässiger Discours* (Mitau, 1740) and Jacob Serenius' *Engelske åkermannen* (Stockholm, 1727), or decreed by royal order as in Prussia, did little to change age-old farming practices and beliefs. William Jacob noted in 1819 that ploughs in East Prussia were still made largely of wood, beasts were tethered to implements by ropes, and sowing drills were virtually unknown. Rationalists might scoff at the idea that bears would not eat oats sown when the wind was in the north or that apple trees planted when the wind was in the south would turn out to be wormy, but the peasants of Livonia continued to abide by such time-honoured folk wisdom.[2]

In the midst of the agricultural depression, Frederick William I embarked upon an ambitious resettlement programme in the Lithuanian border region of East Prussia, designed not only to colonise this remote area, but also to bring it more firmly under central administrative control. Settlers were brought in from Germany, including a large contingent of religious refugees from Salzburg. Not all came willingly, and those who tried to escape were pursued by patrolling hussars. Frederick William was much concerned to introduce 'German' farming methods and techniques into these areas, often ignoring climatic and soil differences, and favouring men from Magdeburg and the Mark over locals in his appointments of bailiffs and stewards. The programme encountered many setbacks, which the choleric monarch was inclined to blame on his subordinates. The towns founded in the

2. As the writer of a textbook on agriculture published in 1753 observed, the young bears would easily be able to grind up the grain: the maxim could thus only apply to toothless old bears. Meder B 1961 *Der Strukturwandel in der baltischen Lebensart um die Mitte des 18. Jahrhunderts* Veröffentlichungen der Ostdeutschen Forschungsstelle im Lande Nordrhein–Westfalen 3. Dortmund, p. 21. See also Transehe–Roseneck A von 1890 *Gutsherr und Bauer in Livland im 17 und 18 Jahrhundert* Abhandlungen aus dem Staatswissenschaftlichen Seminar zu Strassburg 7. Strassburg, pp. 122–7, for the state of agriculture in Livonia; and Jacob W 1826 *Report on the trade in foreign corn and on the agriculture of the north of Europe*. London, pp. 47ff. Blum J 1978 *The end of the old order in rural Europe*. Princeton, is an excellent overview of the general situation.

area were too small to sustain and develop an urban trading economy, and functioned principally as markets for the produce of royal demesnes, which was also channelled in large quantities and at subsidised prices into the royal magazines. The indigenous peasantry were reluctant to adopt the German plough, a measure decreed by law in 1731, fearing this would place even greater demands on their draught animals when they performed boon work. Peasants were ordered to grow potatoes under threat of a beating if they disobeyed, and stewards 'often had to go to the villages to see if the royal edict was being followed, especially in regard to cultivation in the German manner', and to ensure that the peasants were not wasting their time drinking coffee or smoking tobacco. Resettlement and land reclamation helped revive the Prussian agrarian economy, which benefited from the protectionist policy of the crown, designed to keep out cheap Polish grain, and the doubling of the population of Brandenburg–Prussia between 1688 and 1740. But although farming in Prussia showed signs of recovery during a period of general depression, it remained backward and low-yielding.[3]

The agricultural depression had less effect on the largely self-sufficient rural economy of Sweden and Finland. Spared from the terrible crop failures and epidemics which had afflicted the kingdom in the previous century, the population grew steadily, from 1.4 million in 1700 to 2.3 million in Sweden between 1700 and 1800. The rapid recovery began in the 1720s and 1730s. The high surfeit of births over deaths in these years faltered during the bad harvests and war years after 1736, regaining its upward momentum once more from the mid-century onwards. In the eastern half of the kingdom, the demographic recovery was even more remarkable. Reduced to just over 300,000 inhabitants at the end of the Northern War, the population of Finland almost doubled between 1750 (421,537) and 1800 (832,639).

In regions where noble estates were thick on the ground, the number of new leasehold farms (*torpar*), often created out of virgin land, increased significantly. From mid-century onwards, consolidation of land holdings by a process of repartitioning (*storskiftet*) began, initiated by Jakob Faggot. These activities were not however accompanied by any significant general improvement in land management or farming techniques, in spite of the work of enlightened landowners such as Sten Bielke, who introduced new grass strains on his estate at Lövsta,

3. Henning F-W 1969 *Bauernwirtschaft und Bauerneinkommen in Ostpreussen im 18 Jahrhundert* Beihefte zum Jahrbuch der Albertus-Universität 30. Würzburg, pp. 23ff. Terveen F 1952 Das Retablissement König Friedrich Wilhelms I in Preussen-Litauen von 1714 bis 1740 *Zeitschrift für Ostforschung* 1: 500–15.

and scientists such as Pehr Kalm and Carl Linné, who advocated the cultivation of lucerne. Increased cultivation of oats probably led to better provision of fodder for livestock, but attempts to persuade the peasant farmers to grow potatoes met with limited success before the 1770s. Anders Berch, the first professor of economics at Uppsala university, displayed scale models of farm implements in his *Theatrum oeconomico-mechanicum* and attempted to improve plough designs, but few of his ideas were taken up. As late as 1775, sickles were still being used in preference to scythes in the Kalmar area to harvest spring barley and rye. Though Faggot envisaged Skåne as the breadbasket of Sweden, his vision was not to be realised until the enclosure movement was well under way and more rational methods of crop cultivation put into practice by landlords such as Gustav David Hamilton and Rutger Maclean. In Sweden, as in the other lands of northern Europe, real improvements in farming did not get under way until the second half of the century.

The problem of deserted and impoverished farms was to persist in Denmark well into the eighteenth century, though the numbers of smallholders and cottars continued to grow. Increased entry fines, and the burdens of labour service and other obligations made farming an unattractive proposition for the peasant: it has been estimated that up to one-third of tenants were evicted for failing to keep up with their payments and obligations. The plight of landowners hit by the continuing agricultural depression and of their even more unfortunate tenants was not eased by the often contradictory and vacillating policies of governments striving to meet their debts. The Danish state debt in 1719 stood at over four million rigsdaler, with a further million pledged in loans. By 1730, the debt had been cut by a million, but the crown had had to sell off estates at unfavourable prices in a depressed land market. The reintroduction of conscription in 1701, which obliged landowners to furnish recruits according to the size of their holdings, and the abolition of *vornedskab* (thereby allowing peasants to move freely once their period of tenure was up), posed problems in regions where abandoned farmsteads were common. Under pressure from the landowners, the crown restored and even extended the curbs on movement in rural areas in 1733: all males between 14 and 36 years of age were to remain on the estate where they were born (*stavnsbånd*) as long as their lord could provide them with employment. To defend Danish agriculture, a ban on foreign imports of grain into Denmark and southern Norway was also instituted. The principal argument advanced for improving the depressed state of agriculture was fiscal: few advocated more rational farm management or the introduction of new crops. Compulsion was the order of the day for the peasantry: it was even suggested that women should also be subject to the *stavnsbånd* to solve the problem of a lack of milkmaids. Enlightened landowners such as count Hans Rantzau-Ascheberg, who granted his tenants the freehold of their farms in 1739, were rare. In the eyes of most proprietors, the peasants were 'lazy, stubborn, given to smoking tobacco and drinking spirits, rude to those in authority over them... in sum, fear of punishment is the only thing which drives them to do good, or at least, what has the appearance of goodness.'[4] Though peasants did occasionally resort to violence, and more often, to petitioning the king, their principal weapon was dumb insolence and crafty sabotage.

The number of free peasants in Pomerania declined sharply during the eighteenth century. Two-thirds of the rural population were enserfed, and those who were not were obliged to accept fixed-term leases, often for short periods. The average size of peasant holdings declined significantly during the eighteenth century, as the process of engrossment by demesne owners proceeded unhindered. The dispossessed joined the growing ranks of the landless. The ducal demesnes in Swedish Pomerania were mostly pawned to the gentry and not redeemed until the late 1760s, thereafter being leased out. The *Ritterschaft* in Swedish Pomerania, their political position strengthened by the fact that the major towns had passed under Prussian control, and aware of Frederick William's recognition of the allodial claims of the landowners in his domains, were able to negotiate a favourable acknowledgment of their claim that fiefs (*Lehnsgüte*) could only be held by feudal tenure. The Livonian and Estonian nobility also claimed the privilege of exclusive ownership of land, and insisted on their right to redeem estates which had been sold to burghers. Article eleven of the treaty of Nystad promised the revocation of Karl XI's *reduktion* in the Baltic provinces, a measure already set in motion a year earlier by Peter I's commission of restoration. The creation of a closed noble corporation in early seventeenth-century Kurland was finally emulated (in 1747 for Livonia, 1756 for Estonia) with the inclusion of some 120 Estonian and 170 Livonian noble families in the matriculation rolls. The dismantling of the work of the *reduktion* deprived the peasantry of the small degree of protection afforded by the crown; and the declaration of baron Otto von Rosen in 1739, that the nobility had acquired dominion over the peasantry by virtue of the conquest of the

---

4. Cited in Holm E 1894 *Danmark-Norges Historie* (4 vols). Copenhagen, vol. 2, p. 393. See also Bjørn C 1981 *Bonde, herremand, konge. Bonden i 1700-tallets Danmark*. Copenhagen, p. 32.

land by the German knights, was a further reiteration of the Roman law principles which underpinned the system of *Leibeigenschaft*. As in Denmark and the duchies, there was as yet little sign of a more enlightened attitude towards the land question and the peasantry in the ranks of the Baltic nobility.

In the frontier region of Kexholm and the district of Viborg ceded to Russia, crop failure and heavy taxation meant that depopulation was not halted until the end of the 1720s. In the 1730s, a more enlightened policy of tax reliefs and subsidies for agriculture, supported by repopulation measures and helped by good harvests, brought short-term recovery. Timber sawn into deals and planks in sawmills using the Dutch multi-blade frames had already begun to supplant tar as a major export item from the region by 1700. Forty years later, Viborg on the Russian side and Fredrikshamn on the Swedish side of the frontier had overtaken Narva as the principal exporters of sawn timber, though fears of deforestation caused the Russian government to ban the export of beams and to restrict the production of the sawmills. Further crop failures added to the difficulties of the peasantry, whose income from the sale of timber was thus reduced, forcing many into debt.[5]

Although the new frontier with Russia was clearly marked out, it ran through some of the wildest and most inaccessible terrain in the entire Swedish kingdom, where royal proclamations were rarely read in the scattered parish churches, and whose inhabitants received little protection from the robber bands which periodically raided their farms. By 1734, the frontier line was so overgrown that special parties had to be sent out to clear the boundary markers. For the local population, the frontier was a flexible concept, at least in peacetime. The citizens of Lovisa, for example, complained in 1769 of the 'familiarity' of the peasantry and crown officials with illegal trade across the frontier: their outburst was occasioned by the local crown bailiff's attempt to export timber via Viborg from his sawmill on the Swedish side of the frontier.[6]

The loss of territory in Karelia made Finland once more a frontier zone for the Swedish kingdom, as it had been until 1617. At the easternmost extremity of the Gulf of Finland, moreover, a new city was rising on the banks of the river Neva. Within twenty-five years of its

5. Ranta R 1985 *Vanhan Suomen talouselämä 1721–1743* (2 vols) Historiallisia Tutkimuksia 130. Helsinki, vol. 1, pp. 109ff.

6. Cederberg A 1911 *Pohjois-Karjalan kauppa-olot vv. 1721–1775*. Helsinki, pp. 189–90. Wirilander K 1962 Gränsmarken och rikskärnan. Östfinsk förhållanden och opinioner såsom element i Finlands utveckling till autonom stat *Scandia* **28**: 343.

foundation, the population of St Petersburg had reached 40,000, and rose to 90,000 by mid-century. Amongst the new citizens of the city were many immigrants from the surrounding countryside. A Danish visitor in the 1730s observed that servants were as likely to speak Finnish or German as Russian: the Finnish community alone numbered over 1,500 members in the 1730s, more than the number of inhabitants of many of Finland's towns.[7] The city's influence was felt over a wide area, providing the peasants of Ingria and the Karelian isthmus with a market for their produce and an opportunity for seasonal employment. The existence of a growing metropolis, the capital of the Russian empire, on Sweden's Finnish frontier, not only symbolised the shift of political power in the north; it was also a potential alternative to Stockholm for the Finnish economy.

Stockholm, however, remained an important commercial centre for western Finland and the Swedish hinterland. Scores of peasant and small town traders from the Bothnian coast supplied fish, butter, meat and domestic utensils for the needs of the city's population, which grew from 43,000 in 1720 to almost 72,000 in 1757. Stockholm was also a good market for the small producers of specialist goods, such as the stocking-makers of Nådendal and the laceworkers of Raumo. On the other hand, the degree of control over the administration and economic life of the Finnish provinces exercised by the government in Stockholm was irksome, and not only for the town merchants barred from direct trade with foreign markets. In 1738, the peasants of Halikko and Piikkiö petitioned for a governor-general, or at least a special department for Finland in the treasury and commerce board, none of whose members had ever been in Finland or knew anything about the country. This 'strange request' caused some discussion, and although nothing came of it, the ideas it expressed were to resurface. A second occupation of Finland by Russian troops in 1742–3 aroused great concern, which the Finnish deputation at the *riksdag* of 1746–7 was not slow to exploit. On the recommendation of the deputation, a governor-general was appointed, though his primary task was the strengthening of Finland's defences. The prospects for improving the economy of the remaining Finnish provinces were dimmed by fear of renewed invasion and loss of further territory, and a commonly held belief that, lacking all confidence in the crown's ability to defend them, the Finns would throw themselves at the mercy of the Russians. Although Finland's share of the population of the entire kingdom rose

7. Engman M 1983 *St Petersburg och Finland. Migration och influens 1703–1917* Bidrag till kännedom av Finlands natur och folk 130. Helsingfors, pp. 64–94.

from 19.1 per cent in 1750 to 26.2 per cent in 1800, there was a marked disparity between the western and eastern halves of the realm. The lack of inland towns was a severe drawback, especially on the eastern frontier: peasants preferred to cross the frontier to buy and sell in Viborg rather than make the long and tiresome journey to the new town of Lovisa (described by the poet Leopold as a 'scandal of a town' in 1788). Whereas the towns of Sweden proper could support 62,440 craftsmen by 1815, there were just over 3,000 in the Finnish towns. Only 2,000 persons were engaged in manufacturing, mostly in ironworks and sawmills along the southern coast: in Sweden proper, 58,000 were employed in mining and ironworks alone, with a further 17,442 in rural manufactories.[8]

Kongens Nytorv, with its gilded statue of Christian V in Roman attire, was the ceremonial centre of Copenhagen; here the king could review his troops, in a city where almost one-third of the population was employed in the service of the army, navy or court. Vast sums were spent in the reign of Frederik IV (1699–1730) on building palaces, churches and accommodation for the garrison. In spite of improvements, such as paving and street-lighting and the establishment of a fire-fighting service, the outward appearance of the Danish capital still left a good deal to be desired. The city's canals were clogged with filth, the quays of the harbour were in such a bad state of repair that ships could not tie up there, and the many straw-thatched wooden houses were a potential fire hazard. In 1728, much of the city went up in flames. A special tax had to be levied to finance the rebuilding, with tax and excise exemptions for the citizens and would-be settlers. Government efforts to ensure that the town was rebuilt in brick and stone had to be tacitly abandoned, though compulsory fire insurance was decreed by royal order in 1731. The city remained unhygienic, its water supply tainted by the foul waters of the canals and drains. Only through immigration did the population of Copenhagen rise: between 1735 and 1784, deaths in the city exceeded births by over 20,000 though the total population increased by 15,000 to reach 90,000 by the end of the century.

Overshadowed by the capital, whose commercial interests were favoured by the government, the provincial towns of Denmark showed little sign of economic vitality. A report on the state of

8. Sweden proper also had five times as many secondary schools as Finland. Juva E 1947 *Suomen tie Uudestakaupungista Haminaan 1721–1809*. Helsinki, pp. 92–96, 152, 156–9. Castrén G 1958 *Humanister och humaniora* Skrifter utgivna av Svenska Litteratursällskapet i Finland 368. Helsingfors, p. 330. Jutikkala E *et al.* (eds) 1980 *Suomen taloushistoria* (3 vols). Helsinki, vol. 1, p 408. Samuelsson K 1968 *From great power to welfare state. 300 years of Swedish social development*. London, p. 136.

commerce in the provinces of Denmark drawn up in 1735 painted a gloomy picture of local merchants reduced to the role of hawking the goods brought to the towns by Lübeck merchants. The promotion and encouragement of manufactories reaped little reward. The silver mine at Kongsberg in Norway was no longer very productive, and the Norwegian ironworks were hard pressed by Swedish competition, in spite of protectionist measures. High customs duties made smuggling profitable, especially along the Norwegian coastline. The customs at Kristiania and Drammen yielded only a tenth of the estimated amount, and the government at one stage considered farming out the collection of customs to private entrepreneurs. Danish shipping to the Mediterranean was affected by the seizure of ships and crews by pirates, a nuisance which their Swedish rivals were able to reduce by concluding a treaty with the Barbary states. The Greenland trade did not prosper, and the company had to be wound up eight years after its formation. The East India company had also to be refloated in 1729.

The setting up in 1735 of a Board of Trade, the *General Landets Øonomie og Kommercekollegium*, inaugurated a new phase of mercantilist policies in the kingdom and the duchies. The *Kommercekollegium* was a firm believer in encouraging private enterprise, but the state continued to play a leading role. Most manufactories needed considerable financial support, and few made a clear profit. Neither John Beckett nor his successor Charles Maillot could turn a silk-spinning mill into a profitable concern: J. F. Borchholt received a subsidy of 20,000 rdr to build a silk-spinning mill in Altona and to bring workers from Leipzig, but the buildings were never completed and the enterprise had to be taken over by the state. Others simply pocketed the subsidy and failed to appear in the kingdom. There was much resistance from Danish wholesalers and retailers, who considered domestically produced articles to be of inferior quality and of little appeal to the customer. To counter this, a store was set up in the capital to which manufacturers could send their wares for sale. But, in spite of an investment of half a million rigsdaler in the form of subsidies and loans for the promotion of manufactures, the yield to the crown was meagre.

The picture was rather similar in Sweden, where the numbers engaged in manufacturing – mainly in the textile industry – constituted a minute fraction of the population. Retailers complained about the poor quality of native-produced textiles, and the government had to lavish subsidies on the manufactories to keep them going. Home-based crafts (*slöjd*) on the other hand flourished, and were equated with agriculture as a major source of earnings by a speaker in the *riksdag* of 1771. Home crafts flourished in less fertile regions such as the rocky west coast, or Norrland, where flax was grown for linen-weaving. The pedlars of Västergötland travelled all over the kingdom selling the wares of their home district, much to the annoyance of the town traders. Other itinerants performed specialist labour, such as the men from Dalarna who supplied the citizens of Stockholm with their winter fuel, or the gangs of threshers from Halland who went into Skåne every summer. So important was this migrant labour for the local economy that exceptions had to be made in the servant legislation of 1739, which sought to force surplus labour into farm work. The return of the herring shoals to the western Swedish coastal waters in the second half of the century drew large numbers of seasonal workers from Halland, attracted by the prospect of earning more in three months than they could expect to earn in nine months of farmwork. Farmers complained that they were forced to pay higher wages as a consequence of this migration, even though it took place in the slack winter months; officials believed that labour was being diverted from useful projects such as land reclamation; and moralists blamed the overcrowded conditions in which the migrant workers lived for the spread of promiscuity, licence and social diseases. There were fears that the migrants took with them such vast quantities of provisions that there was practically nothing left behind, and the government, suspecting with some justification that the migrants were selling some of what they took with them, attempted to impose restrictions on the amounts taken. The workers for their part complained that they could not subsist on fresh herring alone, which they believed was injurious to the health if eaten constantly – a point contested by the provincial governor, who felt that the deleterious effects of a herring diet were probably neutralised by the 'tender solicitude' of the saltery and fish-oil factory owners, who ensured that their employees were well supplied with *brännvin*.[9]

Mining continued to provide Sweden with its major export commodity, bar-iron, most of which was sent to Britain. Russian competition in the 1730s coincided with a fall in prices, and in an effort to force prices up again, the Board of Mining fixed a maximum production level for each ironworks and a maximum total output of 46,650 tons. The ironmasters were willing to comply with this and formed a cartel to protect their interests, with an executive body (*Jernkontoret*). The creation of a cartel was an indication of the conservatism of the

9. Utterström G 1959 Migratory labour and the herring fisheries of western Sweden in the eighteenth century *Scandinavian Economic History Review* **7**: 3–40.

Swedish ironmasters, who preferred stability and security to unfettered competition; but the technological breakthrough at Abraham Darby's Coalbrookdale works, dismissed by the president of the *Kommerskollegium* in 1724 as a costly failure, was to pose a severe challenge to the Swedish iron industry in the course of time. The fuel problem bedevilled the industry, for rapidly rising transport costs compelled the works to procure charcoal wherever possible from local sources. Tenant-farmers and crofters could produce charcoal at low cost since this was part of their rent agreement, but when fuel had to be bought from outside, it was expensive. The sharp rise in marginal costs may have persuaded the ironmasters to resist the temptation of expanding production when prices began to rise once more. Although the volume of Swedish bar-iron exports to Britain remained fairly constant, Sweden's overall position in terms of iron consumption in Britain fell as rising demand was met by Russian and British producers. Recruitment of workers was hindered by restrictive legislation aimed at keeping competition for labour to a minimum, but the static nature of the industry offered relatively few job vacancies in any case. Jobs were usually filled within the family, and this ensured the preservation of the isolated, homogenous Walloon communities until well into the nineteenth century. All the masters, their assistants and forgehands at Österby had Walloon names as late as 1791, and almost three-quarters of all marriages contracted amongst the families of skilled ironworkers at this forge between 1712 and 1815 were between partners with Walloon names. Many of the workers were also farmers: the hammersmiths' ordinance of 1766 decreed, for example, that masters and their assistants were entitled to a cattle shed and free fodder for their beasts in addition to a cottage or rooms. Works owners also provided food and other necessities on a truck system. In remote forested areas such as Säfnäs, where cultivation was impracticable, something like half of the total income of ironworkers during the eighteenth century was spent on grain. Workers were usually in debt to the truck shop because their wages did not suffice to cover their needs. Though debts were periodically written off by the owners, they served to keep the labour force tied to the plant, for an indebted worker was not entitled to quit his employment.[10]

The marketing of Swedish iron was controlled by the merchant

10. Hildebrand K-G 1958 Foreign markets for Swedish iron in the eighteenth century *Scandinavian Economic History Review* **6**: 3–52. Boëthius B 1958 Swedish iron and steel 1600–1955 *Scandinavian Economic History Review* **6**:144–75. Montelius S 1966 Recruitment and conditions of life of Swedish ironworkers during the eighteenth and nineteenth centuries *Scandinavian Economic History Review* **14**: 1–17.

houses of Stockholm and Göteborg, and these firms played a major role in the financing of the industry, advancing short-term credits to the ironmasters to cover the costs of production. The ironmasters' association also financed the trade from a fund levied on forge production, and advanced loans to the merchant houses. Although these secretive money-lending operations caused political controversy, they were modest in comparison with the activities of the *riksbank*, which was permitted from 1735 to lend money on fixed property and commodities such as iron.

The development of banking and of a domestic credit market facilitated business operations within the northern kingdoms: international trade, however, was heavily reliant on the foreign money markets of Amsterdam, Hamburg and London. During the eighteenth century, both kingdoms participated on an increasing scale in world trade. Unlike his treasury, which strongly upheld the privileges of Copenhagen, Christian VI was prepared to grant favourable customs concessions to the provincial ports, which in the case of Norway stimulated entrepôt trading. Norwegian shipping also seized its opportunity during the Anglo-French war of the 1740s and entered in earnest into the Atlantic trade. The Danish–French commercial treaty of 1742 and the conflict between England and Spain allowed the merchants of Altona to build up their trade in the Mediterranean. A new Danish Asiatic Company was founded by royal octroi in 1732, with rights to use the colony of Trankebar on the Coromandel coast. The king and many high-ranking officials were amongst the leading shareholders of this company. Each shareholder was entitled to contribute to a 'circulating fund', used for fitting out and provisioning the ships bound for the East. This fund was also used as a reserve to counter market fluctuations, and as a means of raising further loans if need be. The outward-bound vessels carried iron, lead and copper as ballast, and some ironware, ships' stores and domestic cloth; but on average, 93 per cent of the value of the cargo destined for China, and 78 per cent destined for India was in specie, obtained until the 1760s through competitive tender. China tea was the most important single import item, both in terms of volume and value, and yielded the greatest profit (as much as 200–300 per cent). Cargoes sold at auction between 1734 and 1745 yielded over nine million rdr, giving an average annual income equivalent to the sale of grain to Norway and abroad. The West Indies trade also began to revive around mid-century. Exports of sugar from the plantations on the Danish island of St Croix increased tenfold between 1755 and 1764. In common with most colonial imports, it was destined for re-export, mostly to Germany and the Baltic region: refined sugar accounted for almost half the value of Copenhagen's exports in the 1760s. In 1745, the Copenhagen merchant fleet totalled 119 ships. With the exception of the seven big East Indiamen and a handful of vessels of more than 100 lasts' capacity, these were small craft, plying the waters of the Baltic. Similar small vessels crossed the Skagerrak with grain for southern Norway, or sailed from the west coast of Slesvig with corn and butter for Holland. Local entrepreneurs such as the Otte family in Eckern-förde built ships for the Mediterranean trade in their yards, and owned tile, faïence and textile factories. In Altona, the van der Smissen, Beets and de Vlieger families, descended from Mennonite immigrants, were major shipbuilders and carriers, operating with Danish licences. Further up the coast, the north Frisians had earned a reputation as whalers, shipping out in Dutch vessels bound for Iceland and Green-land (where they clashed with Danes engaged on the same errand).

The volume of goods exported from the Baltic tripled between 1720 and 1770, though the Dutch share of that trade declined from around half to less than a quarter. In November 1703, the startled skipper of the galiot *d'Juffrouw Anna* was lavishly rewarded by the tsar for having been the first to moor at the quayside of St Petersburg (the captain had expected to find the Swedish town of Nyen, on whose ashes the new town had arisen). This good beginning was not followed up by the Dutch, who were slow to abandon the Archangel route, unlike the English. Peter's ambitions for his new port outstripped its actual potential: an inexperienced bureaucracy, the lack of port facilities and the tsar's own hasty measures to divert trade from Archangel pro-voked protests and caused confusion. When Peter died in 1725, less than a quarter of all shipping from Russia's Baltic ports passing through the Sound was from St Petersburg, and it was not until the end of the century that St Petersburg overtook Riga as the major Russian port. In spite of attempts to develop a merchant fleet, Russia was obliged in 1759 to rely on the Swedes to carry supplies to the army in Prussia from St Petersburg. By the end of the 1770s, the Russian merchant marine consisted of a dozen or so large vessels, mostly captained by foreigners.[11]

Riga remained the major exporter of flax, linseed and hemp from the Baltic, and the city's merchants maintained rigorous quality checks through the institution known as the *brack*. Catherine II's

---

11. See Knoppers J 1976 *Dutch trade with Russia from the time of Peter I to Alexander I.* Montreal, pp. 146–55. Marperger P 1723 *Paul Jakob Marpergers...Moskowitischer Kauff-mann.* Lübeck, pp. 139–9, 162–3, 217.

policy of insisting that custom dues at the port be paid in foreign currency caused great annoyance to the merchants, and may have helped divert trade to Pernau and Reval; but the monopolistic and inflexible trade practices of the merchants also undermined Riga's position as the principal port of the Russian empire. Narva was the major timber-exporting port in the empire during the first half of the century. In 1756, tsarina Elizabeth banned timber exports from Narva as a measure against excessive deforestation. Although this ban was later lifted, the timber trade shifted to the capital, and was also being developed by the Finnish ports. After 1760, demand for building timber in Britain rose steeply, providing an opening for the Prussian port of Memel. In the peak year of 1792, 756 British ships, mostly in ballast, visited Memel to load up with balks and beams from the huge and relatively unexploited forests of the Lithuanian hinterland. Low customs duties added to the attractions of Memel, and drew the timber trade away from Danzig. The Swedish equivalent of the English Navigation Acts, the *produktplakat* of 1724, was designed to restrict imports to native vessels and carriers from the country of origin. It helped stimulate shipbuilding and the growth of the domestic merchant marine, but it also adversely affected Sweden's foreign trade. Foreign merchants preferred, for example, to buy their sawn boards at more advantageous prices and with fewer restrictions at the ports of Viborg and (after 1743) Fredrikshamn, on Russian territory. The amount of boards exported from Swedish Finnish ports in the period 1784–93 was less than a fifth of the amount shipped out of Viborg. To combat competition and falling prices after the Great Northern War, the college of commerce proposed the restoration of the tar company monopoly in 1723, a measure vigorously opposed by the towns along the Gulf of Bothnia. The government also sought to conserve the forests by limiting production. The Ostrobothnian towns were finally allowed to engage in active trade in 1766, and ports such as Uleåborg and Gamlakarleby rapidly became major exporters of pitch and tar. The tar trade of Viborg, on the other hand, suffered serious setbacks from competition, low prices and inept government policies in the first two decades of Russian rule, though the acquisition of further territory in eastern Finland after 1743 led to a revival.

RANK, STATUS AND THE WELL-ORDERED STATE

The subordination of the institutional church to the secular ruler which occurred in Reformation Europe meant that rulers had to assume the responsibility for overseeing man's ethical, social and religious conduct. The task of the ruler now shifted from the passive duty of preserving justice to the active task of fostering the productive energies of society and of providing the appropriate institutional framework. The patrimonial image of the kingdom as the God-given property of the sovereign – a view expressedly stated as late as 1683 by Christian V in his testament – gave way in the eighteenth century to the notion of the ruler as an enlightened leader of the nation – its first citizen, as Gustav III described himself, or, as Frederick II never tired of calling himself, *le premier serviteur de l'état*. The active interventionist policies which rulers adopted in order to promote the maximum use of resources, however, carried the risk of undermining the established socioeconomic order. As a result, policies were often confused and contradictory.[12] The royal council in Denmark, for example, recommended the abolition of most of the gilds in 1719: but even with royal backing, it proved impossible to put this into practice. Town magistrates generally upheld the gilds' complaints against competition from discharged soldiers, whom the king had permitted to practise trades in which they were skilled. By Christian VI's reign (1730–46), soldiers were only permitted to work for military personnel, and the government upheld the restrictive practices of the gilds. At the same time, however, its active promotion of manufactories did little to help the plight of provincial artisans. In attempting to enforce order, the crown also encountered opposition. The bailiffs appointed to round up beggars were unpopular, for the populace still held the medieval view of beggars as bearers of the sins of mankind. In parishes around Kolding, there were complaints in the 1740s that the cattle murrain had been brought to the district because the bailiffs had driven out the beggars, and there were instances of bailiffs being attacked or insulted in the execution of their duty in the capital.

In Prussia, armed police (*Landreuter*) patrolled every district of the state, enforcing a myriad of regulations. Some of these, such as preventive measures against the spread of contagious diseases, were eminently sensible; but others were plainly coercive, reflecting what Otto Hintze saw as the triumph of the cameralist-inspired notion of the state as an instrument of welfare and security, in which *raison d'état* prevailed. Nevertheless, the subjects of the Hohenzollerns frequently resisted the attempts to regulate their lives. Frederick William I soon realised the futility of trying to enforce prohibitions against pack-

12. Raeff M 1975 The well-ordered police state and the development of modernity in seventeenth and eighteenth-century Europe: An attempt at a comparative approach *American Historical Review* **80**: 1221–43.

merchants, demanded by entrenched corporations such as the iron-mongers of Berlin. The travelling pedlar supplied a need which the closed and regulated corporations could not, and his customers not infrequently set upon the policemen who tried to stop his activities. Frederick William was forced to lift restrictions on the import and sale of Bay salt in Königsberg in 1727 because Polish and Lithuanian merchants preferred to go elsewhere rather than buy the dearer and inferior salt from Halle, shipped to Königsberg via Stettin. Rulers were often at odds with their advisers. Frederick II protected and promoted manufactories in Berlin and Potsdam, but his administrators in East Prussia supported the interests of urban trade and sought to persuade the king of the dangers of a restrictive policy. A memorandum submitted to the king in 1753 by the *Kammerkollegium* in Königsberg argued strongly in favour of an unrestricted trade policy which would attract foreign merchants, manufacturers and artisans to the province: if the hindrances upon trade with Prussia's neighbours were not lifted, the entrepreneurial will of the commercial classes would be sapped, and the entire province would be reduced to poverty. Frederick acknowledged the validity of the arguments, but countered by saying his domains were poor and needed protection against competition.[13]

The effective dismantling of royal power in 1720 gave the *riksdag* an important role in the affairs of Sweden, both as a forum for debate and as an initiator of legislation. The draconian state controls instituted by Görtz were rescinded, and although the principles of state regulation were by no means abandoned, they were vigorously challenged and debated in print and in the *riksdag*. Christoffer Polhem and Lars Salvius voiced reservations about restrictions on foreign trade long before the major onslaught launched in the *riksdag* in 1765, for example. Economics was a favoured subject for public debate during the Age of Liberty. The Gothicism of Rudbeck provided an inspiration for many advocates of the new doctrine of 'utilism', the exploitation of the land's resources to the benefit of each estate, the wellbeing of the realm and the glory of the king and fatherland. The philosophy of a benevolent Creator propounded by Leibnitz and Wolff and the work of Linné and his pupils encouraged the utilists to believe that Sweden could be turned into a land 'overflowing with milk, honey and silkworms'.[14] The founding of the Swedish Academy of Sciences in

13. Martineit W 1960 Ostpreussische Manufaktur- und Merkantilpolitik im 18 Jahrhundert *Zeitschrift für Ostforschung* **9**: 491.
14. Lindroth S 1978 *Svensk lärdomshistoria. 3 Frihetstiden*. Stockholm, pp. 91ff.

1739 gave added impetus to the quest for knowledge which could be turned to the benefit and welfare of society and the fatherland. In 1721, the polymath of an earlier age, Christoffer Polhem, had declared that: 'a kingdom without economy, commerce and manufacture is like a human being without a body, feet or hands, and without mechanics, physics and mathematics is like the same person without life, memory or understanding'.[15] Men of the younger generation such as the Carleson brothers, Jakob Faggot, Anders Berch and Pehr Kalm took up that message. Swedish theorists were by no means indifferent or hostile to agriculture: all the gifts of nature were to be utilised for the common good, as Anders von Höpken made clear in launching the work of the Academy in 1739. Sweden was no less well endowed by nature than were other lands, declared Jakob Faggot in 1745, whilst twenty years later, Pehr Gadd could proclaim that the Swedish climate was amongst the most favourable in the world for farming. Students under Gadd's supervision at Åbo academy wrote their dissertations on how to improve agriculture in Finland. The disciples of Carl Linné travelled widely, bringing back seeds and plants from all corners of the world. Pehr Kalm, whose account of his travels in North America appeared in three volumes between 1753 and 1761, spent the remainder of his life as professor of economics at Åbo, busying himself with projects ranging from improving the water-courses of northern Finland to abolishing excessive holidays.

On the whole, Swedish writers tended to eschew closed systems of economic thought. Linné, for example, explicitly repudiated cameral-ism in his thoughts on the foundations of economics. What disting-uished these enthusiastic scholars and scientists was an unbounded faith in the natural sciences; a belief in the benevolence of nature, even in the cold North: and a passion for collecting data, which has left its mark to the present day in Sweden and Finland. Their ideas for the improvement of the kingdom bore distinctly autarkic features, and brought them into conflict with more orthodox mercantilists like Jonas Alströmer, the founder of a large but unsuccessful textile manu-factory at Alingsås, who believed the future prosperity of an infertile kingdom cursed with a wretched climate lay in industry and com-merce. All too often, expectations were not fulfilled: Lidbeck's hopes of rearing millions of silkworms on his mulberry trees in Lund were

---

15. Forsman K 1947 Studier i det svenska 1700-talets ekonomiska litteratur *Skrifter utgivna av Svenska Litteratursällskapet i Finland: Historiska och litteraturhistoriska studier* **23**: 112ff., 119.

dashed, but his failure was not as expensive as that of the silk industry, which imported its raw material from abroad.

Laws designed to conserve and regulate the supply of labour, such as the 1739 servant legislation which restricted the number of sons a farmer might keep on his farm, directed 'superfluous' household workers to take service as hired hands and imposed severe penalties for vagrancy, reflected an anxiety about what was perceived to be a shortage of labour. Restrictions on the subdivision of farms and on colonisation were imposed in much the same spirit. By the middle of the eighteenth century, however, a more optimistic view of the possibilities of increasing the population and hence, augmenting the wealth of the nation, began to make itself heard. In 1749, a central statistical bureau was established on the initiative of Pehr Wargentin, and national censuses were regularly conducted thereafter. A commission on health set up in 1737 worked for thirty years, setting in train a series of preventive measures to curb the epidemics which afflicted the population. The whole principle of restrictive legislation was attacked in a report from the lesser secret deputation of the estates in 1756, which declared that such laws 'render liberty practically unknown to the humbler but no less necessary classes of the nation, and the fatherland nothing more than a harsh stepmother whom they gladly abandon'.[16] Restrictions on the subdivision of farms were relaxed in 1746–7, and the creation of leasehold farms on crown and noble land was encouraged. Various schemes to promote earlier marriages and child-bearing were mooted, and landowners were urged to build cottages for married servants or those who wished to marry.

There was to be something of a Malthusian backlash at the end of the century against the optimism of the Age of Liberty, but the free flow of ideas and debate in mid-century Sweden stands in sharp contrast to the still heavily regulated state system of Prussia, where population increase was largely achieved by a mixture of inducements to settle and coercion. And although the administration between 1738 and 1765 was dominated by the Hats, a party which favoured commercial and industrial interests, the vigorous current of economic thought helped Sweden avoid the kind of dogged commitment to mercantilist principles followed in Christian VI's Denmark, where there was little or no open discussion of economic issues. Swedish writers on economics may have focused their attention on supply rather than demand, and as such, remained wedded to mercantilist

16. Utterström G 1962 Labour policy and population thought in eighteenth-century Sweden *Scandinavian Economic History Review* **10**: 272.

ideas: but they were also pre-eminently concerned with *practical* problems, which enabled them to break free of sterile theory. The struggle to transform Sweden's leading university into a modern institution capable of meeting the needs of state and society was taken up by the Hat-dominated government in the 1740s. The academic community was able to prevent the implementation of all the proposals of the commission on education, though a number of ideas were carried through, such as the introduction of a more career-oriented examination for would-be civil servants, and the creation of new chairs in experimental physics and chemistry. The university at Uppsala was at this time a flourishing institution, with a thousand students in 1740, new buildings such as the observatory and a distinguished list of professors, including the astronomer Anders Celsius and the renowned Carl Linné. On the southern shores of the Baltic, the new spirit of scientific enquiry had also established a foothold at the university in Königsberg, where student numbers rose from around 250 in the 1730s to over a thousand, one-third from other countries, a decade later. 'Moralistic weeklies', usually edited and produced by students, brought the ideas of the Enlightenment to the city. The bookseller J. J. Kanter, who set up business in the city in 1760, could number Kant, Herder and Hamann amongst the regular contributors to his *Königsbergische gelehrte und politische Zeitungen*. Within a few years, Kanter's firm had branches in Mitau, Elbing and Berlin. (The manager of the Mitau shop, Johann Friedrich Hartknoch, moved to Riga to set up his own business in the 1760s, and acquired an even more illustrious clientele than his mentor.) Christian Flottwell, the first holder of the chair of German at the university, joined forces with the court preacher Quandt to found Königsberg's first free bourgeois society in 1741. Modelled on Johann Gottsched's *Deutsche Gesellschaft* in Leipzig, the Royal German Society promoted antiquarian and philological studies.

The university of Copenhagen lagged some way behind Uppsala and Königsberg as a centre of intellectual excellence. Holberg declared it to be little more than a theological school, a view echoed by more than one royal official anxious to secure a more suitably trained personnel for state service. Reform in 1732 brought some slight improvement, though it concentrated on improving and regularising the position of the professors rather than on promoting new subjects. There was no attempt to provide for teaching in economics, nor was the dominance of the precepts of classical humanism challenged to the extent that it was in Sweden. Nevertheless, a chair in natural and public law was established, and a juridicial examination for prospective civil servants was introduced in 1736. The bright start made by Danish theatre in the 1720s was extinguished during the reign of the sombre and reclusive Christian VI, and the development of a distinctively Danish culture was hampered by the prevalence of German as the language of the court and upper classes. The societies set up in the 1740s for the promotion of historical, antiquarian and philological studies were directly influenced by a growing mood of patriotic sentiment: as Jacob Langebek declared in the first issue of his *Danske Magazin*, it was time for the Danish people to begin to love themselves and to acquire a liking for their own heritage.

Danish scholars such as the Bartholins had acquired a European reputation in the seventeenth century: in the eighteenth, the laurels passed to Sweden. The international fame of Swedish scientists, the growth of a book-reading public and the creation of forums for research and debate placed Sweden firmly in the mainstream of European cultural life. Urbane Swedish cosmopolitans such as Carl Scheffer, the tutor of the future Gustav III, moved easily in Parisian society. Their less well-travelled compatriots imbibed French culture, prompting Olof Dalin to complain that if a young man of good family failed to learn French, it was thought that something was lacking in his education. German universities attracted fewer Swedish students than in the previous century, but there was greater awareness of English cultural life than hitherto. Anders Bachmansson, Jonas Alströmer and Mårten Triewald were all deeply influenced by their experiences in England; the academy of sciences was modelled on the Royal Society; and English agriculture had its devoted adherents. The *Spectator* provided the model for Olof Dalin's *Then Swänska Argus*, Swift's satires the inspiration for his *Tale of the horse (Saga om hästan)*.

Provision for the comforts and amusement of the wealthy and leisured classes was an integral feature of the eighteenth-century city, and northern Europe was no exception. Even if towns such as Copenhagen or Danzig fell far short of Paris or London in the range of amusements and services, they could still offer a lively social life. Many of the wealthier merchants of the old-established Hanse towns bought estates and lived the life of country gentlemen. The local aristocracy had their town houses, and mixed in clubs and at assembly rooms with the officers and members of the urban patriciate. The manners of polite society percolated through the social classes: if tea and coffee served no other function, observed Holberg, it had made drunkenness unfashionable. (Unrepentant beer-drinkers retorted that the fashion for hot and spicy drinks had led to an increase in diseases such as gout.) In Königsberg, the bachelor members of the mercantile class gathered in the *Junkerhöfe* to indulge in 'civilised and mannered conversation' (though by the 1740s, they were preferring to mix in a more cosmopolitan society in the masonic lodges), and the barber-surgeons and wigmakers of the town sought to keep pace with their refined clients by upgrading their gilds (*Gewerke*) to societies (*Societäten*). (A young German visiting the town in the 1770s, however, declared that those who understood Low German could hear expressions and terms of abuse 'which one ought not to expect in a civilised town, even from the plebians'.)[17] In Holberg's satire on bourgeois manners, *Barselstuen*, the servant Troels passes a wry comment on the scale of lavishness at weddings. Tailors and shoemakers welcome guests with trumpet fanfares and tables groaning with costly dishes; the middling sort offer only tea, coffee and compliments; whilst the guests at an upper-class wedding are lucky if they get as much as a pinch of snuff.

Life in the provinces was very different, however. The coffee-houses, shops selling exotic and costly foodstuffs and confections, the theatres and assembly-rooms of the capital were a world away from the simple life of the sleepy market town or small port. 'Lackeys, wig-makers, who now comprise a third of the world, are not to be found in Skelskøv', smugly remarked a native of that town, 'balls, assemblies, card-parties and games, banquets and gatherings are unknown here, where everyone lives his own quiet life, filling his pipe from his own pouch'.[18] A Dutch traveller described the Swedish town of Falköping as little more than a collection of wooden huts covered with turf or moss in a large unpaved ditch of a road. Nathaniel Wraxall averred that Åbo, the largest town in Finland, was but 'a wretched capital of a barbarous province', its university not meriting a visit.[19] The livelihood of those who lived in small Danish provincial towns was constantly threatened by travelling pedlars and peasant traders, or artisans protected by powerful landowners. In 1713, the citizens of Kalundborg were obliged to employ a plumber and brick-layer from the nearby Torbenfelt estate to repair their church, and a

17. Glinski G von 1964 *Die Königsberger Kaufmannschaft des 17 und 18 Jahrhunderts* Wissenschäftliche Beiträge zur Geschichte und Landeskunde Ost-Mitteleuropas 70. Marburg, p. 201. Gause F 1968 *Die Geschichte der Stadt Königsberg* Ostmitteleuropa in Vergangenheit und Gegenwart 10/II. Cologne, pp. 32ff. *Briefe einen jungen Reisenden durch Liefland, Kurland und Deutschland.* Erlangen, 1777, pp. 98–9.

18. Steensberg A (ed.) 1971 *Dagligliv i Danmark i den syttende og attende århundrede.* Copenhagen, p. 418.

19. Wraxall N 1775 *Cursory remarks made in a Tour through some of the Northern Parts of Europe, particularly Copenhagen, Stockholm and Petersburgh.* London, p. 194. [Drevon I 1790] *A journey through Sweden.* London, p. 53.

carpenter on the Lerchenborg manor delivered thirty-six new sash windows to a property in the same town in 1760. Many rural craftsmen such as blacksmiths used their trade as a cover for more lucrative activities, such as locksmithing and watch-making. When the townspeople's complaints were heeded, the local sheriff often tipped off these moonlighters of impending investigations. Ruined and deserted houses were a common sight in many of the small towns of Jutland, and most of the burghers, according to one contemporary, were either pedlars or beggars, subsisting as best they could. Even on the more prosperous island of Sjælland, there were only two towns of any consequence outside Copenhagen. Probate settlements for the period 1736–40 show that assets exceeded liabilities only in one-third of the wills proved, and less than 20 per cent left more than 500 rdr. In Helsingør, there were merchants with assets of over one thousand rigsdaler, but this evidence of relative wellbeing pales into insignificance against the twenty thousand left by a supreme court judge or the nine thousand left by a commissary clerk, both resident in Copenhagen.[20]

The diversity of secular amusements and the spread of the ideas of the Enlightenment in the urban centres of the north must also be set against the impact of religious Pietism. With its emphasis on the importance of moral education and the preparation of the young for the world, Pietism contributed significantly to the civilising process. Frederick William I believed that all his efforts to build and improve the fortunes of his country were as nothing if he failed to make his people Christian. His father had offered a refuge to Pietists driven from the strongholds of Lutheranism, and they established a major centre in Halle. August Francke's system of educational institutions, from the orphanages and poor schools up to university level and seminaries for training teachers, was to influence pedagogical thinking throughout northern Europe. Frederick William's efforts to improve elementary education along Pietist lines in East Prussia met with resistance from the orthodox clergy, and a royal commission set up in 1732 also found that the king's wishes could not be fulfilled as long as he expected the impoverished parishes of northern Prussia to finance school building and pay the teachers' salaries. In 1736, the king himself took charge. Schools were to be built with timber provided by the crown, fittings were to be paid for by collections levied in the parishes. A royal fund of 50,000 thaler was set aside for the programme;

20. Jørgensen J 1971 The economic condition of Zealand provincial towns in the eighteenth century *Scandinavian Economic History Review* **19**: 1–11.

within four years, over a thousand schools had been built in East Prussia. Christian VI of Denmark was also an active builder of schools, which were to ensure a basic literacy through the medium of catechisation. His ambition to create a thousand new schools was frustrated by lack of adequate finance, leaving the school-building programme largely in the hands of local estate-owners. The Livonian *Landtag* also agreed in 1737 to create a school in every parish, though this ambition took many decades to fulfil. The quality of education in these elementary schools was variable. There were outstanding teachers, such as Peder Nielsen of Vivild, who was awarded prizes for his work and for his activities in the royal Danish agricultural society; but most were uneducated and often incompetent, struggling to cope in unsatisfactory buildings on an inadequate income. Eight years after the introduction of general elementary education in Denmark there were widespread complaints that many who came for confirmation were unable to read, and the results of Frederick William's educational reforms were likewise rather discouraging.

Rulers sympathetic to Pietism such as Christian VI were also mindful of their authority and the need for good order. Though Christian forbade priests to inveigh against Pietism from the pulpit, he also issued a rescript in 1732 prohibiting assemblies where unauthorised persons claimed to expound holy scripture, and took steps in the 1740s to ensure that no member of the Herrnhut movement was ordained as a priest. The Swedish government also acted against the holding of conventicles, and measures were taken in the Baltic provinces in the 1740s to curb the activities of the Herrnhut movement, which had acquired a strong following amongst the peasantry.[21]

In certain respects, the Pietists and the Herrnhut movement were continuing the work of the earlier generation of reformers, rooting out superstition and replacing the rude habits of the peasant community with prayer, sobriety and piety. In certain other respects, however, the new current posed a challenge to the established church. The Lutheran church had become an institutionalised arm of the state, its clergy upholders of a sterile orthodoxy: in the words of the Swedish clergyman Olof Ekman, who took a mildly critical view of the church in the 1680s, 'we pursue that which seeks to foster an external Christianity, but the inner man we leave untouched and unedified'.[22] It was

21. Lindhardt P 1983 *Kirchengeschichte Skandinaviens*. Göttingen, pp. 56–73. Linderholm E 1966 *Pietismen och dess första tid i Sverige*. Stockholm, p. 113ff. O. Webermann 1956 Pietismus und Brüdergemeinde, in Wittram R (ed.) *Baltische Kirchengeschichte*. Göttingen, pp. 149–65.
22. Linderholm 1966, p. 76.

precisely the inner man (and woman) that Pietism sought to reach, and the glowing of the 'inner light' affected all classes. The spreading of the Word was held to be the task of all Christians. Pietist conventicles and meetings flew in the face of the church ordinances, which decreed that the parish church was the only place of worship. The bringing together of believers from all social classes also challenged the established hierarchy of society. A Swedish commission of enquiry noted with disapproval that people of different classes freely mingled in religious conventicles, whilst in the Baltic provinces, a carpenter and wigmaker led mass rallies of rich and poor, men and women. The active involvement of women was particularly worrying to the upholders of the established order, since women under the law were bound to obedience to the dictates of their fathers or husbands. But unlike the dissenters of seventeenth-century England, the Pietists and their nineteenth-century successors developed no political consciousness, nor did they break with the church or defy the authority of the state. They had more in common with John Wesley than with John Lilburne.

The commingling of the genteel and the unwashed in the fervour of religious emotion did not of course mean that the barriers of status and rank were about to be overthrown, though there was undoubtedly a considerable blurring of distinctions at the upper end of the social ladder. The desire to promote that peculiar status symbol of the mercantilist state, the silk industry, caused rulers to neglect or override sumptuary legislation, though the prohibitions upon dress unsuited to one's station had long been widely ignored. Wealthy burghers, ironmasters and 'persons of quality' wore the same fashionable clothes and expensive periwigs as the nobility, with whom they frequently mixed in assembly rooms and clubs. Conspicuous consumption was even defended as essential for a thriving economy. When the historian Anders Bolin posed the question: 'Why should likeness in estate (*likheten i stånd*) serve any more as a basis for a similar lifestyle as likeness in means (*likheten i förmögenhet*)?' he was challenging the whole ethos which underpinned rank and status.[23]

Rank and social distinction was nevertheless highly valued and jealously guarded, particularly at the lower levels of society. There were innumerable small-town squabbles over seating precedence in church; 'honour' was upheld by gild aldermen and magistrates alike; the nobility increasingly withdrew into private life, engaging tutors

---

23. Wirilander K 1982 *Herrskapsfolk. Ståndspersoner i Finland 1721–1870*. Stockholm, p. 334.

for their children and celebrating services in their private chapels; and there was much concern over the 'purity' of the estates in the Swedish *riksdag*. Even punishment was decreed according to rank. The Björneborg infantry regiment pleaded in 1755 for whipping of non-commissioned officers to be discontinued, since it undermined respect amongst the soldiers. The gentry of St Michel recommended the stocks for the commonalty for breaches of church discipline, though they were convinced that 'every person of quality in the parish is governed by such degree of morality, religion and honour, that all punishments for them in this respect are superfluous'.[24] In the Baltic provinces, the distinctions were even more strenuously maintained. The stream of artisans from Germany were particularly zealous in this regard: 'be they so poor or mean, they insist that the peasant must call them "sir", a laughable conceit', declared A. W. Hupel.[25] Hupel himself poked fun at the peasants who sought to imitate German fashion by cramming shoes on to their feet for Sunday services, and made the point that dress was an outward sign of Germanness and social superiority. The Riga magistrates rejected a request from a mast inspector for burgherage on the grounds that, although he spoke German and was a free man, his parents had been serfs. The *Undeutsche* of the city were all descended from runaway serfs, the magistrates argued, and in order to remind the supplicant and others of like mind of the fact that menial work was their prime function, they rejected the request.

Attempts to maintain barriers were often an indication that they had broken down: this was especially the case of noblemen seeking to prevent non-nobles buying up their estates. Between 1781 and 1784, 86 noble estates at a total value of 592,500 thaler were bought by non-nobles in East Prussia, whilst during the same period, only eight, valued at 94,255 thaler, passed back into noble ownership. The proportion of land in non-noble possession more than doubled during the Age of Liberty in Sweden. Although the high aristocracy retained their dominant landowning status in the central provinces, their lesser brethren on the periphery were losing out: in the western provinces, for example, Göteborg merchants, clergymen and even peasants were active purchasers of land, whilst ironmasters snapped up estates in Värmland. Nearly half of the private estates in Denmark in 1710 were in the hands of non-noble proprietors. The old aristocracy's share had

24. Wirilander 1982, pp. 68–9. Should a gentleman be so unworthy as to commit an offence against church discipline, however, he was to be fined.
25. Hupel A 1777 *Topographische Nachrichten von Lief- und Ehstland* (3 vols). Riga, vol. 2, p. 6.

declined from 95 per cent in 1660 to a mere 38.5 per cent fifty years later. Bereft of political power, the Danish nobility no longer commanded the highest offices of state. Christian V and Frederik IV preferred to create their own administrative apparatus with as little assistance from the old-established families as possible. In his political testament of 1723, Frederik IV urged his son to preserve his power and the welfare of the state by keeping the old nobility out of office. The naval commander Kristian Thomesen Sehested was demoted because Frederik suspected him of being a malicious intriguer, and a number of other members of old Danish families suffered a similar fate. These old families were the most assiduous users of the cloisters which were established for noblewomen, a clear indication that their fortunes were in decline.

The agricultural crisis of the late seventeenth and early eighteenth century was an additional incentive to the aristocracy to seek office. The widespread abandonment of farms and the devastation of war and plague may have pushed many of the Baltic German nobility to seek careers in the service of the Swedish or Russian contenders during the Great Northern War. By the end of the war, over half of the senior officers in Finnish military units and a third of the senior military personnel within the Swedish army as a whole were Baltic Germans. Noblemen from Livonia and Estonia also found employment in the army and administration of the Russian empire. In 1730, roughly a quarter of the Imperial officer corps were Baltic Germans, and one-eighth of all high-ranking officials between 1710 and 1917 hailed from the Baltic provinces. Baltic Germans were also to be found in all the major armies of Europe: of the six brothers of the von Kaulbars family, two served in the Swedish army, two in the Spanish, one in the French and another in the Habsburg forces, and this was by no means untypical.

The Prussian nobility, hard hit by the agricultural depression, found employment for their offspring in Frederick William's army. By the end of Frederick II's reign, the officer corps had become almost exclusively a noble preserve. Frederick II was a good deal more sympathetic towards the aristocracy than his father: Frederick William preferred to appoint men whom he could make or unmake. All of his cabinet secretaries and councillors were commoners, and only 36 of the 118 councillors and directors of the Boards of War and the Domains in 1737 were noblemen. The barriers between the local office-holding magnates and royal officials gradually began to break down. The reforms of Samuel von Cocceji, Frederick II's minister of justice, absorbed the old judicial hierarchy into the ranks of royal service, but also strengthened the privileged position of the nobility, fusing the contesting elites into what Christian Jakob Kraus described at the end of the century as an aristocracy ruling the country in undisguised form as a bureaucracy.[26]

The army was also an important field of employment for the Swedish aristocracy. During the Great Northern War, the proportion of non-noble officers rose significantly, and the aristocracy attempted at the conclusion of peace to augment their privileges in order to prevent further non-noble encroachments. This 'noble reaction' was rather less effective than the scaling-down of the armed forces after the war and the ennoblement of many serving officers, which reduced the proportion of non-noble officers from two-thirds to just over half. By 1757, that proportion had shrunk still further to just over a quarter: as many as 40 per cent of the high-ranking officers were counts or barons. A reverse trend, however, occurred in the ranks of the bureaucracy, as the frequency of ennoblement fell sharply. Aspirants to office of noble birth nevertheless still possessed numerous advantages, such as family connections. Non-noble appointees were in general some ten years older than their noble counterparts, which meant that they were often too old or died before they could reach the highest level of the bureaucracy, which remained essentially an aristocratic preserve. Army officers also enjoyed higher status relative to civilian officials in the table of ranks. In 1735, there were 123 officers or ex-officers, but only 23 civilians in the top eleven ranks. Furthermore, the provision of accommodation, rents or land through the *indelningsverk* system was a valuable asset, particularly when grain prices started to rise. Whereas civilian officials were badly hit by inflation in the 1760s, the real income of officers from their land allotments rose appreciably.[27]

In the scramble for jobs, those on the periphery could lose out. Of the 52 county governors in Finland between 1721 and 1808, just over half were Finnish-born, but these men tended to be appointed to the less attractive and less remunerative posts in the Finnish-speaking hinterland. Swedish-born appointees dominated the higher ranks of the army and the presidencies of the high courts, though three-quarters of the bishops and professors at Åbo university were Finnish-born. The 1755 directory for Åbo university indicated that most of the Swedish-born students had managed to obtain good jobs as tutors in

26. Rosenberg H 1958 *Bureaucracy, aristocracy and autocracy. The Prussian experience 1660–1815* Harvard Historical Monographs 35. Cambridge, Mass, p. 201.

27. Artéus G 1982 *Krigsmakt och samhälle i frihetstidens Sverige*. Stockholm, offers a comprehensive overview of this subject.

the best families of the neighbourhood. Forty years later, professor Henrik Porthan complained of the preference for domestic tutors from Uppsala, who were also paid better, even though just as able men (though less foppish and 'refined') could be found in Åbo.[28] The Finnish estates did on occasion seek to ensure that those appointed to office in Finland should have a knowledge of Finnish, but this aroused the opposition of those such as Samuel Åkerhielm, who complained at the 1738–9 *riksdag* that any insistence on a knowledge of Finnish as a qualification for office might also exclude Finns from office in Sweden, and in the long run, might weaken the principles of a common religion and law which held the nation together. Åkerhielm's appeal to the old adage of *unus rex, una lex, unus grex* harked back to the ideals espoused by Johan Skytte; and it was as misplaced as later attempts to see in these demands the beginnings of national consciousness. The demands for officials with a knowledge of Finnish were essentially pragmatic, as were the attempts by the Finnish peasant delegations to the *riksdag* to obtain an interpreter of their own choosing.

A more intimate link between the state and the people was provided by the clergy. In Finland, the priesthood was largely recruited from within the country, and the language question was therefore not a major problem; but the situation was rather different in the Baltic provinces. Ignorance of the languages of the indigenous peoples had long been a charge levelled against the clergy here. Hostile critics such as Garlieb Merkel also accused the clergy of servility towards the nobility on whom they depended for their livings, and of exploiting the peasantry because they were dependent on their glebeland for their income. Merkel painted a picture of a typical clergyman, more concerned with his economic and social affairs than his religious duties. 'Only on Sunday morning is he reminded by the festive costume of his dear wife that he is a clergyman. Over coffee he searches through the calendar to discover which evangelium he must prattle about today, and then leafs through a concordance for half an hour whilst his wig or his holy pate is being attended to.'[29]

There was a sizeable influx of graduates from German universities into the Baltic provinces during the eighteenth century: as one contemporary remarked, they flocked to Kurland as if to the East Indies

---

28. Suolahti G 1927 *Finlands prästerskap på 1600- och 1700-talen*. Helsingfors, p 153.
29. Merkel G 1797 *Die Letten*. Leipzig, p. 340. Worldly priests were the butt for many satirists: *Den Swenske Patrioten* in 1735 portrayed a society clergyman as 'so neat and well-scrubbed, like a doll, and speaking like an angel: i'faith, I cannot remember much of what he said, but it sounded well'. Suolahti 1927, p. 152.

in search of status and fortune. In Kurland, these *literati* enjoyed the same status before the law as the nobility and freedom from personal taxation. In 1797, there were some 3,000 clergymen, doctors, lawyers and officials in Kurland. Lawyers seemed to have made a good living, but J. L. G. Schwarz's blunt assertion that Kurland was a paradise for preachers was not entirely true. Johann Kant, the rector of the town school in Mitau, married a woman with no dowry and had to seek a country living in 1781, burdened down with debts. Even though he could inform his brother eleven years later that he had at last paid off his debts, his widow still had to ask the illustrious philosopher for financial assistance in 1800. As the author of an article in Krünitz's *Øonomisch-technologische Encyklopädie* observed in 1793, rumour made all priests not evidently living in poverty into wealthy men. Kurland was reckoned to be an expensive place to live, and many clergymen sighed longingly for a country living, where they could live off the income from their glebe. On average, the Kurland pastor had some 156 hectares of land, but not all were good farmers and they often had sizeable households to feed. In general, however, the country parson does seem to have enjoyed a modestly prosperous lifestyle, especially if he contracted an advantageous marriage. The same also appears to have been true elsewhere along the southern shores of the Baltic.[30]

There were undoubtedly many parson Woodfordes in the Baltic lands, content to enjoy good dinners and let the world go by; but there were also tireless advocates of reform, such as Johann Georg Eisen, a native of Franconia who settled in Livonia in 1741. Eisen once confided to a friend that whereas Luther had worked for the heart, and Wolff for the spirit, he worked for the good of the stomach. His plans for drying and conserving vegetables for use as army rations aroused interest throughout Europe, but he was also concerned to improve the material lot of the peasantry (and hence, the landowning class and the state). His description of serfdom in Livonia, written with the encouragement of the empress Catherine and published anonymously in 1764, opened a new era of debate in the Baltic provinces.[31] Elsewhere, too, the 1760s mark a watershed between the world of obligation and rank-determined privilege, regulation and control of subjects, patrimonial perspectives and hierarchical world-views, and the world

30. Bosse H 1986 Die Einkünfte kurländischen Literaten am Ende des 18 Jahrhunderts *Zeitschrift für Ostforschung* **35**: 516–94. Steffen W 1963 *Kulturgeschichte von Rügen bis 1815* Veröffentlichungen der Historischen Kommission für Pommern 5:5. Cologne, pp. 300ff.

31. On the work of Eisen, see Neuschäffer H 1975 *Katherina II und die baltischen Provinzen* Beiträge zur baltischen Geschichte 2. Hannover–Döhren; and Donnert E 1978 *Johann Georg Eisen 1717–1779. Ein Vorkämpfer der Bauernbefreiung in Russland.* Leipzig.

where citizens claimed the right to organise freely to pursue their interests, to assert their political and civic rights and to pursue their livelihoods unhindered by cumbersome and restrictive legislation. As with all watersheds, the dividing line was not sharply defined, and the catalyst for change is not easy to pinpoint. The effects of the Seven Years' War, though less dramatic in northern Europe than elsewhere, certainly played a part, as did the dissemination of ideas propounded by theorists such as Adam Smith or the French physiocrats, which an increasingly self-confident and well-educated elite was prepared to discuss and implement. Much of the ground for the great era of reform which encompassed the whole of northern Europe during the latter half of the eighteenth century had been prepared already.

The welfare of the fatherland was the concern of all self-respecting patriots: it was no longer the sole prerogative of the ruler and his administrators. That much was recognised by Gustav III, who, though believing he held absolute power 'considered it nobler, grander ... and certainly surer for my future government, myself to limit royal authority, leaving to the nation the essential rights of liberty, and keeping for myself only what is necessary to prevent license'.[32] Frederik V of Denmark had also relaxed the censorship laws and encouraged intellectual debate: Catherine II actively encouraged advocates of reform in the Russian empire, and vied with Frederick II in her devotion to the ideas of the French Enlightenment. The transition from the corporatist to the class-based structure of society, from the regulated mercantilist economy to unfettered capitalism was a lengthy process, the contradictions and ambiguities of which were clearly reflected in the thoughts and actions of these rulers. The broad concepts of the 'common good' and the wellbeing of the nation were still contained within the old framework of rank and status, which survived well into the nineteenth century. The four estates of the Swedish *riksdag* were not abolished until 1866, and the Finnish estates survived until 1906. Restrictive legislation governing servants, the use of the forests and watercourses, and the right to exercise one's livelihood remained in force for many decades after 1800. Those who opposed the employment of women in the Swedish telegraphic service in the 1860s advanced arguments which would have earned the approval of seventeenth-century divines such as Haquin Spegel. School administrators in Finland still firmly believed in the 1860s that education should be strictly according to estate, with the grammar schools

---

32. Cited in Barton A 1986 *Scandinavia in the revolutionary era 1760–1815*. Minneapolis, p. 83.

reserved for members of the educated class, the elementary schools for the common people. Official bodies were even punctilious about dress: as late as 1846, an advocate who appeared before Viborg high court was fined for wearing a frock-coat instead of the appropriate dress suit.

The demise of the old order did not occur overnight. There was to be no violent, self-conscious break with the past in Scandinavia, where the process of change initiated from above was already well under way by 1789. The most ardent enthusiasts for the French Revolution were members of the ruling classes: artisans and peasants remained indifferent towards or ignorant of the events in Paris. The pace of reform was slower in the lands along the southern shores of the Baltic, where there was powerful and entrenched opposition to the abolition of serfdom. Radical and reformist ideas won some support amongst the urban population, but the political powers of the old Hanseatic towns had long since been emasculated. Behind the fine buildings and rich urban life of cities such as Danzig, Königsberg and Riga lay a bleak hinterland, where the indigenous peasantry had been reduced to serfdom and the Junkers had remained isolated from the rest of the world in their own petty particularism, until dragged into the military state bureaucracy of Prussia and the Russian empire. Here the contrast with the northern kingdoms is particularly striking, for the absolutist regimes established in Denmark and, more briefly, Sweden never adopted the kind of brutal, coercive methods employed by Peter the Great or Frederick William of Prussia. It may be that the decline of territorial ambition fostered in the Swedish and Danish kingdoms a milder spirit than the harsh militarism and regimentation of society of the ambitious powers striving for hegemony in eastern and central Europe. The liberty of the subject was never extinguished, even though it was seriously compromised in the case of the unfortunate Danish peasantry, and circumscribed by regulations. It is the delicate balance between recognition of these fundamental liberties and a concern for good government which has characterised much of the history of the Nordic countries, and has perhaps preserved them from violent revolution, and the kind of authoritarian regimes their less fortunate neighbours on the southern shores of the Baltic have had to endure.

CHAPTER FOURTEEN

1772 – The End of an Era?

The victory of the Caps in the 1764 elections, the unprecedented and tumultuous proceedings of the 1765–6 *riksdag* and the eventual fall from power of the Caps in 1769 brought strife in Sweden to a new pitch of intensity. An English traveller in 1769 observed that the people were much troubled by their government and he foresaw a great revolution. Crown prince Gustav feared that Sweden resembled a decayed building which threatened to collapse in ruins, and he voiced his concern on numerous occasions that Sweden seemed to be going the way of Poland. Renewed attempts to reform the constitution in 1769 came to nothing. The onslaught against noble privilege mounted by the non-noble estates in the *riksdag* of 1771–2 threatened to divide the nation still further. Gustav III's efforts to reach a compromise between the warring parties was not heeded by the Caps, who packed the committees of the *riksdag* with their own partisans. Rumours of a planned *coup* by the court party had been relayed by foreign ministers since 1768, when Adolf Fredrik had threatened to abdicate if the estates were not convened. The crown prince was in France seeking support for a *coup* when he received news of his father's death in 1771. The dismissal of Choiseul, the most ardent supporter of a restoration of royal power, was a blow to Gustav's hopes. The young king had to rely for the time being on his own powers of persuasion as a Swedish-born patriot, content merely to be 'the first citizen amongst a free people'.[1] At the end of 1771, however, French

---

1. Nordmann C 1971 *Grandeur et liberté de la Suède (1660–1792)*. Paris, p. 283. Hennings B 1957 *Gustav III*. Stockholm, p. 39. Gustav described himself as the 'first citizen' in his speech to the estates in June 1771.

policy shifted. Gustav was urged to stage a *coup*, and French financial support for the Hats was withdrawn. Eager young royalists plotted the restoration of Sweden's greatness in their club, *Svensk botten*, and plans were made for an uprising in Finland and southern Sweden. The fortress of Sveaborg was captured by J. M. Sprengtporten's dragoons on 16 August 1772, but adverse winds delayed the seaborne transportation of these troops to join the king in Stockholm. At this critical stage, the king decided to act on his own initiative. He was able to secure the allegiance of the officers and men of the guards, and proceeded in triumph through the streets of the capital, having the members of the council arrested as they sat in session. There was no resistance to the *coup*, and the assembled estates dutifully acclaimed the constitution already drawn up by the king and his advisers.

Although it has been claimed that the parliamentary regime in Sweden would not have been swept away had not the officer corps perceived it to be a threat to its corporate interests, there is ample evidence to suggest a general weariness with party strife and a wish for the restoration of monarchical power. It was not only royalist officers who hoped that the nation could be reunited and its fortunes restored by the monarchy. Doubts about the viability of the constitution had been expressed by Hats and Caps alike in the 1760s, and the failure to reform the constitution in 1769 had persuaded many others to turn to the court as the only salvation. A dangerous gulf had opened up between the estates and the country in 1771–2, when the *riksdag* showed itself incapable of dealing with the famine which afflicted the land. When the blow fell, there was no popular opposition, and no resistance. The *coup* was hailed by the nobility as putting a stop to the presumptuous claims of the lower estates, and by the non-noble orders as a blow against aristocratic rule.[2] The constitution that the king presented to the estates was shot through with ambiguity. Though the king and no other was to govern, he was to do so within the limits of the law. The king alone was to appoint the council, but he was obliged to consult it on matters pertaining to justice, war, peace and alliances, and if the council was unanimously opposed to the king on matters of foreign policy, the king had to give way. The estates were to be summoned at the king's pleasure, but they retained control over the levying of new taxes, and the king was accountable to them for state expenditure. Moreover, the king was not to declare war

2. Artéus G 1982 *Krigsmakt och samhälle i frihetstidens Sverige*. Stockholm, pp. 360–1. Roberts M 1986 *The Age of Liberty. Sweden 1719–1772*. Cambridge, pp. 185–6, 203–4. Odhner C 1885 *Sveriges politiska historia under konung Gustaf III:s regering* (vol. 1). Stockholm, p. 152ff.

without their consent. Appointments and promotions were to be on the basis of ability and experience without respect to birth, unless associated with ability – a formulation which neatly sidestepped the vexed question of privilege.

Acutely aware of the threat of Russian intervention, Gustav also appears to have been genuinely anxious to avoid confrontation with the estates. The 1772 constitution did indeed restore the equilibrium between king and estates; but that delicate balance was upset by the king's absolutist tendencies. 'Although the new government at its commencement offered favourable prospects for a felicitous present and future, and it was supposed that a divided people would by degrees be restored to the sentiment of patriotism,' wrote a contemporary observer, 'the course of events revealed that the spirit of discord was merely in repose, ready to break out with renewed vigour at a suitable occasion, which the court was not always careful or particular enough to prevent.'[3] The fluctuation of the pendulum between king and estates, the characteristic feature of Swedish constitutional history since the Middle Ages, was to continue for some time yet, taking with it the king (at the hands of a noble assassin) and his successor (forced to abdicate in 1809, when the Gustavian constitution was replaced).

The estates as a representative institution had been removed from the scene in Denmark in 1660, and did not re-emerge until the nineteenth century. Denmark's monarchy exercised absolutist, but not despotic powers, as critics of Montesquieu such as Holberg and Kofod Ancher were not slow to point out. Danish political theorists tended to stress the contractual nature of absolutism. Ancher maintained that the absolute monarch was bound by natural law, and Henrik Stampe believed the law to be the guarantee of the subject's liberty. Jens Schieldrup Sneedorff, professor of jurisprudence at Sorø academy and editor of *Den patriotiske Tilskuer* (The patriotic observer), maintained that Denmark was the only kingdom in Europe founded on trust between ruler and people. In an ingenious adaptation of Montesquieu's ideas, Sneedorff argued that the estates had handed over supreme power to the ruler in order that he might maintain the balance between them. Criticism of the system was at best oblique, and a wave of enthusiastic patriotism was generated by the relaxation

3. Lagerblad E (ed.) 1887 Historiskt-politiska anteckningar från åren 1743–1796 af assessoren Henrik Thomas Adlerkreutz *Skrifter utgivna av Svenska Litteratursällskapet i Finland* **8**: 20.

of censorship and encouragement of intellectual enquiry during the reign of Frederik V (1746–66).[4]

Frederik, a good-natured but idle man, left the governance of the realm to his advisers and officials. Most were German: during the reign, only one Dane and one Holsteiner sat on the royal council. The foreign minister J. H. E. Bernsdorff pursued a policy of cautious neutrality. His efforts to settle the Holstein-Gottorp question by negotiation were ultimately successful, but the threat of war posed by Peter III in 1762 obliged Denmark to mobilise, and left the country with a debt of over twenty million rigsdaler. The financial crisis obliged the crown to sell off land, and to introduce new taxes. A poll tax led to disturbances and open revolt in Norway. The army reforms proposed by Claude Louis de St Germain threatened landowning interests, and although the war chancery was remodelled in 1763 along Prussian lines, most of the plans were quietly abandoned in the face of entrenched resistance. The old order was able to survive Christian VII's initial burst of reformist zeal, returning to office when the king departed on his grand tour in 1768. During that tour, the mental instability of the sovereign became distressingly apparent. The exercise of power slipped from his hands into those of his queen and her lover, the royal physician Johann Friedrich Struensee, who began replacing ministers with their own confidants in the summer of 1770. For a period of eighteen months, Denmark was ruled by the Struensee faction. In December 1770, the council was dismissed and replaced by a conference of heads of government departments. Struensee's main instrument of government was the cabinet order. In July 1771, he was made privy cabinet minister (*Gehejmekabinettsminister*), with authority to sign orders without the royal counter-signature. The stream of reforms, at a time of economic crisis, did little to strengthen Struensee's position. His anti-mercantilist measures were ineffective, arousing the hostility of the Copenhagen merchants, whose privileges were undercut, and causing widespread temporary unemployment as the result of a flood of cheap imports from Germany. The abolition of press censorship led to a flood of scurrilous pamphlets, mostly directed at Struensee and his royal mistress. Unlike the inamorati of the regal person in Russia – and unfortunately for him – Struensee outraged contemporary convention by cuckolding the absolute (if mentally incapable) sovereign. In January 1772, Struensee was overthrown in a palace *coup*, and he ended his life on the scaffold three

---

4. Olsen A 1936 *Danmark-Norge i det 18 Aarhundrede*. Copenhagen, p. 115, argues that excessive loyalty towards the crown was not incompatible with liberal ideas, though he also notes that professions of loyalty were essential for patronage and royal favour.

months later. The council was revived and given a central role in government. All ministerial business was to be discussed by the council, and the king's signature could only be appended to documents in the presence of the councillors. To avoid further abuse of the royal signature, all in possession of orders signed by the king were to report to the relevant office, which had then to give an account of its actions to the council. The system of cabinet orders was retained, however, and effective government of the realm remained in the hands of the cabinet secretary Ove Höegh Guldberg for the next decade.

Although most of Struensee's reforms were either rescinded or abandoned, the impetus for change remained. Journals such as Erik Pontoppidan's *Danmarks og Norges Øonomiske Magazin* (1755–64) and Sneedorff's *Den patriotiske Tilskuer* (1760–64) had ensured the circulation and discussion of enlightened ideas in Denmark. The government had played its part by supporting the publication of suitable essays on economics; after 1750, the volume of literature on trade, manufacturing and above all agriculture rose appreciably.

The life of the Danish peasant was if anything even more tightly circumscribed by the state in the first half of the century. The rights of the village gilds in Denmark were significantly reduced in 1724; the 1733 *stavnsbånd* law was further extended in 1746 and 1764, effectively tying the male peasant to the land from the age of four onwards. The situation was hardly any better elsewhere along the southern Baltic. The extension of demesne land and the diminution in the number of tenants owing labour service, further aggravated by a flight from the land, meant that compulsion was resorted to in Holstein to tie down available labour. As late as 1771, it was specifically decreed that the unfree peasantry were obliged to carry out unlimited labour services and could be physically punished for refusing to do so. Peasants in the Baltic provinces were regularly bought and sold: A. W. Hupel commented in his survey of Livonia and Estonia that they were less expensive than negro slaves in the American colonies. Stupid and insensitive, content if they have enough coarse bread to eat and enough guile to avoid a whipping, the Latvian peasant was, in Garlieb Merkel's words, 'what a nation, whose humanity has been gnawed away by the dragon's tooth of slavery for six hundred years, can become'.[5]

In his polemical attack, as Roger Bartlett has pointed out, 'Merkel

---

5. Hupel A 1777 *Topographische Nachrichten von Lief- und Ehstland* (vol. 2). Riga, p. 127. Merkel G 1797 *Die Letten*. Leipzig, pp. 70–1.

combined the rationalism and moral purpose of the older generation with the passion and overt personal engagement of the age of Rousseau, the French revolution and incipient Romanticism'.[6] Earlier reformists had proceeded from the theories of German cameralists and the physiocrats, who regarded the miserable social conditions of the servile peasantry as an obstacle to prosperity and national wellbeing. This position was clearly enunciated by Hans Rantzau-Ascheberg, one of the pioneers of land reform in Holstein. It was essential, Rantzau argued in his widely read work on improving the conditions of farming and the peasantry in Holstein, that means be devised to ensure that the peasant could realise his private interests, and thereby improve the general wellbeing. The reforms set in motion by Rantzau, and by Caspar von Saldern in the duchy of Holstein-Gottorp, were closely followed by Catherine II in Russia. Catherine also encouraged the Pietist pastor of Torma in Estonia, Johann Georg Eisen, who was given the opportunity to try out his ideas on crown estates and on the Ropsha demesne of the imperial favourite G. G. Orlov. Eisen envisaged a reordering of the relationship of lord and peasant through a 'constitution', which would bind both to the supreme authority of the state, and which would allow the peasant his natural right to pursue happiness by the enjoyment of the fruits of his labours. He proposed the commutation of labour services by cash payment, and the creation of hereditary leaseholds, measures which went much further than those contemplated by the Livonian landowner Karl Friedrich Schoultz von Ascheraden. In his *Bauerrecht* of 1764, Schoultz von Ascheraden fixed the level of labour service and granted a limited degree of hereditary tenure for the peasants on his estates. Schoultz von Ascheraden tried the following year to persuade his fellow-nobles voluntarily to accept his code in preference to one imposed by the empress, but his efforts were brushed aside by the *Landtag*.[7]

6. I am indebted to Dr Bartlett for allowing me to read his unpublished manuscript 'The question of serfdom: Catherine II, the Russian debate and the view from the Baltic periphery (J. G. Eisen and G. H. Merkel)', to be published in: Bartlett R, Hartley J *Russia in the Age of the Enlightenment. Essays for Isabel de Madariaga*, from which this quote is taken.
7. Klose O, Degn C 1960 *Die Herzogtümer im Gesamtstaat 1773–1830* Geschichte Schleswig-Holsteins 6, Neumünster, pp. 221ff. Neuschäffer H 1974 Die livländische Pastor und Kameralist Johann Georg Eisen von Schwarzenberg. Ein deutscher Vertreter der Aufklärung in Russland zu Beginn der zweiten Hälfte des 18 Jahrhunderts *Russland und Deutschland* (ed. U Listkowksi). Kiel Historische Studien 22 Stuttgart, pp. 120–43. Transehe-Roseneck A von 1890 *Gutsherr und Bauer in Livland im 17 und 18 Jahrhundert* Abhandlungen aus dem Staatswissenschaftlichen Seminar zu Strassburg 7. Strassburg, pp. 154–67. Diederichs H 1870 Garlieb Merkel als Bekämpfer der Leibeigenschaft *Baltische Monatsschrift* **19**: 38–83.

The proposals laid before the *Landtag* by the governor-general count George Browne were not so easily ignored, since Browne made it plain that they had imperial backing. The nobility, hard pressed by the burdens of providing horses and fodder for the Russian armies during the Seven Years' War, and suspicious of the ruler's intentions, likened Browne's proposals to the experience of Karl XI's *reduktion*. Faced with the threat of the imposition of the proposals by imperial decree, the *Landtag* agreed to issue a fourteen-point patent which embraced most of Browne's propositions. The peasantry were to be given rights to dispose of personal movable goods they had acquired or inherited; labour services were to be fixed, unless the number of inhabitants of a farmstead increased; the rights of the landowner to administer physical punishment were curbed; the sale of peasants abroad was declared illegal; and peasants were permitted to lodge complaints against unfair increases of taxes and labour service in the lower courts. The terms of the patent were widely ignored; when peasant revolts broke out in 1777, Browne laid some of the blame at the door of the nobility who had failed to observe the patent of 1765.

The peasant question was kept at the forefront of public debate in the Baltic provinces by writers and publicists such as Hupel, H. J. von Jannau and J. C. Petri, and was given added urgency by outbreaks of violent unrest sparked off by the imposition of a poll tax in 1783. Several landowners in Kurland and Estonia followed the example set by Schoultz, but it was not until the reign of Alexander I that serfdom was ultimately abolished in the Baltic provinces. Progress in easing the burden of servitude was also slow and halting in the Prussian lands. In Denmark and the duchies, the emancipation of the peasantry was an integral, if somewhat uneven, part of a general programme of agrarian reform set in motion in the middle of the century. Peasants on some royal estates were allowed to commute their obligations and were given hereditary tenure. The government encouraged landowners to sell tenant farms by allowing them to continue to claim tax exemption on the farm and to exercise manorial rights such as shooting and hunting over the land. The sale of crown estates in the 1760s enabled wealthier peasants to acquire their own farms, though most of the land passed into seigneurial hands.

A number of measures favourable to the peasantry were pushed through in Sweden during the period of Cap ascendancy between 1765 and 1769. *Skatteköp*, the right of crown tenants to buy up the freehold of their farms, suspended in 1763, was renewed and noble (*frälse*) land was allowed to pass into peasant ownership. Many of these measures were suppressed during the brief return to power of the Hats, but during the last *riksdag* of the Age of Liberty, the peasants' estate presented a draft charter of liberties, which comprehended the right freely to exploit and dispose of their land, abolition of hunting privileges outside royal parks, and a relaxation of some of the more obnoxious measures of the statute of servants. The peasants also sought admission to the all-important secret committee of the *riksdag*, from which they had always been excluded, an indication of their growing self-confidence and political maturity. In Denmark, the work of the reformist agricultural commission set up in 1767 was advanced by Struensee. The downfall of Struensee and Gustav III's *coup* ushered in a period of reaction in both the northern kingdoms. Peasant representatives were eased off *riksdag* committees, *skatteköp* was once more suspended in Sweden, the *stavnsbånd* was tightened and the creation of hereditary tenancies virtually ended in Denmark. Poor harvests hindered the extension of freehold purchase by individual peasants or communities, and the forfeiture of tenancies seems to have risen. In the 1780s, however, the Swedish crown adopted a far more conciliatory attitude towards the peasantry, whilst Denmark entered the decisive phase of land reform which was to transform rural society over the next three decades.[8]

Many enlightened writers such as Sneedorff and Jannau believed that emancipation would be a dangerous thing for an immature peasantry. To this end, they urged better provision of schooling and the dissemination of useful practical knowledge. Some Lutheran pastors took up the challenge: the agricultural academy set up in Glücksburg by Philipp Ernst Lüders sought to teach its peasant pupils the virtues of good loaming and the nutritional value of potatoes. (Peasants in northern Europe long regarded potatoes with the utmost suspicion; their resistance was in part overcome when they realised that they could be converted into cheap and potent spirits.) The rural dean of Gingst, on the island of Rügen, set up a school according to Pestalozzi's principles to teach reading, writing and handicraft skills. Clergymen introduced new crops and techniques of cultivation on their own farms, and tried to persuade their parishioners to have their children vaccinated, to dig deeper wells, or to build more efficient ovens. Agricultural societies awarded prizes for the most innovative ideas and published their proceedings for the edification of the general

---

8. Olsen A 1939 Samtidens Syn paa den danske Stavnsbundne Bonde *Scandia* **12**: 99–139. Skrubbeltrang F 1961 Developments in tenancy in eighteenth-century Denmark as a move towards peasant proprietorship *Scandinavian Economic History Review* **9**: 165–75, argues however that the reforms in the 1780s occurred against a background of recent economic decline.

public. The Danish agricultural society, founded in 1769, offered membership to all, irrespective of social status, who strove for the common good. In spite of much footdragging by local landowners and parents (who not infrequently kept their children away from school to attend to work about the farm), progress was made in the provision of elementary rural education.

The economic arguments in favour of a free peasantry were probably decisive; but the changing attitude towards the peasant's position and role in society should not be underestimated. Writers in the second half of the eighteenth century began to view the peasant in a more positive light, either as a valuable and worthy member of society, or as an idealised representative of bucolic innocence and charm. Johann Gottfried Herder's collection of folksongs from various lands, published in 1778–9, was to serve as a model and inspiration for successive generations of poets and scholars, but Herder was only one of many enthusiasts, rediscovering the poetry of the common people. The Norwegian peasant was hailed as a model of independent spirit by Tyge Rothe and apostrophised in poems such as Claus Frimann's 'Songs of the common poeple' and 'Songs of the Norwegian peasantry' by Jens Zetlitz. Breast-feeding and fresh air, claimed the Swede Gustav Dahlgren, endowed peasant children with better health: the virtues of physical labour were also recommended, though as the Finnish peasants wryly remarked, whereas the gentry toiled for pleasure, they themselves did so because they had to.[9]

The improvement of the peasant's situation also implied a general restructuring of society, the freeing of the individual from the fetters of regulations and formal, legalised ranks. For the Danish cameralist Georg Christian Oeder, emancipation meant full civic freedom, the right of every individual to augment and enjoy his own prosperity by whatever means were socially acceptable. Swedish writers of the 1760s such as the Runeberg brothers, Johan Fischerström and Carl Leuhusen were more forthright in their critique of the existing order. Fischerström inveighed against the popular view of the peasant as a dumb, lazy brute who had to be coerced, and advocated the introduction of cash rents in place of labour services. Restrictive laws and the table of ranks were condemned by Leuhusen as a remnant of absolutism, incompatible with the constitution of the Age of Liberty. Freedom of occupation would increase the number of workers, promote enterprise and competition, stimulate consumption, which in turn would create employment and prosperity, encourage marriage and

9. Wirilander K 1982 *Herrskapsfolk. Ståndspersoner i Finland 1721–1870.* Stockholm, p. 59.

thereby increase the nation's population. Each individual, argued the Finnish clergyman Anders Chydenius, is naturally inclined to pursue the occupation which is most profitable. This was the true foundation of national prosperity, and was being hindered by restrictive legislation such as the ban on direct foreign trade imposed on the Bothnian ports, which was finally rescinded in 1766. Chydenius attacked laws such as the Statute of Servants which made marriage and procreation a fearsome burden, with no reward save a beggar's staff:

> 'If farmhands and serving-maids were sexless, like the bee and the ant, only born to slavery, then there would be no need to pity them; but as it is otherwise, compulsion must in all tenderness be reduced. If the saying *patria est, ubi bene est* [where it is good, there is the fatherland] is correct, then is there not good reason to say that these are without a fatherland.'[10]

'Freedom', the watchword of the age, was nevertheless capable of a wide variety of interpretations. The corporatist concept of liberties was still very much alive, nowhere more so than in Poland, where the attachment of the nobility to *złota wolność*, their 'golden freedom', was widely believed by contemporaries to be a principal cause for the anarchy and ultimate demise of the Commonwealth. The nobility of Holstein-Gottorp feared that they would be excluded from the administration after the transfer of the duchy to Danish rule, and the Danes agreed to accept changes in the German Chancery which ensured that the director of affairs in the duchies would be an indigenous nobleman. In his speech at the ceremonial handing over of the duchy of Holstein-Gottorp to the Danish crown in 1773, Caspar von Saldern was careful to emphasise that 'all privileges, liberties and rights, immunities and exemptions, which entire corporations or individual persons have hitherto enjoyed will be maintained in the future through the stipulations of the treaty'.[11] In 1796, the emperor Paul I bowed to the pressure of the Baltic nobility, restoring much of the special autonomous status of the provinces according to their rights and privileges. The nobility of Swedish Pomerania retained their privileged autonomy until the very end of Swedish rule. The Prussian junkers were forged into instruments of the state by Frederick William I and his son, but their proprietary privileges and freedoms were preserved.

10. Cited in *Suomen historian dokumentteja*, vol. 1, Helsinki 1968, p. 395. On Chydenius, see the recent biography by Virrankoski p. 1986. Anders Chydenius: demokraattinen poliitikko valistuksen mosisadalta. Porvoo. See also Forsman K 1947 Studier i det svenska 1700-talets ekonomiska litteratur *Svenska Litteratursällskapet i Finland* **312**. Helsingfors, pp. 205–232.
11. Klose, Degn 1960, p. 86. In fact, the first appointee as director, A. P. Bernsdorff, had to be received into the *Ritterschaft* of the duchies.

The contemporary concept of 'freedom', as employed in the journals and reformist literature of the age, was that which encouraged and promoted the common good; in J. S. Sneedorff's words, it 'always has the effect of making people more reasonable and more active'.[12] It was not generally construed as an inalienable individual right. Thus, the freedom of the press was regarded by Chydenius and others as a means of establishing the truth, a guarantee against an absolutist government, and a form of dialogue between governors and governed. Chydenius' fellow-countryman Petter Forsskål believed that it made more sense for the government to allow the public to voice its dissatisfaction with the pen than with other weapons.[13] Liberties were indeed graciously conceded by the enlightened state, rather than demanded as natural rights of free citizens. Since rulers found it advantageous to the general prosperity of the realm to admit foreign entrepreneurs and workers, religious minorities were tolerated and allowed to build their own places of worship; but the laws enforcing Lutheran orthodoxy remained. Freedom was also masculine: the rights of women were rarely raised. Nor was freedom universally welcomed. The liberalisation of trade and industry introduced by Struensee aroused the hostility of entrenched privileged groups and suddenly exposed the fragile domestic economy to the winds of competition. Many landowners feared the worst consequences of peasant emancipation, and not all peasants viewed the prospect of freedom from their landlord with unalloyed joy. William Jacob recorded in the 1820s that the Polish peasants of West Prussia were worried 'that in age or sickness, or other incapacity, they should be abandoned by their lords and left to perish in want', and although experience had shown that fear to be exaggerated, Jacob nonetheless observed that it was generally acknowledged that the peasants were in a worse condition than under the old system, due to the agricultural depression and lack of capital.[14]

The actions taken to dismantle the constraints upon free and unhindered economic activity were by no means uniform or even consistent. Regulations relating to trade and manufacturing might be relaxed, but those dealing with labour were often tightened. The right freely to choose one's occupation was not fully conceded until the nineteenth century. The sanctions and punishments ordained by the

12. Holm E 1975 *Kongemagt, folk og borgerlig frihed* (reprint of 1883 edn). Copenhagen, p. 56.
13. Zilliacus C, Knif H 1985 Opinionens tryck. En studie över pressens bildningsskede i Finland *Svenska Litteratursällskapet i Finland* **526**. Helsingfors, p. 27.
14. Jacob W 1826 *Report on the trade in foreign corn and on the agriculture of the north of Europe*. London, pp. 64–5.

state and upheld by the church for the better regulation of society, the petty prejudices and snobberies of rank, still remained largely intact. Frederick II, an avowed upholder of aristocratic status, forbade the Junkers to engage in urban trade or enterprises in 1752 on the grounds that this might distract them from the *métier d'honneur* of military service. The legal code of 1794 reasserted the 'natural, inalienable and sacred rights of noblemen' and strictly defined the economic spheres of burghers, peasants and nobles. Artisans and merchants alike still sought to control and restrict entry into their ranks. The memorial laid before the Swedish estate of burghers in 1770 by Alexander Kepplerus did not seek to overthrow the existing social order, though by making property the basis for the rights of the non-noble *odalstån-det* – an archaic term which may loosely be translated as the yeoman estate – the author of the memorial was, however unwittingly, 'an advocate of the approaching class society'.[15] Nevertheless, the non-noble estates in Sweden, although united in demanding the opening up of offices to all men of ability, still jealously guarded their own privileges and sought to preserve their exclusivity. The peasants, who nursed their own grievances against the merchants of the towns, were disinclined to support them in their struggle against the oligarchic magistracy; and apart from a few passionate humanitarians such as Chydenius, none championed the rights of the poor and landless.

Rank and status were indeed important, as the constant invention of new titles and honours and the many publications of manuals of etiquette reveal. Between the old order of closed corporations and prescribed socio-political categories and the new, heterogenous middle class, there existed an uneasy relationship. The highest ranks of the *literati* might be accepted as social equals by the urban patriciate in the Baltic provinces, but musicians and artists were simply regarded as artisans. In the more cosmopolitan atmosphere of the larger cities such as Danzig and Königsberg, lawyers and merchants mingled freely with French refugees and army officers in the clubs and lodges, but the gilds still upheld their strict code of honour. The social structure of the towns resembled the urban topography, where splendid rococo town houses, coffee houses, theatres and parks co-existed alongside the Gothic churches, warehouses and town halls. Entrepreneurs such as Friedrich Saturgus in Königsberg or Johann Friedrich Jürgens in Reval were able to amass fortunes as suppliers of provisions to the armed forces or as bankers and manufacturers; enjoying the patronage

15. Bonsdorff G von 1952 En finländsk insats i frihetstidens statsrättsliga diskussion *Svenska Litteratursällskapet i Finland* **335** Helsingfors, p. 334. There is some controversy about the actual author: *ibid*, pp. 357–8.

of the crown, they were also less likely to identify themselves with the defence of ancient liberties. On the other hand, the long-distance export trade seems to have remained under the control of the old-established firms, many of which reinforced their position through judicious marriages and adaptability to changing circumstances. The wealthy burghers of Stockholm, for example, acquired their own institution for tax adjustment: the *Grosserer-Societetet*, founded in 1742, represented the interests of the wholesale merchants of Copenhagen.

Absolutist monarchs sought to enforce control over the towns, but they were also reluctant to overthrow entirely the established social and political structure. Frederick II's regulations of 1755 clearly defined the exclusive nature of burgherage, for example, and although Catherine II's town ordinance of 1785 sought to transform the estates into organic components of a centralised state, it was ambiguous in its definition of the 'town', which was seen as composed of a community of inhabitants according to occupation and as the place of domicile of an hereditary estate (*Geburtsstand*). The former exclusivity of burgherage was breached, only to be replaced by 'state citizenship' (*Staatsbürgerrecht*) defined on local and corporate lines. Elections replaced co-option to the town council, with six categories of electors according to property, calling and estate. The possibility of non-Germans acquiring burgher rights was significantly reduced by the action of the Imperial Senate and the *Statthalter* (the new title of the governor-general), though three mast inspectors of Latvian origin at least managed to squeeze through the obstacles in Riga. However, this 'pseudo-corporatist' restructuring of urban government did not survive the death of the empress in 1796.[16]

Mere possession of ancient lineage, however, was no longer regarded as sufficient. Fichte characterised the old nobility of Prussia as little more than arrogant flatterers, tolerated only in artistic or mercantile circles if they made an effort to be humble. The new passport

16. Elias O-H 1978 *Reval in der Reformpolitik Katharinas II* Quellen und Studien zur baltischen Geschichte 3. Bonn–Bad Godesberg, pp. 102ff. Elias O-H 1966 Die undeutsche Bevölkerung im Riga des 18 Jahrhunderts *Jahrbücher für Geschichte Osteuropas* **14**: 481–4, Thaden E 1984 *Russia's western borderlands, 1710–1870*. Princeton, NJ, pp. 27–31. According to Marc Raeff (The well-ordered police state and the development of modernity in seventeenth- and eighteenth-century Europe *American Historical Review* 1975, **80**, 1140–3) Catherine was obliged to create estates in order to reform. In 1808, over twenty years after the emperor Paul had rescinded Catherine's legislation, Frédéric-César de la Harpe wrote urgently to his former tutee, the emperor Alexander I, that Russia would never be a civilised country on a par with other nations as long as the bourgeois third estate was excluded from a share in government. Biaudet J, Nicod F 1979 *Correspondance de Frédéric-César de la Harpe et Alexandre I* (vol. 2). Neuchâtel, p. 293.

to social advancement and success was *Bildung*: an ancient name counted for little if its bearer were not refined and educated. The notion of education for a profession was one of the distinctive features of the age. Although the officer corps remained predominantly a noble preserve, it was not enough simply to be a gentleman. Noble cadets had to digest the contents of training manuals and pass through the military academies which were founded during the course of the century. The obsession of the age with scientific enquiry meant that they had to show some familiarity with learned treatises on ballistics and fortifications. In order to keep up with the latest developments, they would have to subscribe to professional military literature, such as the Danish *Militærisk Bibliotek* (1765–6), the second-oldest military periodical in Europe, or its successor, *Den danske Krigsbibliotek*, which had almost a thousand subscribers in its first year, 1794.[17] The increasing demand for qualified personnel to sort out legal problems, design dwellings or carry out a land survey gave the professional a greater degree of social status and independence. Lawyers, as always, were able to command sizeable fees: Hupel contended that it was not unknown for a man to own a house, coach and horses after three years' law practice, and to buy a small estate in the country after a few more years. Land surveyors in eastern Finland were bold enough to defy the government's refusal of passports, and practised their trade across the frontier: Isak Hasselbladt, for instance, was in Russian employ for over a decade, but continued to live in Finland, where he also held a post in the local administration.

The value of the skilled professional was also recognised in the creation of institutions and academies to promote the arts, industry and agriculture. Architects such as Nicodemus Tessin and his son Carl Gustav elevated their calling above the ranks of the artisan masons (and acquired noble title in the process); and if the petty-minded burghers of provincial towns still relegated actors, painters and musicians to the outer margins of polite society, royal and noble patrons did not. Many exalted personages such as the Swedish poets Gustav Philip Creutz and Johan Gabriel Oxenstierna, Frederick II of Prussia and Gustav III were indeed accomplished artists in their own right.

Certain professions also sought to elevate their status. The Danish barber-surgeons, for example, set up their own teaching institute in 1736; reorganised in 1785 as the Royal Chirurgical Academy, it pro-

17. On this question, see Lind G 1986 Den dansk-norske hær i det 18 århundrede *Historisk Tidskrift* **86**: 26–73. Artéus G 1982 *Krigsmakt och samhälle i frihetstidens Sverige*. Stockholm; Busch O 1962 *Militärsystem und Socialleben im alten Preussen 1713–1807* Veröffentlichungen der Berliner Historischen Kommission 30/7. Berlin.

vided Denmark with properly qualified district surgeons, and finally severed the demeaning link with barbering, bringing surgical skills within the ambit of academic medical training and practice. Those whose talents had a scarcity value could command a good price or advance socially, like the Danish barber's assistant who was made a court official because he was adept at shaving and bleeding the local gentry. Not all were successful in obtaining social recognition, however. J. J. Kanter's efforts to secure the title of *Commercienrat* was turned down by Frederick the Great on the grounds that 'bookseller' was an honest enough title. Writers of articles in the many encyclopedias which flourished at the end of the century advocated the provision of a proper training for schoolteachers, which would give them status and respect; but although there were almost 3,000 members of the *nobilitas literariae* in Kurland in 1797, elementary schoolteachers were notable by their absence. The general legal code in 1794 included grammar-school teachers amongst the privileged officials of the Prussian state, but explicitly excluded the elementary schoolteachers from the *Staatsbürgertum*.

'In the past thirty years, our manners and customs have become very refined,' wrote A. W. Hupel in 1777, 'Even the poorest artisan cannot celebrate a wedding without wine, punch and a groaning table; his wife appears on Sunday in a decidedly bourgeois dress; without coffee, she could hardly pass the day in peace.'[18] The cramped, straw-thatched houses in which many of the rural nobility of the Baltic provinces lived in the aftermath of the Great Northern War were torn down and replaced by commodious stone-built mansions; the bucolic dancing and singing to the sounds of the bagpipe were disappearing as the peasantry too adopted the habits of the town-dweller. As early as 1683, the bishop of Visby noted that peasants on the island of Gotland were beginning to forsake their traditional garb for town dress, and peasants on the Norrland coast began buying their clothes in the towns with the money earned from sales of their produce. Painted chests and furniture, porcelain cups, wallhangings and even carpets indicate the growing affluence of a section of the rural population of Scandinavia. The old communal pleasure-gardens of the Hanse towns became amusement parks and Tivolis; the *Junkerhöfe* were turned into rooms to be hired out for concerts or private functions. In their place appeared private clubs, salons and lodges, where members of the urban elite mingled. The transformation of the shooting clubs into voluntary associations (*Freischützen*), not attached to any specific

18. Hupel 1777, p. 40.

gilds, marked the transition from the closed corporation to the voluntary bourgeois organisation. The periodic attempts of the state to curb consumption of luxuries were deeply unpopular amongst all sections of society: the spies employed by the Swedish government to sniff out the places where coffee might be brewing were heartily detested by peasant and noblewoman alike. Significantly, the renewal of the ban on coffee consumption in 1794 merely appealed to the honesty and goodwill of the king's subjects to obey the law.

The spread of comfortable prosperity to the middle classes – a term which came into use during the last two decades of the century – and certain sections of the peasantry should not be allowed to obscure the poverty and wretchedness of the growing numbers of the landless proletariat, nor indeed the generally low standard of living which travellers found in the less fertile regions of the north. Those who would know not to clean glasses with their spittle or beg for a twist of tobacco (experiences recounted by Malthus's travelling companion, Edward Clarke), or could afford to deck their tables with fresh fruit and flowers were still a small minority of the population. Nevertheless, economic wellbeing did foster a self-awareness and self-confidence and sustained the spirit of inquisitiveness – and of acquisition – which contemporaries proudly declared to be the characteristic of their age. It brought good manners to the dining table and 'bon ton' to the assemblies, soirées and balls, it sustained the coffee-houses and debating clubs and the newspapers and periodicals which now appeared in almost every town of any pretension. It even inspired satire and caricature, from Carl Michael Bellman's anti-club for dissolute drunkards, *Bacchi-Orden*, to Frans Michael Franzén's dig at the Swedish press in his satire, *Om Sällskapet Publicum*.

The economic century to some, the philosophical century to others, the age was also profoundly patriotic. Local pride in distinctive features – church towers, fair maidens, fine ales – had existed for centuries, and the tradition still flourished. Inhabitants of Königsberg, for example, stoutly averred that Zerlina was tempted into Don Giovanni's house by promises of *Bratwurst* and Löbenicht ale. Love of the fatherland in societies where the aristocracy was politically dominant, as in Denmark before 1660, or in Poland–Lithuania, was strongly coloured by a corporatist viewpoint; this kind of corporate particularism (*Ständespartikularismus*) still flourished in the Baltic provinces, Kurland, Pomerania and Holstein. On the other hand, the expansion of the state's activities and the superimposition of centralised royal authority over the ancient pattern of semi-autonomous corporations created new loyalties which began to stretch beyond the person of the sovereign to embrace the nation. In a word, the citizen with a stake in the affairs of the country was superseding the subject whose duty it was simply to obey.

In this regard, the events of 1772 raised fundamental questions about the national composition and cohesion of the state. The partitioning of Poland–Lithuania helped unleash a reform movement which did seriously attempt to come to grips with the problems of government and finance which had bedevilled the commonwealth for so long. In its last years, the doomed Polish–Lithuanian commonwealth witnessed a resurgence of patriotism which was kept fiercely alive in the emigration and amongst those who now found themselves under different rulers. The partitioning powers had acted out of suspicion of each others' ambitions, beginning that curious process of reluctant cooperation which was ultimately to disintegrate into hostility and war at the beginning of the twentieth century. To the disparate collection of lands, provinces, duchies and khanates acquired by Austria and Russia as Ottoman power declined was added the truncated residue of a once-great power. The creation of a German empire under king Wilhelm I a century later has perhaps tended to obscure the 'half-German' roots of the Prussian state; and as Rudolf von Thadden notes, it seemed after the third partition of Poland in 1795 as if the fulcrum of the Hohenzollern state was about to shift away from Germany, leading Prussia down the road of the multinational Habsburg monarchy.[19] Although the Prussian state integrated its new acquisitions rather more ruthlessly and efficiently than did its partners in the partitions, it was no more successful in eradicating the Poles' attachment to their past independence.

The impending fate of Poland was viewed with much concern and alarm by Gustav III. In April 1772, he noted that: 'In Sweden, an exaggerated liberty, which has degenerated into self-indulgence and which, as a result of the crown's (perhaps premature) attempts to limit it, has intensified into a state of anarchy; this anarchy, if not as disastrous as that in Poland, is perhaps no less deplorable, since a remedy seems even less likely.'[20] The staging of a bloodless *coup* four months later can only be understood in the light of general weariness with factional party strife, which threatened to reduce a once-great

19. Thadden R von 1981 *Fragen an Preussen. Zur Geschichte eines aufgehobenen Staates.* Munich, p. 29. cited in: Zernack K 1983 Die Geschichte Preussens und das Problem der deutsch-polnischen Beziehungen *Jahrbücher für Geschichte Osteuropas* **31**: 40. See also Biskup M 1983 Preussen und Polen *Jahrbücher für Geschichte Osteuropas* **31**: 1–27.

20. Cited in Konopcynski L 1925 Polen och Sverige i det adertonde århundradet. En historisk parallel *Historisk Tidskrift* **45**: 101.

kingdom to the plaything of foreign powers: the king was hailed as having restored a lost fatherland to its citizens. Within a decade, however, members of the nobility who had backed the king were beginning to drift into opposition, and their discontent was to erupt into mutiny during the war against Russia in the summer of 1788. One most intimately involved in planning the *coup* in 1772 who was to become a bitter opponent of the king was the Finnish officer Göran Magnus Sprengtporten. In a series of letters to a friend, published shortly after the *coup*, Sprengtporten regretted that the law had fallen victim to self-interest, and the fatherland had become a market-place. What was needed was 'a certain unanimity of thought and mode of living', which could inspire enthusiasm and unity in the Swedish nation: laws decreed by a plurality (*mångvälde*) were not enough.[21]

In his letters, Sprengtporten proudly proclaimed that it had been Finns who had supported the throne in its hour of need. Sprengtporten, who had been mocked for his uncouth accent at cadet school, was probably voicing little more than the glee of the provincial at the humbling of the high and mighty in the capital. The regimental district of Savo, in which Sprengtporten was based, was regarded as akin to Siberia by fastidious Swedes: the poet Johan Oxenstierna mockingly asked a lady-in-waiting who became engaged to a captain in the Savo regiment if she would boast of eating fried turnips and pork daubed in bear-grease.[22] There was more than a grain of truth in the frequent accusation made by memoir-writers after 1809 that Swedish indifference and haughtiness had alienated many Finns, though against this must be set the strong loyalty of the people, and their hostility towards those who seemed to be plotting to detach Finland from Swedish rule, during the crisis of 1788.

The resentment felt by Swedish-speaking provincials in Finland towards the grandees of the capital was paralleled in the wave of anti-German sentiment following Struensee's downfall in Copenhagen. It was not only Danish writers such as P. A. Heiberg who satirised the grasping Germans: so did the members of the Norwegian Society. The Norwegian poet Edvard Storm greeted the 1776 law, which restricted entry into state service to native-born and naturalised subjects of the king, in the following manner:

21. Cited in: En finsk officerares bref till sin vän i Stockholm *Historiallinen Arkisto* **17**: 242–3, Helsinki, 1902. See also Carlsson S 1979 Rikets sprängning 1809 *Skrifter utgivna av Svenska Litteratursällskapet i Finland* **483**: 115–27; and Lesch B 1933 Självständighetsmännen och den nationella romantiken på Gustav IIIs tid *Skrifter utgivna av Svenska Litteratursällskapet i Finland* **236**: 283–305.
22. Castrén G 1958 Finland i Sveriges 1700-talsdikt *Skrifter utgivna av Svenska Litteratursällskapet i Finland* **368**: 328, 333.

Lad o, Udlænding af mit Folkes Brød at æde,
Giv fødde Undersaat igien sit eget Sæde.
Kun den, som første Lys i Danske Stater saae
Skal Borgerret og Rang i Christians Rige naae.

(Cease, foreigner, of my people's bread to eat,
Give native subjects again their rightful seat.
To him alone, who first saw light in Danish states
Shall burgher's rights and rank in Christian's realm await.)[23]

In February 1772, Danish was declared to be the official language in all matters concerning Denmark and Norway and the language of command in the army. Three years later, the teaching of Danish was introduced into the grammar schools, and it was also proposed that pupils should study Danish history. Ove Malling's *Store og gode Handlinger af Danske, Norske og Holstenere*, with its selection of heroes from all parts of the realm and society and its notion of the fatherland as the whole state, under the unifying symbol of an absolutist monarch, won official approval; but the Guldberg regime was critical of P. F. Suhm's draft history, which was held to be biased towards the Norwegians. Suhm, who had complained in an anonymous pamphlet published in Germany in 1771 that Norway lacked schools and academies, was obliged to give way before Guldberg's brusque instruction, 'there are no Norwegians. We are all citizens in the Danish state.' In his corrected manuscript, he declared the fatherland to be all the lands ruled over by the king.[24]

The notion of a single state (*helstat*) was indeed little more than a projection of absolutism, devoid of truly integrative features, such as a common parliament or even common laws and customs. The nobility of Holstein still retained a corporate identity and their committee, renamed the 'Perpetual Deputation' after 1773, acted as a link between crown and land. Andreas Peter Bernsdorff, who directed the affairs of the duchy on the crown's behalf, was content to leave alone its peculiar administrative and judicial features. Holsteiners welcomed the exclusion of foreigners from office in Denmark, since it provided new opportunities for them: but their narrow particularism (and their use of German) aroused hostility and provoked unrest in 1790.

The officials and merchants who constituted the upper echelons of Norwegian society identified more closely with the Danish state than did the peasantry, who tended to be on the receiving end of tax burdens and military impositions. There was a rebellion in the Bergen

23. Infødsretten (1778), quoted in Olsen 1936, p. 122.
24. Feldbæk O 1984 Kærlighed til fædrelandet. 1700-tallets nationale selvforståelse *Fortid og Nutid* **31**: 280.

district against the poll tax and the extortions of officials in 1765, and another tax revolt led by Christian Lofthuus some twenty years later. There was nonetheless growing dissatisfaction amongst the mercantile classes with the restrictions placed upon the Norwegian economy. The upsurge in overseas trade as a result of the Anglo-French colonial wars boosted the self-confidence of the Norwegian merchants, who were attracted to the growing campaign for improvements in their country's wellbeing. With their connections overseas, they were also open to new ideas, such as those of Adam Smith, whose *Wealth of Nations* was translated into Danish in 1779. The ideals of the French Revolution seem to have penetrated deeply into Norwegian society. Mary Wollstonecraft tried in vain to persuade the citizens of Moss of the tyranny of Robespierre, and even the clergy introduced fraternity, liberty and equality into their sermons and pastoral letters. In 1790, the crabbed old conservative Ove Guldberg, no longer in high office, voiced his fears that Norway would be lost at the slightest disturbance, though he was of the opinion that the republic which the Norwegians wanted was in the English spirit. Rather more influential in creating a sense of Norwegian identity were the tireless activists for a university and a bank in Norway, poets, pamphleteers and historians, who revealed the special and noteworthy features of Norwegian history and society. The revolutionary and Napoleonic wars were to show that Norway was probably by no means a fully integrated part of the single state (*helstat*) of the absolutist monarchy. There were very real differences of social structure and patterns of land tenure between Norway and Denmark. The populations of the two kingdoms were roughly equal, Norway had a long history of independence and had become united with Denmark through dynastic marriage, not conquest, and yet, during the absolutist era, it had become little more than a peripheral territory whose affairs were all decided in Copenhagen.

The separation of Finland from Sweden, and of Norway from Denmark, will be considered more fully in the next volume: but it is perhaps necessary to say at this stage that these events owed more to the course of international relations than to the volition of the Finnish or Norwegian people. It is certain that the enthusiasm for folksong and the life of the people inspired poets and artists to seek new themes and to express different attitudes. Where versifiers had earlier expressed patriotism in martial terms, extolling the heroic virtues of warrior kings such as Karl XII or lamenting the fate of towns destroyed or conquered by the enemy, poets of the age of Rousseau and Herder such as the Norwegians Edvard Storm, Nordal Brun and Jens Zetlitz or the Finn Carl Michael Franzén looked to man and nature as the inspiration for love of the fatherland. The 'discovery of the people' was to become one of the most vibrant chords of the nationalist movement in the nineteenth century; but it was still in its more idyllic and apolitical phase in the eighteenth. The older traditions of Gothicism still lived on: Gustav Bonde was a tireless disciple of Rudbeck, claiming in 1755 to have identified the Finns as one of the lost tribes of Israel, and lengthy polemics were waged with sceptics such as Olof Dalin, who maintained that the country had been mostly under water when it had been supposedly settled by the Swedes' illustrious ancestors. Loyalty to the monarchy and identification by rank and status, rather than with the people or nation: these were the hallmarks of the age of reason and enlightenment. Admiration for and pride in one's province or region added colour to such sentiments, but did not constitute a desire for separate statehood.

Select Bibliography

This list is primarily confined to works in English, though important books and articles in other languages are also included.

GENERAL

Anderson M 1958 *Britain's discovery of Russia 1553–1825*. London.

Barton A 1986 *Scandinavia in the revolutionary era 1760–1815*. Minneapolis.

Carsten F 1954 *The origins of Prussia*. Oxford.

Christiansen E 1980 *The Northern Crusades. The Baltic and the Catholic Frontier 1100–1525*. London.

Davies N 1981 *God's playground. A history of Poland* (2 vols). Oxford.

Derry T 1979 *A history of Scandinavia*. London.

Eckhardt J 1876 *Livland im achtzehnten Jahrhundert*. Leipzig.

Holm E 1891–1901 *Danmark-Norges Historie fra den store nordiske Krigs Slutning til Rigernes Adskillelse* (7 vols). Copenhagen.

Hovde B 1943, 1948 *The Scandinavian countries 1720–1865* (2 vols). Boston, Ithaca.

Jeannin P 1969 *L'Europe du Nord-Ouest et du Nord aux XVIIe et XVIIIe siècles*. Paris.

Kouri E, Scott T (eds) 1988 *Politics and society in Reformation Europe*. London.

Nordmann C 1971 *Grandeur et liberté de la Suède (1660–1792)*. Paris.

Oakley S 1972 *The story of Denmark*. London.

Roberts M 1967 *Essays in Swedish history.* London.

Roberts M ed 1968 *Sweden as a great power 1611–1697.* London.

Roberts M 1968 *The early Vasas. A history of Sweden 1523–1611.* Cambridge.

Roberts M 1979 *The Swedish Imperial Experience 1560–1718.* Cambridge.

Roberts M 1986 *The age of liberty. Sweden 1719–1772.* Cambridge.

Scott F 1978 *Sweden. The nation's history.* Minneapolis.

Spekke A 1951 *History of Latvia.* Stockholm.

Wittram R 1954 *Baltische Geschichte die Ostseelande Livland, Estland, Kurland 1180–1918.* Munich.

Zernack K 1981 Schweden als europäische Grossmacht der frühen Neuzeit *Historische Zeitschrift* **232**.

BIOGRAPHIES

Andersson I 1963 *Erik XIV* revised edn. Stockholm.

Barudio G 1985 *Gustav Adolf der Grosse. Eine politische Biographie.* Frankfurt-am-Main.

Donnert E 1978 *Johann Georg Eisen. Ein Vorkämpfer der Bauernbefreiung in Russland.* Leipzig.

Erdmann Y 1970 *Der livländische Staatsmann Johann Reinhold von Patkul.* Berlin.

Frey L and M 1984 *Frederick I: The man and his times.* East European Monographs 166, New York.

Hatton R 1968 *Charles XII of Sweden.* London.

Hennings B 1957 *Gustav III. En biografi.* Stockholm.

Madariaga I de 1981 *Russia in the age of Catherine the Great.* London.

Roberts M 1953, 1958 *Gustavus Adolphus. A history of Sweden 1611–1632* (2 vols). London.

Roberts M 1973 *Gustavus Adolphus and the rise of Sweden.* London.

Wittram R 1964 *Peter I. Czar und Kaiser* (2 vols). Göttingen.

ECONOMIC HISTORY

Boëthius B 1958 Swedish iron and steel 1600–1955 *Scandinavian Economic History Review* **6**.

Gille P 1949 The demographic history of the northern European countries in the eighteenth century *Population Studies* **3**.

Hecksher E 1931 Natural and money economy *Journal of Economic and Business History* **3**.

Hecksher E 1935–49 *Sveriges ekonomiska historia från Gustav Vasa.* (2 vols). Stockholm.

Hecksher E 1954 *An economic history of Sweden.* Cambridge, Mass.

Jørgensen J 1971 The economic condition of Zealand provincial towns in the eighteenth century *Scandinavian Economic History Review* **19**.

Kellenbenz H 1954 German aristocratic entrepreneurship. Economic activities of the Holstein nobility in the sixteenth and seventeenth centuries *Explorations in Entrepreneurial History* **6**.

Metcalf M 1982 Challenges to economic orthodoxy and parliamentary sovereignty in eighteenth-century Sweden *Legislative Studies Quarterly* **7**.

Morell M 1987 Eli F Hecksher, the 'food budget' and Swedish food consumption from the sixteenth to the nineteenth century *Scandinavian Economic History Review* **35**.

Utterström G 1955 Climatic fluctuations and population problems in early modern history *Scandinavian Economic History Review* **3**.

Utterström G 1959 Migratory labour and the herring fisheries of western Sweden in the eighteenth century *Scandinavian Economic History Review* **7**.

Utterström G 1962 Labour policy and population thought in eighteenth-century Sweden *Scandinavian Economic History Review* **10**.

Åström S-E 1986 The role of Finland in the Swedish national and war economies during Sweden's period as a great power *Scandinavian Journal of History* **11**.

TRADE

Attman A 1973 *The Russian and Polish markets in international trade 1500–1650.* Publications of the Institute of Economic History of Gothenburg University 26. Göteborg.

Attman A 1979 *The struggle for Baltic markets. Powers in conflict 1558–1618.* Acta Regiae Societatis Scientiarum et Litterarum Gothoburgensis. Humaniora 14. Göteborg.

Attman A 1985 *Swedish aspirations and the Russian market during the 17th century.* Acta Regiae Societatis Scientiarum et Litterarum Gothoburgensis. Humaniora 24. Göteborg.

Bogucka M 1973 Amsterdam and the Baltic in the first half of the seventeenth century *Economic History Review*, Second Series, **26**.

Bogucka 1974 Danzigs Bedeutung für die Wirtschaft des Ostseeraumes in der frühen Neuzeit *Studia Historica Oeconomicae* **9**.

Bogucka M 1984 Danzig an der Wende zur Neuzeit: von der aktiven Handelstadt zum Stapel und Produktionszentrum. *Hansische Geschichtsblätter* **102**.

Christiansen A 1941 *Dutch trade to the Baltic about 1600*. Copenhagen–The Hague.

Doroshenko V, Kahk J, Ligi H, Piirimäe H, Tarvel E. 1974 *Trade and agrarian development in the Baltic provinces 15th–19th centuries.* Tallinn.

Faber J 1966 The decline of the Baltic grain trade in the second half of the seventeenth century *Acta Historica Neerlandica* **1**.

Fedorowicz J 1980 *England's Baltic trade in the early seventeenth century. A study in Anglo-Polish commercial diplomacy.* Cambridge.

Hildebrand K-G 1954 Salt and cloth in Swedish economic history. *Scandinavian Economic History Review* **2**.

Hildebrand K-G 1958 Foreign markets for Swedish iron in the eighteenth century *Scandinavian Economic History Review* **6**.

Hinton R 1959 *The Eastland trade and the common weal.* Cambridge.

Hoszowski S 1960 The Polish Baltic trade in the 15th–18th centuries *Poland at the 11th International Congress of Historical Science at Stockholm.* Warsaw.

Jeannin P 1964 Les comptes du Sund comme source pour la construction d'indices généraux de l'activité économique en Europe (XVIe–XVIIIe siècles) *Revue Historique* **231**.

Jørgensen J 1963 Denmark's relations with Lübeck and Hamburg in the seventeenth century *Scandinavian Economic History Review* **11**.

Kirby D 1974 The Royal Navy's quest for pitch and tar during the reign of Queen Anne *Scandinavian Economic History Review* **22**.

Kirchner W 1966 *Commercial relations between Russia and Europe 1400–1800.* Bloomington.

Knoppers J 1976 *Dutch trade with Russia from the time of Peter I to Alexander I.* Montreal.

Malowist M 1959 The economic and social development of the Baltic countries from the fifteenth to the seventeenth centuries *Economic History Review*, Second Series, **12**.

Reading D 1938 *The Anglo–Russian commercial treaty of 1734.* New Haven.

Willan T 1956 *The early history of the Russia Company 1553–1603.* Manchester.

Zins H 1972 *England and the Baltic in the Elizabethan era.* Manchester and Totowa, NJ.

Åström S-E 1962 *From Stockholm to St Petersburg. Commercial factors in the political relations between England and Sweden 1675–1700.* Studia Historica 2. Helsinki.

Åström S-E 1975 Technology and timber exports from the Gulf of Finland 1661–1740 *Scandinavian Economic History Review* **23**.

Öhberg A 1956 Russia and the world market in the seventeenth century *Scandinavian Economic History Review* **3**.

THE LAND

Abel W 1986 *Agricultural fluctuations in Europe from the thirteenth to the twentieth centuries.* London.

Blum J 1978 *The end of the old order in rural Europe.* Princeton.

Christiansen A 1960 The development of large-scale farming in Denmark 1525–1774 *Scandinavian Economic History Review* **8**.

Dahl S 1961 Strip fields and enclosure in Sweden *Scandinavian Economic History Review* **9**.

Dunsdorfs E 1981 *The Livonian estates of Axel Oxenstierna.* Stockholm.

Jutikkala E 1975 Large-scale farming in Scandinavia in the seventeenth century *Scandinavian Economic History Review* **23**.

Olsen G 1957 *Hovedgård og bondegård: Studier over stordriftens udvikling i Danmark i tiden 1525–1744.* Copenhagen.

Schwabe A n.d. *Agrarian History of Latvia.* Riga.

Skrubbeltrang F 1979 *Det danske landbosamfund 1500–1800.* Copenhagen.

Soininen A 1964 Burn-beating as a technical basis for colonisation *Scandinavian Economic History Review* **12**.

Soom A 1954 *Die Herrenhof in Estland im 17 Jahrhundert.* Lund.

GOVERNMENT AND POLITICS

Back P-E 1955 *Herzog und Landschaft. Politische Ideen und Verfassungsprogramme in Schwedisch-Pommern um die Mitte des 17 Jahrhunderts.* Lund.

Backus O 1963 The problem of unity in the Polish-Lithuanian state *Slavic Review* **22**.

Brolin P–E 1953 *Hattar och mössor i borgarståndet 1760–1766.* Uppsala.

Bøggild-Andersen C 1971 *Statsomvæltingen i 1660* (reprint of 1936 edn). Århus.

Dahlgen S 1964 *Karl X Gustav och reduktionen.* Uppsala.

Ekman E 1957 The Danish Royal Law of 1665 *Journal of Modern History* **29**.

Hintze O 1967 *Regierung und Verwaltung. Gesammelte Abhandlungen zur Staats- Rechts- und Sozialgeschichte Preussens* (3 vols). Göttingen.

Ladewig Petersen E 1975 From domain state to tax state *Scandinavian Economic History Review* **23**.

Ladewig Petersen E 1982 Defence, war and finance. Christian IV and the council of the realm 1596–1629 *Scandinavian Journal of History* **7**.

Ladewig Petersen E (ed.) 1984 *Magtstaten i Norden i 1600-tallet og dens sociale konsekvenser. Rapporter til den XIX nordiske historikerkongres.* Odense.

Lundquist C 1975 *Council, king and estates in Sweden 1713–14.* Stockholm.

Neuschäffer H 1975 *Katherina II und die baltischen Provinzen* Beiträge zur baltischen Geschichte 2. Hannover-Döhren.

Peterson C 1979 *Peter the Great's administrative and judicial reforms: Swedish antecedents and the process of reception* Skrifter utgivna av Institutet för rättshistorisk forskning 1:29. Stockholm.

Rosén J 1946 Statsledning och provinspolitik under Sveriges stormaktstid *Scandia* **17**.

Rosenberg H 1958 *Bureaucracy, aristocracy and autocracy. The Prussian experience 1660–1815* Harvard Historical Monographs 35. Cambridge.

Rystad G 1963 Med råds råde eller efter konungens godtycke? *Scandia* **29**.

Thaden E 1981 Estland, Livland and the Ukraine: reflections on eighteenth-century regional autonomy *Journal of Baltic Studies* **12**.

Thaden E 1984 *Russia's western borderlands, 1710–1870.* Princeton.

Upton A 1987 The Riksdag of 1680 and the establishment of royal absolutism in Sweden *English Historical Review* **403**.

SOCIAL HISTORY

Artéus G 1982 *Krigsmakt och samhälle i frihetstidens Sverige.* Stockholm.

Artéus G 1986 *Till militärstatens förhistoria. Krig, professionalisering och social förändring under Vasasönernas regering* Militärhistoriska studier 8. Stockholm.

Busch O 1962 *Militärsystem und Sozialleben im alten Preussen 1713–1807*. Berlin.

Carlsson S 1949 *Ståndsamhälle och ståndspersoner 1700–1865*. Lund.

Ladewig Petersen E 1980 *Fra standssamfund til rangssamfund 1500–1700* (Dansk social historie, vol. 3). Copenhagen.

Lind G 1987 Military and absolutism: The army officers of Denmark–Norway as a social group and political factors 1660–1848 *Scandinavian Journal of History* **12**.

Montelius S 1966 Recruitment and conditions of life of Swedish ironworkers during the eighteenth and nineteenth centuries *Scandinavian Economic History Review* **14**.

Rystad G (ed.) 1983 *Europe and Scandinavia: aspects of the process of integration in the 17th century*. Lund Studies in International History 18. Lund.

Samuelsson K 1968 *From great power to welfare state. 300 years of Swedish social development*. London.

Wirilander K 1982 *Herrskapsfolk. Ståndspersoner i Finland 1721–1870* Nordiska museets handlingar 98. Stockholm.

Ylikangas 1976 Major fluctuations in crimes of violence in Finland *Scandinavian Journal of History* **1**.

THE PEASANTRY

Berg G, Svensson S 1969 *Svensk bondekultur*. Stockholm.

Bjørn C 1977 The peasantry and agrarian reform in Denmark *Scandinavian Economic History Review* **25**.

Bjørn C 1981 *Bonde, herremand, konge. Bonden i 1700-tallets Danmark*. Copenhagen.

Carlsson S 1948 Bondeståndet i Norden under senare delen av 1700-talet *Scandia* **19**.

Henning E 1969 *Bauernwirtschaft und Bauerneinkommen in Ostpreussen im 18 Jahrhundert*. Würzburg.

Ingers E 1948 *Bonden i svensk historia* (2 vols). Stockholm.

Munck T 1979 *The peasantry and the early absolute monarchy in Denmark 1660–1708*. Copenhagen.

Transehe-Roseneck A von 1890 *Gutsherr und Bauer in Livland im 17 und 18 Jahrhundert* Abhandlungen aus dem Staatswissenschaftlichen Seminar zu Strassburg 7. Strassburg.

THE NOBILITY

Carsten F 1989 *History of the Prussian Junker*. Aldershot.

Elmroth I 1981 *För kung och fosterland. Studier i den svenska adelns demografi och offentliga funktioner 1600–1900*. Biblioteca historica Lundensis 50. Lund.

Fedorowicz J 1982 *A republic of nobles. Studies in Polish history to 1864*. Cambridge.

Ladewig Petersen E 1968 La crise de la noblesse danoise entre 1580 et 1660 *Annales* **23**.

Sjödell U 1976 *Infödda svenska män av ridderskapet och adeln*. Skrifter utgivna av Vetenskapssocieteten i Lund 72. Lund.

Ågren K 1976 Rise and decline of an aristocracy. The Swedish social and political elite in the 17th century *Scandinavian Journal of History* **1**.

URBAN LIFE

Cowan A 1986 *The urban patriciate in Lübeck and Venice 1580–1700*. Quellen und Darstellungen zur Hansischen Geschichte, NF 30. Cologne.

Engman M 1983 *St Petersburg och Finland. Migration och influens 1703–1917* Bidrag till kännedom av Finlands natur och folk 130. Helsingfors.

Gause F 1968 *Die Geschichte der Stadt Königsberg* (2 vols). Cologne.

Glinski G von 1964 *Die Königsberger Kaufmannschaft des 17 und 18 Jahrhunderts* Wissenschäftliche Beiträge zur Geschichte und Landeskunde Ost-Mitteleuropas 70. Marburg.

Johansen P, von zur Mühlen H 1973 *Deutsch und Undeutsch im mittelalterlichen und frühzeitlichen Reval*. Cologne–Vienna.

Pullat R 1983 *Tallinn through the ages*. Tallinn.

Schildhauer J 1985 *The Hanse. History and Culture*. Leipzig.

CHURCH HISTORY

Arbusow L 1964 *Die Einführung der Reformation in Liv-Est- und Kurland*. (reprint edn). Aalen.

Dunckley E 1948 *The Reformation in Denmark*. London.

Lindhardt P 1983 *Kirchengeschichte Skandinaviens*. Göttingen.

Wittram R (ed.) 1956 *Baltische Kirchengeschichte*. Göttingen.

Zins H 1960 The political and social background of the early Reformation in Ermeland *English Historical Review* 75.

EDUCATION AND INTELLECTUAL LIFE

Dahlgren S (ed.) 1967 *Kultur och samhälle i stormaktstidens Sverige.* Stockholm.

Lindroth S 1975–8 *Svensk lärdomshistoria* (3 vols). Stockholm.

Siilivask K (ed.) 1985 *History of Tartu university 1632–1982*. Tallinn.

Tazbir J 1986 *La république nobiliaire et le monde. Etudes sur l'histoire de la culture polonaise à l'époque du baroque* Polish Historical Library 7. Wroclaw.

THE LIVONIAN WARS (1558–1629)

Angermann N 1972 *Studien zur Livlandspolitik Ivan Groznyjs* Marburger Ostforschungen 32. Marburg.

Donnert E 1963 *Die livländische Ordenritterstaat und Russland. Der livländische Krieg und die baltische Frage in der europäischen Politik 1558–1583*. Berlin.

Dow J 1965 *Ruthven's army in Sweden and Esthonia* Historiskt Arkiv 13. Stockholm.

Esper T 1966 Russia and the Baltic 1494–1558 *Slavic Review* 25.

Kirchner W 1954 *The rise of the Baltic question* University of Delaware Monograph Series 3. Newark.

Lepszy K 1960 The union of the crowns between Poland and Sweden in 1587 *Poland at the 11th International Congress of Historical Sciences at Stockholm.* Warsaw.

Tiberg E 1984 *Zur Vorgeschichte des Livländischen Krieges. Die Beziehungen zwischen Moskau und Litauen 1549–1562* Studia Historica Upsaliensia 134. Uppsala.

THE THIRTY YEARS' WAR (1618–48)

Goetze S 1971 *Die Politik des schwedischen Reichskanzlers Axel Oxenstierna gegenuber Kaiser und Reich*. Kiel.

Repgen K (ed.) 1988 *Krieg und Politik, 1618–1648.* Europäische Probleme und Perspektiven. Munich.

Roberts M 1982 Oxenstierna in Germany 1633–1636 *Scandia* **48**.

Rystad G 1960 *Kriegsnachrichten und Propaganda während des Dreissigjährigen Krieges.* Stockholm.

Tandrup L 1979 *Mod triumf eller tragedi* (2 vols). Aarhus.

THE BALTIC IN INTERNATIONAL RELATIONS (1648–1700)

Lossky A 1954 *Louis XIV, William III and the Baltic crisis of 1683* University of California Publications in History 49. Los Angeles.

Stade A, Wimmer J (eds) 1973 *Polens krig med Sverige 1655–1660* Carl X Gustaf-Studier 5. Kristianstad.

THE GREAT NORTHERN WAR (1700–21)

Cavallie J 1975 *Från fred till krig. De finansiella problemen kring krigsutbrott år 1700.* Uppsala.

Chance J 1909 *George I and the Northern War.* London.

Kalisch J, Gierowski J (eds) 1962 *Um die polnische Krone. Sachsen und Polen während des Nordischen Krieges 1700–1721.* Berlin.

Lewitter L 1968 Russia, Poland and the Baltic 1697–1721 *Historical Journal* **11**.

Nordmann C 1962 *La crise du Nord au début du XVIIIe siècle.* Paris.

Murray J 1969 *George I, the Baltic and the Whig split of 1717.* London.

Vozgrin V 1986 *Rossiya i evropeyskie stranyi v godyi severnoy voynyi.* Leningrad.

THE BALTIC IN INTERNATIONAL RELATIONS AFTER 1721

Bagger H 1974 *Ruslands alliancepolitik efter freden i Nystad* Københavns universitets slaviske institutet: Studier 4. Copenhagen.

Kaplan H 1968 *Russia and the outbreak of the Seven Years' War.* Berkeley.

Kent H 1973 *War and trade in northern seas. Anglo-Scandinavian economic relations in the mid eighteenth century* Cambridge Studies in Economic History. Cambridge.

Lind G 1983 The making of the neutrality convention of 1756. France and her Scandinavian allies *Scandinavian Journal of History* **8**.

Mediger W 1968 Russland und die Ostsee im 18. Jahrhundert *Jahrbücher für Geschichte Osteuropas* **16**.

Metcalf M 1977 *Russia, England and Swedish party politics 1762–1766*. Totowa, NJ.

Müller M 1983 *Polen zwischen Preussen und Russland* Einzelveröffentlichungen der Historischen Kommission zu Berlin 40. Berlin.

Müller M 1980 Russland und der Siebenjährige Krieg *Jahrbucher fur Geschichte Osteuropas* **28**.

Rauch G von 1957 Zur baltischen Frage im 18. Jahrhundert *Jahrbücher für Geschichte Osteuropas* **5**.

Reading D 1938 *The Anglo-Russian commercial treaty of 1734*. New Haven.

Roberts M 1980 *British diplomacy and Swedish politics 1758–1773*. London

Tuxen O 1988 Principles and priorities. The Danish view of neutrality during the colonial war of 1755–1763 *Scandinavian Journal of History* **13**.

Maps

THE BALTIC
IN 1500

N

Bergen

JÄMTLAND

HÄRJEDALEN

NORRLAND

GULF

DALARNA

S W E D E N

UPPLAND

ÅLAND

SKAGGERAK

BOHUSLÄN

Göta

VÄSTERGÖTLAND

ÖSTERGÖTLAND

Stockholm

KATTEGAT

GOTLAND

Visby

JUTLAND

D E N M A R K

SMÅLAND

Helsingør

SKÅNE

Kalmar

SJÆLLAND

ÖLAND

Copenhagen

BORNHOLM

BALTIC SEA

Hamburg

Lübeck

Rostock

RÜGEN

Elbe

POMERANIA

Oder

Danzig

Elbing

Vistula

Königsberg

Niemen

EAST
PRUSSIA

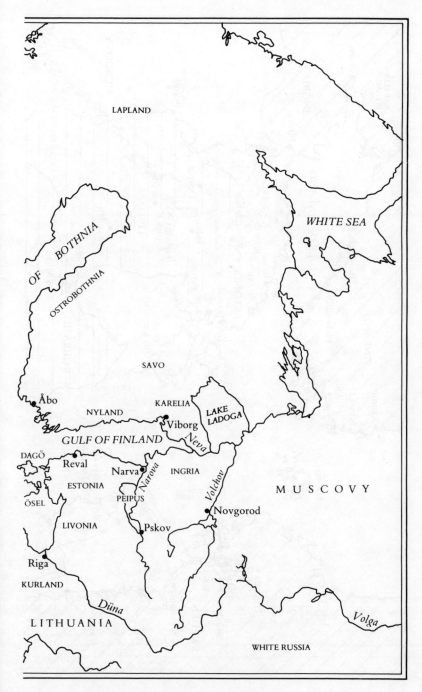

LAPLAND

WHITE SEA

GULF OF BOTHNIA

OF BOTHNIA

OSTROBOTHNIA

SAVO

Åbo

NYLAND

KARELIA

LAKE LADOGA

Viborg

Neva

GULF OF FINLAND

DAGÖ

Reval

Narva

Narova

INGRIA

Volchov

MUSCOVY

ESTONIA

PEIPUS

ÖSEL

Novgorod

LIVONIA

Pskov

Riga

KURLAND

Düna

Volga

LITHUANIA

WHITE RUSSIA

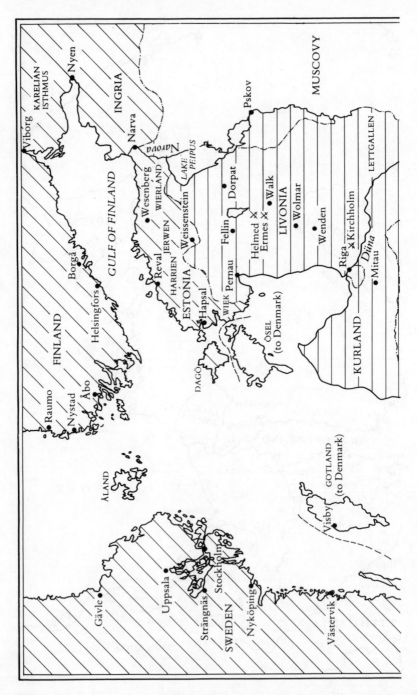

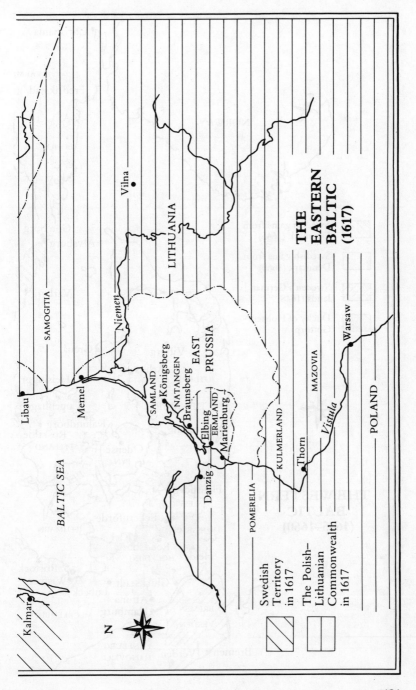

THE
EASTERN
BALTIC
(1617)

BALTIC SEA

Kalmar

Libau

Memel

SAMLAND
Königsberg
NATANGEN
Braunsberg
EAST
PRUSSIA
Elbing
ERMLAND
Marienburg

Danzig

POMERELIA

KULMERLAND

Thorn

MAZOVIA

Vistula

POLAND

Warsaw

Niemen

SAMOGITIA

LITHUANIA

Vilna

N

Swedish
Territory
in 1617

The Polish–
Lithuanian
Commonwealth
in 1617

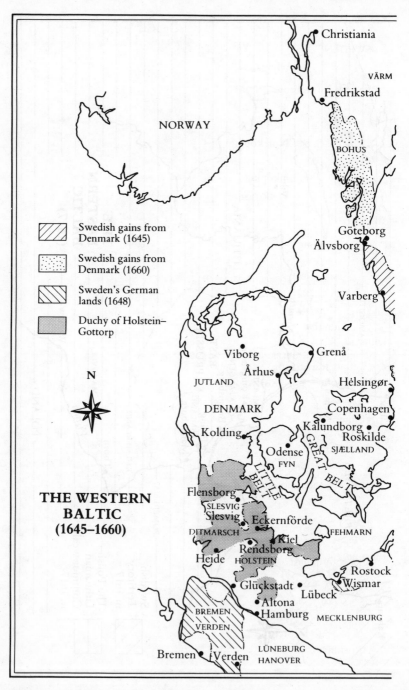

Christiania

VÄRM

Fredrikstad

NORWAY

BOHUS

Göteborg

Älvsborg

Varberg

Swedish gains from
Denmark (1645)

Swedish gains from
Denmark (1660)

Sweden's German
lands (1648)

Duchy of Holstein–
Gottorp

N

Viborg

Grenå

Århus

JUTLAND

Hélsingør

DENMARK

Copenhagen

Kolding

Kalundborg

Roskilde

**THE WESTERN
BALTIC
(1645–1660)**

Odense

SJÆLLAND

FYN

Flensborg

LITTLE
BELT

GREAT
BELT

SLESVIG

Slesvig

Eckernförde

DITMARSCH

FEHMARN

Kiel

Heide

Rendsborg

HOLSTEIN

Rostock

Glückstadt

Wismar

Altona

Lübeck

BREMEN

Hamburg

MECKLENBURG

VERDEN

LÜNEBURG

Bremen

Verden

HANOVER

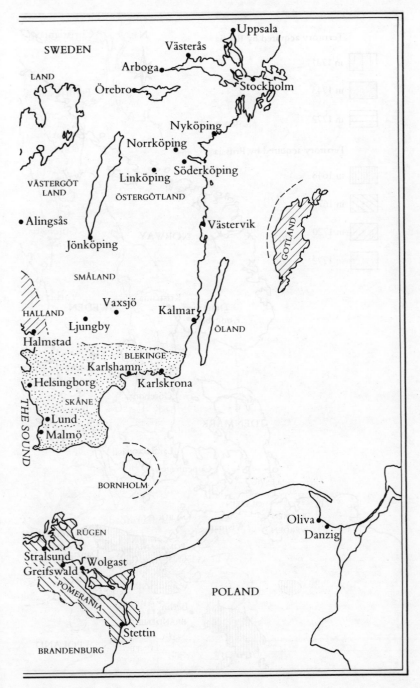

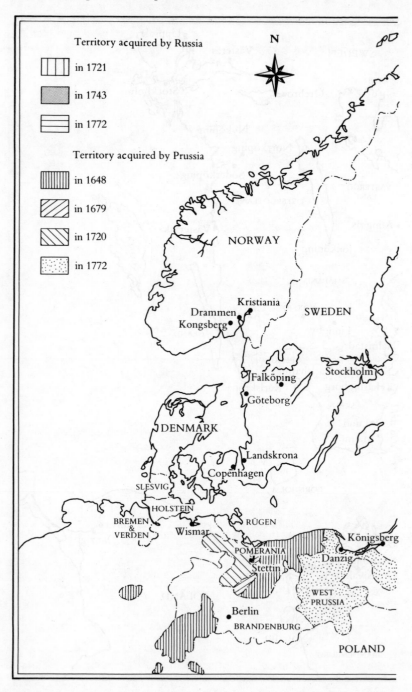

N

Territory acquired by Russia

in 1721

in 1743

in 1772

Territory acquired by Prussia

in 1648

in 1679

in 1720

in 1772

NORWAY

SWEDEN

Kristiania

Drammen
Kongsberg

Falköping

Göteborg

Stockholm

DENMARK

Landskrona

Copenhagen

SLESVIG

HOLSTEIN

BREMEN
&
VERDEN

Wismar

RÜGEN

POMERANIA

Stettin

Königsberg

Danzig

WEST
PRUSSIA

Berlin

BRANDENBURG

POLAND

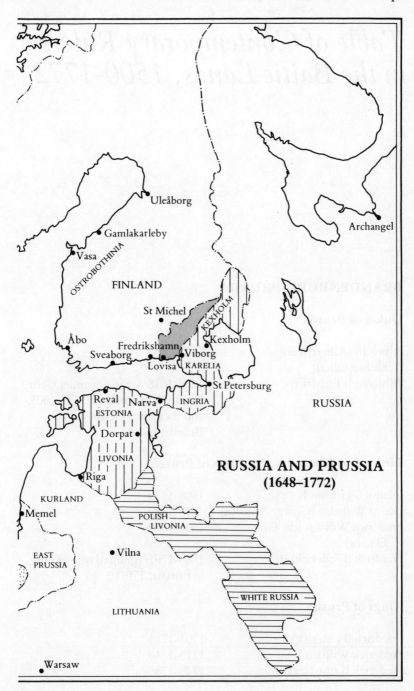

**RUSSIA AND PRUSSIA
(1648–1772)**

Uleåborg

Archangel

Gamlakarleby

Vasa

OSTROBOTHINIA

FINLAND

St Michel

KEXHOLM

Åbo

Kexholm

Fredrikshamn

Sveaborg

Viborg

Lovisa

KARELIA

INGRIA

St Petersburg

RUSSIA

Reval

Narva

ESTONIA

Dorpat

LIVONIA

Riga

KURLAND

Memel

POLISH
LIVONIA

EAST
PRUSSIA

Vilna

WHITE RUSSIA

LITHUANIA

Warsaw

Table of Contemporary Rulers in the Baltic Lands, 1500-1772

BRANDENBURG-PRUSSIA

Dukes of Prussia

Albrecht (Albert) von Hohenzollern	1525–1568
Albrecht II Friedrich	1568–1618 (regency under Georg Friedrich of Ansbach 1578–1603, and thereafter the elector of Brandenburg)

Electors of Brandenburg, dukes of Prussia

Johann Sigismund	1608–1619
Georg Wilhelm (George William)	1619–1640
Frederick William (the Great Elector)	1640–1688
Freidrich (Frederick) III	1688–1701 (granted title of king in Prussia, 1701)

Kings of Prussia

Friedrich (Frederick) I	1701–1713
Frederick William I	1713–1740
Frederick II (the Great)	1740–1786

DENMARK

Hans	1481–1513
Christian II	1513–1523 (deposed)
Frederik I	1523–1533
Christian III	1534–1559
Frederik II	1559–1596
Christian IV	1596–1648
Frederik III	1648–1670
Christian V	1670–1699
Frederik IV	1699–1730
Christian VI	1730–1746
Frederik V	1746–1766
Christian VII	1766–1808 (his son Frederik exercised the regency from 1784 on account of the king's insanity)

POLAND-LITHUANIA

Zygmunt (Sigismund) I Jagiełło	1506–1548
Zygmunt II August Jagiełło	1548–1572
Henri of Anjou	1573–1575
Stefan Batory	1575–1587
Zygmunt (Sigismund) III Vasa	1587–1632
Władysław (Ladislas) IV Vasa	1632–1648
Jan II Kazimierz (John Casimir) Vasa	1648–1668 (abdicated)
Michał (Michael) Korybut Wiśniowiecki	1669–1673
Jan (John) III Sobieski	1674–1696
August II of Saxony	1697–1733 (deposed 1704, restored 1709)
Stanisław I Leszczyński	1704–1709, 1733–1735 (twice elected, twice deposed)
August III of Saxony	1733–1763
Stanisław II August Poniatowski	1764–1795 (last king of Poland)

427

RUSSIA (MUSCOVY)

Grand dukes of Muscovy

Ivan III (the Great)	1462–1505
Vasily III	1505–1533
Ivan IV (the Terrible)	1533–1584
Fedor I	1584–1598
Boris Godunov	1598–1605
Dmitri	1605–1606 (Time of
Vasily Shuisky	1606–1610 Troubles)
Mikhail Romanov	1613–1645
Alexis	1645–1676
Fedor II	1676–1682
Ivan V and Peter	1682–1689 (regency of Sophia)

Emperors and empresses of Russia

Peter I (the Great)	1689–1725
Catherine I	1725–1727
Peter II	1727–1730
Anna	1730–1740
Ivan VI	1740–1741 (deposed)
Elizabeth	1741–1762
Peter III	1762 (murdered)
Catherine II (the Great)	1762–1796

SWEDEN

Regents

Sten Sture	1470–1503
Svante Nilsson	1503–1512
Sten Sture (the Younger)	1512–1520

Kings

Gustav I Vasa	1523–1560
Erik XIV	1560–1569 (deposed)
Johan III	1569–1592

Sigismund	1592–1600 (deposed: duke Karl, regent from 1594)
Karl IX	1604–1611
Gustav II Adolf	1611–1632
Christina	1632–1654 (abdicated)
Karl X Gustav	1654–1660
Karl XI	1660–1697
Karl XII	1697–1718
Ulrika Eleanora	1718–1719 (vacated the throne in her husband's favour)
Fredrik I	1719–1751
Adolf Fredrik	1751–1771
Gustav III	1771–1792 (murdered)

Glossary of Recurrent Terms

Adel (German, Danish, Swedish): noble(man) – see also *frälse*

Amt, Ämter (German) *amt, amter* (Danish): unit(s) of local administration, similar to English county

Amtshauptmann, amtmand: governor of an *amt*

Bauer (German) *bonde* (Danish, Swedish): peasant farmer

frälse(jord) (Swedish): of privileged status; usually applied to land reserved for the nobility

Haken (German): unit of land measurement in the eastern Baltic lands

härad (Swedish), *herred* (Danish): district similar to the English hundred, the area of jurisdiction for the local court (*häradsting, herredsting*)

husmand, husmænd (Danish): cottager, usually employed as farm worker; somewhat better-off than the landless *inderster*

indelningsverk(et) (Swedish): the system of military apportionment perfected in the reign of Karl XI

Indigenatsrecht (German): the right of the native-born, usually to posts and offices

län (Swedish): largest unit of administration within the kingdom

Landrat, -räte (German): councillor, advisor to the ruler in the eastern Baltic lands

Landratskollegium (German): the executive council of the nobility in Livonia and Estonia

Landtag (German): provincial diet or assembly, usually dominated by the noble estate

Leibeigenschaft (German): serfdom

len (Danish): fief, before the 1662 reform transformed these units into *amter*

Oberrat (German): supreme councillor in Prussia and Kurland

(rigs)råd (Danish), *(riks)råd* (Swedish): council of the realm

Rat (German): council, usually municipal

reduktion (Swedish): the resumption of alienated crown lands undertaken during the second half of the seventeenth century

riddarhus (Swedish): house of the nobility for the *riksdag* meetings

riksdag (Swedish): the national diet, or assembly, of four estates

riksföreståndare (Swedish): regent (especially during the period of the Kalmar union (1397–1520)

Ritterbank (German): the corporation of the nobility established in Kurland in 1617

Ritterschaft (German): the collective term for the nobility

Rossdienst (German), *rusttjänst* (Swedish): the obligation of the nobility to provide and equip cavalry for the crown

rzeczpospolita (Polish): the Polish–Lithuanian commonwealth

sejm (Polish): national diet or assembly: provincial or regional diets were called *sejmniki*

skattebonde/bönder (Swedish): tax-paying freehold peasant farmer(s)

stavnsbånd (Danish): eighteenth-century system whereby peasants of military age were not permitted to leave their home district without their lord's permission

vornedskab (Danish): system of peasant bondage in eastern Denmark, abolished in 1702

Index

(Currently-used placenames are given in parentheses)